KEYGuide

The **AA** **KEY**Guide
France

Contents

KEY TO SYMBOLS

- ✚ Map reference
- ✉ Address
- ☎ Telephone number
- 🕐 Opening times
- ✋ Admission prices
- Ⓜ Métro station
- Bus number
- Train station
- Ferry/boat
- Driving directions
- ℹ Tourist office
- Tours
- Guidebook
- Restaurant
- Café
- Shop
- Lavatories
- ⓘ Number of rooms
- 🚫 No smoking
- Air conditioning
- Swimming pool
- Gym
- ❓ Other useful information
- Place to stay
- Place to eat

UNDERSTANDING FRANCE

With memorable meals, world-renowned art collections and magnificent chateaux, France would be worth visiting even without the wonderful scenery. No wonder it is one of the world's most popular holiday destinations, clocking up more than 75 million visitors each year. It is the largest country in Western Europe and has a population of around 60 million. Each part of the country has managed to retain its own character and this regional diversity can be seen especially in French food and wine, which inspire fierce local pride. The diversity is evident in the very landscape itself, with unending rows of vines in one region, followed by flocks of sheep, goats or cattle in the next; olive groves in the southeast and apple orchards in the northwest.

A horse and cart on the beach at Barfleur

Flowers brighten up the courtyard of a farmhouse in Issenhausen

Strolling in the grounds of the Château de Chambord

ECONOMY

Until recently there was a strong division between France's wealthier cities and its poorer industrial and mining areas. But intelligent use of the high-speed rail network and budget air services has diluted the divide. Abandoned mining towns in the north are now home to many major international financial institutions, only an hour from Paris and within two hours of several European capitals. Likewise, workers in Paris can now buy homes near the Mediterranean and commute to the capital, injecting new blood and new money into formerly run down provincial villages. There has also been investment in discount shopping malls and low-rent business complexes far from the principal cities.

Food and wine are key factors in the national economy. Famously, former president Charles de Gaulle bemoaned the impossibility of governing a nation that produced over 350 different cheeses. Bordeaux and Burgundy provide some of the world's top wines—and many of the more distinguished chateau estates are owned and managed by international financial institutions. The Champagne region is the source of the entire global supply of champagne, and the vast vineyards of Languedoc-Roussillon are Europe's principal suppliers of inexpensive and reliable supermarket table wines. Food is also a key lure to visitors, and restaurants and hotels pocket a fair share of the €34 billion spent annually by people coming from overseas.

POLITICS

French presidents manage to stamp their personalities onto the country in a way that most world leaders can only envy. This is because elections are held only once in seven years and a two-term tenure will outspan a decade, giving the incumbent the freedom to implement long-term policies without having to worry about short-term popularity. Thus Francois Mitterrand was able to implement policies that brought about enormous social change and monumental architectural projects with only one interruption in the name of democracy. This can also lead to voter apathy, with the population feeling impotent mid-term. Thus, the extreme right candidate Jean-Marie Le Pen nudged his way into second place in the first round of the 2002 presidential elections. Accordingly, socialists had to vote for conservative Jacques Chirac at the final poll, in order to keep the extremists out of the Elysée Palace. Extremism is usually kept at bay by parliamentary elections held mid way through a presidential term, where opposition to the president is often reflected in the appointment of a prime minister from a rival party. This 'cohabitation' leads to workmanlike compromise. The other important elected official in France is the local mayor, whose powers are wide ranging. Even a village mayor can decide to reduce the working hours of local police, and personally intervene to stop house purchases, and Paris mayors are major political figures on the national stage. However, politicians may grab the headlines, but true power lies with the workers, whose lightening strikes are greeted philosophically by a population used to days without rail and air travel.

LANGUAGE AND SOCIETY

France was originally many kingdoms and the regions retain the languages and cultures of other times. But there is fierce pride in the French language itself—remember the many campaigns to remove English words from the national vocabulary (*Le Weekend*, *Le Sandwich* and others). This pride is maintained by the Académie Française, who insist that email is called *mél*, with an accent to disguise its American origins. Other tongues are fiercely defended in various corners of the country. Brittany celebrates its heritage with an annual gathering of Celts from Ireland, Wales, Scotland

sunbathe or both. There are six mountain ranges (including the Alps, Jura, Vosges and Pyrenees) and 5,500km (3,418 miles) of coastline on the Channel, Atlantic and Mediterranean. Some dramatic river gorges cleave through the country and there are 15 million hectares (37 million acres) of forest. The landscape is both typically northern and typically southern European—lush hedgerows in Normandy, huge tracts of dusty scrubland in Languedoc, rich verdant undulating hills in Auvergne and heady fields of lavender in Provence.

VISITING FRANCE

France is a large country so don't be over-ambitious when deciding what to see during your visit. It is probably best to base yourself in one region—and they are all quite different—and

Pinot Noir grapes

The game of boules is a popular pastime in France

A field of bright sunflowers

and even farther afield at the Interceltic fortnight in August. It is said that a Breton fisherman and his counterpart from Cornwall, England, can converse freely in their native tongues. In the southwest, French Basques are less volatile than the ETA activists across the Spanish border, but their language and rituals are celebrated with pride. On the southern side of the Pyrenees, another cross border culture, Catalan, is almost a national identity in its own right. Across the southwest, bilingual road signs include place names in Occitan—the Langue d'Oc that gives a region its name. In most of modern France, multiculturalism refers more to new communities than the old kingdoms. This stirs up notorious agitation from the right-wing National Front, whose support in the south stems from both immigration from North Africa (in the cities) and scaremongering about European regulation (in the agricultural and fishing communities). Conversely, Montpellier, with its large Arab population, has been a haven of tolerance for centuries and even houses its Islamic and Jewish cultural facilities in the same building. One poster in the Arab Quarter wryly announced during election year 'Send us home and we take the Cup with us', a reference to the multi-ethnic team that won France the soccer World Cup in 1998.

LANDSCAPE

France's distinctive borders give it the nickname The Hexagon. The sheer scale of it—the country is the size of Texas—means that for part of the year visitors can choose to ski,

really get to know it, rather than travel up and down the *autoroutes* ticking off as many sights as possible. In addition to the must-see sights, each region offers its own blend of leisure activities—do you want a weekend of culture and style in Paris, or a week of walking in the Pyrenees, skiing in the Alps or relaxing on a beach on the Côte d'Azur?

If you're taking your car (see pages 50–54), it's a good idea to plan an overnight stop on longer drives. If you're moving around by train, consider buying a rail pass before you leave home, as this can save you money (see page 58). Regions can vary greatly depending on the season, so bear this in mind when planning your trip. For example, Paris is quiet but stiflingly hot in August, while much of the south of France is packed with people and traffic; some of the trails in the breathtaking Pyrenees are impassable during the colder months, while this, obviously, is an ideal time for skiing in the Alps.

The shimmering white basilica of Sacré-Cœur is a Paris landmark

PARIS AND THE ÎLE DE FRANCE

Paris is a seductive capital, with its legendary style, romance, art and architecture. It is the heart of France's political, economic, social and cultural life and has a population of just over two million.
The Île de France region, with Paris at its heart, has a population of 11 million—and plenty of chateaux, including Versailles and Fontainebleau.

NORTHWEST FRANCE

Normandy, west of Paris, has timbered manor houses, abbey ruins and seaside resorts. It is famous for Camembert, Calvados and its links with the Impressionists.
Brittany, west of Normandy, has a long coastline of golden beaches, dotted with small fishing ports. The region's richly decorated churches are often surrounded by 'parish closes'—enclosed cemeteries with imposing gateways and elaborate calvaries.

A snowy track through the Col du Coq

A farm trail leads through the high pastures of the Pyrenees

A steep, cobbled lane in a Corsican village

NORTH AND NORTHEAST FRANCE

Nord-Pas-de-Calais, at the northern tip of France, has the busy ports of Boulogne, Calais and Dunkerque, as well as Lille, capital of the north.
Picardie, south of Nord-Pas-de-Calais, has Amiens as its ancient capital, sitting on the banks of the Somme.
Champagne-Ardenne, to the east, shelters the chalk hills and escarpments of champagne country.
Lorraine, farther east, includes Nancy, former capital of the independent Duchy of Lorraine, and Metz, Lorraine's current capital.
Alsace borders Germany and you can see German influences in its food, wine and architecture. Strasbourg sits on its eastern edge.

LOIRE

Centre, south of Paris, is renowned for its Renaissance chateaux, historic towns, and beautiful river and valley scenery.
Pays de la Loire, farther west, has the lively city of Nantes, a stretch of Atlantic coastline, and the towns of Angers, Saumur and Le Mans—famous for its 24-hour sports car race.

CENTRAL FRANCE AND THE ALPS

Franche-Comté, in the east of France and bordering Switzerland, has the Jura woods and mountains, which are popular with walkers and cross-country skiers.
Bourgogne (Burgundy) is a gastronomic hub known for mustard, *boeuf bourguignon* and snails. It has the wine towns of Dijon and Beaune.
The Auvergne has the Massif Central mountain range, with its distinctive volcanic cones.
Rhône-Alpes includes Lyon, with its Renaissance old quarter. The region has the highest peak in Europe—Mont Blanc—and some of the best skiing.

FRANCE'S REGIONS

(Map of France showing its regions: NORD-PAS-DE-CALAIS, PICARDIE, HAUTE-NORMANDIE, BASSE-NORMANDIE, BRETAGNE, ÎLE-DE-FRANCE, CHAMPAGNE-ARDENNE, LORRAINE, ALSACE, PAYS DE LA LOIRE, CENTRE, BOURGOGNE, FRANCHE-COMTÉ, POITOU-CHARENTES, LIMOUSIN, AUVERGNE, RHÔNE-ALPES, AQUITAINE, MIDI-PYRÉNÉES, LANGUEDOC-ROUSSILLON, PROVENCE-ALPES-CÔTE-D'AZUR, MONACO, CORSE, with border markers GB, B, L, D, CH, I, E, AND)

SOUTHEAST FRANCE

Provence-Alpes-Côte-d'Azur borders Italy and has miles of Mediterranean coastline. There are the great cities of Marseille and Nice and the area's Roman past is evident in the amphitheatres and arches at Orange and Arles.

Languedoc-Roussillon also has a long Mediterranean coastline and its Roman legacy is the wonder of Roman engineering, the Pont du Gard. The main city, Montpellier, is vibrant and cosmopolitan.

Monaco is the tiny principality that thinks big.

SOUTHWEST FRANCE

Poitou-Charentes, north of Aquitaine, includes historic Poitiers, the sophisticated coastal town of La Rochelle and the offshore islands of Ré and Oléron. There is also La Venise Verte—a huge area of greenery and waterways.

Limousin, east of Poitou-Charentes, is home to Limoges, famous for its fine porcelain.

Midi-Pyrénées, south of Limousin, shares its southern border with Spain and Andorra and includes part of the Pyrenees mountain range, the cultural city of Toulouse and the pilgrimage site of Lourdes.

Aquitaine, west of the Midi-Pyrénées, is famous for its wine in Bordeaux and the surrounding area, its sandy beaches and resorts, such as Biarritz, on the Atlantic coast, the caves and gastronomy—including foie gras and truffles—of the Dordogne area, and the Pyrenees mountains to the south.

CORSICA

This Mediterranean island lies off the coast of Provence. You can walk in the mountains, relax on the beach, spot the diverse birdlife and admire the architecture of Pisan and Genoese rulers.

PARIS AND THE ÎLE DE FRANCE

Eiffel Tower (see page 93): Test your nerves on the viewing platforms of this Paris landmark.

Musée du Louvre (see pages 82–83): One of the world's most famous art galleries.

Musée d'Orsay (see page 85): A wonderful collection of Impressionist paintings and other art, in a former Belle-Époque rail station.

Notre-Dame (see page 87): Admire the cathedral's magnificent architecture, then climb the towers for wonderful views.

Fontainebleau (see page 74): This chateau is just as lavish as Versailles but less crowded.

Fountains at Versailles (see page 94): Pick a day when the famous fountains are flowing to experience Versailles at its best.

Views from Sacré-Cœur (page 91): Sunset is a great time to appreciate the breathtaking views from the front terrace of this basilica.

The Louvre's striking Pyramid (above).
The wonderful station clock at the Musee d'Orsay (top left).
Looking across to Mont St-Michel (below)

NORTHWEST FRANCE

Côte d'Albâtre (see page 290): Start at Étretat for a cliff walk with breathtaking views along this coastline, named after its chalky cliffs and milky waves.

Bayeux (see page 97): See the famous 11th-century tapestry.

D–Day Beaches (see page 103): Visit the beaches where Allied forces landed on 6 June 1944.

Honfleur (see page 107): A picturesque fishing port and artists' colony.

Mont St-Michel (see page 110–111): Cross to this mystical abbey on its rocky mount and enjoy wonderful views of the bay.

Océanopolis (see page 98): See 10,000 marine creatures at one of Europe's best aquariums.

Rouen (see pages 116–119): Normandy's capital has an attractive old town, good shopping and a cathedral made famous by Monet.

Sables-d'Or-les-Pins (see page 120): Relax on the golden sands of this beach, backed by pine trees.

St-Thégonnec (see page 122): Brittany's most spectacular parish close.

NORTH AND NORTHEAST FRANCE

Battlefields of Picardie (see page 125): See the fields where so many soldiers lost their lives during World War I and pay your respects at the immaculate war cemeteries.

The coastline of the Côte d'Opale

Champagne-tasting (see pages 138–139): Visit a Maison du Champagne at Reims and remind yourself why bubbly has been prized for centuries.

The splendid spire of St-Maurice church, in Lille

Lille (see pages 132–135): France's fourth-largest city has a prestigious art gallery, vast shopping mall and 17th-century Citadelle.

Nancy (see page 131): Immerse yourself in the art nouveau architecture and fabulous glassware.

Nausicaa (see page 126): An imaginative aquarium at Boulogne.

Strasbourg (see pages 140–143): This city, near the German border, is seat of the European Parliament.

Sand sports on the Côte d'Opale (see pages 129, 240): Take a lesson in sand-yachting on the beaches north of Boulogne.

Troyes (see page 137): An attractive village of half-timbered houses, cobbled streets and vivid stained-glass windows.

THE LOIRE

Chartres (see page 146): See the awesome Notre-Dame-de-Chartres cathedral.

Chateaux of the Loire (see pages 145–154): This scenic region is dotted with fairytale chateaux.

A pop art sign for the entrance to Le Mans 24-hour circuit

Le Mans (see page 152): Not just for car enthusiasts—as well as the racetrack and automobile museum there is a lovely old town, with cobbled streets, medieval timber-framed houses and a 12th-century cathedral.

Saumur (see page 154): This town, a World Heritage Site, has half-timbered houses, chic boutiques and wonderful views.

Tours (see page 154): A thriving city, between the Loire and Cher rivers, with a rich historical, cultural and architectural heritage.

Walking in the Loire Valley: For a walk around Langeais and the valley of the River Roumer, see pages 302–303.

CENTRAL FRANCE AND THE ALPS

The Alps (see page 252): The most exhilarating way to experience these mountains is on skis or a snowboard.

Dijon (see pages 160–161) This easily walkable, historic town is a hub of the Burgundy wine trade.

The Gorges de l'Ardèche (see page 162): Canoe along the river and underneath the natural archway, the Pont d'Arc.

Lac d'Annecy (see page 156): For boat trips, water sports and outdoor activities in a beautiful mountain setting, Annecy is hard to beat.

Lyon (see pages 164–167): A must-see city, great for culture and nightlife.

Parc des Volcans: This park is ideal for walkers, with volcanic peaks such as the Puy de Dôme (see page 168) giving views of the Auvergne.

A skier weaves around the red-flagged gates in the slalom at La Tou (right)

Canoeists gather on the shingle beach beneath the Pont d'Arc, in the Gorges de l'Ardèche (above)

SOUTHEAST FRANCE

Aix-en-Provence (see page 172): An elegant town with fine Renaissance mansions and links with the painter Paul Cézanne.

Avignon (see page 174): The main draws are the magnificent Palais des Papes, once the seat of the Pope, and the huge drama and dance festival held in July.

The Camargue Delta (see pages 318–321): Great for long, wild walks, peace and quiet, and bird-watching.

Cannes (see page 176): Shop 'til you drop in Provence's most glamorous destination.

Gorges du Tarn (see pages 316–317): Drive, walk or take a boat along the river for spectacular gorge views.

Marseille (see pages 182–185): Soak up the history in the Vieux Port and Le Panier districts of this ancient city.

Montpellier (see page 181): Visit in the summer to enjoy one of the city's many arts festivals.

Nice (see page 188): Experience the city's hectic nightlife.

Nîmes and Pont du Gard (see page 189): Marvel at the Romans' engineering skills at the amphitheatre in Nîmes and at the Pont du Gard aqueduct.

A handprint of film director Franco Zeffirelli, on the boardwalk at Cannes

SOUTHWEST FRANCE

Biarritz (see page 195): A chic resort, with fantastic beaches.
Bordeaux (see pages 196–199): Sample the city's fine wines or enjoy its architecture.
Caves: See the prehistoric cave paintings at Lascaux (see page 201) or Les Eyzies (see page 200).
Drive through the vineyards of Bordeaux (see pages 330–331): Don't miss the picturesque wine town of St-Émilion.
Futuroscope (see page 201): This leisure park, with its high-tech visual effects, has something to entertain the whole family.
Périgueux (see page 203): Shop for truffles, foie gras, walnuts, wine and cheese in the markets—the biggest in the area.
La Rochelle (see page 204): A sophisticated coastal resort, with lively cafés, interesting architecture and a vast marina.
Toulouse (see pages 206–207): Great for art and history.

A view over the bright sun umbrellas at Biarritz

CORSICA

Réserve Naturelle de Scandola (see page 214): This coastal nature reserve has abundant birdlife.
Beaches: Take your pick from the island's many beaches.
Cap Corse (see page 212): For white villages, sandy coves and peace and quiet, head to this mountainous peninsula.

A boat at Erbalunga village, on the eastern shore of Cap Corse (left)

TOP 15 ACTIVITIES

Be cosmopolitan Take in one of France's great cities: Choose from Paris, Lille, Lyon, Bordeaux, Toulouse or Marseille.
Discover France's history Visit the Roman amphitheatre in Orange, the D-Day Landing beaches in Normandy or the megalithic standing stones at Filitosa, in Corsica.
Drink red wine from Bordeaux, champagne from Reims, Calvados from Normandy or beer from St-Omer.
Drive from chateau to chateau in the Loire, through the mountains in the Pyrenees or along the Mediterranean coastline (but not after drinking!).
Eat whatever the locals are eating, whether it's snails in Bourgogne, *sauerkraut* in Alsace or *bouillabaise* in Provence.
Get on your bicycle Options include Bordeaux, a nature reserve in the Camargue or the vineyards of Champagne.
People-watch with a coffee in your hand at a town-square café.
Shop at a market, in a Parisian boutique or in a village *charcuterie*.
Ski, snowboard or simply enjoy a *vin chaud* in the Alps.
Swim in the sea. Try the Mediterranean in Corsica or Provence, or the Atlantic by Arcachon.
Take in some culture Try the Musée d'Orsay in Paris, Les Abattoirs in Toulouse or the Palais des Beaux-Arts in Lille.
Visit a cathedral and learn more about France's architectural history. Choices include Notre-Dame in Paris, Bordeaux's 1,000-year-old cathedral and Chartres.
Wander around a chateau For a fairytale Loire palace try the Château d'Ussé and for excess go to the sumptuous Versailles.
Walk in the countryside. Follow a mountain trail in the Alps, a coastal path in Brittany or a peaceful canal towpath such as the Canal de Bourgogne.
Watch sport The endurance event of the year is the Tour de France. International rugby or soccer matches take place at the Stade de France, in Paris.

A market stall on the cours Massena, Antibes

Notre-Dame cathedral, in the heart of Paris

Living France

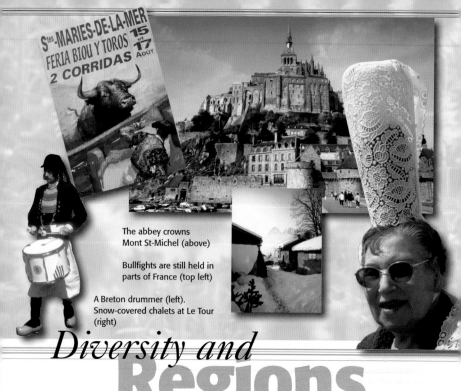

The abbey crowns
Mont St-Michel (above)

Bullfights are still held in
parts of France (top left)

A Breton drummer (left).
Snow-covered chalets at Le Tour
(right)

Diversity and Regions

Gypsies and cowboys by the sea

Gypsies dance with the Camargue's cowboys during one of the most lively events of the Provençal calendar, the *Pèlerinage des Gitans*. The village of Saintes-Maries-de-la-Mer is where, legend has it, Maria Jacobé and Maria Salomé, half sisters of the Virgin Mary, arrived with their maid Sarah, patron saint of gypsies. Every year in late May, gypsies from all over Europe make their pilgrimage to the coast. Dressed in vibrant, traditional costumes, gypsies and *gardiens* (local cowboys who look after wild black bulls) carry jewel-encrusted statues of St. Sarah and the Marias into the sea to be blessed. During the evening and into the night, the beach echoes to the sound of celebrations.

In a nation once made up of kingdoms and principalities, duchies and counties, there is no such thing as 'typically French'. The annual parades of model giants through the streets of the north would be as out of place in Provence as the traditional bullfighting of the south would be if it were transported to the Alps. Regional identity matters to the French—when a local talks patriotically of *mon pays* (my country) the reference is most likely to be the region rather than France itself. While food and drink most commonly define a region, games and traditions also play their part. Essentially, each area and its culture is determined by its landscape and geography. The story of how a rock or cave got its shape will provide cautionary bedtime tales for generations. Regions have their own slang, patois and even languages. Occitan (from Languedoc) and Breton (from Brittany) are languages that are being preserved and cultivated like endangered species. Even in conventional French-speaking towns, listen to older generations in conversation and you may find it hard to recognize the language of your school textbooks.

The Basque logo (right)

A wacky character from Nice carnival (below)

Raking the salt pans (above)

The azure Mediterranean, viewed from Èze (right)

The Breton *bigoudène* headdress (above left)

A shoe nailed to a farm door in Hunspach (right)

Silly skiing

The Olympic resorts in the Alps are known for serious sport, yet once a year, bathtubs are cooler than snowboards and scrap metal is sharper than skis. In late April, La Clusaz hosts the Défi-Foly waterslide challenge. Around 150 participants from across the region take part in the daredevil event around the Confins lake. The fun begins at dawn as racers slide down the slope and try to cross the waters or, at any rate, beat Freddy Quenet's 1998 record of 140m (460ft). This inventive combination of downhill and waterskiing is then followed by the Unidentified Sliding Object contest to find the most bizarre object used on the course. Previous contestants have used car parts and baths to glide down the slopes to the waters.

Puffed up parade

Should you feel a sudden gust of wind around your nether regions in Périgord Vert, don't worry—it means that you have been accepted as a local. The worthy citizens of Nontron put on clogs, masks and nightshirts, and take to the streets armed with a pair of bellows for the annual *Soufflaculs* parade, when residents joyfully shoot air up each others' nightshirts and pump up their petticoats to chase out evil spirits that might be lurking within. The custom dates from an Ash Wednesday tradition at the nearby abbey of St-Sauveur, when monks used bellows to purify each nook and cranny before Lent. In the Middle Ages, townsfolk adopted the Bellows Festival as a cue for much debauchery and licentiousness. The modern-day parade is now seen as a bit of harmless fun.

Cabins in the sun

While New Yorkers have their summerhouses in the Hamptons, the good people of Marseille have their *cabanons*. Most casual visitors may well pass through the coastal area south of Marseille unaware of its unique *cabanon* lifestyle. This is focused around weekend and holiday houses where families decamp to party and play boules or cards with their friends in huts, cabins, shacks and boathouses. The Route des Cabanons takes you through the enchanting yet little-known villages of Montredon, Madrague, Sormiou and Morgiou, as well as more well-known fishing ports such as Vallon des Auffes. The tourist office in Marseille can suggest an early evening driving itinerary through this hinterland of the south.

Menton citron

Forget understated style—the Riviera has a gaudy party for a glorious fortnight, when the international visitors are looking the other way. Mardi Gras on the Riviera is the way to party out of winter and into spring sunshine. Shrove Tuesday ends more than two weeks of merry-making. In Nice, massive papier mâché heads join the marching bands and dancing crowds following gigantic floats parading daily through the streets and along the Promenade des Anglais to the sea. The giant King of the Carnival reigns supreme until he is finally set alight and put to sea, bringing the carnival to its dramatic close. Along the coast, the usually genteel folk of Menton provide a rival assault on the senses, with the added fragrance of citrus fruits when 130 tonnes of oranges and lemons are transformed into massive floats for the Fête du Citron.

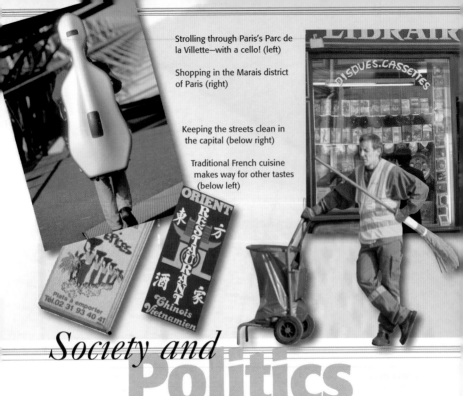

Strolling through Paris's Parc de la Villette—with a cello! (left)

Shopping in the Marais district of Paris (right)

Keeping the streets clean in the capital (below right)

Traditional French cuisine makes way for other tastes (below left)

Society and Politics

There is a lot of talk in France about voter apathy, though this should not be confused with political apathy, as the French are prone to voicing their opinions. Even the most staid of weekly markets is likely to have at least one small protest somewhere. In the rural communities of the south, pamphlets and banners made from bedsheets issue dire warnings about the powers of the European Union, while in liberal university cities, foreign affairs will inspire a protest march or a well-mannered yet lively chorus will take up human rights and immigration issues. The downside is that official strikes and unsanctioned industrial action are a way of life. The French resign themselves to changing travel plans around railway strikes but get angry when industrial action affects their children's education. Politicians may not always get the votes, even if they can rely on popular support, but the ones who get it right have streets named after them for generations to come.

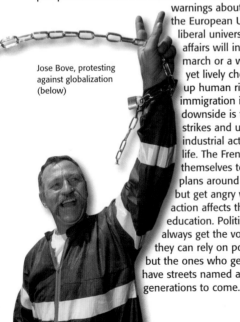

Jose Bove, protesting against globalization (below)

City of protest

Parisians feel it a matter of pride to pour into the streets to express their grievances by rallying, marching and erecting barricades. But while the Left demonstrates on the streets, when it is time to step into the polling booths it is the Right which has consistently won control of the capital. The election of a Socialist mayor in 2001 meant that for the first time for nearly 100 years Paris was to be governed by the Left. The new mayor, Bertrand Delanoë, proudly declared 'For the first time since 1909, the forces for progress hold the majority. Paris is still the capital of the movement...a city that will neither conform nor submit'.

Mending fishing nets at St-Vaast-la-Hougue (left)

Harvesting the grapes (below)

Jean-Marie Le Pen, of the National Front party, gave many people a shock by coming second in the 2002 Presidential elections

A street hero named *Désir*

Members of the European Parliament do not usually find their way to Strasbourg on a wave of support from an otherwise disaffected youth. However, Harlem Désir owes his parliamentary seat in part to his charismatic turning of the tide against the National Front racism of the 1980s, when attacks on cemeteries and offensive graffiti were rife. The organization SOS Racisme, fronted by the media-friendly Monsieur Désir, celebrates the nation's multiculturalism with its simple logo, a yellow palm daubed with the words *Touche pas à mon pote* ('hands off my mate'). What could otherwise have led to inner-city rioting has become a cause for partying in the streets, with jeering mob culture subdued by a cheering mass of humanity

Thank you for the music

Question: How does a politician transcend party lines to become a national institution? Answer: He gets the country singing. As corny as it may sound, in 1982 the then Minister for Culture, Jack Lang, did just that. Today, the Fête de la Musique that he founded is almost as important a part of summer as Bastille Day. Both amateurs and professionals alike stage 10,000 free concerts across the country, with many famous musicians returning to their home towns for the night of 21 June. In Paris, salsa bands and accordionists mingle with crowds, orchestras perform outside the Palais Royal, rock stars fill the place République and indie bands take over place Denfert-Rochereau. In every other city, town and village, musicians claim every spare paving stone and café terraces become stages for a night.

Cheeseman vs. the world

France loves a hero, especially if he has a moustache and speaks for the working man. So when sheep farmer and Roquefort cheesemaker Jose Bove led a protest against a fast-food outlet in 1999 he was hailed as a popular hero. Since the nation holds dear traditional country cuisine, it was unlikely to welcome the spread of fast-food restaurants. Bove soon became a national icon and his pronouncements on a range of issues, from genetically modified crops to globalization, are readily reported by the media. Despite appearing in the dock for his beliefs and militant actions, Bove is one farmer who hardly needs to knock on the door if he wants to speak to the prime minister.

Black Spartacus

Two hundred years after he was jailed, France has paid tribute to its first black general and leader of the world's first successful black revolt against slavery. A memorial has been erected at the Château de Joux prison, where Toussaint Louverture, who was born a slave, died in 1803. A founding father of Haiti, he earned the name Louverture after winning several cities for France on St-Domingue, for which he was proclaimed Governor for Life in 1801. He declared slavery illegal but was arrested for alleged treachery and taken to prison in France. Popularly hailed as the 'Black Spartacus', Toussaint Louverture is remembered with other freedom campaigners in the Franche-Comté region and the prison where he died is on the so-called Abolitionist Road along which lie the towns of Pontarlier and Champagney, which formally condemned slavery in 1789.

High-speed TGV trains (above) link cities across France

Marseille's busy streets (above) contrast with the slower pace of village life (left)

A brimstone butterfly on a flower in the Auvergne (right)

Urban vs. Rural

The day the sheep came to town

Spring sees the *transhumance*, when shepherds take their flocks from winter to summer grazing grounds. As the sheep are driven through the narrow streets of historic towns, it is a time for thanksgiving, music and wine. From little known Vaucluse villages such as Jonquières to more established visitor destinations including St-Rémy-de-Provence and ski resorts in the Alps, thousands of sheep, dogs, donkeys and shepherds parade along the streets. Mass is said, tambourines are shaken and copious quantities of wine are quaffed until the animals are well on their way. Then, in autumn, the locals get ready for the return journey.

The arrival of the TGV (super-fast trains) cut journey times for travel around France. But move from the city to the countryside and your journey will still be measured in decades not hours. While cities such as Lille, Lyon, Toulouse and Montpellier vie with each other to outdo Paris as the ultimate contemporary city, away from the urban buzz, rural France eschews the cult of internationalism, choosing instead a celebration of all things rural. People of all generations nod and bid each other a friendly *bonjour* or *bonsoir* when passing in the street or when entering a shop. Of course time does leave its mark, and those same fast trains that are making France smaller are nudging away at those differences. Paris is now only three hours from the Mediterranean, and as the local rail networks link up with TGVs, city families are finding it increasingly easy and attractive to leave behind the cosmopolitan life and move to the country. These families are buying houses in the country not simply for weekends and holidays (a trend which had seriously threatened many rural communities), but as their principal homes. They believe their children will receive a better education away from the metropolis, and so the breadwinner opts for a daily or weekly two-hour commute to the city and staying in a studio pied-à-terre, while the rest of the family lives the country life.

Hectic traffic on the Champs-Élysées, in Paris (left)

The Camargue's distinctive white horses (below)

A graffiti-covered mailbox in Paris (below)

14 July festivities

Nothing highlights the difference between small country towns and big cities more than the different regional ways to celebrate the national holiday, Bastille Day, on 14 July. Paris lets its hair down with plenty of *bals publics* (free parties) hosted by the city's firemen, and in principal towns around France fireworks light up the sky. However, in smaller towns the French Revolution knows its place, with local celebrations taking precedence. Villages in the *département* of Gard celebrate the feast of Volo Biou, with dramatic processions based on the legend of a flying cow. The Hippodrome de Pompadour racecourse forsakes horses to become enamoured of an ass as the people of Corrèze celebrate the Day of the Donkey. Meanwhile at the ponds of St-André-le-Bouchoux, a lavish dinner-dance rounds off the annual frog fishing competition.

A stroll with your snorkel

Ten per cent of France is protected parkland. However, should you fancy a ramble in the park of Port Cros, opposite Toulon, in a unique corner of Provence, don't forget your snorkel. The nature trail here, in Europe's most unusual national park, takes visitors underwater more than a third of a mile along the seabed. This 687 hectare (1,700 acre) island nestles in amazingly clear waters and was designated as a national park in 1963, with the protected zone extending around the coast, some 600m (654 yards) out to sea. Signposted visitor trails continue from the island's pathways down into the unspoiled waters and to protect the wildlife, boats are not allowed to moor on the sandy beaches. Underwater guided tours from La Palud beach are free, but you should bring your own snorkel.

Beware of the beast

Just when parents in Auvergne had finally got the children to sleep after 300 years, out came a movie about the legendary Beast of Gévaudan. For city folk, the gory film *Brotherhood of the Wolf* (2001) was just a gothic yarn, but locals still talk in hushed whispers about the creature that devoured at least 100 women and children between July 1764 and June 1767. The attacks were so vicious that the beast makes the Hound of the Baskervilles seem like a playful puppy. Yet, more than 200 years after his notorious reign of terror, little is known about the Beast. Werewolf or madman? Or simply the result of mass hysteria? City scepticism and legend are explored in a *son-et lumière* (sound and light show) at the Musée Fantastique de la Bête du Gévaudan, at Saugues.

An original gallery

You don't need an urban gallery to create a contemporary art space, just a castle, a park and the help of a countess. At Drulon, in the heart of the Centre-Val-de-Loire, Piet and Nanou Hendriks have transformed their chateau into a space to rival any city gallery. In 1998, the chateau and grounds were run down and overgrown, so the Hendriks married the skills of avant-garde artists with those of respected gardeners, such as Countess Alix de Saint-Venant, who designed the classical rose gardens and neatly laid-out formal borders. You haven't seen a water feature until you come across the strange figures rising through the marsh mists here. Nor will any other parterre or rose garden have prepared you for the lifelike figures created by Martine Salavize and Djanashvili Amiran emerging from bushes and wetlands.

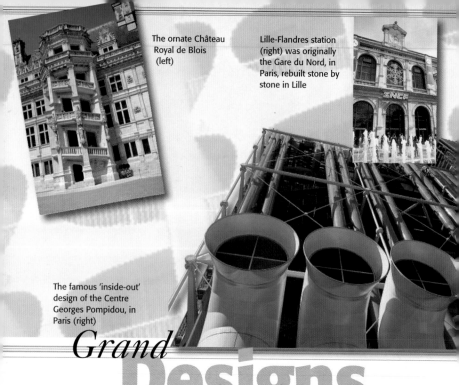

The ornate Château Royal de Blois (left)

Lille-Flandres station (right) was originally the Gare du Nord, in Paris, rebuilt stone by stone in Lille

The famous 'inside-out' design of the Centre Georges Pompidou, in Paris (right)

Grand Designs

More than a pinch of salt

Modern presidential and mayoral schemes may be better known, but grand-scale utopian visions have been around for years. Listed by UNESCO, yet still hardly featuring among the best-known attractions in the land, are the royal salt works at Arc-et-Senans. It's hard to believe that Claude-Nicolas Ledoux's beautiful classical architecture was actually an industrial plant, but this monument, built between 1775 and 1779, was used to extract salt from the water from the old mines of Salins les Bains. The Saline Royale was more than merely a factory—it was a template for a new utopian city, a vision of town planning, centuries ahead of its time.

In most European countries and in the US, political leaders keep a close eye on the polls and an ear open for the latest whisper of public opinion. But in the 20th century, some French presidents preferred to listen out for the reverberation of posterity and instigated grand-scale projects with which their names would be associated long after any election result was forgotten. They thus followed the tradition set by the great French kings and emperors. Louis XIV dotted the country with buildings reflecting the glory of the Sun King and Napoleon commissioned an imperial statue on top of a column to commemorate his successful invasion of Britain, long before he called off the planned attack. So, after Charles de Gaulle's La Défense and President Georges Pompidou's Beaubourg, was it any wonder that François Mitterrand should have ended his reign with a cornucopia of *Grands Projets* that redrew the map of Paris in a manner hardly seen since Baron Haussmann laid out the boulevards? The Pyramid of the Louvre, the Opéra Bastille and the national library that bears his name ensure that the word Mitterrand becomes part of the city itself. How long before a Métro station is renamed?

The huge station clock at the Musée d'Orsay, in Paris (right)

20th-century pyramids at the Louvre (right)

The glistening stained glass of Paris's Sainte-Chapelle, commissioned by St. Louis in the 13th century (below right)

The mammoth Grande Arche, one of Paris's newest monuments (below)

Too much design?

The 21st century is the era of the designer hotel. Where once it was enough to have French designer Philippe Starck come up with a new chair or waiters' uniforms, France's newest hotels vie for the most outrageous concepts. In traditional Nice, the palatial elegance of the Negresco has a new rival in Matali Crassel's multiconcept Hi-hôtel on avenue des Fleurs, where you can choose the space that best suits your mood and personality. You can take a shower behind a plant screen in a room with an indoor terrace theme, relax on furniture created from computer monitors or sing along to the Sofablaster with its built-in music. Other options include a bathroom with lava rock-pool and, for total luxury, a champagne vending machine.

Ideas above their station

As the TGV stretches its superfast way across the country, linking up with similar high-speed rail networks in Germany, Belgium and Spain, the arrival of a dedicated rail station in each town and city is cause for celebration. When Rem Koolhaas created the futuristic Europe quarter in Lille, with its famous 'ski-boot' Credit Lyonnais skyscraper above the station, it was a case of history repeating itself. The old Flandres station along the road was in fact the original Gare du Nord from Paris, donated to the town when the 19th-century railway reached Lille. The people of Lille were unimpressed by the capital's hand-me-downs and commissioned a second level to the façade.

Antigone without the antagonism

When a city has a thousand years of cultural integration, building a brand new district risks upsetting the equilibrium of the place. France, like many other countries, has its share of the snaking concrete blight that mars the outskirts of many decent towns, creating social divisions and losing its lustre after just a couple of rainy winters. It helps when the architect and the politician creating the dream share the same vision. Thus architect Riccardo Bofill was perfectly able to reflect the harmonious aims of Mayor Georges Freche in his grand scale Antigone district, which spills out of the Roman, medieval and Belle-Époque heart of Montpellier into a high-tech homage to classical harmony. The district, with its Ancient Greek-style lines and curves on an epic scale, is built for the future but celebrates the past.

Upstaging nature

The end of the 20th century saw a plethora of building projects with grand ideals. Surely the most ambitious must have been the dream of upstaging real volcanoes. The stunning green, panoramic landscape of the Auvergne is a living legacy to the great volcanoes that shaped the region. The Parc des Volcans has long been a well-loved spot for those wishing to escape into lush and vibrant nature, but now man goes beyond nature with Vulcania, European Park of Volcanism, on a 57-hectare (141 acre) site at St-Ours-les-Roches. Here you can take a trip along simulated lava flows, burning rivers and ground that appears to crack beneath your feet. The attraction also presents a tour of the world's most beautiful volcanoes and even re-creates momentous events like the eruption of Mount St-Helens in Washington state in May 1980.

A market stall in La Rochelle (above).
A traditional French bakery (far right).
A road sign to delight wine-lovers (below)

Fresh oysters (above)

Dijon is famous for its mustard (below)

Wine and Food

Food and wine are not merely important to the French, they define the nation, its regions and its people. At its most simple level, the fresh produce of a village or a region is the essence of communication. Every wedding, confirmation, harvest festival or good-news day is likely to be celebrated with the uncorking of a bottle of the district's finest, be it champagne in Champagne, wine in the south or a potent calvados in Normandy, served with the pick or catch of the day. On the coast, this might be a *bruscade* (seafood barbecue), in the east perhaps plums and *charcuterie* (cooked pork meat). The best way to get to the heart of a region is to visit during one of the many hundreds of local food and wine festivals. The bonus is that an olive festival, for example, is as much an excuse for the makers of cheeses, wines, pâtés and jams for miles around to offer tastings in the streets as for the olive growers to sell their oils and soaps. Food is the great equalizer in this republic, with budget, not class, determining who eats where. The rich may be able to afford to dine out every night of the year, but even those on low incomes will appreciate the rarer treat of a fine meal at a good restaurant. A gastronomic menu of five, six or seven courses in a decent restaurant may be beyond the budget of many, but the same establishment's inexpensive set *menu du terroir*, using good local ingredients, will be no less carefully considered and prepared.

One man and his melons

Cavaillon, in the Vaucluse region, is the heart of melon country. One man who has more than a passing respect for the rich succulent summer fruit is restaurateur Jean-Jacques Prévot. Not only does it feature on every menu from mid-May until the end of September (try the melon cocotte with lobster), but it is the heart of a local aperitif, *délice de melon*. Monsieur Prévot even makes paint from the pips and skins and these contribute to the restaurant's exhibition of 600 melon-related arts and crafts. The town itself hosts an annual melon parade in July, with music in the streets and melon tasting late into the night.

A foie gras sign in
Cahors (below)

Advertising cheese in Roquefort-sur-Soulzon
(above) and wine in St-Émilion (left)

Open-air eating in Agen (below)

A market stand (above)
in Caudebec-en-Caux

Vine therapy

Au revoir lettuce leaves,
adieu pills and potions,
and *bonjour* and
bienvenue to the grape
and its bounty. Doctors
may concede that a
glass of red wine can
be beneficial, but in
Bordeaux locals extol
the virtue of a bathtub
full of grapey goodness
for true well-being.
Vinothérapie is a system
of anti-ageing and
slimming treatments
based on vine and wine
extracts, in particular
grape seed polyphenols.
The first *vinothérapie*
facility, in the heart of
the Graves vineyards,
opened in 2000 and
has inspired imitators
at deluxe spas. Half-day
or week-long pampering
sessions are available
and after a grapeseed
Jacuzzi in a barrel
bath or a wine and
honey wrap, you
may feel ready to
sample the stuff in the
region's vineyards and
wine cellars.

Basque-ing in chocolate country

The town that gave the
world the bayonet and
some of France's most
celebrated cured hams,
Bayonne, was the
unlikely sanctuary for
Jews fleeing the
Spanish Inquisition. In
return, the grateful
refugees offered France
the gift of chocolate.
The delights of the
confection were
unknown on the French
side of the Pyrenees
until the arrival of the
refugees in the capital
of the French Basque
country, and people still
come to Bayonne to
taste the treats
introduced by these
Jewish chocolatiers. At
quaint tea rooms on
rue Neuf, chocolate is
most popularly enjoyed
as a mid-morning or
mid-afternoon snack.
However, the genteel
nibble makes way
for several days of
chocoholic over-
indulgence during the
annual Chocolate
Festival in midsummer.

A Provençal Christmas

If you dine out in
Provence at the end of
December you'll find
that Christmas dinner is
both a sweet and
savoury occasion. The
table is decked with
symbolism and tradition
in mind. The *Gros
Souper* (Big Supper) on
Christmas Eve is one
of the South's most
cherished rituals. With
its 13 desserts, the
meal is known for its
abundance of sweets
and, paradoxically, for its
so-called austerity.
Dishes include modest
marinated vegetables,
anchoïade (anchovy
paste), salt-cod and
escargots à l'aioli (snails
in garlic), through to the
finale of a spread of
platters representing
Christ and the apostles,
with nougats, nuts and
raisins, and plenty of
fruit dishes, from
delicious figs to sweet
confits (candied fruits).
The table is draped with
three white cloths and
set with bowls and
candles symbolizing
the Holy Trinity.

Floral bouquets

You know you have
probably had enough to
drink when you see
roses blooming in
January. Burgundy's
greatest wine festival
takes place in midwinter,
as one of the legendary
villages around the wine
town of Beaune hosts
the annual St-Vincent
Tournante. It is the
festival that rotates, not
the patron saint of
winegrowers, as each of
the 50 villages takes its
turn in hosting the
prestigious event. A
cuvée speciale is
created for the occasion
and then poured freely
into the glasses of the
thousands of visitors
who wander through the
streets. Visitors and
locals enjoy two days
of some of the finest
wines in the region, all
for the price of a wine
glass. While the wine-
makers are preparing
the vintages, children
spend weeks making
imitation flowers for the
village gardens to
give the winter event
the appeal of a
summer celebration.

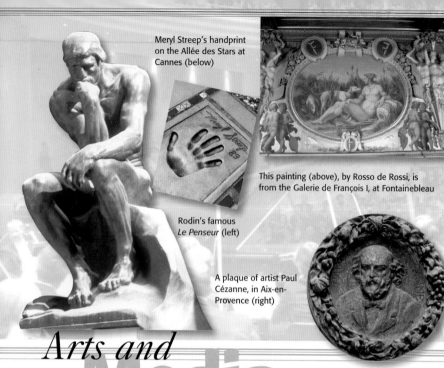

Meryl Streep's handprint on the Allée des Stars at Cannes (below)

This painting (above), by Rosso de Rossi, is from the Galerie de François I, at Fontainebleau

Rodin's famous *Le Penseur* (left)

A plaque of artist Paul Cézanne, in Aix-en-Provence (right)

Arts and Media

The Europa Jazz Festival, in Le Mans (below)

Reims' season

Around 120 free concerts throughout July and August make Reims a very special place in summer. The Flâneries Musicales d'Été, established in 1990 by Yehudi Menuhin, provide many of the season's true delights. Events take place in parks and public spaces around the city, with international performers such as Montserrat Caballe, Helen Merrill and Wilhelmenia Fernandez among the legends topping the bill in recent years. As effervescent as the fizz that made the city famous, the event offers an eclectic selection of concerts. You can expect to find jazz in a park, baroque on the street corner or even George Gershwin being sung on the cathedral steps.

When the Canadian pianist and singer Diana Krall played Paris in 2001, the concert became a best-selling album and video, seen by millions. When she played Montauban in summer 2002, it made the local paper and was a fantastic piano accompaniment to excellent local wines. France embraces the arts and so the world's artists return the compliment, with even the smallest town's art gallery offering a spectacular surprise. A village church in Limousin might have unheralded stained-glass windows by Marc Chagall, simply because the artist liked the place, just as a classical music festival in the heart of Perigord might attract a dozen world class soloists. The same season that Diana Krall came to play, you might have seen opera's golden couple Roberto Alagna and Angela Gheorghiu in Orange in Provence. The following summer offered the British band Supergrass in a field in Brittany and Elton John in the Roman arena at Nîmes. The high point of the arts year is the Avignon festival, when the world's art critics decamp to the walled city to report on what will be making headlines in Paris in the year to come, with each hotel lobby commandeered by the media as makeshift TV studios.

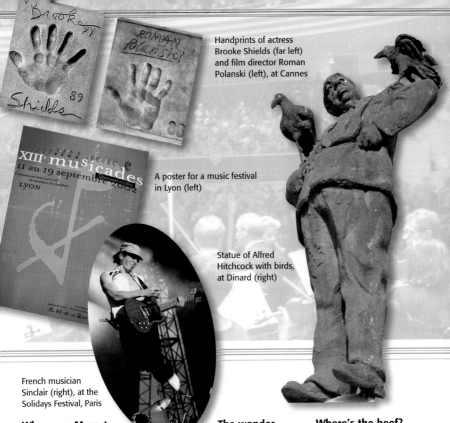

Handprints of actress Brooke Shields (far left) and film director Roman Polanski (left), at Cannes

A poster for a music festival in Lyon (left)

Statue of Alfred Hitchcock with birds, at Dinard (right)

French musician Sinclair (right), at the Solidays Festival, Paris

When one Mozart is not enough

Some people can never have too much sun, nor too much Mozart. Thus Provence in summer reverberates to the sound of popular arias in historic settings. To add to Provence's festivals of music, such as the pageantry of Orange's epic productions and concerts at Aix-en-Provence's open-air theatre in the grounds of the Archbishop's palace, a new venue arrived in 2002, when fashion designer Pierre Cardin launched his own opera festival in the ruins of Château Lacoste. The opening star-studded production was Mozart's condemnation of loose morals and licentiousness, *Don Giovanni*. This was apt because the chateau's most famous resident before Pierre Cardin was the Marquis de Sade.

Getting ready to rock

While many children have to make do with a poster on the bedroom wall and a sticker on an exercise book, their French cousins are inducted into the world of live popular music at a young age. France hosts Europe's premier outdoor rock festival aimed squarely at the under 12s. Rockyssimômes is a day-long music event for children whose tastes run more towards Glastonbury than computer games. About 6,000 youngsters turn up at Sable-sur-Sarthe every July for six hours of rock and world music, face painting and even an open-mike session. Rockyssimômes is now in its 22nd year and its security and supervision have been honed to a fine art.

The wonder of wood

If you go down to the woods around the Alpine destination of Les Gets in midsummer, you'll be sure of a big surprise. The skis and snowboards are stacked away for the winter and the resort turns its attention to the arts. But it's macho arts for the true outdoors type, as Les Gets hosts the French National Chainsaw Sculpting Championships. There's music and drama extolling the glories of wood, and you can revel in the one true art form for the tattoo and plaid-shirt set, when real lumber reigns supreme with Billes de Bois, a festival of the wonder of wood. Highlights include the chainsaw art battle, a game of Mikado played with huge painted telegraph poles and exhibitions of wood-carving staged in village streets and shops.

Where's the beef?

More vegetarians are venturing into the abattoirs of France than ever before. Perhaps it has something to do with city slaughterhouses turning away from carcasses in preference for the arts. Just as the meat-packing and processing halls of Calais are being turned into performance spaces, so the former abattoirs of Toulouse are bringing culture vultures to the left bank of the Garonne. Les Abattoirs is an exciting modern art gallery devoted to the second half of the 20th century and housed in Urbain Vitry's former slaughterhouses. Inside there's no meat, but rather 2,000 works by 667 artists from 44 countries. From a slightly earlier period than the main collection, the gallery displays Pablo Picasso's massive stage backdrop from Romain Rolland's *14 Juillet*.

White-water rafting (right)

The traditional Basque game of *pelota* (left)

The arduous Tour de France bicycle race (below)

Activities and Sport

Even as the bid went in to stage the 2012 Olympic Games, and long before the first beach volley-ball match took place under the Eiffel Tower, France based its Olympic hopes around the hosting of another world class sporting event. The Stade de France in St-Denis, Paris, built for the 1998 soccer World Cup, was the setting for the 2003 World Athletics Championships. The 2,000 athletes stayed in the players' village near the Parc de Montsouris, and journeyed to their events on the excellent bus and Métro system used by half a million spectators. When France hosts (and wins) major sporting events, the world soon knows about it, thanks to the sounds of car horns blaring down the Champs-Élysées. But one-off events apart, the nation has a packed sporting calendar, with the Le Mans 24-hour race and the French Open tennis tournament at Roland Garros the best-known summer events. The Tour de France brings with it its own road show, making every stage of the route a day to remember for visitors. Likewise, when it's Burgundy's turn for Formula One, around 100,000 spectators turn up at Magny-Cours. Golf is a popular participatory game and rugby and horse-racing are the principal topics of conversation at the *Bar des Sports* in every town. Out of season, fans are not averse to trying other sports. Thus, Toulouse hosts the Paintball World Cup and Biarritz swaps high-fashion for wetsuits and a surfboard as the international surfing set hit the Bay of Biscay.

Rugby in the fast lane

Rugby-mad southwest France has used top international players to lure drivers off the *autoroutes* in peak holiday season. Just as free jazz concerts, massages and baby changing facilities have persuaded motorists in central France to take a break every two hours, so Sporting Stopovers at 18 rest areas on the *autoroutes* in the south have been organized by athletes and the national Olympic committee to ensure cars pull over for a while. So, instead of a sandwich and comfort break, motorists have been treated to exhibition rugby matches at Narbonne, a chance to try their hands at kendo at Montelimar, tennis at St-Rambert d'Albon on the A7 *autoroute* and canoeing alongside the A61 at Port-Lauragais.

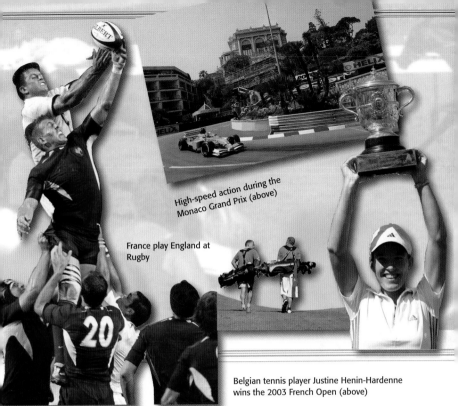

High-speed action during the Monaco Grand Prix (above)

France play England at Rugby

Belgian tennis player Justine Henin-Hardenne wins the 2003 French Open (above)

Paragliding with donkeys

Question: What do you get when you cross a donkey with a parachute? Answer: Les Randonnées Paramules. The donkey has long been the rambler's friend, with much of the countryside open for exploration by walkers accompanied by a faithful pack-mule. The newest adventure for the donkeys and their guests is paramuling. Fear not, for the donkeys keep four hooves firmly on the ground—they simply carry the paragliding kit up to the least accessible crannies of the mountains so that sportsmen and women can make the most spectacular dives. As sensation-seekers skim the skies over the dramatic scenery of the alpine Portes du Soleil area, best known for its winter sports resorts including Avoriaz and Morzine, the donkeys walk back to base.

Bicyclists on the right track

For three weeks each summer, the nation is gripped by the thrill of the Tour de France. However, France's love of two-wheeled travel is a year-round affair. In 2003, Aquitaine launched a pilot scheme to create a sporting resort designed for bicyclists, along the lines of the mountain ski villages. Créon, which is among the vines of Entre-Deux-Mers and just 20 minutes from Bordeaux, has green, blue and red routes depending on the skill level of the bicyclist, with the main tourist office and bicyclists' rendezvous in Créon's former railway station. To get there, a stretch of disused railway line 56km (35 miles) long has been turned into a cycle route with seven former stations serving as rest areas and restaurants.

Jousting on water

Forget medieval re-enactments—the sport of jousting is alive and thriving on the waterways of Languedoc-Roussillon. Horses are unnecessary as the combatants ride on opposing boats, lances and shields at the ready, to do battle and topple the loser into the water. While many summer challenges take place in towns and villages along the coastline, the sport's principal home is on the busy canals of the port of Sète, where water jousting has existed since Roman times and the present sport dates back to 1666. Hand-painted wooden *pavois* are both shields and trophies and local fishermen and dockers take the games very seriously. The season opens on 29 June with weekend skirmishes on brightly painted barges, and ends with the celebrated St-Louis contest in late August.

Stunt of the century

The Tour de France has been going for more than a century, which is not bad for a marketing stunt. Originally staged in 1903 as a campaign to publicize *l'Auto* magazine, the first Tour saw 60 riders covering 2,500km (1,550 miles) over 19 days. There were only six stages however, so riders had to pedal their boneshakers through the night, whereas these days, not only are comfortable hotels provided as standard, but vast tracts of the country are crossed by luxury train or plane between stages. The event has been dogged by tabloid headlines and intrigue almost since the first. Dirty tricks of previous years included nails scattered on the road and allegations of poisoning.

You'll get noticed wearing these shoes (above)

Vivid catwalk designs (left)

Style and Fashion

In bed with Gaultier

Top models won't get out of bed for less than a dazzling fee and in Paris, top shoppers can indulge themselves in the same way. After all, the city is as AbFab as you can get (the French were the first to turn the cult British TV series into a big screen movie). Instead of braving the crowds, fashionistas can sip champagne and browse the designer aisles of Printemps department store from the comfort of their hotel bed, with just a laptop and a credit card. Through the store's website, a personal shopper on roller blades, armed with a webcam, will skate through the racks of Bulgari, Hermès and Gaultier, showing the goods from all angles, so that the buyer never has to stir from the duvet.

Prêt-à-porter shows staged four times a year at the Carrousel du Louvre remind the world what real people will be wearing in the coming season, and the couture shows of Paris Fashion Week reveal what no-one beyond the glare of a flashbulb would even think of wearing. Paris retains its rightful global reputation for chic, and France gets its own ideas as to how to keep one step ahead of the rest of the world. Every year another nation is hailed as the next world leader in fashion, but the glamour and style of the French is never really threatened. After all, when a new *enfant terrible* from outside the borders threatens to steer international attention away from the country, the French fashion houses manage to lure the new talent.

Choccy couture

Between the prêt-à-porter shows and Paris Fashion Week, there is one event where all the critics agree that every item of clothing is good enough to eat. Edible couture is the highlight of the autumn *Salon du Chocolat* at the Carrousel du Louvre, a catwalk show combining the talents and skills of the finest chocolatiers with the city's more daring designers.

In the fast lane

The Champs-Élysées is packed with traffic even in the small hours, but once a month the famous avenue closes to cars. To benefit, pack your in-line skates. Pari-Roller is the social event of the week in Paris, as tens of thousands gather near Montparnasse station on Friday evening. At 10pm the crowd becomes a parade and sets off to explore the city. Strictly for experienced skaters, the route varies each week. Itineraries are posted on the website before the event. Once a month, two hours after the skaters have left the starting point, they turn into place Charles-de-Gaulle for the high-speed descent down the Champs-Élysées.

The Story of France

Gaul, Rome and France

Celtic tribes ruled Gaul from around 1500BC, but they fought each other so much that the Romans had little trouble adding them to the Empire. Julius Caesar's defeat of the Celtic leader Vercingetorix in 52BC consolidated Roman rule and 200 years of peace and prosperity followed. After the fall of the Roman Empire in the 5th century, a Germanic tribe called the Franks overran the country and renamed it Francia. The Merovingian dynasty ruled until the 8th century, with King Clovis making Paris his capital. He converted to Christianity in 497 and extended his influence over the Christian provinces. After Clovis, Merovingian power declined and it was the turn of the Carolingian kings to rise to power. In 754, Pepin the Short took the throne, although it was his son, Charlemagne, who became one of the most remarkable men in the history of France. His reign lasted for almost 40 years, during which time he advanced his country's culture and military power. In 800 he was crowned Holy Roman Emperor by the Pope, ruling territory equivalent to present-day Germany and France. But this golden age did not last: Squabbles among Charlemagne's heirs split the Empire and the provincial counts and bishops appointed by Charlemagne became increasingly powerful. When the last Carolingian king died in 987, the counts elected one of their own as king, Hugh Capet, the founder of the dynasty that dominated France well into the Middle Ages.

Vercingetorix or Asterix?

Vercingetorix is a French national hero, symbolizing resistance to tyranny. He led an uprising against the Romans in 52BC but was eventually captured and put to death in Rome by Julius Caesar. The legendary scene of Vercingetorix laying his arms at Caesar's feet is a key moment in French history, but in the hugely popular *Asterix* cartoon, Vercingetorix drops the lot with a clatter on Caesar's big toe and the Emperor hops about shrieking. In fact, René Goscinny and Albert Uderzo, the creators of Asterix, based their anarchic little hero on Vercingetorix. French myth has it that Vercingetorix (pictured below) escaped a terrible death in Rome and stayed behind to make life difficult for the occupiers, incidentally becoming a symbol of the French Resistance.

190BC

A statue of a Roman warrior at Vaison-la-Romaine (above)

Relief carving on a building in Arles (above).
A Celtic chieftain (right)

Crossing the Rubicon

Once Julius Caesar had subdued Gaul in 52BC, he was Governor of the whole province and a powerful man. Three years later, he was forced to take the greatest decision of his life—whether to stay, or leave Gaul and conquer his rival, Pompey, for control of the Roman Empire. Caesar gathered a force to invade and as he drew nearer to the Rubicon river, which separated Gaul from Italy, he went more slowly and his doubts grew. He ordered a halt as he could not decide what to do—stay where he was or risk everything. Then, with the famous words, 'Let the die be cast', he crossed the river. Caesar left the fledgling state of Gaul behind him and went into Italy.

Julius Caesar (below)

Urbicus, Bishop of Clermont-Ferrand c.AD250

Conversion to Christianity brought its own struggles and temptations for Urbicus, from a Roman senatorial family and the first Bishop of Clermont-Ferrand. After his conversion, he and his wife decided to live apart, in religious contemplation. But growing tired of this restraint, the Bishop's wife ran to his church and started banging on the doors, demanding her conjugal rights. Urbicus let her in and she stayed the night. When Urbicus discovered that his wife was pregnant he was horrified and retreated to a monastery to ask forgiveness for his sin. But all went well as his new daughter became a nun like her mother, the bishop returned to his post, and in death they were all united by being buried in the same crypt.

Charlemagne (far right) and his horn (right)

Charlemagne and the fasting bishop

A truly great king, Charlemagne chastized by example rather than punished outright. A bishop once criticized him for eating early each day in Lent, which was not strictly allowed. Keeping calm, Charlemagne told the bishop he was right, but then informed him that he would be the last person to be served during his stay at the palace. The bishop had to wait until the nobles, the commanders, the courtiers and the officials had all been served, before he was finally given his food. After many hungry days, Charlemagne asked the bishop, 'Do you now understand that I eat early not from greed, but in consideration for those who have to wait?'

Carolingian miniscule

Charlemagne tried hard to learn how to write but he left it very late. So it is extraordinary that the form of writing we still use today owes its existence to him. Until about AD800, writing was all in capital letters with no punctuation and with the words all running together, which created a great deal of confusion. Under guidance from his teacher, Alcuin, Charlemagne set up writing schools in the monasteries. There, the monks developed Carolingian miniscule—capital and lower case letters, punctuation and separated words—the form of script you are reading at this moment. The monks had to practise their new skills on something, and it's thanks to the writing schools that 90 per cent of the Latin works we have now survived at all.

AD987

The exterior of Les Arènes in Nîmes (above).
The Pont du Gard is a masterpiece of Roman design and engineering (left)

The Roman arena in Nîmes, Les Arènes (left), is still used for perfomances

GAUL, ROME AND FRANCE 29

The Middle Ages

The kings of the new Capetian dynasty had little real power and did not venture much beyond their stronghold of the Île de France. William of Normandy became their rival when he conquered England in 1066, and the marriage of Eleanor of Aquitaine to Henry II of England in 1152 provoked territorial wars that lasted for 300 years. However, the Capets gradually came to dominate France through a network of marriages and treaties. The Crusades, instituted in 1095 by Pope Urban II, benefited the dynasty when an internal crusade, the Albigensian Heresy, allowed them to crush their opponents in southern France.

Many of the great cathedrals of France were constructed in the 13th century, the University of Paris opened and the country prospered. However, the 14th century witnessed the twin disasters of the Black Death (1348–49), which killed 30 per cent of the population, and the Hundred Years War (1337–1453), provoked by English claims to the French throne, a legacy of Eleanor of Aquitaine's marriage. The war went badly for the French and by 1422 Henry IV had been crowned King of France in Paris. Joan of Arc turned the fortunes of France, but was betrayed by Charles VII, who eventually drove the English out by 1453.

987

A sea battle during the Hundred Years War (left).
King Henry IV (below)

A miraculous cure for baldness
Bernard, a nobleman of the Auvergne, lost his hair after an illness and was so ashamed that he hid himself away. Around the year 1000, St. Foy came to him in a dream and told him to go to her shrine in Conques. She told Bernard to stand on the left side of the shrine and wait until the abbot had finished his prayers and washed his hands. The abbot would then wash Bernard's head with the water. Putting his faith in this dream, Bernard rushed to Conques where the abbot refused to do anything so silly. But Bernard wouldn't leave and the abbot gave in. Legend has it, the next day Bernard's head was covered in shiny curls.

French knights embark on a crusade (above)

'The Fortress of Faith' (right), defended against heretics by the Pope and his bishops

A carved medieval head (far right) on the Batelle Europe building in Troyes

The rules of courtly love

Eleanor of Aquitiane and her daughter Marie de Champagne had a great influence on the medieval notions of love, some which are still with us today. Troubadours at their courts in the south of France wrote the first romantic love poems. Courts were full of young, unmarried men, so elaborate rules of love were imposed to restrain them. A knight was supposed to love his lady with the same feudal obedience he paid his lord.

Since noble marriages were dynastic, affairs were common, but usually chaste.

Eleanor of Aquitaine (below) married Henry II of England

The popes at Avignon 1309–1418

After years of violence at the hands of the citizens of Rome, the pope fled to the safety of Avignon in 1309, after an invitation from King Philip, who lusted after papal money and influence on French soil. The popes lived in a fortress-like palace, which the poet Petrarch called 'a sewer where all the filth of the universe had gathered', and by 1377 the court was so threatened by thieves and swindlers that Gregory XI returned to Rome. The sovereigns of Europe then sponsored their own candidates, and by 1414, there was the spectacle of three popes, each vying for pre-eminence. The prelates of the Sorbonne, among others, put a stop to this, and in 1418 a sole pope again sat in Rome.

Joan of Arc's arrival at the Château de Chinon in 1428 (right). The Great Seal of William the Conqueror (below)

Christine de Pisan 1365–c.1430

Christine de Pisan was an Italian lady widowed in Paris in 1390. She had a family to support and, daringly for the time, decided to make her living by writing. She produced biographies, histories and poetry, all on a heroic scale. De Pisan soon gathered a list of wealthy patrons and became one of the most popular writers in France. As the lone female voice of the time, she protected women from attacks by male writers, particularly in the debate on *The Romance of the Rose*, a famously misogynistic poem. 'Why do you hate women?' she asked simply. 'You have mothers and wives. Are they evil?'

Joan of Arc

A peasant girl called Joan wrote to the King of England in 1429 with breathtaking confidence and in the words of a born leader: 'Duke of Bedford, who call yourself the regent of France for the King of England, the Maid asks you not to make her destroy you,' she said. Joan of Arc broke down the boundaries of gender and class, in an age when women were subservient to men. But a more creative act of hers was the idea of patriotism. She gave her country a sense of itself as a nation. 'You have no rights in France from God,' she lectured Bedford, '…go home to your own country.' As Europe emerged from the Middle Ages others followed her example.

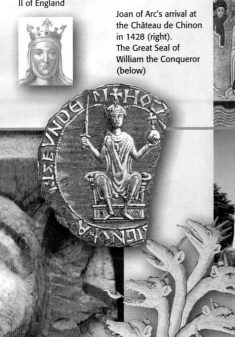

1453

Construction of the Château de Luynes (above) began in the 11th century

Detail (left) of one of the *Tapestries of the Apocalypse*, commissioned in the 14th century and now in the museum at the Château d'Angers

The Renaissance

France's long war with Italy lasted from 1494 to 1559 and was an attempt to curb the power of the Habsburg Empire. It had one fortunate result: the splendid influx of ideas and art from the Italian Renaissance. The kings of the time, especially François I, imported artists and architects, sculptures, jewels and paintings to add to the glory of the French monarchy. Some of France's finest chateaux, books and paintings were created during this period. Alongside this spectacular flowering of culture, Protestantism grew quickly after the Reformation of the 1530s. It was strengthened by the influence of the exiled John Calvin, and became a powerful force in the country. Catholic-Protestant wars, eight in all between 1562 and 1598, soon split the state, and their cruelty and violence brought it to breaking point. One of the worst incidents was the Massacre of St. Bartholomew's Eve of 1572, when nearly 3,000 Protestants were murdered in Paris and up to 20,000 more throughout the country. After assassinations and the threat of civil war, the troubles started to diminish only when the protestant Henry IV converted to Catholicism to gain entry to Paris in 1593. The Edict of Nantes of 1598, which granted rights and protection to Protestants, brought about an uneasy truce.

Bronze of a stag held at bay by four dogs at the entrance to Château d'Anet (right)

François Rabelais

In his fantasy novels *Gargantua* and *Pantagruel*, recounting the adventures of a father and son, comic genius François Rabelais symbolizes the energy of the French Renaissance. As a doctor, monk, writer and student of botany, astrology, philosophy, archaeology and history, who invented new devices for setting fractures while creating two immortal characters in world literature, Rabelais was Renaissance man. His novels are funny and raunchy, but more importantly they come out of the Humanist tradition of the times and are daring in their criticism of the Church and the powerful. No-one was spared from his satire and in the process he wrote some of the greatest works in French literature.

1453

Château de Chenonceau, in the Loire (above)

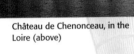

Catherine de Medici (right; 1519–89) married the future King Henri II of France

Visitors stroll through the formal gardens of Château d'Azay-le-Rideau (right)

Diane de Poitiers

Diane de Poitiers, the mistress and great love of Henri II, was a remarkable woman in looks and mind. In an age when teeth blackened and wrinkles formed early, Diane kept her beauty intact well into her fifties. She was a strong influence on Henri during his reign and was instrumental in ending the war with Italy in 1559. But it was in Henri's relations with his wife, Catherine de Medici, that Diane revealed her true mettle and cunning. On agreed nights, Henri would spend the first hours with his mistress, then go to his wife. After a while with Catherine, Henri would return to his beloved Diane. Catherine, not unreasonably, hated her rival even more.

Leonardo da Vinci in France

François I was a collector of paintings, jewels and chateaux, but his great prize was Leonardo da Vinci. In 1516 the King lured the 70-year-old Leonardo to Amboise, where he treated the artist and inventor with true respect. Leonardo was given a house and a generous pension and, although he was paralysed in his left arm, he designed court entertainments, made drawings, investigated anatomy and the nature of water, and invented machines. He didn't stop until he died, perhaps, as legend has it, in the King's arms. François I certainly had a real affection for the old man and in return received a magnificent gift from Leonardo. He had brought the *Mona Lisa* with him from Italy and it still hangs in the Louvre today.

French cuisine

Great French cuisine owes its existence in part to Catherine de Medici, who brought Florentine chefs to France when she married the Dauphin in 1533. French cooking was still medieval, heavy and limited, but Catherine's chefs used delicate sauces instead of thick spices, refined sugar instead of honey and a wide variety of pastries, vegetables and fowl unknown in France. Catherine also brought the fork, although the French resisted this for a century. She expected richly dressed ladies to join banquets, and set her table with crystal and gold. Under her influence, feasting became a spectacle. Catherine's kinswoman, Marie de Medici, arrived from Italy in 1600, bringing with her the recipe for puff pastry which has resulted in that most famous of French foods, the croissant.

The essayist

Michel de Montaigne (1533–1592) created the essay as a literary form. Born near Bordeaux into a wealthy family, Montaigne was educated in Latin and French as well as the arts. He studied law, and while involved in the Bordeaux *parlement* he was hugely influenced by his friend Etienne La Boétie. Etienne's own work *Discours de la servitude volontaire* is an outspoken attack on absolute monarchy. Le Boétie's death in 1563 in his early 30s troubled Montaigne and in 1570 he moved to the chateau he inherited from his father. There he lived with his wife and started writing his *Essais*. The first collection of essays was published in 1580 and covered an eclectic range of subjects while demonstrating tolerance, wit and wisdom. Montaigne was elected mayor of Bordeaux in 1581. He died at home in 1592.

Portraits (left to right): François I, Leonardo da Vinci, Henry IV and John Calvin (below)

1598

The St. Bartholomew's Eve Massacre (below), when thousands of Protestants were killed

J. CALVIN

Grand Siècle

This period was dominated by two great men, Cardinal Richelieu (1585–1642), minister to Louis XIII, and the Sun King himself, Louis XIV (ruled 1643–1715). Richelieu set about centralizing power under the monarch. He crushed a revolt by Louis XIII's brother, destroyed the Protestant stronghold of La Rochelle and tried to protect France's borders. His wars with Holland, Austria and England continued throughout the 17th century. Richelieu built up the navy and the textile industry, creating a vibrant economy.

Louis XIV was fortunate to be served by a brilliant finance minister, Jean-Baptiste Colbert (1619–83). He worked to reform France's chaotic tax system and managed to provide the economy with a surplus. Louis spent this freely on his twin obsessions, the Palace of Versailles (the glory of France and the envy of other monarchs who tried to copy it) and foreign wars. However, Louis's belligerence and intolerance did not serve his country well when he revoked the Edict of Nantes in 1685, thereby losing France a huge population of hardworking Protestants. His wars drained the treasury, and although he gained the throne of Spain for his grandson, the ensuing war did not help France's finances. Just two years after the war ended in 1713, Louis died.

Richelieu—the roots of royal power

Cardinal Richelieu was an extraordinary man who laid the foundations of royal authority so ruthlessly perfected by Louis XIV. Richelieu dominated Louis XIII's reign, which still suffered from many of the problems of the medieval monarchy— ambitious nobles, a Catholic Church hungry for power, and belligerent Protestants, the Huguenots. Richelieu set about establishing royal power by crushing the Huguenots and reducing the power of the Church, even making it pay taxes. The popular view, much of it from Alexandre Dumas' novel *The Three Musketeers*, is that Richelieu was a devious and ruthless politician. While this may be true, he also rebuilt the Sorbonne and founded the Académie Française in 1634.

1598

The Neptune fountain, at Versailles (above).
The chateau at Versailles, framed by a fountain (below)

Vaux-le-Vicomte

On 17 August 1661, the young Louis XIV went to a house-warming party at the chateau of his finance minister, Nicolas Fouquet. Vaux-le-Vicomte was a miniature palace, full of gold, silk and fine furniture, where guests received horses and diamond tiaras as gifts. Louis was furious at Fouquet's impertinence and would not tolerate a subject building a power base with public money. The chateau was certainly the model for Versailles, and Louis appropriated the furniture and silver, along with the architect Le Vau, the garden designer Le Nôtre and the painter Le Brun, a brilliant trio. They started work on Versailles immediately, and Louis started to make it clear who was the master of France.

Versailles—a palace fit for the Sun King

When the French think of a palace, they probably think of Versailles. It is the physical embodiment of Louis XIV's iron will, but only his monstrous ego makes sense of it. To build and run Versailles swallowed five per cent of the national tax revenue. Up to 20,000 staff serviced it, with the cooks and the gardeners inheriting their positions, like the princes above them. Marie-Antoinette was mistaken when she treated the palace as a playground; it had been the Sun King's seat of power for nearly 50 years. However, after Louis XIV, Versailles began to lose its power and the mediocre rulers who followed the Sun King could never impose themselves on France as he did.

Louis's friend, Molière

Louis XIV liked and protected the playwright Molière (1622–1673). He funded his plays, was godfather to his son and dined alone with him, which was unheard of at the time. No doubt Molière regarded this with some caution, as Claud le Petit, a writer who satirized the King, had his hand cut off before being burned alive in 1662. When Molière's *Tartuffe* (1664), a satire on hypocrisy, was attacked by the Church and the Queen Mother, he quickly withdrew the play; it was restaged in 1669. Louis appeared unconcerned, but as a consummate politician, he let others do his dirty work—up to 60 censors worked on Molière's plays. The reworked version of *Tartuffe* ends with the King praised to the skies and Molière keeping his hand.

Three dauphins die within a year

At the beginning of 1711, Louis XIV felt that the succession to the throne had never been so secure. His son was in good health and his grandson already had two sons of his own. However, within 12 months three generations would be dead. The Grand Dauphin died first, of smallpox, in April 1711. His son, the new heir to the throne, was a clever young man, well-educated and the great hope of many courtiers, who saw in him a professional politician who might make the country work. However, he succumbed to measles in February 1712, along with his wife and eldest son. A sickly two-year-old child was left, the future Louis XV, who reigned for a long time, but to little effect.

Cardinal Richelieu (left)

The Église du Dôme (below), in Paris, built for Louis XIV

The playwright Molière (left)

Louis XIV (far left)

1715

A procession by knights across the courtyard of the Château de Fontainebleau (above)

Jean-Baptiste Colbert (left), foreign minister to Louis XIV

Revolution and Napoleon

This spectacular era in French history started with the long, stultifying reign of Louis XV (1715–1774). He failed to notice the revolutionary ideas of the Enlightenment espoused by the writer Voltaire (1694–1778) and the philosopher Jean-Jacques Rousseau (1712–1778), or sympathize with a country languishing under a cumbersome, outdated government. Louis fought disastrously expensive wars, and French aid to the Americans in their War of Independence only helped spread ideas of revolution and liberty throughout the country.

Under the hapless Louis XVI (ruled 1774–1793) and Marie-Antoinette, the economy disintegrated and by the time Louis called a meeting of the Estates General in 1789, France was almost ungovernable. Royal authority soon collapsed and a succession of increasingly fanatical groups took control of the ensuing Revolution, with thousands of people executed during the Reign of Terrror in 1794. The more rational Directory followed, but the country was ripe for a coup d'état by the shrewd young soldier, Napoleon Bonaparte. He carried through some of the aims of the Revolution, mainly with the *Code Civil*, but his government was reactionary and dependent on military victories. The French became disillusioned with his Imperial dictatorship when he started losing wars after the Moscow campaign of 1812. His downfall came three years later, and in 1815, Louis XVI's brother, Louis XVIII, was made king.

The Bastille (above).
Jean-Jacques Rousseau (top).
Napoleon's retreat from Moscow (right)

Flying over Versailles

On 19 September 1783, from the courtyard at Versailles, Louis XVI and Marie-Antoinette witnessed one of the first balloon flights, organized by the Montgolfier brothers. The Montgolfiers were paper manufacturers and had only discovered the principles of flight the year before. By 1785, men were flying across the Channel, and balloons floated over France like visitors from the future.

On that day in 1783, 100,000 citizens gathered at Versailles, not to see the King (royal etiquette and grandeur meant little to them), but to witness the powers of freedom and invention, hardly the stuff of the French monarchy. These crowds were sinister forebears of the crowds who arrived at Versailles six years later to put an end to royal authority.

Marie-Antoinette and her follies

The teenage Queen Marie-Antoinette felt stifled by the etiquette of Versailles—she was once left shivering while duchesses squabbled over who had the right to hand the queen her chemise. She rebelled and indulged herself by building a fantasy village, Le Hameau, lined with silk and lit by diamond candelabra, where she played peasant in cotton dresses and straw hats, while cows were led past on ribbons and milked into fine porcelain Sèvres pots. Her excesses were costly but were dwarfed by the cost of wars at the time. Stuffy courtiers were shocked by the Queen's antics and the people ridiculed her by calling her Madame Deficit. She was playing shepherdess while people, not far away on the streets of Paris, were starving to death.

Patriote Palloy and the Bastille

The Fall of the Bastille on 14 July 1789 was the symbolic start of the French Revolution. But in a large country like France, where news still moved slowly, the Revolution needed quick, entertaining propaganda. An enterprising businessman, Pierre-Francois Palloy, hit on the idea of revolutionary kits, objects made from the remains of the Bastille such as keys, medals and models of the prison itself, which could be taken to all corners of the country. 'Apostles of Liberty', unemployed actors, roamed over France, shouting out slogans and revolutionary tales while waving souvenirs from the Bastille in front of the crowd. Its novelty waned when the people had a new spectacle to occupy them—the guillotine.

Code Civil of 1804

This set of laws is Napoleon's enduring achievement, in which he brought about one of the great aims of the Revolution—the equality of all citizens before a rational code of laws. Under the *ancien regime*, laws could vary from region to region, or were simply the will of the monarch. Napoleon ordered the Code to be drawn up in 1800 and it came into effect in 1804. Under his influence, the Code destroyed feudalism and although it ignored the rights of women, it united a France on the verge of anarchy and was exported throughout the Napoleonic Empire. It is a civil, not a criminal, code and is the basis of modern notions of liberty and civil rights throughout much of the Western world.

Madame de Pompadour (far left).
The Montgolfier fire balloon (left).
Philosopher and writer Voltaire (right)

Napoleon Bonaparte (right), the general who became an emperor

1821

The execution of Robespierre (above), a leading Revolutionary who fell out of popularity with the people

Marie-Antoinette (left) and the chateau at Versailles (above left) that she enjoyed with Louis XVI until the Revolution

The 19th Century

This century swung between royalty and Revolution. The Bourbon Louis XVIII and Charles X were caught in the struggles between vengeful monarchists and those determined to maintain the Revolution. Charles's attempts at repression resulted in the Revolution of 1830 and his nephew, the 'Citizen King' Louis-Phillipe took the throne. In turn he was deposed in 1848, the year that revolutions swept Europe. The following presidential elections were won by Louis Napoleon Bonaparte, Napoleon's nephew. In 1851 he proclaimed himself Emperor Napoleon III, but corruption led to instability. War with Prussia in 1870 destroyed both him and the French monarchy. After the agonies of the Commune in 1871, a bloodbath that killed more than 20,000 people, France entered the stable Third Republic and the glorious years of the Belle Époque.

The achievements of this era are magnificent: the Suez Canal, the scientific advances of Pasteur and the establishment of Paris as Europe's capital of pleasure. Worth and Paquin created haute couture, Cesar Ritz invented the luxury hotel, Cartier and Boucheron covered Europe in jewels and Escoffier cooked up the cuisine that, although modified, still dominates. By 1900, France, although no longer the military power of Europe, was the heart of luxury, taste and art.

Napoleon III (left)

1800

Les Misérables

Victor Hugo chronicled 19th-century France the way Charles Dickens chronicled Victorian England, and his best-known novel, *Les Misérables* (1862), still has a hold on the public imagination. It sold out on the first day, plays and films followed, and the musical is still one of the most popular in the world. As with all great stories, it meshes the personal (the struggles of Jean Valjean and Cosette) with the public (the 1830 Revolution). Hugo wrote his book not about the poor, but for them, and in so doing gave them a voice and dignity they did not have in real life. In return they loved him—Hugo's funeral in 1885 was attended by three million people, more than the population of Paris.

Novelist and poet Victor Hugo (below)

Poster advertising winter in Nice (above right).
Cover of *La France* picturebook (right).
Red Republicans barricading the streets in 1848 (below)

The Côte d'Azur

British people of a certain class in the 19th century often went on the Grand Tour in Europe. In 1834, Lord Brougham, a member of the English aristocracy, was forced to spend the night in the village of Cannes and loved the place so much he built a villa there. His wealthy friends soon followed him and over the years British aristocrats opened up the rest of the coast, resulting in a rail line connecting London directly to Menton (via a ferry) by 1868. Royalty were not averse to the Riviera's charms—Queen Victoria spent winters at Nice in the 1890s, away from the chills and fogs of England. Even today there is a little bit of Nice that is forever England—the seafront is named Promenade des Anglais.

The Suez Canal

The first Suez Canal, which opened in 1500BC, was maintained by the Persians and had Cleopatra's barge sailing through its waters. In 1869, the French engineer Ferdinand de Lesseps stood beside Empress Eugénie at the opening of his modern version. It was at the same time a triumph of French engineering and evidence of European imperialism. To make the canal, 2 million cubic metres of earth were dredged by 1.5 million Egyptians, 125,000 of whom died of cholera. The British hated the idea of France owning the Canal, and quickly bought the Egyptian government's shares in 1879, and then moved troops in to guard it in 1882. Only in 1956 did the Egyptian government take control of the canal, after the Suez War.

Life and death by Louis Pasteur

Joseph Meister owed his life and his death to Louis Pasteur. Besides the famous discovery of pasteurisation (the heating of milk to make it safe to drink), Pasteur discovered the cure for rabies in 1885. He had tested it only on dogs when, in July 1886, nine-year-old Joseph came to Pasteur's laboratory, badly mauled by a rabid dog. Joseph's mother pleaded with the reluctant scientist to treat her son. Pasteur eventually agreed, and Joseph made a complete recovery. As Pasteur's fame grew and grew, Joseph remained attached to the Pasteur Institute and became concierge. In 1940, during World War II, the occupying Germans ordered Joseph to open Pasteur's crypt and rather than perform this sacrilege, he committed suicide.

Diamonds at Maxim's

The frivolity of the Belle Époque is summed up in this anecdote from Hugo, maître d'hôtel at the fashionable restaurant Maxim's. La Belle Otero and Liane de Pougy were courtesans with many rich lovers who had splendid collections of jewellery and were great rivals. One evening Otero, determined to humiliate Liane, arrived at Maxim's wearing her entire, astonishing collection of jewels, including a bolero of diamonds. Later, Liane arrived dressed in severe black without even a ring on. Following behind her was her dowdy maid in a cloak that Liane dramatically ripped off with a swirl, to huge applause. The girl was wearing every piece of Liane's jewellery. Spitting and cursing, La Belle Otero was carried out by her supporters.

Louis Pasteur (above).
Côte d'Azur ticket (left)

The Riviera coast began attracting visitors in the 19th century

The Eiffel Tower and the Paris Exhibition of 1889 (left)

The 20th Century

After a decade of prosperity, World War I brought devastation to France. With one million people dead, three million wounded and industrial output down by 60 per cent in 1918, the nation was vengeful and bitter. The inter-war years saw some Socialist gains, with the Front Populaire of 1936 frightening employers into agreeing to many reforms. During World War II, France was occupied from 1940–44 by the Germans and this left its scars on society. When the war ended, General de Gaulle briefly became leader of the Free French and acted as a unifying influence. The ensuing Fourth Republic witnessed an exhausted country grow and prosper hugely throughout the 1950s. The Republic collapsed in 1958, when the brutal colonial war in Algeria almost provoked a right-wing coup. De Gaulle was brought back to become President of the Fifth Republic. He dominated France in the 1960s, but the revolutionary events of 1968, which brought society to a standstill, showed how much dissatisfaction there was.

In the final decades of the 20th century France, with Germany, was driving the European Union.

A moveable feast
'J'ai deux amours, mon pays et Paris,' sang Josephine Baker in the 1920s. Many of her fellow Americans agreed. Wealthy ones, like Winaretta Singer, married French noblemen. When movie star Gloria Swanson brought her trophy husband, Marquis de la Falaise, back to the States she telegraphed her studio 'Arrange the ovation'. Ernest Hemingway found US dollars bought plenty of French wine and good food, but while he thrived, nervy F. Scott Fitzgerald was almost destroyed. Gertrude Stein, who bought paintings by Paul Cézanne and Picasso while they were going cheap, dubbed her compatriots the Lost Generation. The fallout of the alcohol (banned in Prohibition America) and parties was often realized in insanity and burned-out careers.

A British tank in France in 1917 (left)

The popular cabaret artist Josephine Baker (right)

1900

Wartime advertisement for Michelin (above). *Art Goût Beauté* front cover (right), September 1922

US troops prepare to land on the shores of Normandy in 1944 (above).
A print of the arrival of a transatlantic liner at Le Havre (left)

20th century logos—Chanel

Coco Chanel, quintessential Frenchwoman and fashion designer, created great clothes. She also invented the branding, corporate identity and core values practised in business today. Chanel dreamed up a simple, instantly identifiable look that has hardly changed. Her list of successes is formidable: the little black dress, the tweed suit, the handbag, the perfume. Each of them carried her name, relentlessly repeated, until it was reduced to two interlinked Cs, one of the top-10 most-recognized logos. Chanel predicted what women wanted, then gave it to them with a sparkling finish.
Today, the look is still effortlessly reproduced.

Occupation and resistance—the Vichy Government

From 1940 to 1944, under the German Occupation, the Vichy Government of Marshal Pétain ran the southern part of France. It's a painful episode that still divides French society. Klaus Barbie was convicted of war crimes in the 1980s. Vichy is remembered for deporting 70,000 Jews and 650,000 workers to Germany. But Vichy did not spring solely from Nazi Occupation. Far right politicians in 1930s France had spoken out against foreigners and pushed through the Family Code in 1939, setting down strict laws for women and sexual morality.

Philippe Pétain (below)

The Cannes Film Festival

Fights, booing and mass walkouts at screenings, scantily-clad starlets posing on the beach, and anarchy in 1968 when Truffaut and Godard invaded the stage—these are all events that have made the Cannes Film Festival a uniquely French occasion. The first festival, scheduled for September 1939 as a riposte to Mussolini's fascist affair in Venice, was halted by the war. But since 1947, it has been up there with the Oscars as one of the most exciting events in the movie calendar. As usual with the film industry, behind all the glitz and excess a great deal of hard-headed business is undertaken. From romantic comedy to arthouse, 50 per cent of all the movies in the world are bought and sold at Cannes.

Franglais, qu'est-ce que say?

In 1964, Rene Etiemble, author of *Parlez-Vous Franglais?*, recommended severe punishments for those degrading French with English words, as words such as *le cheeseburger* and *le rip-off* found their way into the French language. 'People were shot during the war for treason,' he added.

No-one has been executed yet, but in 1992 the French parliament altered the constitution, solemnly informing the country that, 'the language of the Republic is French.' Parliament passed a law in 1994 insisting that French be used all the time. But then the Constitutional Council informed them that they couldn't tell people how to speak. As ever, official interference has resulted in confusion. *Un e-mail*, for example, is now supposed to be *un mèl*, which doesn't exist in either French or English.

General de Gaulle (left)

2000

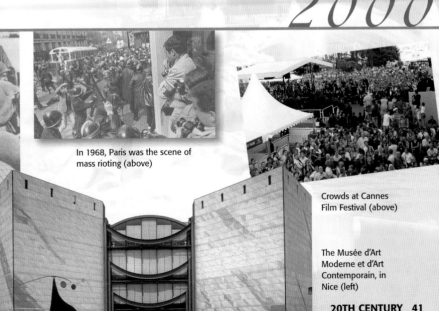

In 1968, Paris was the scene of mass rioting (above)

Crowds at Cannes Film Festival (above)

The Musée d'Art Moderne et d'Art Contemporain, in Nice (left)

The 21st Century

In January 2002, France, along with 11 European Union partners, embraced the euro and the French franc became history. After 80 years of enmity with Germany, the two countries now have a friendship more determined than affectionate, and it is generally admitted that they fuel much of the policy of the European Union.

Jean-Marie Le Pen

He is reported to have described immigration as the biggest problem facing Europe, but Le Pen is not some fanatic on the fringes of French politics. He is the leader of the far right National Front and in April 2002 the unthinkable almost happened. Anti-immigration sentiments and voter apathy allowed him to defeat the then Prime Minister Lionel Jospin and enter the second round of the Presidential elections. This rude awakening brought voters out to re-elect Jacques Chirac by a vast majority of almost 82 per cent.

Le Train à Grande Vitesse

The high-speed TGV (it can reach 321mph/515 kph) breaks down barriers and busts borders. Extremely expensive, the TGV soon paid for itself with enormous numbers of passengers. Since 1981, it has been shooting from Paris to Lyon in two hours and today it reaches great swathes of France. A planned link with the Spanish rail system could cut the Paris–Barcelona trip to four hours. In 2006, politicians will get to Strasbourg from Paris in just over two hours and from there to Stuttgart and Frankfurt.

Paris Plage

Paris Plage, the beach by the Seine, is set to become a summer must-see in Paris. From mid-July to mid-August, when most Parisians desert the city, part of the Right Bank is transformed into a seaside. Palm trees (Parisian-style, in a chic row) sway over 100m of imported sand, along with 300 deckchairs, 150 parasols and striped changing tents.

Paris Plage was introduced in summer 2002 and Mayor Bertrand Delanoë has promised that it will be around for years to come.

Summer heat

Summer 2003 took a tragic turn when thousands of elderly people in France died of hyperthermia and dehydration, as a result of a heatwave. In July, the heatwave was assumed to be nothing more than a national hot spell, but by mid-August the crisis had grown, with waits of up to two weeks for funerals. Many people died on the same night, 12 August, when the temperature hit 37.8°C (100°F) in northern France. About half of those who died across the country lived in retirement homes, some of them with fewer members of staff on duty because of the holiday season. As well as causing public outcry about the lack of medical facilities available in holiday periods, the tragedy raised broader questions of how France is coping with its ageing population.

2000–today

A rally for Jean-Marie Le Pen (above). His success in the first round of the 2002 elections shocked many

A jazz musician in Montpellier (left). Tour de France sculpture in Pau (right). Paris Plage (top right), when the beach comes to the capital

On the Move

ARRIVING

By Air

Many visitors to France arrive by air and the numbers are increasing with the availability of inexpensive flights and the popularity of short breaks from other European countries. Paris has two airports, Roissy–Charles de Gaulle and the smaller Orly, and is also served by Beauvais Tillé airport, farther north. Other French cities with airports include Marseille, Toulouse, Lyon, Strasbourg and Bordeaux.

● Paris's busiest airport is **Roissy–Charles de Gaulle**, 23km (14 miles) from the heart of the city. It has three terminals: T1, T2 and T3 (formerly T9). Terminal 2 is subdivided into 2A, 2B, 2C, 2D and 2F. Airlines operating out of T1 include Aer Lingus, British Midland, KLM and United Airlines. T2 serves Air France, British Airways and American Airlines, among others. Airlines using T3 include EasyJet. Terminals can change, so always check before setting off.

You'll find information desks, shops, restaurants, banks, bureaux de change, car rental firms and a first aid station in T1 and T2. T3 has shops, cafés, a bureau de change and car rental outlets. For security reasons there is no left luggage office.

GETTING TO THE CITY FROM THE AIRPORT		
AIRPORT	**TAXI**	**TRAINS**
Roissy–Charles de Gaulle (CDG) (Paris)	Cost: €38–€43. Journey time: 30 min–1 hour.	RER line B takes you into the heart of Paris (Gare du Nord, Châtelet or St-Michel). Trains leave roughly every 5–15 min, from 5am to 11.40pm. Cost: €7.70. Journey time: 35 min.
Orly (ORY) (Paris)	Cost: around €25. Journey time: 15–30 min.	The Orlyval train (Mon–Sat 6am–10.30pm, Sun 7am–11pm) takes you two stops to Antony, where you pick up RER line B. Cost: €8.80. Journey time: 35 min.
Beauvais Tillé (BVA) (North of Paris)	Cost: around €120. Journey time: 1 hour 20 min.	None.
Marseille-Provence, also called Marseille-Marignane (MRS)	Cost: around €37 day, €46 night. Journey time: 30 min.	None.
Toulouse-Blagnac (TLS)	Cost: around €20 day, €25 night. Journey time: 20 min.	None.
Strasbourg (SXB)	Cost: around €25 day, €30 night. Journey time: 15 min.	Trains leave from Gare Entzheim, which is a 5-min walk from the airport. They run from 5.30am–8.30pm. Journey time: 15 min.
Lyon St-Exupéry (LYS)	Cost: around €33 day, €47 night. Journey time: 30 min.	None.
Bordeaux (BOD)	Cost: around €25 day, €35 night. Journey time: 40 min.	None.

● The smaller **Orly** airport, 14km (8.5 miles) south of central Paris, has domestic flights and some international flights. Its two terminals—Orly Sud and Orly Ouest—are connected by shuttle buses and the Orlyval train. The airport has shops, restaurants, bureaux de change and car rental companies.

● **Beauvais Tillé** airport, 90km (56 miles) north of Paris, is used by low-cost airlines. Facilities include a news-stand, restaurant and car rental desks.

● **Marseille-Provence** airport is 30km (19 miles) northwest of the city. Terminals 1 and 4 have restaurants, cafés, shops and information desks. Terminal 1 also has a pharmacy, first aid point and bureau de change and terminal 4 has a bank and car rental desks.

● **Toulouse-Blagnac** airport is 8km (5 miles) northwest of the city. In Departures, halls 1 and 2 have a restaurant, a bar, shops and a bureau de change. In Arrivals there are car rental companies, a café and a bureau de change.

● **Strasbourg** airport is 12km (7 miles) southwest of the city.

There is a restaurant and café in Departures and a first aid point, car rental companies, a cafe, shops, and information desk in International Arrivals.

● **Lyon St-Exupéry** airport is 28km (17 miles) east of Lyon. Facilities include restaurants, bars, shops, a post office and a bureau de change.

● **Bordeaux** airport is 10km (6 miles) west of Bordeaux. In Departures there are shops, bars and restaurants.

● See the chart below for information on reaching the cities from the airports.

BUS	CAR
The Air France bus runs from Terminals 1 and 2 to Montparnasse and Gare de Lyon every 30 min, 7am–9pm. Cost: €11.50. Journey time: 45 min–1 hour. Another Air France bus runs to the Arc de Triomphe every 15 min, 5.45am–11pm. Cost: €10. Journey time: 45 min–1 hour. The Roissybus runs every 15 min from Terminals 1, 2 and 3 to Opéra, 6am–11pm. Cost: €8.20. Journey time: 50 min.	Take the A1 south to Paris. Journey time: 30 min–1 hour.
Air France runs from Orly Sud and Ouest to Les Invalides and Gare Montparnasse every 15 min, 6am–11pm. Cost: €7.50. Journey time: 30 min. The Orlybus runs from Orly Sud and Ouest to Denfert-Rochereau Métro station every 15–20 min, 6am–11.30pm. Cost: €5.70. Journey time: 30 min.	Take the A106, then A6A or A6B into Paris. Journey time: 15–40 min.
Bus to Porte Maillot. Cost: €10. Journey time: around 1 hour 15 min.	Take the N1, A16, N1 then A1 to Paris. Journey time: 1 hour 20 min.
Buses to the Gare St-Charles train station run from 6.10am–10.50pm and leave every 20 min. After 10.50pm they coincide with flight arrivals. Cost: €8.50. Journey time: 30 min.	Take the D20, D9, then A7 to Marseille. Journey time: 30 min.
Buses leave every 20 min. They run Mon–Sat 7.30am–12.15am and Sun and public hols 9.15am–12.15am. Cost: €3.70. Journey time: 20 min.	Take the D901 then A620 to Toulouse. Journey time: 20 min.
Buses to the Baggersee train station leave every 20 min; from there you can take tram line A to downtown. They run Mon–Fri 5.30am–10.50pm, Sat 5.30am–10.45pm (11.30pm July–end of first week of September) and Sun 6.45am–10.50pm. Cost: €4.80. Journey time: 30 min.	Take the D221 and then D392 to Strasbourg. Journey time: 15 min.
Buses leave every 20 min. They run daily from 6am–11.20pm from the airport to Lyon, and from 5am–9pm from Lyon to the airport. Cost: €8.20. Journey time: 40–50 min.	Take the A432, A43 then N383 to Lyon. Journey time: 35 min.
Buses leave from Terminal B every 45 min. They run daily from 7am–10.45pm from the airport to Bordeaux and from 6am–9.45pm from Bordeaux (train station) to the airport. Cost: €6. Journey time: 45 min.	Take the N563 then D106 to Bordeaux. Journey time: 40 min.

AIRPORT CONTACTS

Roissy–Charles de Gaulle	01 48 62 22 80
	www.adp.fr
Paris Orly	01 49 75 15 15
	www.adp.fr
Beauvais Tillé	0892 682 066
	www.aeroportbeauvais.com
Marseille-Provence	04 42 14 14 14
	www.marseille.aeroport.fr
Toulouse-Blagnac	05 61 42 44 00
	www.toulouse.aeroport.fr
Strasbourg	03 88 64 67 67
	www.strasbourg.aeroport.fr
Lyon St-Exupéry	04 72 22 72 21
	www.lyon.aeroport.fr
Bordeaux	05 56 34 50 50
	www.bordeaux.aeroport.fr

OTHER USEFUL CONTACTS

General airport information www.worldairportguide.com
Information on all French airports www.aeroport.fr
Air France 0820 820 820 **www.airfrance.fr**
American Airlines 1 800 433 7300 (US number)
www.aa.com
British Airways 0870 850 9850 (UK number) **www.ba.com**
British Midland 0870 60 70 555 (UK number)
www.flybmi.com
Delta 1 800 241 4141 (US number) **www.delta.com**
Easyjet 0870 6000 000 (UK number) **www.easyjet.com**
Ryanair 0871 2460 000 (UK number) **www.ryanair.com**
United 1 800 538 2929 (US number) **www.ual.com**
Orlybus 01 40 02 32 94
Paris Métro and RER information 0892 687 714
www.ratp.fr
Air France bus to Paris 0892 350 820
www.cars-airfrance.com

AIRPORTS AND PORTS

By Train

There are good train links between France and other European countries. If you are starting from the UK, you can take the Eurostar from London Waterloo, through the Channel Tunnel to Paris, where you can connect to services to destinations across France. The Eurostar also travels direct to Disneyland Resort Paris, Bourg St-Maurice and Moutiers (during the ski season only), and Avignon (weekly in summer). The Channel Tunnel rail link has revolutionized travel to Paris, allowing you to reach Paris from London in less than three hours, without leaving the ground or boarding a boat. The tunnel opened in 1994, almost 200 years after the first designs were submitted for an undersea link between England and France. It is the longest undersea tunnel in the world, with 39km (24 miles) of its 50km (31 miles) length under the Channel.

BOARDING EUROSTAR

● Up to 16 trains per day travel to Paris from London; some stop en route at Ashford International (UK) and Calais (France). The introduction of upgraded track has cut the journey time to Paris to 2 hours 35 minutes.

● Trains leave from Waterloo International Station, in central London, which is on the Northern, Bakerloo, Jubilee, and Waterloo and City underground lines. Several mainline train services also run to Waterloo.

● The terminal is separated from the hubbub of the rest of the station. You can check-in automatically with certain types of tickets, otherwise check in at the desks. You must do this at least 30 minutes before your train is due to leave.

● Before you reach the departure lounge you must go through airport-style security checks and passport control (French passport control is actually carried out at Waterloo). Once in the departure lounge there are newspaper and gift shops, cafés, lavatories, Internet points and a mail box.

● Boarding begins around 20 minutes before departure. Information screens tell you where and when to board. Each train has 18 carriages (cars) so you could face a long walk along the platform. Trolleys (carts) for luggage are available, although you need a £1 coin as a deposit. Once on board, large cases must be stored on the luggage racks at the end of each carriage, but you can put smaller bags in the racks above your seat.

THE JOURNEY

● A buffet car serves drinks, snacks and light meals. There are lavatories and a designated place where you can change your baby on board. The journey through the tunnel itself takes around 20 minutes and an announcement is made just before you enter.

ARRIVING

● When you arrive in Paris's Gare du Nord station you do not need to go through passport control as this has been carried out at Waterloo. Watch for pickpockets at the station.

● The covered taxi stand is well signposted. Don't be too depressed at the long queue, as it moves fairly quickly. A taxi into the middle of Paris costs between €10 and €15, although there are extra charges for each piece of luggage and for travel after 7pm and on Sundays.

● Gare du Nord is on Métro lines 4 (purple) and 5 (orange). Line 4 (direction Porte d'Orléans) will take you across the river to the Left Bank. If your hotel is on the Right Bank, you can change lines at Gare de l'Est, Strasbourg St-Denis, Réaumur Sébastopol or Châtelet. Line 5 (direction place d'Italie) is handy if you're heading to the Bastille area.

● Gare du Nord is also on two RER lines, D (green) and B (blue). Line B takes you to Châtelet, then on to the Left Bank (St-Michel-Notre-Dame and Luxembourg). The RER can be a confusing rail system to the uninitiated (see page 63). If it's your first time in Paris, it may be better to take the Métro or a taxi.

TIPS

● You'll pay less for your Eurostar ticket if you reserve it in advance. It is highly recommended that you do this, since non-booked seats are limited. The train is split into Premium, First and Standard class. Premium and First class give you a meal, extra legroom, a reclining seat and free newspapers. Certain tickets also allow admission to the business lounge at Waterloo and Gare du Nord.

● Remember that you need your passport to travel between Britain and France (see Visas, page 403).

● The official luggage allowance is two suitcases and one piece of hand luggage. Luggage must be clearly labelled with your name and seat number.

● Trolleys (carts) are available on the platforms at Waterloo and Gare du Nord, but you need a £1 or €1 coin (refundable). If you have a heavy case a trolley is a good idea as the walk along the platform can be long if your carriage (car) happens to be the last of 18.

USEFUL NUMBERS

Eurostar: 08705 186 186 (UK number); www.eurostar.com
Lost luggage at Waterloo: 020 7928 0660 (UK number)
Lost luggage at Gare du Nord: 01 55 31 58 40

By Ferry, Car or Long-Distance Bus

If you want to drive from the UK to France you can use either the Eurotunnel, which takes you to Calais, or a ferry, with a choice of ports on France's northwestern coast. Driving to France from countries on mainland Europe is straightforward.

ON THE MOVE

There is a choice of ferry routes between England and France

BY FERRY
● Numerous ferries link France with the UK. The cost of crossings varies widely according to time, day and month of travel. Most companies require you to check in at least 30 minutes before departure, although extra security checks may mean you have to arrive earlier.
● P&O Ferries and Seafrance sail from Dover to Calais (journey time: 70 to 90 minutes). The Hoverspeed catamaran cuts the journey to 50 minutes, although it is more prone to cancellations owing to bad weather. On board there are shops, cafés, a bureau de change and lounges. Once in Calais, it takes around 3 hours 15 minutes to drive to Paris (for directions see Eurotunnel, right).
● Hoverspeed operates a Newhaven to Dieppe service (journey time: 2 hours).
● Brittany Ferries sail from Portsmouth to Caen (journey time: 6 hours).
● P&O Ferries sail from Portsmouth to Le Havre (day journey time: 5 hours 30 minutes).
● Brittany Ferries sail from Poole to Cherbourg (journey time: approximately 4 hours; Fastcraft 2 hours 15 minutes, summer only). P&O Ferries operate a Portsmouth to Cherbourg service (day journey time: 5

hours; Fastcraft 2 hours 40 minutes, summer only).
● Brittany Ferries sail from Portsmouth to St-Malo (journey time: approximately 8 hours 30 minutes).

Ferry Contact Details
Brittany Ferries: 08703 665 333 (UK); www.brittany-ferries.com
Hoverspeed: 0870 240 8070 (UK); www.hoverspeed.com
P&O Ferries: 08705 20 20 20 (UK); www.poferries.com
Seafrance: 08705 711 711 (UK); www.seafrance.com

BY EUROTUNNEL
● Load your car onto the Shuttle train at Folkestone for the 35-minute journey under the Channel to Calais/Coquelles.
● To reach the terminal at Folkestone, leave the M20 at junction 11A and follow signs to the Channel Tunnel.
● There are up to four departures per hour, 24 hours a day, and the price is charged per car (reserve ahead).
● French border controls take place on the UK side, saving time when you arrive in Calais.
● You stay with your car during the journey, although you can go to the lavatory or walk about within the air-conditioned carriage. During the journey you can listen to the on-board radio station and staff are available if you need any help.
● To reach Paris from Calais you can take the A16 (E40) in the direction of Dunkerque, then join the A26 (E15). At the intersection with the A1, head southbound on the A1 (E15), which will take you all the way to Paris. You will have to pay *autoroute* tolls.
● If you are driving from Calais to the south of France allow at least 11 hours. The journey time will

vary depending on traffic, season and weather conditions. It is probably best to break up the journey with an overnight stop. You will have to pay toll charges if you use the *autoroutes*.
● See pages 50–54 for more information on driving in France.

Eurotunnel Contact Details
08705 35 35 35 (UK); www.eurotunnel.com

BY LONG-DISTANCE BUS
● Going to France by long-distance bus can be a useful option if you're on a tight budget, although the journey from London to Paris takes almost eight hours.
● Eurolines runs services from Victoria coach station to Paris up to five times a day, with pick-up points at Canterbury and Dover. They also serve more than 60 other destinations in France. The Channel crossing is made either by Eurotunnel or ferry.
● Book your ticket at least 30 days in advance for the least expensive fares.

Eurolines Contact Details
08705 143219 (UK); www.eurolines.co.uk

TIPS
● Look out for inexpensive ferry deals in British newspapers.

● It is often less expensive to book Eurotunnel tickets online rather than by telephone.
● LPG vehicles cannot use the Eurotunnel.
● The phone numbers given on this page are UK-based. To call from the US, dial 011 44, then omit the initial zero from the number. To call from European countries, dial 00 44, then omit the zero.

GETTING AROUND FRANCE

France is a relatively large country, but its excellent network of trains and *autoroutes* means you can usually travel between regions quickly and easily.

BY ROAD

Driving in France is made easier by the country's extensive network of *autoroutes* (motorways/expressways). However, you'll have to pay a toll to use them. Journey times can be affected by weather conditions, traffic and the season—the roads, especially in the south of France, can get very busy in the summer.

BY TRAIN

The train is one of the best ways of getting around France—it is fast, comfortable and usually runs on time. France's state railway, the Societé Nationale des Chemins de Fer (SNCF), runs the services. The high-speed train service—the TGV *(Train à Grande Vitesse)*—links large cities and towns, while TER trains do regional journeys.

BY BUS

Long-distance bus travel is not an ideal option for crossing the country. Buses are really only useful for short trips in areas not served by the rail network, such as some destinations in Brittany, Normandy and the Côte d'Azur. Long-distance bus stations *(gares routières)* are usually close to railway stations and major train and bus services usually coincide. Smaller towns without train stations are usually linked by bus service to the nearest station. Bus services in cities are generally excellent and inexpensive, but rural areas tend to be less well served.

DOMESTIC FLIGHTS

The train system is so efficient in France that air travel is not particularly time-saving, although the national airline, Air France, still has an extensive network of flights linking most large towns to Paris, as well as connections between regional towns. Air

France operates flights to 16 French destinations from Paris Roissy-Charles de Gaulle and 14 from Paris Orly airport. Most routes have several flights a day, with an average flight time of just one hour. For information and reservations on Air France contact agencies in France *(tel 08 20 82 08 20; www.airfrance.fr)*, the UK *(tel 0845 0845 111; www.airfrance. co.uk)* or in the US *(tel 1 800 237 2747; www.airfrance.com)*. For information on all of the French airports look up www.aeroport.fr.

Buses are useful for travel within a city

France has an excellent rail system

MAPS

Good quality regional maps are invaluable in planning a trip. The AA (UK) publishes four France atlases as well as a series of France sheet maps. The AA website, www.theAA.com, has a helpful route planner.

You can find town and city maps *(plans)* in France at *maisons de la presse* news-stands, bookshops and some newspaper kiosks. Every city and town, and many villages, have an *office de tourisme, syndicat d'initiative,* or town hall that will provide a local map.

Driving in France

France has a comprehensive system of *autoroutes* (motorways/expressways) fanning out from Paris, enabling you to cross the country with relative ease. From the capital, the A1 leads to the north, the A13 to Normandy and the northwest, the A4 to the east, the A6 to the Alps and the Riviera, and the A10 to the west and southwest. Driving is the best way to tour smaller villages and towns, but is not so convenient in some of the bigger cities, especially Paris, where the traffic is heavy, the one-way systems confusing and parking difficult and expensive.

BRINGING YOUR OWN CAR
Legal Requirements
● Private vehicles registered in another country can be taken into France for up to six months without customs formalities.
● You must always carry the following documentation: a current passport or national ID card, a full (not provisional), valid national driver's licence (even if you have an International Driving Permit), a certificate of motor insurance, and the vehicle's registration document (as well as a letter of authorization from the owner if the vehicle is not registered in your name).

● You should always tell your insurer before you take your car abroad. Third-party motor insurance is the minimum requirement in France but fully comprehensive cover is strongly advised.
● Check that your insurance covers you against damage in transit, for example on the train

AUTOROUTES

ON THE MOVE

or ferry when your car is not being driven.
● There are spot checks on cars and you may be asked to produce your documents at any time. To avoid a police fine and/or confiscation of your car, be sure that your papers are in order.
● Display an international sticker or distinguishing sign plate as near as possible to the national registration plate at the rear of your car. If you don't, you will risk an on-the-spot fine. Since March 2001, registration plates (Euro-Plates) displaying the Euro-symbol of an EU

Use the chart below to work out the distance in km (green) and estimated duration in hours and minutes (blue) of a car journey

country mean displaying a conventional sticker or plate is unnecessary when driving in the EU, but it is always safer to display one.
● To avoid dazzling oncoming drivers you should adjust the headlights of left-hand-drive vehicles for driving on the right. On older cars, use the simple black headlamp beam converters that stick onto the glass. But don't use these on cars with halogen headlamps—check in your car handbook or with your dealer. If your vehicle has Xenon or High Intensity Discharge (HID) headlamps, check with your dealer who may need to make the adjustment.
● Remove the converters or have your headlamps reset as soon as you return home.

Some autoroutes are relatively uncrowded

Breakdown Cover
If you are taking your own car, make sure you have adequate breakdown cover for your trip to France. For information on AA breakdown cover, call 0800 444 500 or visit www.theAA.com.

From \ To	Amiens	Bordeaux	Brest	Calais	Clermont-Ferrand	Dijon	Grenoble	Lille	Limoges	Lyon	Marseille	Montpellier	Nantes	Nice	Paris	Poitiers	Reims	Rennes	Rouen	Strasbourg	Toulouse
Amiens	—	724	705	140	554	439	717	133	542	616	928	920	533	1059	158	507	150	448	139	511	846
Bordeaux	723	—	640	843	438	750	730	802	301	648	622	444	327	755	557	231	702	449	653	1023	223
Brest	634	630	—	745	851	856	1115	822	706	1014	1247	1109	323	1419	631	533	736	247	545	1057	848
Calais	161	879	722	—	713	535	826	115	701	725	1037	1028	633	1207	316	626	246	528	219	607	1005
Clermont-Ferrand	567	359	804	723	—	350	303	632	256	212	450	358	604	620	427	357	532	613	528	654	434
Dijon	473	761	868	574	349	—	302	454	520	201	513	504	640	643	329	533	253	618	443	332	720
Grenoble	746	776	1127	876	295	303	—	745	546	114	311	303	845	442	549	637	543	837	702	544	519
Lille	119	809	767	111	653	504	806	—	620	644	956	947	620	1126	235	545	205	558	257	517	924
Limoges	539	228	609	695	177	436	545	625	—	456	717	539	353	850	415	150	520	515	516	824	318
Lyon	639	542	1020	769	179	196	109	699	429	—	317	308	754	447	448	547	442	736	601	505	524
Marseille	972	652	1278	1102	479	529	310	1032	714	318	—	154	933	207	800	824	754	1041	913	811	410
Montpellier	954	488	1114	1085	344	511	293	1015	550	300	169	—	756	327	751	700	746	918	905	802	233
Nantes	518	330	300	599	483	656	764	611	309	648	978	814	—	1106	414	220	519	126	426	840	535
Nice	1127	810	1436	1258	635	684	466	1188	872	473	205	327	1136	—	930	955	925	1211	1044	816	543
Paris	143	582	596	294	426	312	571	224	398	464	797	779	384	952	—	340	143	353	148	504	719
Poitiers	478	249	524	634	318	516	599	564	121	482	783	733	224	938	337	—	445	342	436	806	439
Reims	177	718	732	278	562	298	601	208	534	494	827	809	520	982	144	473	—	458	304	324	824
Rennes	443	445	245	532	556	620	879	575	424	772	1021	929	106	1176	348	339	484	—	328	819	657
Rouen	123	620	504	211	513	461	720	256	485	613	946	929	384	1102	141	375	284	313	—	625	820
Strasbourg	520	1061	1076	621	661	341	541	523	748	508	824	807	863	792	488	816	346	827	628	—	1018
Toulouse	840	245	871	996	384	753	535	926	307	542	411	247	571	569	699	490	835	686	785	1049	—

RENTING A CAR

● Most major car rental agencies have offices at airports, main railway stations and in large towns and cities throughout France.

● Renting a car in France can be expensive due to high taxes. Arranging a fly-drive package through a tour operator or airline from home could be a less expensive option. SNCF, the national railway company, has inclusive train and car-rental deals from mainline stations.

● To be able to rent a car in France you must be at least 20 years old and have held a full driver's licence for at least a year. However, some companies either do not rent to, or else add a surcharge for, drivers under the age of 25. The maximum age limit varies, but the average is 70.

● You will have to show your licence and passport or national ID card.

● As a guide, companies should include the following in their rental agreement: unlimited mileage, comprehensive insurance cover, theft protection and 24-hour emergency roadside assistance.

● Some agencies include mileage in the cost but others may charge you extra above a certain distance, so check before you rent.

● Most international rental companies will let you return your car to other French cities, and even other countries, but there may be an extra charge for this. Always agree the drop-off point with the company first.

● Make sure you have adequate insurance and that you are aware of what you are covered for in the event of an accident.

● Bear in mind that low-cost operators may have an extremely high excess charge for damage to the vehicle.

● Most car-rental companies supply vehicles with breakdown cover, so refer to your documentation or to the information regarding breakdowns in the car, which is often kept in the glove compartment or under the sun visor.

● If your car breaks down on an *autoroute*, look for emergency telephones on the roadside. You can contact the breakdown services from here.

RENTING AUTOMATIC CARS

If you are keen to rent an automatic, rather than manual, car it is best to reserve in advance, as there are fewer available in France than in countries such as the US. You may also have to pay a premium for the vehicle.

CAR RENTAL COMPANIES

Company	Telephone number	Website
Avis	0820 050 505	www.avis.com
Budget	0825 003 564	www.budget.com
Europcar	0825 352 352	www.europcar.com
Hertz	01 41 91 95 25	www.hertz.com
Sixt	0820 007 498	www.sixt.com

GENERAL DRIVING
Roads

● The *autoroute* is the French counterpart of the British motorway or American expressway and is marked by an 'A' on maps and road signs. A few sections around key cities are free of charge, but tolls are charged on the rest (*autoroutes à péage*). Tolls are expensive but are often worth it to get to destinations quickly. Always have some cash available as foreign credit cards may not be accepted. For information on *autoroute* conditions throughout France call 01 47 05 90 01 or look up www.autoroutes.fr.

● There is a comprehensive network of other roads, with surfaces that are generally good. A highway or trunk road is called a *Route Nationale* (N). The next level down is the *Route Départementale* (D), which can still be wide and fast. There are also quieter country roads.

The Law

● In France you drive on the right (*serrez à droite*).

● The minimum age to drive is 18, although to rent a car you must be at least 20.

● In built-up areas vehicles should give way to traffic coming from the right (*Priorité à droite*), unless signs advise otherwise. At roundabouts (traffic circles) with signs saying *Cédez le passage* or *Vous n'avez pas la priorité*, traffic already on the roundabout has priority. On roundabouts without signs, traffic entering has priority. A priority road can also be shown by a white diamond-shaped sign with a yellow diamond within it. A black line through the diamond indicates the end of priority. A red-bordered triangle with a black cross on a white background, with the words *passage protégé*, also shows priority.

● Holders of EU driver's licences who exceed the speed limit by more than 25kph (16mph) will

have their licences confiscated by the police on-the-spot.

● You must wear a seatbelt. Children under 10 must travel in the back, with a booster seat, except for babies under nine months with a specially adapted rear-facing front seat (but not in cars with airbags).

● Do not overtake where there is a solid single central line on the road.

● There are harsh penalties if the level of alcohol in the blood is 0.05 per cent or more. If you drink, don't drive.

● You must always stop completely at STOP signs, or you may be fined.

Road Signs

● Road signs are split into three categories. Triangular signs with a red border are warnings, circular signs are mandatory (such as speed limits or No Entry) and square signs display text information.

● Signs include: *déviation* (diversion), *attention travaux* (roadworks), *sortie* (exit), *gravillons* (loose chippings), *chaussée déformée* (uneven road and temporary surface) and *nids de poules* (potholes).

SELECTED ROAD SIGNS

No entry except for buses and taxis

Road-toll pay station

A yellow diamond (top) indicates priority

Speed limits for various road types, in kph

Give way to traffic

Parking 150m to the left

Parking only for those with disabilities

No left turn

A town sign, with the road number displayed above

SPEED LIMITS

Urban roads	50kph (31mph)
Outside built-up areas	90kph (56mph); 80kph (49mph) in wet weather
Dual carriageways (divided highways), and non-toll motorways	110kph (68mph); 100kph (62mph) in wet weather
Toll motorways (*autoroutes*)	130kph (80mph); 110kph (68mph) in wet weather

Visiting drivers who have held a licence for less than two years are not allowed to exceed the wet-weather limits, even in good weather.

● Before you take to the road, familiarize yourself with the French highway code on www.legifrance.gouv.fr.

● For more information on road signs see www.permisenligne.com.

Equipment

● Carry a red warning triangle in case you break down. Even if your car has hazard warning lights, a triangle is still strongly advised as a breakdown may affect the electrics in your car.

ROAD SIGNS

Allumez vos phares	Switch on your lights.
Cédez le passage	Give way
Chantier	Road works
Péage	Toll
Priorité à droite/gauche	Priority to the right/left
Rappel	Reminder (continue with the previous instruction)
Route barré	Road closed
Sens interdit	No entry
Sens unique	One way
Serrez à droite/gauche	Keep to the right/left
Stationnement interdit	No parking
Travaux	Roadworks

- Keep a spare-bulb kit (buy before you go) to hand as it is illegal to drive with faulty lights.
- Snow chains must be fitted to vehicles using snow-covered roads, in compliance with road signs. You could be fined for non-compliance. Snow chains

Filling stations do not always open late and many close on Sunday

can be rented from most tyre specialists in France or you can buy them from hypermarkets, especially in mountain areas.

Fuel

- Fuel (*essence*) comes as unleaded (95 and 98 octane), lead replacement petrol (LRP or *supercarburant*), diesel (*gasoil* or *gazole*) and LPG.
- Many filling stations close on Sundays and at 6pm the rest of the week. You may find it difficult to locate a 24-hour station and some may not accept foreign credit cards.
- Prices are high at filling stations on *autoroutes*.
- Filling stations can be far apart in rural areas, so never let your tank get too low.

Parking

- Authorized parking spaces are indicated by road markings (white dotted lines). In those marked *Payant,* you have to pay.
- Charges usually apply from 9am to 7pm, Monday to Saturday. Sundays and holidays are generally free, but always check before parking your car.
- To pay for parking, buy a ticket from a machine at the side of the road and display it in your car.
- Some towns also have multi-level or underground parking areas.

Car Breakdown

- If your car breaks down on an *autoroute*, look for an emergency telephone along the roadside that will connect you with the breakdown services.
- If you break down on the Paris *périphérique* or an *autoroute*, you must call the police or the official breakdown service operating in that area, rather than your own breakdown/insurance company.

Road Conditions

- To find out about traffic conditions visit www.bison-fute.equipement.gouv.fr (in French only).
- For the National Road Information Centre (voice service in French) call 0836 682 000.
- For road conditions on *autoroutes* call 0892 681 077.
- For information on regional road conditions, call 0826 022 022.
- Autoroute FM provides useful and up-to-date traffic bulletins.

HINTS FOR DRIVING AND PARKING IN PARIS

- The speed limit in central Paris is 50kph (31mph). On the ring road (*périphérique*) the limit is 80kph (49mph).
- Give way to traffic approaching from the right (*priorité à droite*), unless signs advise you otherwise.
- Don't use the bus lanes.
- Don't park or stop on any of the *axes rouges* (key routes through the city).
- Avoid the rush hour (generally from 7 to 9.30am and 4.30 to 7.30pm, weekdays).
- The city's roads are least congested in August, when many Parisians escape to the coast. But August is also when most road repairs take place.
- The network of narrow streets in Paris can be confusing, so plan your route in advance.
- Useful maps include *Plan de Paris par Arrondissement*, published by Grafocarte, and *Paris par Arrondissement*, by Editions L'Indispensable.
- On most of Paris's streets you must pay to park from 9am to 7pm Monday to Saturday.
- Parking tickets are usually dispensed by Pay-and-Display meters. They accept coins or cards that you can buy in tobacconists. Two hours is the maximum stay and hourly rates vary from less than a euro to more than two euros.

USEFUL WEBSITES	
Website address	**What you can find**
www.iti.fr	Route planner
www.autoroutes.fr	Information on *autoroutes*
www.equipement.gouv.fr	Road and traffic information
www.afp.com	French and international news
www.sytadin.tm.fr	Traffic reports around Paris
www.bison-fute.equipement.gouv.fr	Road conditions information

Trains

France has a good rail network and travel between cities and other European countries is relatively simple. The system is run by the Societé Nationale des Chemins de Fer (SNCF) and has *Grands Lignes* (long distance services) and *Lignes Régionals* (regional services). *Grands Lignes* have regular CORAIL trains and faster TGV trains (which can travel up to 300kph/186mph). The *Lignes Régionals* have TER trains (*Trains Express Régionaux*), called Transilien trains in Paris. Paris has six mainline stations, each serving different regions in France and the rest of Europe.

TICKETS

● Most trains have first and second classes, both of which are perfectly acceptable.

● Fares are split into blue (normal) and red (peak). Reduced-rate fares are generally available for normal travel on mainline routes, excluding TGV and couchette services.

● Ticket prices vary according to the level of comfort (first or second class; called Comfort Level 1 and Comfort Level 2 on Thalys) and departure time. First class fares are roughly 50 per cent more expensive than second class.

● You can buy tickets in the stations, at SNCF offices and through some travel agents. Tickets for TGV trains must be reserved. You can do this up to a few minutes before departure, although in peak season it is best to book well in advance. Couchettes must be booked at least 75 minutes before the train leaves its first station.

● Make sure you stamp your ticket in the orange machines on the platforms before you start your journey. You'll risk a fine if you forget to do this. If leaving from a suburban rail station in the Paris region to take a connection from one of the main Paris stations, you have to stamp your ticket twice, once at the departure station and once in Paris.

● If you are under 26, you can get a 25 per cent discount (called *Découverte 12–25*) on train travel. Seniors also receive discounts (called *Découverte Senior*).

● When you travel second class, there are lower rates for booking more than eight days in advance (ask for *Découverte J8*) and more than 30 days in advance (ask for *Découverte J30*).

● A variety of rail passes are available, which allow travel either within France only, or within France and certain other countries, or within the whole of Europe. You should buy these before you enter France, either

The busy Gare du Nord, in Paris

through travel agents or Rail Europe (see page 56).

● Ticket machines, with instructions in English, accept notes, coins and credit cards. They can also be used to collect tickets you have ordered on the Internet, by telephone or Minitel.

CATERING SERVICE

● Catering facilities—ranging from sandwiches and salads to hot meals—are available on most TGV and Corail services, but can be quite expensive.

● A benefit of first-class travel is that you can have food served at your seat during meal times on most TGV trains. You'll need to reserve in advance, except on TGV *Méditerranée* trains.

● You can reserve meals when you purchase your train ticket. Ticket machines dispense meal vouchers.

● Hot and cold drinks,

sandwiches and snacks are served on most trains.
- Overnight trains (and some day services) have vending machines dispensing hot and cold drinks and sweets (candy).

OVERNIGHT TRAINS
- Most overnight trains offer either reclining seats, couchette berths or a sleeper car.
- Reclining seats are available only in second class. They have adjustable head- and foot-rests and a reinforced foam seat for sleeping.
- In first class, couchettes are in four-berth compartments; in second class they are in six-berth compartments.
- Sleeper car compartments are for up to two people in

FASTEST JOURNEY TIMES FROM PARIS (APPROXIMATE)
Amsterdam
4 hours 10 min
Bordeaux
3 hours
Brussels
1 hour 20 min
Lille
1 hour
Marseille
3 hours

first class and up to three people in second class.
- Overnight trains operate between Paris and Toulouse; Paris, Irun and Tarbes; Paris, Port-Bou and Latour de Carol; Strasbourg and Vintimille; Luxembourg, Metz, Reims and Nice; Bordeaux and Nice; Lille and Vintimille; Paris and Nice-Vintimille; Paris and Briançon; Paris and Bourg St-Maurice; Paris and St-Gervais; Metz and Port-Bou; Strasbourg and Port-Bou; Hendaye and Geneva; and Hendaye and Nice.

SNCF
www.sncf.com
www.voyages-sncf.com
www.tgv.com
Tel 0892 353 535

Thalys
Trains to cities in northern Europe.
www.thalys.com
Tel 0892 353 536

Rail Europe
Sells a variety of European rail passes.
www.raileurope.com (for US visitors)
www.raileurope.co.uk (for UK visitors)

- Trains also travel to other European countries.

STATION ASSISTANCE
- Larger stations have an information kiosk, which is usually easy to find.
- If you need assistance, look for a member of the station staff, identifiable by their red waistcoats.
- You'll need a €1 deposit to use the luggage trolleys (carts).
- Porters are on hand to help with your luggage in main stations. They wear red jackets and black or navy caps.

The chart on the left shows the duration in hours and minutes of a train journey between these destinations in France

Distance chart (cities: Amiens, Bayonne, Bordeaux (St-Jean), Brest, Clermont-Ferrand, Dijon, Grenoble, Lille (Europe/Flandres), Limoges (Bénédictins), Lyon (Part Dieu), Marseille (St-Charles), Montpellier, Nantes, Nice (Ville), Paris, Poitiers, Reims, Rennes, Rouen (Rive Droite), Strasbourg, Toulouse (Matabiau)):

642
456 144
730 952 809
556 1001 548 920
359 742 534 703 348
509 1222 710 839 424 326
120 648 501 642 513 245 448
504 441 203 822 341 521 656 431
325 908 545 648 238 136 120 251 509
505 744 529 841 436 320 220 431 643 134
538 605 400 909 455 327 229 447 514 143 126
420 559 358 401 548 452 623 355 508 424 602 622
727 1039 804 1217 718 602 507 724 918 414 218 401 925
107 450 303 422 324 141 257 100 250 157 302 320 215 537
330 322 138 623 527 357 540 308 208 410 615 627 242 831 126
225 819 531 711 630 340 540 250 607 455 617 612 448 807 136 424
423 745 548 206 622 444 600 347 626 414 609 630 116 908 203 350 439
121 736 513 648 558 335 453 254 550 346 514 537 418 807 106 341 349 413
612 1049 839 641 840 356 652 541 754 437 705 723 711 950 356 651 328 736 643
711 315 158 1030 546 543 457 720 303 359 326 156 605 607 514 355 751 755 735 939

LEFT LUGGAGE
● Some stations have a left-luggage office or coin-operated lockers. Electronic locks issue a printed ticket with a code number. You'll need to keep this ticket for when you return to collect your items.
● Don't store valuables in lockers.
● Security concerns mean that left-luggage facilities are not always available.

UNDERSTANDING RAILWAY TIMETABLES
● You can pick up free timetables (*horaires*) at stations.

● SNCF timetables are usually published twice a year—the summer one lasts from late May to late September, and the winter one from late September to late May.
● There are two styles of timetable: one for the *Grandes Lignes*, covering high-speed TGV and other mainline services, and another for the regional TER trains.
● Be prepared to decipher French railway terminology. On *Grandes Lignes* timetables, two rows of boxed numbers at the

Ticket machines (right) save time

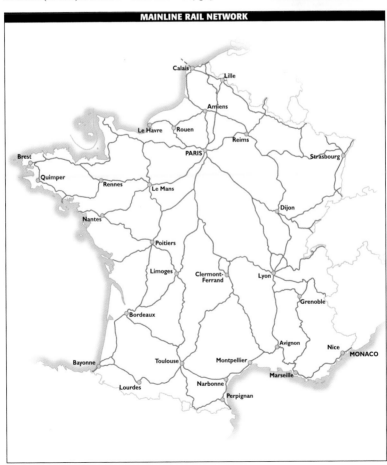

MAINLINE RAIL NETWORK

The railway departures board

top refer to the *numéro de train* (train number) and to the *notes à consulter* (footnotes). In TER timetables, the train number is not listed.

● Footnotes at the bottom explain when a particular train runs (*circule*). *Tous les jours* means it runs every day; *sauf dimanche et fêtes* means it doesn't run on Sundays and holidays. *Jusqu'au,* followed by a date, indicates the service runs only up until that date.

RAIL PASSES

● If you are staying in France for a long time, consider buying a rail pass that is valid for a year. This entitles you to a 50 per cent discount and is available to those aged 12 to 25 (*Carte 12–25*), those with a child under 12 (an *Enfant+* card) and the over 60s (senior card).

● For foreign visitors using the rail network in France there are many attractively priced rail passes. You should buy these before you enter France. To buy certain passes you must have been resident in Europe for at least six months, and have a valid passport with you.

● Rail Europe sells a variety of rail passes (*www.raileurope.com* for US visitors; *www.raileurope.co.uk* for UK visitors).

● Once you are in France it may be difficult to change reservations made abroad.

CAR TRANSPORTER SERVICES

● You can take your motorcycle or car on board the *Auto-Train*. Your vehicle is loaded onto the train and you pick it up at your destination, or you can travel with your car by sleeper accommodation or couchette. The most useful services run from Calais to the south of France (Brives, Toulouse, Narbonne, Avignon and Nice).

● The *Guide auto/train*, with timetable, service and practical information, is available from SNCF stations and outlets.

TIMETABLE, FARE AND OTHER INFORMATION

● Timetable, fare and service information is available from SNCF train stations, ticket outlets and travel agencies, by telephone (*tel 08 91 67 68 69; 24 hours; €0.23 per minute*), the Internet or Minitel.

● Timetable booklets are published for 180 different mainline rail routes.

● Five brochures provide fare, service and timetable information for the Atlantique Ouest, Atlantique Sud-Ouest, Sud-Est, TGV-Méditerranean and Nord high-speed TGV rail services. A sixth, *Province–Île de France–Province*, has details on connections in Paris for travel between the French regions.

● Ask for the *Guide Train+Velo* for information on taking your bicycle on the train.

TIPS

● If you plan to travel by train during peak times (mid-June to early September, holiday periods and during rush hours), reserve your tickets well in advance.

● At train stations you must validate (*composter*) your ticket or pass before boarding the train.

● Bar and at-seat services on most long distance trains are expensive. You may prefer to bring your own snacks.

● Pick-up and delivery of luggage from your hotel to your final destination can be arranged 24 hours in advance. Contact the SNCF Baggage Service (*tel 0825 845 845*). Luggage is picked up and delivered Monday to Friday from 8am to 5pm.

● If you wish to travel on a TGV on which all the seats have been reserved, you can be placed on standby. Your ticket entitles you to board the train but does not guarantee you a seat, so if all reserved passengers do take the train, you will have to stand.

TRAIN PASSES

France Railpass

Unlimited first or second class rail travel in France for any three to nine days within one calendar month. Youth (under 26) and senior (first class only) versions are also available.

Euro Domino Pass

Unlimited first or second class rail travel in France for any three to eight days within one calendar month. There is also a youth (under 26) version for second class travel only.

ON THE MOVE

Long-Distance Buses and Taxis

France's excellent train service means that long-distance buses are not the most convenient option for moving from city to city. Eurolines operates services from Paris and other French cities to destinations in Europe, with stops en route in major French towns and cities. SNCF runs a bus service as an extension of rail links. If you do wish to travel by bus, they are generally clean, comfortable and punctual. Large towns generally have a *gare routière* (bus station), which is often next to the *gare SNCF* (railway station).

ON THE MOVE

LONG-DISTANCE BUSES

● You can buy tickets for short distances on board, but for greater distances buy tickets in advance at the bus station. You must reserve your seat on most long-distance buses.
● Buses are slightly less expensive than trains, but significantly slower.
● If you are taking a bus operated by SNCF, you may be able to use an SNCF rail pass, if you have one. Check before you travel.
● Timetables tend to be constructed to suit working, market and school hours, so there will often be one bus in the morning and one in the evening.
● For information on SNCF-run buses, telephone 0891 676 869 (24 hours; €0.23 per minute).
● Few bus stations have a left-luggage office but some have information desks that can double as luggage rooms.

Eurolines Contact Details
Gare Routière Eurolines,
28 avenue Général-de-Gaulle,
Bagnolet
Tel 0836 695 252;
www.eurolines.fr

TAXIS
● Taking a taxi is not the most cost-effective way of getting about but you may consider it worthwhile for convenience.
● There is a pick-up charge and a charge per kilometre (0.6 mile), plus an extra charge for luggage and journeys during the evening or on Sundays. All taxis use a meter (*compteur*).
● The best way to find a taxi is to head to a taxi stand,

These taxi stands in Paris are hard to miss

marked by a blue Taxis sign. You can phone for a taxi but this can be more expensive as the meter may start running as soon as the taxi sets off to collect you.
● Smoking is allowed in some taxis—look for the sign.
● Always check the meter is reset when you enter the taxi.
● Some taxis accept bank cards, but it is best to have cash available. It is usual to leave a tip of around 10 per cent.
● If you want a receipt, ask for *un reçu*.

Taxis in Paris
● You can hail a taxi in the street, if you can find one that is free. A white light on the roof indicates the taxi is available. When the light is off, the taxi is already occupied.
● Taxi charges are based on area and time—it is more

expensive in the suburbs and at night. The tariff is shown on the meter.
● Journeys in central Paris average €6–€12. The meter starts at €2, with a minimum charge of €5. There is a surcharge of €1 for each piece of luggage and an extra €0.70 if you are picked up at a mainline station.
● Most drivers will not take more than three people.
● If you have any complaints, contact the Préfecture de Police, Service des Taxis, 36 rue des Morillons, 75015; tel 01 55 76 20 00.

Taxi companies in Paris include:
Alpha Taxis: tel 01 45 85 85 85
Artaxi: tel 01 42 06 67 10
Taxis Bleus: tel 0891 701 010;
www.taxis-bleus.com
Taxi G7: tel 01 47 39 47 39;
www.g7.fr

Getting Around in Paris

Paris has an efficient and relatively inexpensive transportation network and you should have few problems finding your way around the city. The Métro (underground/subway) is the backbone of the network. Other useful options include buses, riverboats and the suburban RER trains. Finally, don't forget your own two feet—central Paris is compact and walking is a great way to get your bearings.

TICKETS
- The Métro and buses use the same tickets and travel cards, and these can also be used on the RER within central Paris.
- The city is divided into fare zones. Most of the key sights are in Zone 1, although the Grande Arche is in Zone 3, Orly airport is in Zone 4 and Roissy–Charles de Gaulle airport is in Zone 5.
- Buy tickets at Métro stations, on buses (one-way tickets only) and at some news-stands.
- Children under four travel free, and children between the ages of four and nine travel for half price.

TICKETS			
TYPE	**PRICE**	**VALID**	**EXTRA INFORMATION**
Single ticket	€1.30	Tickets are valid on the Métro, the RER (within central Paris) and most buses. You don't have to use them on the day of purchase, but once you have stamped a ticket (by slotting it through the automatic barrier at Métro stations or in the machine on buses) it is valid for that journey only.	You can change Métro and RER lines within one journey on the same ticket, but you can't change from the Métro to a bus on the same ticket, or from one bus to another.
Carnet	€10 for 10 single tickets	As single tickets, see above.	This is cost-efficient if you are planning eight journeys or more. If you are with a friend, you could buy 10 tickets and share them.
Mobilis	Zones 1–2: €5.20 Zones 1–3: €6.95 Zones 1–5: €12	Valid for one day on the Métro, buses and RER, within the relevant zones.	A less expensive option than the one-day Paris Visite card (see below).
Paris Visite, Zones 1–3	1 day : €8.35 2 days: €13.70 3 days: €18.25 5 days: €26.65 Children's passes (4–11 year-olds) are roughly half-price	Valid for an unlimited number of journeys on the Métro, bus, RER and Transilien services, within zones 1–3. The ticket is valid from the first occasion you use it.	If you need to travel for one day only or if you are staying within zone 1, the Mobilis pass (see above) is a less expensive option. But with the Paris Visite card you also receive special offers for various sights. Buy the ticket at Paris tourist offices or at stations.
Paris Visite, Zones 1–5	1 day: €16.75 2 days: €26.65 3 days: €37.35 5 days: €45.70	Valid for an unlimited number of journeys on the Métro, bus, RER and Transilien services within zones 1–5 (including Versailles, Disneyland Resort Paris and Orly and Roissy–Charles de Gaulle airports).	An expensive option.
La Carte Orange-Coupon Hebdomadaire Zones 1–2	€14.50	Valid for a week on the Métro, buses and RER within zones 1–2.	The card is officially intended for residents of the Île de France, and runs from Monday to Sunday. So the earlier in the week you purchase it, the better the value. You'll need a passport-size photo.

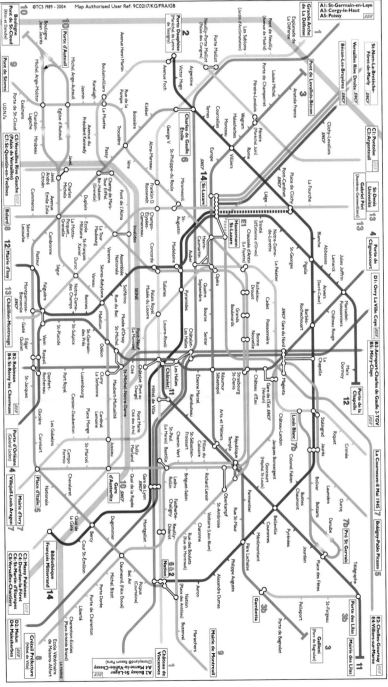

PARIS MÉTRO

- The Métro (*Métropolitain*) is the quickest way to travel for most journeys within the city. It runs from 5.30am to around 12.30am.

The Métro is one of the best ways of getting around Paris

- Each line is colour-coded and numbered (1–14, 3b and 7b).
- Stations are identified either by a large M or by the famous art nouveau Métro signs.
- Steps, or occasionally escalators, lead down into a lobby, where you can buy tickets from either a manned booth or a machine. Larger stations have shops and cafés.
- To reach the platforms, validate (*composter*) your ticket by slotting it into the machine at the automatic barrier, then collect it and keep it with you—inspectors make random checks.
- You'll often have a fairly long walk to the platform, so follow direction signs carefully. Signs will show the line number and colour. You also need to know the final destination of the train in the direction you wish to travel.
- Trains are frequent but get crowded during rush hour.
- An orange *correspondance* sign on the platform gives directions to connecting lines. Blue *sortie* signs show the exits.

Travel Information

- You can pick up free Métro maps at every station.

- For 24-hour recorded information (in English, Italian, Spanish and German), call 0892 684 114.
- To speak to an advisor (in French only) call 0892 687 714.
- The major stations have information desks, although communication can sometimes be limited if you don't speak French.
- The RATP website (*www.ratp.fr*) has a helpful route planner and also gives up-to-date traffic and travel information. Click on Paris Visite for advice for visitors.

How to survive the Métro

- When planning your route, don't confuse Métro lines with the suburban RER lines—both are usually shown on Métro maps. RER lines have letters rather than numbers and will usually flow off the map.
- To estimate your journey time, allow two minutes between each station. Bear in mind that it could take five minutes to walk from the station entrance to the actual platform (especially in warrens such as Châtelet).
- To save time, use the ticket machines rather than the manned ticket booths.
- Cash is more useful than credit cards when buying tickets.
- Always keep your ticket with you, in case you come across an inspector.
- If you need to change lines, don't exit the interchange station or you will invalidate your ticket.
- Keep your bags close to you and watch out for pickpockets.
- If you find you're going in the wrong direction, come off at the next station and double back. Follow directions to the correct platform, but stay within the automatic barriers or you'll invalidate your ticket.
- Street maps of the local areas are posted up in most station entrances.
- You may feel uncomfortable using the Métro alone late at night.

BUSES

Paris has a comprehensive network of buses, with more than 1,300 vehicles fighting their way through the traffic. Taking the bus is a good idea if you want to

Paris's buses move slowly, but allow you to see the sights

see the streets and sights rather than simply passing under them on the Métro, but don't expect to get anywhere quickly—the average speed is less than 13kph (8mph)!

- Most buses are painted easy-to-see turquoise and run from 7am to 8.30pm, although some continue into the evening, until around 12.30am. You're unlikely to have to wait more than 5 or 10 minutes from Monday to Saturday, but services are reduced or, on some routes, non-existent, on Sunday.
- The route number is displayed on the front of the bus, along with the final destination.
- Hold out your hand to stop the bus.
- If you need to buy a ticket, have the exact change ready as drivers don't carry much change.
- Enter at the front of the bus and show your travelcard or *carnet* ticket (see page 60) to the driver. *Carnet* tickets or single tickets must be stamped in the machine next to the driver.
- In rush hour, you are unlikely to get a seat. Be prepared for a long and uncomfortable stand.
- Just before your stop, press

the red button to alert the driver that you want to get off. You'll see the *arrêt demandé* (stop requested) sign light up.
● Leave by the central doors.

Tickets
● Buses use the same tickets as the Métro. A single ticket is valid for most central routes but you are not allowed to change buses on one ticket.
● You can buy single tickets on board, but not travelcards or *carnets* of 10 tickets.
● Always stamp single tickets (including *carnet* tickets) in the machine near the driver, but not *Paris Visite, Mobilis* or *Carte Orange* passes. Keep your ticket until you have left the bus.

Finding Information
● The *Grand Plan Lignes et Rues*, available from Métro stations, has a useful bus map.
● www.ratp.fr has bus information in French and English, as well as a handy route planner.
● Call 0892 684 114 for a recorded message in various languages or 0892 687 714 to speak to an advisor (in French).

Night Buses
Night buses, called Noctambus, link Châtelet with the suburbs from 1am to 5.30am. Buses are identified by a letter and tickets cost €2.60. Stops have a black-and-yellow owl logo. With waits of up to one hour, you may prefer to take a taxi.

TIPS
● Try to avoid the rush hour (roughly 7–9.30am and 4.30–7.30pm).
● Smoking is banned on buses, the Métro and the RER.
● Buying a *carnet* of 10 tickets is better value than buying tickets separately for each journey, and also saves time waiting at the ticket office.

RER
RER (Réseau Express Régional) trains travel through the city en route to the suburbs and can be a good time-saver if you are going from one side of

The RER is the best way to get out to the suburbs

town to the other. But reaching the correct platform can be a lengthy and confusing process, so for a short trip you're usually better off taking the Métro.

Tickets
● A single Métro ticket is valid for RER journeys in central Paris and you can change lines (including Métro lines) on the same ticket. For journeys farther afield, you'll need to buy a separate ticket valid for the destination.
● Travelcards (see page 60) are valid if they cover all the zones you are going through.
● Keep hold of your ticket as you'll need to slot it through the automatic barrier to exit the station.

Using the RER
● Trains run from around 5.30am to 12.30am.
● The RER has five lines, named A to E. Each line breaks into offshoots, which bear a number after the letter.
● The RER lines in central Paris are on the Métro map on page 61.
● Information screens in the lobby should tell you which

platform you need; or you could ask at the ticket desk.
● Slot your ticket into the automatic barrier and remember to retrieve it when it emerges.
● An increasing number of platforms have screens with information on arrival times for the next five trains.
● When leaving the train, follow blue *sortie* signs if it is the end of your journey, or orange *correspondance* signs if you need to change to another RER or Métro line.
● You'll need to slot your ticket into the automatic barrier to leave the station.

TIPS
● Few visitors use the RER outside central Paris (unless they are going to Versailles, Disneyland or the airport) so you may feel conspicuous. Be aware that some of the suburbs the RER passes through are somewhat run-down, and the trains and platforms tend to have more graffiti than on the Métro. Outside peak periods, the trains may also be quite empty.
● Trains run fairly frequently in central Paris, but less so in the outlying areas.

Getting Around in Major Cities

Public transportation in large French cities is usually excellent, with a variety of modes available, from Métros and buses to trams and funiculars. If you decide to drive, you'll find that cars are often positively discouraged with high parking rates.

GETTING AROUND LYON

www.tcl.fr

Lyon is a manageable size and the network of buses, trams, funiculars and Métros, run by TCL (Transports en Commun Lyonnais) is extensive, easy to use and covers the city and the outlying districts. You can get a map (plan de réseau) from the tourist office or any TCL branch.

Métro

Lyon's four Métro lines—A (red), B (blue), C (orange) and the futuristic driverless line D (green)—criss-cross the middle of the city, stopping at 40 stations. They serve most major squares and streets and connect with buses, trams and funiculars. Trains run from 5am to 12.15am and are easy to use. The main Métro stations are Bellecour, Perrache and Part-Dieu. You'll need to stamp your ticket at the start of your journey.

Buses

Buses cover every corner of Lyon, with 100 routes, running generally from 5am to 9pm (but check individual services). Remember to stamp your

Lyon (below) is well served by public transportation

ticket in the machine at the start of your journey.

Trams

There are two tram (streetcar) lines, T1 and T2, both starting from Perrache SNCF and Métro station. Trams run almost silently, so be careful when stepping into the street.

Funiculars

Two *funiculaires* (funiculars) depart every 10 minutes until 10pm from Vieux Lyon Métro station. One goes to Fourvière, to the hilltop basilica, and the other goes to Minimes, for the Roman ruins, or St-Just.

Tickets

You can use a one-way ticket on the Métro, bus or tram. They cost €1.40 for one hour, €1.90 for two hours or €11.20 for a *carnet* of 10 tickets, although you can buy only one-hour tickets on the bus. A one-day travel pass, *Ticket Liberté*, costs €4 and gives unlimited access. The funicular costs €2.20 return.

GETTING AROUND MARSEILLE

Régie des Transports de Marseille (RTM) is responsible for the city's Métro. The main office is at Espace Infos, 6–8 rue des Fabres

(*Mon–Fri 6.10am– 6.30pm, Sat 9am–12.30pm and 2–5.30pm; tel 04 91 91 92 10*).

Métro

The city has two fast, well-maintained Métro lines. Métro 1 runs from La Timone in the eastern suburbs through the northeast suburbs to La Rose and is due for extension by 2006. Métro 2 runs roughly north to south, from Bougainville in the north to Sainte-Marguerite Dromel in the south and is due to be extended east one station to St-Loup between 2005 and 2006. The Métro runs Monday to Thursday from 5am to 9pm, and on Friday to Sunday until 12.30am.

Tickets

Tickets cost €1.40 and can be used on any combination of Métro, bus and tram. Your ticket is valid for one hour after you have stamped it. There are no return tickets.

GETTING AROUND TOULOUSE

Métro

The high-tech, driverless Métro, is clean, comfortable and efficient. There is just one line, with 15 stations. It runs from Jolimont to Basso-Cambo, taking

18 minutes. Construction is underway on a second line. There is a Métro stop at the railway station (Marengo-SNCF). Other useful stops include Jean Jaurès (for place Wilson and the Boulevards) and Capitole (for place du Capitole and rue Alsace Lorraine). The system operates from 5am to around midnight (12.42am on Fridays and Saturdays). Trains run every two minutes during rush hour, every four minutes outside the rush hour and every six minutes at night.

Tickets

You can buy tickets at machines in Métro stations, which have instructions in English and give change. Many stations do not have a ticket office so make sure you have cash. Tickets are valid for 45 minutes and can be used on both the Métro and buses.

GETTING AROUND LILLE
Métro

The VAL is a driverless two-line Métro system with trains that run both above and below ground.

Buses and trams

The regional bus network serves all districts of Lille and its surrounding towns, and even goes into Belgium. Most leave from place des Buisses, between the two train stations (Lille-Flandres and Lille-Europe, the Eurostar station). There are two routes from the underground terminus at Lille-Flandres station to Tourcoing and Roubaix. There is a limited night bus network.

Tickets

You can buy a one-way ticket, a *carnet* of 10 or a one-day pass, which you can use on the bus, tram (streetcar) and Métro. Services run from around 6am to midnight and there is no service at all on 1 May. Get tickets and information at Lille-Flandres station.

GETTING AROUND STRASBOURG

www.cts-strasbourg.fr
Services are run by CTS (Compagnie des Transports Strasbourgeois). Call 03 88 77 70 70 for information.

Buses and trams

The city has four efficient, modern tramlines which run daily from 4.30am to 12.30am. There is also a good bus network.

Tickets

Tickets for buses and trams are the same and are valid for an hour. For unlimited travel, get a *Tourpass* (€3 per day). You must stamp your ticket before your journey. For trams, insert your ticket into the machine on the platform. For buses, use the machine on board.

Many French cities can be explored by tram

Lille's futuristic-looking Métro runs above and below ground

GETTING AROUND BORDEAUX
Buses and trams

The city is installing a state-of-the-art tram system, with the first sections (25km/16 miles) due to start running in 2004. The work has caused major disruptions to traffic in the city, but this should improve when the trams are ready. Buses are run by Connex-CGFTE (www.netbus-bordeaux.com). For information call 05 57 57 88 88.

Tickets

On the buses, a one-way ticket costs €1.15 and a *carnet* of 10 tickets costs €8.60. A one-day *Découverte* card gives unlimited travel and costs €3.75. You can also buy *Découverte* cards which last up to six days.

VISITORS WITH A DISABILITY

Getting around the country is becoming easier, thanks to improvements to buses and trains. Most airports have facilities for people with disabilities and Eurostar trains are accessible to wheelchair-users. But you'll still find challenges when getting around France, especially in historic towns, with their narrow, cobbled streets. Before you travel, it's worth checking what facilities are available at your arrival airport (look up www.aeroport.fr) and your hotel, as older buildings may not have an elevator.

ON THE MOVE

ARRIVING IN FRANCE
By Air
In Paris, both Roissy–Charles de Gaulle and Orly airports are well equipped for people with reduced mobility. Shuttle buses between terminals have ramps for wheelchairs, as well as voice announcements for people with visual impairments. The terminals have adapted lavatories, low-level telephones and reserved parking spaces. For more information, ask for the leaflet *Guide—Passager à Mobilité Réduite (fax requests to: 01 49 75 58 78 or email: DCCMP3@adp.fr)*. There are organizations that offer specialist services from the airports into Paris, which you'll need to reserve in advance, such as Airhop *(tel 01 41 29 01 29)*. Taxis are also an option. The Orlyval train (see page 44) is accessible to wheelchairs.

For information on facilities at other airports in France, contact Aeroguides editions *(tel 01 46 55 93 43; www.aeroguide.fr)*.

If you are a wheelchair-user, tell your airline when you reserve your ticket.

By Train
Eurostar trains and terminals are wheelchair-friendly and wheelchair-users can also benefit from discounted tickets.

GETTING AROUND IN FRANCE
By Train
France's long-distance trains are equipped for people with reduced mobility. On TGV and CORAIL trains, spaces for wheelchair-users are reserved in first class, although only a second class fare is payable. Reserve at least 24 hours in advance. There are also adapted lavatories. Most large stations have elevators or ramps to the platform. If you need assistance, request it at the time of reserving your ticket. For more information, look up SNCF's website *(www.sncf.com)*.

Facilities on regional trains tend to be more varied. It is always best to check before you travel. For more information, call 0800 154 753.

In Paris
The Métro is virtually inaccessible to wheelchair-users, due to countless steps, a warren of passageways and inflexible automatic barriers. The exception is Line 14. Some RER stations on Lines A and B have elevators to the platforms, although some can be operated only by a member of staff (press the *Appel* button for assistance). Most stations have a ticket office fitted with induction loops for people with hearing impairments. Some buses have ramps for wheelchair-users and voice announcements of the next stop for passengers with visual impairments. There are plans for 59 bus routes to be accessible to wheelchair-users by 2006.

USEFUL WEBSITES AND ORGANIZATIONS

Access Project
39 Bradley Gardens, West Ealing, London, W13 8HE, UK
www.accessproject-phsp.org/paris/about.htm
Advice on getting around in Paris.

Les Compagnons du Voyage
Tel 01 45 19 15 00
An accompaniment service for the Métro, RER trains and buses in Paris.

Holiday Care Service
Tel 08451 249 971 (from UK)
www.holidaycare.org.uk
Travel and holiday information for people with disabilities.

RATP Mission Accessibilité
Tel 01 49 28 18 84
19 place Lachambaudie, 75570, Paris Cedex 12
Set up by the Paris Métro operator RATP to improve access for people with disabilities.

Infomobi
www.infomobi.com
Travel information for people with disabilities in the Île de France area.

Maison de la France
www.franceguide.com
The website of the French tourist office has useful information for people with disabilities.

Mobile en Ville
www.mobile-en-ville.asso.fr
A website packed with information on disability access and related issues.

Mobility International USA
www.miusa.org
Promotes international travel and exchange schemes for people with disabilities.

Paris Tourist Office
Tel 0892 683 000
25–27 rue des Pyramides, 75001
www.paris-touristoffice.com
Useful information about wheelchair access in the city's museums, on buses, the RER and at airports.

Society for Accessible Travel and Hospitality (SATH)
Tel 212 447 7284 (from US)
www.sath.org
A US-based organization offering advice for visitors with disabilities and promoting awareness of their travel requirements.

This chapter is divided into eight regions of France. Places of interest are listed alphabetically in each region. A contents page at the front of each regional section gives the key sights. To see where the sights are located turn to the atlas on pages 423–444.

The Sights

PARIS AND
THE ÎLE DE FRANCE

France's capital city draws millions of visitors to its world-famous monuments, top-class museums and romantic bridges, parks and squares. It sits within the Île de France, with its chateaux and theme parks.

MAJOR SIGHTS

The Arc de Triomphe viewed from the Champs-Élysées

ARC DE TRIOMPHE AND CHAMPS-ÉLYSÉES

Paris's most famous avenue is crowned by the mighty Arc de Triomphe.

The wide, leafy Champs-Élysées is a focal point for the French nation, witness to momentous events such as De Gaulle's triumphal Liberation march in 1944 and the soccer World Cup celebrations in 1998. The bustling avenue, over 2km (1.2 miles) long and 71m (232 ft) wide, is packed with cinemas, shops, cafés and car show-rooms. Go there on 14 July (Bastille Day) and most of the French army will roll past you. Another good time to visit is during the Christmas illuminations.

THE EARLY DAYS
The Champs-Élysées dates back to 1616, when Marie de Medici turned the area into a fashionable driveway. Then landscape designer André Le Nôtre (of Versailles fame) added alleys of trees and gardens, prompting the name 'Elysian Fields'. Walkways and fountains were installed in 1824 and the avenue soon became crowded with cafés, restaurants and a smart clientele.

ARC DE TRIOMPHE
The Arc de Triomphe crowns the western tip of the Champs-Élysées, standing on a hectic roundabout known as L'Étoile (the star). Within its grounds are the Tomb of the Unknown Soldier, installed in 1920 after World War I, and a poignant Memorial Flame. There are wonderful views from the rooftop, 50m (164ft) above street level. From here you can admire the geometry of Baron Haussmann's web-like street design and look along the so-called Grand Axis towards place de la Concorde in one direction and the Grande Arche in the other. At night the city shimmers with lights. Back at ground level, save some time to admire the magnificent sculpted façade, the work of three different artists. Don't miss the fearsome winged figure of Liberty on François Rude's sculpture *La Marseillaise,* calling the French to defend their nation (northeastern pillar, facing the Champs-Élysées).

Napoleon commissioned the arch in 1806, wanting an awesome memorial to the French army. In 1810 a full-size model was installed to celebrate the emperor's marriage to Marie-Louise of Austria but the real thing was not ready until 1836, 15 years after his death.

RATINGS	
Historic interest	●●●○
Photo stops	●●●○
Shopping	●●○○
Walkability	●●●○

TIPS
● It takes at least 30 minutes to walk from one end of the Champs-Élysées to the other and, with the heavy traffic, it is not a restful stroll. You may prefer to take the Métro—line 1 (yellow) runs underneath the entire length of the avenue.
● Most of the cafés and restaurants are at the Arc de Triomphe end, although you may find better value in establishments in the side streets.

BASICS
ARC DE TRIOMPHE
✚ 424 B1 • Place Charles-de-Gaulle, 75008 ☎ 01 55 37 73 77
◉ Daily 9.30am–11pm, Apr–end Sep; 10am–10.30pm, rest of year
🏛 Free to wander around the base. Rooftop: adult €7, under 18 free
🚇 Charles de Gaulle–Étoile
🚌 22, 30, 31, 52, 73, 92
🚉 RER line A, Charles de Gaulle–Étoile
🏬 Gift shop 🎧 €6
📞 Call Monum on 01 44 54 19 30
www.monum.fr

AVENUE DES CHAMPS-ÉLYSÉES
✚ 424 C1 • 75008
🚇 Charles de Gaulle–Étoile, Georges V, Franklin D. Roosevelt, Champs-Élysées-Clemenceau 🚌 32, 42, 73 and others
🚇 Charles de Gaulle–Étoile

The bustling lobby of the Centre Georges Pompidou

RATINGS

Cultural interest	● ● ● ● ●
Good for kids	● ● ●
Photo stops (exterior and views)	● ● ●

TIPS

● If you're a traditionalist when it comes to art, let yourself in to the Museum of Modern Art (relatively) gently by starting with the 5th floor (1905–1960) before tackling the more bemusing 4th floor (1960 to the present day).

● If your mind is spinning from a day of modern art, enjoy a calming concert at the nearby church of St-Merri, Saturdays at 9pm and Sundays at 4pm.

BASICS

Centre Georges Pompidou
✛ 426 H3 • Place Georges-Pompidou, 75004 ☎ 01 44 78 12 33
⊙ Centre Georges Pompidou: Wed–Mon 11–10. Musée National d'Art Moderne and exhibitions: Wed–Mon 11–9 (last ticket one hour earlier; late nights Thu, Fri until 11pm for some exhibitions).
✋ Full ticket €10; Musée National d'Art Moderne, Atelier Brancusi and Children's Gallery: adult €5.50, under 18 free; free to all 1st Sun of month; Exhibitions: prices vary
Ⓜ Rambuteau, Hôtel de Ville
🚌 29, 38, 47, 75
Ⓡ Châtelet-Les-Halles
☕ Café on first floor
🍴 Georges restaurant on 6th floor
📚 Bookshops, boutique, post office
📖 €12 🎧 Audiotours €4.50
www.centrepompidou.fr

CENTRE GEORGES POMPIDOU

Paris's wackiest building has one of the largest collections of modern art in the world.

You'll either love or hate the brazen design of the Centre Georges Pompidou, and you may well feel the same about the contemporary art it contains. The venue has sparked controversy since it opened in 1977, gracing the historic heart of Paris with an incongruously modern building that resembles a giant air-conditioning system. But while its design may not please everyone, the arts complex attracts around six million visitors each year—roughly the same as the Louvre—with its canny, ever-changing mix of visual, performance and new-media art.

THE CONCEPT

Georges Pompidou, President of France from 1969 until his death in 1974, wanted a venue where people could enjoy contemporary film, drama, dance, music and visual art. The outlandish building took five years to construct and was a controversial addition to Beaubourg, a run-down district of 18th- and 19th-century town houses. Designers Renzo Piano and Richard Rogers turned the building 'inside out' by placing its 'guts' (all the piping) on the outside. This piping was coded: yellow for electrics, blue for air-conditioning, green for water and red for the elevators. Pompidou did not live to see the opening in 1977, but his vision proved sagacious—the venue was soon attracting 22,000 visitors a day, rivalling the Louvre in popularity. The site closed for two years for extensive renovation work in the autumn of 1997, re-opening just in time for the new millennium.

MUSÉE NATIONAL D'ART MODERNE

The Museum of Modern Art takes over where the Musée d'Orsay leaves off, featuring works from 1905 to the present day. Up to 2,000 pieces from the 50,000-strong collection are on display at any one time, ranging from Cubism by Georges Braque and Pablo Picasso to Pop Art by Andy Warhol and video art by Korean artist Nam June Paik.

The Centre Pompidou's temporary exhibitions, on the first and sixth floors, are as much of a draw as the permanent museum. Other attractions include children's activities, two cinemas and a library.

Don't miss The surreal *Stravinsky Fountain* (pictured right) is round the corner from the main entrance, in place Igor Stravinsky.

The grave of the composer Rossini, in Père Lachaise

CIMETIÈRE DU PÈRE-LACHAISE

➕ 427 L2 • Boulevard de Ménilmontant, 75020 ☎ 01 55 25 82 10 🕐 Mon–Fri 8–6, Sat 8.30–6, Sun 9–6 (closes 5.30 early Nov to mid-Mar) 🎟 Free 🚇 Père Lachaise, Gambetta 🚌 61, 69

Visit the graves of luminaries such as Frédéric Chopin, Marcel Proust and Oscar Wilde at this vast cemetery on the eastern edge of the city. Père-Lachaise covers 44 hectares (108 acres) and contains 70,000 tombs.

The cemetery is named after Louis XIV's confessor, Père La Chaise, who once owned the land here. It was designed by Brongniart in 1803 to echo an English-style garden. At first, it was not popular, but once the graves of writers Molière and Jean de La Fontaine and tragic lovers Abélard and Héloïse had been transferred here, it soon became the most fashionable place to be buried in Paris.

Now the cemetery has become a place of pilgrimage—among the famous people buried here are composers Frédéric Chopin and Georges Bizet, Paris town planner Baron Haussmann, artists Amedeo Modigliani and Eugène Delacroix, singers Edith Piaf and Maria Callas, writers Marcel Proust, Honoré de Balzac and Oscar Wilde, actresses Simone Signoret and Sarah Bernhardt, actor Yves Montand and dancer Isadora Duncan. One of the most visited graves is that of Jim Morrison, lead singer of The Doors, who died in Paris in 1971.

The Mur des Fédérés, in the eastern corner, marks the site of the Communards' tragic last stand in 1871, when the 147 survivors of the Commune were lined up against the wall and executed by a government firing squad.

CONCIERGERIE

The horrors of the French Revolution linger on in this dimly lit Gothic palace, where prisoners spent their final days before being led to the guillotine.

Sailing past the Conciergerie's beautifully floodlit towers on an evening boat cruise, it is hard to imagine the fear that lurked within its walls for more than five centuries. The former palace played a gruesome role in the Revolution, housing more than 4,000 inmates, up to 600 at a time. Marie-Antoinette, wife of Louis XVI, was among the most famous prisoners and you can see a poignant re-creation of her cell during your visit.

The Conciergerie was originally a palace, part of a royal complex that included Sainte-Chapelle and the Palais de Justice. The oldest parts of the building date from the early 14th century, although a governor's palace and fortress probably stood on the Île de la Cité as far back as Roman times. In the late 14th century, Charles V chose to live else-where, and the site became a law court and prison, with occasional use for royal functions. It was around this time that the Conciergerie gained its name, from the Concierge who oversaw the site.

Entering from the boulevard du Palais, you are plunged into semi-darkness in a vast Gothic chamber said to be Europe's oldest surviving medieval hall. The Salles des Gens d'Armes, 63m (206ft) long and 8.5m (28ft) high, dates back to the 14th century, when it formed the lower floor of the Grand'Salle. The king's staff ate in here, up to 2,000 at a time, while royal banquets and marriage celebrations were held upstairs. A spiral staircase leads up to the kitchens, where there are four walk-in fireplaces, each big enough to roast a couple of sheep.

RATINGS	
Historic interest	●●●●
Photo stops (from the Seine)	●●●

TIPS

● Signage in the rooms isn't particularly clear. Pick up a leaflet at the entrance to help navigate your way around.
● If you intend to visit Sainte-Chapelle as well, buy a joint ticket at the Conciergerie.

BASICS

➕ 426 H3 • 2 boulevard du Palais, Île de la Cité, 75001
☎ 01 53 40 60 97; 01 53 73 78 52
🕐 Daily 9.30–6
🎟 Adult €5.50 (€8 for combined ticket with Sainte-Chapelle), under 18 free
🚇 Cité, Châtelet
🚌 21, 24, 27, 38, 58, 81, 85, 96
🚊 RER line B, C St-Michel-Notre-Dame
📖 Bookshop 🎧 Daily guided tours in French, English, Italian 🎫 €6
www.monum.fr

Sleeping Beauty's castle

© Disney

DISNEYLAND RESORT PARIS

Experience the magic of Disneyland—a must for kids of all ages.

Disneyland Resort Paris attracts millions of visitors to its two theme parks—Disneyland Park and Walt Disney Studios Park. The site, in the countryside east of Paris, opened in 1992 to a blaze of publicity.

DISNEYLAND PARK

You can visit five different 'lands', each with its own themed rides, restaurants and shops. Main Street USA takes you back in time with its nostalgic scenes from an American town at the turn of the 19th century. Seasonal parades (check the website for dates and times) bring scenes from Disney's animated films to life with jugglers, clowns, dancers and well-known characters. Fantasyland, especially popular with younger children, includes Sleeping Beauty's Fairytale Castle, the 'It's a Small World' ride and the enchanting 'Pays de Contes de Fées' (Fairystory Land) canal cruise. Adventureland boasts the swashbuckling Pirates of the Caribbean Adventure Isle and the high-speed 'Indiana Jones and the Temple of Peril' ride. Frontierland, with its canyons, gold mines and rivers, offers two thrill-seeker attractions—the 'Big Thunder Mountain' runaway train ride and the ghostly Phantom Manor. Discoveryland was inspired by Jules Verne's visions of the future, and the 'Mystery of the Nautilus' ride is based on the film *20,000 Leagues Under the Sea*. Reaching top speeds of 70kph (43 mph), the 'Space Mountain—from the Earth to the Moon' roller coaster is not for the faint-hearted. The spectacular Star Tours flight simulator whisks visitors on an interplanetary journey.

WALT DISNEY STUDIOS PARK

The Walt Disney Studios Park opened in 2002, based on the concept of Disney–MGM Studios in Florida. Four zones each aim to create the atmosphere of a real film studio—Front Lot, Animation Courtyard, Production Courtyard and Backlot. The 33m (108ft) water tower, crowned with Mickey Mouse's black ears, dominates the Front Lot.

DISNEY VILLAGE

Between the two parks and the Disney hotels you'll find the Disney Village entertainment complex, open until the early hours and bustling with themed restaurants, bars, shops, street artists and cinemas.

RATINGS

Good for kids	●●●●●
Photo stops	●●●
Walkability	●●●●

BASICS

🏠 441 J5• BP 100, Marne-la-Vallée, 77777 Cedex 4

☎ 01 60 30 60 30

🕐 Times vary

🚇 RER line A to Marne-la-Vallée/Chessy station

🚗 A4 motorway (Autoroute de l'Est), direction 'Metz/Nancy', and take exit 14 to Parcs Disneyland

🎟 1-day Theme Park ticket (valid for either Disneyland Park or Walt Disney Studios Park): adult €39, child (3–11) €29, under 3 free.
3-day Theme Parks Hopper Ticket (valid for both Theme Parks): adult €107, child (3–11) €80, under 3 free. Prices may vary according to season.

🅿 €8 per day; free if you are staying at a Disneyland Resort Paris hotel

🛍 Shops and boutiques

❓ Height and age restrictions apply to some rides

www.disneylandparis.com

TIPS

● Information points at City Hall in Disneyland Park and Studio Services in Walt Disney Studios Park provide maps and event details.
● A free FASTPASS time-saving system is available on some of the more popular rides, cutting down queuing.

Galerie François I overlooks the Cour de la Fontaine

RATINGS

Historic interest	●●●○
Photo stops (exterior)	●●●○
Walkability	●●●○

TIP

● Holders of a *Carte Musées-Monuments* receive free entry to the chateau.

BASICS

✚ 441 J5 • Château de Fontainebleau 77300 ☎ 01 60 71 50 70/60
🕐 Renaissance Rooms, Sovereigns' State Apartments and Napoleon I's Imperial Apartment: Wed–Mon 9.30–6, Jun–end Sep; Wed–Mon 9.30–5, rest of year. Last admission 45 minutes before closing. Petits Appartements and Napoleon I Museum: guided tour only. Gardens: daily 9–7, May–end Sep; 9–6 Mar, Apr and Oct; 9–5 Nov–end Feb
💶 Adult €5.50, under 18 free, free to wander in the grounds; Petits Appartements and Napoleon I museum: adult €3
🚆 From Gare de Lyon to Fontainebleau-Avon; from here, the A/B bus takes you to the castle
🚗 Take the A6 motorway from the Porte d'Orléans and leave at the Fontainebleau exit
🍴 There is no café; picnics are allowed in the park, but not the gardens. There are cafés and restaurants in the town
ℹ See the notice board at the ticket desk for times. Audioguides cost €2.20
🏠 4 rue Royale (next to the Château de Fontainebleau bus stop), tel 01 60 74 99 99
www.musee-chateau-fontainebleau.fr

CHÂTEAU DE FONTAINEBLEAU

This former royal residence has 1,900 opulent rooms and exquisite landscaped gardens. Napoleon signed his deed of abdication here.

The Château de Fontainebleau rivals Versailles in grandeur and history but has the bonus of fewer crowds. Louis XIII was born here and Napoleon I signed his abdication papers within these walls.

REMINDERS OF NAPOLEON

You enter the chateau through the stately Cour du Cheval Blanc (Courtyard of the White Horse), also known as the Cour des Adieux. Napoleon Bonaparte bade farewell to his Imperial Guard at the horse-shoe staircase here before being exiled to the island of Elba. Inside, your tour begins on the first floor. Look out for the dazzling Renaissance Salle de Bal (ballroom), with its wood panels and frescoes illustrating mythological and hunting themes, and the Galerie François I, with frescoes painted by the Florentine artist Rosso, a pupil of Michelangelo. Farther on, highlights in Les Grands Appartements des Souverains (Sovereigns' State Apartments) include the ornate Empress's Bedchamber, with a bed made for (although not used by) Marie-Antoinette, and Napoleon's preposterously extravagant Throne Room. L'Appartement Intérieur de l'Empereur (Napoleon I's Imperial Apartment) offers a glimpse into some of the more personal aspects of the emperor's life, although this is not his private apartment (Petits Appartements), which can be seen only on a guided tour, along with the Napoleon Museum. The Abdication Room has the unassuming round table where Napoleon signed his deed of abdication on 6 April 1814. Save time to wander around the stunning grounds, with the elegant Grand Parterre and vast Carp Pond.

ORIGINS

Fontainebleau has attracted kings since the 12th century, keen to hunt in the surrounding forest. Much of the chateau dates from the Renaissance, when François I built a sumptuous royal residence. He employed the cream of Italy's artists and craftsmen to decorate the interior and laid out the garden with lakes and canals. A century later, the gardens were re-landscaped by André Le Nôtre, who also designed Versailles's stately parterres. Various kings commissioned modifications to the chateau and Napoleon I refurnished it in 1804.

Galerie Vivienne (above).
La Grande Arche (right)

LES GALERIES

Galerie Vivienne ✚ 426 G2 • 4 rue des Petits-Champs/6 rue Vivienne/5 rue de la Banque, 75002 ⓜ Bourse
Galerie Colbert ✚ 426 G2 • 6 rue des Petits-Champs, 75002 ⓜ Bourse
http://passagescouverts.free.fr

These elegant covered passage-ways, with their glass skylights and decorative floors, were the stylish shopping malls of early 19th-century Paris. Less than 30 of the original 140 passages survive—relics of pre-department store days. The elegant Galerie Vivienne, built in 1823, is one of the most fashionable, with its ornate cast-iron entrance gates, high glass roofs, chandeliers and splendid mosaic floors. Running parallel to it is the Galerie Colbert, dating from 1826. Others include the Passage des Panoramas, off boulevard Montmartre, and the Galerie Véro-Dodat, near the Louvre.

GRAND PALAIS

Grand Palais ✚ 425 D2 • Avenue Winston-Churchill, 75008 ☎ 01 44 13 17 30; reservations 01 42 31 32 28 ⓞ Wed–Mon 10–8 (also Wed 8–10pm) 🎟 Varies ⓜ Champs-Élysées-Clemenceau 🚌 42, 73, 83, 93
Palais de la Découverte ✚ 424 D2 • Avenue Franklin Roosevelt, 75008 ☎ 01 56 43 20 21 ⓞ Tue–Sat 9.30–6, Sun 10–7 🎟 Adult €5.60, child €3.70; €3.05 extra for Planetarium
www.palais-decouverte.fr

The Grand Palais, with its soaring glass and iron domes, was built for the 1900 Universal Exhibition. A striking mix of art nouveau and neoclassical, it hosts high-profile art exhibitions. On the western side, the Palais de la Découverte is a science museum, with a Planetarium.

An art installation (right) in La Défense, near La Grande Arche

GRANDE ARCHE
Paris's most striking modern monument.

The Grande Arche is best admired from below, looking up into the vast chasm that is greater than the height of Notre-Dame and the width of the Champs-Élysées.

The futuristic monument-cum-office-block was designed as a symbolic western gateway to Paris and focal point of the new business district, La Défense. It was completed in 1989 in time for the bicentenary of the French Revolution.

Standing below the Grande Arche is a rather unnerving experience, as you look up at 300,000 tonnes of concrete, marble-cladding and glass rising 110m (360ft). But if you think that's daunting, wait until you take the glass elevator that climbs up the cavity of the arch on what looks disconcertingly like a piece of scaffolding. At the top, walk outside to see the view, up some steps onto a viewing platform. The panorama is partly obscured by wire fencing and the office blocks of La Défense—if you climb only one of Paris's tall buildings, the Grande Arche is probably not the one to choose. However, if you have already seen the view from the Eiffel Tower and the Arc de Triomphe, the Grande Arche offers a new perspective.

The arch was the culmination of many unsuccessful attempts to find a nucleus for La Défense in the 1970s. The design, by Danish architect Johan Otto von Spreckelsen, was finally chosen in 1983.

RATINGS	
Photo stops	● ● ● ○

TIPS

● The best view of the Arc de Triomphe is not from the roof of the Grande Arche but from the top of the 54 marble steps leading up to the elevators.
● To experience the atmosphere of business-focused La Défense, visit on a weekday.

BASICS

✚ 424 off A1 • 1 parvis de la Défense, 92044 Paris-La-Défense
☎ 01 49 07 27 57
ⓞ Daily 10–7 (Sat until 8, Apr–end Sep; last entry 30 min before closing)
🎟 Adult €7, child (6–17) €6
ⓜ Grande Arche de la Défense 🚌 73
🚆 RER line A, La Défense 🍴 ♿
📷 €6
www.grandearche.com

Île St-Louis (above) and the larger Île de la Cité (below right)

The historical heart of Paris, packed with must-see sights and offering wonderful views of the Seine.

The Île de la Cité is where the Paris story began, when the Celtic Parisii tribe moved in more than 2,000 years ago. The Romans arrived 200 years later, and in the Middle Ages the island gained a royal palace (now the Palais de Justice and Conciergerie).

Today it is still a key part of the city, packed with visitors, traffic and fabulous architecture. One of the best ways to appreciate its beautiful buildings is by boat, taking one of the trips that start from below the Pont Neuf, Paris's oldest bridge. From the water you'll see the elegant Notre-Dame rising high above the banks and the stern façade of the Conciergerie, once Paris's most notorious prison.

On foot, the Île de la Cité's charms may be harder to appreciate at first, thanks to the heavy traffic and crowds of visitors. But persevere. When you have ticked off the don't-miss sights of Notre-Dame (see page 87), the Conciergerie (see page 72) and Sainte-Chapelle (see page 91) there are quieter spots where you can relax and enjoy the views. The grassy square Jean XXIII is a good place to sit and admire the architecture of Notre-Dame, while square de l'Île de France, at the eastern tip of the island, gives lovely views of the Seine and the Île St-Louis. It is also home to the haunting Mémorial des Martyrs de la Déportation, commemorating the French citizens deported to concentration camps during World War II.

When your legs just won't take you any farther, give in and enjoy a coffee or crêpe in one of the cafés—although you may find yourself paying tourist prices for the privilege.

Don't miss The flower market in place Louis Lépine (*Mon–Sat 8–7*) sells anything from delicate blooms to trees 1.8m (6ft) high.

RATINGS			
Good for kids	● ● ●		
Historic interest	● ● ● ● ●		
Photo stops	● ● ● ● ●		

BASICS
⊞ 426 H4 • Île de la Cité, 75001 and 75004
Ⓜ Cité (also Pont Neuf, St-Michel, Châtelet, Hôtel de Ville)
🚌 21, 24, 27, 38, 47, 58, 70, 85, 96
🚆 RER line B, C, St-Michel-Notre-Dame
🍴 A selection on Île de la Cité, as well as on the nearby Île St-Louis and in the Latin Quarter
🏨 A selection

THE SIGHTS

ÎLE ST-LOUIS

⊞ 427 J4 • Île St-Louis, 75004 Ⓜ Pont Marie, Sully Morland 🚌 67, 86, 87

This peaceful, leafy island sits discreetly behind the Île de la Cité and offers wonderful views of Notre-Dame from its western tip. Visitors pack its main road, the narrow rue St-Louis-en-l'Île, to browse in the shops and try the famous ice cream at Maison Berthillon (*closed Mon, Tue and Aug*). Architect Le Vau designed many of the town houses on the tiny island in the 17th century. Residents have included the poet Baudelaire, sculptress Camille Claudel and the painter and caricaturist Honoré Daumier.

INSTITUT DU MONDE ARABE

⊞ 427 J5 • 1 rue des Fossés-St-Bernard, 75005 ☎ 01 40 51 38 38 🕐 Tue–Sun 10–6 💰 Adult €4, child (12–18) €3, under 12 free Ⓜ Jussieu, Cardinal-Lemoine, Sully-Morland 🚌 24, 63, 67, 86, 87, 89 🔖 Guided tours daily, €6.10 🍴 Le Ziryab panoramic restaurant ☕ Café Littéraire, Le Moucharabieh cafeteria 🏨 www.imarabe.org

The Arab World Institute is in a stunning aluminium and glass building that combines modern materials with the spirit of traditional Arab architecture. The southern façade consists of 240 metal panels, adjusted every hour to filter the sunlight as it enters the building. Their design is inspired by traditional carved wooden screens called *moucharabiehs*. The Institute, designed by Jean Nouvel, Pierre Soria, Gilbert Lezenes and Architecture Studio, opened in 1987. Exhibits in its museum range in origin from Spain to India and from prehistory to the 19th century.

Don't miss The views from the 9th floor are wonderful.

Napoleon's grand tomb (above).
The golden Église du Dôme (right)

LES INVALIDES

See Napoleon's tomb and an absorbing army museum.

Although its architecture is pompous, severe and authoritarian, Les Invalides was actually built to house wounded and elderly soldiers. Louis XIV was thinking of others for once when he commissioned Libéral Bruant to design the imposing building, with its 195m (640ft) façade. In 1674 the first soldiers moved in and were welcomed by the king himself. It took another 32 years before the gold-encrusted Église du Dôme (Church of the Dome) was completed. Today, visitors come to see a later addition, the tomb of Napoleon I, as well as the impressive Army Museum. On entering the stately grounds you'll be following in the footsteps of many a military hero, including General de Gaulle and Winston Churchill.

REMEMBERING PAST CONFLICTS

The Musée de l'Armée is one of the largest of its kind in the world, and among the extensive collections of weapons, armour, flags, uniforms and paintings are some real gems. The museum is in three wings, although renovation work means the west wing will be closed until summer 2005. As you would expect, Napoleon I features prominently, and you can see his frock coat, hat, coronation saddle and even his actual horse, Vizir (not for the squeamish). Don't miss the evocative World War II exhibition, which uses film footage, photos and day-to-day objects to convey the horrors of the war and the bravery of those who fought against Hitler. On the fourth floor of the east wing, the Musée des Plans-Reliefs displays huge scale models of fortresses and French towns, which were used to plan sieges in the 17th and 18th centuries.

ÉGLISE DU DÔME

The golden dome of this stunning church rises 107m (350ft) above the ground, a glistening monument to two of France's most influential and charismatic rulers, Louis XIV and Napoleon. The church, dedicated to St. Louis, was designed by Versailles architect Jules Hardouin-Mansart and was completed in 1706. Its inauguration was a grand affair, attended by Louis XIV and members of the royal family.

Don't miss Napoleon's tomb is in a grandiose crypt directly below the dome. His remains were brought back to France in 1840, but it took another 21 years to create a mausoleum fit for an emperor.

RATINGS

Good for kids	● ● ●
Historic interest	● ● ● ●
Photo stops (exterior)	● ● ●

TIPS

● The best way to appreciate the grandeur of Les Invalides is to approach the site from Pont Alexandre III.
● The Army Museum is busiest between 11am and 1pm.
● As an antidote to the war focus of Les Invalides, unwind in the nearby gardens of the Musée Rodin (see page 86).

BASICS

✚ 425 D4 • Hôtel National des Invalides, 129 rue de Grenelle, 75007
☎ 01 44 42 37 72
🕐 Daily 10–6, Apr–end Sep (also 6–7pm, mid-Jun to mid-Sep for the Église du Dôme); daily 10–5, rest of year. Closed 1st Mon of each month. (The west wing is closed for renovation until summer 2005.)
💶 Adult €7, under 18 free
🚇 La-Tour-Maubourg, Invalides, Varenne
🚌 28, 63, 69, 82, 83, 93
🚆 RER line C, Invalides
▯
🏪 Gift shop/bookshop
📷 €12
🎧 Guided tours available
www.invalides.org

Jardin du Luxembourg is especially popular on sunny days (above). Feeding the birds (left)

JARDIN DU LUXEMBOURG

This is one of Paris's most popular parks, with a boating pond, fabulous flower displays and an Italianate palace.

The Jardin du Luxembourg forms an attractive southern boundary to St-Germain and the Latin Quarter. Students come here to relax after lectures and visitors catch some breathing space between sightseeing. It is a popular haunt of chic Montparnasse residents and their offspring, who make the most of the many children's attractions.

ATTRACTIONS
The 24ha (60-acre) park has some of the most beautiful public flower displays in Paris and is landscaped in an appealing mixture of French, English and Italian styles. The focal point is a large octagonal pond, elegantly encircled by stone urns and statues of French queens and other notable women. On the northern side, the Italianate Palais du Luxembourg is a reminder of the park's Florentine origins and is now home to the French Senate. In good weather the park is full of Parisians sunbathing, playing boules or jogging along the shady paths. Other attractions include tennis courts, a bandstand and even a bee-keeping school. The Musée du Luxembourg, in the former orangery, stages temporary art exhibitions. The Fontaine Médicis is a popular romantic spot on the eastern side of the Palais du Luxembourg.

Children are well catered for, with donkey rides (during French school holidays), puppet shows in the Théâtre du Luxembourg (*Wednesday, Saturday and Sunday from 2pm*) and swings and slides. They can also rent remote-control yachts to sail on the pond.

RATINGS
Good for kids	●●●○
Photo stops	●●●○
Walkability	●●●○

BASICS
✚ 426 G5 • Rue de Vaugirard/rue de Médicis/boulevard St-Michel, 75006
☎ Park: 01 42 34 23 89. Senate: 01 42 34 20 00. Musée du Luxembourg: 01 42 34 25 95
🕐 Times vary depending on season; generally dawn to dusk
💶 Free
Ⓜ Odéon
🚌 21, 27, 38, 58, 82, 83, 84, 85, 89
🚆 RER line B, Luxembourg
☕ Open-air cafés, kiosk restaurant
🍴 Kiosk
🚩 Guided tours of the Palais du Luxembourg take place on the first Sat of each month. To book a place call 01 44 54 19 49. To sit in on a Senate debate call 01 42 34 20 01
www.senat.fr

MEMORIES OF HOME
Bored with the Louvre, Marie de Medici commissioned the gardens and palace in 1615, hoping for a reminder of her native Florence. She bought the land from Duke François of Luxembourg and asked architect Salomon de Brosse to use the Pitti Palace as inspiration. Work finished in the mid-1620s but Marie, widow of Henri IV, did not have long to enjoy it. She was exiled from France by the powerful Cardinal Richelieu and died penniless in Cologne. During the Revolution, the Palais du Luxembourg became a prison, then in 1799 it became the seat of France's Upper Chamber.

Wandering in the arcades of the Jardin du Palais Royal

JARDIN DU PALAIS ROYAL

➕ 426 G2 • Place du Palais-Royal, 75001 🕐 Daily 7am–11pm, Jun–end Aug; 7am–10.15pm, Apr, May; 7am–9.30pm, Sep; 7.30am–8.30pm, Oct–end Mar 🎟 Free
🚇 Palais Royal–Musée du Louvre
🚌 21, 48, 67, 69, 72, 81
🍴 Restaurants and tea rooms around the outside
🏪 Small shops in the arcades

This tranquil garden is the perfect place to recharge your batteries after a visit to the Louvre. The flower-filled enclave is separated from the 21st century by a cordon of handsome 18th-century arcades, sheltering quirky shops and traditional *salons de thé*. In good weather the garden is full of Parisians resting, reading and playing boules. Children come to roller-skate around the incongruous striped columns in the Cour d'Honneur, a controversial 1986 addition by artist Daniel Buren. The courtyard's sleek water features blend more easily with the rest of the garden.

It's worth wandering through the arcades, with their small shops selling anything from art and clothes to silverware and model soldiers. There is a choice of places to stop for a drink.

The Palais Royal was commissioned by Louis XIII's advisor, Cardinal Richelieu, in the 17th century and was originally called the Palais-Cardinal. Louis XIV spent part of his childhood in the palace. Molière and his troupe of actors used to perform in the Théâtre du Petit Cardinal, which once stood at the southern corner of the palace. The nearby Comédie Française still stages Molière's plays today.

The arcades and apartments surrounding the palace garden were constructed in the 18th century.

JARDIN DES TUILERIES

A chic park offering great views of Paris's most famous landmarks.

The Tuileries is dominated at one end by the place de la Concorde and at the other by the mighty Louvre—there are also views of the Eiffel Tower, Arc de Triomphe and Musée d'Orsay. The park runs alongside the Seine and the grandest way to enter is through the gilded gates at the Concorde end. This brings you to the first of the two large ponds. Art galleries stand on terraces either side of this first pond—the Jeu de Paume and the Orangerie (*due to reopen in autumn 2004*).

Follow the wide central avenue towards the Louvre and the gravel gradually gives way to grass and well-tended flower beds. You pass allegorical statues, open-air cafés and children's playgrounds. At the eastern end, the neoclassical Arc du Carrousel forms a symbolic gateway to the Louvre and is also the first arch in Paris's Grand Axis, the imaginary straight line linking the Louvre, the Arc de Triomphe and the Grande Arche.

The Tuileries was the inspiration of Catherine de Medici, who wanted an Italian-style garden to complement the palace built in 1564. Lavish balls, concerts and fireworks ensured her garden remained an important social venue. The park as we know it today dates from 1649, when Louis XIV asked landscape architect André Le Nôtre to redesign it in the formal French style. The palace went up in smoke at the hands of the Communards in 1871 but the garden survived. After years of neglect in the 20th century, it received a makeover in time for the new millennium.

RATINGS	
Good for kids	🔵🔵🔵🔵
Historic interest	🔵🔵
Photo stops	🔵🔵🔵
Walkability	🔵🔵🔵🔵

TIPS
● Children can hire model yachts to sail on the pond at the eastern end of the park. ● Free guided tours take place during the summer months. For more information see the notice boards or call 01 44 54 19 34.

BASICS
➕ 425 F2 • Place de la Concorde, 75001 ☎ 01 49 26 07 59 🕐 Daily 7am–9pm, Apr–end Sep; 7.30am–7pm, rest of year 🎟 Free 🚇 Tuileries, Concorde 🚌 24, 68, 72, 73, 84, 94 ☕ Open-air cafés 🏪 Bookshop at Concorde end

The obelisk and the Arc de Triomphe are just two of the landmarks you can see from the Jardin des Tuileries

A Marais bookshop (above).
Rides in Montmartre (right)

MAISON EUROPÉENNE DE LA PHOTOGRAPHIE

427 J4 • 5–7 rue de Fourcy, 75004
01 44 78 75 00 Wed–Sun 11–8.
Closed during exhibition changeovers
Adult €5, child €2.50, under 8 free;
free to all Wed 5–8 St-Paul 67,
69, 76, 96
www.mep-fr.org

Stylish Maison Européenne de la
Photographie hosts dynamic
exhibitions of contemporary
photography. The galleries are
spread over five floors of the
18th-century Hôtel Hénault de
Cantobre, as well as in a newer
wing that opened in 1996. A
100-seat auditorium shows films
relating to the exhibitions.

LE MARAIS

427 J3 • Le Marais St-Paul,
Rambuteau, Hôtel de Ville 29, 69,
75, 76, 96

The Marais district, on the
eastern side of the Right Bank,
has ornate architecture and
trendy restaurants, boutiques and
art galleries. There's a bustling
Jewish quarter and Paris's oldest
square—place des Vosges (see
page 90). The area was once
low-lying marshland, hence its
name *marais* (marsh). For
two centuries sections were
controlled by the powerful
religious and military order, the
Knights Templar. During the 17th
century aristocrats competed to
build the most elegant mansions,
but the area later fell into neglect.
Then, in 1962, Culture Minister-
cum-writer André Malraux
pointed out the historic value of
the many crumbling mansions
and restoration began. Many of
these impressive buildings
(called *hôtels*) now house
museums, including the Musée
Picasso (see page 86), the
Musée Carnavalet (see page 81),
the Musée d'Art et d'Histoire du
Judaïsme (see page 81).

MONTMARTRE

**This village within a city has cobbled streets,
stunning views and the mighty Sacré-Cœur basilica.**

Hilltop Montmartre, north of
central Paris, has a split
personality. There are the
teeming tourist traps, including
place du Tertre and the front
steps of Sacré-Cœur, but
venture a few minutes off the
beaten track and you'll find
quiet cobbled streets, whitewashed cottages and all the
charm of a small village. It's
hard to remember you are
still in France's capital city.
The area earned an almost
mythical status at the end of
the 19th century, thanks to
its bohemian community of
artists and its raunchy nightlife.
Henri Toulouse-Lautrec immortalized scenes of dancing girls
at the world-famous cabaret
venue Moulin Rouge, where
you can still see shows today.

Montmartre is crowned by
the Sacré-Cœur basilica (see
page 91), a dazzling white
neo-Byzantine creation whose
domes look stunning against a
blue sky. The nearby place du
Tertre is Paris's highest point
and swarms with visitors and
street artists. A short walk away
are quieter, picturesque streets (see walk, page 276–277).

In Roman times, Montmartre's hill hosted a temple to Mercury.
It was renamed Mont des Martyrs after the murder of Paris's first
bishop, St. Denis, in the 3rd century. By the end of the 17th
century around 30 windmills stood on the hill and Montmartre
prospered with the production of wine, flour and gypsum (plaster
of Paris). Only two of these windmills still stand.

RATINGS	
Good for kids	●●●
Historic interest	●●●●
Photo stops	●●●●●

TIPS

● Montmartre's Métro stations
are on the edge of the district,
leaving you with an uphill walk
to reach many of the main
sights. If your legs are suffering, take the Montmartrobus,
which runs a circular route
from place Pigalle, past Sacré-
Cœur, and north to the Métro
station Jules Joffrin.
● You can avoid walking up
the daunting steps to Sacré-
Cœur by taking the funicular
from square Willette.

BASICS

427 L1 • 75018 Anvers,
Abbesses, Blanche, Lamarck
Caulaincourt Montmartrobus
(buses 30, 54, 68, 74, 80 have stops
around the edge) Plenty of restaurants and cafés, some of them very
touristy A selection For a
Montmartre walk, see page 276–277
www.montmartrenet.com

Exhibits at the Musée d'Art et d'Histoire du Judaïsme

Musée Carnavalet conveys the atmosphere of Paris in ages past

MUSÉE DES ARTS DÉCORATIFS

✚ 426 F2 • 107 rue de Rivoli, 75001
☎ 01 44 55 57 50 🕐 Tue–Fri 11–6
(until 9pm on Wed), Sat, Sun 10–6
💶 Adult €5.40, under 18 free
🚇 Palais-Royal–Musée du Louvre,
Tuileries 🚌 21, 27, 39, 48, 69, 72, 81,
95 🏛
www.ucad.fr

This museum displays decorative arts from the Middle Ages to the present day. More than 150,000 items cover almost every aspect of the genre, from ceramics, glass and embroidery to wood and metalwork. Periods covered include the Middle Ages and Renaissance, art nouveau, art deco, Modern and Contemporary and a further five specialist departments: Glass, Toys, Drawings, Wallpaper and Jewellery.

Only the Middle Ages and Renaissance galleries have been open to the public for the past few years, because of renovation work. The 17th–20th century collections are due to reopen at the end of 2004.

MUSÉE D'ART ET D'HISTOIRE DU JUDAÏSME

✚ 427 J3 • Hôtel de St-Aignan,
71 rue du Temple, 75003 ☎ 01 53 01
86 60 🕐 Mon–Fri 11–6, Sun 10–6.
💶 Adult €6.10, under 18 free
🚇 Rambuteau, Hôtel de Ville 🚌 29,
38, 47, 75 🚹 🏛 Bookshop
🎧 Audioguide included in entry price
www.mahj.org

This museum paints a vibrant picture of the development of Jewish culture from the Middle Ages to the present day, in France and beyond. It also highlights the contribution members of the Jewish community have made to European art.

The museum opened in 1998 in the Hôtel de St-Aignan, a restored 17th-century mansion that became home to Jewish immigrants from Eastern Europe in the 19th century.

MUSÉE DES ARTS ET MÉTIERS

✚ 427 J2 • 60 rue Réaumur, 75003
☎ 01 53 01 82 00 🕐 Tue–Sun 10–6
(Thu until 9.30pm) 💶 Adult €6.50,
under 18 free 🚇 Arts et Métiers,
Réaumur-Sébastopol 🚌 20, 38, 39, 47
🚹
www.arts-et-metiers.net/

Art meets science at this quirky museum, with its collection of early scientific machinery, vintage cars and mechanical toys. The exhibits pay tribute to humanity's quest for scientific achievement, as well as highlighting the absurd beginnings of some key inventions. Exhibits include a primitive calculating machine invented by Pascal and one of Edison's phonographs. Closer to today, a Formula 1 racing car sits incongruously in the former chapel. The museum, set up by the Revolutionary government back in 1794, is in a medieval priory with a 13th-century chapel.

MUSÉE CARNAVALET

✚ 427 J3 • 23 rue de Sévigné, 75003
(also an entrance on rue des Francs-
Bourgeois) ☎ 01 44 59 58 58
🕐 Tue–Sun 10–6 💶 Free (except for
temporary exhibitions) 🚇 St-Paul
🚌 29, 96 🏛 Bookshop 🔹 In French
Tue, Wed, Sun 3pm; in English on first
Sun in month at 3pm
www.paris.fr/musees/musee_carnavalet

Immerse yourself in the turbulent history of Paris at this intriguing museum, housed in two 16th- and 17th-century mansions. Paintings, memorabilia and sumptuous re-creations of period rooms evoke the spirit of the city in previous eras, including the French Revolution and the reign of Napoleon I. The emphasis is on conveying an atmosphere rather than listing historical facts, so if you're expecting a detailed account of each era you may be disappointed. But if you want a taste of the high life during Louis XV's rule or a glimpse of the terrors of the Revolution, this is the place to come.

The main entrance takes you into the Hôtel Carnavalet, where exhibitions on two floors lead you up to the reign of Louis XVI. The adjoining Hôtel Le Peletier moves on to the Revolution (second floor), 19th century (ground and first floors) and 20th century (first floor).

MUSÉE JACQUEMART ANDRÉ

✚ 425 D1 • 158 boulevard
Haussmann, 75008 ☎ 01 45 62 11 59
🕐 Daily 10–6 💶 Adult €8, child €6;
under 7 free 🍴 Daily 11.30–5.30
🚇 St-Philippe-du-Roule, Miromesnil
🚌 22, 28, 43, 52, 80, 83, 84, 93
🚉 RER line A, Charles de Gaulle–Étoile
www.musee-jacquemart-andre.com

Wealthy banker Edouard Jacquemart and his painter wife Nélie André were ardent collectors of European art and amassed an impressive private collection of European master-pieces. In 1875 they built a stately mansion on the boulevard Haussmann to display their acquisitions, complete with a ballroom, picture gallery and ornate swirling staircase. Nélie outlived her husband, but when she died she respected his wishes to donate the mansion and its contents to the Institut de France. It opened as a museum in 1913. The collection includes paintings and sculptures by Italian artists (including Canaletto, Botticelli and Della Robbia), Flemish and Dutch masters (Van Dyck, Rembrandt and Hals) and French artists (Boucher, David and Fragonard).

Musée du Louvre

**The Louvre is one of the world's largest museums.
Legendary works of art include the *Mona Lisa, Venus de Milo* and a
4,000-year-old Egyptian sphinx.**

One of the lower galleries

Mona Lisa, by Leonardo da Vinci, is one of the must-see exhibits

Wandering past dramatic sculptures

RATINGS	
Cultural interest	●●●●●
Historic interest	●●●●○
Shopping (art books)	●●●●○

TIPS

● The museum is least crowded first thing in the morning and during late-opening on Mondays and Wednesdays. Sunday is the busiest day.

● Remember the museum is closed on Tuesdays.

● The entrance fee is reduced to €5 after 3pm and on Sundays

● To avoid queues, use a *Carte Musées-Monuments* or pre-book your ticket by phone, Internet, FNAC (*tel 01 42 31 32 28; small commission charged*) or at some department stores. This allows you to use the passage Richelieu entrance.

● Staff shortages mean that certain rooms are not open every day. If there are particular exhibits you want to see, check the website for the schedule of closures.

● If you visit on Monday evening, ask at the information desk for the *Nocturnes du Lundi* leaflet which takes you on a tour of 26 key exhibits.

SEEING THE LOUVRE

The Louvre is one of the most famous art galleries in the world, with a vast collection spanning thousands of years, from ancient civilizations to mid-19th century European paintings. The main entrance is through I. M. Pei's striking glass pyramid (1989) in the Cour Napoléon. Escalators take you down to a subterranean foyer, where you can pick up a museum plan and decide which of the three wings will be your first port of call. Don't be too ambitious—there is no way you'll be able to see all 35,000 works on display in one visit. If you don't know where to begin, you could take one of the *Visite-Découverte* guided tours or rent an audioguide. When it's time for a break, the museum has a choice of cafés and restaurants.

HIGHLIGHTS

MONA LISA

When Leonardo da Vinci set up his easel in Florence in the early 16th century to paint the *Mona Lisa*, little did he know he was creating what was to become one of the world's most famous works of art. The diminutive painting, only 77cm (30in) tall and 53cm (20in) wide, is on the first floor of the Denon wing, surrounded by bullet-proof glass and a constant crowd of admirers. The identity of the woman is not known for certain, although she is believed to be the wife of Francesco del Giocondo, hence the portrait's other name, *La Gioconda*. Da Vinci painted the work between 1503 and 1506. François I obtained the painting soon after its completion. In 1911 an Italian stole the portrait, wanting to return it to its native Florence. It was recovered two years later, after a police hunt that won it worldwide fame.

VENUS DE MILO

The eternally serene *Venus de Milo* is the most famous of the Louvre's ancient Greek exhibits, discovered on the island of Melos in 1820. As Aphrodite, the goddess of love, she portrays the Greek image of perfect beauty. The marble statue was created around 100BC, during Greece's Hellenistic period, although its simple style harks back to Classical Greek sculpture.

BASICS

✚ 426 G3 • 99 rue de Rivoli, 75001

☎ 01 40 20 50 50. Recorded information in 5 languages: 01 40 20 51 51. Auditorium: 01 40 20 51 86

🕐 Wed–Mon 9–6 (last entry 45 min before closing); late opening until 9.45pm Mon (Richelieu wing only) and Wed (whole museum)

💶 Adult €7.50 (€5 after 3pm and on Sundays), under 18 free. Tickets are valid all day, so re-entry is allowed. Free 1st Sun of month and 14 July. Temporary exhibitions in the Hall Napoléon €7.

🚇 Palais Royal–Musée du Louvre

🚌 21, 27, 39, 48, 67, 68, 69, 72, 74, 75, 76, 81, 85, 95

🚆 Châtelet-les-Halles

📖 Range of guidebooks on sale. Free leaflet (in 9 languages) available at information desk to guide visitors around the museum

🍴 Cafés and restaurants

🏪 Large bookshop

▪ A variety of guided tours are available in English and French, including *Visite-Découverte* (Discovery Visits) in English at 11, 2 and 3.45 (11.30 only on Sun; not 1st Sun of month) and in French at 11.30. Audiotours are available in French, English, German, Spanish, Italian and Japanese. Pick them up from the entrances to the three wings of the museum (€5)

❓ Special tours are available for those with reduced mobility. Wheelchair loan is available on request. There is a special sculpture gallery for the blind. Ask for a leaflet at the information desk about disability access

www.louvre.fr (in French, English, Spanish and Japanese; see the works, have a virtual tour, find out about tours and browse the online shop)

THE EGYPTIAN COLLECTION

The Egyptian collection is the largest of its kind outside Egypt, containing 55,000 items, around 5,000 of which are on show. Don't miss the pink granite *Grand Sphinx*, part pharaoh, part lion, that once protected the corridors of a holy shrine. Stylistic details suggest it could be more than 4,600 years old. The collections are presented thematically on the ground floor of the Sully wing, where topics include fishing, funerals, writing and jewellery. On the first floor the displays are chronological, starting with prehistory, tracing the rule of the pharaohs and ending just before the arrival of the Romans in 333BC. To see how Egyptian culture developed under Roman rule you can continue your tour in the lower floor of the Denon wing.

FRENCH HISTORICAL/ALLEGORICAL PAINTINGS

These vast paintings, on the first floor of the Denon wing, draw you into the action not only by their immense size but also the vivid detail. Look out for Delacroix's *Liberty Leading the People* (1830), where the presence of the allegorical figure of Liberty brings a sense of triumph to the destruction and chaos of the 1830 Uprising it portrays. David's neoclassical *The Coronation of Napoleon I* seems rather cold when set against the passion of Delacroix's work, although the detail is compelling. Almost 10m (33ft) wide, it was commissioned by the Emperor himself and completed in 1807.

The stunning entrance foyer (top)

One of the sculptures on display in the Cour Marly

BACKGROUND

Charles V transformed Philippe-Auguste's 12th-century fortress on the Louvre site into a medieval castle in the 14th century. The wily Renaissance King François I ordered considerable rebuilding nearly two centuries later, and also launched an art collection. During the Revolution, an art museum opened to the public in the Grand Galerie. Napoleon celebrated his marriage to Marie-Louise in the Louvre in 1810 and lived in the nearby Tuileries Palace. He set about creating a courtyard dominated by the Arc du Carrousel and building a new wing. His victories overseas, and the subsequent looting, added to the Louvre's stock. The 1980s and 1990s saw extensive renovations to the galleries.

Promenade near Argenteuil by Claude Monet

MUSÉE MARMOTTAN MONET

🗺 424 off A3 • 2 rue Louis-Boilly, 75016 ☎ 01 44 96 50 33 🕐 Tue–Sun 10–6 💶 Adult €6.50, child €4, under 8 free 🚇 La Muette (then a 10-minute walk; follow signs from the station) 🚌 22, 32, 52 🚆 RER line C, Boulainvilliers 🏬 Gift shop/bookshop ♿ Wheelchair access to ground floor and basement only www.marmottan.com

It's a bit of a trek out to this museum in the leafy 16th *arrondissement* but you'll be rewarded with the world's largest collection of Monet paintings, as well as significant works by his contemporaries. The intimate setting in a discreetly elegant 19th-century town house makes a pleasant change from Paris's larger, more impersonal museums. And if the Impressionist works fail to satisfy your appetite, there are paintings and furniture from the Napoleonic period, as well as more than 300 illustrated pages from medieval and Renaissance manuscripts. It's a curious but compelling combination.

The main draw for visitors is the Monet collection, built up over the last 50 years from donations from the artist's son, Michel, and various other collectors. Many of the paintings are displayed in the purpose-built basement gallery, remarkably light and airy considering its underground location.

The museum takes its name from art historian Paul Marmottan, who left his house and collection of Empire paintings and furniture to the nation in 1932. The collection also includes paintings from the Flemish, Italian and German primitives.

Don't miss Monet's influential *Impression—soleil levant* (c1873) gave the Impressionist movement its name.

MUSÉE NATIONAL DU MOYEN ÂGE–THERMES DE CLUNY

This enchanting collection of medieval paraphernalia takes you back to the days of courtly love and feudal living.

In an intimate Gothic mansion, the Cluny Museum provides an intriguing glimpse into medieval life. Tapestries, jewellery, headless statues and religious items are among the 23,000 exhibits. What makes the collection so compelling is that you get a close-up view of objects that can usually only be admired from a distance. Vivid stained-glass windows you would normally crane your neck to see are down at eye level, while altarpieces created to sit imposingly at the far end of a church are right there, in front of you. The detail is stunning. The concert hall has a surreal collection of heads knocked off 13th-century statues on the west front of Notre-Dame by zealous Revolutionaries, who thought they represented French kings.

The museum is on the site of Paris's most ancient Gallo-Roman baths, the ruins of which can still be seen. The turreted, 15th-century Hôtel de Cluny is one of the city's oldest mansions.

Don't miss *La Dame à la Licorne (The Lady and the Unicorn)* tapestries are a highlight.

RATINGS			
Cultural interest	●	●	● ●
Historic interest	●	●	● ●
Photostops (exterior)	●	●	

TIPS

● Pick up a plan of the site at reception, which highlights the key exhibits.
● You don't have to pay to enter the Gothic courtyard off place Paul-Painlevé. It's a calming spot to sit for a few minutes and the turrets and gargoyles are worth a look.
● After your visit, take a break in the medieval gardens on the corner of boulevards St-Michel and St-Germain.

BASICS

🗺 426 G4 • 6 place Paul-Painlevé, rue du Sommerard, 75005 ☎ 01 53 73 78 16; 01 53 73 78 00 🕐 Wed–Mon 9.15–5.45

💶 Adult €5.50, under 18 free, free to all on 1st Sun of month 🚇 Cluny-La-Sorbonne 🚌 21, 27, 38, 63, 85, 86, 87, 96 🚆 RER line B, C St-Michel 🏬 🎧 Guided tours in English www.musee-moyenage.fr

The Musée d'Orsay started life as a Belle-Époque railway station and the ornate station clock still hangs in the main hall

MUSÉE D'ORSAY

A magnificent former railway station houses this collection of world-famous Impressionist paintings, as well as other art from the mid-19th century to early 20th century.

The collections here span 1848 to 1914, a crucial period in Western art that witnessed such giants as Monet, Renoir, Degas and Cézanne. Chronologically, the museum fits neatly between the Louvre (see pages 82–83) and the Centre Georges Pompidou (see page 70).

YOUR VISIT

Most people come to see the breathtaking Impressionist collection, which includes Monet's *Blue Waterlilies* (c1916–1919), Van Gogh's *The Church at Auvers-sur-Oise* (1890) and Renoir's *Ball at the Moulin de la Galette* (1876). But Impressionism forms less than a third of the vast display, which also includes sculpture, Symbolist and historical paintings, photography and art nouveau furniture. To see the works chronologically, start with the ground floor, then take the escalators to the Impressionist works on the upper floor, before finishing on the middle floor. Even if your sole reason for visiting the museum is the Impressionist collection, don't leave without wandering through the central aisle on the ground floor, displaying 19th-century neoclassical sculpture. This is the best place to catch the feel of the building—part museum, part Belle-Époque railway station—with its ornate clock and magnificent glass roof.

THE BUILDING

The imposing Orsay station and its accompanying hotel were built along the banks of the Seine in time for the Exposition Universelle in 1900. Victor Laloux designed the soaring glass and iron roof, together with the wildly ornate Belle Époque restaurant and ballroom, all still intact. But in 1939 the advent of longer electric trains forced the station to close for long-distance travel (it was still used for suburban trains), less than 40 years after its completion. Public protest saved it from demolition, and approval was given to turn it into a museum in 1977. Italian architect Gae Aulenti masterminded the conversion of the interior, encasing both the walls and floors with stone, and President François Mitterrand opened the museum in December 1986.

Don't miss Seek out the lavishly mirrored Salles des Fêtes (Room 51).

RATINGS	
Cultural interest	● ● ● ● ●
Historic interest	● ● ●

TIPS

● A *Carte Musées–Monuments* allows you to skip the queues, which can be long.

● Thursday evening is the quietest time to visit.

● The museum is closed on Mondays, unlike the Louvre and Centre Georges Pompidou, which close on Tuesdays.

● For more Impressionist paintings, visit the Musée Marmottan (see page 84).

BASICS

✚ 425 F3•62 rue de Lille, 75007. Entrance on place de la Légion d'Honneur ☎ 01 40 49 48 14; 01 40 49 48 48 🕐 Tue–Wed, Fri–Sat 10–6, Sun 9–6, Thu 10–9.45 (the museum opens at 9 from late-Jun to late-Sep). Last ticket 45 min before closing.

💶 Adult €7, under 18 free, free to all on 1st Sun of month. Temporary exhibitions cost extra.

🚇 Solférino

🚌 24, 63, 68, 73, 83, 84, 94

🚊 RER line C, Musée d'Orsay

🍴 On the middle level (11.30–2.30, 3.30–5.30; dinner 7–9.15 on Thu)

☕ Café des Hauteurs on upper level, with wonderful view of the old station clock; self-service café just above it

🏬 Giftshop and bookshop

🎧 Tours in English Tue–Sat 11.30; in French Tue–Sat 11 (€6). Audioguides (€5).

www.musee-orsay.fr

Just one of the many paintings at the Musée Picasso

MUSÉE PICASSO

🔲 427 J3 • Hôtel Salé, 5 rue de Thorigny, 75003 ☎ 01 42 71 25 21 🕐 Wed–Mon 9.30–6, Apr–end Sep; 9.30–5.30, rest of year. Last admission 45 minutes before closing 🎟️ Adult €5.50, under 18 free 🚇 St-Paul, Chemin Vert, St-Sébastien Froissart 🚌 29, 69, 75, 96 🎧 Mon and Fri 2.30pm, €6 per person ☕ Summer café in the garden, open mid-Apr to mid-Oct. 📚 Bookshop and gift shop www.musee-picasso.fr

The grand opening of this museum in 1985 put an end to 11 years of legal wrangling over Pablo Picasso's death duties. Thanks to a law allowing payment of these duties in the form of works of art, the French State received one quarter of Picasso's collection. The huge collection was enhanced even further after the death of his wife in 1990, and the museum now holds around 203 paintings, 158 sculptures, 16 collages and more than 1,500 drawings and prints. Also on display is Picasso's personal collection of works by his mentors and contemporaries, including Cézanne, Renoir, Miró, Braque and Matisse.

The museum is arranged chronologically, taking you on a journey from Picasso's early 1900s 'Blue' and 'Pink' periods through his years of Cubist experimentation with Braque and his classical period to the 1930s and beyond.

The collection is housed in the Hôtel Salé, a stunning 17th-century mansion in the heart of the Marais district, with a grand staircase, ornate chandeliers and beautiful old wooden doors. A small room dedicated to the history of the mansion displays black-and-white photographs and information on the building and its occupants over the years.

MUSÉE RODIN

This museum has soothing gardens, where you can wander past Rodin's sculptures or simply relax among the roses.

The Musée Rodin's open-air gallery, spread over nearly 3 hectares (7 acres) of beautiful gardens, makes a great escape from more intensive sight-seeing. Once you've recharged your batteries strolling through the grounds, see more of Rodin's works in the airy 18th-century mansion where he once lived, the Hôtel Biron.

Outside, don't miss the brooding bronze *Le Penseur (The Thinker)*, supposedly representing the Italian poet Dante and originally placed outside the Panthéon, or the gruesome doorway *La Porte de l'Enfer (The Gates of Hell)*, inspired by Dante's *Divine Comedy. Les Bourgeois de Calais (The Burghers of Calais)* depicts six burghers who gave up their lives to save their townsfolk during a siege by the English in the 14th century, while *Balzac* is a rather unflattering portrayal of the writer in his dressing gown. There are few information boards, so rent an audioguide or pick up a free leaflet from the Hôtel Biron.

Inside the elegant rococo

RATINGS

Cultural interest	● ● ● ●
Good for kids (garden)	● ● ●

TIPS

● The garden-only ticket allows you to admire some of Rodin's most important works for only €1. The garden also has a play area for children.
● If the Rodin Museum has whetted your appetite for open-air sculpture, try the riverside Musée de la Sculpture en Plein Air, on quai St-Bernard, which has around 40 avant-garde works. (The gallery is open 24 hours, but is best avoided at night.)

BASICS

🔲 425 D4 • 77 rue de Varenne, 75007 ☎ 01 44 18 61 10 🕐 Tue–Sun 9.30–5.45, Apr–end Sep (gardens open until 6.45pm); Tue–Sun 9.30–4.45, rest of year 🎟️ Adult €5, under 18 free. Garden only: €1 🚇 Varenne 🚌 69, 82, 87, 92 🚆 RER line C, Invalides ☕ Garden café 📚 Book/gift shop 🎧 Audiotours €4. Guided tours once a week.
www.musee-rodin.fr (in French and English)

mansion, you can follow Rodin's artistic evolution chronologically, from his early academic sketches and paintings to his vigorous watercolours. The highlight is the passionate white marble *Le Baiser (The Kiss)*. There are also works by Rodin's contemporaries, including Camille Claudel, Renoir, Van Gogh and Monet.

Notre-Dame at night, bathed in floodlights (above).
The west façade of the cathedral (right)

NOTRE-DAME

This beautiful Gothic cathedral is one of France's most visited religious sites.

Notre-Dame is as famous a symbol of Paris as the Eiffel Tower and around 10 million people enter its doors each year. The crowds are smallest in the early morning, when the cathedral is also at its brightest. Save some time for wandering around the outside to admire the architecture, including the flying buttresses. One of the best views is from the Seine, on a boat trip that circles the Île de la Cité. Finally, if your legs will agree to it, there are wonderful views from the top of the 69m (226ft) towers.

HIGHLIGHTS INSIDE THE CATHEDRAL

The south rose window, in the transept, is especially glorious when the sun shines through, adding extra vibrancy to the purple hues. Christ stands in the heart of the 13m (42ft) diameter window, encircled by angels, apostles, martyrs and scenes from the New Testament. The intricately carved and painted choir screen, created in the 14th century and restored in the 1960s, has enchanting depictions of Gospel scenes. In contrast, the bronze altar at the heart of the cathedral is strikingly modern. It depicts Gospel writers Matthew, Mark, Luke and John, as well as Old Testament prophets.

OUTSIDE AND UP THE TOWERS

The symmetrical west façade is packed with statues and sculptures, originally painted and intended as a Bible for the illiterate. It's a tough climb, but it's well worth tackling the 69m (226ft) towers for views over Paris and a closer look at the grotesque gargoyles.

MORE THAN 800 YEARS OLD

Notre-Dame owes its existence to the 12th-century bishop Maurice de Sully, who decided that Paris needed its own cathedral. Pope Alexander III laid the foundation stone in 1163 and the choir was built in just under 20 years. Guilds of carpenters, stone-carvers, iron forgers and glass craftsmen worked on the grand project but it took almost 200 years to complete the building, which was finally ready in 1345. By the time Napoleon was crowned in the cathedral in 1804 the building was in a state of disrepair. Victor Hugo, author of *The Hunchback of Notre-Dame,* campaigned fervently for its restoration.

RATINGS	
Historic interest	● ● ● ●
Photo stops (views)	● ● ● ● ●

TIP

● Try to visit just before a service, when you feel a sense of anticipation as lights are gradually turned on and people gather to worship.

BASICS

Cathedral
✚ 426 H4 • Place du Parvis Notre-Dame, 75004 ☎ 01 42 34 56 10
🕐 Daily 8–6.45 🎫 Free
Ⓜ Cité, St-Michel, Châtelet
🚌 21, 24, 38, 47, 85, 96
🚆 RER lines B, C, St-Michel
📖 In the cathedral and up the tower
🎧 Guided tours: in French, daily at 12 (Mon, Sat 2pm); in English, Wed, Thu 12, Sat 2.30pm
🎵 Organ recitals at 5.30pm on Sun

Towers
🕐 Daily 9–7.30, Jul, Aug (also 7.30–11pm Sat, Sun); 9.30–7.30, Apr–end Jun, Sep; 10–5.30, Oct–end Mar. Last admission 45 min before closing
🎫 Adult €5.50, under 18 free
www.monum.fr

A full-size boat, exhibited in the Musée National de la Marine

OPÉRA PALAIS GARNIER

⊞ 426 F1 • Place de l'Opéra, 75009
☎ 01 40 01 22 63. Box office: 08 92 89
90 90. Museum: 01 47 42 07 02
🕐 Daily 10–5 (until 6, mid-Jul to
mid-Sep). Closed during matinées;
auditorium closed during rehearsals
💶 Adult €6, child €3, under 10 free
🚇 Opéra 🚌 20, 21, 22, 27, 29, 42, 52,
53, 66, 68, 81, 95 🎧 Guided tours, €10
www.opera-de-paris.fr

The sumptuous Opéra Palais
Garnier, commissioned by
Napoleon III, was the largest
theatre in the world when it
opened in 1875. Charles Garnier
beat 171 hopefuls in the
competition to design the
prestigious building. The stage
can accommodate up to 450
performers and the opulent
auditorium holds around 2,200
spectators under a domed ceiling
painted by Marc Chagall in 1964.
Even if you don't see one of the
ballets staged here, take a look at
the splendid marble and gilt
Grand Staircase. Outside, notice
Carrier-Belleuse's lamp-bearing
statues and a copy of Carpeaux's
sculpted group *La Danse,* to the
right of the front arcade. A small
museum explains the history of
the Opéra house.

PALAIS DE CHAILLOT

⊞ 424 B3 • 17 place du Trocadéro et
du 11 Novembre, 75016 🚇 Trocadéro
🚌 22, 30, 32, 63, 72, 82

There are breathtaking views
across the Seine to the Eiffel
Tower from the terrace of the
Palais de Chaillot. The colon-
naded palace was built for the
Exposition Universelle of 1937.
Its curved wings are dotted with
gleaming bronze statues, and its
wide terraces overlook the foun-
tains of the Jardins du Trocadéro.
The palace houses the Théâtre
National de Chaillot, the Musée
National de la Marine and the
Musée de l'Homme.

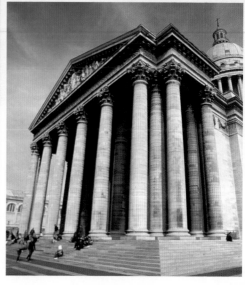

PANTHÉON

**Originally a basilica, this striking monument is now the
final resting place of some of France's greatest citizens.**

The neoclassical grandeur of
the Panthéon is an arresting
sight after you have wandered
through the warren-like streets
of the Latin Quarter to reach it.

The colossal mausoleum
contains the tombs of many
illustrious citizens, including
writers Victor Hugo, Émile Zola
and Voltaire, scientists Marie
and Pierre Curie, Braille inventor Louis Braille, and World
War II Resistance martyr Jean
Moulin. To be 'pantheonized'
is one of the greatest honours
in France and arguments still
ignite periodically about who
merits a reburial here.

The monument was
commissioned by Louis XV
as a basilica dedicated to
St. Geneviève, patron saint of
Paris, in thanks for his recovery
from gout. The king laid the
foundation stone in 1764 and
work finally finished in 1790,
by which time the original
architect, Soufflot, had died. Only a year later, in 1791, the
Revolutionaries seized the building, bricking up the windows and
changing its function to a secular Temple of Fame.

You enter the building through an imposing columned area
(peristyle), based on the grandiose frontage of Rome's Pantheon.
Inside, the cross-shaped chamber feels austere.

To climb to the circular colonnade beneath the dome you
must take a guided tour (and tackle 206 steps). But you'll be
rewarded with panoramic views of the city from 35m (115ft)
above street level. Downstairs in the huge, shadowy crypt you
can see the tombs of Rousseau, Voltaire, Victor Hugo, Émile Zola,
Marie Curie and others.

RATINGS	
Historic interest	● ● ●
Photo stops (exterior and views)	● ● ●

TIPS

● See the notice board outside
for times of guided tours up to
the dome's circular colonnade.
● If you don't feel like climbing
to the colonnade, you can still
enjoy lovely views of the Eiffel
Tower from the top of the
Panthéon's steps.

BASICS

⊞ 426 H5 • Place du Panthéon, 75005
☎ 01 44 32 18 00 🕐 10–6.30,
Apr–end Sep; 10–6, rest of year; last
admission 45 minutes before closing
💶 Adult €7, under 18 free
🚇 Cardinal-Lemoine 🚌 21, 27, 84, 85,
89 🚊 RER B, Luxembourg
📖 Small bookshop/gift shop
🎧 Guided tours in French. Ring ahead
for tours in other languages
www.monum.fr

Walking near the modern Opéra Bastille

PLACE DE LA BASTILLE

🔲 427 K4 • Place de la Bastille, 75004/75012 🚇 Bastille 🚌 20, 29, 65, 69, 76, 86, 87, 91 🍴 A good selection of cafés and restaurants

Frenetic place de la Bastille, now bustling with street cafés and traffic, witnessed one of the pivotal events in France's history. Where in-line skaters and pedestrians now jostle for space, a Revolutionary mob stormed the Bastille prison in 1789 in a violent riot that signalled the start of the French Revolution.

The Bastille was built in 1380 as a fortress guarding the eastern entrance to Paris. It later became a jail for political prisoners, including the Marquis de Sade and Voltaire. Nothing remains of the building, although paving stones mark its outline. A visual reminder of Paris's turbulent past is the Colonne de Juillet (July Column), which stands 50m (164ft) tall on place de la Bastille's busy roundabout. It was constructed in 1840 to commemorate victims of another revolt, the 1830 uprising, and is topped by the winged *Spirit of Liberty*.

Bastille has been spruced up and is now a lively nightspot, with many restaurants and bars. During the day you can shop in the streets that radiate from the Colonne de Juillet. There is also a marina, galleries and the ultra-modern Opéra Bastille. Walk down the rue de Lyon and you'll come to the Viaduc des Arts, a railway viaduct converted into craft workshops and showrooms (9–129 avenue Daumesnil). **Don't miss** To escape the noise and traffic of the Bastille, head down rue St-Antoine, then turn right into the peaceful rue de Birague. Here, browse in the shops, then walk back in time through an archway to place des Vosges (see page 90).

PARC DE LA VILLETTE

An urban park that combines arts, science and nature.

This ultra-modern park, formerly the city abattoirs, was transformed in the 1980s into 55ha (136 acres) of water features, themed gardens, children's playgrounds and cultural venues. The site, northeast of central Paris, is dotted with trademark red metal follies and the Canal de l'Ourcq runs through the middle. The renovated former cattle hall, La Grande Halle, is now used for trade fairs, exhibitions and concerts and the Zénith concert hall, seating over 6,000, hosts pop and rock events. A covered walk-way links the two main cultural venues at either end of the park, the Cité des Sciences et de l'Industrie to the north and the Cité de la Musique to the south.

The futuristic Cité des Sciences et de l'Industrie is a giant science and technology

RATINGS

Cultural interest	● ● ●
Good for kids	● ● ● ● ●
Photo stops	● ● ●

BASICS

Cité des Sciences et de l'Industrie
🔲 427 off J1 •30 avenue Corentin-Cariou, 75019 ☎ 01 40 05 80 00
🕐 Explora: Tue–Sat 10–6, Sun 10–7. Planetarium: Tue–Sun, shows every hour from 11–5 (except 1pm)
🚇 Porte de la Villette
🚌 75, 139, 150, 152, PC2, PC3
www.cite-sciences.fr
www.lageode.fr

Cité de la Musique
🔲 427 off J1 •221 avenue Jean-Jaurès, 75019 ☎ 01 44 84 45 45 (information); 01 44 84 44 84 (reservations)
🕐 Tue–Sat 12–6, Sun 10–6 (until 8 for concerts).
🚇 Porte de Pantin
🚌 75, 151, PC2, PC3
www.cite-musique.fr

museum, packed with high-tech, interactive displays. Highlights include the Explora exhibition, on levels 1 and 2, which has five main themes: The Universe, Water and the Earth, Challenges of the Living World, Industry and Communication. There is a planetarium (level 2) and the excellent Cité des Enfants, for 3- to12-year-olds. The spherical Géode cinema is just south of the Cité des Sciences, across the moat. This 400-seater cinema has a 1,000 sq m (10,765sq ft) hemispheric screen, producing images that are 10 times larger than in a normal cinema.

The Cité de la Musique, designed by Christian de Portzamparc opened in 1995 and is home to a concert hall, the Conservatoire National Supérieur de Musique de Paris and the Musée de la Musique.

Two fountains flank the obelisk in place de la Concorde

Peaceful place des Vosges was once a busy marketplace

Shakespeare and Company bookshop, in the Latin Quarter

PLACE DE LA CONCORDE

⊞ 425 E2 • Place de la Concorde, 75008 🚇 Free 🚇 Concorde 🚌 24, 42, 72, 73, 84, 94

Paris's largest square boasts the city's oldest monument and wonderful views of the Arc de Triomphe, the ornate gates of the Jardin des Tuileries, and across the river to the Assemblée Nationale and Eiffel Tower. It played a gruesome role in the Revolution, witnessing the execution of more than 1,300 people.

The square, originally called place Louis XV, was designed by architect Jacques-Ange Gabriel and laid out between 1755 and 1775 to accommodate an equestrian statue of the reigning king. During the Revolution it was renamed place de la Révolution, the statue of Louis XV was removed and the guillotine erected in its stead. Louis XVI and his queen Marie-Antoinette were among its victims. With the cooling of Revolutionary passions in 1795, the square was renamed place de la Concorde, in the hope of a less troubled future. Soon after, Coustou's magnificent *Chevaux de Marly* were added to the entrance of the Champs-Élysées (the horses you see today are replicas, the orginals are now in the Louvre). **Don't miss** The 230-tonne pink granite obelisk, around 3,300 years old, was presented to France by Mohammed Ali, Viceroy of Egypt, in 1883.

PLACE DES VOSGES

⊞ 427 K4 • Place des Vosges, 75004 🚇 Bastille, St-Paul 🚌 29, 96

Picturesque place des Vosges is only minutes from the busy, modern Bastille district but a world away in character. Its charming arcades shelter galleries, boutiques and cafés where you can while away a half hour enjoying a cup of hot chocolate to the sounds of street musicians.

The square consists of a central formal garden, with trees, gravel paths, a children's play area and a statue of Louis XIII, ringed by a road and surrounded by 36 red-brick and stone-faced houses. The north and south façades retain a royal touch, as each has a larger, central house, respectively the *Pavillon de la Reine* (Queen's pavilion), and the *Pavillon du Roi* (King's pavilion).

Place des Vosges was one of the first examples of town planning in Paris, when it was commissioned by Henri IV. It opened in 1612 amid spectacular celebrations, under the name place Royale. In 1800, it was renamed place des Vosges in tribute to the first French *département* to pay its new taxes.

Throughout history many famous characters have lived in the square's mansions and apartments. Princesses, duchesses, official mistresses, Cardinal Richelieu, the Duc de Sully, the writer Alphonse Daudet and, more recently, the painter Francis Bacon and the architect Richard Rogers have all gazed out at its perfect symmetry. Victor Hugo penned many a manuscript at No. 6, his home from 1832 to 1848 and now a museum.

QUARTIER LATIN

⊞ 426 H5 • On the Left Bank, between the Carrefour de l'Odéon and the Jardin des Plantes, 75005
🚇 St-Michel, Cluny-La Sorbonne, Odéon 🚌 21, 24, 27, 38, 63, 84, 85, 86, 87, 89 🚇 RER line B, C, St-Michel-Notre-Dame
🍴 A wide selection of restaurants and cafés 🛍 Plenty of clothes stores and bookshops, including Shakespeare and Co.

The Latin Quarter's picturesque narrow side streets take you back to the Middle Ages, while the presence of many students gives the area a refreshing vibrancy. No other district of Paris claims so many bookshops or colleges, and there are cinemas, jazz clubs, restaurants and historic churches. You'll find a relaxed and youthful atmosphere compared to the frenetic, business-focused Right Bank. Here, the cliché of students and artists lingering for hours in cafés is actually true.

If you're arriving from the Right Bank or Île de la Cité, your first taste of the Latin Quarter is likely to be the chaotic place St-Michel, with its imposing fountain symbolizing St. Michael slaying a dragon. The busy boulevard St-Michel (or 'Boul Mich' to students) runs from here along the length of the district and teems with students, visitors and magazine kiosks. Unless you want to browse in its clothes stores and bookshops it is best to venture off this traffic-ridden highway onto the winding, historic side streets.

Sights worth seeing include the mighty Panthéon (see page 88) and the Musée National du Moyen Âge (see page 84). The flower-filled Jardin du Luxembourg (see page 78) is the perfect place to rest your aching feet after a day exploring.

The Latin Quarter is Paris's intellectual heart, a title it has held since the Middle Ages. It owes its scholarly, literary and artistic reputation to the founding of the Sorbonne University in the 13th century, in an area known as the Montagne Ste-Geneviève. Other colleges soon grew up around it and the area gained the new name of 'Latin Quarter', after the language used by the students for everyday conversation.

The glorious upper chapel of Sainte-Chapelle

SAINTE-CHAPELLE

🗺 426 G4 • 4 Boulevard du Palais, Île de la Cité, 75001 ☎ 01 53 73 78 52
🕐 9.30–6 💳 Adult €5.50, under 18 free 🚇 Cité, Châtelet 🚌 21, 24, 27, 38, 85, 96 🚉 RER line B, C St-Michel-Notre-Dame 📅 🎫 Daily 11, 3
www.monum. fr

Stunning stained-glass windows turn this 13th-century royal chapel into a shimmering jewel. It's not quite heaven, but the celestial rays of blue, red and golden light streaming through the windows of Sainte-Chapelle certainly seem out of this world. The chapel was commissioned by Louis IX (St. Louis) to house holy relics and to promote the king's authority as a divinely appointed leader. It was constructed within the royal palace complex (now the Palais de Justice) in less than six years. Fifteen windows, up to 15m (49ft) tall, and a glorious rose window depict more than 1,100 biblical scenes, from the Creation to the Apocalypse. The only downside is the crowds, which, as with Rome's Sistine Chapel, can detract from what should be an awe-inspiring experience.

Before reaching the brilliance of the upper chapel you walk through the dark lower chapel, originally used by palace staff and dedicated to the Virgin Mary. When you step into the upper chapel you are immediately hit by colour coming at you from all directions, not only from the glorious windows but also from the patterned floor, the golden columns and the painted lower walls. Two-thirds of the windows are 13th-century originals, the oldest stained glass in Paris. The panels start with Genesis in the window on the left as you enter and work clockwise round the chapel to the Apocalypse in the rose window.

SACRÉ-CŒUR

You'll get stunning views over Paris from this gleaming white neo-Byzantine basilica.

The mighty Sacré-Cœur basilica is one of Paris's most prominent landmarks, shimmering at the top of Montmartre's hill. Its eastern-inspired dome is the second-highest point in the city and the views from the top stretch as far as 50km (30 miles). This sweeping panorama is the main attraction for many visitors. But walk into the hushed interior, especially during Mass, and it is an altogether more spiritual experience.

Sacré-Cœur was commissioned as atonement for the 58,000 people who died in the Franco-Prussian war of 1870–1871 and the bloody events of the Commune. Citizens from across France donated the money and the first stone was laid in 1875. Various problems hampered the project and the basilica was not ready until 1914. Then World War I intervened, and Parisians had to wait until 1919 for the consecration. More than 130 years after the vow to build Sacré-Cœur, priests still work in relays to maintain constant prayer for forgiveness for the horrors of war.

Joan of Arc and St. Louis guard the entrance to the basilica, on horseback in sculpted bronze. A stone statue of Christ stands high above them, in an arched recess. Inside, the striking golden mosaic over the choir is one of the largest of its kind, covering 475sq m (5,113sq ft). Christ stands in the middle, with outstretched arms and a golden heart. The Virgin Mary, Joan of Arc, St. Michael, the Pope and a figure representing France are among those immediately surrounding him. God the Father and the Holy Spirit are represented on the ceiling.

You'll get great views over Paris from the front terrace. If you have the time (and energy), it is worth climbing the dome for another panorama. The best view of the basilica itself is from below, in place St-Pierre.

Youngsters play in the shadow of Sacré-Cœur (above)

RATINGS	
Historic interest	● ● ● ○
Photo stops (views)	● ● ● ●

BASICS

🗺 427 L1 • Place du Parvis du Sacré-Cœur ☎ 01 53 41 89 00
🕐 Basilica: daily 6am–11pm. Dome and crypt: daily 9.15–5.30 (until 7 in summer)
💳 Basilica: free. Dome and crypt: €5
🚇 Anvers or Abbesses, then walk to base of funicular
🚌 Montmartrobus
🏢 Small bookshop/gift shop
www.sacre-coeur-montmartre.com

*It's worth the wait (above) to climb the Eiffel Tower.
Souvenirs of Paris's most famous sight (right)*

TOUR EIFFEL

The Eiffel Tower is the symbol of Paris and one of the world's most famous monuments.

The sleek iron silhouette of the Eiffel Tower, rising 324m (1,063ft) high, finds its way into many of the city's best views. Gustave Eiffel's extraordinary construction is a feat of late 19th-century engineering, weighing more than 10,000 tonnes and made up of 18,000 iron parts. It was a controversial addition to the city skyline in 1889 and was only intended to last 20 years. More than a century on, it has clocked up 200 million visitors.

VISITING THE TOWER

The view is the reason for climbing the Eiffel Tower, whether to take in the magnificent sweep across the city or to test your nerves peering down 120m (395ft) through the glass window on the floor of level 2. From the viewing gallery on level 3 you can see up to 75km (46 miles) on a clear day. If the vertigo-inducing top level is too much for you, the panoramas are equally stunning on level 2, where you can see the city in more detail. There is also a viewing gallery on level 1, with information boards. The views are often at their best in the run-up to sunset, when the light is kinder to cameras. At night, a totally different picture unfolds, as hundreds of thousands of lights sketch out the city. Once you have soaked up the view, you can learn more about the history of the tower from the short film shown at Cineiffel (level 1). Other attractions on the first floor include the Observatory, where you can monitor the sway at the top of the tower (measured at 9cm/3.5in during the storms of 1999), and the Feroscope, focusing on all things iron. You can also see the original hydraulic lift pump and a piece of the original spiral staircase, as used by Monsieur Eiffel himself. If you want to boast of your whereabouts to your friends back home, you can have your postcards franked with 'Tour Eiffel' at the post office (*daily 10–7.30*).

CONSTRUCTION

Construction of the unconventional monument took only two years, finishing just in time for the Exposition Universelle of 1889. For 40 years the tower basked in the glory of being the highest structure in the world until New York's Chrysler building usurped the title. It gained another 20m (66ft) in 1957 when television antennae were added.

RATINGS
Good for kids	● ● ●
Historic interest	● ● ●
Photo stops	● ● ● ● ●

TIP
● Book well ahead if you want to splash out at the plush Jules Verne restaurant.

BASICS
🗺 424 B3 • Quai Branly, Champs de Mars, 75007 ☎ 01 44 11 23 23
🕐 Daily 9am–midnight, mid-Jun to end Aug; 9.30am–11pm, rest of year (stairs close at 6.30)
🎫 By lift: level 1 €3.70, level 2 €7, level 3 €10.20. By stairs: €3.30. Children: level 1 €2.30, level 2 €3.90, level 3 €5.50
Ⓜ Bir-Hakeim 🚌 42, 69, 82, 87
🚆 RER line C, Champ-de-Mars/Tour Eiffel
🍴 Altitude 95 on level 1, Jules Verne on level 2 ☕ Snack bars on ground floor, level 1 and level 2 🎁 Gift shops on levels 1 and 2. Post office on level 1
📷 Monum organizes occasional guided tours. Call 01 44 54 19 30
www.eiffel-tower.com

Looking across the Jardins du Trocadéro to the Eiffel Tower (left)

RATINGS

Historic interest	●●●●
Photo stops (grounds)	●●●●
Walkability	●●●●

TIPS

● The busiest days at Versailles are Tuesdays, Sundays, and holiday weekends. The palace is closed on Mondays.
● A *Carte Musées-Monuments* or a combined rail/palace *passeport* allows you to avoid some of the queues.

BASICS

✚ 441 J5 • Versailles, 78000
☎ 01 30 83 78 00
🕐 Grands Appartements: Tue–Sun 9–6.30, May–end Sep; Tue–Sun 9–5.30, rest of year. Grand Trianon: daily 12–6.30, Apr–end Oct; 12–5.30, rest of year. Gardens: daily 9–6. Fountains (play): Sun 11–12, 3.30–5, Apr–end Sep (also Sat Jul–end Sep and other occasional days). Park: daily dawn–dusk
✋ Adult: State Apartments €7.50; Gardens €3 Mar–end Oct, free Nov–Feb, €6 when fountain show is on; Grand Trianon and Petit Trianon €5; *Passeport* (combined train travel and entrance ticket) €20.80 Apr–end Oct, €14.50 rest of year; under 18 free; free to all on 1st Sun of the month, Oct–Mar
🚆 RER line C to Versailles Rive-Gauche; mainline train from Gare Montparnasse to Versailles Chantiers; mainline train from Gare St-Lazare to Versailles Rive Droite
🚗 Autoroute A13 to the Château Versailles exit, then follow signs
🍴 🛍
www.chateauversailles.fr

The Hall of Mirrors at Versailles, designed by Jules Hardouin-Mansart

VERSAILLES

Versailles is France's ultimate royal palace, an opulent monument to the super-ego of the Sun King, Louis XIV.

More like a town than a chateau, Versailles was the seat of French power for more than 100 years and kept members of the royal family safely cushioned from their subjects in Paris—until the invasion of the bloodthirsty revolutionary mob.

PACE YOURSELF

It's ambitious to try to see everything in one visit so you may prefer to limit yourself to the majestic, fountain-filled gardens and the Grands Appartements (State Apartments), which include the Appartement du Roi (King's State Apartment), the Galerie des Glaces (Hall of Mirrors) and the Appartement de la Reine (Queen's Apartment). The Hall of Mirrors, 73m (240ft) long, was designed by Jules Hardouin-Mansart. The Treaty of Versailles was ratified here in 1919, ending World War I. More than 350 mirrors catch the light pouring in through the huge arched windows, which in turn give spectacular views of the gardens and canal. The gardens were tamed by the king's preferred landscape architect, André Le Nôtre, and form part of the largest palace grounds in Europe, at 100 ha (247 acres). The fountains are renowned, and it is a pity that on most days they remain still. To catch them in full flow, visit during one of the *Grandes Eaux Musicales*. Louis XIV sailed a flotilla of ships and gondolas on the 1.6km (1 mile) Grand Canal—nowadays, you can hire rowing boats. If you have more time, other parts to visit include the Petits Appartements (guided tour only), the Grand Trianon and Petit Trianon, and the Chambre du Roi.

ROYAL COURT

Versailles had relatively humble beginnings, as a hunting lodge for Louis XIII. In 1661, Louis XIV decided to move his court to the deserted swamp, 20km (12.5 miles) southwest of Paris, an astute way of isolating the nobility and his ministers while keeping an eye on his not-too-distant capital. Building work continued right up to his death in 1715. The smaller palaces of the Grand Trianon and the Petit Trianon were later created as a royal love-nest. The building project put a severe strain on France's finances but the palace remained the seat of power until 1789, when a revolutionary mob seized Louis XVI and forced him to return to Paris.

NORTHWEST FRANCE

Visitors are drawn to Normandy by its sandy beaches, renowned Bayeux Tapestry and mystical Mont St-Michel. The rich countryside is known for Camembert cheese and for apples—made into cider, Calvados brandy and delicious desserts. To the west, Brittany's rugged coastline yields superb seafood and surrounds a land of legends and intriguing parish closes.

MAJOR SIGHTS

There are plenty of historic buildings in Alençon

ALENÇON

🗺 440 G5 🏛 Maison d'Ozé, place de la Magdeleine, 61003, tel 02 33 80 66 33; Mon–Sat 9.30–12, 2–6.30, Apr–end Jun, Sep; Mon–Sat 9.30–7, Sun, public hols 10–12.30, 3–6.30, Jul, Aug
🚉 Alençon
www.paysdalencontourisme.com

Normandy's southern gateway is a handsomely restored old market town and the heart of the region's lace-making industry. Royal lace works were introduced here by Colbert, Louis XIV's finance minister, uniting various lace techniques already established in the town. Two museums pay homage to the craft. One, the Musée des Beaux Arts et de la Dentelle *(daily 10–12, 2–6, Jul–end Sep; Tue– Sun 10–12, 2–6, rest of year)*, is in a former Jesuit college in the Cour Carrée de la Dentelle. The other, the Musée de la Dentelle au Point d'Alençon, rue du Pont-Neuf *(Mon–Sat 10–noon, 2–6)*, doubles as a museum to Maréchal Leclerc, who liberated the town in 1944 and used the building as his headquarters.

Lace apart, there is plenty to see in Alençon, including the Halle au Blé (corn exchange), opposite the town hall, with its stunning glass dome. The town's religious heritage includes the birthplace of St. Thérèse of Lisieux, at 50 rue St-Blaise, and the Flamboyant Gothic Notre-Dame church, in place de la Magdeleine. The tourist office is in the Maison d'Ozé, a splendid turreted 16th-century house. Alençon's oldest building is believed to be the medieval Café des Sept Colonnes, in Grande Rue, a high-gabled, timbered building once home to the town executioner.
Don't miss The library of the Musée des Beaux Arts et de la Dentelle is a former chapel, with a wooden ship-shaped roof. The conservatory is filled with plants.

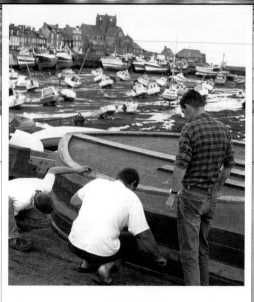

BARFLEUR

This pretty fishing port attracts visitors for its excellent seafood and its historical links with the kings of England.

Just a short drive from the more commercial ferry port of Cherbourg, Barfleur sits on the eastern side of the Cotentin peninsula on a stretch known as the Viking coast. The town has been putting boats to sea since the days of the Vikings and in the Middle Ages it was the peninsula's principal port. A plaque at the port entrance reminds you that the boat that took William the Conqueror to England in 1066 was built in Barfleur's shipyards. The town's tradition in supplying England with monarchs continued in 1194, when Richard the Lionheart set sail from here to be crowned king. Meanwhile, the notoriously treacherous currents have claimed many vessels.

RATINGS	
Historic interest	●●●
Photo stops	●●●
Walkability	●●●

TIPS
● Don't leave without trying the famous local mussels, known as *blondes de Barfleur*.
● Visit on Saturday mornings to enjoy the small market.

BASICS
🗺 439 E3 🏛 2 Rond-point Guillaume le Conquérant, 50760, tel 02 33 54 02 48; Mon–Sat 10–12.30, 2.30–6.30, Jul, Aug; Tue–Sat 10–12, 3–6, Mar–end Jun, Sep to mid-Nov; Tue–Sat 10–12, 2.30–4.30, Feb; closed mid-Nov to end Jan
🚌 Regular service from Cherbourg
www.ville-barfleur.fr

The neat granite and slate buildings around the port are modest and simple. The prettiest and oldest district is Cour Sainte-Cathérine, with its arched stone entrance by the harbour. A gentle stroll through the unpretentious harbour and along the seaside paths takes in a couple of small lighthouses, dwarfed by the massive Gatteville Lighthouse at Pointe de Barfleur, 4km (2.5 miles) north of the town. It is the second tallest in France, at 75m (246ft), and the light can be seen for 56km (35 miles). A small museum at the foot of the lighthouse recounts its history and explains modern lighthouse technology *(closed Jan, mid-Nov to mid-Dec)*. Barfleur is home to France's first lifeboat station and there is a lifeboat museum at the harbour.

Don't miss The Gatteville Lighthouse offers stunning views of the coast.

THE SIGHTS

The village of Le Bec-Hellouin

LE BEC-HELLOUIN

Abbaye du Bec-Hellouin 440 G4 • 27800 ☎ 02 32 43 72 60 Daily 7am–9pm Free Mon–Sat 10.30, 3, 4 (also 5 Mon–Fri), Sun and public hols 12, 3, 4, Jun–end Sep; Mon, Wed–Sat 10.30, 3, 4, Sun and public hols 12, 3, 4, Oct–end May (not during services) Adult €4, under 12 free
www.abbayedubec.com
www.ateliersdubec.fr

The history of this village's peaceful walled abbey has been intertwined with England's for the best part of a millennium. The Abbey was founded in the Middle Ages as a place of learning. Lanfranc, later Archbishop of Canterbury, taught here in the 11th century and his successor in England, Anselm, was another alumnus of Le Bec. The abbey continued to maintain strong links with England even beyond Henry VIII's break with Rome in the 16th century.

During the French Revolution, the monks were expelled, books and tapestries looted and the 13th-century church and chapter house demolished. Even the bells were melted down. Monks returned in 1949 and the church today is in the former refectory wing of the newer 17th- and 18th-century buildings.

The central cloister remains calm and spiritual and the water-side Cour de France is another good place for quiet reflection. A walk through the tranquil grounds is revitalizing. The monk's workshop is famous for producing stylish tableware, including plates, bowls and vases, all brightly painted and for sale in the Abbey shop.

The public are welcome to attend services at the abbey—Matins is daily at 7am.

Don't miss The 15th-century St-Nicolas tower is the abbey's only surviving medieval building.

BAYEUX

Bayeux's 11th-century tapestry is world famous, depicting in fresh and vivid detail William the Conqueror's triumph at the Battle of Hastings, and the events leading up to it.

RATINGS	
Historic interest	●●●●●
Specialist shopping (needlework)	●●●

BASICS

439 F4 Pont St-Jean, 14400, tel 02 31 51 28 28; Mon–Sat 9–7, Sun 9–1, 2–6, Jun–end Aug; Mon–Sat 9.30–12.30, 2–5.30, Jan–end Mar, Oct–end Dec; daily 9.30–12.30, 2–6, Apr, May, Sep Bayeux
www.bayeux-tourism.com

Bayeux Tapestry
Centre Guillaume Le Conquerant, rue de Nesmond ☎ 02 31 51 25 50 Daily 9–6.30, mid-Mar to end Apr, Sep, Oct; 9–7, May–end Aug; 9.30–12.30, 2–6, rest of year Adult €7.40, child (10–18) €3, under 10 free

Clean streets, timbered buildings and the gentle sound of watermills in the medieval quarter make Bayeux a welcome diversion on the Battle of Normandy route. The principal lure is, of course, the tapestry, but the place has more recent historical significance, being the first town liberated from German occupation in 1944. The Musée Mémorial de la Bataille de Normandie (*daily 10–12.30, 2–6, mid-Sep to end Apr; 9.30–6.30, rest of year; closed 2nd and 3rd weeks in Jan*) focuses on the 1944 battle. Bayeux's less violent heritage is displayed in the Hôtel du Doyen (*daily 10–12.30, 2–7, Jul, Aug; 10–2.30, 2–6, rest of year*), where you can see art, porcelain and lace exhibitions. The 11th- to 15th-century cathedral (*daily 8.30–6, Oct–end Jun; 8.30–7, rest of year*) has a carved fresco over the south entrance depicting the murder of Archbishop Thomas Becket in Canterbury by soldiers of England's King Henry II.

THE BAYEUX TAPESTRY

The tapestry, 70m (230ft) long but only 50cm (20in) high, is a masterpiece of political propaganda and cartoon storytelling. Commissioned by William the Conqueror's half-brother Odo, Bishop of Bayeux, it was stitched by nuns over 10 years, from 1070 to 1080. The frame-by-frame drama of how William, Duke of Normandy, won the crown of England in 1066 is punctuated by Latin captions, dramatic scenes of Halley's Comet, shipwrecks and banquets. Multilingual audioguides provide a running commentary and an exhibition explains the needlecraft.

Port Palais, Belle-Île (above).
Océanopolis, Brest (right)

BELLE-ÎLE

➕ 438 C7 ℹ️ Quai Bonnelle, BP30, 56360, tel 02 97 31 81 93; Mon–Sat 8.45–7.30, Sun 8.45–12.30, 3–6.30, Jun–end Aug; Mon–Sat 9–12.30, 2–6, Sun 10–12.30, rest of year 🚢 From Quiberon (tel 0820 056 000). Seasonal services from Lorient, Vannes, Port-Navalo and La Trinité ❓ Several shops in Le Palais rent out bicycles www.belle-ile.com

Belle-Île is the largest of Brittany's islands and has some wonderful scenery, especially on the Côte Sauvage in the west, where the mighty waves of the Atlantic Ocean pound the cliffs. The island's capital and main port, Le Palais, lies on the more sheltered eastern side, at the mouth of a small river. Sauzon, the second port, is smaller, with painted cottages and a harbour lined with fishing nets. Bicycle tracks make the island perfect to explore on two wheels. The landscape is dotted with prehistoric menhirs (standing stones), including two in the northwest known as Jean and Jeanne, lovers turned to stone as punishment for a pre-wedding night of passion. **Don't miss** The view of Les Aiguilles de Port-Coton, a series of sharp rocks off the western cliffs, was painted by Monet.

BRIONNE

➕ 440 G4 ℹ️ 1 Rue du Général de Gaulle, 27800, tel 02 32 45 70 51; Mon–Sat 2.30–6.30, Sun 9.30–12

Brionne became part of Normandy in 1050 when Duke William's three-year siege ousted the Duke of Burgundy. The remains of a Norman keep stand high above the town, with good views over the river and valley. The remaining broad walls are an impressive reminder of William's military might. The 15th-century Église St-Martin and the doll museum are also worth visiting.

BREST

The Océanopolis mega-aquarium here is one of the best in Europe.

Brest's most important visitor attraction lies on the water-front a little way out of the city heart. Océanopolis is a theme park on a Disneyesque scale, based on life in the oceans. More than 10,000 marine creatures live in aquariums varying in size from 50 litres (11 gallons) to 1,000,000 litres (220,000 gallons). The park is divided into three sections—Polar, Tropical and Temperate—and you'll see everything from octopuses and sharks to seahorses and electric eels. There are film shows and feeding displays, as well as a re-created penguin environment.

Brest is one of France's largest cities and has been a significant settlement since Roman times. Its natural deep-water port is home to a large naval base. Despite its long history, the city is not particularly enticing—much of

RATINGS			
Good for kids (Océanopolis)	●	●	● ●
Historic interest			● ●
Photo stops			● ● ●

BASICS
➕ 438 B5 ℹ️ Place de la Liberté, BP24, 29266, tel 02 98 44 24 96; Mon–Sat 9.30–7, Sun/hols 10–12, Jul, Aug; Mon–Sat 9–12, 2–6, Sep–end Jun 🚌 The city bus system (BIBUS) is well organized. There are also bus services around the Brest region 🚢 Ferry or pleasure boat links with the Crozon Peninsula from the Port du Commerce

Océanopolis
Port de Plaisance du Moulin Blanc, BP411 ☎ 02 98 34 40 40 ⊙ Daily 9–6, Apr to mid-Jul; 9–7 mid-Jul to end Aug; Tue–Sat 10–5, Sun 10–6, Sep–end Mar (also Mon 10–6 during French school holidays). Closed 2 weeks in Jan 💶 Adult €14.50, child (4–17) €10, under 4 free www.oceanopolis.com

its older architecture was destroyed during World War II. Inland from Océanopolis, on the Allée du Bot, the Conservatoire Botanique National de Brest is a fine botanical garden (*garden: daily 9-6; greenhouses: times vary*). The Musée des Beaux-Arts, at 24 rue Traverse, (*Wed–Sat and Mon 10–12, 2–6, Sun 2–6*) is noted for its collection of works from the Pont-Aven school. The Château, at the tip of the old town, has commanding views along the Rade de Brest and inland along the Elorn river.

Don't miss The Pont de Recouvrance is a huge lift-bridge said to be the highest in Europe.

98   NORTHWEST FRANCE

A gargoyle on a city roof (above).
One of Caen's shopping streets (right)

CAEN

This city was William the Conqueror's base in the 11th century. Today, people come to see the poignant peace museum, the Mémorial de Caen.

Caen is a working city with a busy river port and several top-class attractions, inevitably associated with tumultuous moments in history. After the massive bombardments of 1944 it rebuilt itself as a business-focused city; sadly what older architecture remains is now encircled with unimaginative concrete estates.

REMEMBERING WORLD WAR II
The Mémorial de Caen, on Esplanade Eisenhower, in the north-western outskirts, immerses you in a century of global conflict (*daily 9–7, Feb–end Jun, Sep, Oct; 9–8 Jul, Aug; 9–6 Nov–end Jan; closed two weeks in Jan*). The museum starts with the peace pledges of 1919, then moves through newsreels and scenes of daily life to the horrors of the Holocaust and occupation. Multi-screen special effects recount the Battle of Normandy and a harrowing film, *Espérance*, hammers home the empty truth of post-war peace, with painful images of conflicts in Europe, Africa and the Middle East. Sections of the Berlin Wall mark out a huge new Cold War exhibit, and an observatory reveals current locations of global disorder and suffering.

WILLIAM THE CONQUEROR
Highlights in Caen itself include the restored ramparts of the ducal castle, founded by William the Conqueror in the 11th century. The Musée des Beaux Arts, within the castle walls, has a splendid collection of Dutch, Italian and French works from the Renaissance to the 20th century (*Wed–Mon 9.30–6*). The castle is flanked by two abbeys—St-Étienne for men and La Trinité for women—founded by William and his cousin-bride Matilda to regain admission to the Church after being excommunicated following their incestuous marriage. These are known as the Abbaye-aux-Hommes and the Abbaye-aux-Dames. You can see William the Conqueror's tomb at the Renaissance-Gothic abbey church of St-Étienne, although only his thighbone remains after a raid by Huguenots in the 16th century. The abbey itself is now the Hôtel de Ville, while the ladies' convent is home to the regional council. Guided tours allow you to see Matilda's tomb, the grand staircase and the cloister.

RATINGS	
Historic interest	● ● ●
Photo stops	● ● ●
Shopping	● ● ●

TIPS
● The *Ticket 24h* bus and tram pass costs €2.70 and is valid for 24 hours from the time of your first journey. It is sold on buses and trams.
● If you need some soothing surroundings after your visit to the peace museum, head for the nearby avenue Amiral Mountbatten, where you'll find the Colline aux Oiseaux, a former rubbish tip reinvented as a floral park for the 50th anniversary of D-Day.

BASICS
✚ 440 F4 ▪ Place St Pierre, 14000, tel 02 31 27 14 14; Mon–Sat 9.30–7, Sun and public hols 10–1, 2–5, Jul, Aug; Mon–Sat 9.30–1, 2–6, Sun and public hols 10–1, Sep–end Jun
▪ The restaurants of the Vaugueux quarter are known for excellent seafood
▪ Buses and a new tramway
▪ Caen
▪ Caen-Carpiquet Airport, 9km (5.5 miles) west of the city

www.ville-caen.fr (tourist information)

Oysters for sale at Cancale

CANCALE

🔲 439 E5 🛈 44 rue du Port, 35260, tel 02 99 89 63 72; daily 9–5.30, Jul, Aug; Mon–Sat 9–12.30, 2–5.30., Sep–end Jun 🚌 TIV, the departmental bus line, runs to Cancale from St-Malo and Dol-de-Bretagne www.ville-cancale.fr

Cancale is Brittany's oyster capital and you can sample the shellfish at either a seaside stall or one of the finer restaurants in the port area (La Houle). The town's muddy beaches, on the western flank of the wide, shallow Baie du Mont-St-Michel, aren't ideal for seaside activities, but provide perfect conditions for oysters.
Don't miss The panoramic cliff views are typically Breton.

CAP FRÉHEL

🔲 439 D5 🚌 The most picturesque approach to Cap Fréhel is along the D34 coast road

Cap Fréhel is one of Brittany's most dramatic promontories, offering spectacular views of the frothing waves below and the ragged scenery of the Emerald Coast. On a clear day you can see as far as the Channel Islands. Where land meets water, the red sandstone, porphyry and schist rocks break into jagged towers, battered by incoming waves.

The headland, 70m (230ft) above the sea, crowns 400ha (1,000 acres) of gorse and heather moorlands. This Fauconnière area is now a natural reserve, protecting the breeding grounds of several species of seabirds. The area is also good for walking. In summer, you can visit the Cap Fréhel lighthouse (*daily 2–7, Jul, Aug*).
Don't miss The best views of the cliffs are from the water rather than the land, and you can take boat trips around the cape from St-Malo and Dinard.

CARNAC

Carnac shelters one of the most spectacular concentrations of prehistoric monuments in the world.

The first sight of Carnac's fields of standing stones is breathtaking—if only for the sheer numbers involved. There are more than 3,000 menhirs and other megalithic structures within a 4.5km (3-mile) radius and nobody knows for sure who put them there. What most experts agree is that the monuments—mostly long lines (*alignements*) of standing stones (menhirs)—were erected between 4500 and 1800BC and were used during a religious or ritual activity.

There are three main groups of *alignements* just north of the town. Conservation measures mean it is no longer possible to wander at will among them, although you can walk around one small section at Kermario. The information point here (*daily 9–8, Jul, Aug; 10–5.15, Sep–end Apr; 9–7, May, Jun*) has a model that helps you appreciate the scale of the site.

Le Musée de Préhistoire, 10 place de l'Église (*Mon–Fri 10–6, Sat, Sun and public hols 10–12, 2–6, Jun–end Sep; Wed–Mon 10–12, 2–5, Oct–end May*) uses more than 6,000 prehistoric items to create a vivid picture of the people who may have erected the stones.

Some 300m (1,000ft) east of the town, the tumulus of St-Michel is a prehistoric burial mound that looks so much like a natural hill that a chapel was built on it in the 16th century. The mound, 12m (40ft) high, 125m (400ft) long and 60m (200ft) wide, is thought to date from around 4500BC.

Don't miss Relax on the beach at nearby Carnac-Plage.

RATINGS				
Good for kids	●	●	●	
Historic interest	●	●	●	●
Photo stops	●	●	●	●

BASICS

🔲 438 C7 🛈 Carnac: Place de l'Église; Carnac-Plage: 74 avenue des Druides, tel 02 97 52 13 52; Carnac: Mon–Sat 9–1, 2–7, Sun 9–1 Apr–end Sep and French school hols. Carnac-Plage: Mon–Sat 9–1, 2–7, Sun 2–7 Jul, Aug; Mon–Sat 9–12, 2–6, Sep–end Jun 🚆 No. 1 runs from Vannes. A bus connects Carnac-Plage and Carnac town with the main *alignements* several times a day, Jun–end Sep. 🚂 A *Petit-Train* links Carnac-Plage with Carnac *alignements* and La Trinité-sur-Mer in summer 🎟 Combination tickets (€10) are available for the megaliths at Carnac, those at Locmariaquer and the Musée de Préhistoire. www.ot-carnac.fr

Cherbourg's seafaring history continues to the present day

A section of the ramparts surrounding Concarneau

CHÂTEAU DE KERJEAN

🔲 438 B5 • 29440 St-Vougay ☎ 02 98 69 93 69 🕒 Daily 10–7, Jul, Aug; 10–6, mid-Jun to end Jun, early Sep; Wed–Mon 2–5, late Sep–end Oct; Wed, Sun 2–5, Nov–end Mar; Wed–Mon 2–6, Apr to mid–Jun; Wed–Mon 2–5, French school hols 💰 Adult €4, child (7–17) €1, under 7 free 🔳 The chateau is signposted off the D30 between Plouescat and Landivisiau 🎁 Gift shop with books and postcards www.chateau-de-kerjean.com

This fortified manor was built in the 16th century, when Louis Barbier decided to commission a home that would outdo that of his rival and one-time overlord at nearby Lanhouarneau. The building was damaged by fire in 1710 and suffered again during the Revolution, when the last feudal lord was guillotined. In 1911 it passed into state ownership and was restored and filled with antique furnishings. It sits in 20ha (50 acres) of parkland and hosts a museum of Breton daily life. Unlike many of the chateaux in this area, it is relatively easy to find.

Don't miss The lovely Renaissance well in the second courtyard comes complete with Corinthian columns.

CHERBOURG

🔲 439 E3 🛈 2 quai Alexandre III, 50100, tel 02 33 93 52 02; Mon–Sat 9–6.30, Sun 10–12.30 Jul, Aug; Mon–Sat 9–12.30, 2–6.30, Jun; Mon–Sat 9–12.30, 2–6, Sep–end May 🚉 Cherbourg www.ot-cherbourg-cotentin.fr

Cherbourg has flourished as both a military and passenger port. Today the imposing art deco Gare Maritime Transatlantique passenger terminal has been reinvented as Cité de la Mer (daily 9.30–7, Jun to mid-Sep; 10–6, mid-Sep to end May), a celebration of Cherbourg's seafaring heritage. The biggest

attraction is *Le Redoutable*, France's first nuclear submarine, and the largest submarine in the world open to the public. There's also a museum of naval history and an aquarium with an impressive 'undersea' trail that brings you face to face with marine life. Give yourself at least three hours to see everything.

Non-aquatic attractions in Cherbourg include the Musée de la Libération, in the Fort du Roule, with World War II exhibits (*Tue–Sat 10–12, 2–6, Sun, Mon 2–6, May–end Sep; Wed–Sun 2–6, Oct–end Apr*).

COMBOURG

🔲 439 E5 🛈 Maison de la Lanterne, 23 place Albert Parent, 35270, tel 02 99 73 13 93 www.combourg.org

Château • 23 rue des Princes ☎ 02 99 73 22 95 🕒 Daily 11–5.30, Jul, Aug; Sun–Fri 2–5.30, Jun, Sep; Sun–Fri 11–5, Oct. Gardens: daily 10–6, Jul, Aug; Sun–Fri 10–12.30, 2–6, Jun, Sep; Sun–Fri 10–12, 2–5, Oct; Sun–Fri 10–12.30, Apr, May

The chateau at lakeside Combourg is where the French Romantic writer François-René de Chateaubriand (1768–1848) spent a short but gloomy period of his youth. The edifice rises well above the maze of stone cottages surrounding it. Founded in the 11th century by the Archbishop of Dol (Dol-de-Bretagne), it underwent many expansions and changes throughout the Middle Ages before coming into the hands of the Comte de Chateaubriand, father of the writer. The period the author spent here is recalled in his book *Memoires d'Outre-Tombe*, and in one room you can see some of his papers and furniture.

Don't miss There are lovely views from the chateau.

CONCARNEAU

🔲 438 B6 🛈 Quai d'Aiguillon, BP529, 29185 ☎ 02 98 97 01 44 🕒 Mon–Sat 9–7, Sun 10–4, Jul, Aug; Mon–Sat 9–12.30, 2–5.30, Sep–end Jun 🚌 20 to the main train line at Rosporden; 21 to Port Manech; 14 to Pont-Aven and Quimper; 15 to la Forêt-Fouesnant and Beg-Meil 🛥 To the Glénan Islands or along the Odet river with Vedettes Glenn 🛈 The Blue Nets Festival is held in late Aug www.ville-concarneau.fr

Concarneau combines all that is best about Brittany. It is one of France's key fishing ports and hosts great fish auctions (*criées*). The bustling town has plenty of shops and restaurants and a historic walled town (Ville Close) sits on an island within the port. There are also beaches and boat trips to enjoy.

The town was first fortified in the 11th century and was at its most formidable in the 14th. The Ville Close, linked to the rest of the town by a bridge and gateway, was fortified by the military strategist Vauban during Louis XIV's reign. There are excellent views from his ramparts. The main street, rue Vauban, is flanked by 16th- to 18th-century buildings filled with souvenir shops. The Musée de la Pêche (Fishing Museum) is at the start of this street (*daily 9.30–8, Jul, Aug; 9–12, 2–6, Sep–end Jun*).

Concarneau's modern marina sits on the seaward side of the Ville Close, while the main fishing port, with its utilitarian buildings, is on the land side. The fish auction at quai de la Criée (arrive by 6.30am) is the largest in Brittany and the catches are dispatched across France. If you prefer to see live fish, visit the Marinarium, on the seafront at the place de la Croix (*daily 10–7, Jul, Aug; 10–12, 2–6, Apr–end Jun, Sep; 2–6, Oct–end Dec, Feb–end Mar*).

THE SIGHTS

A fishing boat returning to Le Conquet

An artist perched above the beach at Barneville-Carteret, on the west coast of Normandy's Cotentin peninsula

THE SIGHTS

LE CONQUET

🞧 438 A5 🛈 Parc de Beauséjour, 29217, tel 02 98 89 11 31; Mon–Fri 9–5.20, Sat, Sun 10–4, Jul, Aug; Mon–Fri 9–12.30, 2–5.30, Jun, Sep; Tue–Sat 9–12.30, Oct–end May 🚌 31 to Brest 🚢 To Molène and Ouessant
www.leconquet.fr

Le Conquet is perhaps the prettiest of Brittany's many attractive coastal villages, with its whitewashed cottages hugging the hillside and its lively fishing harbour. There are beautiful beaches nearby and you can take a ferry to the islands of Ouessant and Molène.

The small square above the port is flanked by fishermen's stone cottages and is full of the trappings of fishing—lobster pots, baskets and nets. Casting a protective eye over the port entrance is La Maison des Seigneurs, part of a larger fortress dating from the 15th century and now a private home. The tiny Dom Michel chapel, at the top of rue Dom Michel le Noblezt, makes an interesting contrast to Brittany's larger, more ornate, churches.

Offshore from the town lie the waters of the Parc Naturel Régional d'Armorique (Armorique Natural Park), now classed as a Biosphere Reserve by UNESCO. You can take trips out by glass-bottomed boat. **Don't miss** The town itself has very little in the way of sandy beaches but it is only a 2km (1-mile) walk from the harbour, via a footbridge, to the Plage des Blancs-Sablons, one of the finest beaches in Brittany.

Sand-yacht racing at Vauville, on the Cotentin Peninsula

CÔTE DE GRANIT ROSE

🞧 438 C4 🛈 Offices at Trébeurden, Perros-Guirec (see page 112), Tréguier and Paimpol

The Pink Granite Coast is one of the most dramatic stretches of Brittany's shoreline and the region's most northerly area. Here, land meets sea in an unending visual spectacle of high cliffs, narrow inlets, fjord-like river valleys and sheltered coves. The coastline gets its name from the granite rocks—pinkish-brown in harsh sunlight, mellowing to a deep rosy hue at sunset. The granite has been a popular building material all along the coast, making a stark contrast to the grey stone or white-painted stucco in other areas of Brittany.

The best places to see the rocks lie between Trébeurden in the west and Paimpol in the east. There is no easy-to-follow driving route. Instead, mazes of narrow lanes carry you past tiny settlements to high, windblown promontories such as Pointe du Château or Le Gouffre. **Don't miss** The stretch around Ploumanac'h is good for walking, with the added benefit that you are never too far from a good restaurant at Ploumanac'h or Perros-Guirec.

COTENTIN PENINSULA

🞧 439 E4 🛈 Cité de la Mer, Gare Maritime Transatlantique, 50100, Cherbourg-Octeville, tel 02 33 20 26 26; daily 10–7, Jun to mid-Sep; 10–6, mid-Sep to end May. Closed 2nd and 3rd week in Jan 🚊 Cherbourg
www.ot-cherbourg-cotentin.fr

This unspoiled peninsular landscape suggests a remote region far removed from Normandy's commercial towns and the fairytale quaintness of the hinterland. The Cotentin Peninsula offers an authentic glimpse of French rural life, with farming and fishing very much to the fore. On the west of the peninsula, the stark rugged coastline around Cap de La Hague and Nez de Jobourg is almost Breton in its craggy majesty, perfect for windswept walks and views out to the Channel Islands. In contrast, the eastern side has a lusher more verdant landscape. The green fields and rich woodland marking the countryside around the Val de Saire stretch to the dunes of the D-Day beaches.

Highlights of the region include the views from the top of the Gatteville Lighthouse at Barfleur (see page 96) and the tiny island of Tatihou, with its Vauban fort, off the coast of the oyster fishing port of St-Vaast-la-Hougue. Strict environmental-protection rules limit visitors to no more than 500 a day. Arrive on foot at low tide or take the amphibious boat, included in the admission charges to the fort and maritime and marine heritage museum.

COUTANCES

🞧 439 E4 🛈 Place Georges Leclerc, 50200, tel 02 33 19 08 10; Mon–Sat 10–12.30, 1.30–7, Sun 10–12.30, 2–6, Jul to mid-Sep; Mon–Fri 10–12.30, 2–6, Sat 10–12.30, 2–5.30, mid-Sep to end Jun 🚊 Coutances

Hailed as a masterpiece of Norman Gothic architecture, the cathedral at Coutances is cunningly grafted on to the remains of an earlier Romanesque church. The 13th-century construction is beautifully proportioned, with strong buttresses anchoring it to the ground, elegant spires and an octagonal lantern tower. Stained-glass windows tell the story of St. Thomas Becket. The nearby Jardin des Plantes is a pleasant spot for a walk or picnic on a summer's day. If you're here in spring, catch the jazz festival *Jazz Sous les Pommiers*.

Four thousand boats took Allied soldiers to the D-Day beaches

D-DAY BEACHES

From the Bay of the Seine to Cherbourg, Normandy is a vast open-air museum commemorating the events of *Le Débarquement*, 6 June 1944.

Eight well-signposted routes take you through the invasion, battles and liberation of Normandy—and the beginning of the end of World War II. For veterans and their families, the respect with which the sacrifices of a generation are treated is uplifting. For younger people, the lessons of the past are recounted in a simple yet powerful way.

LIBERATION PLAN
A year before D-Day, Winston Churchill and Franklin D. Roosevelt began planning *Operation Overlord*, the Allied invasion of Normandy. On the night of 5 June 1944, 4,000 landing craft set sail from England for the Cotentin and Calvados coast in preparation for the dawn raids. Aircraft silently targeted key defences at either end of the invasion front, with gliders and parachutists of the 6th Airborne Division taking Pegasus Bridge on the Caen-Ouestreham Canal at Benouville. Next, several hundred Rangers captured the Pointe du Hoc, before the landings at the five key beaches, where 135,000 men and 20,000 vehicles came ashore between 6.30 and 7.30am. British, French and Commonwealth forces, aiming to capture Caen, landed at beaches code-named Sword (Bella Riva, Lion-sur-Mer and St-Aubin), Juno (Bernières and Courseulles) and Gold (Ver-sur-Mer and Asnelles). Farther west, American troops landed at Omaha (St-Laurent, Colleville and Vierville) and Utah (the Cotentin coast towards Cherbourg). Losses were heavy, but the Germans lacked air support and the Allies won a vital toehold.

SEE WHERE IT HAPPENED
At Arromanches, remains of the prefabricated Mulberry Harbour towed across the Channel can still be seen off shore. Learn more about the landings at the Musée du Débarquement (*Feb–Dec*) and the Arromanches 360° circular cinema. Pegasus bridge sits in the grounds of the Mémorial Pegasus museum (*Feb–end Nov*), in Ranville.

Rows of neatly tended war-graves provide an indelible memory, whether the small plot of 40 British graves at Chouain, the classical Commonwealth memorial at Bayeux or the precision alignment of 9,387 white crosses of the American cemetery at Colleville-sur-Mer.

Quinéville's Musée de la Liberté (*mid-Mar to mid-Nov*) contains a street scene of life in occupied Normandy.

RATINGS
Historic interest	●●●●●
Photo stops	●●●

TIPS
● Ask at the tourist office for the free booklet *The D-Day Landings and The Battle of Normandy*. If you buy a full-price ticket at any of the museums listed here, you can gain free entry to most of the others over the next 30 days.
● Many museums close from November to spring. During May and June, arrive early or at lunchtime to avoid noisy school parties.
● Most museums and memorials have excellent access for people with disabilities.

BASICS
✚ 439 F4
Calvados ✚ 440 F4 🚹 8 rue Renoir, 14000, Caen, tel 02 31 27 90 30; Mon–Fri 8.30–12.30, 1.30–5.30
www.calvados-tourisme.com
Manche ✚ 439 E4 🚹 Maison du Département, Route de Villedieu, 50008, St-Lô, tel 02 33 05 98 70; Mon–Fri 8.30–12.30, 1.30–6
www.manche-tourisme.com
Orne ✚ 440 G5 🚹 88 rue St-Blaise, 61002, Alençon, tel 02 33 28 88 71; Mon–Fri 8.45–12, 1.30–5.30
www.cg61.com
❓ For the Mémorial de Caen, see page 99; for Bayeux's Musée Mémorial de la Bataille de Normandie, see page 97

Relaxing on the beach at Deauville

THE SIGHTS

DEAUVILLE

➕ 440 G4 🛈 Place de la Mairie, 14804, 02 31 14 40 00; Mon–Sat 9–7, Sun 10–1, 3–6, Jul to mid-Sep; Mon–Sat 9–12.30, 2–6.30, Sun 10–1, 2–5, mid-Sep to end Jun 🚉 Deauville-Trouville www.deauville.org

Deauville is the summer playground of the north, with huge mock-Norman hotels and the weekend homes of rich Parisians. Popular pastimes include looking stylish on the seafront, betting on the races, gambling at the casino and seeing a cabaret. The season ends with an American Film Festival in September. If it is all very artificial, then that is the point—the resort is an upscale beach party.

Don't miss The boardwalk is inscribed with names of stars who have graced the promenade.

DIEPPE

➕ 444 H3 🛈 Pont Ango BP152, 76204, 02 32 14 40 60; Mon–Sat 9–1, 2–8, Sun 10–1, 3–6, Jul, Aug; Mon–Sat 9–1, 2–7, Sun 10–1, 3–6, May–end Jun, Sep; Mon–Sat 9–12, 2–6, Oct–end Apr 🚉 Dieppe ⛴ From Newhaven, UK (4 hours); 2-hour fast ferry in summer www.dieppetourisme.com

Dieppe is a lively port town and a popular destination for day-trippers from the UK. The 15th-century Château-Musée (*daily 10–12, 2–6, Jun–end Sep; Wed–Mon 10–12, 2–5, rest of year*), with its round turrets, has paintings by Renoir, Boudin and Pissarro and an ivory collection, witness to the city's historic trade links with Africa. Other attractions include the timbered 17th-century Maison Miffant, the Cité de la Mer maritime museum and aquarium (*daily 10–12, 2–6*) and, on a clifftop above the port, the church of Notre-Dame-de-Bon-Secours, built in 1876 in memory of sailors lost at sea. For lunch, head for the quai Henry IV.

DINAN

Walk along the oldest and most extensive ramparts in Brittany, high above the Rance valley.

Medieval Dinan is one of Brittany's best preserved old towns. Many sections of the 600-year-old ramparts are walkable, such as Duchess Anne's walk that brings you out into the Jardin Anglais, with panoramic views of the valley.

RATINGS	
Historic interest	●●●●
Photo stops	●●●●

BASICS

➕ 439 D5 🛈 9 rue du Château, 22105, 02 96 87 69 76; Mon–Sat 9–7, Sun 10–12.30, 2.30–6, Jun–end Sep; Mon–Sat 9.30–12.30, 2–6.30 rest of year 🚉 Dinan ⛴ From St-Malo www.dinan-tourisme.com (containing historical information, two virtual tours and places to visit in the Rance valley)

You can find out more about local history at the Musée du Château, in the ruined 14th-century castle keep (*daily 10–6.30*). In the 12th century, Dinan crusader Rivallon le Roux pledged that, if he survived, he would return to his home town and pay for a church dedicated to Christ. The Gothic and Romanesque St-Sauveur basilica (*daily 10–5*) was built between the 12th and 18th centuries. It contains relics from every period, including the heart of another local knight, Bertrand du Guesclin, whose equestrian statue stands in place du Guesclin. This square hosts the Thursday-morning market.

The old town is perfect for exploring on foot. The narrow, cobbled rue du Petit-Fort winds its way (steeply) from the port to the heart of the town. It's lined with medieval merchants' houses, *crêperies*, arts and crafts shops and the Maison du Gouverneur (*open 10–6.30, Jun–end Sep*), a spectacular three-floor, half-timbered house containing a display of regional furniture. Head to the place des Merciers to see the town's most beautiful half-timbered houses. The Gothic Église St-Malo has a superb English organ, dating from the Romantic period, and beautiful stained-glass windows illustrating great moments in the town's history.

A pleasant walk from central Dinan you'll find Léhon, a pretty hamlet with a 9th-century priory. You can take boat trips up the Rance from St-Malo to Dinan from April to September.

Don't miss There are good views of the town and the Rance valley from the Tour de l'Horloge.

Dinard is a popular seaside resort

A fishing boat at Douarnenez

The chalk cliffs of Étretat

DINARD

⊞ 439 D5 ⓘ 2 boulevard Féart, 35802, tel 02 99 46 94 12; daily 9–6, Jul, Aug; Mon–Sat 9–12.30, 2–6, Sep–end Jun 🚌 From St-Malo, La Richardais, St-Lunaire, St-Briac-sur-Mer and Lancieux. No. 11 links with Dinan 🚢 From St-Malo ✈ Dinard-Pleurtuit airport is 6km (4 miles) south of the town ❓ During summer the Promenade du Clair de Lune is floodlit after dark and there are concerts in the gardens
www.ville-dinard.fr

Dinard occupies a rocky outcrop across from St-Malo (see page 121), and has several small but sandy beaches. High tides and regular sea breezes provide excellent yachting conditions, and the tempering effects of the Gulf Stream encourage lush subtropical vegetation.

Dinard was a typical Breton fishing port until the 19th century, when it was discovered by the American and British moneyed classes. During the Belle Époque it was the place for yachting, gambling and other upper-class leisure activities. Today it is an upscale resort, popular with French visitors.

The Plage de l'Écluse, with its distinctive blue-and-white striped cotton beach huts, is the largest beach. Overlooking it is the Casino Barrière du Dinard, in boulevard Wilson (*gambling daily 9pm–4am; dining daily 12–2.30, 7.30–10.30*). Nearby is an Olympic-size, covered, heated seawater swimming pool (*daily 10–12.30, 3–7.30*) and the modern Palais des Arts et Festivals.

A public footpath, the Chemin de Ronde, leads along the coast. The central section, from Plage du Prieuré in the south to the Pointe du Mulinet, is called Promenade du Clair de Lune and is popular for an afternoon or evening stroll.

DOMFRONT

⊞ 440 F5 ⓘ 12 place de la Roirie, 61700, tel 02 33 38 53 97; Mon–Sat 9.30–12.30, 2.30–6.30 🚉 Flers, 23km (14 miles) away, then bus to Domfront ❓ In early Aug the town stages a medieval fair, with music, markets and feasting
www.domfront.com

Unrivalled views over the landscape of Lower Normandy make this pretty town an essential stop on a clear day.

Dominated by the remnants of an 11th-century fortress perched high on the hilltop overlooking the Varenne river, the town has clusters of typical stone and timber houses lining its cobbled streets. At the foot of the hill stands the church of Notre-Dame-sur-l'Eau, where Thomas Becket is said to have celebrated Mass in 1166.

In spring and summer brick-bordered flower beds, pots and hanging baskets justify Domfront's reputation as one of Normandy's *Villes Fleuries*.

The town is in the heart of Camembert country and also produces the brandy *Calvados Domfrontais* (made with apples and pears), *Pommeau*, a fortified apple drink, and *Poiré* (perry). In spring, the white blossom of the pear orchards outside Domfront provides an unforgettable sight and scent.

A stone sculpture at the entrance to the Port-Musée, Douarnenez

DOUARNENEZ

⊞ 438 B6 ⓘ 1 rue du Dr Mével, BP216, 29172, tel 02 98 92 13 35; Mon–Sat 10–12, 2–6 🚌 Links to Quimper, Pont-Croix, Audierne and the Pointe du Raz ❓ Some of the beaches in Douarnenez bay can be dangerous for swimming
www.douarnenez-tourisme.com

Douarnenez is Brittany's second fishing town after Concarneau, but it lacks the refined air of its larger sibling. Unlike Concarneau's Ville Close (see page 101), it was never touched by royalty; instead, its heritage is humble fishermen's cottages. The town has several sheltered harbours—one reason for its long success as a fishing port. Today, fish is canned in factories alongside the docks.

You can learn more about local links with the sea at the Port-Musée, in place de l'Enfer (*daily 9–7, Apr–end Oct*).

The town's history pre-dates Roman times. In the Dark Ages, Douarnenez was associated with King Mark and the Tristan legend and it is also one of the disputed sites of Brittany's mythical 6th-century Atlantis—the Lost City of Ys. In the 16th century, residents were plagued by the notorious pirate La Fontenelle, who ransacked the houses and stole the stone to build his own chateau on the Île d'Tristan, just offshore.

Don't miss There are excellent views over Douarnenez's eastern port from Les Plomarc'h, 500m (1,500ft) to the east.

ÉTRETAT

See page 290.

The Grande Porte, main entry to the upper town at Granville

THE SIGHTS

EVREUX

⊞ 440 H4 ℹ Place Général de Gaulle, 27000, tel 02 32 24 04 43; Mon–Sat 9.30–12.30, 1.30–6.15 🚉 Evreux
www.ot-pays-evreux.fr

Evreux has risen from the ashes many times over the centuries, most recently after the World War II air raids that melted the spire of its cathedral, Notre-Dame. A replacement spire topped with a golden rooster was installed in 1973. Parts of the church date back to the 12th century, and the blend of Early and Flamboyant Gothic styles is testament to the town's stoic rebuilding plans following each fresh battle. Stained-glass windows from the 13th to 17th centuries are well worth a look. The ornate Gothic Tour de l'Horloge chimes the hour from the last vestige of the town's medieval fortifications.

GRANVILLE

⊞ 439 E5 ℹ 4 cours Jonville, 50400, tel 02 33 91 30 03; daily 9–1, 2–7.30, Jul, Aug; Mon–Sat 9–12.15, 2–6.30, Sep–end Jun 🚉 Granville
www.ville-granville.fr

On the bay of Mont St-Michel, this busy port and lively summer resort retains its 15th-century battlements, built by Englishman Thomas Scales. The main entrance to the upper town is still via the original drawbridge of the Grande Porte. Climb to the Musée de Vieux Granville (*Wed–Mon, 10–12, 2–6.30, Apr–end Sep; Wed, Sat, Sun 2–6, rest of year*) to see local crafts and learn about the history of the fishing port. Modern art at the Musée Richard Anacréon (*Wed–Mon 11–6, Jul–end Sep; Wed–Sun 2–6, rest of year*) includes works by Picasso. **Don't miss** The Musée Christian Dior is in the designer's childhood home (*daily 10–12.30, 2–6.30, Jun–end Sep*).

GIVERNY

Visit the home of Impressionist painter Claude Monet and the gardens that inspired his famous Water Lily series.

Thousands of visitors leave the main sightseeing trail in Normandy to visit this modest town in the Seine Valley. Ironically, there are no original works by Monet in the pretty pink-and-green house where he lived until his death in 1926. Plenty of prints and copies adorn the rooms, but it is the garden and the famous lily pond and bridge that lure the crowds. Gardeners keep the scene as close as possible to the way things were in Monet's day.

The painter bought the house in 1895, having rented it as a family home since 1883. It was here that he painted the irises and lily pond scenes that were his final obsessions. You can see his walled garden—Le Clos Normand—and the lily pond. A main road separates the gardens, but an underpass takes visitors safely to the pond. Wonderful though the gardens are, the press of people means they are not a place for quiet contemplation.

RATINGS	
Cultural interest	●●●●
Photo stops	●●●●

TIPS

• Arrive early to see the lily pond without the crowds.
• Visit in early summer to see the gardens at their very best.

BASICS

⊞ 440 H4 ℹ Office de Tourisme de Vernon, 36 rue Carnot, 27201, tel 02 32 51 39 60; Tue–Sat 9.30–12.15, 2.15–6.30, Sun 10–12, May–end Aug; Tue–Sat 10–12, 2–5, rest of year
🚉 Vernon station, then taxi or cycle 5km (3 miles) to Giverny
www.giverny.org (in French and English; see photos of Monet's gardens and find out what's on in the area)

Fondation Claude Monet
Rue Claude Monet, 27620 ☎ 02 32 51 28 21 🕐 Wed–Mon 9.30–6, Apr–end Oct 💶 Adult €5.50 (house and garden), €4 (garden) €1.50 (house); child (8–11) €3; under 7 free
www.fondation-monet.com

The art trail spills over onto the nearby streets, and rue Claude Monet is filled with artists' workshops and galleries. The Musée d'Art Américain Giverny (*Tue–Sun 9.30–6, Mar–end Nov*) has works by Monet's American contemporaries in France, as well as temporary exhibitions.
Don't miss The Hôtel Baudy, a former boarding house and bar in rue Claude Monet, is where Monet met with Renoir, Sisley, Pisarro and Rodin and the American artists who followed them.

Children learning to sail, off the coast of Le Havre

LE HAVRE

🔲 440 G4 ℹ️ 186 boulevard Clemenceau, 76600, tel 02 32 74 04 04; Mon–Sat 9–7, Sun 10–12.30, 2.30–6, Easter–end Sep; Mon–Sat 9–6.30, Sun 10–1, rest of year 🚊 Le Havre www.lehavretourisme.com

Le Havre is Normandy's premier industrial port, bounded by the English Channel and the Seine estuary. Claude Monet grew up here and his painting of the boats here, *Impression—soleil levant* (*c*1873), gave the Impressionist movement its name. You can see works by Monet and his contemporaries at the Musée des Beaux Arts André Malraux, on the boulevard Clemenceau (*Mon, Wed–Fri 11–6, Sat, Sun 11–7*), as well as other art from the 17th to 20th centuries. The showpiece glass building is as close as an indoor space can get to bathing in the natural light that launched Impressionism. Two local artists represented in the gallery are Le Havre's Raoul Dufy and Honfleur's Eugène Boudin.

For a glimpse of how Le Havre used to be, visit the Musée de l'Ancien Havre, on rue Jerome-Bellarmato (*Wed–Sun 10–12, 2–6*). It is in one of the few 17th-century timbered and brick houses to have survived the World War II air raids that destroyed around 80 per cent of Le Havre's buildings.

HUELGOAT

See page 282.

A fisherman mending his nets at Le Havre

HONFLEUR

Art and the business of the sea combine in this much-painted Normandy fishing port.

Honfleur is one of France's most attractive working ports and a familiar sight in art galleries across the world. Painters who have captured the town on canvas include J. M. W. Turner and local man Eugène Boudin. Honfleur continues to attract artists seeking seascape inspiration, as well as visitors in search of a seafood supper at the quayside.

You can see some of the art inspired by the town at the Musée Eugène Boudin (*Wed–Mon 10–12, 2–6, mid-Mar to end Sep; Mon, Wed–Fri 2.30–5, Sat, Sun 10–12, 2.30–5, rest of year. Closed Jan to mid-Feb*), in place Erik Satie. The local painter's works are hung alongside pieces by Corot, Dufy and Boudin's student, Monet. Less conventional, but highly stimulating is the Maisons Satie, in boulevard Charles V (*Wed–Mon 10–7, May–end Sep; Wed–Mon 11–6, rest of year. Closed Jan to mid-Feb*). This modern museum experience celebrates the life and work of another son of Honfleur, the eccentric composer and artist Erik Satie (1866–1925). Art and music join forces as you walk past surreal images, while headphones play Satie's music.

The town also has a strong maritime tradition, as a plaque on the wall of the 16th-century Lieutenant building at the Vieux Bassin (Old Dock) reminds you: It was from here that French pioneer Samuel de Champlain set sail for Quebec in the early 17th century. The Vieux Bassin itself is packed with fishing boats and pleasure craft. Tall, slate-fronted, oak-tiled and timber-framed buildings surround the port—their ground floors now house ship's chandlers, art galleries and restaurants. The 15th-century church of Ste-Cathérine, built by shipbuilders, has its 18th-century bell tower built across the square as a precaution against fire. Buskers and craft stalls inhabit the pedestrian-only streets nearby.

RATINGS		
Cultural interest	● ● ●	
Historic interest	● ● ●	
Photo stops	● ● ● ●	

BASICS
🔲 440 G4 ℹ️ Place Arthur Boudin, 14602, tel 02 31 89 23 30; daily 9.30–7, Jul, Aug; 10–12.30, 2–6.30, Sep; Mon–Sat 9.30–12.30, 2–6.30, Sun 9.30–12.30, 2–5, Easter–end Jun; Mon–Sat 9.30–12, 2–6, Oct–Easter 🚌 20 and 50 from Pont-l'Évêque www.ot-honfleur.fr (in French and English; see photos of the town and find practical information)

The haunting ruins of Abbaye de Jumièges

Lisieux, where St. Thérèse lived from the age of four

ÎLE DE BRÉHAT

➕ 438 C5 🛈 Le Bourg, 22870, tel 02 96 20 04 15; Mon, Tue, Thu–Sat 10–12, 2–5.30 🚢 Vedettes de Île de Bréhat operate year-round services from Pointe de l'Arcouest, just north of Paimpol. There are summer crossings from Binic, Erquy and St-Quay-Portrieux

Île de Bréhat is a tiny traffic-free rural idyll, criss-crossed with dry-stone walls, granite cottages and myriad species of flowers. It makes a good day trip from the mainland and is ideal for walking or bicycling.

Only 2km (1 mile) off the north Brittany coastline, Bréhat is in fact two tiny islands connected by a 16th-century bridge. Each of the low-lying islands is less than a kilometre (half a mile) long and is surrounded by a ring of treacherous reefs. These form a natural protection for its many bays and coves. Most of Bréhat's 470 residents live in the south island, where the mild Gulf Stream climate has encouraged a profusion of Mediterranean plants in the gardens of the pretty painted cottages. Ferries dock at the tiny Port Clos, on the south coast. The Plage de Gerzido, the island's best beach, is to the east, facing the mainland. From Port Clos it is a 500m (545 yard) walk north to the main village, Le Bourg. West of here is the Chapelle St-Michel. Nearby, the Moulin à Marée du Birlot (*Sun, Jul, Aug, depending on the tide*) is a 17th-century tidal watermill whose restoration has won numerous awards.

According to legend, the fishermen of Île de Bréhat passed on their knowledge of sea routes to the New World to Christopher Columbus before his 'discovery' of those lands to the west.

Don't miss There are lovely views from the Chapelle St-Michel.

ÎLE DE GROIX

➕ 438 C6 🛈 Quai de Port-Tudy, 56590, tel 02 97 86 53 08; daily 9.30–1, 2–7 Jul, Aug; Mon–Fri 9–12, 2–5, rest of year 🚢 From Lorient

This island, a 50-minute ferry ride from Lorient, is a raised plateau fringed by steep cliffs. The sheltered eastern coast has the best beaches, including the fine Plage des Grands Sables. The force of the Atlantic has left its mark on the western Côte Sauvage (wild coast).

The island, 8km (5 miles) by 2km (1 mile), has little in the way of visitor facilities. But it is a good option if you want to escape the bustle of the mainland, and there are 25km (15 miles) of footpaths to explore. Rare minerals are found here and there is a geological reserve near Locmaria.

During the 1930s Groix had the largest tuna fishing fleet in France. You can learn more about the history of the fleet at the *Écomusee* (*daily 9.30–12, 3–7 Jul, Aug; 10–12.30, 2–5 May, Jun, Sep; Tue–Sun 10–12.30, 2–5 Apr, Oct, Nov; Wed, Sat, Sun 10–12.30, 2–5 Dec–end Mar*) at Port-Tudy. The last tuna fishing boat, the *Kevano*, sits in retirement in the port. Most of the island's 3,000 residents live in the capital, Groix, just inland from Port-Tudy.

JOSSELIN

➕ 439 D6 🛈 Place de la Congrégation, 56120, tel 02 97 22 36 43; daily 10–6 Jun–end Aug; Mon–Sat 10–12.30, 1.30–6, Sun 2–6, rest of year 🚌 From Pontivy, Rennes and Ploermel **www.paysdejosselin.com**

This inland Breton town has a fantastic medieval castle, whose rounded turrets make a memorable sight mirrored in the river Oust. The castle (*daily 10–6, mid-Jul to end Aug; 2–6, Jun to*

mid-Jul, Sep; 2–6 Sat, Sun and French school hols, Apr, May, Oct*) dates from the 14th century, with the Renaissance screen added between 1490 and 1510. It was restored in the 19th century. A sober wall of stone overlooks the river, with three circular towers topped by witch's-hat turrets. Once you enter the courtyard, the inland façade offers a riot of Renaissance detail on its 10 upper gables and exquisite carving over each of its door and window openings on the lower floor. A magnificent carved frieze links the two elements at roof level. Inside, there is 17th- and 18th-century style decoration. Nearby, the Musée de Poupées has a family collection of around 600 dolls, dating from 1880.

A maze of cobbled alleyways links the courtyard to Josselin's main town square, where you'll find the late-15th-century Notre-Dame-du-Roncier (Our Lady of the Brambles).

Don't miss The best views of the castle are from across the river in the Quartier Sainte-Croix.

JUMIÈGES

➕ 440 G4 ☎ 02 35 37 24 02 🕐 Daily 9–7 Apr–end Sep; 9.30–1, 2.30–5.30, rest of year 💶 Adult €4.60, under 10 free

Jumièges was the greatest of the Seine Valley abbeys and its haunting ruins are worth a visit. The earliest remains, from the Église St-Pierre, date from the 10th century. The nearby (roofless) church of Notre-Dame, with its white twin towers, was built a century later. The abbey suffered in the 17th century, when much of its stone was used for other buildings. Its ruins stand in well-maintained parkland, and from April to September *son-et-lumière* shows add to the romantic atmosphere.

This square, in Lisieux, conjures up a quieter, less mechanized world

A shingled house with pretty flower boxes in Morlaix

LISIEUX

🏠 440 G4 🛈 11 rue d'Alençon 14100, tel 02 31 48 18 10; Mon–Sat 8.30–12, 1.30–6, Oct to mid-Jun; Mon–Sat 8.30–6.30, Sun 10–12.30, 2–5, mid-Jun to end Sep 🚂 Lisieux www.ville-lisieux.fr

Pilgrims flock here in summer to pay homage to St. Thérèse of Lisieux, whose touching autobiography proved particularly popular during the hard days of World War I. Born Thérèse Martin, she moved with her family to Lisieux at the age of four. Throughout her childhood she begged her father to allow her to enter the Carmelite convent with her sister; aged only 15, Thérèse received papal dispensation to join the order.

Always a frail young woman, she developed tuberculosis in the draughty convent. She died in 1897, aged just 24, shortly after completing her memoirs *History of a Soul*. She was canonized in 1925 and her relics are displayed in the Carmelite chapel. In summer, a mini-train shuttles visitors between the chapel, Thérèse's family home at *Les Buissonnets*, and the domed basilica of Sainte-Thérèse.

The Gothic cathedral of St-Pierre contains the tomb of Bishop Cauchon, who executed Joan of Arc; it is also said to be where Eleanor of Aquitaine married England's Henry II. **Don't miss** On Saturday morning (and Wednesdays in summer) you can buy delicious cheeses and cider at the weekly market.

LOCRONAN

🏠 438 B6 🛈 Place de la Mairie, 29180, tel 02 98 91 70 14; Mon–Sat 10–1, 2–7, Sun 2–7 mid-Jun to end Aug; Mon–Fri 10–12, 2–6, Apr to mid-Jun, Sep; Mon–Fri 2–6, mid-Dec to end Mar; closed Nov to mid-Dec 🚌 Route 10 from Quimper to the Crozon peninsula runs through

Locronan 🅿 There are several car parks on the outskirts www.locronan.org

Locronan is one of the prettiest towns in Brittany, with its stone houses decked in flowers. It was a sacred site for the Druids, then a place of Christian pilgrimage after the death of the Irish missionary St. Ronan in the 5th century. The town's golden age in the 17th century was based on the production of hemp sailcloth, but when Louis XIV abolished its monopoly in hemp, Locronan's economy quickly collapsed. In the ensuing centuries, money was never available to update the buildings, leaving the architecture much as it was in the town's heyday.

At the heart is the old town square, place de l'Église, chosen by Roman Polanski as a film set for *Tess* (1979). The 15th-century church of St-Ronan (*daily 9–6*) is in a style known as Ogival Flamboyant. It is surrounded by 17th- and 18th-century buildings, once the homes of rich merchants, along with an office of the East India Company and the Canvas Office. Rue Moal, with more humble weavers' homes, leads to the 15th- and 16th-century church of Notre-Dame-de-Bonne-Nouvelle (Our Lady of Good News; *daily 9–6*), with stained glass by Alfred Manessier (1911–93).

The Musée Municipal, in place de la Mairie, is a good venue to continue your historical explorations (*open same hours as tourist office*).

The Surrealist painter Yves Tanguy (1900–55) had a home on rue Lann, and various potters, painters and sculptors work and have gallery space in the town. **Don't miss** Enjoy panoramic views from Plas ar Horn, 289m (948ft) high.

MORLAIX

🏠 438 B5 🛈 Place des Otages, 29600, tel 02 98 62 14 94; Mon–Sat 9–12, 2–7, Sun 10.30–12.30, Jul, Aug; Mon–Sat 9–12, 2–6, rest of year 🚌 51 to Loccuirec; 52 and 61 to Huelgoat; 53 to Carantec-sur-Mer, St-Pol-de-Léon and Roscoff; 55 to Plougasnou and le Diben 🚂 Morlaix

Morlaix sits in a ravine at the head of a large estuary, in the shadow of a towering viaduct. It was once Brittany's third city, prospering on fishing, shipbuilding, linen, paper and a little piracy. This made it a target for reprisals. The worst came in 1522, when the English attacked in retaliation for French corsairs' ransacking of Bristol. Morlaix's citizens took their revenge when they found the English sleeping off hangovers after helping themselves to the town's wine.

The huge viaduct was built in the 1860s to carry the Paris–Brest railway. Below it, Morlaix rises up the steep valley sides in a series of narrow lanes. In the old town there are many Breton *maisons à lanterne* (lantern houses), characterized by a central hall and a fireplace that carries through to the top of the house. You can visit the Maison à Pondalez, at 9 Grand Rue (*Tue–Sat 10.30–12.30, 3–7, Jul, Aug; varies rest of year*). The Maison de la Reine Anne, in the rue du Mur, is where Anne of Brittany stayed in 1505 (*Mon–Sat 10–6.30, Jul–end Sep; Mon–Sat 11–6, May, Jun*). **Don't miss** See Léon furniture and Breton paintings at the Musée Jacobin, in the Église Jacobin. The building is part of a 13th-century Dominican and Jacobin monastery, in place des Jacobins (*daily 10–12, 2–6.30, Jul, Aug; Mon, Wed–Fri 10–12, 2–6, Sep, Oct; Mon 10–12, 2–5, Wed–Fri 10–12, 4–5, Sat 2–5, Nov–end Jun*).

THE SIGHTS

Mont St-Michel

**One of the truly essential sights of France, Mont St-Michel is a living reminder of 1,000 years of religious history.
It's also a place of stillness, despite the crowds.**

A distant Mont St-Michel shimmers above the water

Mont St-Michel's narrow streets throng with visitors

RATINGS	
Good for kids	● ● ●
Historic interest	● ● ● ●
Photo stops	● ● ● ● ●

TIPS

● When the main street is packed with people, climb the steps to the less crowded ramparts to look down on the village and across the sea.
● Rather than pay the €7 admission charge to visit the Abbey, you could time your visit to coincide with the midday mass, when tickets are free. You can take your time walking through the monument after the service.
● Son et lumière shows are staged at the Mount in summer.

SEEING MONT ST-MICHEL

Mont St-Michel is more than a church on a rock in a bay. The silhouette of the walled Abbey rising from the mists was the very symbol of France and French ingenuity long before the Eiffel Tower was even a stack of rivets and girders. This fortified religious community, separated from the mainland by quicksands and tides, is a surreal sight, especially through the early morning sea mists. Reached via a causeway, just north of Pontorson, the Mount was originally an island in the sea between Normandy and Brittany. It is now a UNESCO World Heritage Site.

Although, in peak season, the Mount is one of the most crowded visitor attractions in the country, it is well worth making the effort to cross the causeway from the mainland. Don't venture onto the mudflats unless you are part of a guided walk, as tides can sweep in quickly. If you're visiting during the peak summer months, arrive at around 8am or after 5pm to miss the crowds. Never mind your aching calf muscles—continue climbing the steps of the Abbey once you have reached the summit of the Mount itself. Views of the protected Baie de Mont St-Michel from the very top of the Abbey are stunning.

HIGHLIGHTS

THE ABBEY

☎ 02 33 89 80 00 ◔ Daily 9–7, May–end Aug; 9.30–6, Sep–end Apr
▣ €7 ◻ Audioguides €4 for 1 person or €5.50 for 2
www.monum.fr

You can join a guided tour around the Abbey and discover the huge treadmill in which prisoners once trudged to work a system of pulleys to haul building materials up the side of the Mount. The Abbey is often referred to as *La Mervielle* (the wonder), but this epithet actually applies to a Gothic extension commissioned by King Philippe Auguste of France in the 13th century to celebrate his conquest of Normandy. The name reflected the amazing feat of the architects and builders who created it in just 20 years. The *Merveille*, with its three floors of dining rooms for pilgrims, nobles and monks, is topped by a tranquil cloister garden, with a window looking out to sea.

MAISONS DE LA BAIE

☎ Courtils: 02 33 89 66 00; Le-Vivier-sur-Mer: 02 99 48 84 38; St-Léonard: 02 33 89 06 06 🕐 Daily 2–6, Apr, May; 10–6, Jun, Sep; 10–7, Jul, Aug; 2–6 school hols; www.maison-baie.com

Back on the mainland, you can enjoy wonderful views of the Mount from the Maison de la Baie vantage points at Le-Vivier-sur-Mer, Courtils and St-Léonard. These individually themed mini-museums offer a perspective on the daily life of the Abbey in past times, along with excellent displays of local wildlife. They also organize escorted treks across the sands to the Mount, on foot and horseback.

BACKGROUND

The Mount has drawn pilgrims since 708, when St. Aubert, Bishop of Avranches, built a modest chapel on the 79m (260ft) granite Mont Tombe, after seeing a vision of the Archangel Michael. Benedictine monks settled here and a village soon formed around them. A Romanesque church was constructed on the site in the 11th century, and work continued on other buildings over the following years. The Mount was fortified against the English during the Hundred Years War (mid-14th to mid-15th centuries) and managed to resist attack. Work continued on the Abbey from the 15th to the 17th centuries, and the site spent time as a prison after the Revolution. It opened to visitors as a national monument in 1874 and in 1897 Emmanuel Frémlet's gilded statue of St. Michael was placed on top of a new steeple, 157m (515ft) high. A monastic community returned to the site in 1969, and monks and nuns continue to provide a spiritual anchor within what might otherwise be merely a hub of tourism and history. Although 3.5 million visitors come to Mont St-Michel each year, the resident population is just 35.

A project (due to finish in 2007) is under way to surround the Mount with the sea at high tide to combat generations of silting, 5m (16ft) deep. The causeway will be replaced by a footbridge.

BASICS

✚ 439 E5 🚹 BP4, Mont St-Michel 50170, 02 33 60 14 30; Mon–Sat 9–7, Sun 9–1, 2–7, Jul, Aug; Mon–Sat 9–12.30, 2–6.30, Sun 9–12, 2–6, May, Jun, Sep; Mon–Sat 9–12, 2–6, Sun 10–12, 2–5, Apr, Oct; Mon–Sat 9–12, 2–5.30, Sun 10–12, 2–5, Nov–Mar www.ot-montsaintmichel.com

Le Mont

🍴 At *La Mère Poulard*, world-famous omelettes, beaten in age-old copper bowls, have fortified pilgrims and visitors alike for years

🚌 From Rennes, St-Malo

🚆 You could take the TGV to Rennes, which connects with a morning bus-link to the Mount. There is also a station at Pontorson, 9km (6 miles) from the Mount, from where you can take a bus

🅿 The visitors' car park alongside the present causeway is to be replaced with parking for 4,200 cars 2km (1 mile) south of the coast road, on the mainland. Parking will cost €6, but a free eco-friendly shuttle-bus service (eventually to be replaced by a dedicated railway line) will take visitors from their vehicles to the Mount.

🎫 €0.35

The abbey of Mont St-Michel (top) towers over the village

The lighthouse off the rugged coast at Pointe du Raz

THE SIGHTS

PERROS-GUIREC

438 C5 21 place de l'Hôtel de Ville, tel 02 96 23 21 15; Mon–Sat 9–7.30, Sun, public hols 10–12.30, 4–7, Jul, Aug; Mon–Sat 9–12.30, 2–6, Sep–end Jun 15 to Trégastel and Lannion To the Sept-Îles (seasonal only), from the Gare Maritime at Plage de Trestraou or Port de Ploumanac'h www.perros-guirec.com

This is a good place for a family beach holiday or as a base for exploring. The resort encapsulates what is most attractive about Brittany's Pink Granite Coast, with fine sandy bays interspersed with rose granite rocky outcrops. The houses are made from the local rose granite, giving the town a beautiful pink hue, especially at sunset. Just offshore are the Sept-Îles, among France's best bird reserves.

Don't miss The town beaches—Plage de Trestraou and Plage de Trestrignel—and the scenic coastal paths are superb.

POINTE DU RAZ

438 A6 Pointe du Raz, tel 02 98 70 67 18; daily 10.30–6, Apr–end Jun, Sep; daily 9.30–6.30, Jul, Aug; Sun 2.30–5.30, Oct–end Mar (daily 10.30–6 in school hols) 7, 8 to Quimper www.pointeduraz.com

Pointe du Raz is the most dramatic of Brittany's wild peninsulas. Here the land meets the untamed Atlantic Ocean in a crescendo of breaking waves, charging wind and screeching gulls. The point sits on the western tip of the Cap Sizun, and the views down to the sea and across to the Île-de-Sein are breathtaking. You can't drive to the tip, but you can park at a welcome area with exhibition space, cafés and shops. In July and August a shuttle-bus takes you out to the tip, otherwise it is a walk of 1.5km (1 mile) along a paved footpath to the lighthouse.

PARC NATUREL RÉGIONAL NORMANDIE-MAINE

Here you'll find delightful villages, good food and drink, and a wilderness to explore.

This huge area is one of 32 regional natural parks that preserve 10 per cent of France's countryside from the ravages of modern life. Straddling two regions, Normandy and the Western Loire, the 134,000ha (331,130-acre) protected zone is home to 160,000 people as well as numerous winged and four-legged inhabitants. The forests of Ecouves, Andaines, Perseigne and Sillé, covering 60,000ha (148,000 acres), shelter deer and boar.

Tributaries of the Orne river flow north towards the English Channel, while the waters of the Sarthe, Mayenne, Egrenne and Varenne head west to the Atlantic. In some places these seem little more than brooks; elsewhere, such as at Villiers, the natural gorges are dramatic. For height, head to the Mancelles Alps and the highest point in western France,

RATINGS			
Activities	●	●	● ○
Good for kids		●	● ●
Photo stops		●	● ●

TIPS

● Head to Domfront (see page 105) for three of Normandy's 10 listed gourmet products—*Calvados Domfrontais*, *Pommeau* and *Poiré*.
● Sées, by the source of the Orne, has a stunning cathedral with superb stained glass and a museum of religious art.
● The Maison de la Pomme et de la Poire museum and orchard, in Barenton, promotes the history of local fruits.

BASICS

440 F5 Maison du Parc, Le Capitre, 61320, tel 02 33 81 75 75; Mon–Fri, 9–12, 2–6 www.paysdalencontourisme.com (in French and English; click on 'tourism', then 'nature' for details about the park)

Mont des Avaloirs. On lower ground the Passais country is lush farmland covered with apple and pear orchards, where the still of the night is punctuated by the sounds of owls hunting. Castles stand guard over this timeless region, some in ruins.

Forest rangers take escorted groups on nature rambles, mushroom hunts and deerstalking expeditions. Anglers fish for trout in the rivers and streams, while other visitors enjoy canoeing, hiking and climbing. The spa town of Bagnoles-de-l'Orne is a good base, as are Alençon (see page 96), Sées, Carrouges, La Ferté-Macé or Domfront (see page 105). Some hotels offer themed breaks.

China plates on a shopfront in Quimper

Yachts and canal boats moored in Redon, where the Vilaine river and Nantes-Brest Canal converge

QUIBERON

🚏 438 C7 🛈 14 rue de Verdun, 56174, tel 02 97 50 07 84; Mon–Sat 9–1, 2–7, Sun 10–1, 2–5, Jun–end Aug; Mon–Sat 9–12.30, 2–6, rest of year 🚌 1 to Vannes 🚂 In Jul and Aug the Quiberon line links with Auray, from where there are regular trains to Vannes or Lorient ◼ The tourist office organizes walking tours of Quiberon in Jul and Aug (Wed 10.30) 🅿 There is a park-and-ride on the main road, just before you reach town (Jul, Aug only) ❓ Bathing is forbidden on the Côte Sauvage (the western coast of the peninsula) because of dangerous currents and sharp rocks www.quiberon.com

Quiberon is one of Brittany's most popular holiday resorts, at the tip of a long, slim peninsula, surrounded by sublime sandy beaches. It makes the perfect base for exploring Belle-Île (see page 98), offshore, and inland to Carnac and Auray. But on a long summer day it is the sands that have most pulling power—the one access road can be clogged with traffic as day-trippers from surrounding towns join longer-stay visitors in the rush for the beach.

Quiberon has long made a living from the sea, traditionally sardine fishing and processing. Today, the commercial port and ferry services are in the main town, while the pleasure port, Port Haliguen, is to the northeast. **Don't miss** The state-of-the-art-thalassotherapy venue has a covered swimming pool and a range of relaxation treatments.

QUIMPER

🚏 438 B6 🛈 Place de la Résistance, 29000, tel 02 98 53 04 05; Mon–Sat 9–7, Sun 10–1, 3–6, Jul, Aug; Mon–Sat 9.30–12.30, 1.30–6.30, Sun 10–1, Jun; Mon–Sat 9.30–12.30, 1.30–6.30, mid-Mar to end May; Mon–Sat 9.30–12.30, 1.30–6.30, Sep; Mon–Sat 9.30–12.30, 1.30–6, Oct to mid-Mar 🚌 1 to Brest via Plougastel-Daoulas, le Faou, Pleyben and Châteaulin; 2a and 2B to Pont l'Abbé and Île-Tudy; 4 to Pont l'Abbé, Lechiagat and le Guilvinec; 8 to Pointe du Raz; 9 to Douarnenez; 10 to Camaret-sur-Mer, Locronan, Pentrez-Plage, Argol, Crozon and le Fret; 15 to Beg Meil; 16 to Bénodet 🚂 Quimper ◼ The tourist office organizes guided tours of the cathedral and the old town 🎉 The Festival de Cornouaille (Jul) attracts Celts from across Europe www.quimper-tourisme.com

Quimper is the spiritual heart of lower Brittany, a hub of Breton culture with a wonderful old quarter. It was an influential city throughout Brittany's independence but lost its power after the union with France in 1532. The city suffered relatively little damage during World War II, despite its links with the French Resistance.

Today, the old quarter shelters pretty, half-timbered houses. Look out for the ornate Maison des Cariatides on rue Gueodet. The magnificent Cathédrale St-Corentin dates from the 13th to 19th centuries (daily 9–6). Stained glass in the nave depicts local Cornouaille nobility along with their patron saints—a veritable Who's Who of Breton feudal luminaries.

The highlight of the Musée Départemental Breton, in rue du Roi Gradlon, is the collection of Breton costumes (daily 9–6, Jun–end Sep; Tue–Sat 9–12, 2–5, Sun 2–5, Oct–end May).

Quimper has been connected with the production of ceramics (faïence) for three centuries. True Quimper ware, with its blue-and-yellow flower and bird pattern, is handmade, with a potter's or decorator's signature. You can see more than 500 examples in the Musée de la Faïence, 14 rue J. B. Bousquet (Mon–Sat 10–6, mid-Apr to mid-Oct).

Don't miss The Musée des Beaux-Arts, at 40 place St-Corentin, is one of the best art galleries in Brittany (daily 10–7, Jul–end Sep; Wed–Mon 10–12, 2–6, Apr–end Jun, Oct; Mon, Wed–Sat 10–12, 2–6, Sun 2–6, Nov–end Mar).

REDON

🚏 439 D6 🛈 Place de la République, 35600, tel 02 99 71 06 04; Mon–Sat 9–12.30, 2–6, Sep–end Jun; Mon–Sat 9–7, Sun, public hols 10–1, 4–6, Jul, Aug 🚌 10g to la Roche Bernard 🚂 Redon www.ville-Redon.fr

Rivers, roads, railways, regions and a canal all converge at Redon, which sits on the border of Brittany and the Pays de la Loire. The small town is popular with boating people, who can sail along the river Vilaine or the Nantes–Brest canal. The river Oust adds its own tortuous course to this watery complexity.

Redon is not particularly touristy, lacking the charm of other Breton towns, although its summer festivals are popular. It was first settled in 832, with the founding of what was to become an important Benedictine abbey. Later the town developed as a river port for Rennes to the north and grew prosperous on the trade this brought. As canal trade declined in importance, the town replaced it with light industry.

The Romanesque remains of the Abbaye St-Sauveur are a town landmark. They include a nave and tower dating from the 12th century.

Don't miss The Musée de la Batellerie (Waterways Museum), at quai Jean-Bart, concentrates on daily life on the canals at the height of their importance (daily 10–12, 3–6, mid-Jun to mid-Sep; Sat–Mon, Wed 2–6, mid-Sep to mid-Jun).

Rennes

**Brittany's cosmopolitan capital city is a modern metropolis with a lively medieval heart.
In previous centuries, the city played an important role in the region's political struggles.**

Taking a break in a café on rue St-Georges

The 18th-century town hall, with its impressive clock tower

RATINGS	
Cultural interest	●●●○
Historic interest	●●●○
Photo stops	●●●○
Shopping	●●●○

TIPS

● Place Railier du Baty, a pleasant square near the cathedral, is a good place to sit and enjoy a coffee.
● Beware of traffic, even in streets or squares that appear to be pedestrian-only.

A statue in the Parc du Thabor

SEEING RENNES

Rennes is often compared negatively with some of the more picturesque destinations in Brittany, but a day spent here can be rewarding. Inside the modern, industrial shell are some fascinating medieval streets in the old town, along with excellent museums and grand civic architecture. The tourist office is a good place to start a visit, as you can pick up a map marked with a walking route covering the main sights (French only), and a leaflet on the city's history (English). After exploring the old town, wander through the Parc du Thabor for a change of pace. These large gardens were once the grounds of a Benedictine abbey.

HIGHLIGHTS

MUSÉE DES BEAUX-ARTS

• 20 quai Émile Zola, 35000 ☎ 02 99 28 55 85 🕓 Wed–Mon 10–12, 2–6
🚇 République 🎫 Adult €4, under 18 free
This art gallery has paintings ranging from 14th-century Primitives to Impressionists and members of the Pont-Aven school. Artists represented include Leonardo da Vinci, Rubens, Paul Gauguin and Pablo Picasso. Look out for a powerful canvas by the 19th-century artist Luminais, depicting the legend of Ys (see page 105). The Musée de Bretagne currently stages exhibitions in the same building, although it is due to move to the city's Nouvel Espace Culturel in 2005. Exhibitions focus on Brittany's culture and history and range from archaeological finds to displays about the *corsaires* (pirates).

CATHÉDRALE ST-PIERRE

• Rue du Griffon 🕓 Daily 9.30–12, 3–6; closed Sun pm and Mon in Jul, Aug
Rennes's cavernous cathedral, with its vast dark marble pillars, dates from the 19th century. Don't miss the 16th-century Flemish retable in the fifth chapel on the right. Its 10 panels, full of human interest, depict scenes including the birth of Mary and the marriage of Mary and Joseph. The delightful rue de la Psalette, curving behind the cathedral, is a medley of beautiful half-timbered 15th-century houses. Psalette was the local word for the cathedral choir, and it is said that the street resounded with their singing.

Attractive timberwork on 17th-century town houses (left)

The Musée des Beaux-Arts and Musée de Brétagne will share the same building (below) until 2005

PLACE DES LICES

This square once hosted jousts, although since the 17th century its main focus has been as a market place. Today, there's an open-air Saturday vegetable market (ends 1pm), and a meat market in the impressive covered hall. Near here, on the edge of the old town, is Portes Mordelaise, a fine gateway with a restored drawbridge. It dates from 1440, when the city walls were enlarged, and was intended as a ceremonial entrance to the city.

PLACE DE LA MAIRIE

In the spacious place de la Mairie you can admire the magnificent Hôtel de Ville (town hall), designed by Jacques Gabriel in the 18th century. The huge clock tower, known as *Le Gros,* links two curving side wings. From here, look down towards the elegant Palais de Commerce in place de la République.

BACKGROUND

Rennes shared parliamentary power with Nantes and Vannes during the Middle Ages, becoming the undisputed Breton capital during the time of Anne de Bretagne (1477–1514). From then on it played a key role in Brittany's political struggles, including rebellions against the heavy taxation imposed during Louis XIV's reign, the Revolutionary Terror and the German occupation in World War II. The city was almost entirely demolished by fire in 1720—only the area between the market square (place des Lices) and the city's two waterways escaped. It was subsequently rebuilt in severe classical style.

The city's population has doubled since World War II to nearly 250,000. The figure is boosted by students at the two universities and the prestigious medical school. Commerce and industry flourish, and the headquarters of car manufacturers Citroën lie just outside. The city feels more French than other Breton towns.

BASICS

➕ 439 E6 ℹ️ 11 rue St-Yves, CS 26410, 35064, tel 02 99 67 11 11; Mon–Sat 9–7, Sun 11–6, Apr–end Sep; Mon–Sat 9–6, Sun 11–6, rest of year
🍽 There are plenty of bars around place Ste-Anne; most close Sat lunch
Ⓜ Métro system, with one line
🚌 Good bus links
🚆 Trains to St-Malo, Fougères, Dinan, Vitré, Nantes
www.tourisme-rennes.com

CITY GUIDE

CHAPELLE ST-YVES

The converted Chapelle St-Yves now houses the tourist office, where you'll find a permanent exhibition on the history of Rennes and its trading links. It is also worth visiting for its impressive beams and the restored carvings in the chapel.

PALAIS DU PARLEMENT DE BRETAGNE

The former seat of the Breton parliament is north of place de la Mairie. Ironically, having survived the fire of 1720, it almost totally burned down in a fire in 1994. Restoration has now finished and its intricate timber-framed roof and beautiful coffered ceilings look as impressive as before. Look up to see the gilded figures that top the building.

Rouen

●

Normandy's capital is a city of cobbled streets, tall timbered houses and Gothic churches, captured by the painter Monet in his Rouen Cathedral series. Joan of Arc was executed here, and the heart of Richard Coeur de Lion is held in the cathedral's crypt.

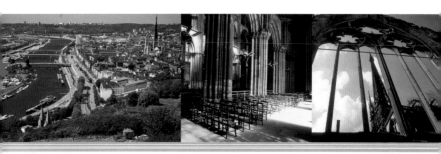

A view across Rouen from Vista Point

Inside Rouen's Notre-Dame cathedral

Notre-Dame seen through the remains of the Bishop's Palace

RATINGS	
Cultural interest	● ● ●
Historic interest	● ● ● ●
Shopping (ceramics)	● ● ● ●
Walkability	● ● ●

TIPS

● If you are visiting at a weekend, take advantage of the *Bon Weekend en Ville* promotion, offering two nights' hotel accommodation for the price of one. There are similar deals at museums.

● Visit Rouen during the last week in May to take part in the Joan of Arc festival, which usually coincides with the city's main cultural festival. On the Sunday closest to 30 May local children throw flowers into the Seine from the Boïeldieu Bridge, the spot where Joan's ashes were scattered on the water.

● A good time to experience the Abbey of St-Ouen is during one of the many concerts held there. The organ is one of the most famous in France.

SEEING ROUEN

Rouen rises on the horizon as a blur of steeples above the grandly Gothic Notre-Dame Cathedral and nearby Abbey of St-Ouen. This makes for a memorable first view, especially if you are lucky enough to arrive at dawn or dusk. Don't be misled by the sprawling perimeter—the historic core is quite compact. Although there are bus and Métro systems, the city is best explored on foot, as all the major sights are walkable from the main station. Any trip should begin opposite the cathedral with a visit to the tourist office, housed in Rouen's oldest Renaissance building, the former tax collector's office, dating from 1509.

HIGHLIGHTS

CATHÉDRALE DE NOTRE-DAME

✚ 118 B3 • Place de la Cathédrale ☎ 02 35 89 73 78 🕐 Mon 2–7, Tue–Sat 8–7, Sun 8–6

Rouen cathedral is one of the great churches of France, known across the world thanks to Impressionist painter Claude Monet's *Cathédrales de Rouen* series (1892–1893). Monet worked on the paintings from the second floor of what is now the tourist office. The cathedral's Gothic architecture spans 400 years, from the mid-12th to early 16th centuries. The dark, shadowy interior is offset by flashes of bright blue light through the stained-glass windows, dating from the 13th century. The choir contains tombs of many Dukes of Normandy, while the crypt holds the heart of Richard the Lionheart of England. The 151m (495ft) spire, the tallest in France, was built in the 19th century.

AÎTRE ST-MACLOU

✚ 118 C2 • rue Martainville 🕐 Courtyard: daily 8–8 🎫 Free

A short walk from the Gothic Église St-Maclou, in place Barthélemy (*Mon–Sat 10–12, 2–5.30, Sun 3–5.30*), is its unusual annexe, the Aître St-Maclou. This pretty courtyard of timbered buildings is now home to the School of Fine Arts. A more macabre history is hinted at by the skulls that adorn the woodwork. This was a plague cemetery, built to house the remains of the victims of the Great Plague of 1348, which claimed the lives of 75 per cent of the population.

GROS HORLOGE

118 B3 • rue du Gros-Horloge

No visit to Rouen is complete without a stroll under the 14th-century Gros Horloge, a huge, one-handed, ornamental clock mounted on a sumptuously carved Renaissance arch straddling the road of the same name. Once part of a nearby belfry, the remarkable timepiece was moved to its present position in the 16th century, after locals complained that it was impossible to see the clockface in the narrow streets.

JOAN OF ARC

This is the city of Joan of Arc, and the tales surrounding France's greatest folk heroine would alone be lure enough for visitors. On the place du Vieux Marché, a short stroll from the Gros Horloge, a large cross marks the spot where Joan of Arc was executed. The nearby Église Jeanne-d'Arc (1981) is a stunning combination of modern slate and copper work on the outside, with light from Renaissance stained-glass windows within. The windows were salvaged from the earlier church of St-Vincent, destroyed during World War II. The wonderful contemporary sculpture was inspired by the saint's martyr's pyre.

The remains of the two towers in which Joan was imprisoned from Christmas 1430 until her execution in 1431 can be seen on rue du Donjon. These vestiges of Philippe-Auguste's castle, built in 1204 and scene of Joan of Arc's trial, incorporate the Tour Jeanne d'Arc and traces of the Tour de la Pucelle. You can learn more about the medieval heroine at the Musée Jeanne d'Arc, on place du Vieux Marché (*daily 9.30–1, 1.30–7, mid-Apr to mid-Sep; 10–12, 2–6.30, mid-Sep to mid-Apr*).

440 H4 25 place de la Cathédrale, BP 666, 76008

02 32 08 32 40

Mon–Sat 9–7, Sun and public hols 9.30–12.30, 2–6, May–end Sep; Mon–Sat 9–6, Sun and public hols 10–1, Oct–end Apr

Rouen: good connections to Paris
www.rouen.fr (in French only. Information about the city and its attractions, as well as photos)

The tower of St-Ouen, seen from rue Damiette (top)

LITERARY CONNECTIONS

There is the chance to pay homage to Rouen's literary heritage at museums dedicated to *Madame Bovary* author Gustave Flaubert (1821–1880) and playwright Pierre Corneille (1606–1684). The Musée Flaubert et d'Histoire de la Médecine is in the house where Flaubert was born, at 51 rue de Lecat (*Wed–Sat 10–12, 2–6, Tue 10–6*). Flaubert's father was a surgeon and the museum contains not only displays about the novelist's life but also medical implements from the 19th century. The Musée Pierre Corneille is in the playwright's birthplace, at 4 rue de la Pie (*Thu–Mon 10–12, 2–6, Wed 2–6*).

MUSÉE DES BEAUX-ARTS

✚ 118 B2 • Esplanade Marcel-Duchamp ☎ 02 35 71 28 40 🕓 Wed–Sun 10–6
💶 Adult €3, child (6–18) €2, under 6 free
This gallery has an impressive collection of paintings, drawings, sculptures and objets d'art from the 16th century to the present day. Highlights include Caravaggio's *Flagellation of Christ* and works by Pierre-Auguste Renoir and Monet.

MUSÉE DE LA CÉRAMIQUE

✚ 118 B2 • 1 rue Faucon ☎ 02 35 07 31 74
🕓 Wed–Mon 10–1, 2–6 💶 Adult €2.30, child free
Learn more about the distinctive blue-patterned Rouenware (*faïence*), which rose to popularity in the 17th and 18th centuries. If you want to buy some, you'll also find it in the antiques quarter of the old town.

Rouen's tall, timbered houses, with pretty flower displays

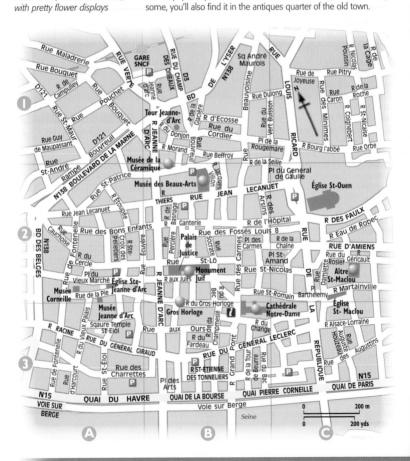

BACKGROUND

The Romans established a settlement on the site of today's Rouen in the 1st century AD, calling it Rotomagus. In the Middle Ages, Rouen became the seat of the Dukes of Normandy, who won the English throne in 1066. Later, it was at the heart of the Hundred Years War between the French and the English. One of the most famous episodes of the war took place in May 1431, when Joan of Arc, after reviving French fortunes in the siege of Orléans, was burnt at the stake at the insti- gation of the English.

Merchant trade has been key to Rouen's development over the centuries, funding many of the timbered and gabled tradesmen's houses in the city. Later buildings, including 19th-century stores, art deco shop fronts and post-World War II blocks, run down to the port. The city was heavily bombed during World War II and many historic buildings needed meticulous renovation.

Today, Rouen has the fourth largest port in France, despite being so far inland. The city sits on the Seine, 86km (53 miles) from the estuary at Le Havre. The contrast between the working docks along the river and the Gothic spires and quaint old streets of the city heart is striking.

Strolling along the riverfront

L'ARMADA
Every four years (make a date for 2007) the world's greatest sailing ships gather along the quays for L'Armada, eight days of celebrations in June or July.

JEWISH MONUMENT
✚ 118 B2 • Rue aux Juifs ❓ You can't enter the courtyard, but you can see the monument from outside

The Jewish Monument, in the courtyard of the 16th-century Palais de Justice, is in fact the remains of the oldest surviving Jewish building in France. Believed to date from the 12th century, the site is the last remaining vestige of the city's ghetto, destroyed after the expulsion of the Jews in 1306. Although it was originally thought to have been a synagogue, experts now believe it was a religious school.

A statue on rue d'Amiens

Carved face decorating an old house in Rochefort-en-Terre

The long golden curve of beaches at the seaside resort of St-Cast-le-Guildo, viewed from Pointe de St-Cast

ROCHEFORT-EN-TERRE

439 D6 Place des Halles, 56220, tel 02 97 43 33 57; Mon–Fri 10–12.30, 2–6, Sat, Sun, public hols 2.30–6.30, mid-Jun to mid-Sep; Mon–Fri 10–12.30, 2–5.30, mid-Sep to mid-Jun 9 to Vannes Parking in the heart of the village is for residents only, but there are several parking areas for visitors around the edge of the village The village is floodlit in the evenings (nightly, Apr–end Sep; Sat only, Oct–end Mar)
www.golfedumorbihan.com
www.rochefort-en-terre.com

Rochefort-en-Terre wins award after award in 'most beautiful village' competitions and it is easy to see why. The setting is one of the most spectacular in Brittany, on a high spur overlooking the Arz valley and surrounded by dense woodland.

A maze of cobbled lanes tumbles down from the castle and you'll find interesting architectural details in every nook and cranny. The main street (in fact several streets linked by small squares) is lined with sturdy granite houses and halls, now home to souvenir shops, bookstores, restaurants and *crêperies*.

The castle, a true 'rock fort'—the origin of the town's name—was originally built in the Middle Ages but was destroyed in the Revolution and rebuilt by two American brothers in the early 20th century (*daily 10–6.30, Jul, Aug; daily 2–6.30, Jun, Sep; Sat, Sun, public hols 2–6.30, Apr, May*).

The church of Notre-Dame-de-la-Tronchaye, off rue du Pelican, has a façade of unusual Gothic windows under ornate gables. Inside you'll find one of the most important religious relics in Brittany—a revered statue of Our Lady of Tronchaye, discovered in a tree in the 12th century.

SABLES-D'OR-LES-PINS

439 D5 A wooden kiosk on the main street, tel 02 96 41 51 97 Mon–Sat 9–7, Sun 10–12, 4–6, Jul, Aug Swimming in the sea can be dangerous because of strong currents

The long stretches of golden sand and verdant pines that give this resort its name are the main draw here. You can rent a beach buggy to carry you around or take in a round of golf at the links course, but most people come simply to enjoy the beach.

Sables-d'Or-les-Pins is essentially an artificial resort. Work began in the early 1920s but the project was abandoned after the financial crash of 1929, before it had been completed. As you arrive in town, a wide but neglected central boulevard hints at the grand design originally envisaged. This is flanked by ornately designed parades of shops and cafés, topped by apartments.

Just south of Sables-d'Or-les-Pins, the village of Plurien adds some historical gravitas, with a Knights Templar church and the remains of a Gallo-Roman villa.

ST-CAST-LE-GUILDO

439 D5 Place Charles de Gaulle, BP 9, 22380 02 96 41 81 52 Mon–Sat 9–7.30, Sun, public hols 10–12.30, 3–6.30, Jul, Aug; Mon–Sat 9–12.30, 2–6.30, Sep, Jan–end Jun; 9–12, 2–5 Oct–end Dec 1 to Lamballe; 14 to St-Malo; 13 to Dinan At the port Fête de l'Huître (oyster festival) is at the end of Jun
www.ot-st-cast-le-guildo.fr

This is one of the liveliest bucket-and-spade resorts on Brittany's Emerald Coast, popular for its wide sandy beach. It is ideally situated for excursions to Dinard, Dinan and St-Malo or for walks along the wild footpaths of Cap Fréhel.

The resort has several separate districts and its geography takes some fathoming. Le-Guildo is an old seaport on the Arguenon river. Its associated market town is called Notre-Dame. Here you'll find humble stone cottages set near the ocean, and the ruined chateau of Gilles de Bretagne overlooking the bay. St-Cast consists of L'Isle (the port), Les Mielles (the resort area, with a beautiful wide sandy beach) and Le Bourg (the administrative hub). L'Isle is a popular stop for yachts during the summer, although the islets of Rocher de la Feuillade, Rocher du Bec Rond and Rocher de Canavez make navigation a challenge.

The Grand Plage (Large Beach) at Les Mielles has a fairground in summer, and a small square at the northern end has shops, bars and restaurants. The southern tip of the beach is marked by the small chapel of Notre-Dame-de-la-Garde, on a headland of the same name.

Between St-Cast and Le-Guildo is the tiny settlement of Pen-Guen, with its own fine beach. It is renowned in French golfing circles for its links course, one of the oldest in the country.

This column, in St-Cast-Le-Guildo, was built to celebrate the failure of a British naval attack in 1758

Pleasure boats at St-Malo (above)

ST-MALO

A lively port, with a proud maritime past and a magnificent walled citadel.

The Breton port of St-Malo has had a rumbustious nautical past, peopled by explorers, merchants, fishermen (the Newfoundland fishing fleets sailed from here in the 16th century) and ruthless *corsaires* (pirates). Today it is quieter. Fishing and freight are still important, but the harbours also shelter pleasure craft.

CITADEL

The town's main attraction is its citadel, known as Intra Muros ('within the walls'), faithfully restored after destruction by bombs in 1944. Towering walls frame inviting glimpses of the elegant shopping streets and outdoor cafés within. Many of the streets are quite steep and paved with large cobbles. You can walk around the ramparts, originally constructed in the 14th century, with views of the sea on one side and the old town on the other. Pass through one of the gaps to cross the causeway to the island of Grand Bé to see the tomb of the writer Chateaubriand (1768–1848) and for great views of the islands, the mainland, the mountains and Dinard. Children are likely to enjoy this walk as there are rocks to clamber on and pools to explore. Don't get stranded by the tide: If you do, there's a six-hour wait before you can walk back! Sights in the Intra Muros district include the Cathédrale St-Vincent (*9.45–12, 2–6*), with its modern stained-glass window and diamond-shaped mosaic commemorating Jacques Cartier's interior exploration of Canada in 1535. The aquarium concealed in the ramparts has an extraordinary range of tropical fish (*daily 9.30–8, early Jul and late Aug; 10–7, Apr–end Jun, mid-Jul to mid-Aug; 10–6, Feb, Mar, Oct–end Dec. Closed Jan*).

CASTLE MUSEUM

The Musée d'Histoire Château de St-Malo (*daily 10–12.30, 2–6, Apr–end Sep; 10–12, 2–6, Oct–end Mar*), within St-Malo's old castle, has some fascinating exhibits. On the second floor, look out for the carved figurehead destined for the prow of a *corsaire* vessel, depicting a 17th-century sailor. One room describes the life of St-Malo fishermen in Newfoundland. Another floor deals with great men of St-Malo, including the naval commander Robert Surcouf (1773–1827) and the ubiquitous Chateaubriand (see page 101).

RATINGS	
Good for kids	●●●
Historic interest	●●●●
Photo stops	●●●

TIP

● Hotels and cafés within the Intra Muros are often more expensive than those outside.

BASICS

439 D5• Esplanade St-Vincent, 35400, tel 02 99 56 64 48; Mon–Sat 9–12.30, 1.30–6, Oct–end Mar

St-Malo

Access to the ramparts is by steps only

www.saint-malo-tourisme.com (in French and English; with photos and practical information)

The fine 1610 Calvary in St-Thégonnec

A window box on an old house in Vannes

The central square in the old quarter of Vitré

THE SIGHTS

ST-THÉGONNEC

🕂 438 B5 🕙 Daily 9–6 (no visits during Sunday mass at 10.30) 🚃 St-Thégonnec

St-Thégonnec is the epitome of the Breton 'parish close', a highlight of this curiously specialized form of Breton art.

In 16th- and 17th-century Brittany, as in nowhere else in France, the buildings around the village graveyard developed into an elaborate architectural complex called the *enclos paroissial*. At first these were simple affairs, but as lower Brittany grew richer, they developed into highly ornate structures and their calvaries (the elaborate crucifix that stood outside the church) became the storybooks of the time.

St-Thégonnec was one of the richest parishes in Brittany during the 17th century. Its multi-branched calvary, constructed in 1610, shows Christ's tormentors carrying out their sadistic work with gusto (one was alleged to be the Protestant French king Henry IV), while angels mop up the Redeemer's blood. The little-known St. Thégonnec himself puts in an appearance on a low niche. The church interior is equally sumptuous, with statues adorning every nook, and altar-pieces alive with detail.

Don't miss The tour de force is the wooden pulpit, encrusted with saints, angels, evangelists, Cardinal Virtues and God himself, giving Moses the tablets of stone inscribed with the Ten Commandments.

Vannes and his wife, above the House of Vannes

VANNES

🕂 439 C/D6 🛈 1 rue Thiers, 56009, tel 02 97 47 24 34; daily 9–7, Jul, Aug; 9.30–12.30, 2–6, Sep–end Jun 🍴 Cafés in place Gambetta 🚃 Links with Quimper, Carnac, Auray and surrounding towns in the Golfe du Morbihan 🚃 Vannes, links with Auray, Quimper, Brest, Rennes, Paris 🚗 The Animation du Patrimoine department at the Hôtel du Roscanvec runs several guided walks throughout the summer 🅿 By the pleasure port
www.mairie-vannes.fr

Vannes, on the western coast of the Golfe du Morbihan, has a wonderful old town full of 16th- and 17th-century architecture. Its narrow streets are perfect for strolling, and it has a livelier, more cosmopolitan feel than many Breton towns.

Throughout the Middle Ages Vannes shared the accolade of being the Breton capital with Nantes and Rennes. It is where Brittany was formally signed over to the French crown in 1532.

Its port played an important trading role in times past, but today it caters only to pleasure traffic. You can take excursions from it around the Golfe du Morbihan.

The Cathédrale St-Pierre is a mixture of architectural styles from the 13th to the 19th centuries. The Rotunda Chapel contains the remains of the city's patron, St. Vincent-Ferrier. Almost opposite the cathedral, La Cohue dating from the 16th century, was once a market building and hall of justice. It now houses the Musée des Beaux-Arts (*daily 10–8, Jul–end Sep; 1.30–6, Oct–end Jun*).

The Parc du Golfe, on the waterfront, has exhibition areas, a butterfly garden, aquarium, funfair and parkland for picnics.
Don't miss A famous carved corbel peers out from the corner of rue du Rogues. The ruddy-

faced figures are known as *Vannes et sa femme* (Vannes and his wife).

VITRÉ

🕂 439 E6 🛈 Place Charles-de-Gaulle, 35500, tel 02 99 75 04 46; Tue–Fri 9.30–12.30, 2.30–6; Sat 10–12.30, 3–5, Mon 2.30–6 🚃 To Fougères and Rennes 🚃 Vitré 🚗 The tourist office organizes guided walking tours of the town in French only, but has audioguides in English 🅿 Up to 4 hours' free parking in place du Château
www.ot-vitre.fr

Half-timbered, slate-hung houses lurch in all directions on Vitré's hilly, cobbled streets, watched over by a turreted castle. The town is best seen from a view-point known as the Tertres Noirs, by the bank of the river Vilaine: a silhouette of bristling turrets, drum towers and ramparts.

The chateau played a vital role in the Middle Ages when Vitré sat on the border between Brittany and France and was a constant target. (*daily 10–6, Jul–end Sep; 10–12, 2–5.30, Apr–end Jun; Wed–Fri 10–12, 2–5.30, Sat–Mon 2–5.30, Oct–end Mar*).

The church of Notre-Dame sits within the town ramparts. Dating from the 15th and 16th centuries, its Flamboyant Gothic south façade contrasts with the plainer, late 16th-century west façade. Between the chateau and the church is the Poterne St-Pierre, leading to the remains of the city ramparts, a pleasant stroll with far-reaching views.
Don't miss The 17th-century author Madame de Sévigné lived at 9 rue Sévigné. The Gothic manor Les Rochers-Sévigné, 7km (4 miles) southeast of town, was said to be her best-loved Breton residence (*daily 10–6, Jul–end Sep; Wed–Fri 10–12, 2–6.30, Sat–Mon 2–6.30 rest of year*).

NORTH AND NORTHEAST FRANCE

Stretching from the English Channel to the German border, this region takes in sandy beaches, the Somme valley, champagne country, Alsace, the Vosges mountains and the great cities of Lille, Reims, Metz and Strasbourg.

MAJOR SIGHTS

A brass band plays in place des Héros, Arras

THE SIGHTS

LES ARDENNES

✛ 444 L3 🚹 Comité Départemental du Tourisme, place Ducale, 08107, Charleville-Mézières, tel 03 24 56 06 08; Mon–Sat 9–7, Sun 10–7, Jul, Aug; Mon–Sat 9–12.30, 1.30–7, Sun 2–7, rest of year
www.ardennes.com

The densely wooded uplands of the Ardennes, most of them on Belgian territory, form a high plateau penetrated by the deep valley of the meandering river Meuse. They are a paradise for walkers and for hunters hoping to spot deer or boar. Other activities include horse-riding, bicycling and canoeing. A good way of exploring is by boat—you can take a *bateau-mouche* from Charleville-Mézières (see page 127) or Monthermé. There are fortresses at Rocroi, Sedan and Charleville-Mézières.

ARRAS

✛ 444 J2 🚹 Hôtel de Ville, place des Héros, 62000, tel 03 21 51 26 95; Mon–Sat 9–6.30, Sun 10–1, 2.30–6.30, May–end Sep; Mon–Sat 9–noon, 2–6, Sun 10–12.30, 3–6.30, rest of year
🚉 Arras
www.ot-arras.fr

Arras has a Flemish feel, thanks to houses embellished with wonderfully curly gables. The town was renowned for its tapestries in the late Middle Ages and spent its resulting wealth on its 16th-century town hall (rebuilt after World War I) and on adorning its two main squares with dignified town houses. The Grand' Place and the smaller Petite Place (or place des Héros) were created more than 800 years ago as market places. Underneath are the extensive cellars that sheltered local people during the bombardments of World War I. The British War Cemetery is on the western edge of town.

AMIENS

The ancient capital of Picardie is dominated by France's largest cathedral.

This lively city, along the banks of the river Somme, suffered much damage in both world wars but has been extensively rebuilt. At its heart is the magnificent 13th-century Cathédrale Notre-Dame, now a World Heritage Site. The Gothic cathedral, 145m (476ft) long, 70m (230ft) wide and 42m (139ft) high, has a glorious west façade with a famous statue of Christ known as *Le Beau Dieu*. The

RATINGS	
Historic interest	● ● ●
Photo stops	● ●
Walkability	● ● ●

BASICS
✛ 444 J3 🚹 6 bis rue Dusevel, BP 1018, 80010, tel 03 22 71 60 50; Mon–Sat 9.30–7, Sun 10–12, 2–5, Easter–end Oct; Mon–Sat 9.30–6, Sun 10–12, 2–5, rest of year 🚉 Amiens www.amiens.com/tourisme

serenely simple interior is enhanced by the richness of the 16th-century choir stalls. Southeast of the cathedral, in a 19th-century mansion in rue de la République, is the Musée de Picardie, displaying archaeological finds and 19th-century sculpture *(Tue–Sun 10–12.30, 2–6)*. The Musée de l'Hôtel de Berny, in rue Victor Hugo, focuses on art and local history, including furniture from the Louis XV and Louis XVI eras *(Thu–Sun 2–6, May–end Sep; Sun 10–12.30, 2–6, rest of year)*.

You can still see shows at the 19th-century Cirque Municipal, on place Longueville, a curious drum-shaped building dedicated to the science-fiction writer Jules Verne. Just east of here, the Maison de Jules Verne, in rue Charles-Dubois, *(Tue–Fri, Sun 10–12, 2–6, Sat 2–6, Apr–end Sep; Tue–Sun 2–6, rest of year; closed Jan)* was the writer's home for 18 years. Near the rail station look out for La Tour Perret, an unusual skyscraper, 104m (341ft) high, built between 1948 and 1954.

Amiens's watery *hortillonnages*, in the flood plain of the Somme, form a strange area of market gardens threaded by little channels. You can reach parts on foot on the Chemin de Halage (towpath) and others by boat *(departing from 54 boulevard de Beauvillé daily from 2–5, Apr–end Oct)*.

Don't miss The picturesque Quartier St-Leu, ('Little Venice of the North'), was once the weavers' and dyers' district. Here there are canals and narrow islands with painted leaning houses.

A poignant reminder of the cost of war

BATTLEFIELDS OF PICARDIE

The *Champs de Batailles* (battlefields) of the Somme were at the front line during World War I and now contain poignant war cemeteries and memorials.

Many of the most dramatic struggles in French history have taken place in the Picardie region, whose gently rolling countryside offers few natural barriers to invasion from the northeast. The savage Battle of the Somme, in World War I, led to more than one million casualties. After the war, memorials arose all over the now silent battlefields to commemorate the unprecedented slaughter.

REMEMBRANCE TOUR
A good way to visit the key sites is to follow the 60km (37-mile) *Circuit de Souvenir* that starts at the rebuilt town of Albert. This tour takes you past timelessly serene war cemeteries, former battlefields and museums. Pick up a leaflet at a local tourist office or follow the roadside poppy symbols.

TRENCH LIFE
Before you set off, visit the underground Musée des Abris Somme 1916, in rue Anicet Godin, which re-creates the conditions facing the soldiers in the trenches *(daily 9.30–6, Jun–end Sep; 9.30–noon, 2–6, Feb–end May, Oct to mid-Dec)*. A stretch of trenches has been preserved at Beaumont-Hamel, at the Mémorial Terre-Neuvien, watched over by a statue of a caribou, insignia of the Royal Newfoundland Regiment *(permanently open; visitor facility daily 10–6 May–end Oct; 9–5 mid-Jan to end Apr, Nov to mid-Dec)*.

A rare semicircular concrete German shelter survives in a field outside Martinpuich.

MEMORIALS
At Thiepval, the imposing Mémorial Franco-Britannique (Franco-British Memorial) remembers the 73,367 British and French men who died between July 1915 and March 1918 but have no known grave. The triumphal arch, 45m (150ft) high and designed by Sir Edwin Lutyens, can be seen for miles. Close by, the Tour d'Ulster (Ulster Tower) commemorates the soldiers from the 36th Ulster Division who lost their lives during the war. To the north of the *Circuit de Souvenir*, near Arras, the Canadian Vimy Parc Memorial dominates the hilltop at Vimy Ridge.

● Tourist offices provide useful leaflets, including *The Visitor's Guide to the Battlefields of The Somme*, *Le Circuit du Souvenir* and *The Somme Remembrance Tour of the Great War*.
● Remembrance ceremonies are held on 1 July, the date the Battle of the Somme began in 1916.
● Guided tours are available by reservation. A list of guides is available from the Somme Tourist Board, local tourist offices and at the main places of interest.

Albert
✚ 444 J3 🛈 9 rue Léon Gambetta, BP 82, 80300, tel 03 22 75 16 42; Mon–Fri 9–12.30, 1.30–6.30, Sat 9–noon, 2–6.30, Sun 10–12.30, Apr–end Sep; Mon–Fri 10–12.30, 1.30–5, Sat 9–noon, 3–5, rest of year
🚉 Albert
www.ville-albert.fr

Comité du Tourisme de La Somme
🛈 21 rue Ernest-Cauvin, 80000 Amiens, tel 03 22 71 22 63
www.somme-tourisme.com

The medieval cathedral, in Beauvais

THE SIGHTS

BEAUVAIS

➕ 441 J4 ℹ️ 1 rue Beauregard, BP 537, 60005, tel 03 44 15 30 30; Mon 10–1, 2–6, Tue–Sat 9.30–6.30, Sun 10–5, May–end Sep; Sun 10–1.30, rest of year 🚉 Beauvais
www.mairie-beauvais.fr

The bulky medieval cathedral of Beauvais rises above the nearby roofs in the flat Picardie landscape. Work started in 1227 but soon after completion the choir area collapsed under the weight of its ambitious design. The 14th-century replacement remained roofless for two centuries. More disaster struck in 1573, when the new spire collapsed.

Much of Beauvais was rebuilt after World War II, but you can still see remains of the 3rd-century Gallo-Roman town walls.

CALAIS

➕ 444 H1 ℹ️ 12 boulevard Clemenceau, 62102, tel 03 21 96 62 40; Mon–Sat 9–7, Sun 10–1, 3–6, Jun–end Aug; Mon–Sat 10–1, 2–6.30, Sun 10–noon, 3–6, Sep–end May 🚉 Calais Ville for Paris; Calais Fréthun for Eurostar to London ⛴ To Dover, UK 🏬 Shops close Sun, Mon; hypermarkets Sun
www.ot-calais.fr/

Calais is worth exploring, despite an undistinguished reconstruction after World War II. The belfry of the Hôtel de Ville guides you to the town's heart, where Auguste Rodin's sculpture *The Burghers of Calais* stands. Some of Rodin's bronze studies are in the Musée des Beaux-Arts et de la Dentelle, in rue Richelieu *(Mon, Wed–Fri 10–noon, 2–5.30, Sat 10–noon, 2–6.30, Sun 2–6.30).*

The Plage-Blériot, on the edge of town, is named after Louis Blériot, who flew from Calais to Dover in 1909.

For the Cité Europe complex see page 240.

BOULOGNE-SUR-MER

A busy port and shopping hub, with a picturesque walled old town.

This attractive Channel-port town is a treat for shoppers looking for something different from the hypermarkets up the coast at Calais. Unlike Calais, the historic heart of Boulogne emerged unscathed from World War II, although the port and much of the lower town were devastated by bombs.

The cobbled narrow streets and historic buildings of the old town are enclosed by 13th-century ramparts. The tree-lined walls make a great summer stroll, with views over the Channel. The medieval Château-Musée is linked to the ramparts by a drawbridge and displays eclectic exhibits, from Egyptian mummies to a bronze by Auguste Rodin; look out for the seascapes by Eugène Delacroix *(Wed–Mon 10–5, summer; Wed–Mon 10–12.30, 2–5, rest of year).* At the foot of the hill, place Dalton hosts a bustling market on Wednesday and Saturday mornings.

The symbol of Boulogne, the slightly ungainly dome of the 19th-century Basilica of Notre-Dame, replaced an earlier cathedral destroyed during the Revolution.

Don't miss The Nausicaà aquarium, on the quayside, is an imaginative attempt to re-create hidden worlds under the sea *(daily 9.30–8, Jun–end Sep; 9.30–6.30, rest of year).*

RATINGS			
Good for kids	● ● ●		
Historic interest	● ● ●		
Shopping	● ● ● ●		
Walkability	● ● ●		

TIPS

● Save money by buying a combined ticket for Nausicaà and the Château-Musée.
● Visitors with disabilities can telephone Nausicaà in advance to arrange an alternative circuit, avoiding steps and crowds.
● France's premier fishing port offers the freshest catch at its tables.
● Philippe Olivier's shop, on rue Thiers, is a must for cheese lovers.

BASICS

➕ 444 H2 ℹ️ 24 quai Gambetta 62200, tel 03 21 10 88 10; daily 9–12.30, 1.30–6.30, Apr–end Jun; 9–7, Jul, Aug; 9.30–12.30, 1.30–6.30, Sep to mid-Nov; 9.15–12.30, 1.45–6, mid-Nov to end Mar 🚉 Boulogne-Ville
⛴ There are proposals for services between Dover (UK) and Boulogne to resume some time in 2004
www.tourisme-boulognesurmer.com

Place Ducale in Charleville-Mézières

CHARLEVILLE-MÉZIÈRES

⊞ 442 L3 ❗ 4 place Ducale, Charleville-Mézières, tel 03 24 55 69 90; Mon–Sat 9.30–noon, 1.30–7, Sun 9.30–noon, 1.30–6, Jun to mid-Sep; Mon–Sat 9.30–noon, 1.30–6, rest of year ▣ Charleville-Mèzières www.mairie-charlevillemezieres.fr

Charleville-Mézières makes a good base for touring the forested Ardennes region (see page 124). It was originally two separate towns—Charleville and Mézières—that merged in 1966. Mézières was an important medieval trading town. Charleville is known internationally for puppetry and the Grand Marionnettiste clock on place Winston Churchill gives a puppet show on the hour. You can take boat trips down the river Meuse or head to quai Arthur Rimbaud to visit the museum dedicated to the poet Arthur Rimbaud (1854–1891), who was born here *(Tue–Sun 10–noon, 2–6)*. **Don't miss** Visit the splendid Renaissance square in Charleville.

CHAUMONT

⊞ 442 M6 ❗ Place du Géneral de Gaulle, 52000, tel 03 25 03 80 80; Mon–Sat 9.30–12.30, 2.30–6 (also Sun 10–noon, 2–5, Jun–end Sep) ▣ Chaumont www.ville-chaumont.fr

Chaumont, capital of the Haute-Marne *département,* sits on a ridge in the south Champagne region. Its stone, turreted houses are interspersed with modern buildings, and to the west a huge 19th-century railway viaduct crosses the Suize valley. The town began as a fortress built for the Counts of Champagne, but all that remains of the castle is the 12th-century keep, where you'll find the Musée d'Art et d'Histoire and the Musée de la Crèche *(Wed–Mon 2.30–6.30, summer; 2–6, rest of year)*.

CHANTILLY

Famous for its forests, racecourses and whipped cream, Chantilly also has a fairytale chateau with outstanding art and a horse museum.

Château de Chantilly sits in forests north of Paris and has an appealing mix of architecture dating from the 14th to the 19th centuries. The Condé family became the owners in the mid-17th century and commissioned landscape architect André Le Nôtre to add lakes and canals to the grounds. During the Revolution, much of the chateau was destroyed and what remained was used as a prison. It was restored in the 19th century. The 115ha (285-acre) grounds are ideal for strolling, and in spring and summer you can travel on the canals in an electric boat or take a trip in a horse-drawn carriage.

The Musée Condé opened in April 1898, and now has a magnificent collection of art and furnishings dating from the Italian and French Renaissance to the 19th century. Look out for works by Raphael, Fouquet, Fra Angelico, Poussin, Delacroix, Corot and Clouet, as well as a facsimile of the medieval manuscript *Les Très Riches Heures du Duc de Berry*.

The stables (Grandes Écuries) were built for Louis-Henri, Duke of Bourbon, in the 18th century and could accommodate 240 horses and over 400 hounds used in stag and boar hunts. Today, they contain the Musée Vivant du Cheval (Living Horse Museum; *Mon, Wed–Fri 10–6.30, Sat, Sun 10.30–7, Apr–end Oct; also Tue 10–5.30, May, Jun and 2–5.30 Jul, Aug; Mon, Wed–Fri 2–6, Sat, Sun 10.30–6.30, rest of year)*.

RATINGS	
Cultural interest	●●●●
Historic interest	●●●
Photo stops	●●●●

BASICS
⊞ 441 J4 • Château Chantilly/Musée Condé, BP 70243, 60631 ☎ 03 44 62 62 62 🏛 Musée Condé and park: daily 10–6 Jul, Aug; Wed–Mon 10–6, Mar–end Jun, Sep, Oct; Sat, Sun 10.30–5, Wed–Mon 10.30–12.45, 2–5, Nov–end Feb. Park: daily 10–6, Mar–end Oct; 10.30–12.45, 2–5, rest of year 💶 Musée Condé and park: adult €7, child (13–17) €6, (4–12) €2.80. Park only: adult €3, child (13–17) €3, (4–12) €2 ▣ Chantilly-Gouvieux, then a 30-min walk 🚗 Autoroute du Nord (A1) and take the Survilliers-St-Witz exit. Alternatively take the N16 or N17 🏬 Gift shop 🍴 Several to choose from, prices vary 🎫 Guided tours need to be booked in advance, tel 03 44 62 62 60 www.chateaudechantilly.com (French, some English; with historical and practical information)

The waterways of Colmar's Krutenau district (above). Night-time entertainment (left)

COLMAR

Experience the character of Alsace in this delightful place, with its immaculately restored old town.

Colmar lies at the southern tip of the wooded Vosges mountains and is the main town in Alsace's vineyard-rich Rhine valley. It attracts large numbers of visitors to its carefully restored old town and to the Musée d'Unterlinden, with the dramatic *Isenheim Altarpiece*.

RATINGS

Historic interest	● ● ●
Photo stops	● ● ●
Walkability	● ● ●

EXPLORE

It's a pleasure to stroll the narrow cobbled streets of the old town, with their timber-framed houses and red-tinged Gothic churches. In place de l'Ancienne Douane you'll see the striking Ancienne Douane or Koïfhus (Customs House), once Colmar's economic and political hub. Colmar's oldest house, Maison Adolph (c1350), is on place de la Cathédrale, to the north. The Maison Pfister, on rue des Marchands, is a bourgeois residence dating from 1537; its painted panels depict emperors and biblical characters. On the same road, the Musée Bartholdi is in the birthplace of 19th-century sculptor Frédéric Auguste Bartholdi, creator of the Statue of Liberty *(Wed–Mon 10–noon, 2–6, Mar–end Dec)*. The quartier des Krutenau is a picturesque area, where the pastels of old fishing cottages are reflected in the river Lauch. The district, nicknamed *La Petite Venise* (Little Venice), is where gardeners brought their produce in flat-bottomed boats.

TIPS

● Pick up a copy of the free *Discovery Trail* leaflet from the tourist office to follow a 90-minute self-guided walking circuit of the old town.
● Visit Colmar between late November and the end of December for the town's five Marchés de Noël (Christmas Markets) at place des Dominicains, place de l'Ancienne Douane, inside the Koïfhus (place de l'Ancienne Douane), place Jeanne d'Arc and the children's market in Petite Venise.
● The old town is illuminated on Friday and Saturday evenings and during special events like the Festival International de Colmar, Advent and Christmas.

FINE ARTS MUSEUM

The town's greatest treasure is indoors, in the tranquil chapel of the Musée d'Unterlinden, in rue d'Unterlinden *(daily 9–6, Apr–end Oct; Wed–Mon 9–noon, 2–5, rest of year)*. This museum, in a 13th-century Dominican convent, houses the *Isenheim Altarpiece*, masterwork of Matthias Grünewald (c1475–1528). The eight panels of the altarpiece were painted between 1512 and 1516 for the church of the Monastery of St. Anthony, at nearby Isenheim. They open to reveal vivid religious scenes including the *Crucifixion*—the best-known panel, with its emaciated, agonized Christ—the *Resurrection,* the *Angelic Concert* and the *Temptation of St. Anthony*. Few fail to be gripped by its emotional impact. A rather calmer view of the Christian story is seen in the *Orlier Altarpiece,* attributed to Martin Schongauer (c1445–1491). The museum also has local archaeological finds, Alsatian popular art and decorative art.

BASICS

✚ 443 P6 🛈 4 rue d'Unterlinden, 68000, tel 03 89 20 68 92; Mon–Sat 9–7, Sun 9.30–2, Jul, Aug; Mon–Sat 9–6, Sun 10–1, Apr–end Jun, Sep, Oct; Mon–Sat 9–noon, 2–6, Sun 10–1, Nov–end Mar 🚆 Colmar
www.ot-colmar.fr (French)

Dinghies at the village of Ambleteuse on the Côte d'Opale

Houses fronting on to the Scarpe river in Douai

COMPIÈGNE

✠ 441 J4 🛈 Place de l'Hôtel de Ville, BP 9, 60321, tel 03 44 40 01 00; Mon–Sat 9.15–12.15, 1.45–6.15, Apr–end Sep; Mon 1.45–5.15, Tue–Sat 9.15–12.15, 1.45–5.15, rest of year (also Sun 10–12.30, 2–5, Easter–end Oct) 🚆 Compiègne
www.mairie-compiegne.fr

The elegant town of Compiègne was a retreat for French kings from the 14th century. It is surrounded by the glorious Forêt de Compiègne and has one of France's largest castles. The Château de Compiègne (*Wed– Mon 10–6*) has more than 1,000 lavish rooms and Louis XIV threw some spectacular parties here. His successor, Louis XV, commissioned architect Jacques Gabriel to carry out rebuilding work in the 18th century, and Napoleon I and Napoleon III both spent time here. There are three museums within the grounds—the Museum of the Second Empire, the Museum of the Empress, and the National Museum of the Car and Tourism.

In a clearing in the forest along the route de Soissons, at Rethondes, you can see the spot where the Armistice was signed on 11 November 1918, ending World War I. A railway carriage similar to the one in which the historic event took place houses a small museum (*Wed–Mon 9–12.15, 2–6.15, Apr to mid-Nov; Wed–Mon 9–noon, 2–5.15, rest of year*).

CÔTE D'OPALE

✠ 444 H1 🛈 12 boulevard Clemenceau, 62102 Calais, tel 03 21 96 62 40; Mon–Sat 9–7, Sun 10–1, 3–6, Jun–end Aug; Mon–Sat 10–1, 2–6.30, Sun 10–noon, 3–6, rest of year 🚆 Calais Ville, Calais Fréthun 🚌 Take the D940 coast road

The cliffs, dunes and beaches of the Opal Coast stretch from the Belgian border down to the Bay of the Somme. The most visited section is between Calais and Boulogne-sur-Mer (see page 126). On a clear day you can see the English coast from the top of the 45m (148ft) Cap Gris-Nez, midway between the two ports.

The key resort is Le Touquet, nicknamed 'Paris-Plage' because of the stream of well-to-do Parisians who flocked here for hotel pampering at the beginning of the 20th century. The village of Wissant, 16km (10 miles) southwest of Calais, is famous for round boats known as *flobarts*, from which fishermen sell their catch in the market square.

Many visitors drive inland or south from Calais, and so miss out on the very Flemish final stretch of the Côte d'Opale, which is a pity as the port of Dunkerque (see right) is well worth a visit.

DOUAI

✠ 444 K2 🛈 Place d'Armes, tel 03 27 88 26 79; Mon–Sat 10–1, 2–7, Sun 3–6, Apr–end Oct; Mon–Sat 10–12.30, 2–6.30, rest of year 🚆 Douai
www.ville-douai.fr

Douai was a prosperous town in the Middle Ages, with thriving commerce in textiles and cereals. In the 17th century, it became a refuge for English Roman Catholics. Despite suffering damage in both world wars, the town still has a good number of historic buildings, including the Gothic bell tower, 64m (210ft) tall. The Musée de la Chartreuse (*Wed–Mon 10–noon, 2–6*), on rue des Chartreux, displays Flemish, Dutch and Italian paintings from the 15th to the 17th centuries and French works from the 18th and 19th centuries.

Douai was the administrative town for France's great northern coalfield, and you can learn more about mining life at the Centre Historique Minier in an old mine in nearby Lewarde (*daily 9–5.30, Mar–end Oct; Mon–Sat 1–5, Sun 10–5, rest of year*).

DUNKERQUE

✠ 444 J1 🛈 Rue de l'Amiral Ronarc'h, 59140, tel 03 28 66 79 21; Mon–Sat 9–12.30, 1.30–6.30, Sun 10–noon, 2–4 🚆 Dunkerque ⛴ To Dover, UK
www.ot-dunkerque.fr

Once a small fishing village, Dunkerque ('the church of the dunes') has grown to become France's third-largest port. The Dutch, Spanish and English fought over it down the centuries, until France bought it back from England in the mid-17th century. For many, the name Dunkerque is synonymous with the events that took place between 26 May and 3 June 1940, when 350,000 Allied troops, cut off by the German advance, were evacuated to England from the port and the beaches of nearby Malo-les-Bains. You can learn more about the evacuation at the modest Mémorial du Souvenir, in rue des Chantiers de France (*daily 10–noon, 2–5.30, May–end Sep*). Around 90 per cent of the town was destroyed near the end of World War II.

The port's seafaring history, from privateers to conventional trade, is told in the Musée Portuaire, in a 19th-century tobacco warehouse on the quai de la Citadelle (*Wed–Mon 10–12.45, 1.30–6*). You can take boat trips around the port and to the lighthouse (summer weekends only). The wide sandy beaches of Malo-les-Bains are a short stroll away from the port. **Don't miss** The Musée des Beaux-Arts, in place Charles-de-Gaulle, has Dutch, French and Flemish works from the 17th to the 20th centuries (*Wed–Mon 10–12.15, 1.45–6*).

Interior of the Château de Haut-Koenigsburg

A cobbled street leads to the Port d'Ardon

ÉPERNAY

🗺 442 L4 🛈 7 avenue de Champagne, 51201, tel 03 26 53 33 00; Mon–Sat 9.30–12.30, 1.30–7, Sun 11–4, mid-Apr to mid-Oct; Mon– Sat 9.30–12.30, 1.30–5.30, rest of year 🚉 Épernay www.epernay.net

Épernay, surrounded by vine-covered hills, is a must for lovers of champagne. You can take a guided tour of some of the 28km (17 miles) of cellars belonging to Moët et Chandon, and sample their product at the *dégustation*, at 18 avenue de Champagne *(daily 9.30–11.30, 2–4.30, Apr to mid-Nov; Mon–Fri 9.30–11.30, 2–4.30, rest of year)*. Champagne production began in Épernay in 1743 and the wealth it brought can be seen in the mansions along avenue de Champagne. Other *maisons de champagne* nearby include Mercier, at 70 avenue de Champagne *(daily 9.30–11.30, 2–4.30, Apr to mid-Dec; Thu–Mon 9.30–11.30, 2–4.30, early Jan to Mar)* and De Castellane, at 57 rue de Verdun *(daily 10–6, Jul, Aug; daily 10–noon, 2–6, Apr–end Jun and Oct–end Dec)*.

HAUT KŒNIGSBOURG

🗺 443 P5 • Château du Haut-Kœnigsbourg, 67600 Orschwiller ☎ 03 88 82 50 60 🕐 Daily 9.30–6.30, Jun–end Aug; 9.30–5.30, Apr, May, Sep; 9.45–5, Mar, Oct; 9.45–noon, 1–5, Nov– end Feb 💰 Adult €7, under 18 free; free first Sun of month, Oct–end Mar www.haut-koenigsbourg.net

The formidable silhouette of the pink sandstone Château du Haut-Kœnigsbourg rises over the forested slopes above Sélestat. It is the highest castle in Alsace, at more than 700m (2,300ft) above sea level. The castle was reconstructed in the early 20th century for Kaiser Wilhelm II, when Germany ruled Alsace.

LAON

This historic medieval city has one of the great Gothic cathedrals of France.

More than 80 of Laon's buildings have been classed as *Monuments Historiques* and there are proposals to make this walled city of winding medieval streets and attractive sandstone architecture a UNESCO World Heritage Site.

The city clings to a narrow ridge more than 100m (330ft) above the plains of Picardie and Champagne. Two abbeys once stood here and over the years so many churches sprang up that the site was named the Montagne Couronnée (Crowned Mountain). At one point it was capital of the Carolingian Kingdom.

The picturesque Ville Haute (upper town) is surrounded by 7km (4 miles) of ramparts with splendid views. Rising grandly over the rooftops are the five towers of the 12th- to 13th-century Cathédrale Notre-Dame, each 75m (245ft) high. While the west front epitomizes the excitement and drama of the new Gothic style, the interior impresses by its simple grandeur. Look for the figures of oxen high up in the towers, commemorating the beasts that hauled the heavy stone up the hill to build the cathedral.

The Cité Médiévale district surrounding the cathedral includes the Palais Épiscopal, now the law courts, and the 12th-century Hôtel-Dieu, currently housing the tourist office. Nearby, the Musée Archéologique de Laon, in rue Georges Ermant *(Tue–Sun 11–6, Jun–end Sep; Tue–Sun 2–6, rest of year)* has classical antiquities, 18th-century earthenware and 15th- to 19th-century paintings.

The less scenic Ville Basse (lower town) is linked to the upper town by an innovative overhead tram known as the *Poma*.

Don't miss There are wonderful views from the Promenade de la Couloire, a footpath around the ramparts.

RATINGS

Historic interest	●●●○
Photo stops	●●●○

BASICS

🗺 441 K4 🛈 Hôtel-Dieu, place du Parvis Gauthier de Mortagne, 02000, tel 03 23 20 28 62; Mon–Sat 9.30–6, Sun 10–6, Jul, Aug; Mon–Sat 9.30–12.30, 2–6, Sun 1–6, Apr–end Jun, Sep, Oct; Mon–Sat 10–12.30, 2–6, Sun 1–5, Nov–end Mar
🚉 Laon station is in the Ville Basse www.ville-laon.fr

The Musée National de l'Automobile, Mulhouse

The rivers Moselle and Seille run through Metz

MULHOUSE

443 P6 Place de la Réunion, tel 03 89 66 93 13; daily 10–7, Jul, Aug; Mon–Sat 10–6, Sun 10–noon, 2–6, rest of year Mulhouse www.ot.ville-mulhouse.fr

Mulhouse, a dynamic industrial town near France's border with Germany and Switzerland, is home to the lofty Tour de l'Europe and some outstanding museums. Highlights include the Musée National de l'Automobile (daily 9–6, Apr–end Oct; 10–6, rest of year), on avenue du Colmar. At the open-air Éco-musée d'Alsace, off the D430 to the north, traditional buildings show daily life in Alsace as it was in past years (Mon–Sat 10–5, Sun 9.30–7).
Don't miss The views from the revolving restaurant at the top of the Tour de l'Europe are super.

NANCY

443 N5 Place Stanislas, BP 810, 54011, tel 03 83 35 22 41; Mon–Sat 9–7, Sun 10–5, Apr–end Oct; Mon–Sat 9–6, Sun 10–1, rest of year Nancy www.ot-nancy.fr

Nancy prides itself on its classical townscape, the product of the urban planning of its enlightened rulers. It was the capital of the Duchy of Lorraine before joining the kingdom of France on the death of the last duke, Stanislas, in the mid-18th century. Stanislas was responsible for the elegant square (now place Stanislas), linking what was then the new town to the old. You can learn more about Lorraine's history at the Musée Lorrain, in the Ducal Palace (Wed–Mon 10–12.30, 2–6). Nancy was an important place for art nouveau and you can see a fascinating collection of decorative arts at the Musée de l'École de Nancy, on rue du Sergent Blandan (Wed–Sun 10.30–6).

METZ

The architecture of this picturesque city reveals its French and German heritage.

Metz (pronounced 'Mess') is the capital of Lorraine and the oldest city in the region. It is a picturesque settlement, on the banks of the rivers Moselle and Seille, with buildings in the dark yellow stone known as *pierre de jaumont,* and an abundance of parks.

There was a town here in Roman times, and during the Middle Ages Metz was a wealthy independent city-state. It became part of France in the mid-16th century but was taken by Germany in 1871 after the Franco-Prussian War, not returning to France until 1918. It has developed into a modern city and is now home to software and communications companies.

You can see examples of German architecture in the area around the huge neo-Romanesque railway station, but the city's Gothic Cathédrale St-Étienne is characteristically French, with a lofty interior and a vast amount of sumptuous stained glass. The windows cover an impressive 6,500m sq (70,000sq ft) and date from the 13th to the 20th centuries. Look for the biblical scenes by Marc Chagall in the north transept and ambulatory.

The cathedral dominates the 18th-century place d'Armes, also home to the Hôtel de Ville. On nearby rue du Haut-Poirier, a 17th-century convent houses three museums known as Les Musées de la Cour d'Or—the Musée Archéologique, Musée d'Architecture and Musée des Beaux-Arts (Mon, Wed–Fri 10–5; Sat, Sun 11–5). The Ancienne Église St-Pierre-aux-Nonnains, on rue de la Citadelle, is one of the oldest churches in France. The main shopping area is south of the cathedral, around place St-Louis.

Metz's riverside is worth seeking out, not least for the formidable Porte des Allemands on boulevard Maginot. The four towers on this gateway guarded the eastern entrance to the medieval city. From the Moyen Pont there are good views.

RATINGS	
Historic interest	● ● ●
Photo stops	● ● ●
Shopping	● ● ●

BASICS
443 N4 2 place d'Armes, BP 80367, 57007, tel 03 87 55 53 76; Mon–Sat 9–9, Sun 11–5, Jul, Aug; Mon–Sat 9–7, Sun 11–5, Mar–end Jun, Sep, Oct; Mon–Sat 9–6.30, Sun 11–5, Nov–end Feb Metz www.mairie-metz.fr

Lille

European City of Culture in 2004, Lille has one of France's most prestigious art museums—the Palais des Beaux-Arts—as well as a citadel built for Louis XIV and a cobbled old town.

Place du Général de Gaulle   *A florist on rue Lepelletier*   *Busy market stalls in the street*

RATINGS	
Cultural interest	● ● ● ● ●
Historic interest	● ● ●
Photo stops	● ● ●
Shopping	● ● ● ●

TIPS

● If you are using the Métro, buses or trams, remember to punch your ticket at the start of your journey.

● A City Pass gives you unlimited use of the buses, Métro and trams within Lille, as well as entry to some museums (1 day €15, 2 days €25, 3 days €30).

● For a weekend hotel bargain, contact the tourist office (at least 8 days in advance) for details of the two-for-one Bon Weekend offers

● Town stewards, wearing yellow jackets, give advice and directions to visitors.

An antiques store in Lille's old town (right)

SEEING LILLE

Lille is a thriving city with a compelling mixture of old and new. It is the fourth-largest city in France, capital of the Nord-Pas-de-Calais region, with a population of 1.5 million. Attractions include the Palais des Beaux-Arts, the vast Centre Euralille shopping mall and the warren of cobbled streets in the old town. Here, the 17th-century buildings are built of Lezennes white stone and Armentières brick, with intricately carved wheat sheaves and cherubs crowning the doorways. The heart of the city is the Grand' Place, officially known as place du Général de Gaulle. This square is often used for city celebrations, and the fountain is a popular meeting point. There are many bars and restaurants on the streets between here and nearby place Rihour and place du Théâtre. Lille's newer part is farther east, in the Euralille district.

Getting to Lille is simple: There are good train links with Brussels (40 minutes), Paris (one hour) and London, which is only two hours away on the Eurostar. The city has an efficient Métro, bus and tram system.

HIGHLIGHTS

PALAIS DES BEAUX-ARTS

✚ 134 B2• Place de la République ☎ 03 20 06 78 00 🕐 Mon 2–6, Wed, Thu, Sat, Sun 10–6, Fri 10–7. Closed public hols and first weekend in Sep 🚇 République 🚌 14 💶 Adult €4.60, child (12–18) €3, under 12 free

This magnificent late 19th-century palace, enlarged in the 1990s, houses France's second national museum after the Louvre in Paris, with a collection of masterpieces spanning more than 400 years. Artists represented range from Flemish and Dutch masters to the Impressionists, including Monet, Renoir and Van Gogh. There's 19th-century French sculpture in a hall on the ground floor, while the basement contains the medieval and Renaissance collection, including 40 sketches by Raphael and Donatello's bas-relief *Herod's Feast*. Other highlights are 18th-century relief maps of northern France's fortified cities, and Vauban's models for his Citadelle. Look out for the stained-glass windows near the main staircases. When it's time for a break, relax in the airy atrium with a coffee.

BASICS

🕂 444 K2 🛈 Palais Rihour, place Rihour, BP 205, 59002, tel 03 20 21 94 21; Mon–Sat 9.30–6.30, Sun 10–noon, 2–5

🚇 Two Métro lines serve the city and surrounding area

🚌 Most buses leave from place des Buisses, between Lille's two rail stations. There are also two tram routes

🚆 Lille-Europe station has Eurostar trains from London and Ashford (UK), TGV trains from Paris and all over France, and Thalys trains from Brussels. Regional services arrive at Lille-Flandres station

✈ Lille Lesquin airport, 12km (7 miles) from the city heart, has international and domestic flights

www.lilletourism.com (French and English; a lively site with information on getting to Lille, eating out, visiting the sights, shopping and more)

CITADELLE

🕂 134 A1 • Avenue du 42ème Régiment d'Infantrie ☎ Tourist office: 03 20 21 94 21 🕐 Guided tours only, Sun 3–5, May–end Aug and various other dates. You must reserve in advance at the tourist office 🚌 14 💶 Adult €7, child (under 16) €6

The architecture in Lille's historic heart is an appealing mix of Flemish and French, but the Citadelle, just outside Vieux Lille, is entirely French, built by Louis XIV's military engineer Vauban. The vast fortress—a mini-town—is in the shape of a five-sided star and inspired the design for the US Pentagon. It was completed in 1670, after only three years of building work. The main entrance, the Porte Royale, was intended to reflect the grandeur of Louis XIV, but security was another key concern—the gateway is at an angle to the drawbridge to avoid enemy fire and the walls are 4m (13ft) thick. The Citadelle is still home to 1,000 soldiers.

EURALILLE

🕂 134 C1 • Avenue Le Courbusier ☎ 03 20 14 52 20 🕐 Euralille: Mon–Sat 10–8. Hypermarket: 9am–10pm. Restaurants: 10am–midnight 🚆 Gare Lille-Europe

This futuristic shopping, business and leisure district opened in 1994 to coincide with the launch of the Eurostar rail service. It sits on 70ha (170 acres) of land on the eastern side of the city, sandwiched between Lille's two rail stations, and was laid out by Dutch architect Rem Koolhaas. You can choose from around 140 shops at the Centre Euralille mall or attend a concert in the 5,000-seat Grand Palais, and there are restaurants, a hypermarket, a hotel and holiday apart-

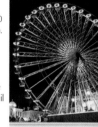

Christmas rides

ments. The modernistic Gare Lille-Europe is crowned by Christian de Portzampac's Tour Credit Lyonnais, popularly known as the 'ski boot'.

MUSÉE DE L'HOSPICE COMTESSE

🕂 134 B1 • 32 rue de la Monnaie ☎ 03 28 36 84 00 🕐 Wed–Sun 10–12.30, 2–6, Mon 2–6 🚆 Rihour 💶 Free

This former hospital takes you back to the 15th to 17th centuries, with French, Flemish and Dutch paintings, period furniture and rare musical instruments. Don't miss the tapestries by local weaver Guillaume Werniers and the kitchen decorated in Dutch style. The museum sits discreetly behind the shopfronts of the rue de la

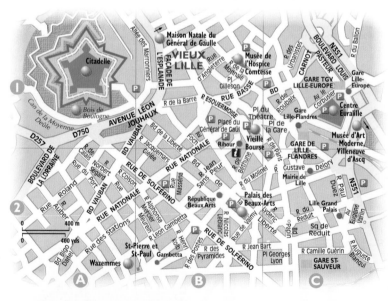

Monnaie, one of Lille's oldest streets. A hospital was founded here in 1237 by Jeanne de Constantinople, Countess of Flanders.

WAZEMMES

✚ 134 A2 • Place de la Nouvelle Aventure ⏰ Sun, Tue, Thu 7am–2pm
🚇 Gambetta

There is a carnival atmosphere at the Sunday morning Wazemmes market, which is more an event than a shopping opportunity. The sound of accordions and the aroma of Sunday lunch wafts past stands selling anything from puppies and kittens to bric-a-brac. You'll find the pet market near Gambetta Métro station and antiques and bric-a-brac on the streets around the church of St-Paul-et-St-Pierre. Toys, clothes, fruit and vegetables are sold on place de la Nouvelle Aventure, and cheese, meat and fish in the market hall.

Try Euralille for retail therapy   *The 'ski boot' building*

BACKGROUND

Lille began life as a village surrounded by tributaries of the river Deûle, giving rise to its name (l'Île—the island). Gradually, canals and a river port were created from the waterways, attracting merchants and prosperity to the burgeoning market town. From the Middle Ages onwards Lille passed from kingdom to kingdom, belonging to France, Spain, Burgundy, Flanders and the Netherlands. Louis XIV captured the city in 1667 and it was officially handed over to France as part of the Treaty of Utrecht in 1713. The Germans invaded in World War I, and again in World War II. More recently, in 1994, the launch of the Eurostar linked Lille with London, making the city an attractive day-trip destination for visitors from the UK. Lille's status was further enhanced by its designation as European City of Culture in 2004.

Lille's most famous sons are the pioneering microbiologist Louis Pasteur (1822–1895), who came to the city in 1854 as Dean of the university's Science Faculty, and Charles de Gaulle (1890–1970), who was born on rue Princesse.

This huge tower rises up from behind the Grand' Place

BOIS DE BOULOGNE

✚ 134 A1 ⏰ Daily 🚌 14

This park is wrapped around the Citadelle and bordered by the canal of the river Deûle. It is popular with bicyclists and joggers and there is also a zoo.

MAISON NATALE DU GÉNÉRAL DE GAULLE

✚ Off 134 B1 • 9 rue Princesse
☎ 03 28 38 12 05 ⏰ Wed–Sun 10–noon, 2–5 (closed for refurbishment until summer 2004) 🚌 3, 6 💶 €3

War hero and first president of the Fifth French Republic Charles de Gaulle was born here, in his grandmother's house, on 22 November 1890. It is now a museum of his life.

MUSÉE D'ART MODERNE

✚ Off 134 C1 • 1 allée du Musée, Villeneuve d'Ascq ☎ 03 20 19 68 68
⏰ Wed–Mon 10–6 🚇 Pont de Bois, then bus 41 to Parc Urbain–Musée
💶 Adult €6.50, child (12–18) €1.50, under 12 free

The modern art museum, a short Métro and bus ride out from the city, displays works by Picasso, Modigliani, Braque and others in its light, airy galleries. Sculptures embellish the gardens.

VIEILLE BOURSE

✚ 134 B1 • Place du Général de Gaulle ⏰ Tue–Sun 1–7 🚇 Rihour
💶 Free

The opulent 17th-century trading exchange is the most beautiful building in Lille, with its intricate carvings and cloistered courtyard. Merchants once traded here—today you can browse the second-hand book market or watch the chess players.

THE SIGHTS

Half-timbered houses and pink sandstone towers in Riquewihr

A canal boat at Claimarais, St-Omer

THE SIGHTS

PARC ASTÉRIX

🗺 441 J4 • Parc Astérix, 60128, Plailly
☎ 03 44 62 34 34 🕐 Apr–end Oct; days and times vary 💶 Adult €31, child (3–11) €23, under 3 free 🚉 RER Roissy-Pôle 🚗 A1 Paris-Lille Highway
www.parcasterix.fr

Parc Astérix is a witty, essentially French theme park with animated attractions based on the antics of the Gallic cartoon hero Astérix. The park, only 30km (19 miles) north of Paris, is packed with replica Roman monuments, gladiators, slaves and an imaginative range of related games, funfair rides and food. All the heroes from the famous cartoons are here, along with their great enemies, the Romans. Attractions include the Zeus Thunder roller coaster, water rides and shows. At the Gauls' village, a scale model depicts Paris through the centuries.

There are hotels on site and plenty of souvenir shops.

The park makes more sense to children (and adults) who know something about the comic-strip hero, but in any event it will provide a lively day out.

RIQUEWIHR

🗺 443 P6 ℹ 2 rue de la 1ière Armée, 68340, tel 03 89 49 08 40; Mon–Sat 9.30–noon, 2–6 (also Sun 10–1, 2–5, May–end Oct)
www.ribeauville-riquewihr.com

Riquewihr is a picturesque village on the Alsace Route du Vin, with timbered houses, cobbled streets and flower-filled window boxes. It is surrounded by vineyards, 300m (1,000ft) above sea level, and you can try the delicious wines they produce at many of the local bars and restaurants. The village dates from medieval times—two 13th-century gate towers and part of the old ramparts survive. In one of the

gate towers, the Tour des Voleurs, you can see a reconstruction of a torture chamber (daily 10.15–12.30, 2–6.30, Apr–end Oct). The village has four other museums, covering topics ranging from stagecoaches to local history.

Be aware that Riquewihr can be extremely crowded in the height of summer.

RONCHAMP

🗺 443 N6 ℹ Place du 14 Juillet, 70250, tel 03 84 63 50 82; Mon 2–5.30, Tue–Fri 10–noon, 2–6, Sat 9–noon, 2–4, May–end Aug; Mon 2–5, Tue–Fri 9–noon, 1.30–5.30, Sat 9–noon, rest of year
www.tourisme-ronchamp.fr.st

Ronchamp's highlight is the modern chapel that sits on a hill to the northwest. Notre-Dame-du-Haut was designed by Le Corbusier in 1955 and is as much a sculpture as a building. A billowing roof covers the mysterious interior and stained-glass windows are deeply set into the massive concrete walls. There are works by Marc Chagall and Henri Matisse inside. The chapel was built in memory of French soldiers killed here in 1944, replacing an older church wrecked during the battle. From the hill, you can see the Jura and Vosges mountains.

Ronchamp itself is a former mining town and you can visit the mining museum on place de la Mairie (Wed–Mon 10–noon, 2–7, Jun–end Aug; Wed–Mon 2–6, rest of year).

ST-OMER

🗺 444 J2 ℹ 4 rue du Lion d'Or, 62500, tel 03 21 98 08 51; Mon–Sat 9–6, Sun 10–1, Easter–Sep; Mon–Sat 9–12.30, 2–6, rest of year 🚉 St-Omer
www.tourisme.fr/saint-omer

This attractive market town in the marshes makes a civilized first break for visitors arriving from the Channel ports. It has fine old 17th- and 18th-century houses and you can take boat trips on its network of canals (watergangs). The town is dominated by the 13th-century cathedral, which has a 16th-century white tower in English Perpendicular style and an impressive art collection that includes Rubens' Deposition of Christ. St-Omer is one of the seven largest towns in Flanders, and was known for cloth trading and brewing: Beer continues to be its best-known export.

The German V2 rocket base at nearby Helfaut-Wizernes is now La Coupole, a museum focusing on rocket science and occupied France (daily 10–7, Jul, Aug; 9–6, rest of year).

Le Corbusier's Notre-Dame-du-Haut, at Ronchamps

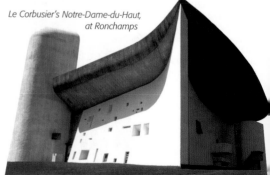

Iron screens in Sélestat's Bibliothèque Humaniste

SÉLESTAT

✠ 443 P5 ℹ Commanderie St-Jean, boulevard du Général Leclerc, BP 184, 67604, tel 03 88 58 87 20; Mon–Fri 9.30–12.30, 1.30–6.45, Sat 9–12.30, 2–5, Sun 11–3, Jul, Aug; Mon–Fri 9–noon, 2–5.45, Sat 9–noon, 2–5, rest of year ℝ Sélestat
www.selestat-tourisme.com

Sélestat may have lost its medieval walls but it retains an attractive network of narrow medieval streets. On place du Marché Vert, the 12th-century Sainte-Foy church is one of the finest Romanesque buildings in Alsace (Mon–Fri 8–6, Sat 8–7, Sun 8–6.30).

You can see books and manuscripts dating back to the seventh century in the Bibliothèque Humaniste, on rue de la Bibliothèque (Mon, Wed–Fri 9–noon, 2–6, Sat 9–noon, 2–5, Sun 2–5, Jul, Aug; Mon, Wed–Fri 9–noon, 2–6, Sat 9–noon, rest of year).

To find out more about local bread-making, visit the Musée de la Maison du Pain, on rue du Sel (daily 10–7, Dec; Tue–Fri 10–6, Sat, Sun 10–5, Jul, Aug; Tue, Fri 10–noon, 2–6, Sat, Sun 2–6, early to mid-Jan, Feb–end Jun and Sep– end Nov).

The Fonds Régional d'Art Contemporain d'Alsace (FRAC), at Espace Gilbert Estève, hosts temporary art exhibitions.
Don't miss The Château d'Eau water tower, built in 1905, is a town landmark.

A solemn marble bust looks over the collection of books at the Bibliothèque Humaniste, in Sélestat

A carved medieval head decorating the exterior of the Batelle Europe building

TROYES

The churches of this well-preserved old town are famed for their stunning stained glass.

A stroll around the old town in Troyes evokes the atmosphere of medieval times, when merchants came from all over Europe to attend the great fairs held here. The town, on the banks of the Seine, was relatively unharmed during both world wars, so its medieval streets are still lined with half-timbered houses. Troyes has an exceptional heritage of stained-glass windows in its nine churches—so much so that it is known as the Ville Sainte du Vitrail ('holy town of stained-glass windows'). The windows date from the 13th to 19th centuries and on-site restoration laboratories use methods that have hardly changed over the years.

Troyes's last great master was the 17th-century Linard Gontier, who specialized in a technique of shading known as grisaille. You can see his work in the Église St-Martin-ès-Vignes on avenue Marie de Champagne. The Gothic Cathédrale St-Pierre-et-St-Paul (daily 10–noon, 2–7, Jul to mid-Sep; Tue–Sun 10–noon, 2–5, Mon 2–5, rest of year) is in the old Cité district, north of the Canal de la Haute Seine. It is one of the largest cathedrals in France and its interior is bathed in light streaming through the magnificent stained-glass windows.

Troyes has almost as many museums as churches, all housed in venerable buildings. The Musée d'Art Moderne (Tue–Sun 11–6), in the former bishop's palace next door to the cathedral, focuses on French art from 1850 to 1950, including works by Rodin, Soutine and Derain. South of the Cité district, in the Vauluisant quartier, the Église St-Pantaléon has a vast collection of statues rescued from various churches during the Revolution.

Reims

The great Gothic cathedral of Notre-Dame has hosted the coronations of many of France's kings.
Reims's other claim to fame is its champagne production.

City statues   *Reims's Cathédrale Notre-Dame*   *Open-air cafés in place d'Erlon*

RATINGS

Cultural interest	● ● ●
Good for wine (champagne)	● ● ● ●
Historic interest	● ● ● ●

TIP

● The tourist office rents out audioguides that take you round the key sights.

BASICS

✚ 442 L4 🛈 2 rue Guillaume de Machault, 51100, tel 03 26 77 45 25; Mon–Sat 9–7, Sun 10–6, mid-Apr to mid-Oct; Mon–Sat 9–6, Sun 11–5, rest of year

🚉 Reims

www.tourisme.fr/reims (French, English)

CITY GUIDE

MUSÉE-HÔTEL LE VERGEUR

✉ 3b place du Forum ☎ 03 26 47 20 75 🕐 Tue–Sun 2–6 (also 10–noon in summer) 💶 Adult €3.90, child (10–18) €1, under 10 free
This museum has a fascinating collection of decorative arts.

MUSÉE DE LA REDDITION

✉ 12 rue Franklin Roosevelt ☎ 03 26 47 84 19 🕐 Wed–Mon 10–noon, 2–6 💶 Adult €3, under 18 free
See the room in Eisenhower's headquarters where the German army signed its surrender (*reddition*) on 7 May 1945. There is also a World War II exhibition.

SEEING REIMS

Reims is a modern, dynamic city with an impressive history—the coronations of 25 French rulers have taken place here since St. Rémi baptized Clovis, the heathen king of the Franks, in 498. But despite this, be aware that your first impression of Reims may be of a large, industrial city rather than a historical treasure. The best place to head for is the *centre ville*, where most of the key attractions can be found. You may find it worthwhile buying the *Pass Citadine Reims en Champagne* from the tourist office (1-day €12, 2-day €23, 3-day €29) as this gives you entry to six museums and a champagne house, as well as local bus travel and a small box of local biscuits.

HIGHLIGHTS

CATHÉDRALE NOTRE-DAME

• Place du Cardinal-Luçon 🕐 Daily 7.30am–7.30pm; no visits during services
The 13th-century cathedral is the city's best-known monument. World War I destroyed much of the Gothic building but it has been expertly restored, and now has three beautiful stained-glass windows by Marc Chagall. The west front is particularly inspiring, with its vivid rose window, Gallery of the Kings and famous statue of the 'Smiling Angel'. Next to the cathedral, the late 17th-century Palais du Tau was formerly the Archbishop's palace (*Tue–Sun 9.30–6.30, Jul, Aug; Tue–Sun 9.30–12.30, 2–6, mid-Mar to Jun, Sep to mid-Nov; Tue–Fri 10–noon, 2–5, Sat–Sun 10–noon, 2–6, mid-Nov to mid-Mar*). Now it contains the cathedral museum, where you can see exhibits ranging from sculptures to coronation paraphernalia. Look out for the striking Salle du Tau, where lavish royal banquets were held after coronations.

BASILIQUE ST-RÉMI

• Place St-Rémi 🕐 Daily 8–dusk or 7pm at the latest; no visits during services
The vast Romanesque St-Rémi Basilica dates from 1007 and shelters the tomb of St. Rémi and a wonderful collection of 12th-century stained-glass windows. Next to the basilica is the Musée St-Rémi (*Mon–Fri 2–6.30, Sat–Sun 2–7*), in the Benedictine abbey of St-Rémi. Exhibits here range from prehistory to Renaissance.

The Palais du Tau displays original stonework from the cathedral

CHAMPAGNE

Reims's status as a champagne producer owes much to the geology underlying the city. The chalk rock has been worn into caves, vast natural cellars for maturing and storing the precious sparkling wine that is synonymous with celebration. Dom Perignon, a 17th-century monk, invented the process that gives champagne its sparkle. No visit to Reims would be complete without a visit to a *maison du champagne* (champagne house), where you can tour the *caves* (cellars) and indulge in a *dégustation* (tasting). Most *maisons du champagne* have English-speaking guides, although at some you need to book tours in advance. Those that don't require pre-booking include Champagne Maxim's, Champagne G. H. Mumm & Cie, Champagne Piper-Heidsieck and Champagne Taittinger.

MUSÉE DES BEAUX-ARTS

• 8 rue Chanzy ☎ 03 26 47 28 44 ⓒ Wed–Mon 10–noon, 2–6
🎟 €3, under 18 free, free to all first Sun of month
This is the city's main arts museum, close to the cathedral in part of the 18th-century Abbaye St-Denis. Its collection ranges from the Renaissance to today. Highlights include 27 paintings by the 19th-century artist Corot.

BACKGROUND

Reims is named after the 5th-century saint St. Rémi. A thriving textiles industry made the city wealthy in the Middle Ages, culminating in the construction of Notre-Dame cathedral, one of the biggest building projects in France at the time. Later, champagne production added to Reims's success. But the city was close to the front line during World War I and much of the historic heart was reduced to rubble. More destruction came in World War II. Expert restoration and rebuilding work followed and in 1991 four monuments were listed by UNESCO as World Heritage Sites—Notre-Dame, Tau Palace, the basilica of St-Rémi and the St-Rémi museum.

CHAMPAGNE HOUSES
CHAMPAGNE MAXIM'S
• 17 rue des Créneaux
☎ 03 26 82 70 67 ⓒ Daily 10–7

CHAMPAGNE G. H. MUMM & CIE
• 34 rue du Champ de Mars
☎ 03 26 49 59 70 ⓒ Daily 9–11, 2–5, Mar–end Oct; Mon–Fri 9–11, 2–5, Sat, Sun 2–5, rest of year

CHAMPAGNE PIPER-HEIDSIECK
• 51 boulevard Henry Vasnier
☎ 03 26 84 43 44 ⓒ Daily 9–11.45, 2–5.15, Mar–end Nov; Thu–Mon 9–11.45, 2–5.15, rest of year

CHAMPAGNE TAITTINGER
• 9 place St-Nicaise ☎ 03 26 85 84 33 ⓒ Mon–Fri 9.30–noon, 2–4.30, Sat, Sun 9–11, 2–5, Mar–end Nov; Mon–Fri 9.30–noon, 2–4.30, rest of year

A bottle of Laurent Perrier champagne

Strasbourg

**Strasbourg sits at the crossroads of Europe and is one of the powerhouses of the European Union.
At its heart is a medieval island, dominated by a lofty cathedral spire.**

A boat tour is a good way to see the city

A narrow street leading to the cathedral

Strasbourg's Christmas market, outside the cathedral

TIPS

- Pick up a copy of the *All Strasbourg in your pocket!* leaflet from the tourist office.
- The Strasbourg-Pass, available from the tourist office, gives free admission and reductions at various sights over three days (€9.90).
- Christmas markets take place in late November and December in place Broglie, place de la Cathédrale and place de la Gare.
- For a break from city life, have a walk on the banks of the river Ill or take a boat trip.

BASICS

➕ 443 Q5 ℹ 17 place de la Cathédrale, 67082, tel 03 88 52 28 28 (also offices at place de la Gare and Pont de l'Europe); Mon–Sat 9–7, Sun 9–6

🚋 Trams and buses

🚉 Strasbourg

www.ot-strasbourg.fr (in French and English; packed with information)

Notre-Dame cathedral (right)

SEEING STRASBOURG

Strasbourg is the capital of Alsace and seat of the European Parliament and European Commission of Human Rights. It is an attractive and wealthy city, which combines the benefits of a modern metropolis with the charms of a medieval core. The central part of the city is an island, encircled by the river Ill, and much of it is traffic-free, making it well suited to exploration on foot. Listed as a UNESCO World Heritage Site, it is dominated by the single soaring spire of the superb medieval cathedral. Head to the western tip of the island to see the picturesque area known as Petite France, where fishermen, millers and tanners once congregated; today you'll find craftsmen. The winding streets, half-timbered houses and turreted bridges are best observed from the top of the 17th-century Barrage Vauban (Vauban Dam) to the southwest. Also in Petite France are the Ponts Couverts, built in the 13th century as wooden roofed bridges, but replaced by uncovered stone versions in the 19th century. The area surrounding the island is modern Strasbourg. The Quartier Européen lies in the northeast, the university campus in the southeast, and the main rail station in the west.

HIGHLIGHTS

CATHÉDRALE DE NOTRE-DAME

➕ 142 B2 • Place de la Cathédrale ☎ 03 88 43 60 32 🕐 Mon–Sat 7–11.30, 12.40–7, Sun 12.40–7

You can see the 142m (466ft) spire of Strasbourg's pink sandstone Gothic cathedral wherever you are in the heart of the city. The cathedral took more than 250 years to build, with work finishing in 1439. It is rich in sculptural decoration, especially the west façade. Inside, in the south transept, the three-tiered Pilier des Anges (Pillar of Angels) depicts the Last Judgement in a triumph of carving. Nearby, don't miss the 19th-century Horloge Astronomique, a vast, intricate astronomical clock. Be there at 12.30 to see the 12 Apostles parading before Christ. If you're feeling energetic, climb the 332 steps up the tower to the viewing platform *(Mon–Fri 9–5.30, Sat, Sun 10–5.30, Jan–end Oct; Mon–Fri 9–4.30, Sat, Sun 10–4.30, Nov, Dec)*.

The European Parliament building

HEART OF EUROPE

Strasbourg's location on the border between western and central Europe makes it an ideal base for various European institutions, clustered together in the Quartier Européen. The European Parliament has a purpose-built, curvaceous glass and steel home, constructed just in time for the new millennium *(one-hour visits, Mon–Fri, by reservation only, tel 03 88 17 20 07)*. Opposite, the sizeable Palais de l'Europe is home to the Council of Europe *(one-hour visits for groups only, Mon–Fri, by reservation)*. The European Commission of

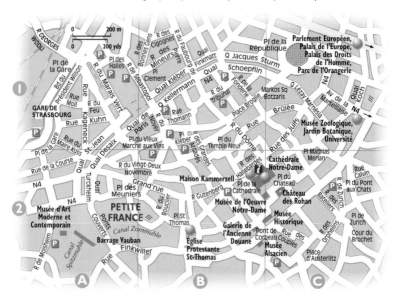

Human Rights and the European Court of Human Rights are in the Palais des Droits de l'Homme (Human Rights Palace), which overlooks the canal, designed by Sir Richard Rogers and opened in 1995.

MUSEUMS

South of the cathedral in place du Château, the Musée de l'Oeuvre Notre-Dame *(Tue–Sun 10–6),* displays cathedral-related sculptures, stained glass, paintings and furniture. These buildings were used by the cathedral architects in the 14th and 15th centuries.

Next door, the 18th-century Palais Rohan, built for the Bishop of Strasbourg, houses three key museums *(all open Wed–Mon 10–6):* In the Musée Archéologique, in the basement, you can learn more about life in Alsace from prehistory to AD800. On the ground floor, the Musée des Arts Décoratifs features the lavish apartments of the

ÉGLISE PROTESTANTE ST-THOMAS

➕ 142 B2 • rue Martin Luther
☎ 03 88 32 14 46 🕐 Daily 10–noon, 2–6, Apr–end Oct; 10–noon, 2–5, Mar, Nov, Dec; Sat, Sun 2–5, Jan, Feb. No visits during services
Strasbourg's second-largest church was started in the 12th century and finally finished in the 16th, resulting in an exquisite piece of Alsatian Gothic architecture. Highlights

A local band entertaining diners   *The Council of Europe*

The European Court of Human Rights

cardinals as well as decorative arts from the 17th to the 19th centuries. On the first floor, the Musée des Beaux-Arts displays European paintings from medieval times to the 19th century.

To the south, near the pont du Corbeau and overlooking the river Ill, is the Ancienne Boucherie (Old Butchery). This houses the Musée Historique, which highlights Strasbourg's political, economic and military history *(re-opening mid-2004).* Nearby, the 14th-century former customs house is now the Galerie de l'Ancienne Douane, with temporary exhibitions.

Across the bridge, three 17th- and 18th-century Alsatian houses in quai St-Nicolas form the Musée Alsacien *(Wed–Mon 10–6),* focusing on local folk culture.

The Musée d'Art Moderne et Contemporain, in place Hans-Jean Arp, *(Tue, Wed, Fri, Sat 11–7, Thu noon–10, Sun 10–6)* overlooks Vauban's Dam and includes works by Monet, Picasso and other painters, as well as photography and graphic art.

South of the Botanical Gardens, in the heart of the university campus, the Musée Zoologique *(Wed–Mon 10–6)* has lively exhibitions on animal-related topics.

BACKGROUND

Strasbourg is France's seventh-largest city, with a population of more than 250,000. Its river port, on the Rhine, is one of the busiest in the country. The city's strategic location on what is now the border of France and Germany is responsible for much of its wealth, but has also been a source of conflict. Strasbourg was forced to switch allegiances many times over the years. It joined France in the 17th century, but after the Franco-Prussian War it formed part of the annexed territory of Elsass-Lothringen. The city moved back to France at the end of World War I, only to be retaken by Germany from 1940 to 1944. A poignant war memorial in place de la République highlights the city's plight during this time—a mother mourns her two dying sons, one who fought for Germany and the other for France. Now indisputably French, Strasbourg nevertheless retains reminders of its German connections.

include the mausoleum of Maréchal Maurice de Saxe, by 18th-century Parisian sculptor Jean-Baptiste Pigalle.

JARDIN BOTANIQUE

➕ Off 142 C1 • rue Goethe ☎ 03 90 24 18 65 🕐 Mon–Fri 8–11.45, 2–5; also open certain weekends 🅿 Free
More than 6,000 species of plants grow in these 3.5ha (9-acre) botanical gardens. The former observatory is now a planetarium.

MAISON KAMMERZELL

➕ 142 B2 • Place de la Cathédrale
This is arguably the most beautiful house in Strasbourg. Goods were once sold from the stone arcades of the 15th-century ground floor. The half-timbered upper floors were added in the 16th century, where there is now a restaurant.

PARC DE L'ORANGERIE

➕ Off 142 C1 • Avenue de l'Europe/avenue du Président Edwards ☎ 03 88 61 62 88 🕐 Daily
This leafy park has floral displays, a boating lake, waterfall, small zoo, children's playground, bowling alley and restaurants. Its pavilion was built in 1804 for Napoleon's wife, Josephine.

The Monument aux Enfants de Verdun war memorial, in place de la Nation

A fountain with gardens beyond, in the spa town of Vittel

VERDUN

442 M4 Maison du Tourisme, place de la Nation, BP 232, 55106, tel 03 29 86 14 18; Mon–Sat 8.30–7, Jul, Aug; Mon–Sat 8.30–6.30, May, Jun, Sep; Mon–Sat 9–noon, 2–6, Mar, Apr, Oct, Nov; Mon–Sat 9–noon, 2–5, Dec–end Feb. Also Sun 9.30–5, Apr–end Sep; 10–1, rest of year
Verdun
www.verdun-tourisme.com

The name Verdun seems fated to be forever associated with the Battle of Verdun in World War I, during which hundreds of thousands of troops died in the trenches under German bombardment. The battlefield extends along the river Meuse, either side of this small country town, and a visit is a powerful reminder of the futility of war. Tour buses, with commentary, leave daily from the tourist office between May and September.

The most evocative monuments are on the right bank, in the forest that now covers the scenes of devastation. Among them is Fort Douaumont, captured almost accidentally in February 1916 by a German platoon in the early stages of the long battle. The nearby tall, white Tower of the Dead, rises over countless graves.

The Citadelle Souterraine, in avenue du 5ième R.A.P., was used as a command facility by the French during the war. Today you can tour the underground corridors and see reconstructions of daily life during the battle (daily 9–6.30, Jul, Aug; 9–6, Apr–end Jun, Sep; 9.30–noon, 2–5, Oct, Nov; 10–noon, 2–4.30, Dec–end Feb).

In 1914, French troops heading for the front line would have passed under the arch of the 14th-century Tour Chaussée, on the left bank. The Monument aux Enfants de Verdun war memorial, across the bridge in place de la Nation, depicts one soldier from each of the five armies. Around 10km (6 miles) northeast of the city, the Mémorial de Verdun museum (daily 9–6, May–end Aug; 9–noon, 2–6, Sep–end Nov; 9–noon, 2–5, early Dec, Mar, Apr; closed mid-Dec to end Feb) stands on the site of the village of Fleury, destroyed in battle.

Aside from its World War I connections, Verdun has an appealing medieval heart, a Romanesque and Gothic cathedral and pleasant riverside quays ideal for a stroll.

VITTEL

442 N6 Maison du Tourisme, 136 avenue Bouloumié, BP 11, 88801, tel 03 29 08 08 88; Mon–Sat 9–6.30, Sun 10–1, 2–6, May–end Sep; Mon–Sat 9–noon, 1.30–6.30, Nov–end Mar; Mon–Sat 9–6.30, Apr, Oct Vittel
www.ville-vittel.fr

Lorraine is world-famous for its water and Vittel is one of a number of luxurious spa towns in the south of the province. Relaxing is the main aim for most visitors, who soothe body and mind in the Thermes de Vittel spa or stroll and bicycle in the surrounding countryside. In the heart of Vittel are elegant late 19th-century buildings and grand hôtels from the early 20th century. Charles Garnier, architect of Paris's lavish Opéra Garnier, designed some of the buildings, including the old thermal baths. Here you'll find 'L'Eau et la Vie', a permanent exhibition focusing on the water industry (Wed–Mon 10–12.30, 1.30–6.30, Apr–end Sep).

You can see the water-bottling process first-hand at the Usine d'Embouteillage, in avenue Georges Clemenceau, part of Perrier Vittel France (tours Tue–Thu, Sat, Sun 9.30–10.30, 2–3.30, Mon 2–3.30, Fri 9.30–10.30, Apr–end Sep).

WISSEMBOURG

443 Q4 9 place de la République, BP 120, 67163, tel 03 88 94 10 11; Mon–Sat 9–12.30, 2–6, Sun 2–5.30, May–end Sep; Mon–Sat 9–noon, 2–5.30, rest of year
Wissembourg A mini-train tours the town, departing from the tourist office (daily at 2, 3, 4, 5, Jun–end Oct; Fri–Sun at 2, 3, 4, 5, rest of year)
www.ot-wissembourg.fr

This border town is one of the most charming little places in Alsace—its name means 'white castle'. Here you can wander through the cobbled Vieille Ville (old town), past old timber-framed houses and the 13th-century Abbatiale St-Pierre-et-St-Paul. The church, on the site of a seventh-century Benedictine monastery, has some lovely stained-glass windows. The 15th-century Maison du Sel, near the pont du Sel, has had various roles over the years, ranging from hospital to salt warehouse to abattoir. Its huge roof is an impressive sight.

The local history museum, Musée Westercamp, is on the northern edge of the town, on rue du Musée (Mon, Wed, Thu 2–6, Fri, Sat 9–noon, 2–6, Sun 10–noon, 2–6, Apr–end Oct). Here you'll find Gallo-Roman items, local costumes and furniture, among other displays. A surviving stretch of Wissembourg's medieval, red-sandstone walls follows the banks of the river Lauter from the Tour des Husgenossen to the Porte de Haguenau.
Don't miss When you've explored the town, it's worth visiting the picturesque villages of northern Alsace, including Oberseebach, Hoffen and idyllic Hunspach. The rugged, forested country of the northern Vosges is to the west, with ruined medieval castles such as Fleckenstein.

THE LOIRE

The Loire is known for its magnificent chateaux, with their turrets, towers, galleries and gardens, set in the lush and picturesque Loire Valley. But the region isn't just about castles—seek out some history in Tours, Saumur, Nantes or Orléans, or, if cars are more your style, head for Le Mans.

MAJOR SIGHTS

The chateau and the Cathédrale de St-Maurice, in Angers

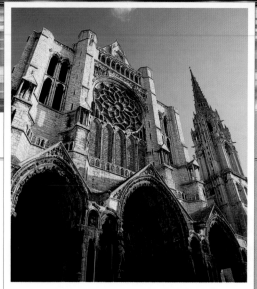

Awesome Chartres cathedral

CHARTRES

Notre-Dame de Chartres is one of France's most famous cathedrals, with its wonderful spires, stained-glass windows and flying buttresses.

The mismatched spires of Chartres's Gothic cathedral rise above the surrounding wheatfields of the Beauce plain.

Notre-Dame de Chartres was built to house the Virgin Mary's *sacra camisia* (tunic), a relic donated by Charles the Bald in the late 9th century. The present cathedral dates from the early 13th century and was built in only 25 years, after fires destroyed its five predecessors. Miraculously, Mary's tunic survived, leading to a revival of religious enthusiasm. The lower half of the façade survived from the earlier church and is pure 11th-century Romanesque. The right-hand octagonal spire, crowning the south tower is 105m (345ft) high and dates from the 12th century. The north tower, 115m (377ft) high, was decapitated by lightning and rebuilt in the early 16th century.

The 176 stained-glass windows cover an area of 2,500sq m (26,900sq ft). Most are 13th-century, although the three crowning the façade predate the fire of 1194. The three rose windows represent the Apocalypse, the Virgin Mary and the Last Judgement.

The circular labyrinth on the nave floor is a unique medieval survivor symbolizing good and evil, with its core representing paradise. The choir, one of the widest in Europe, is surrounded by a lace-like wall of stone sculpture, with 200 statues.

RATINGS	
Cultural interest	●●●○
Historic interest	●●●○
Photo stops	●●●○

BASICS
🔲 440 H5 ℹ️ Place de la Cathédrale, BP 289, 28005, tel 02 37 18 26 26; Mon–Sat 10–6, Sun 10–1, 2.30–4.30 🚆 Chartres www.ville-chartres.fr **Cathedral** 🕐 Daily 8.30–7.30

TIPS
● You can visit Chartres on a day trip from Paris. By car, take the A10 from the Porte de St-Cloud. Trains run from Gare Montparnasse. The journey should take around an hour. ● Save time for wandering around the town itself, with its river and historic churches. ● Visit in July and August for the Organ Festival (see page 248).

ABBAYE ROYALE DE FONTEVRAUD

🔲 434 F7 • BP 24, 49590 Fontevraud-l'Abbaye ☎ 02 41 51 71 41 🕐 Daily 9–6.30 Jun–end Sep; 10–5.30, Oct–end May 💳 Adult €6.10, under 18 free 🅿️ 100m (100 yds) from abbey 💻 www.abbaye-fontevraud.com

Fontevraud Abbey is the resting place of the Plantagenet king of England Henry II, his queen, Eleanor of Aquitaine and their son Richard the Lionheart. Established in the 12th century, the abbey originally housed nuns of the Order of Fontevraud. In 1804 the few buildings that survived the Revolution were turned into a prison. This role ceased in 1965, and since then the abbey has undergone much restoration. Completion is due in 2008.

AMBOISE

See page 306.

ANGERS

🔲 440 F7 ℹ️ 7 place Kennedy, 49051, tel 02 41 23 50 00; Mon–Sat 9–7, Sun 10–6, May–end Sep; Mon 2–6, Tue–Sat 9–6, Sun 10–1, rest of year 🚆 Angers St-Laud www.angers-tourisme.com

This university town is on the river Maine, in the area known as Black Anjou, after the local rock.

The black-and-white striped walls of the Château d'Angers, with its 17 drum towers, shelter a superb 14th-century tapestry series illustrating the Apocalypse of St. John the Divine *(daily 9.30–6.30 May–end Sep; 10–5.30 Sep–end Apr)*.

The early Gothic Cathédrale de St-Maurice is surrounded by old houses, including the 16th-century Maison d'Adam. On the other side of the river is the Doutre district (the old quarter), and the Musée de la Tapisserie Contemporaine, on the boulevard Arago.

Château d'Azay-le-Rideau

BOURGES

🗺 435 J7 ℹ 21 rue Victor Hugo, BP 126, 18003, tel 02 48 23 02 60; Mon–Sat 9–7, Sun 10–7, Apr–end Sep; Mon–Sat 9–6, Sun 2–5, rest of year www.ville-bourges.fr/tourisme

Prosperous Bourges has a long history of trade and industry. Dominating the skyline is the Cathedral of St-Étienne. Stand in front of its west façade to admire the 15 wide steps leading up to five doorways, flanked by two towers. Inside are stained-glass windows dating from the 12th to the 17th centuries, and a restored astronomical clock.

The Musée des Arts Décoratifs, in a superb Renaissance mansion in rue Bourbonnoux, has a fine collection of art and furniture. **Don't miss** The richly decorated Palais Jacques Coeur, in rue Jacques Coeur *(daily 9–12, 2–6)*, was built in the 15th century.

CHÂTEAU D'AZAY-LE-RIDEAU

🗺 434 G7 • 37190 ☎ 02 47 45 42 04 🕐 Daily 9–7, Jul, Aug; 9.30–6, Apr–end Jun, Sep; 10–12.30, 2–5.30, rest of year 💶 Adult €5.50, under 18 free 📷 www.monum.fr

This small, graceful Renaissance chateau sits on an island in the river Indre. Highlights include the superb furniture, a portrait gallery, and French and Flemish tapestries from the 16th and 17th centuries. The chateau was commissioned by Gilles Berthelot, treasurer to Louis XII, in 1518. Later, King François I set up an audit to investigate where the funds for such sumptuous buildings were coming from—an excuse to rid the government of the former king's 'old guard'. Berthelot narrowly escaped the death penalty and his property was confiscated.

CHAUMONT-SUR-LOIRE

See page 306.

CHÂTEAU DE CHAMBORD

The largest chateau in the Loire region, with an extraordinary roofscape of spires, turrets, dormer windows and chimneys.

Not only is the monumental Château de Chambord the largest chateau in the Loire Valley, with 440 rooms, but its parkland is surrounded by the most extensive walled forest in Europe: A 32km (20-mile) wall encloses 5,440 hectares (13,440 acres).

The Renaissance chateau fires the imagination with scenes of 16th-century hunting parties, balls and banquets. King François I, who had most of the chateau built in the 1520s, wanted to divert the river Loire itself to run around it. The architects dissuaded him, diverting a small tributary instead, which caused sufficient flooding to fill the moats. The roof originally doubled as a viewing terrace from which to observe the start and finish of hunts.

Inside, is a famous double-turn spiral staircase, by which people can ascend and descend simultaneously without meeting each other. It is believed to have been designed by Leonardo da Vinci. As if that wasn't enough, there are 14 large and 60 small staircases, although you are not allowed access to all of them. A lot of the furniture and furnishings inside the chateau were destroyed during the Revolution, but some remarkable paintings and tapestries remain.

Various events take place in the chateau, park and forest. The chateau is incredibly popular in summer—there can be up to 8,000 visitors a day.

RATINGS	
Historic interest	● ● ● ○
Photo stops	● ● ● ○

BASICS

🗺 440 H7 • Château et Domaine National de Chambord, Maison des Réfractaires, 41250 ☎ 02 54 50 40 00 🕐 Thu–Tue 9–6.15, Apr–end Sep; 9–5.15, rest of year 💶 €7, under 17 free; free to all 1st Sun of the month Oct–end Mar 🚇 Mer 🎧 Guided tours, in English available everyday Jul, Aug 🍴 Small restaurant serves excellent food at reasonable prices 🏬 Large shop for souvenirs and books 🅿 Two free parking areas a short walk from the chateau www.chambord.org

TIPS

● If you only have time to visit one chateau in the Loire Valley Château de Chambord is an excellent choice.
● There are plenty of picnic areas in the park.
● The chateau and grounds are at their busiest when there is an event on.

A picturesque balcony in the pretty village of Luynes

The 18th-century Château de Montgeoffroy

A pedalo ride past the riverbank gardens of Montreuil-Bellay

CHÂTEAU DE CHENONCEAU

✚ 440 H7 • 37150 Chenonceaux
☎ 02 47 23 90 07 ⏰ Daily 9–7, 16 Mar to 15 Sep; 9–6.30, 16–30 Sep; 9–6, 1–15 Oct and 1–15 Mar; 9–5.30, 16–31 Oct and 16–28 Feb; 9–5, 1–15 Nov and 1–15 Feb; 9–4.30, 16 Nov to 31 Jan
🎟 Adult €7.60, child (7–18) €6.10
🚉 Chenonceaux station is a short walk from the chateau 🍴 Two restaurants in the outbuildings, open mid-Mar to Nov
🏬 Gift shop
www.chenonceau.com

One of the most beautiful of the Loire chateaux, Chenonceau enjoys a stunning position, built over the gently moving waters of the Cher river.

The history of this elegant chateau is entwined with that of the several powerful women who were largely responsible for its construction, beginning with Catherine Briçonnet in the early 16th century. Henri II later gave Chenonceau to his mistress, Diane de Poitiers, and she laid out a fine garden and built a bridge from the chateau over the river Cher. Catherine de Médicis, regent after Henri II's death, forced Diane out, then laid out the park, built a two-floor gallery on the bridge, and added the large outbuildings. She bequeathed the chateau to Louise of Lorraine, her daughter-in-law and wife of Henri III. The days of royal grandeur passed, and in the mid-19th century the chateau was bought by Madame Pelouze, who made it her life's work to restore it to its former glory.

Today you can see the richly furnished interiors, including tapestries and some old masters, as well as the kitchen and wine cellar, where chateau wines are sold. A wax museum presents 'La Galérie des Dames', with historic scenes featuring the ladies. The gardens and park include a maze, and there is a floral workshop and boutique. You can view the chateau from the water by taking a boat tour on the Cher, departing from Chisseaux, 2 km (1 mile) upstream (*La Bélandre: tel 02 47 23 98 64; May–end Oct*).

CHÂTEAU DE LUYNES

✚ 440 G7 • 34 avenue de Clos Mignot, 37230 ☎ 02 47 55 67 55
⏰ Daily 10–6, 1st weekend in Apr to end of Sep 🎟 Adult €6.90, under 15 €3 🏬 Small shop

This chateau is in an elevated position overlooking the pretty town of Luynes and offers wonderful views over the Loire Valley. It is 12km (7.5 miles) west of Tours, on the north bank of the Loire. The chateau has been a private residence since the 17th century and a visit here shows the grandeur in which noble Touraine families have lived. Today, you can see furniture, paintings and tapestries inside, and there are formal gardens to enjoy below the castle walls.

The chateau was originally built in the 12th century, and a warm and elegant family residence developed over the centuries behind the impressive fortified walls. At least two kings of France are known to have been invited here for hunting and banquets. More recently, British royalty—the late Queen Elizabeth (the Queen Mother) and the Prince of Wales—has visited.

One of the lesser-known castles in the region and only opened to the public in recent years, this is a good choice for those seeking to escape the crowds.

The 15th-century collegiate chapel in the chateau grounds is sometimes used for classical music concerts.

CHÂTEAU DE MONTGEOFFROY

✚ 440 F7 • Mazé, 49630 Beaufort-en-Vallée ☎ 02 41 80 60 02 ⏰ Daily 9.30–noon, 2.30–6.30, mid-Mar to mid-Jun and mid-Sep to mid-Nov; 9.30–6.30, mid-Jun to mid-Sep 🎟 Adult €8.50, under 15 €4.60, under 5 €1
🎫 Daily guided tours in season

In beautiful countryside 22km (13.5 miles) east of Angers, the 18th-century Château de Montgeoffroy is a model of proportion, elegance and harmony. The chateau has remained in the same family since it was built and part of it is still privately occupied today. Montgeoffroy was one of the last *grandes demeures* (stately homes) to be built before the French Revolution. Designed by the Parisian architect Nicolas Barré for Maréchal de Contades, governor of Strasbourg, it was built around a chapel and two towers of a former castle. It was completed in 1776 and survived the Revolutionary years.

The interior remains unchanged and some of the furniture, furnishings and paintings are by leading craftsmen and artists of that time. The Louis XVI furniture, wood panels and wall hangings are all original. Guided tours cover some of the most beautiful rooms in the house, the magnificent kitchen and kitchen garden, the saddle room and stables, and the chapel with a stained-glass window dating from the 16th century.

CHÂTEAU DE MONTREUIL-BELLAY

✚ 434 F7 • 49260 ☎ 02 41 52 33 06
⏰ Wed–Mon 10–noon, 2–5.30, Apr–Oct 🎟 Adult €7, child (6–15) €3.50
🎫

The Château de Montreuil-Bellay was built at the beginning of the 11th century by one of the most

The protruding staircase of the Château Royal de Blois

An aerial view of the Château d'Ussé; its fairy-tale appearance is said to have inspired the story of Sleeping Beauty

fearsome of the Anjou counts, Foulques 'the Black'. This large medieval fortress, 17km (10.5 miles) south of Saumur, later withstood attacks by the Plantagenet rulers of England.

The pyramid-shaped kitchen, still has its cooking utensils.

The chateau offers wine tastings and you can also buy estate wines.

CHÂTEAU ROYAL DE BLOIS

➕ 440 H7 • Place du Château, 41000 ☎ 02 54 90 33 33 ⏰ Daily 9–7.30, Jul, Aug; 9–6, mid-Mar to end Jun and Sep, Oct; 9–12.30, 2–5.30, Jan to mid-Mar and Nov, Dec. Closed 25 Dec and 1 Jan 💶 Adult €6, under 18 €4 www.loiredeschateaux.com

Blois, on the north bank of the river, is the visitor capital of the Loire valley. Its skyline is dominated by the immense structure of the Château Royal de Blois.

The chateau has a blood-filled history of royal intrigue and a mix of architectural styles spanning four centuries.

From the 13th century onwards, a succession of buildings was erected around a central courtyard. The most impressive is the elegant François I Italianate wing, with its famous spiral staircase tower. The guided tour includes the royal apartments where, in 1588, Henri III orchestrated the murder of his rival the Duc de Guise. As you walk round, look for Louis XII's royal emblem, the porcupine, and François I's symbol, the salamander, both used as decorative motifs.

A visit here is good value for money, as your ticket also includes entrance to the Musée des Beaux-Arts, Gaston d'Orléans wing, St-Calais chapel, gem-cutter's museum, archaeology rooms, temporary exhibitions and the St-Saturnin churchyard on the other side of the river.

A son et lumière show takes place every evening in the chateau courtyard from the end of April to mid-September (in English on Wednesdays).

CHÂTEAU D'USSÉ

➕ 434 G7 • Château d'Ussé, 37420 ☎ 02 47 95 54 05 ⏰ Daily 9–6.30, Apr–Sep; 10–noon, 2–5.30, mid-Feb to Mar and Oct to mid-Nov 💶 Adults €9.80, child (8–16) €3 🎁 Gift shop www.tourisme.fr/usse

The Château d'Ussé is promoted as Sleeping Beauty's castle and is said to have inspired Charles Perrault to write the story after a visit in the 17th century. With its multitude of turrets and spires, set against the wooded background of the Forêt de Chinon, it certainly has the most fairy-tale appearance of all the Loire chateaux.

One of few chateaux still in private hands and open to the public, it is building a reputation for its annual exhibition of period costumes, which changes as various loaned collections come and go.

Visits to the chateau are by guided tour, lasting around an hour and a half. Written translations are available in English and six other languages.

The outside of the chateau is more captivating than its interior, so you may prefer merely to wander through the formal gardens designed by André Le Nôtre (who also designed the gardens at Versailles) rather than take the guided tour inside.

The chateau is compact, but be prepared to climb up and down the many stairs. It is popular with children—those under ten in particular will appreciate the Sleeping Beauty displays.

CHÂTEAU DE VALENÇAY

➕ 435 H7 • Château de Valençay, 36600 ☎ 02 54 00 10 66 ⏰ Daily 9.30–7.30, Jul, Aug; 9.30–6, 30 Mar–end Jun and Sep–3 Nov 💶 €8.50, child (7–17) €4.50, under 7 free 🎧 A free audioguide, lasting 90 minutes, is available in several languages, including English 🍴 Tea room ■ Shop, selling various souvenirs www.chateau-valencay.com

The vast Château de Valençay is a little way off the usual Loire tourist routes, around 45 minutes' drive southwest from Blois. It was built in the 16th century on the site of a former feudal castle and is surrounded by 150ha (370 acres) of parkland and 19,000ha (47,000 acres) of grounds and woods.

The politician Prince Talleyrand purchased the chateau in 1803, on the orders of Napoleon. The emperor held Ferdinand VII, King of Spain, prisoner here from 1808 to 1814.

The building is a fine example of the classical Renaissance style and has impressive roof turrets.

Today, you can enjoy various attractions on site. You can visit the 100-room, fully furnished interior (with a free 90-minute audioguide) and watch a historical film. Then wander through the formal gardens. For children there is a small farm, a play area with a castle-shaped climbing frame, a picnic area and the largest maze in France, made of wooden panels.

At weekends and public holidays from Easter to the beginning of November, and every day during July and August, you can watch actors in period costumes act out various tableaux around the chateau and the grounds, helping you to imagine former times.

The dining room at the Château de Villandry

Rabelais Festival Weekend in the hillside town of Chinon

Pleasure craft moored beneath the breakwater at Le Croisic

CHÂTEAU DE VILLANDRY

🚩 440 G7 • Château de Villandry, 37510 ☎ 02 47 50 02 09
🕐 Daily 9–6, May–end Sep; 9–dusk, Oct to mid-Nov and mid-Feb to end Apr; gardens open daily, all year
💶 Gardens only: adult €5, child (8–18) €3.50; château and gardens: adult €7.50, child (8–18) €5, under 8 free
🍴 La Doulce Terrasse restaurant and salon de thé 🛍 Gift shop and gardening shop
www.chateauvillandry.com

Local people say that the best way to appreciate Villandry is to visit at least once during each of the four seasons. The gardens are indeed stunning all year round. Early in the morning in February, the sculpted yews have an icing-sugar dusting of frost; in April the jardin d'amour (garden of love) is filled with tulips; June is the month for roses; and in October, fat pumpkins sit in the kitchen garden. Anyone not able to make several visits can see photographs of the gardens on the excellent website or take in the slide show in the chateau.

The gardens are a re-creation of a formal Renaissance garden à la française (French style). They include a water garden, hedges sculpted into the shapes of a Maltese cross and a Basque country cross, a child-friendly maze, and the Jardin de la Musique. Even the vegetable garden is sculpted to perfection, with the many crosses betraying the fact that it was once tended by monks.

The chateau was built in the Italian Renaissance style by Jean le Breton (who also supervised the construction of Chambord, see page 147). He razed a 12th-century castle to make way for Villandry. The only remnant of the older structure that remains is the tower behind the main courtyard.

The interior of the chateau dates from the 18th century and most of the rooms are open to the public. Highlights are works of art by Goya and Velázquez and a beautiful Moorish mosque ceiling. Special events include a tulip festival, art and photography exhibitions, and various classical music concerts.

CHINON

🚩 434 G7 ℹ Place Hofheim, 37500, BP 141, tel 02 47 93 17 85
www.chinon.com

Chinon, on the north bank of the Vienne river, is overlooked by the ruins of an imposing medieval fortress, the Château de Chinon. In the Middle Ages, the town had various links with England—the castle and surrounding area were popular with the Plantagenet kings and Henry II died here in 1189.

Joan of Arc met the Dauphin Charles in Chinon in 1429, reputedly assuring him of his rightful place as king of France and outlining her plans for the relief of Orléans—under siege by the English at that time.

Wander around the lovely old town or visit the Musée du Vieux Chinon, in rue Haute St-Maurice, with its statues, ceramics and local history exhibits (daily 11–1, 3–8 Apr–end Oct).

For music lovers, the town offers free open-air jazz concerts on Thursdays in June. For wine buffs, the wine museum in rue Voltaire (daily 10.30–2.30, 2–6.30 Apr–end Oct) includes a tasting in the entry price. From early July to mid-September, the local wine syndicate offers guided tours (with tastings) of the caves beneath the chateau (tel 02 47 93 30 44).
Don't miss There is a Joan of Arc museum in the Clock Tower (daily 9–7, Apr–end Sep; 9.30–5, rest of year).

LE CROISIC

🚩 439 D7 ℹ Place du 18 Juin 1940, BP 41, 44490, tel 02 40 23 00 70; Tue–Sat, 9–12.30, 2–6.30 🚉 Le Croisic

A successful fishing port for centuries, the pretty town of Le Croisic still has a working fleet and a renowned fish market. The picturesque huddle of streets in the old town is packed with humble stone fishermen's cottages. Take a stroll along the quaysides among the trawlermen and yachtsmen who crowd the popular pleasure marina during the summer—the atmosphere is busy but friendly. In the town, narrow streets are full of souvenir shops and small galleries.

The main visitor attraction is the Oceanium du Croisic, on avenue de St-Goustan (daily 10–7, Jun–end Aug; 10–noon, 2–6, Sep, Oct and Feb–end May; 2–6, Nov, Dec; closed Jan). Walk through the perspex tunnel in the vast aquarium to see sharks, rays and barracudas. There are also penguins, a coral reef display and a touch pool.

The coast of the Le Croisic peninsula is characterized by rocky inlets with small beaches, but just west of the town, the plage de Saint-Goustan offers a good stretch of sand, perfect for relaxing.

DOUÉ-LA-FONTAINE

🚩 434 F7 ℹ 30 place des Fontaines, 49700, tel 02 41 59 20 49
www.journesdelarose.com

The small town of Doué-la-Fontaine, 16km (10 miles) southwest of Saumur, has an abundance of troglodytic sites. You can visit around half a dozen, including the caves at Dénezé-sous-Doué (daily 10–7, Jun–end Aug; daily10–6, Sep; Tue–Sun 2–6, Apr, May), where you can admire some remarkable 16th-century sculptures.

A troglodyte bedroom near Dénezé-sous-Doué

The imaginatively run Zoo de Doué (Parc Zoologique), on route de Cholet *(daily 9–7 in summer; otherwise varies; closed mid-Nov to early Feb)* has more than 500 animals and is a labyrinth of caves, waterfalls and tropical vegetation.

Doué-la-Fontaine has superb public rose gardens and an annual rose exhibition is held in mid-July. At Les Chemins de la Rose, you can stroll through the Parc de Courcilpleu, on route de Cholet, discover the history of roses in France and get advice on how to grow roses in your own garden *(daily 9.30–7, mid-May to mid-Sep and last two weekends in Sep)*.

LOCHES

🗺 434 G7 🛈 Place de la Marne, BP 112, 37601, tel 02 47 91 82 82 www.lochesentouraine.com

Loches lies on the banks of the Indre river, 42km (26 miles) southeast of Tours and surrounded by the Indre-et-Loire countryside. The major sight is the medieval fortress, with its dungeons and torture chambers, *(daily 9–7, Apr–end Sep; 9.30–5, rest of year)*. There are also video reconstructions and computer animations depicting the keep in the 11th century.

The Logis Royal de Loches (Royal Residence) on place Charles VII contains the tomb of Agnès Sorel, the Gothic chapel of Anne of Brittany, and fine Flemish tapestries *(daily 9–7, Apr–end Sep; 9.30–5, rest of year)*. Walk around the exterior ramparts to appreciate the forti-fied camp as a whole.

The family home of landscape artist Emmanuel Lansyer (1835–1893), on rue Lansyer, is now a museum exhibiting over 100 of his works, *(daily 10–12.30, 2–6.30, Apr–end Sep; Mon–Sat, 10–1, 2–5, rest of year)*.

LE MANS

Best known for its world-renowned 24-hour motor race, Le Mans also has a delightful old town.

Motor-racing enthusiasts will love the Musée Automobile de la Sarthe, in rue de Laigné, near the main entrance to the racetrack *(daily 10–7, Jun–end Sep; 10–6, Oct–end Dec and Mar–end May; weekends only, Jan, Feb)*. Around 150 vehicles are on display, including motorcycles, historic racing cars and 11 previous winners of the 24-hour race. You can also see an art gallery, working models, and video-screen depictions of the evolution of motorized transportation.

RATINGS	
Historic interest	● ● ●
Special interest (cars)	● ● ● ●

BASICS
🗺 440 G6 🛈 Hôtel des Ursulines, rue de l'Étoile, 72000, tel 02 43 28 17 22; Mon–Sat 9–6, Sun 10–12.30, 2–5 Jun–Sep; Mon–Fri 9–6, Sat 9–12, 2–6, Sun 10–noon Oct–May 🚇 Le Mans 🎧 Guided tours are available; contact the tourist office for details www.ville-lemans.fr

As well as the famous 24-hour race, the 24-Hour Circuit hosts motorcycle races, a 24-hour lorry race, and other trials during the year *(tel 02 43 40 24 24 for race dates; tel 02 43 40 24 75 or 02 43 40 24 77 for ticket reservations)*.

Le Mans' old town is within the walls of the original Roman fortress, built in AD280. The cobbled streets are packed with tastefully restored medieval timber-framed houses, now bijoux restaurants, top-class boutiques and art galleries. The Musée de la Reine Bérangère, covering local history, ethnography and ceramics, is in a beautiful building classed as a Historic Monument, in rue de la Reine Bérangère *(Tue–Sun 10–12.30, 2–6.30, May–Sep; Tue–Sun 9–12, 2–6 Oct–Apr)*. It is named after Queen Berangeria, wife of Richard the Lionheart, who lived nearby at the beginning of the 13th century. The St-Julien cathedral in place St-Michel *(daily 8–7, May–end Sep; 8–noon and 2–7, Oct–Apr)*, dating from 1134, has some very early stained glass and a rose window that is almost as beautiful as the one in Chartres. Steps to the right of the Mairie lead to the heart of the town. Here, in narrow lanes dating from Roman times, there are bakeries, restaurants and small boutiques catering to workers in the surrounding streets.

A 1960 French DB Pannhard Type D13 (top), on display in the Musée Automobile de la Sarthe

Passage Pommeraye, a mid-19th-century glass-roofed arcade

RATINGS	
Cutural interest	● ● ●
Historic interest	● ● ● ●

BASICS

✚ 433 E7 ℹ Palais de la Bourse, place du Commerce, 44000 ☎ 02 40 20 60 00/02 40 35 25 94 (Sat pm, Sun)
🕐 Mon–Sat, 10–7
🚉 Nantes
🎫 Guided tours available, contact the tourist office for details.
🚢 There are pleasure cruises on the Loire during the summer months
www.nantes-tourisme.com

TIPS

● Nantes tourist office sells *Le Passport Gourmand,* which entitles the holder, plus a guest, to 50 per cent off their meals at over 90 restaurants in the city and surrounding area. The passport lasts for one year and costs €50.

● You can rent bicycles from outside the railway station and at several other locations around the city.

NANTES

Capital of the Pays de la Loire region, the lively city of Nantes has many treasures surviving from its long history.

Once described as the Venice of the West because of its waterways, Nantes was the historic capital of Brittany during the city's golden age in the 15th century. The town grew rich through shipbuilding and commerce and by 1704 it was the busiest port in France.

CASTLE AND CATHEDRAL

Dominating the upper (old) town is the Château des Ducs de Bretagne *(daily 10–7 Jul, Aug; Wed–Mon 10–6 Sep–end Jun).* This was home to the Dukes of Brittany during the golden age of François II and his daughter Anne. Henri IV's Edict of Nantes, giving freedom of worship to the Huguenots, was signed here in 1598. The castle is undergoing restoration work and will become a regional historical museum (due to open in 2006). In the cathedral *(daily 9–6),* don't miss the beautiful Renaissance tomb of François II and Marguerite de Foix.

OTHER HIGHLIGHTS

West of the cathedral, at 10 rue Georges Clemenceau, is the Musée des Beaux-Arts, in an exceptional neoclassical building *(Mon, Wed, Thu, Sat, Sun 10–6, Fri 10–8).* There are rich 15th- and 16th-century collections, and the 20th-century gallery includes works by Monet, Kandinsky and Picasso. Surrounding the heart of the old town are 18th- and 19th-century districts. Streets of fine houses are best viewed around place Graslin, where the Théâtre Graslin is one of the major performing arts venues in the city. The Musée Dobrée, on rue Voltaire, is in a palace designed by Viollet-le-Duc and has an eclectic range of items including medieval ivories, illuminated manuscripts and a gold casket said to contain the heart of Anne of Brittany *(Tue–Fri 9.45–5.30, Sat, Sun 2.30–5.30).* Other sights worth visiting include the Jardin des Plantes, at the north end of rue Clemenceau, established as a botanical garden as early as 1688; Île Feydeau—for its architecture—with 18th-century mansions decorated with wrought-iron balconies; and the Musée Jules-Verne, at 3 rue de l'Hermitage, dedicated to the science-fiction author born in Nantes in 1828.

Don't miss The Passage Pommeraye is a three-floor, glass-roofed arcade with wonderful neoclassical features and statuary.

A bronze statue of Joan of Arc, outside the Hôtel de Ville

ORLÉANS

Visit the house of French heroine Joan of Arc and see her story told in the cathedral's stained glass.

Joan of Arc recaptured Orléans from the English in 1429 after an eight-month siege, and the city is now strongly associated with her name. But even before this, Orléans was the site of decisive battles. From the early days, when the city stopped the hordes of Attila, through the Wars of Religion and the Revolution, and finally during World War II, Orléans suffered much destruction. Its focus is now on industry, but it is also a lively university city.

FOLLOWING IN THE FOOTSTEPS OF A SAINT

References to Joan of Arc abound in Orléans—in road names, house names, statues and museums. You can visit the heroine's house, the Maison Jeanne d'Arc, in place du Général de Gaulle, which is now a museum dedicated to her life *(Tue–Sun 10–noon, 2–6)*. The annual festival celebrating Joan of Arc's lifting of the siege takes place from 1 May to 8 May, with a medieval market, a folklore parade, concerts and fireworks. Stained-glass windows in the dramatic Cathédrale Sainte-Croix tell the story of St. Joan. The cathedral, overlooking the river Loire, took more than 600 years to build and has some fine carved panels *(daily 9.15–noon; also 2.15–7, Jul, Aug; 2.15–6, May, Jun and Sep; 2.15–5, Oct–end Apr)*. For more about Joan of Arc, see page 31.

ART AND ARCHITECTURE

Orléans was badly damaged during World War II, so much of it is relatively new. But there are still plenty of examples of impressive Renaissance architecture and half-timbered buildings. In the Renaissance Hôtel Groslot, on place de l'Étape *(daily 9–6),* the sumptuous interior includes several remarkable pieces of furniture. The Musée des Beaux-Arts, at 1 rue Fernand Rabier, is also worth a visit.

PARK LIFE

To the south of the city is the Parc Floral de la Source *(daily 9–6 Apr–11 Nov; 2–5, 12 Nov–end Mar)*. There are many attractions for children here, including an outdoor play area, an animal park and a small train.

RATINGS	
Cultural interest	● ● ●
Historic interest	● ● ● ●

BASICS

➕ 441 H6 ℹ 6 place Albert Ier, 45000, tel 02 38 24 05 05; daily 9.30–1, 2–6 (closes 5.30 in winter) 🚇 Orléans www.ville-orleans.fr (in French and English; packed with historical, cultural and practical information, as well as details of local events)

TIPS

● The best time to visit Orléans is the end of April and beginning of May, just as the weather is getting warmer and before the full flood of visitors. You can also enjoy the Joan of Arc festival (1 May–8 May).
● Parking in town can be tricky. Electronic signs tell you which parking areas still have spaces.

The imposing Château de Saumur

SAUMUR

434 F7 Place de la Bilange, BP 241, 49418, tel 02 41 40 20 60
www.saumur-tourisme.com

Saumur is a pretty town with half-timbered houses and elegant boutiques. It is within the Regional Nature Park of Loire-Anjou-Touraine and is a UNESCO World Heritage Site.

The 13th-century Château de Saumur dominates the skyline when you approach the town from the north. The chateau *(daily 9.30–6, Jul, Aug; 10–1, 2–5.30, Sep–end Jun; closed Tue, Nov–end Mar)* stages medieval pageants during high season and there are floodlit tours on Wednesday and Saturday evenings.

Saumur is well known for its wine, especially a sparkling white which many people prefer to champagne for its lightness in both taste and price.

You can also visit the stables of the national riding school, L'École Nationale d'Équitation et Cadre Noir, in Terrefort.

VENDÔME

See page 304.

A statue in Saumur

TOURS

This thriving city has a lively old town and excellent shopping facilities.

The middle of Tours is sandwiched between the Loire and Cher rivers, with the oldest area between Pont Napoléon and Pont Wilson. Here, in the narrow pedestrian-only lanes, are beautifully preserved timber-framed medieval buildings.

Rue des Halles and rue Nationale are very popular for high-class shopping, while rue Colbert is lined with antiques shops, small restaurants and art galleries.

St-Gatien cathedral, on rue Colbert, has magnificent stained-glass windows dating from the 13th to 15th centuries and, on the north side, the Psalette Cloister featuring three galleries and a remarkable spiral staircase. Next to the cathedral is the popular Musée des Beaux-Arts *(Wed–Mon, 9–12.45, 2–6)*. In the splendid former Palace of Archbishops, its exhibits include works by Mantegna, Rubens and Rembrandt. Spare a look for the massive 200-year-old, 30m (100ft) cedar of Lebanon in the front courtyard. Its trunk has a circumference of 7.5m (25 feet). In an outbuilding opposite the main entrance you can see Fritz, a stuffed elephant who died in Tours in 1904.

Don't miss There is a flower market on Wednesday and Saturday on the central island of Boulevard Béranger. Farther east, there is a street market on Boulevard Heurteloup, on Tuesday morning.

RATINGS

Cultural interest	●●●
Historic interest	●●●●
Shopping	●●●●

BASICS

440 G7 78/82 Rue Bernard Palissy, BP 4201, 37042 Tours Cedex 1, tel 02 47 70 37 37; Mon–Sat 8.30–7, Sun and public hols10–12.30, 2.30–5, mid-Apr to mid-Oct; Mon–Sat 9–12.30, 1.30–6, Sun and public hols 10–1, mid-Oct to mid-Apr Guided tours Apr–end Oct; contact tourist office for details
www.ligeris.com

TIPS

- **A combined ticket costing €7.62, available from the tourist information office, allows entry to six of the town's museums and includes a guided tour of the town.**
- **Parking in the middle of town can be a problem. If you approach from the north, there are large parking areas along the south bank of the river (between the four major bridges from the northern suburbs). Or park north of the river and walk across.**

CENTRAL FRANCE AND THE ALPS

Here you can ski at Chamonix, canoe in the Ardèche gorges and hike in the Auvergne. Less sporty visitors might prefer to discover Roman history in Vienne and Lyon, or visit the wine towns of Burgundy.

MAJOR SIGHTS

St-Germain abbey overlooks the old buildings at Auxerre

THE SIGHTS

AUTUN

🗺 436 L8 🛈 2 avenue Charles de Gaulle, 71400, tel 03 85 86 80 38; Mon–Sat 10–7, Sun 10–5 Jul–end Sep; 10–12, 2–5 rest of year 🚉 Autun www.autun.com

Autun's great treasure is the 12th-century cathedral of St-Lazare. Look out for the lively carvings on the capitals inside and the wonderful tympanum. Large information panels, in several languages, guide you around the building. The town's main museum, the Musée Rolin *(Wed–Mon 9.30–12, 1.30–6 Apr–end Sep; 10–12, 2–5 Oct–end Mar)*, is near the cathedral. Its Roman and medieval items shed light on the town's history. It also has a collection of contemporary and modern art. On the eastern outskirts of town is the Plan d'Eau du Vallon, a huge lake with watersports such as windsurfing.

AUXERRE

🗺 441 K6 🛈 1/2 quai de la République, 89000, tel 03 86 52 06 19; Mon–Sat 9–1, 2–7, Sun 9.30–1, 3–6.30 Jun–end Sep; Mon–Fri 9.30–12.30, 2–6, Sat 9.30–12.30, 2–6.30, Sun 10–1 Oct–end May 🚉 Auxerre www.ot-auxerre.fr

Auxerre, a relaxed town on the river Yonne, was awarded 'City of Art and History' status in 1995. You can take a cruise along the river or a leisurely stroll around the historic quarter. Pick up the brochure *Follow the thread of history in Auxerre* from the tourist information office. This guides you along an orange line on the ground that takes you past all the major sights, including the Gothic cathedral of St-Étienne, with its medieval frescoes. The trail also passes an old British red telephone box at the bottom of rue Michelet, and the Clos de la Chaînette vineyard.

ANNECY

A pretty town in a magnificent setting on the banks of mountain-fringed Lac d'Annecy.

Annecy lies at the head of a lake of the same name, flanked by gardens, villas and smart hotels. The heart of town is a delightful canal zone, where the Thiou river flows from the lake, overlooked by the towers of the 16th-century Château d'Annecy. This ancient power base of the Counts of Geneva now houses the Musée d'Annecy *(daily 10–6 Jun–end Sep; Wed–Mon 10–12, 2–6 rest of year)*. Exhibits range from Alpine anthropology to fine art. The museum's Observatoire Régional Alpine des Lacs explains the geology, flora and fauna of the region.

The town's old quarter sits below the castle, separated from the lake by a road. In passage de l'Île, the Palais de l'Île *(daily 10–6, Jun–end Sep; Wed–Mon 10–12, 2–6, rest of year)* is Annecy's most photographed building and a symbol of the town. Built in the 12th century on a natural islet, it was originally a prison, as well as a mint for the *Genevois* currency when the area was independent. Today it houses the Musée d'Histoire d'Annecy *(daily 10–6, Jun–end Sep; Wed–Mon 10–noon, 2–6, rest of year)*. The narrow streets either side of the islet form the heart of old Annecy. The houses have geranium-filled window boxes and wooden balconies. On place St-Maurice is Église St-Maurice, a 15th-century former Dominican church with a splendid trompe l'oeil painting.

Don't miss Cruise boats leave for lake trips from quai Perrière at the mouth of the Thiou. A one- or two-hour trip is the perfect way to see more of the magnificent mountain views.

RATINGS			
Activities	●	●	●
Historic interest	●	●	●
Photo stops	●	●	●	●

BASICS
🗺 437 N9 🛈 Centre Bonlieu, 1 rue Jean Jaurès, 74000, tel 04 50 45 00 33; Mon–Sat 9–12.30, 1.45–6; Sun and public hols 10–1; closed 5 Jan–20 Mar and 2 Nov–28 Dec 🚉 www.lac-annecy.com (in French and English, with webcam views of the lake, local weather reports, town maps and museum opening hours and prices)

TIPS
● Go up chemin des Remparts to the Jardin des Senteurs for wonderful views over the old town.
● Cafés in rue St-Claire, rue de l'Île or the quai de l'Île are good places to enjoy an ice cream and watch the world go by.

Bridges over the river Doubs, at Besançon

BESANÇON

⊞ 437 N7 🛈 2 place de la 1ère Armée Française, 25000, tel 03 81 80 92 55; Mon–Sat 9.30–7, Sun 10–5, Jun–end Sep; Mon–Sat 9.30–6, Sun 10–12.30, rest of year 🚊 Viotte www.besancon-tourisme.com

Capital of the Franche-Comté region, Besançon is a dignified city with handsome buildings, plenty of fountains and a 17th-century citadel. It sits on a peninsula almost encircled by the river Doubs, and you can admire the city from a different angle by taking a *bateaux mouches* boat trip.

On a hilltop 100m (300ft) above the town is La Citadelle, built in the 17th century by Louis XIV's great military engineer, Vauban. The walls of this fort enclose 11ha (27 acres) of grounds, with zoological gardens, an aquarium focusing on river life, an insectarium, a noctarium and a museum dedicated to the Resistance movement during World War II *(daily 9–6 Easter–end Jun, Sep, Oct; daily 10–5 Nov–end Mar; daily 9–7 Jul and Aug)*.

Besançon has a history of clock- and watch-making and you can learn more at the Musée du Temps, in the 16th-century Palais Granvelle *(Wed–Sun 1–7 May–end Sep; Wed-Sun 1–6 Oct–end Apr)*. Save some time (and euros) for the boutique selling wonderful wooden clockwork toys. The Musée des Beaux-Arts et Archéologie *(Wed–Mon 9.30–12, 2–6)*, in place de la Révolution, is also worth visiting. **Don't miss** The astronomical clock at St-Jean cathedral has 57 faces and gives the time in 16 places around the world.

An attractive jug in Beaune's Musée du Vin (right)

BEAUNE

The historic capital of Burgundy, in the heart of the area's most celebrated vineyards.

Beaune's manicured streets, chic boutiques and opulent cellars reflect the wealth brought to the town by trade in some of the world's most expensive wines. Learn more about the wine business at the Musée du Vin, in a former mansion of the dukes of Burgundy, in rue d'Enfer *(daily 9.30–12.30, 1.30–6 Jan–end Feb, Apr–end Nov; 9.30–12.30, 1.30–5 Mar, Dec)*.

As the wine capital of Burgundy, it is no surprise that Beaune has 15 cellars offering tastings. The tourist office can help you arrange tours.

Beside the tourist office is the 15th-century Hôtel-Dieu, with its distinctive tiled roof. It began life as a hospital, founded in 1443 by Nicolas Rolin, Chancellor of Burgundy and a great art patron. It is now a museum *(daily 9–6.30 Mar to mid-Nov; 9–11.30, 2–5.30 mid-Nov to end Feb)*, where you can see the old pharmacy, kitchens and the vaulted 70m (230ft) ward.

RATINGS			
Good for wine	●	●	● ○
Photo stops	●	●	● ○
Shopping	●	●	●

⊞ 436 M8 🛈 1 rue de l'Hôtel-Dieu, 21200, tel 03 80 26 21 30; Mon–Sat 9.30–8, Sun 10–12.30, 2–6 Jun–end Sep; Mon–Sat 10–6, Sun 10–12.30, 2–5 Oct–end May 🚊 ❓ As well as a wine festival in November, the town hosts a summer baroque festival and a three-day jazz festival in September www.ot-beaune.fr (in English, German and French)

TIPS

● The Beaune Pass scheme, run by the tourist office, gives discounts on wine cellar tours and tastings, leisure activities (including hot-air balloon rides, helicopter flights, tours by horse and carriage and excursions on the *petit train*) and heritage sites. There are greater reductions the more activities you book.
● Pick up local cheese and pâté at the Wednesday and Saturday morning markets.
● Hotels in Beaune get busy in September and October because of the grape harvest, so reserve ahead or stay outside the town.

The Hôtel-Dieu, with its decorative roof (top)

Briançon is the highest town in Europe

La Fontaine des Elephants, erected in Chambéry in 1838

Wooded hills below the snowy peak of Mont-Blanc

BRIANÇON

🔲 437 P11 ℹ️ 1 place du Temple, 05100, tel 04 92 21 08 50; daily 9–7, Jul, Aug; 9–noon, 2–6, rest of year 🔲 Briançon
www.ot-briancon.fr

Briançon is the highest town in Europe, at 1,320m (4,330ft), and is surrounded by mountain peaks. Two national parks, the Parc National des Écrins and Parc National Régional du Queyras are in the surrounding area.

The town is on the Col de Montgenèvre, one of the major Alpine passes linking France and Italy, and has been settled since pre-Roman times. It now promotes itself as a ski station of the Serre Chevalier ski area, with more than 250km (155 miles) of ski runs between four villages.

At the end of the 17th century Louis XIV's military planner, Vauban, turned Briançon's old medieval town into an impenetrable walled city. Now known as Cité Vauban, this area is traffic free and the focus of visitor interest. Go through Porte de Pignerol into Grande rue, which has some impressive houses.

Other highlights include the Maison des Templier (which houses the tourist information office), the 14th-century Église des Cordeliers and the Fort du Château, where 19th-century

A cross-country skier with a well-wrapped-up dog

defences replaced the last vestiges of the original chateau, built in the 11th century. The 18th-century Collégiale (Notre-Dame de St-Nicolas) was built to Vauban's design, with its strong walls as much for protection as for worship.

CHAMBÉRY

🔲 437 N10 ℹ️ 24 boulevard de la Colonne, 73000, tel 04 79 33 42 47; Mon–Sat 9–12.30, 1.30–7, Sun and public hols 9–12.30, Jul, Aug; Mon–Fri 9–noon, 1.30–6, Sun 9.30–12.30, closed public hols, rest of year 🔲 Chambéry
www.chambery-tourisme.com

The historic capital of the Savoie dukedom, Chambéry has some imposing historic buildings and an impressive 15th- and 16th-century old quarter to explore. Its most famous landmark is the amusing Fontaine des Elephants, at the base of rue du Boigne.

The ancient residence of the dukes, the Château des Ducs, dominates the town and is now home to the Prefecture of the Savoie region. You can visit some parts (guided tours only; tel 04 79 33 42 47 for times). Highlights include the 14th-century Tour Trésorie, the Salles Basses and the 15th-century Sainte-Chapelle. From 1453 to 1578 this chapel housed the Holy Shroud, now in Turin. The carillon of Sainte-Chapelle is one of the most impressive in Europe, with 70 bells (concerts Sat at 3pm).

At the foot of the chateau, the old quarter fans out in a series of pedestrian-only streets with elegant mansions from the Renaissance through to the 18th century. The 15th-century Cathédrale St-François contains a vast collection of trompe l'oeils, covering more than 2,000sq m (21,500sq ft), and a rare 12th-century Byzantine-style ivory

diptych. The Musée Savoisien, in an old Franciscan monastery, presents the history, archaeology and art of the Savoie (Wed–Mon 10–noon, 2–6).

CHAMONIX-MONT-BLANC

🔲 437 P9 ℹ️ 85 place du Triangle de l'Amitié, 74400, tel 04 50 53 00 24; daily 8.30–7.30 🔲 Chamonix
www.chamonix.com

The ski resort of Chamonix-Mont-Blanc lies in the heart of the French Alps and is one of France's principal and most enduring playgrounds. It is backed by the spectacular Mont Blanc, the highest peak in Europe, at 4,810m (15,777ft). The mountain straddles the French/Italian border, with the Mont Blanc road tunnel, 22km (13.5 miles) long, connecting the two countries.

Chamonix is among the smartest resorts in France, its rise dating from the time when mountaineering and skiing began to attract the wealthy crowd. It provides a comprehensive range of winter sports, including skiing, snowboarding, snow-shoeing, ski-du-fond (cross-country skiing) and luge, as well as summer activities such as hiking, mountaineering, parapenting and rafting.

Chamonix's less energetic attractions include its casino and chic shops selling designer clothes. For panoramic views, footpaths and a restaurant where you can enjoy the high Alpine air, take the Aiguille du Midi cable car. The heart-stopping views from here also come with a heart-stopping ticket price. The Mont Blanc tramway, the highest in Europe, climbing to 2,372m (7,780ft), carries passengers through some exceptional landscapes and terminates at the base camp for Mont Blanc.

A bird's-eye view of the industrial city of Clermont-Ferrand

Évian-les-Bains, reflected in the blue waters of Lac Léman

CLERMONT-FERRAND

🔲 435 K10 🚹 place de la Victoire, 63000, tel 04 73 98 65 00; Mon–Fri 9–7, Sat, Sun and public hols 10–7, May–end Sep; Mon–Fri 9–6, Sat 10–1, 2–6, Sun and public hols 9.30–12.30, 2–6, rest of year 🚉 Clermont-Ferrand www.clermont-ferrand.fr

Once two separate towns, industrial Clermont-Ferrand is ironically the capital of one of France's great remaining rural areas. It sits at the meeting point of the Auvergne and the Massif Central. The city's heart is the old Clermont, with the much smaller Montferrand a couple of kilometres (around a mile) to the northeast. In between, the Michelin factory is like a third town and the economic lifeblood of the city.

Much of the old town is built from dark volcanic stone quarried in the hills to the west. The Éspace Art Roman in the tourist office is a free display about the Romanesque art and architecture in the city and its environs. The most important Romanesque building is the UNESCO-listed 12th-century Notre-Dame-du-Port, in the northeast corner of

The octagonal Holy Water Tower at the Abbaye de Cluny

the old quarter, which has an exceptional raised choir supported by finely carved pillars and elegant arches. The stained-glass windows in the choir of Cathédrale Notre-Dame-de-l'Assumption, in the heart of town, are said to be from the same workshops as those of Sainte-Chapelle in Paris. **Don't miss** For excellent views over the city, climb the Tour de la Bayette.

CLUNY

🔲 436 L8 • Palais Jean de Bourbon, 71250, tel 03 85 59 15 93; daily 9.30–6, May–end Aug; 9.30–12, 1.30–5, rest of year 💶 Adult €6.10, under 18 free 🏛 Souvenir shop www.monum.fr

The Cluniac order was founded in 910 by William the Pious, Duke of Aquitaine, with 12 monks who moved from another abbey to the village of Cluny, near Mâcon. As reformers of the Benedictine Rule, the Cluniacs' influence spread quickly and hundreds of dependent houses were founded throughout Europe.

Cluny Abbey's third church, 177m (580ft) in length, was built between 1080 and 1130 at the height of Cluniac power. It was the largest and most splendid church in Christendom until St-Peter's was built in Rome. Cluny later fell into decline under absentee abbots and was dismantled after the Revolution. Only a single tower of the transept remains. The former abbey's palace is now the Musée d'Art et d'Archéologie, housing a collection of capitals.

Cluniac churches were designed to glorify God—and the more ornate they were, the better. Of many examples of Cluniac architecture in Burgundy, Paray-le-Monial's church, contemporary with Cluny, is

almost a replica of the lost original, on a reduced scale. A chapel at Berzé-la-Ville has a series of early frescoes, probably by the same artists employed at Cluny itself.

ÉVIAN-LES-BAINS

🔲 437 P8 🚹 Place d'Allinges, 74501, tel 04 50 75 04 26; Mon–Fri 8.30–12.30, 2–7, Sat 9–12, 2–7, Sun 10–12, 12.15–6, Jul–end Aug; Mon–Fri 8.30–12.30, 2–6.30, Sat 9–12, 2–6.30, rest of year 🚉 Évian-les-Bains 🚢 Several ferries daily to and from Lausanne, in Switzerland www.eviantourism.com

Évian-les-Bains sits on the banks of Lac Léman (Lake Geneva), in the lee of Alpine hills to the south and with wonderful panoramas north across to Lausanne and the Swiss countryside. In 1789, the water of the Sainte-Catherine fountain was found to have an excellent taste and beneficial qualities. Trading on this, the town went on to become a leading spa of the Belle Époque. Visitors have included Greta Garbo, Winston Churchill and the Aga Khan. Today wealthy visitors are still catered for, with a casino and a thalassotherapy facility.

The Hall d'Exposition des Eaux Minérales d'Évian, on rue Nationale, has information on the water sources and their properties, as well as films and a gift shop. To visit the main Évian factory, 5km (3 miles) out of town, reserve ahead at the Hall (tickets include transportation).

A good way to see the area is to take a boat trip on the lake—the town is one of the stops on trips linking the French section of the lake with the Swiss towns of Lausanne, Geneva and Montreux. Along the French side towards Thonon-les-Bains there are good views of the medieval village of Yvoire.

THE SIGHTS

Dijon

A key town in the Burgundy wine trade, Dijon is known for its cassis, mustard
and delicious *pain d'épice* gingerbread cake.
The pleasantly walkable old town has more than 150 listed
historical monuments.

Dijon mustard stacked up in a
grocery store

If you tire of sightseeing, there are plenty of shops in Dijon

RATINGS	
Historic interest	● ● ●
Food and Drink	● ● ● ●
Shopping	● ● ● ●
Walkability	● ● ●

BASICS

✚ 442 M7 ℹ Place Darcy and 34 rue
des Forges, 21000, tel 03 80 44 11 44;
Place Darcy: daily 9–7, Jun–end Aug;
10–6 rest of year; rue des Forges:
Mon–Sat 9–12, 2–6
🚉 Dijon-Ville
www.dijon-tourism.com (information,
in English and French, on guided
tours and wine villages nearby, plus a
photo gallery)

TIPS

● The Jardin Botanique de
l'Arquebuse, on avenue Albert
1er, about 15 minutes on foot
from the middle of town, is
ideal for a sandwich lunch.
There's a children's play area,
and the paths have been
designed with wheelchair-
users in mind.
● The tourist office sells a
guidebook for €2 called *The
Owl's Trail*, which gives details
of the main sights along a
route marked on the ground
by red arrows. Information
panels in French, German
and English are attached to
historic buildings.

SEEING DIJON

Dijon is a busy industrial city and regional capital, with a core of
picturesque medieval streets. It is great for gourmets, but you'll
also find historic buildings, boutiques, bars, museums, parks,
churches and galleries. All this, plus effective traffic control and—
often—plenty of sunshine. Buses are inexpensive, but as there are
no steep slopes and most major sights are within walking distance of each other, the best way to get around is often on foot.
Dijon à la Carte is an excellent-value visitor ticket that covers
entry to all the main museums, all guided tours organized by the
tourist office (available in nine languages) and unlimited use of
the buses (1-day card €8, 2-day €11, 3-day €14). The tourist
information office at place Darcy is bigger and has a more
extensive range of literature than the one at 34 rue des Forges.

HIGHLIGHTS

MUSÉE DES BEAUX-ARTS

• Palais des Ducs et des États de Bourgogne, 21000 ☎ 03 80 74 52 70
🕐 Wed–Mon, 9.30–6, May–end Oct; 10–5, rest of year. Modern and contemporary
art section closed 11.45–1.45 💶 Adult €3.40, under 18 free; free to all on Sun
The Palace of the States-General, an extension to the Palace of the
Dukes of Burgundy next door, houses the town hall as well as this
fine arts museum—one of the oldest museums in France. Level 1 has
an outstanding collection of sculpture, as well as Italian, French and
Flemish paintings, mainly from the 15th to the 18th centuries. Levels
2 and 3 are devoted to modern and contemporary art, including the
School of Paris and French 19th-century paintings.

MEDIEVAL ZONE

Some of the most interesting streets behind the palace are rue
Verrerie and rue des Forges, where you'll find the tourist office in
Hôtel Chambellan, a pretty half-timbered building off an interior
courtyard. In rue de la Chouette (Owl Street), you'll find evidence of
the town's strong association with the owl. There's an owl sculpted
on a side wall of the Église Notre-Dame and it is considered good
luck to rub the owl with your left hand while making a wish.

Two 17th-century towers frame the façade of Église St-Michel (above)

Concerts are held at the Auditorium de Dijon (left)

PLACE DE LA LIBÉRATION

The semicircular place de la Libération was originally place Royale because it was designed to enhance a statue of Louis XIV. When the statue was melted down for cannon during the Revolution, the site was renamed place d'Armes. Most of the arches outlining the square shelter boutiques, bars and restaurants. A few have small streets or passages underneath them, such as rue Vauban, which leads to the area around the Palais de Justice, with its many old buildings.

SHOPPING

Les Halles, the immense covered market, was built in 1875 by Gustave Eiffel's company, based on the design of the former market of the same name in Paris. Markets are held here both inside and outside, on Tuesdays, Thursdays, Fridays and Saturdays, and there are plenty of cafés, restaurants and food shops to choose from. Past the triumphal arch is the start of rue de la Liberté, the town's semi-pedestrianized main shopping street, home to the superb Moutarde Maille—a mustard-lover's dream. Pretty place François Rude, on the left, has fountains and seats, and is a good place for a coffee stop.

BACKGROUND

Dijon's history goes back to Roman times. In place St-Chapelle, a plaque indicates that the walls of the Gallo-Roman castrum, from which the town was developed, were 10m (32ft) high, 4.5m (14ft) thick and enclosed an area of 11ha (27 acres). Built in AD273 for defence against barbarian invasions, the castrum had four gates and 33 towers. In the 14th century, Philip the Bold made Burgundy a great independent power at the heart of Europe by marrying the heiress of Flanders. Dijon became his capital.

CITY GUIDE

CATHÉDRALE ST-BÉNIGNE
• Place St-Bénigne, 21000
☎ 03 80 30 39 33 ⓘ Daily 9–7
The interior of this Gothic cathedral is a delicate light gold, with straw-seated chairs.

ÉGLISE NOTRE-DAME
• Place Notre Dame, 21000
☎ 03 80 28 84 99
A good example of Burgundian Gothic architecture, this church has rows of grimacing monsters on its façade and a 14th-century mechanical clock.

ÉGLISE ST-MICHEL
• Place St-Michel, 21000
☎ 03 80 63 17 80
This church is Flamboyant Gothic, with a Renaissance façade.

TOUR PHILLIPE LE BON
• Palais des Ducs et des États de Bourgogne, 21000 ☎ 03 80 74 52 71
🎫 Tours: daily every 45 min from 9–12.30 and 1.45–5.30
You'll get great views from the top of this tower, 52m (160ft) high.

Gorges de l'Ardèche, carved out of the limestone over millennia

GORGES DE L'ARDÈCHE

⊞ 431 L12 🛈 Vallon-Pont-d'Arc, place de l'Ancienne Gare, 07150, tel 04 75 88 04 01; Mon–Sat 9–1, 3–7, Sun 9–12.30 Jul, Aug; Mon–Fri 9–noon, 2–5.30, Sat 9–noon, rest of year
www.vallon-pont-darc.com

One of France's most dramatic natural attractions, the Gorges de l'Ardèche have been carved over hundreds of thousands of years by the power of the Ardèche river. The sheer sides of the limestone gorge reach 30m (100ft) in height and the water has sculpted various cave systems, their interiors decorated with fantastic stalactites and stalagmites. The Grotte de la Madeleine and Grottes de St-Marcel, are the largest in the area, with more than 40km (25 miles) of caves and tunnels.

It's easy to admire the gorge, as the D290 runs along its northern edge and links the main villages. You'll get several panoramic views along the route, particularly at the Belvédères de la Haute Corniche. Just south of Vallon-Pont-d'Arc is the Pont-d'Arc, a natural bridge cut through the rock by the power of the water and one of the most photographed sights in southern France. Look out, too, for Aiguèze, the tiny medieval stone village on the gorge's northern bank, with its ruined chateau.

A popular way to enjoy the gorge is by taking to the water. You can go on an escorted kayak trip between Vallon-Pont-d'Arc and St Martin-d'Ardèche to the southeast, which lasts anything from two to five hours and takes you into the natural cathedrals of the gorge sides and past riverside beaches. If you prefer to go at your own pace, you can rent a canoe at Vallon-Pont-d'Arc and ask the rental company to pick you up later from the village of Sauze, downstream.

GRENOBLE

The cultural capital of the French Alps and a year-round base for outdoor activities.

Grenoble is said to be the flattest city in France—a surprising fact given that it's surrounded by mountain peaks. As an Alpine city, it draws outdoor enthusiasts year round. It also styles itself as the cultural capital of the French Alps and has several major museums and many temporary exhibitions. It was the birthplace of the author Stendhal. The historic quarter of town is compact, with good shopping along the traffic-free streets around place Grenette.

The Musée de Grenoble *(Wed–Mon 10–6)*, in a modern building in place de Lavalette, has an outstanding collection of art from the 13th to 20th centuries. For avant-garde art, head to the Centre National d'Art Contemporain, in cours Berriat *(Tue–Sun 12–7, exhibitions only)*. It is in a factory built for Gustav Eiffel's workshops.

RATINGS	
Activities	●●●●
Cultural interest	●●●
Historic interest	●●●

BASICS
⊞ 437 N10 🛈 14 rue de la République, 38019, Grenoble, 04 76 42 41 41; daily Mon–Sat 9–6.30 all year; Sun 10–1, 2–5 May–end Sep; Sun 10–1 Oct–end Apr 🚊 Grenoble www.grenoble-isere.info (in English and French, with information on watersports, ski resorts and the city)

TIPS
● *Multipass Grenoble* covers entry to one museum, use of public transportation, one return trip on the cable car and a guided tour of Grenoble. Buy it from the tourist office.
● Watch out for trams on streets that are otherwise vehicle-free—they move almost silently.

The Musée Dauphinois *(Wed–Mon 10–7 Jun–end Sep; 10–6, rest of year)*, in a 17th-century convent on rue Maurice Gignoux, has two permanent exhibitions, 'People of the Alps' and 'The Great History of Skiing', plus temporary displays. To the north, the Romanesque Église St-Laurent is now the Musée Archéologique *(Wed–Mon 9–6)*, incorporating a 3rd-century AD necropolis, sarcophagi from the 6th to the 8th centuries, and the remains of a 9th-century Carolingian church and an 11th-century monastery.

Don't miss For good views over the city and mountains, take the gondola cable car (pictured above) to the 16th-century Bastille.

Selecting fine wines at the Maison des Vins, Mâcon

A decorative feature at the Palais Idéal

A brightly painted sundial in the market square at Pérouges

MÂCON

✚ 436 M9 **🛈** 1 place St-Pierre, 71000, tel 03 85 21 07 07; daily 10–7 Jun–end Sep; Mon–Sat 12–12.30, 1.30–6.30 Mar–end May, Oct; 10–12.30. 2–6.20 Jan, Feb
www.macon-bourgogne.com

Mâcon, on the river Saône, is one of the most important of the Burgundy wine towns, but retains a quiet and relaxing atmosphere. The river's importance to the town is symbolized by the much-loved Pont St-Laurent, dating from the 11th century but altered over the years. The bridge is one of few in the area to survive World War II undamaged. Huge catfish appeared in the river during the 1970s and you can arrange fishing expeditions at the Centre de Pêche au Gros, on rue de la Liberté. If your preference is for wine, try a tasting at the Maison des Vins, on avenue de Lattre de Tassigny.

Rue Carnot is a short pedestrian-only lane lined with boutiques and old buildings, including the 16th-century Maison du Bois, overlooking the market square, place aux Herbes. Where rue Carnot meets place Poissonnière, fish designs in the ground indicate the fishmongers' area.

The Musée des Ursulines, in rue des Ursulines, was a 17th-century convent and, during the Revolution, a prison. Today it exhibits wine-making antiques,

Carvings on the Renaissance Maison de Bois, in Mâcon

sculpture and fine arts of the French and Flemish schools *(Tue–Sat 10–12, 2–6, Sun 2–6)*. The Musée Lamartine, in rue Sigorgne, is in Mâcon's Academy of Arts, Sciences and Literature *(Tue–Sat 10–12, 2–6, Sun 2–6)*. Mâcon-born 19th-century Romantic poet Lamartine was once president here. As well as Lamartine memorabilia, there are tapestries and 18th-century objets d'art.

PALAIS IDÉAL

✚ 436 M10 • Le Palais Idéal du Facteur Cheval, 26390, Hauterives ☎ 04 75 68 81 19 🕐 Daily 9–12.30, 1.30–7.30, Jul, Aug; 9–12.30, 1.30–6.30, Apr–end Jun, Sep; 9.30–12.30, 1.30–5.30, Oct, Nov; 9.30–12.30, 1.30–4.30, Feb, Mar and Dec to mid-Jan **✋** Adult €4.90, child (6–16) €3.40
www.facteurcheval.com

Le Palais Idéal du Facteur Cheval (The Palace of Postman Cheval) is 50km (31 miles) south of Vienne, in hills east of the Rhône valley. It was built between 1869 and the early 1900s by the local postman with stones he collected on his daily rounds. Although not popular with locals at first, it is now a national monument.

The palace is enormous—a remarkable achievement given that it is the creation of just one man, working without formal plans (apparent in the fact that the walls are not straight). Without any training, Cheval managed to incorporate a variety of architectural features, creating, at the same time, the feel of a medieval castle, Gothic cathedral, Hindu temple and mosque. He also incorporated his own philosophical thoughts on life in a number of inspirational poems inscribed on plaques in the building. Both Pablo Picasso and André Breton visited the Palais Idéal, drawing inspiration for their

surrealist revolution. Classical and jazz concerts are held in the evenings throughout the summer.

PÉROUGES

✚ 436 M9 **🛈** Syndicat d'initiative de Pérouges, 01800, tel 04 74 61 01 14; daily 10–6, May–end Sep; 11–12, 2–5, rest of year 🚉 Meximieux then 1km (0.6 mile) walk
www.perouges.org

Voted one of the most beautiful villages in France, Pérouges is a tiny stone settlement seemingly transported from the 15th century to the present day. It sits on a small rocky outcrop 290m (950ft) above the Ain valley and 35km (22 miles) northeast of Lyon. Perfectly preserved, it has been used in numerous period films and TV shows. It now thrives as an enclave for artists and has several small galleries. It is also known for its production of the sweet, thin biscuits called *les galettes de Pérouges*.

The main entrance to the village is the 11th-century Porte d'En Haut. It is marked by the Église-Forteresse (fortified church), built into the ramparts, the circle of fortified houses that form the outer layer of village buildings. The rue des Rondes follows the lines of the ramparts inside, encircling the heart of Pérouges, place des Halles. This square is also known as place de Tilleul, and its medieval houses are now souvenir shops or cafés. In the corner of the square is the entrance to the Musée de Vieux Pérouges *(daily 10–12, 2–6, Easter–end Sep)*, where your ticket also gives admission to the remains of the old chateau, the Maison des Princes.

Be aware that the old, cobbled streets are very uneven—not ideal for wheelchairs or high-heeled shoes.

Lyon

Lyon was once the Roman capital of Gaul and is now France's third-largest city (by population). Its Renaissance old quarter is listed as a UNESCO World Heritage Site and the city is known for its gastronomy.

Basilique Notre-Dame de Fourvière

Detail of carving on a building in place Bellecour

Cathédrale St-Jean

RATINGS	
Cultural interest	●●●○
Good for food	●●●○
Historic interest	●●●○

TIPS

● A Lyon City Card (€7.50 for one day, €12.50 for 2 days and €15 for 3 days), available from the tourist office, entitles you to entry to 19 museums, guided and audioguided city tours, river cruises, lunchtime classical concerts and public transportation within the city.

● Lyon's modern Métro system has four lines, running from 5am until midnight. In Vieux Lyon the Métro links with a funicular to the top of the Fourvière hill.

● Parc de la Tête d'Or, by the Musée d'Art Contemporain, has plenty of places to stroll and sit in the sunshine. There's a lake, rose garden, glasshouses, playground, small zoo, 'petit train' and mini-golf

● River cruises with Naviginter include lunch or dinner and depart from bis quai Rambaud. Tours without meals leave from quai des Célestins, where there is also a ticket office.

Relaxing in the sun at Lyon's amphitheatre (right)

SEEING LYON

The city sits at the confluence of the Rhône and Saône rivers, with the medieval quarter on the west bank of the Saône, the modern suburbs on the east bank of the Rhône, and the heart of the city on the narrow peninsula (the Presqu'île) between the two. Like Paris, Lyon is divided into administrative *arrondissements*. Its Métro system makes it easy to get around. A trip to Lyon isn't just about what to see—its unique *bouchon* eateries serve some of the world's best food, and the city has a lively social scene, with clubs, drama and live performance. It is also known for a type of puppet theatre known as *guignol*.

HIGHLIGHTS

FOURVIÈRE AND VIEUX LYON

Head across the river Saône to find Vieux Lyon, the wonderfully atmospheric old quarter. Its pedestrian-only streets cover three districts (St-Georges, St-Jean and St-Paul), lined with four-floor mansions, the whole constituting one of the most complete Renaissance towns in Europe. The main streets, rue St-Jean and rue du Boeuf, run parallel to the river, and here you'll find the typical *traboules* of Lyon—the arched galleries, courtyards and vaulted walkways that cut under the Renaissance mansions to make a warren of hidden alleyways. This side of the river is great for browsing in antiques shops and galleries and has some of the best-value *bouchon* bistros in the city. *Lugdunum,* the Roman capital of Gaul, was set above here on top of the hill now known as Fourvière. You can walk or take the funicular to the Roman remains.

CATHÉDRALE ST-JEAN

✚ 166 B3 • Place St-Jean, 69005 🕐 Mon–Sat 8–12, 2–7.30, Sun 8–12, 2–7 🚇 Vieux Lyon

The cathedral anchors Vieux Lyon. Built on the site of an earlier church, the oldest part is the cloister wall, dating from the 11th century, although building went on throughout the 13th century. The resulting church is one of the finest examples of a transitional Romanesque/Gothic building. The vaults of the apse, for instance, are

BASICS

➕ 436 M9 🛈 Place Bellecour, 69002, tel 04 72 77 69 69; Mon–Sat 9–7, Sun 9–6, mid-Apr to mid-Oct; Mon–Sat 10–6, Sun 10–5.30, rest of year

Ⓜ Lyon's Métro system has four lines

🚉 There are two main stations in Lyon. Gare de la Part-Dieu is where most TGV services from Paris terminate, but some trains go on to the more central Perrache station

✈ Lyon St-Exupéry airport, 24km (15 miles) east of Lyon.

www.lyon-france.com

Romanesque at the base and topped with classic Gothic vaulting. There's some stunning stained glass, such as the rose windows in the transepts, and a rare astronomical clock dating from the 14th century. Pope John XXII was crowned here in 1316 and Henri IV married Marie de Medici here in 1600. The church received a visit by Napoleon in 1805 and was the site of the world's first recorded organ recital in 1928.

MUSÉE DE LA CIVILISATION GALLO-ROMAINE

➕ 166 A3 • 17 rue Cléberg, 69005 ☎ 04 72 38 81 90 🕐 Tue–Sun 10–6 👋 Adult €3.80, under 18 free; free to all on Thu

This museum, on Fourvière hill, is in an innovative subterranean building. Its 17 rooms display objects found in Lyon and the Ain and Isère regions. Highlights include the 'Claudius Tablet', part of a bronze

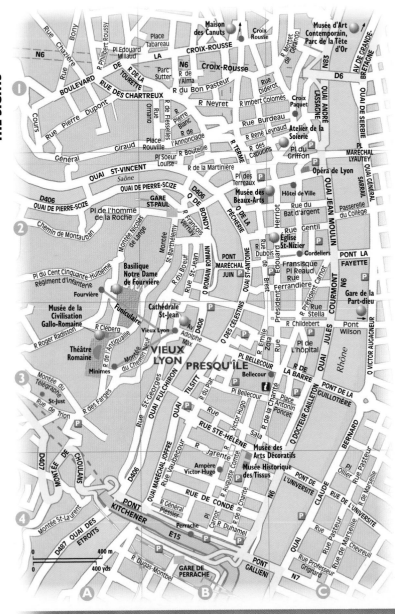

tablet inscribed with a speech given by Emperor Claudius to the Senate in AD48, in which he put forward the rights of the Gallic people to take part in the magistrature. Don't miss the rare mosaic showing a Roman circus, along with a vivid depiction of a chariot race.

BASILIQUE NOTRE DAME DE FOURVIÈRE

🟦 166 A2 • Esplanade de Fourvière 🕐 Daily 8–7 🚊 Vieux Lyon then Funiculaire Fourvière

Despite its Roman connections, Fourvière is today famous for a much more modern edifice, the Basilique Notre Dame de Fourvière, built on the site of the Roman forum and an 11th-century chapel. Its white marble façade, with four turrets and a rounded apse, can be seen from much of the city. In 1870 the people of Lyon, threatened by Prussian forces, prayed to the Virgin Mary (the city's patron) to spare their city. The enemy never breached the city walls and the grateful public donated enough money to build this magnificent basilica. The interior has exceptional Belle-Époque mosaics and vividly detailed stained glass depicting scenes from the life of the Virgin. The church's primary treasure is a golden statue of Mary in the 18th-century chapel adjoining the basilica.

MUSÉE DES BEAUX-ARTS

🟦 166 C2 • 20 place des Terreaux, 69001 ☎ 04 72 10 17 40 🕐 Permanent collections: Sat–Mon and Wed–Thu 10–6, Fri 10.30–6. Closed 1–8 May, Easter Mon, Pentacost Mon, Ascension Day, 14 Jul and 15 Aug. First-floor rooms closed noon–1.15; Second-floor rooms closed 1.15–2.15 🚇 Hôtel de Ville 💶 Permanent collection: adult €3.80, child €2. Temporary exhibitions: adult €8, under 18 free

In the Presqu'île district, the Palais St-Pierre, a former Benedictine monastery, now houses the fine arts gallery—one of the best in France outside Paris. There are more than 1,800 paintings, shown in chronological order. Look for the fine altarpiece of *The Ascension of Christ* by Perugino from the Italian Quattrocentro, and works by 17th-century Dutch and Flemish artists including Rembrandt and Rubens. The 18th-century Italian gallery has works by Tintoretto and Veronese. The museum is particularly strong on paintings by 19th- and early 20th-century artists including Dégas, Gauguin, Manet, Monet and Picasso. There are 16 rooms devoted to ancient civilizations, with outstanding collections of Greek, Roman and Egyptian items. A further 17 rooms have varied collections, including Byzantine ivories, Limoges enamels, Islamic art and rare Japanese tea sets. The interior courtyard of the museum is now a formal garden.

BACKGROUND

The Gallo-Roman settlement on the hill of Fourvière was founded by Julius Caesar in 44BC and became the Roman capital of Gaul. But with the fall of the Roman Empire, the town moved down to the riverside, to what is now Vieux Lyon. An episcopal complex was established in the fifth century and power stayed in the hands of the bishops until the 14th century, when the monarchy introduced a secular government and law courts. In the 15th century, Lyon became an important European hub for currency dealing and printing, and began hosting huge trade fairs. The silk trade came into its own at this time and the city entered a golden age, leading to the building of the Renaissance town. Today Lyon is still at the forefront of architecture, with the ultramodern TGV station and the dramatic St-Exupéry airport, by Santiago Calatrava.

ATELIER DE LA SOIERIE

🟦 166 C1 • 33 rue Romarin, 69001 ☎ 04 72 07 97 83 🕐 Mon–Sat 10–12, 2–6 Jul, Aug; 2–7 rest of year 🚇 Hôtel de Ville

This is one of the few working silk workshops left in the city. Watch the material being screen printed and made into scarves, then browse the shop.

ÉGLISE ST-NIZIER

🟦 166 C2 • Place St-Nizier 🕐 Daily 10–7.45 Jun to mid-Sep; Mon–Sat 8.30–7.45, Sun 2.30–6, rest of year

This church sits on the site of a 5th-century basilica. Begun in the early 14th century, its exterior is an excellent example of Flamboyant Gothic architecture.

MAISON DES CANUTS

🟦 Off 166 B1 • 12 rue d'Ivry, 69004 ☎ 04 78 28 62 04 🕐 Mon–Fri 8.30–12, 2–6, Sat 9–noon, 2–6 🚇 Croix Rousse 💶 Adult €3.82, child €2.29

This museum re-creates the old system of silk production in an original house with working handlooms. Dyeing and spinning took place on the ground floors of the tall 18th- and 19th-century houses in the Croix Rousse district, while the workers' families lived above.

MUSÉE D'ART CONTEMPORAIN

🟦 Off 166 C1 • 81 quai Charles des Gaulle, 69006 ☎ 04 72 69 17 18 🕐 Wed–Sun noon–7 🚌 4 and 47 💶 Adult €3.80, under 18 free

In a spectacular building designed by Renzo Piano, this museum concentrates on 20th- and 21st-century art forms. It leans strongly towards installation art and computer-generated art.

MUSÉE DES TISSUS AND MUSÉE DES ARTS DÉCORATIFS

🟦 166 B4 • 34 rue de la Charité ☎ 04 78 38 42 00 🕐 Musée des Tissus: Tue–Sun 10–5.30. Musée des Arts Décoratifs: Tue–Sun 10–noon, 2–5.30 💶 €4.60 for both

These textiles and decorative arts museums are in the 17th-century Hôtel de Villeroy. Learn about the use of silk and other textiles in clothing and soft furnishings.

A quiet side street in Lyon (above left)

The imposing Puy de Dôme

Blue-and-white bunting hangs along a street in Le Puy-en-Velay

An outdoor café in front of the Cathédrale St-Étienne, in Sens

THE SIGHTS

PUY DE DÔME

➕ 435 K10 • Off route N89, 10km (6 miles) west of Clermont-Ferrand
☎ Peage: 04 73 62 12 18; welcome venue: 04 73 62 21 46
🕐 Daily 7am–10pm, Jun–end Aug; 7am–9.30pm, Sep, May; 8–8, Apr; 8–7.30, Oct; 8–7, Mar; 8–6, Nov. Closed Dec–end Feb 🚗 Car €4.50, motorcycle €3 🚌 In Jul and Aug a shuttle bus runs daily 10–6: adult return €3.50, child (4–16) €1.40, under 4 free 🍴 🎁 Gift shop 🚻 ❓ Visitors possessing disabled badges can travel to the summit in their own vehicles at all times. The welcome venue is wheelchair accessible, with elevators to all areas.
www.puydedome.com

Le Puy de Dôme is the highest of a series of 80 ancient volcanic peaks in the southern Massif Central. The almost circular dome of laval rock rises 1,465m (4,805ft) and offers wonderful views of the Auvergne national park and the city of Clermont-Ferrand.

Leave your car in the parking area at the foot of the *puy* and walk or take the *navette* (shuttle bus), which runs in July and August to the summit. Another *navette* leaves from the rail station in Clermont-Ferrand four times a day and links directly with the parking area.

The welcome venue at the summit has an explanation in French and English of how the site and other volcanic features of the surrounding Auvergne hills were formed. *'Tables d'orientation'* on the terraces help you get your bearing and there are footpaths around the summit. You can also see the remains of the first-century Roman Temple of Mercury and the huge Tele de France antenna (off-limits to the public), but the stunning views alone make a trip to the top worthwhile.

You can learn more about how volcanoes work at Vulcania, 5km (3 miles) from the Puy de Dôme (*9–7 Apr–end Aug; 9–6 rest of year*). This state-of-the-art attraction is cut out of underground volcanic basalt and is linked to Puy de Dôme by the Clermont-Ferrand *navette*.

LE PUY-EN-VELAY

➕ 436 L11 ℹ Place du Breuil, 43000, tel 04 71 09 38 41; daily 8.30–7.30, Jul, Aug; 8.30–12, 1.30–6.15, Easter–end Jun, Sep; Mon–Sat 8.30–12, 1.30–6.15, Sun and public hols 10–noon, Oct–Easter 🚉 Le Puy-en-Velay
www.ot-lepuyenvelay.fr

In the heart of the wooded Auvergne region, Le Puy-en-Velay is one of France's most important religious sites. During the Middle Ages it was one of the main gathering points for pilgrims en route to Santiago de Compostela in Spain. Thanks to the pilgrims, the town grew rich and the streets of the old quarter are lined with buildings dating from the 15th to the 18th centuries. The Romanesque Cathédrale de Notre Dame is built on the site of an alleged apparition of the Virgin Mary. Pilgrims still flock to the church to venerate the 18th-century statue of the Black Virgin. The adjoining cloister, classed a national monument, has a riot of Romanesque arches in the courtyard and several frescoes inside.

The oldest and most appealing church is tiny Chapelle St-Michel d'Aiguilhe, built high on a tufa rock in the 10th century and reached by a steep stone staircase. The 16m (52ft) statue of the Virgin Mary on another tufa column was forged from 213 cannons captured at the Siege of Sebastopol during the Crimean War.

SENS

➕ 441 K6 ℹ Place Jean-Jaurès, 89100, tel 03 86 65 19 49; Mon–Sat 9–12.30, 1.30–7, Sun 10–12.30, 2–5.30 Jun–end Aug; Mon–Fri 9–12, 1.30–6.15, Sat 9–12, 1.30–5.15, rest of year
🚉 Sens
www.office-de-tourisme-sens.com

Known as 'Burgundy at the gates of Paris', Sens makes a good first port of call for visitors heading southeast from the capital.

The main attraction is the Cathédrale St-Étienne and its associated museums. In the Middle Ages, the cathedral held sway over a vast ecclesiastical province that included the dioceses of Paris and Chartres. Its museums, in the former Archbishop's Palace, hold a rich collection of religious items, plus rare silks and tapestries, ivory pieces, archaeological discoveries and more than 800 pieces of bronze jewellery. A more recent addition is the Collection Marrey, a private collection of 19th and 20th century art that includes ceramics, paintings and some bronzes by Rodin. There are also Flemish and Dutch paintings from the 16th and 17th centuries (*daily 10–6 Jul, Aug; daily 10–noon, 2–6 Jun, Sep; Mon, Thu, Fri 2–6, Wed, Sat, Sun 10–noon, 2–6, rest of year*).

Across place de la République from the western end of the cathedral is the massive covered market (*all-day market on Mon*), with rooms used for art exhibitions. Outside town to the south, the Parc du Moulin à Tan (*daily 8–dusk*) has 10ha (25 acres) of parkland with various botanical zones, trails and animal enclosures. Vast greenhouses contain more than 1,500 species of tropical plants, including the astonishing giant aquatic Victoria Cruziana.

Water lilies on the moat surrounding Château de Tanlay

Harvested fields and vineyards stretch towards houses in the town of Vézelay

TANLAY

442 L6 • Château de Tanlay, 89430
03 86 75 70 61 45-min tours
Wed–Mon 9.30, 10.30, 11.30, 2.15, 3, 3.45, 4.30, 5.15, Apr to mid-Nov
Adult €7, child (7–15) €3; entry to chateau grounds €2.50 Tonnerre

The magnificent Renaissance Château de Tanlay, near Tonnerre, has elegant round towers and bell-shaped domes. Inside, there are sculpted chimney pieces, period furniture and a *trompe l'oeil* gallery. The highlight is the School of Fontainebleau painted ceiling in the Tour de la Ligue, which depicts courtiers as divinities. Entry to the interior is by guided tour only. The grounds are ideal for a picnic lunch and there is a surprisingly large supermarket in the village for provisions.

The castle, surrounded by a moat, was built on the foundations of an old fortress. In 1533 the property was left to Louise de Montmorency, widow of Gaspard de Coligny. Her son, François de Coligny d'Andelot, began major reconstruction work.

In the 17th century Michel Particelli d'Hémery, finance minister and associate of Cardinal Mazarin, bought Tanlay and, with the services of the architect Le Muet, completed the main chateau, the petit chateau, the outbuildings, stables, grounds and the moat.

At the beginning of the 18th century, the chateau passed into the hands of Jean Thevenin, who was made Marquis de Tanlay by Louis XIV, and it has remained in the family ever since.

THIERS

436 K9 Château (Hôtel) du Pirou, 63300, 04 73 80 65 65; Mon–Sat 9–1, 1.30–7, Sun 10–noon, 2–6, mid-Jun to mid-Sep; Mon–Sat 9.30–12, 2–6, rest of year Thiers

Thiers, on a hillside above the river Durolle, is in the heart of the Parc Naturel Régional Livradois-Forez. It was capital of the French knife-making industry from the Middle Ages and there are still small artisan workshops where cutlery is made by hand. In the middle of the modern town is a tiny old quarter preserving the 15th-century street-plan and architecture, including the Hôtel du Pirou, an impressive half-timbered building dating from 1410 and now home to the tourist office.

The surrounding narrow streets have fine old corbels, lintels and doorways. It's worth taking a look inside the Église St-Genès which has one of the largest Romanesque domes in France and a simple stone interior dating from 1016. St. Genès is said to have been martyred in the town and the first church erected here in 575 was allegedly on the exact site of the saint's grave.

The excellent Musée de la Coutellerie (Cutlery Museum) is at 23 and 58 rue de la Coutellerie (*daily 10–6.30 Jul–end Aug, 10–12, 2–6.30 Jun and Sep. 10–12, 2–6 rest of year. Closed Jan*). Number 23 concentrates on the history of the industry with demonstrations by craftsmen, while number 58 re-creates a 16th-century cutler's house. Other interesting buildings on this street include the 'house of the wild man', named after the sculpture on the façade.

VÉZELAY

441 K7 Rue St-Pierre, 89450, tel 03 86 33 23 69; daily 10–1, 2–6 Jun–end Oct; Fri–Mon, 10–1, 2–6, rest of year
www.vezelaytourisme.com

People visit Vézelay for its UNESCO-listed Basilique Sainte-Madeleine. The hilltop site was a major stop on the Santiago de Compostela pilgrimage route. Reminders of this pilgrimage link can be seen in the brass scallop shells set into rue St-Étienne as it climbs the hill, past picturesque houses. The entrance to the basilica is impressive: A pair of immense wooden doors, each about 3.5m (11ft) wide, are left open to welcome the continuous stream of visitors. The view from here along the length of the 62m (203ft) nave is stunning. The interior is sparsely furnished and very bright, with the sun beaming through the high windows on the south side. The crypt and cloister are open to visitors and you can climb the tower (200 steps) for excellent views over the village and surrounding area. The basilica hosts summer concerts.

In the village, there are art galleries and souvenir shops. For the more active, the Morvan countryside—Burgundy's wilderness—is ideal for walking and mountain biking.

A detail of the magnificent tympanum of the central doorway of the Basilique Ste-Madeleine

The magnificent interior of Vichy's opera house

VICHY

🗺 436 K9 🅸 19 rue du Parc, 03204, tel 04 70 98 71 94; Mon–Sat 9–12.30, 1.30–7, Apr–end Jun and Sep; Mon–Sat 9–7.30 Jul, Aug; Sun 2.30–12,30, 3–7 Apr–end Sep; Mon–Fri 9–12, 1.30–6, Sat 9–12, 2–6, Sun 2.30–5.30 Oct–end Mar

🚉 Vichy

www.vichy-tourisme.com

www.ville-vichy.fr

Vichy has been a therapeutic base since Roman times. Julius Caesar came for treatment during his wars of conquest in Western Europe. In the 19th century, the patronage of Napoleon III and his family led to a golden age for the spa, which continued into the early 1900s.

Today, Vichy is one of France's principal spa resorts, with state-of-the-art therapy facilities. The leading venue is Grand Établissement Thermal, whose shimmering oriental domes have become a symbol of the town.

Historic Vichy revolves around the huge neoclassical Palais des Congrès, designed by the architect Badger at the behest of Napoleon III in 1865. In 1903 the whole complex was expanded when the Opéra de Vichy was added by the Belle-Époque architect Lecoeur. Regular ballet, opera and classical music concerts take place in its magnificent art nouveau interior.

The Congrès is linked to the main thermal source by the Parc des Sources, which has formal gardens and wide walkways with ornate iron and glass arcades designed to protect visitors from the rain. Les Halles des Source, housing a number of specialists in therapeutic water treatments, is in the same style.

Napoléon III's influence can again be seen in the 20ha (50 acre) park named after him, and in the neo-Gothic Église St-Louis, whose stained glass depicts members of the ruling family.

VIENNE

One of the richest concentrations of historic buildings in France, with exceptional examples from the 1st century BC to the present day.

Vienne, on the eastern bank of the Rhône, is not to be missed. Its Roman remains and the Romanesque architecture in its early Christian churches are exceptional, and it's a wonderful place to wander.

The Gaulish settlement here became one of the largest towns in Roman Gaul. You can see the remains of a Gallo-Roman town at Jardin Archéolgique de Cybèle, off place François Mitterrand, but there are better remains at the Musée et Sites Archéologique de St-Romain-en-Gal *(Tue–Sun 10–6, Mar–end Oct; 10–5, rest of year)*. The remains of streets, houses, public baths and workshops form an open-air exhibition here. A glass and steel structure houses the main body of the museum, with excellent mosaics.

RATINGS	
Historic interest	●●●○
Photo stops	●●○

BASICS

🗺 436 M10 🅸 Cours Brillier, 38200, tel 04 74 53 80 30; Mon–Sat 9–12, 1.30–6; Sun 10–12, 2–5.

📷 2-hour guided city tours throughout the year on the first Sun of the month and twice a week in Jul and Aug

🚉 Vienne

www.vienne-tourisme.fr (in French with information on sights and museums)

TIPS

● You can buy a multi-entry ticket to six attractions at museums or the tourist office.
● Book tickets and lodgings early if coming for the jazz festival in early June.
● A *petit train* runs through the town in summer, linking the major attractions.

The Théâtre Romain *(daily 9.30–1, 2–6, Apr–end Aug; Tue–Sun 9.30–1, 2–6, Sep–end Oct; Tue–Sat 9.30–12.30, 2–5, Sun 1.30–5.30, rest of year)* was one of the largest in the world when it was completed around AD50. Restored in 1930, it now hosts summer concerts. The Musée des Beaux-Arts et d'Archéologie *(Tue–Sun 9.30–12.30, 2–6, Apr–end Oct; Tue–Fri 9.30–12.30, 2–7, Sat–Sun 2–6, rest of year)*, in a 19th-century grain store, displays domestic items used in Roman daily life. The Musée Archéologique, in the Église St-Pierre, has a fine statue of Tutela, the Gallo-Roman goddess and guardian of Vienne.

Vienne's Théâtre Romain (above)

SOUTHEAST FRANCE

Experience the glitz of St-Tropez and the wildlife of the Camargue. Relive the region's Roman past at the amphitheatre at Nîmes and its Roman Catholic history in Avignon. Learn about perfume in Grasse and modern art in Céret.

MAJOR SIGHTS

Aix-en-Provence's enticing fruit and vegetable market

RATINGS	
Cultural interest	● ● ● ○
Historic interest	● ● ● ○
Photo stops	● ● ○

BASICS

➕ 431 N13 ℹ️ 2 place Général de
Gaulle, 13100, tel 04 42 16 11 61;
Mon–Sat 8.30–8, Apr–end Sep; 8.30–7,
rest of year; Sun 10–1, 2–6, all year
🚇 Aix-en-Provence
www.aixenprovencetourism.com
(in English and French, with many
photographs)

TIPS

● Reserve lodgings as far
ahead as possible at festival
time (June and July).
● To see fine Renaissance
mansions, explore the Quartier
Mazarin south of Cours
Mirabeau.
● Aix has more than 100
fountains. The moss-covered
Fontaine d'Eau Thermale is a
natural hot spring, with water
pouring out at 34°C (93°F).

AIX-EN-PROVENCE

**This elegant, historic town has an impressive array of
Renaissance buildings.**

Aix is one of Provence's most pleasing towns, with a quintessentially
southern feel. In Roman times it was known as *Aquae Sextiae*, a
prosperous spa resort. Later it became a place of learning, culture and
art. It is famous as the home of painter Paul Cézanne, who was born,
and did most of his work here, and for its university, founded in 1409.

COURS MIRABEAU AND VIEIL AIX

Vieil Aix, the old quarter, is enclosed by a ring of avenues and
squares that have replaced the town's ramparts. One of these
avenues, the bustling Cours Mirabeau, is Aix's main attraction. Its
double row of leafy plane trees shades hundreds of café tables on
the north side; one café, Les Deux Garçons, dates from the 1790s.
Across the road are banks and offices in fine 17th- and 18th-century
hôtels (private mansions), some with elaborate façades, balconies
and doorways supported by huge atlantes. For more grandiose
Renaissance architecture, turn south into the quieter Quartier Mazarin.

ART

You can visit Cézanne's studio, on the avenue named after him (*daily
10–12, 2–5*). It is preserved as it was in the 1900s, but doesn't
contain any of his work. The Musée Granet, in place St-Jean de Malte
(*reopening in 2006*) has some of his early paintings. The Musée des
Tapisseries, in the former archbishops' palace in place des Martyrs de
la Résistance, has magnificent 17th- and 18th-century tapestries, as
well as modern pieces (*Wed–Mon 10–12.30, 1.30–5.30*).

THE CATHEDRAL

The Cathédrale St-Sauveur is an interesting mix of styles from
Romanesque to Baroque, spanning the fifth to the 17th centuries.
Look for the 16th-century Flemish tapestries in the chancel, which
were stolen from Canterbury Cathedral during the English Civil War.
The ancient baptistery, off the right-hand nave, contains traces of the
main street of the Roman town. There are superb pieces of medieval
art, notably Nicolas Froment's triptych of the *Burning Bush* in the
central nave, painted for King René in 1476; the king and his queen
are depicted kneeling in prayer.

The arched courtyard of the Espace Van Gogh (above).
Les Arènes (right), the Roman amphitheatre,

THE SIGHTS

ARLES

Arles is a lively, arty, market town with exceptionally well-preserved Roman remains.

Founded by the Greeks in 600BC as a trading outpost of Massalia (Marseille), Arles was later taken over by the Romans, who built it up as a sea and river port, linked by canal to the Mediterranean.

ROMAN ARLES

At the heart of town is the spectacularly well-preserved Roman amphitheatre, Les Arènes, which held more than 20,000 spectators (*9–6.30, May–end Sep; 9–5.30, Mar–end Apr, Oct; 10–4.30, Nov–end Feb.*). It was converted into a medieval fortress and later into a town within a town, and is now regularly used for bullfights and performances. The remains of the nearby Théâtre Antique are used to stage concerts and for Arles's folk culture festival in July. Roman Arles extends to the banks of the Rhône, where you can see what remains of the vast Thermes de Constantin spa baths. On the other side of the N113 expressway, is the extraordinary modern building of the Musée de l'Arles Antique (*daily 9–7, Mar–end Oct; 10–5.30, rest of year*), an airy, spacious museum displaying ancient items found at Arles .

OTHER HIGHLIGHTS

The Romanesque Église St-Trophime, on place de la République, has one of France's most beautiful cloisters (*daily 9–6.30 May–end Sep; 9–5.30, Mar–end Apr, Oct; 10–4.30, Nov–end Feb*). Don't miss the reliefs of the *Last Judgement* on the façade. On rue de la République, the Museé Arlaten focuses on Provençal culture and was set up by the poet Frédéric Mistral using his 1904 Nobel Prize money (*daily 9–1, 2–6.30 Jun–end Aug; 9–12, 2–6, Sep; Tue–Sun 9.30–12.30, 2–6, Apr, May; Tue–Sun 9.30–12.30, 2–5, Oct–end Mar*).

VINCENT VAN GOGH

Van Gogh dreamed of establishing an artists' colony in Arles, and several locations in and near the town are the subjects of some of his paintings. The hospital where he went to recuperate after the severed ear incident is now Espace Van Gogh, a study facility in place Félix Rey. The Fondation Van Gogh, near Les Arènes, doesn't contain any of his paintings, but has works by modern artists such as Francis Bacon (*daily 10–7, summer; Tue–Sun 10–12, 2–5.30, winter*).

RATINGS	
Cultural interest	●●●○
Historic interest	●●●●
Walkability	●●●

BASICS

🚹 431 M13 🛈 Esplanade Charles de Gaulle, boulevard des Lices, 13200, tel 04 90 18 41 20; Mon–Sat 9–7, Sun and public hols 9–1
www.tourisme.ville-arles.fr (in English, German, Italian and Spanish, with information on galleries and Van Gogh, and with links to other sites)

TIPS

● A single ticket (*Pass Monuments*) covering all the major sights in Arles is good value if you visit more than three.

● The town's huge Saturday morning market is on boulevard des Lices. The second-hand market is on the same street on the first Wednesday of every month.

Visitors are dwarfed by the vast square towers of the Palais des Papes (above). An antique carousel in place de l'Horloge (left)

AVIGNON

Avignon has a fine walled city, once the home of popes, with a long tradition of art and culture.

Massive ramparts enclose the whole of Avignon's old city, on the left bank of the Rhône. In 1309 the papal court moved here from Rome and the city grew in size and importance. The area remained in papal hands for centuries, only becoming part of France again in 1791. During its time under papal control, the city attracted a large wealthy clerical class, but also political refugees and outcasts on the run from their own communities, who were given refuge. Something of that dichotomy survives today—there are many luxury shops and well-to-do inhabitants but also people begging. At festival time in July, hundreds of thousands of visitors arrive from all over Europe.

THE PALAIS DES PAPES
The Papal Palace was the home of the popes from 1309 to 1403 and is Avignon's principal sight *(daily 9–9, Jul; 9–8, Aug, Sep; 9–7, Apr–end Jun, Oct; 9.30–5.45, rest of year)*. The vast and rather bleak fortress-like building dominates the town. Inside, largely unfurnished, you can go round on your own or join a guided tour in English. The Pope's Bedroom has a decorated ceiling and walls adorned with birds and golden vines on a blue background. The Grand Tinel banqueting hall has Gobelin tapestries, and there's a good view from the Terrasses des Grands Dignitaires. Across the huge, empty place du Palais is the Petit Palais *(Wed–Mon 10–1, 2–6, Jun–end Sep; 9.30–1, 2–5.30, rest of year)*, which served as a guest room for visiting royalty and nobility. The Rocher des Doms park, on the hill rising beside the Palais des Papes, offers dramatic views over the Rhône.

ART
The Fondation Angladon Dubrujeaud *(Wed–Sun 1–6; also Tue, May– end Nov)*, on rue Laboureur, has the personal collections of Jacques Doucet and Jean et Paulette Angladon-Dubrujeaud. It focuses on late-19th and 20th-century art, including works by Paul Cézanne and Pablo Picasso.

Don't miss Pont St Bénézet (Le Pont d'Avignon) is the picturesque narrow cobbled medieval bridge that features in the nursery rhyme. Today only a few arches survive after floods in the 17th century.

RATINGS
Cultural interest	● ● ● ○
Historic interest	● ● ● ●
Walkability	● ● ● ●

BASICS
✚ 431 M12 🛈 41 cours Jean-Jaurès 80400, tel 04 32 74 32 74; Mon–Sat 9–6, Sun 10–5, Apr–end Sep; Mon–Fri 9–6, Sat 9–5, Sun 10–noon, rest of year
🚉 Main station in boulevard St-Rochand; TGV station 5km (3 miles) from the middle of the city
www.ot-avignon.fr (in English and French, with information on shopping, river cruises, hotels and museums)

TIP
● The *Avignon Passport* gives reductions on entry tickets to the main sights.

Dining in the shade of canopies in the old town of Antibes

ANTIBES

⊞ 432 P13 🛈 11 place Général de Gaulle, 06600, tel 04 92 90 53 00; daily 9–7, Jul, Aug; Mon–Fri 9–12.30 1.30–6, Sat 9–noon, 2–6, rest of year ⓡ www.antibesjuanlespins.com

Antibes, east of Cannes, is one of the most rewarding and important smaller towns on the Riviera. It is densely packed and attracts its fair share of millionaires, as can be seen from the size of the yachts moored in Port Vauban. The attractive historic central quarter, Vieil Antibes, is still enclosed by Vauban's 17th-century ramparts and there's a busy open-air market on Cours Masséna, in the middle of town, every morning except Monday.

The world-class Musée Picasso *(Tue–Sun 10–6, summer, Tue–Sun 10–noon, 2–6, rest of year; closed Nov)* is in a striking medieval fortress on the cliff edge, once owned by the Grimaldi family, the rulers of Monaco. The gallery contains many ceramics and other works by Picasso (who had a studio here), and also work by Antibes-born Nicholas de Staël, as well as Fernand Léger, Modigliani and Joan Miró.

The Musée Archéologique, at Bastion St-André *(Tue–Sun 10–noon, 2–6; closed public hols, Nov)*, contains many items from the area—Antibes was founded by the Greeks and became a busy Roman port.

Nearby Cap d'Antibes, a promontory of land extending south, has some sandy beaches and seafront restaurants that are good for lunch. There's a long public beach—surprising given that this area is a haven of secluded palatial villas and expensive hotels.

CAMARGUE

See pages 318–321.

LES BAUX-DE-PROVENCE
A ruined citadel among the jagged Alpilles hills.

This stunningly picturesque medieval fortress-village is in the Alpilles hills 25km (15 miles) south of Avignon. The village, with its atmospheric alleyways, sits dramatically poised on a sheer stony crag. This eagles-nest inaccessibility once deterred invaders but now attracts thousands of visitors.

Les Baux first came into being as a refuge during the 8th-century Arab raids. It became an important fortress in the Middle Ages, under the control of ambitious and aggressive local lords. They claimed, improbably, direct descent from the Magi king Balthazar, and to prove the point put the star of Bethlehem on their crest. The village as seen today is a narrow strip outside the original fortress, and dates largely from the 16th and 17th centuries. It has few permanent residents, having been almost entirely taken over by seasonal artists and craftspeople. Many of the restored old houses contain galleries, shops and cafés.

The principal sight is the ruined walled enclosure of the medieval Citadel (the entrance is at the Musée d'Histoire des Baux). A large and bleak ruined area, evocatively known as the Ville Morte (Dead City), it offers fantastic views of the countryside.

As you walk through the pretty streets look out, among the ice cream outlets and crêperies, for the 16th-century town hall, which has a façade of mullioned windows, a lovely Renaissance courtyard and, inside, a museum of Nativity scene figurines *(santons)*. There's also a 12th-century church, Église St-Vincent, partly carved out of the rock, with a Lanterne des Morts tower (the lamp was lit when someone died) and windows designed by the 20th-century stained glass master Max Ingrand.

Don't miss Val d'Enfer, at the foot of the village, is a spectacular gorge of wild rocks and caves, where you can see the Cathédrale des Images, a huge cave with a sound and light show.

RATINGS			
Historic interest	●	●	●
Photo stops	●	●	● ●

BASICS

⊞ 431 M13 🛈 Maison du Roi, 13520, tel 04 90 54 34 39; daily 9–7, Apr–end Sep; 9–12.30, 2–6 rest of year www.lesbauxdeprovence.com

TIP

● In summer, the parking areas can be full and the access road closed. No parking is allowed on the surrounding roads. It is best to visit early in the morning or at sundown.

The famous Carlton Hotel, in Cannes

CANNES

🔲 432 P13 ℹ️ Palais des Festivals, 1 boulevard de la Croisette, 06403, tel 04 93 39 24 53; daily 9–8, Jun–end Sep; 9–7, rest of year 🚉 Cannes
www.cannes.fr
www.cannes-festival.fr

THE SIGHTS

Cannes is a fairly small town with a big reputation. Its name conjures up luxury, glitz and big money, an image stemming partly from the International Film Festival held here in May, but also from its impeccable pedigree as an aristocratic winter resort. Be warned that you should make reservations a long way ahead for any hotel in Cannes, whether budget or de luxe—and don't even think about it during the film festival.

The lively hub of activity is the wide promenade la Croisette, which runs around the beautiful curve of the bay beside a sandy beach, most of which is divided up into pay-to-use or private sections. The latter are largely for the use of guests at the pre-war hotels on the other side of the boulevard. La Croisette begins at the Palais des Festivals et des Congrès, where you can see the handprints of film stars in the concrete of the plaza in front, although most are now a few decades old. Lined by designer shops, the promenade is especially attractive at night thanks to floodlighting.

Inland, rue d'Antibes is the narrow main shopping street, with boutiques, jewellers and art specialists. West of La Croisette is a more 'real' Cannes, with a relaxed air and lower prices. The esplanade La Pantiero, with its cropped plane trees, attracts strollers and boules players, and there are hundreds of café tables. Farther west still is Le Suquet, the small, older area of narrow lanes that was fortified by the monks of the Îles de Lérins.

CARCASSONNE
The medieval Cité is the largest fortified town in Europe and never fails to amaze.

The old walled city of Carcassonne (the Cité) takes your breath away. Thanks to its elevated position, if you visit late in the day, the walls and turrets are often bathed in the soft, red glow of the setting sun.

More than 3 million visitors a year pass through the city's gates. Once inside, many visitors are content to stroll the narrow lanes lined with the inevitable souvenir shops interspersed with boutiques selling high-quality gifts and local produce. In the bars and restaurants around place Marcou the prices are not as high as you might expect.

The more energetic can explore the Château Comtal and the inner western ramparts *(guided tour only)*, dating from the 12th century. In July and August, jousting displays are sometimes held in the Lices Hautes, the grassy area between the inner and outer ramparts. The Romanesque and Gothic St-Nazaire basilica has beautiful stained-glass windows and statues, and is the venue for occasional concerts.

The lower town, the Ville Basse or Bastide St-Louis, has a partly pedestrianized area, fine town houses and excellent small shops. Its central square, place Carnot, is the main meeting place and has been the site of the market *(Tue, Thu, Sat mornings)* since the Middle Ages. For older children, the Im@ginarium brings the Middle Ages to life in a multimedia/interactive show within the Cité, while for small children an old-fashioned merry-go-round is outside the Porte Narbonnaise.

RATINGS			
Historic interest	●	●	●
Photo stops	●	●	● ●
Walkability	●	●	●

BASICS

🔲 430 J14 ℹ️ 15 boulevard Camille Pelletan (opposite place Gambetta), 11890, tel 04 68 10 24 30; daily 9–7, Jul, Aug; Mon–Sat 9–6, Sun 9–1, rest of year 🚉 Carcassonne 🔲 Château Comtal tour: adult €6.10, under 18 free www.carcassonne-tourisme.com (in English and French; pictures, photos and information on the town's sights)

TIPS

● The roads enclosing the Ville Basse form a busy one-way system, and parking can be difficult in season, even though there are several large parking areas around the exterior.
● A good place for a walk is by the Canal du Midi—a UNESCO listed World Heritage Site.

Taking to the water in Castres

The old town bridge at Céret

Châteauneuf-du-Pape has been produced since the 14th century

CASTRES

🏠 430 J13 ℹ️ 3 rue Milhau Ducommun, 81100, tel 05 63 62 63 62; Mon–Sat 9.30–12.30, 1.30–6.30, Sun 10.30–noon, 2.30–5, Jul, Aug; Mon–Sat 9.30–12.30, 2.30–6, rest of year (closed Sun Nov–end Jan). Closed 1 Jan, 1 May, 1 Nov and 25 Dec
🚉 Castres
www.ville-castres.fr

Castres is a pleasant town with something of a Venetian feel. It makes an ideal stop on the route between Albi and Toulouse (once you have passed the extensive industrial estates that surround the town and negotiated the busy approach roads). The small historic part of town is easily explored in an hour or two, and you can see an impressive collection of Spanish paintings in the Musée Goya (daily 10–6, Jul, Aug; Tue–Sat 9–12, 2–6, Sun 10–12, 2–6, rest of year). This is the town's top sight and has France's second most important collection of Spanish paintings outside the Louvre. The works range from the Middle Ages to today, and include three Goya paintings and an important series of his engravings. The collection is in the beautiful Hôtel de Ville, the former Bishop's Residence, designed by Mansart. The small but exquisite garden was designed by André Le Nôtre.

Ask at the tourist office for a leaflet detailing 11 sights in a tour with an easy-to-follow map.

The walls of the old houses on the stretch of river along the eastern bank of the Agout descend directly into the water on either side of ancient stairwells, and the river contains many fish. From June to September, a passenger barge, Le Coche d'Eau, makes a 45-minute round trip between the quay opposite the tourist office and La Gourjade park.

CÉRET

🏠 430 J15 ℹ️ 1 avenue Georges Clemenceau, 66400, tel 04 68 87 00 53; Mon–Sat 9–12.30, 2–7, Sun 10–1 Jul, Aug; Mon–Fri 9–12, 2–5, rest of year www.ot-ceret.fr

Céret nestles close to the Spanish border, in a sheltered spot on the northern slopes of the Pyrenees. Its exceptionally mild climate produces mimosa and almond blossom in January and cherries (for which it is famous) by mid-April. The pretty town is an ideal base for hiking in the Pyrenees.

The unmissable Musée d'Art Moderne, on boulevard Maréchal Joffre (daily 10–7, mid-Jun to mid-Sep; Wed–Mon 10–6, rest of year), was created in 1950 to collect together some of the works by artists drawn to the region because of the special Mediterranean light. The stunning collection now includes pieces by Matisse, Miró, Dufy, Cocteau, Dalí, Picasso and Braque. The museum also hosts temporary exhibitions.

CHÂTEAUNEUF-DU-PAPE

🏠 431 M12 ℹ️ Place Portail, 84230, tel 04 90 83 71 08; Mon–Sat 9.30–7, Sun 10–1, 2–6, summer; Mon–Sat 9.30–12.30, 2–6, rest of year

Châteauneuf is a picture-book restored medieval fortified village, handsomely set on a riverside. The village, a popular visitor destination, is totally dedicated to producing, providing tastings of, and selling its celebrated red wines. The tourist office has a list of vineyards and can arrange tours and tastings for you. One of the winemakers has a free museum in an old wine cellar in the heart of the village: Musée Père Anselme is all about traditional winemaking techniques, with displays of tools and equipment. At the end of your visit you can taste the wine and, of course, buy a couple of bottles to take home.
Don't miss There are lovely views from the hilltop vantage point of the castle ruins.

ÈZE

🏠 432 Q13 ℹ️ Place Général de Gaulle, 06360 (on N7 below medieval village), tel 04 93 41 26 00; Mon–Sat 9–7, Sun 2–7, May–end Sep; Mon–Sat 9–6.30, Sun 9.30–1, 2–6.30, rest of year
🚉 Èze Bord de Mer
www.eze-riviera.com

Èze is one of the most perfect examples of a village perché, a fortified medieval village perched on a rocky hilltop for defensive reasons. It is also one of the easiest of all the perched villages to visit, being beside the Corniche Moyenne, midway between Nice and Monaco.

The village is poised 430m (1,410ft) high on the summit of a soaring pinnacle that looks straight down onto the sea. It is exceptionally pretty, with its narrow medieval lanes and steps. Its proximity to some of the smartest coastal towns has made Èze a chic, arty, sometimes crowded little place, yet on the whole it remains surprisingly uncommercialized and very rewarding to visit. There are a couple of pricey luxurious hotels in the old village.

Walk up the steep road to enter the medieval village through an imposing 14th-century fortified gateway, which takes you into a maze of old lanes dotted with flowers. The café terrace of the Eza hotel is open to the public for drinks and has wonderful views. If you head upwards, following signs to Jardin Exotique, you'll reach the ruins of a fortress, which is surrounded by an unusual cactus garden and has unforgettable views along the Riviera coast.

THE SIGHTS

The Fondation Maeght

An old working water wheel, at Fontaine-de-Vaucluse

FONDATION MAEGHT

✚ 432 P13 • Route de Pass-Prest, 06750 St-Paul de Vence, tel 04 93 32 81 63; daily 10–7, Jul–end Sep; 10–6, Oct; 10–12.30, 2.30–6, Oct–end Jun

🎫 Adult 11, child (10–18) 9, under 10 free

www.fondation-maeght.com

This large and unusual art gallery in an interesting modern building has one of Europe's leading collections of 20th-century and contemporary art. It is hidden away down a country lane in Mediterranean pinewoods, outside the perched village of St-Paul-de-Vence, close to Nice.

The gallery was launched by Marguerite and Aimé Maeght, successful art dealers, in 1964 to house their private art collection and as a memorial to their son, who died in childhood. It is still financed entirely by their foundation.

The building, designed by Catalan architect Josep-Lluis Sert, is a low, simple, mainly brick structure with a pair of strange curved shapes resting on the roof. Several large sculptures stand in the grounds and there are quasi-natural outdoor spaces devoted to particular artists, including Giacometti, Joan Miró and Marc Chagall. These artists also feature prominently inside the building, together with Bonnard, Kandinsky, Calder and Léger, among many others. The

Greenery at Fontaine de Vaucluse

interior is gloriously lit from above. A tiny chapel contains Georges Braque's *White Bird on a Mauve Background* in memory of the Maeghts' son. Other highlights include the Miró *Labyrinth* with sculptures and ceramics, Chagall mosaics, and stained glass by Braque.

FONTAINE-DE-VAUCLUSE

✚ 431 M12 🛈 Chemin de la Fontaine, 84800, tel 04 90 20 32 22; times vary

This pretty little riverside village is named after the nearby spring that has long fascinated both visitors and locals because the actual source of the water has never been located. Water gushes from beneath a sheer cliff into a strange, still and very deep pool, surrounded by rocks and vegetation and often by a dense, dripping spray. At its height, the Fontaine-de-Vaucluse is among the world's most powerful natural flows of fresh water: 630 million cubic metres (22,260 million cubic feet) of water emerge from it each year, flowing down the narrow valley to become the river Sorgue.

In springtime, the water at full flow is truly spectacular. In summer, the flow is less and the number of visitors greater, so come in March, April or May for maximum effect. To reach the spring, walk for around 15 minutes along a signposted, traffic-free lane which has several

stalls selling souvenirs. On the way there's an underground museum of rocks and minerals, Le Monde Souterrain de Norbert Casteret, which deals vividly with efforts to discover the source of the water. In the village, there's a perfectly restored traditional paper mill which, in its day, made use of the fast-flowing water.

FONTFROIDE

✚ 430 K14• RD613, 11100, Narbonne, tel 04 68 45 11 08; 9.30–6, mid-Jul–end Aug; 10–noon, 1.45–5.30, Apr to mid-Jul, Sep, Oct; 10–noon, 1.45–5, rest of year 🎫 Adult 6.25, child (7–15) 3 🎧 Guided tours all year in English, German and Spanish

www.fontfroide.com

The Abbaye de Fontfroide, a 10-minute drive southwest of Narbonne (see page 189) in *Le Pays Cathar* (Cathar country), is one of the largest and best preserved Cistercian abbeys in Europe. It was founded by Benedictines at the end of the 11th century in a wooded area with its own water source. The abbey was affiliated to the Cistercian order in 1145, and was a bastion of orthodoxy during the period of the Albigensian crusade against the Cathar heretics in the 13th century. It became prosperous, with 20,000 sheep and agricultural land spanning Roussillon and Catalonia.

The 12th-century abbey church of ochre sandstone stands at the end of a little road edged with scrub and cypress trees. It is as big as a cathedral and is known for its chapter house and cloister. You can explore various gardens, including the monks' kitchen garden and the *jardin des senteurs*, planted with sweet-smelling flowers. Visit between May and September to see 30,000 bushes in the rose garden in bloom.

Stepped and terraced buildings of the small town of Gordes

Kayaking on the river at the Gorges du Tarn

Buying local produce at a market in Grasse

FRÉJUS

432 P13 325 rue Jean-Jaurès, 83600, tel 04 94 51 83 83; Mon–Sat 9–7, Sun 10–noon, 3–6, Jul, Aug; Mon–Sat 9–noon, 2–6, Sun 10–noon, 3–6, rest of year Fréjus/St-Raphael www.ville-frejus.fr

Fréjus, on the east bank of the river Argens estuary and its flood plain, is an animated and long-established little beach resort, popular with families. It is close to the Esterel hills and makes a good base for coastal drives.

The middle of the town, 3km (2 miles) inland, consists of 17th- to 20th-century districts around an old quarter of narrow streets, many now traffic free or with restricted traffic. At the heart of the old town is the lovely Cité Épiscopale (cathedral close), with a medieval cathedral, cloisters and fifth-century baptistery. Nearby, there are considerable Roman ruins, including the remnants of an aqueduct, an army base, a fortified quay and a small amphitheatre, where concerts are still held. Out of town, on the D4, there is a surprising African mosque in red stone, a perfect replica of a mosque in Mali, built by African sailors based at Fréjus in the 1920s. Other attractions out of town include a zoo and Aquatica, a huge water park on the N98.

Fréjus is big on events and festivals: As well as a market on Wednesdays and Saturdays, there are special summer markets, a *bravade* (religious festival and procession) at Easter, and a grape festival in August.

GORDES

431 M12 Place du Château, 84220, tel 04 90 72 02 75; daily 9–12.30, 2–6.30, summer; 9–noon, 2–6, rest of year www.gordes-village.com www.gordes.enprovence.com

The houses appear to be built one on top of the other as they climb the steep hill on which this picturesque old village stands. Medieval Gordes, in the southern part of the Vaucluse plateau, was abandoned during the early 20th century, but was quickly discovered and restored by artists and well-to-do visitors. Now a rather chic place to have a second home, it is popular with media people. As a result, it is well served with shops and restaurants at the expensive end of the scale.

Narrow stairways and covered passages wind steeply around the hill, which is topped by a medieval chateau fancifully restored by modern artist Victor Vasarely. It now contains a gallery of the work of another modern artist, Pol Mara. Around the village are numerous *bories*, windowless dome-shaped drystone dwellings, many of them centuries old. They were used as shepherds' huts, storage sheds, animal shelters and seasonal or even permanent residences; some were inhabited until the 19th century. To see a restored museum village of these structures, follow the signs to *Village des Bories,* which is off the D2, 4km (2.5 miles) from Gordes. Also nearby is the Cistercian abbey of Sénanque.

GORGES DU TARN

See pages 316–317.

GRASSE

432 P13 Palais de Congrès, 22 cours Honoré Cresp, 06130, tel 04 93 36 66 66; Mon–Sat 9–7, Sun 9–1, 2–6, Jul–end Sep; Mon–Sat 9–12.30, 2–6, Oct–end Jun www.grasse-riviera.com

Grasse, about 17km (10 miles) inland from Cannes, is known as the 'Perfume Capital of the World', as the essences prepared here are turned into perfumes for the great fashion houses such as Dior and Chanel. Although a tour of a perfume factory is why many visitors come, the town is worth visiting in its own right and makes a good pause on the *Route Napoléon*. There's an evocative restored medieval quarter, with narrow traffic-free streets and many fine old mansions. The terrace at the top of the old quarter has great views of the sea and flower-filled Provençal countryside.

Long-established as a leather-tanning town, Grasse specialized in luxury gloves. The perfume industry arose by chance, when there was a brief fashion for scented gloves in the 16th century. The essences for perfuming the leather were made using local jasmine, lavender and other flowers that grew abundantly around the town. Glove-making declined but the 17th and 18th centuries saw perfume-making go on to an industrial scale. The three major perfumeries are Molinard, Galimard and Fragonard. All have tours in English, where you can learn how perfume is made.

Perfume from Fragonard, at Grasse

Canoeing in the spectacular
Gorges du Verdon

The terraced gardens of Villa
Sainte-Clare, overlooking Hyères

The observatory at the summit
of Mont Ventoux

GORGES DU VERDON

🔲 432 N13 🛈 Hôtel-Dieu, rue de la
Bourgade, Moustiers-Sainte-Marie,
04360 (western edge of canyon),
tel 04 92 74 67 84; daily 10–12.30, 2–7,
summer; 2–4.30, rest of year
www.ville-moustiers-sainte-marie.fr

At the foot of the Maritime Alps
in inland Provence is one of
the most spectacular natural
phenomena in France, known as
the *Grand Canyon,* mainland
Europe's deepest river gorge.
Sheer cliffs rise 700m (2,300ft)
above the flowing river, with
panoramic views down the
21km (13-mile) length of this
rocky corridor. A winding, difficult
road—little more than a country
lane for most of the way—runs
along the top of each side of the
ravine. A succession of
belvédères close to the edge
provide fantastic viewpoints that
give a broad look along the
ravine and across the surrounding rocky terrain.

The road on the south side, the
Corniche Sublime, has grander
scenery and better viewpoints—
the best stretch being the
Balcons de la Mescla. The
north side is also extremely
impressive, but the road is more
hair-raising and there are fewer
viewpoints. At either end of the
gorge are interesting small towns,
Castellane and pretty Moustiers-
Sainte-Marie.

The drive is best done outside
the peak months of July and
August, when nose-to-tail traffic
crawls along the road. In fact,
there's no great advantage in
driving the whole route—a short
drive along the Corniche Sublime
is impressive enough. For keen
walkers, there's a path running
the full length of the canyon at
the foot of the gorge.

The first survey of the gorge
was carried out in 1905. The
gorge was designated a Parc
Naturel Régional in 1997.

HYÈRES

🔲 432 N14 🛈 Forum du Casino, 3
avenue Ambroise Thomas, 83400,
tel 04 94 01 84 50; daily 8–8, Jul, Aug;
Mon–Fri 9–6, Sat 10–4, rest of year
🚉 Hyères
www.ot-hyeres.fr

Hyères sits on a fertile part of the
Provençal coast and is known for
its vast quantities of flowering
shrubs and palm trees. This has
led to its alternative name,
Hyères-les-Palmières.

The atmospheric old quarter
rises on a hill set well back from
the sea. A fortified Gothic
gateway stands at the entrance
and Italianate buildings, several
with Renaissance doorways, line
steep lanes. Place Massillon is
the focal point, a triangular-
shaped market place alongside
12th-century Tour St-Blaise.
Other remnants of the medieval
period include the Église St-Paul,
with its Romanesque tower, and
the Église St-Louis, part of a
former Franciscan monastery.

At the top of the hill, in Parc
St-Bernard, are the extensive
vestiges of a chateau, with
superb views. Next to the park is
the Villa de Noailles where, in the
1920s, the Noailles family gave
parties attended by illustrious
guests such as Picasso and
Salvador Dali. Southeast of the
town, the Olbius Riquier tropical
gardens, set around a Moorish-
style villa, have palms and cacti,
an animal enclosure and a
greenhouse with exotic plants
(daily 9–dusk).
South of town,
along a narrow
sandbar 4km
(2.5 miles)
long, is Giens,
where you
can catch a
ferry to one of
the Îles d'Or
(Golden
Isles).

MENTON

See page 326.

MONT VENTOUX

🔲 431 M12 🛈 Rue Portail Olivier,
Bédoin, 84410, tel 04 90 65 63 95

Rising high above the rest of the
region, the neatly conical summit
of Ventoux makes a distinctive,
mysterious landmark. In spring
and winter, the 1,909m
(6,262ft) peak is covered in
snow; at other times of the year
it is often shrouded in cloud
while the rest of Provence basks
in sunshine.

There is something irresistibly
compelling about Ventoux, and
many people have wanted to get
closer to this 'Giant of Provence'.
The 14th-century Italian poet
Petrarch was the first person to
write about his ascent of the
mountain, which took him two
days. Now, there is a tarmac road
all the way to the summit. The
Tour de France bicycle race
sometimes includes this road. It is
the most feared section of the
race, and one where a competitor
died of heart failure in 1967.

At the top, the winds are rarely
light and the temperature is
generally around 11°C (51°F)
lower than at the foot of the
mountain. Check the weather
forecast and don't go up in
stormy or windy weather, or without adequate preparation. The
view from the top is worth the
ascent, as it takes in the Alps, the
Rhône Valley, the Vaucluse
plateau, the Cévennes and
the Mediterranean.

*A granite memorial,
commemorating
a bicyclist who
died on Mont
Ventoux*

Place de la Comédie, in the stylish old town (above).
A statue in the Antigone district (right)

MONTPELLIER

A dynamic city of high-tech industry, bold new architecture and buzzing student life.

Montpellier's immediate appeal lies in the whiteness of its buildings (it is sometimes referred to as 'the white city'), the modernity of its architecture, the spaciousness of its squares, parks and walkways, and its multitude of fountains. The city is the ultimate young person's destination, offering 24-hour entertainment, especially during the hot summer days and nights, and festivals that cover cinema, dance, music and drama.

SEEING THE TOWN

People congregate around place de la Comédie in the fashionable old town, where elegant mansions and museums line narrow winding streets. The 17th- and 18th-century promenade du Peyrou is an impressive ensemble of a triumphal arch, a regal statue (of Louis XIV) and the water tower at the head of the aqueduct. The tourist office organizes guided tours that explore some sights and buildings not normally open to the public. They include a climb to the top of the triumphal arch and a visit to the university's faculty of medicine. Getting around Montpellier is easy thanks to the inexpensive, quiet and sleekly designed trams. Vill' à Vélo, on rue Maguelone, rents out bicycles, tandems and motorized cycles, and offers secure parking for them with 1,200 attachment points throughout the city. This is an excellent way to see Montpellier as there are 120km (75 miles) of bicycle routes, 11km (7 miles) of which follow the tramway. Cars are positively discouraged by high parking charges.

THE ARTS

Montpellier has a policy of making the arts available to as many people as possible, with very reasonably priced tickets. In the summer you will be spoiled for choice with the Montpellier Dance Festival, circus performers in June and the Radio France modern and classical music festival in July The city also has an opera house, where enjoying the music is more important than dressing up. Montpellier's best art gallery, and one of the biggest in France, is the Musée Fabre, at 39 boulevard Bonne Nouvelle (*closed for renovation until 2006*), with works by 16th- to 18th-century painters, contemporary paintings, ceramics and sculpture.

THE SIGHTS

RATINGS	
Cultural interest	●●●○
Shopping	●●●○
Walkability	●●○○

BASICS

🚩 430 L13 🛈 Place de la Comédie, 30 allée Jean de Lattre de Tassigny, 34000, tel 04 67 60 60 60;
Mon–Fri 9–7, Sat 10–6, Sun 10–1, 2–5
🚊 Montpellier
www.ot-montpellier.fr (information on guided tours, festivals, museums and the City Pass)

TIPS

● A City Pass admits two for the price of one to certain visitor attractions.
● A flea market is held under the aqueduct on Saturdays.

Marseille

This ancient yet dynamic city is a Mediterranean melting pot, with an intriguing atmosphere and exhilarating joie de vivre.

The Cathédrale de la Major soars above the cars

Relaxing in the sunshine in the heart of Marseille

View of Marseille, looking across the port

RATINGS	
Cultural interest	● ● ●
Good for food (fish)	● ● ● ●
Historic interest	● ● ● ●

BASICS

✚ 431 M13 ℹ 4 La Canebière, 13001, tel 04 91 13 89 00; Mon–Sat 9–7, Sun 10–5; longer hours in peak season

🚆 Gare St-Charles

www.marseille-tourisme.com (in English and French, with information on sights, guided tours and the City Pass)

SEEING MARSEILLE

On the west coast of Provence, close to the Camargue, Marseille is an energetic city with a long history. It is France's premier Mediterranean sea gateway and has a distinctive mix of ethnic and cultural influences. The city has plenty to offer, including many museums and art galleries, and boat trips to offshore islands. There are two Métro lines. The grandly beautiful Vieux Port (Old Port) and its surrounding streets form Marseille's focal point. Here are bars, art galleries, music venues and scores of little restaurants. You can walk or drive the shore road a few minutes south from Le Vieux Port to the old-fashioned little harbour at Anse des Auffes, where bright fishing boats are pulled up in front of a choice of fish restaurants. And the city makes a good base for some out-of-town sightseeing on the western Provence coast. While there are areas where you should be careful, on the whole the 'crime and drugs' image of the city is exaggerated.

HIGHLIGHTS

VIEUX PORT

✚ 184 A3

Visitors and residents alike tend to gravitate to the large, rectangular, westward-facing Old Port. It is fortified, enclosed by Italianate 17th-century quays and surrounded by pale stone façades and red roofs. Thousands of boats jostle one another. Steep hillsides slope down to the waterside, overlooked on the south side by the Fort St-Nicolas defences *(no entry to visitors)* and the powerfully fortified Basilique St-Victor, which has a 5th-century crypt. North of the Vieux Port, the extensive modern docks extend along the shore.

A massive gilded Madonna crowns the belfry of the basilica of Notre-Dame-de-la-Garde

THE SIGHTS

MUSÉE D'HISTOIRE DE MARSEILLE

🕂 184 B2 • Square Belsunce, Centre Bourse, 13001 ☎ 04 91 90 42 22
🕐 Mon–Sat noon–7 🎫 Adult 2.2, under 5 free

The fascinating Musée d'Histoire de Marseille stands alongside the
Jardin des Vestiges. It sets out the complete history of the city, with a
3rd-century Roman ship as its focal point. The Jardin des Vestiges
is an archaeological site now transformed into a pretty garden. A
walkway enables an overview of the ruins of the original Greek
ramparts, traces of a roadway and parts of the dock as it was in the
1st century AD. Many of the items found in the excavations are now
in the museum.

LE PANIER

🕂 184 A2

Stepped alleys and rundown tenements with washing lines strung
between windows climb the Panier hill from the docks. In 1943
the occupying Nazi regime destroyed 2,000 buildings here and
expelled or murdered around 25,000 residents. Among the buildings
that survived is the 16th-century Maison Diamanté, so-called for a
façade of stones carved into diamond-like points. It houses the
Musée du Vieux Marseille *(closed until 2006)*, with sections

*Fresh produce at the daily fish
market on the quai des Belges*

● Street parking is difficult so use the big, reasonably priced parking areas. There are five in the Vieux Port area.

● The monthly *Marseille Poche* and weekly *Ventilo* list hundreds of events in the city.

● *Bouillabaisse*, the classic Provençal fish stew, can only be made correctly in Marseille according to gourmets, so try it in a restaurant on the streets around le Vieux Port.

dedicated to Provençal furnishings, *santons* (Nativity scene figurines), and the esoteric playing cards called the Tarot Marseillaise. Another survival, in Grand Rue, is the 16th-century Hôtel de Cabre. After World War II, it was taken apart and rebuilt in a different street, which is why it says Rue de la Bonneterie on the wall. At the top of the Le Panier district is the former 17th-century hospice called La Vieille Charité, a rectangle of lovely, three-floor arcaded galleries, set around a large courtyard with a small baroque chapel. Originally a place of detention and shelter for vagrants, La Vieille Charité now hosts art exhibitions and the Musée de l'Archéologie Mediterranéenne (*Tue–Sun 11–6, Jun–end Sep; 10–5, rest of year*). Beyond is the 19th-century neo-Byzantine Cathédrale de la Major, with its domes and striped façade. The sad, damaged little building beside it is the 12th-century Romanesque Ancienne Cathédrale de la Major (*closed*).

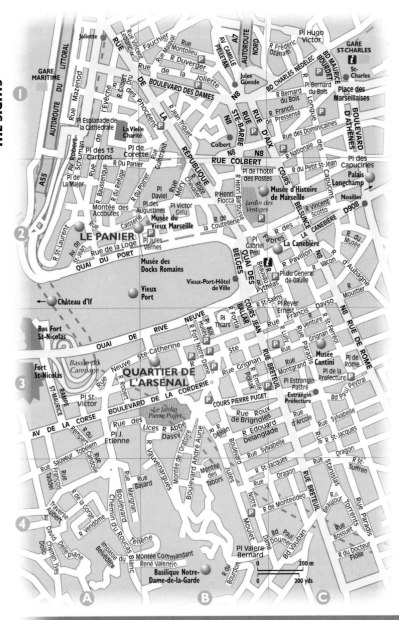

The Marché aux Capucins (left)

LA CANEBIÈRE
✚ 184 B2

Leading through the heart of the city in a majestic straight line directly from the Vieux Port's quai des Belges is the broad central avenue called La Canebière. Built in the 17th century, the street was for a long time rather seedy, but today it is an inspiring sight. Most of the main shopping streets are turnings off La Canebière.

MUSÉE CANTINI
✚ 184 C3 • 19 rue Grignan, 13006
☎ 04 91 54 77 75 🕙 Tue–Sun 11–6, Jun–end Sep; 10–5, rest of year
🎫 Adult €3, under 5 free
🚇 Estangin-Préfecture

This modern art gallery, with a good Surrealist collection and works by Matisse, Dufy, Miró, Kandinsky and Picasso, was a private home in the 17th century.

MUSÉE DES DOCKS ROMAINS
✚ 184 A2 • 28 place Vivaux, 13002
☎ 04 91 91 24 62 🕙 Tue–Sun 11–6, Jun–end Sep; 10–5, rest of year
🎫 Adult €2, under 5 free

At the foot of the Le Panier district are several important relics and museums of the Classical period. The Musée des Docks Romains (Museum of the Roman Docks) displays a collection of first- to third-century Roman objects discovered during post-war rebuilding work. It has a good collection of Roman *dolia* (large ceramic storage jars).

NOTRE-DAME-DE-LA-GARDE
✚ 184 B4

About 1km (half a mile) south of the old port is the hilltop Notre-Dame-de-la-Garde, a 19th-century basilica with a huge gilded Virgin, strikingly lit at night, believed by locals to give divine protection to the city.

QUARTIER DE L'ARSENAL
✚ 184 A3

Close to the port (to the south), behind quai de Rive Neuve, is the grid of streets called the Quartier de l'Arsenal. Once a notorious shipyards area where galley slaves were housed among the workshops, it is now full of restaurants.

PALAIS LONGCHAMP
✚ Off 184 C2 • 142 boulevard Longchamp, 13004 ☎ Palais: 04 91 14 59 50; Musée des Beaux-Arts: 04 91 62 21 17 🕙 Musée des Beaux-Arts: Tue–Sun, 11–6, Jun–end Sep; 10–5, rest of year 🚇 Longchamp-Cinq Avenues

This palace is home to the Musée d'Histoire Naturelle *(Tue–Sun 10–5)*, which has a zoo behind it, and the Musée des Beaux-Arts. The latter has 16th- and 17th-century French and Italian paintings, a room devoted to local architect, sculptor and painter Pierre Puget, and another room dedicated to local cartoonist Honoré Daumier.

CHÂTEAU D'IF
✚ Off 184 A2 ☎ 04 91 59 02 30 🕙 Daily 9.30–6.30, May–end Sep; Tue–Sun 9.30–5.30, rest of year 🎫 Adult €4, under 18 free ⛴ Ferries leave from quai des Belges

It's a 15-minute ferry journey to the island of If, with its nightmarish prison fortress, made famous by Alexandre Dumas in *The Count of Monte Cristo*. The journey gives great views of the city and guided tours take you to the cells once occupied by the 'Man in the Iron Mask' and other aristocratic prisoners.

BACKGROUND

Founded as the trading port of Massalia by the Greeks 2,600 years ago, Marseille has been the western Mediterranean's main port ever since. After the Roman conquest of Provence, the port was sacked and stripped of its fleet, although excavations reveal that Marseille remained a busy town. A period of decline followed the Saracen and other raids of the 7th century, which curtailed all Mediterranean trade. By the 11th century, the city had revived and continued to develop until the plague arrived in 1720, killing 50,000 residents. By the 1760s, the city was the major port trading with the Caribbean and Latin America. The republican zeal of Marseille's oppressed workers proved a backbone of the Revolution, the city giving its name to the new national anthem, *La Marseillaise*, even though it was composed in Alsace. The city sustained extensive damage during World War II. In the second half of the 20th century, large numbers of people from Africa, particularly North Africa, moved to the city. Today, Marseille has a total population of around one million.

THE SIGHTS

Monaco

Big yachts and big money epitomize the tiny principality, which is also the site of one of Europe's best aquariums.

Luxury boats in the marina

Shop in the most exclusive boutiques in Monaco

The Grimaldi coat of arms on the Palais du Prince

RATINGS	
Cultural interest	● ● ●
Photo stops	● ● ● ●
Shopping (luxury)	● ● ● ●

BASICS

✚ 432 Q13 ✇ 2a boulevard des Moulins, 98000, tel 92 16 61 16 (country code 377); Mon–Sat 9–7, Sun 10–noon

🚉 Monaco–Monte Carlo

❓ Tourist information kiosks are set up at the railway station and main sights in summer.

www.visitmonaco.com (information on the major sights, and you can order a free brochure on the principality)

SEEING MONACO

By a historical anomaly, this beautiful patch of rock hanging off the Provençal coast never became part of France. Instead, it has grown into a super-rich city, tax haven and millionaires' playground. It's a place that deserves to be seen, if only for the clever way it has made use of the limited space available. To accommodate the 32,000 people who live here (only 6,000 of whom are native Monégasques), the mini-state has expanded upwards in the form of skyscrapers and outwards into the sea on artificial platforms. Some streets, sitting almost on top of one another, are connected by lifts. Despite being just under 2km sq (0.75sq miles) in area, Monaco has several districts. Monaco-Ville is the original town on Le Rocher (the Rock); Monte Carlo is the larger new town, with a beach; La Condamine, the harbour district, lies between Monaco-Ville and Monte Carlo; on the steep slope between Monaco-Ville and the French border is the residential district Moneghetti; and Fontvieille is the area west of Monaco-Ville, which has been artifically extended into the sea.

HIGHLIGHTS

MONACO-VILLE

A bronze statue of Princess Grace

Walk through the pretty, spotlessly clean, narrow streets, with their well-kept, pastel-shaded houses to get to Monaco's cathedral. It has a Louis Bréa altarpiece, some fine paintings and the tombs of all Monaco's past princes as well as that of Princess Grace. The main sight in Monaco-Ville, however, is the small, but sturdily fortified 13th- to 17th-century Palais du Prince (*daily 9.30–6.30, Jun–end Sep; 10–5 Oct*), whose rooms are adorned with frescoes, tapestries and paintings. The palace also contains a museum devoted to Napoleon, with an assortment of objects, including one of his hats. In the courtyard you can watch the guardsmen, in their elegant uniforms (white in summer and black in winter), perform the Changing of the Guard (*daily at 11.55*). The Musée Océanographique, carved into the edge of the Rock, has superb aquariums holding 350 species (*daily 9–8, Jul, Aug; 9–7, Apr–end Jun, Sep; 9.30–7, Oct, Mar; 10–6, Nov–end Feb*). There are fantastic views from the terrace.

MONTE CARLO

East of the Rock is Monte Carlo, a glitzy area of restaurants, luxurious hotels, beautifully kept palm and flower gardens, and the lavishly ostentatious Belle-Époque Casino. The Salons Européens and Salons Américains (*daily, from noon*) in the Casino have slot machines, roulette and gaming tables. To get into the more lavish Salons Privés (*daily, from 3pm*), which are the real Casino, not much frequented by ordinary visitors, you have to pay a fee and be appropriately dressed. A grand staircase goes down to a money-no-object nightclub. For those who have not blown all their cash at the gaming tables, there's plenty of expensive shopping for jewellery and designer clothes around the casino and on boulevard des Moulins.

FONTVIEILLE

Fontvieille is a residential and business quarter standing on artificial platforms of rock, with a yachting marina alongside. Its Roseraie Princesse Grace is an exquisite rose garden with more than 3,500 varieties, dedicated to Princess Grace of Monaco, the former film star Grace Kelly, who died in a car accident in 1982. There are several museums here—the Musée des Timbres et des Monnaies (stamps and currency), the Musée Naval (model ships), and the Collection des Voitures Anciennes (gleaming classic cars).

BACKGROUND

Monaco was originally a medieval perched fortress village, its castle a possession of Barbarossa. In the 13th century, the powerful aristocratic Grimaldi family of Genoa acquired the Rock and made it their headquarters, refashioning themselves as the Princes of Monaco. Under Napoleon, most of the many independent fiefdoms of Provence were incorporated by force into France, but the Grimaldi influence in Provence and Italy was so strong that Napoleon decided to make an ally of the Grimaldis instead of seizing their lands. Monaco's income had come from high taxes on its domains, but the principality found a role for itself as a refuge for the aristocracy, and in the 19th century Prince Carlo III created the glamorous zone called Monte Carlo, where the casino raised more funds for the royal family. It did so well that taxes were eventually abolished.

Flowering cacti and tropical plants in the Jardin Exotique

TIPS

● Law enforcement is rigorous in Monaco, with 24-hour surveillance of the entire principality, including inside public buildings. All driving laws (and most other laws), road signs and drink-driving limits are the same in Monaco as in France.
● Unless you are into motor racing, don't come during the Monaco Grand Prix in the second week in May, when tens of thousands of visitors cram into the principality and many roads are closed.
● Near the Larvotto beach area is the Jardin Japonais, a Shinto garden and a quiet, meditative refuge from the glitz that is Monaco.

The baroque Hotel Negresco, on promenade des Anglais

NICE

The capital of the Riviera is a hectic town and an art lover's dream, with several major art galleries.

Nice was developed in stages by different civilizations, including the Ligurians, Greeks and Romans. It was part of Italy until 1860, evident by the beautiful Italianate architecture of the old quarter. Artists began to arrive in the 1920s and there are several important galleries.

ART AND HISTORY

At the western end of the stony beach, a handsome 19th-century mansion contains the town's prestigious Musée des Beaux-Arts *(Tue–Fri 10–6, Sat, Sun 10–1, 2–6)*. It has extensive collections of 17th- to 19th-century French and Italian paintings and sculpture. Close to the luxurious pink-domed Hotel Negresco, the Musée d'Art et d'Histoire *(Sat, Sun 10–1, 2–6)* traces the history of Nice through painting, sculpture, jewellery and tapestries. On the Paillon promenade that divides the old town from the new, there are several galleries, including the famously avant-garde Musée d'Art Moderne et d'Art Contemporain *(Wed–Mon 10–6)*, which has the definitive collection of works from the Nice school of 1960s modern artists, including Andy Warhol's *Campbell's Soup Can*. At the foot of Cimiez hill, the Musée Marc Chagall/Musée du Message Biblique *(Wed–Mon 10–6, Jul–end Sep; 10–5, rest of year)* has a phenomenal collection of Chagall's work, including stained glass, mosaics and vivid, dream-like canvases. Farther up the hill, the Musée Henri Matisse *(Wed–Mon 10–6, Apr– end Sep; 10–5, rest of year)* shows the artist's exquisite line drawings and vivid gouaches. Matisse and Dufy are both buried in the cemetery nearby.

VIEUX NICE

The old quarter is a delightful tangle of picturesque narrow lanes, with bars, restaurants and little shops. There are also some interesting small baroque churches.

ROMAN REMINDERS

The Cimiez hill has the ruins of a Roman city and a Musée Archeologique *(Wed–Mon 10–6, Apr–end Sep; Wed–Mon 10–5, rest of year; closed for a week in Dec)*. The oval arena is a venue for open-air performances.

In-line skating along the promenade des Anglais

RATINGS

Cultural interest	● ● ● ●
Photo stops	● ● ●
Shopping	● ● ●

BASICS

✚ 432 Q13 🛈 5 promenade des Anglais, 06000, tel 0892 707 407; Mon–Sat 8am–8pm, Sun 9–6, summer; Mon–Sat 9–6, rest of year 🚆 Nice
www.nice-coteazur.org
www.nicetourisme.com

TIPS

● Visit the big flower market *(Tue–Sun)* on Cours Saleya.
● Stroll the Nice waterfront along the Promenade des Anglais—a long, wide walkway edged by mimosa and palms.

Narbonne has a long history and a lively present

NARBONNE

✠ 430 K14 ❒ Place Salengro, 11100, tel 04 68 65 15 60; Mon–Sat 8–7, Sun 9.30–12.30, mid-Jun to mid-Sep; Mon–Sat 8.30–12, 2–6, rest of year
🚉 Narbonne
www.mairie-narbonne.fr

Narbonne is a delightful small town, with a Roman past. The Canal de la Robine, which links the town to the Canal du Midi on its north side, is a good place for a walk, with its pretty bridges, shady trees and picturesque walkways. There are several parking areas along its banks, and it's a good idea to park here and then walk the short distance to the middle of town.

Traffic-free lanes full of small shops lead off the quai Dillon on the canal's right bank. On the left bank is place de l'Hôtel de Ville, the town's central square, where a section of the Roman Via Domitia, which linked Italy to Spain, was revealed in 1997.

On the square's northern side is the Passage de l'Ancre, an entrance to the town's major historical attractions. These include the Cathédrale-St-Just-et-St-Pasteur and the Palais des Archevêques, which houses the Musée Archéologique and the Musée d'Art et d'Histoire *(daily 9.30–12.15, 2–6, Apr–end Sep; Tue–Sun 10–12, 2–5, rest of year)*. The latter has impressive collections of paintings, faïence and tapestries.

Less than an hour's drive to the south are some of the Mediterranean's sandiest beaches, at resorts such as Gruissan-Plage, Narbonne-Plage and St-Pierre-sur-Mer. At Sigean, farther round the coast towards Perpignan, is the Réserve Africaine de Sigean safari park, and only a 10-minute drive away is the Cistercian Abbaye de Fontfroide (see page 178).

NÎMES

A town of wonderful Roman remains, including one of the best-preserved amphitheatres of the ancient world.

RATINGS				
Historic interest	●	●	●	●	●
Photo stops	●	●	●		
Walkability	●	●	●		

BASICS
✠ 431 L13 ❒ 6 rue Auguste, 30000, tel 04 66 58 38 00; Mon–Fri 8.30–7, Sat 9–7, Sun 10–5, Oct–Easter; Mon–Fri 8–7, Sat 9–7, Sun 10–6, Easter–end Sep; Mon–Wed and Fri 8–8, Thu 8–9, Sat 9–7, Sun 10–6 Jul–end Aug 🚉 Nîmes www.ot-nimes.fr/ (in French and English, with guide to the sights and history of Nîmes, and accommodation)

TIPS
● Look out for the brass studs in the city's walkways, which bear the city symbol of a crocodile and a palm tree. ● At Les Arènes note that the topmost tier has no safety rails.

Nîmes and the Pont du Gard—the amazing Roman aqueduct 20km (12 miles) to the northeast (see page 190)—are rightly classed as 'must-see' destinations in the southeast. On the border of Languedoc and Provence, Nîmes is large enough to offer visitors plenty to see, yet small enough, especially in the tastefully preserved old city, to generate a feeling of intimacy.

The top attraction is Les Arènes, one of the best preserved arenas of the Roman world *(9–7, mid-Mar to mid-Oct; 10–5, rest of year)*. Once inside, you are free to climb up and over the tiers and wonder at the scale of the 2,000-year-old monument, which could hold more than 20,000 spectators in its heyday. Today it is used for bullfighting and events such as trade fairs. In winter, a dome-shaped inflatable cover is added.

A short walk away, the Maison Carrée dates from the 1st century BC and is the only fully preserved temple of the ancient world *(daily 10–7, summer; 10–6, rest of year)*. Inside, panels describe the history of the temple and there are some beautiful small examples of Roman mosaic work.

Overlooking the temple is the Musée d'Art Contemporain *(Tue–Sun 10–6)*. The spacious, bright Carrée d'Art (as it is known) displays art from the 1960s to the present. There are occasional touring exhibitions and an excellent third-floor bar/restaurant, with a terrace overlooking the Maison Carrée.

Don't miss There are excellent views over Nîmes from the Magne tower, in the beautiful Jardin de la Fontaine.

Place de la Loge, Perpignan

Diving into the Gard river, below the Roman aqueduct

ORANGE

➕ 431 M12 ℹ Cours A. Briand.
Summer office: place Frères Mounet, tel
04 90 34 70 88; Mon–Sat 9.30–7, Sun
and public hols 10–12.30, 2.30–6,
Apr–end Sep; Mon–Sat 10–1, 2–5, rest
of year 🚉 Orange
www.provence-orange.com

In medieval times, Orange was a
small independent principality,
but it became a possession of
the Dutch Prince of Nassau in
the 16th century, eventually
giving its name to the Dutch
ruling house. The town has a
splendidly preserved Roman
theatre, unique for its remarkable
surviving backdrop wall, 103m
(338ft) long. The Théâtre
Antique hosts many performances during the year, including
the town's world-class Chorègies,
an international choral music
festival. Rising behind the theatre
is the Colline St-Eutrope, which
gives a great view over Roman
and medieval Orange. The
theatre is in effect cut into the
side of this hill, and many Roman
objects were found here. Near
the theatre, the Musée Municipal
displays some of the important
Roman and medieval relics from
Orange, notably a Roman land
survey, carved on marble.
  On the north side of
town, standing rather
forlornly with traffic
whirling round it, is the
Arc de Triomphe, a
grandiose three-arched
monument erected in the
1st century BC to mark the
Romans' defeat of the local
tribes. Rich carvings on the
monument tell the story
of Augustus' victory and
the founding of the
Roman town here.

*A statue of
Augustus, at
Orange's
Théâtre Antique*

PERPIGNAN

➕ 430 K14 ℹ Palais des Congrès,
place Armand Lanoux, 66002, tel 04 68
66 30 30; Mon–Sat 9–7, Sun 10–4,
mid-Jun to mid-Sep; Mon–Sat 9–6, Sun
9–noon, rest of year 🚌 Free minibus
service follows a circular route around
some of the central parking areas and
pedestrian-only areas (not Sun or public
hols) 🚉 Perpignan
www.perpignantourisme.com

Perpignan, the capital of the
Roussillon region, has plenty to
draw visitors: a glorious
Mediterranean climate, the
region's largest shopping mall,
many events with a Catalan
accent, and an old quarter ideal
for a day's strolling. Going south,
the town is France's last major
conurbation on the Mediterranean
seaboard before Spain.
  Le Castillet, a small fort that
has become the town's emblem,
is now a museum of Catalan
folk arts and traditions *(Wed–
Mon 9–6, May–end Sep, 10–6,
rest of year)*.
  Quai Vauban is a good place
for a walk along the banks of the
river Basse; it passes place Arago
where you can find the busiest
bars and brasseries.
  The Palais des Rois de
Majorque is the star historical
attraction *(daily 10–6,
May–end Sep, 9–5, rest
of year)*. Built on a
small hill, it offers
good views of the
town from its
ramparts and from
the top of the
Homage tower. The
Cathédrale St-Jean
has a monumental
organ and a peal of 46
bells. Behind it is
Campo Santo,
the oldest
and largest
cloister
cemetery
in France.

PONT DU GARD

➕ 431 L12 ● Exhibition Centre, Pont
du Gard, 30210, tel 04 66 37 51 10.
Exhibition hall: 9.30–7, Easter–end Sep;
10–6, rest of year. Site: 7am–1am, all
year 🚉 Parking ticket (€5) gives
entrance to the Pont du Gard.
Exhibition hall: €5. 25-minute film: €3.
Ludo, children's discovery zone: €4
🍴 🏪 ♿

A UNESCO World Heritage Site,
this aqueduct was built in the
1st century BC to channel huge
amounts of water to the Roman
settlement at Nîmes. City
engineers carved out the
aqueduct from a source near
Uzès, 50km (30 miles) away,
which necessitated spanning the
Gardon river gorge at a height of
48m (156ft). Details such as the
fact that no mortar was used, or
that the average drop over the
entire length of the aqueduct
was only 24cm (10in) per
kilometre, add to the fascination
and interest of the site.
  On the left bank, there is a
huge parking area, information
panels and a pathway leading
directly to the exhibition hall,
which has been carefully
designed and positioned so
as not to detract from the site.
The exhibition shows how water
was used to enrich the civilized
lifestyle of the Romans—wealthy
households had their own piped
supply, public baths were
constructed, fountains graced
public areas and water powered
industry. It also deals with the
geological challenges that were
overcome during construction.
Various multimedia and
participative displays add up to
an excellent facility.
  Although people are no longer
allowed onto the Pont itself, you
can walk over the bridge that
runs alongside it at the same
level as the first tier of arches.
By so doing you fully realize the
size and weight of the building

St-Rémy-de-Provence has a wealth of Roman monuments

blocks used in the aqueduct's construction, but to appreciate it fully, you'll need to go up- or downstream for an unimpeded view from a distance.

ST-RÉMY-DE-PROVENCE

🔲 431 M13 🅸 Place Jean-Jaurès, 13210, tel 04 90 92 05 22; Mon–Sat 9–12.30, 2–7, Sun 10–12, 3–6, Jun–end Sep; Mon–Sat 9–noon, 2–6, rest of year www.saintremy-de-provence.com

South of Avignon, St Rémy-de-Provence attracts artists and art-lovers. It's a busy, well-kept, wine-making town with a small old quarter full of fine 16th- to18th-century mansions, pleasant narrow streets and quiet tree-shaded squares and fountains. There are some small art galleries and museums, including the Centre d'Art Présence Van Gogh, on rue Estrine, which hosts art exhibitions and displays various items of memorabilia relating to the artist's time here, including letters and full-size prints of his works. Part of the house where Nostradamus was born in 1503 can be seen in rue Hoche, although it is not open to the public.

Around 1km (half a mile) south is the beautiful old monastery of St Paul-de-Mausole, where Van Gogh voluntarily committed himself for a year's rest and treatment after mutilating his ear. It was one of the most productive periods of his life as he turned out 150 paintings and 100 drawings in 12 months. You can visit the monastery's Romanesque church and cloisters on avenue Vincent van Gogh. Nearby is the archaeological site of the Graeco-Roman town of Glanum. For interesting finds from Glanum, visit the Collection Archéologique in rue du Parage.

ST-TROPEZ

Once a Provençal seaside village, St-Tropez has become a playground of the rich and famous.

The small town of St-Tropez is world-famous—it symbolizes a certain rich, classless, glamorous but unconventional, hedonistic lifestyle. You only need to look at the luxury yachts moored along the quayside to see that the town attracts wealth and celebrities. But it is also packed with lesser mortals, who come to imbibe the atmosphere, pretend to be stars for a day, admire the enormous luxury yachts parked along the quay-side—or maybe just enjoy St-Tropez for what it originally was and still is, a pretty, fortified harbour village.

The Vieille Ville (old quarter) has managed, despite the huge numbers of visitors, to retain its charm. It has narrow streets of small old houses, with several chic boutiques. Outside the old quarter is the large main square, place des Lices, with boules players and shady plane trees. The quay curves along the edge of a beautiful blue bay with remnants of the old fortifications at one end. Beyond them is the tiny quarter called La Ponche, once a fishermen's district. There are no proper beaches in town, so for a sandy beach head to the Cap de St-Tropez, on the peninsula.

On a hilltop to the east, clothed with pine and oleander, the Citadelle is an untidy area of ruined 16th- to17th-century defences. The fortress houses the Musée de la Citadelle, dedicated to the history of St-Tropez, with an interesting section on the 1944 Allied invasion (*daily 10–noon, 1.30–6*).

RATINGS			
Photo stops	●	●	●
Specialist shopping	●	●	● ●

BASICS

🔲 432 P13 🅸 Quai Jean-Jaurès (main part of harbour front), tel 04 94 97 45 21; daily 9.30–8.30, Jul, Aug; 9.30–12.30, 2–7, Apr–end Jun, Sep, Oct; 9.30–12.30, 2–6, Nov–end Mar www.saint-tropez.st (includes 360° photographs of the town's sights/views)

TIPS

● Don't try to drive to St-Tropez—traffic is terrible, with waits of an hour or more to get into town, and nowhere to park. Instead, use the large public parking areas at Port Grimaud and take the passenger ferry across the bay.
● If you visit in May, you'll catch the spectacular annual *bravades* festival.
● Minutes away from the crowds of St-Tropez are the beautiful unspoiled villages of the St-Tropez peninsula.

The massive restored citadel looms over Sisteron

Detail of the Atlantes sculptures on Toulon's town hall doorway

Roman ruins in the town of Vaison-la-Romaine

SISTERON

431 N12 Place de la République, 04200, tel 04 92 61 36 50; Mon–Sat 9–7, Sun 10–noon, 2–5, Jul, Aug; Mon–Sat 9–noon, 2–6, rest of year
Sisteron
www.sisteron.fr

In Provence's mountainous interior, Sisteron is an unusual fortified town that once marked the border between Provence and Dauphiné. Its curious setting is a *clue,* a narrow valley edged by high, almost vertical cliffs, dramatically scored with the hues of various geological strata.

The old quarter is a labyrinth of stepped alleys, narrow streets and covered passageways called *andrônes,* where you'll find Notre-Dame des Pommiers, a 12th-century Romanesque church. A signposted route leads past some fine houses, ending up in place de l'Horloge on the north side, where there's a lively market on Wednesday and Saturday mornings.

Sisteron's gaunt citadel, narrowing as it follows a rocky ledge, stands 500m (1,600ft) above the waters of the Durance, on a high ridge overlooking the town. It survived until World War II, when the Germans used it as a garrison, strategic base and prison, but it was destroyed by Allied bombers in August 1944. Now it's a mere shell of ramparts enclosing the former fortress site, although the remaining gates, towers and 12th-century keep are impressive, as is the view.

TOULON

431 N14 place Raimu, 83000, tel 04 94 18 53 00; Mon–Sat 9–6, Sun 10–noon, Jun–end Sep; Mon–Sat 9.30–5.30, Sun 10–noon, rest of year
Toulon
www.toulontourisme.com

France's second largest naval port, Toulon is often bypassed in preference for more glamorous locations farther to the east. The city was transformed into a naval base soon after Provence became part of France in 1481, and under Louis XIV it became the strategic base for the Mediterranean fleet, a role that it maintains today. The port's surroundings (a huge natural harbour backed by a ring of hills) and Toulon's lively atmosphere make it worth a visit if you are nearby.

The Atlantes figures by the baroque sculptor Pierre Puget, on either side of the old town hall doorway, are powerful figures, based on stevedores Puget had seen unloading ships in Marseille. Boats leave regularly for trips around the harbour from quai Stalingrad and, for those interested in maritime history, there's the Musée National de la Marine on quai de Norfolk *(daily 10–6.30, Apr to mid-Sep; Wed–Mon 10–noon, 2–6, rest of year)*. The excellent Musée d'Art de Toulon *(daily 1–6.30)* has an extensive collection of over 500 Provençal paintings from the 17th century onwards. The cours Lafayette is the setting every morning for Toulon's well-known Marché de Provence, a huge market selling some of the best produce that Provence has to offer.

A matelot doll, *handmade locally and sold in Toulon*

VAISON-LA-ROMAINE

431 M12 Place Sautel, 84110 (between the two Roman sites), tel 04 90 36 02 11 Mon–Fri 9–noon, 2–7, summer; Mon–Fri 9.30–5.45, rest of year
www.vaison-la-romaine.com

In northeast Vaucluse, close to Mont Ventoux, this small town has a spectacular setting with the Dentelles peaks rising behind. Its large numbers of visitors come for the exceptional Roman ruins. The town also has an interesting medieval area on the other side of the Ouvèze river, reached by crossing a Roman bridge which has seen hardly any repairs and has not been widened in 2,000 years. The Ville Haute (Upper Town) is a picturesque area of lanes and alleys, overlooked by the ruined chateau, built in the 12th century and redesigned in the 15th. There's a large street market on Tuesdays.

Since 1907, the Roman town has been partially exposed in two large sites. In the larger and more interesting site, Quartier du Puymin, you can see streets, walls, patches of fresco, mosaics, statuary and a restored theatre which is still in use. The smaller Quartier de la Villasse has a remarkable street of shops and fine mosaic floors. The Musée Archéologique *(museum and Roman sites: daily 9–12.30, 2–6.45, Jun–end Aug; 9.30–noon, 2–5.45, Mar–end May, Sep, Oct; 10–noon, 2–4.30, rest of year; ruins closed Tue am Nov–end Apr)* is well laid out and easy to follow, and has an impressive collection of Roman sculpture.

SOUTHWEST FRANCE

The Southwest has something for everyone: Surfers ride the waves at glitzy Biarritz, wine lovers pick up rich reds at St-Émilion and birdwatchers head to the Arcachon basin. For peace, relax in the Venise Verte and for city culture take in the museums and architecture of Bordeaux and Toulouse.

MAJOR SIGHTS

Towers of Albi's austere
Cathédrale Sainte-Cécile

An oyster park in Arcachon

A shop window in Bayonne
displays a Basque cross

THE SIGHTS

ALBI

➕ 430 J12 ℹ️ Palais de la Berbie, place Sainte-Cécile, 81000, tel 05 63 49 48 80; Mon–Sat 9–7, Sun 10–12.30, 2.30–6.30, Jul–end Sep; Mon–Sat 9–12.30, 2–6, Sun 10–12.30, 2.30–6.30 rest of year 🚆 Albi
www.tourisme.fr/albi

This pleasantly untouristy town has lovely pink-brick architecture, superb shopping and views. The magnificent river Tarn adds a quiet grace.

The tourist office has a useful, free brochure in English, which gives routes for three cultural heritage walks, as well as details of religious heritage sites and the town's arts and crafts shops.

The Cathédrale Sainte-Cécile (daily 9–noon, 2–6.30 Oct–end May; 9–6.30 Jun–end Sep) has an austere, fortress-like Gothic exterior which belies the sumptuous Renaissance decoration of the interior. In the 16th century, Italian artists covered the walls and ceiling of the nave with frescoes, and on the west wall is a huge, grisly 15th-century mural depicting The Last Judgement.

Beside the tourist office, the former archbishop's palace, the Palais de la Berbie, is now the Musée Toulouse-Lautrec. Here you can see more than 600 paintings and prints by Henri Toulouse-Lautrec, who was born in the town in 1864 (daily 6–6, Jul, Aug; 9–noon, 2–6, Jun, Sep; 10–noon, 2–6, Apr, May; Wed–Mon 10–noon, 2–5.30, Mar, Oct; Wed–Mon 10–noon, 2–5, Nov–end Mar).

ARCACHON

➕ 428 E11 ℹ️ Esplanade Georges Pompidou, 33311, tel 05 57 52 97 97; Mon–Sat 9–7, Sun 9–1, 2–5 Jul; Aug; Mon–Sat 9–6.30, Sun 10–1, 2–5, Apr–end Jun, Sep; Mon–Fri 9–6, Sat 9–5, Oct–end Mar 🚆 Arcachon
www.arcachon.com

The Bassin d'Arcachon, a huge natural bay 90km (55 miles) in circumference, is ideal for families seeking seaside holidays. Its sandy beaches and calm waters are protected from the waves that pound the Atlantic coast just beyond Cap Ferret. It's a great place for outdoor activities such as sailing, kayaking, parasailing, bicycling and walking. The only drawback is that car parking in high season can be difficult.

In town, the Observatoire Sainte-Cécile (Le Belvédère), built by the young Gustave Eiffel, is a spiral staircase suspended on cables inside a metal lattice tower, which sways as you ascend. Although only 15m (50ft) high, it gives a good view over the town, the surrounding villas and the Bassin d'Arcachon.

The best way to see the bay is on a boat trip. Aim for a trip that visits both the Île aux Oiseaux and several of the small oyster-fishing ports around the bay.

Eleven kilometres (7 miles) south of Arcachon, the energetic can hike up Europe's largest sand dune, the Dune du Pilat, nearly 3km (2 miles) long and 110m (360ft) high. There are superb views from the top.

BAYONNE

➕ 428 E13 ℹ️ Place des Basques, 64108, tel 05 59 46 01 46; Mon–Sat 9–7, Sun 10–1, Jul, Aug; Mon–Fri 9–6.30, Sat 10–6, rest of year 🚆 Bayonne
www.bayonne-tourisme.com

The unofficial capital of the French Basque country (you may well hear the Basque language, Euskara, spoken), Bayonne sits on the confluence of the Adour and Nive tidal rivers and makes a good day trip from Biarritz.

In the 18th century the town was a major port, with whaling, shipbuilding, cod fishing and

trade with the West Indies bringing in wealth. It also had a reputation for fearless pirates (corsaires). You can see the results of that wealth in the magnificent town houses overlooking the rivers, and the arcaded traffic-free shopping streets, such as rue du Port-Neuf, with its many chocolate boutiques.

There are two excellent museums, both in the 'Petit Bayonne' area. The Musée Bonnat (daily 10–6.30, May–end Oct; Wed–Mon 10–12.30, 2–6, Nov–end Mar), on rue Jacques-Laffitte, has a nationally recognized art collection, with works by El Greco, Goya, Delacroix and Degas. The Musée Basque, on the quai des Corsaires, covers every aspect of Basque culture, from its earliest history to modern times, and includes a history of the town (daily 10–6.30, Jul–end Aug; Wed–Mon 10–6.30, May, Jun, Sep, Oct; Wed–Mon 10–12.30, 2–6 rest of year).

The town's festival, in the first week of August, has everything from bull fighting and carnivals to Basque music and dancing.

A café in Bayonne

Surfers at Grand Plage, Biarritz

The 14th-century Valentre Bridge, at Cahors

An old van carries barrels of Martell cognac

BIARRITZ

🔲 428 D13 🔲 Square d'Ixelles, 64200, tel 05 59 22 37 10; daily 8–8, Jul, Aug; Mon–Sat 9–6, Sun 10–5, rest of year 🔲 Biarritz–La Négresse
www.biarritz.fr

In 1854 Empress Eugénie persuaded her husband Napoleon III to holiday here. He built Villa Eugénie for her and the rest of Europe's glitterati soon followed, turning Biarritz into the most chic seaside resort in southwest France. This is testified by the town's streets, many of which are named after famous visitors. Biarritz built a reputation for balls and banquets, and casinos, golf courses, smart restaurants, boutiques and exquisite food shops all followed.

Other attractions include the Musée de la Mer (daily 9.30–7, Jun, Sep; 9.30–midnight, Jul, Aug; 9.30–12.30, 2–6, rest of year; closed 1–15 Jan), where you'll find an aquarium, shark tank, and seals, with feeding times at 10.30 and 5. The nationally important Musée de l'Art Oriental, on rue Guy-Petit, has more than 1,000 works of art from India, China, Nepal and Tibet (Mon–Fri 10.30–7, Sat,

A shop display in Biarritz

Sun 2–8; public hols 2–7). For chocoholics, the Musée du Chocolat (daily 10–noon, 2.30–7, Jul–end Aug; Mon–Sat 10–noon, 2.30–6, rest of year), on avenue Beaurivage, offers tastings. For shopping, try Les Halles covered market (mornings only).
Don't miss Most visitors come to Biarritz for its three beaches: the Grande Plage, the most fashionable; the small beach in le Port-Vieux, popular with locals; and the Plage de la Côte des Basques, beloved of surfers.

CAHORS

🔲 429 H12 🔲 Place François Mitterrand, 46000, tel 05 65 53 20 65; Mon–Fri 9–12.30, 1.30–6.30, Sat 9–12.30, 1.30–6, Apr–end Jun, Sep, Oct; Mon–Sat 9–6.30, Sun 10–12.30, Jul, Aug; Mon–Sat 9–12.30, 1.30–6 Nov–end Mar 🔲 Cahors
www.mairie-cahors.fr

Cahors has a beautiful setting, on a south-facing isthmus, formed by a loop in the meandering river Lot. The town is known for its dark red wine, the product of the vineyards that cover the steep terraces to the south and west. The heart of the town splits into two parts, with the main street, boulevard Gambetta (named after Léon Gambetta, one of France's most admired republicans, a native of Cahors), running between the medieval quarter on the east side and the newer streets and buildings on the west. The English besieged Cahors during the Hundred Years War (without actually attacking it), and the old town bears this legacy, with ramparts, battlements, barbicans and fortified towers.

In the west is the symbol of the town, Pont Valentré. The curious proportions of this medieval bridge are emphasized by three pointed towers from

which missiles could be fired at intruders. In the old town, the 12th-century Cathédrale St-Étienne is a mix of Flamboyant Gothic, Gothic and Romanesque, with Périgord-style Byzantine domes, a fine, carved north doorway and frescoes. Near the cathedral is the Maison de Roaldès, Henri IV's mansion.

COGNAC

🔲 434 F10 🔲 16 rue du XIV Juillet, 16100, tel 05 45 82 10 71; Mon–Sat 9–7, Sun 10–4, Jul, Aug; Mon–Sat 9.30–5.30, May, Jun, Sep; Mon–Sat 10–5, rest of year 🔲 Cognac
www.tourism-cognac.com

Cognac's old town retains its medieval layout and several references to the salt trade on which its economy once depended. In its narrow streets, half-timbered buildings jostle for position alongside fine 15th- to 17th-century stone town houses. The Tours St-Jacques, on rue du Château, a solid fortified gateway, is all that remains of the ramparts. You can also admire the 15th-century rose window in the Église du Prieuré St-Léger (daily 9–6).

Smart shops and cafés radiating from place François I represent the Cognac of today: Lively and prosperous, it is a hub of commerce, gastronomy and tourism and the heart of the global cognac business. Telltale black stains on pale stonework reveal the places where barrels of the famous spirit are ageing. The vast cellars of the Château François I (birthplace of the king who succeeded to the throne in 1515) are now the home of Otard cognac (daily 10–noon, 2–6; 10–7 Jul, Aug; times vary Apr–end Oct; Mon–Fri, Nov–Dec; group visits only, Jan–Mar).
Don't miss Among the cognac houses you can visit are Camus, Martell, Hennessy and Rémy Martin.

Bordeaux

This elegant city is world famous for the quality of its wines.
Other attractions include a superb 18th-century theatre, a 1,000-year-old
cathedral and a fine arts museum.

Pont St-Pierre, spanning the Garonne river

An eye-catching art installation in a parking area

Looking across Bordeaux from the Basilique St-Michel

RATINGS

Cultural interest	● ● ● ●
Historic interest	● ● ● ●
Good for wine	● ● ● ●

BASICS

✚ 434 F11 ⓘ 12 cours 30 Juillet, 33080, Bordeaux, tel 05 56 00 66 00; Mon–Sat 9–7, Sun 9.30–6.30, May, Jun, Sep, Oct; Mon–Sat 9–7.30, Sun 9.30–6.30, Jul, Aug; Mon–Sat 9–6.30, Sun 9.45–4.30, rest of year
🚉 Gare St-Jean
www.bordeaux-tourisme.com

TIPS

● The Maison du Vin, opposite the tourist office, has information on vineyard tours.
● On the last Friday of each month, in-line skaters take over the allée de Bristol, on the north side of Esplanade des Quinconces, for *La Nuit du Roller*.
● Discover the city with a bicycle that comments on the main sights in English—contact the tourist office for information.

Medoc (right), produced in the Bordeaux area. Taking a break in place Gambetta (far right)

SEEING BORDEAUX

Bordeaux is an elegant city with a long history and enough attractions to keep you entertained for several days. The principal sights are relatively close together and most are easily reached from the magnificent Grand Théâtre or from the huge central square, Esplanade des Quinconces. A new tram system promises to make the city's main attractions even more accessible, although the works have caused major disruptions, with road diversions and the closure of some sights. The first section is due to open in 2004, but work will continue into 2007.

If it is your first visit to Bordeaux, be sure to walk out onto the Pont de Pierre, Bordeaux's oldest bridge, for great views of the Porte de Bourgogne and the stone buildings lining the quayside, where a regeneration project is bringing new life. If the sun is shining, it will be obvious why the city was often called Bordeaux la Blonde.

HIGHLIGHTS

GRAND THÉÂTRE

✚ 198 C3 • Place de la Comédie ☎ 05 56 00 75 20; tours 05 56 00 66 00 🕐 Depends on rehearsal schedules
This striking venue, with its 12 lofty Corinthian columns topped by statues of nine Muses and three goddesses, dominates place de la Comédie. It was built between 1773 and 1780 by Victor Louis, the restorer of Chartres cathedral, and is almost 90m (295ft) long and 50m (165ft) wide. Restored to its original glory in 1991, its auditorium is known for its exceptional acoustics and the tiered boxes drip with gold leaf. The sweeping grand staircase was a model for Garnier's lobby in the Opéra Palais Garnier in Paris. You won't be able to see inside if a rehearsal is under way, so it's worth checking earlier in the day for any scheduled break in rehearsals later.

CATHÉDRALE ST-ANDRÉ AND TOUR PEY-BERLAND

✚ 198 B4 • Place Pey-Berland ☎ 05 56 52 68 10 🕑 Mon 10–11.30, 2–6.30,
Tue–Sat 7.30–11.30, 2–6, Sun 8–12.30, 2–5.30 (closed Sun in winter)

This 1,000-year-old cathedral, whose delicate twin spires can be seen
from all over the city, is a UNESCO World Heritage Site. The huge nave
is said to be where Eleanor of Aquitaine married the future Henry II of
England in 1152. The north and south doors of the transept, the choir
and the Porte Royale on the north wall are decorated with medieval
sculptures and scenes from the Last Judgement. Next to the cathedral
is the 15th-century Tour Pey-Berland. On its pinnacle, 50m (165ft) up,
is the statue of Notre-Dame-d'Aquitaine. The view from the top is
tremendous, as is the noise if you're up there when the 11-tonne bell,
Ferdinand-André, is tolling.

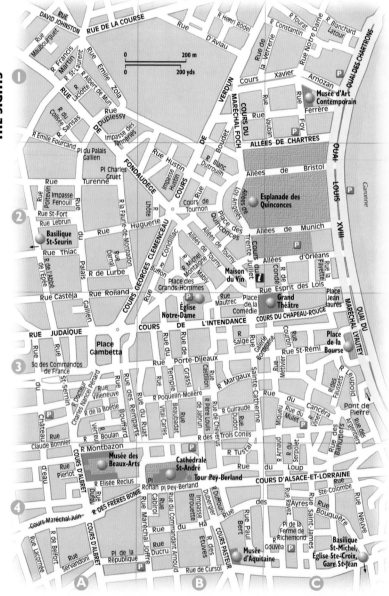

THE SIGHTS

A fountain at the Esplanade des Quinconces

MUSÉE DES BEAUX-ARTS

⊞ 198 A4 • 20 cours d'Albret ☎ 05 56 10 20 56 ⏰ Wed–Mon 11–6 📷 Guided tours Wed 12.30 and other times by arrangement

The fine arts museum is in the gardens of the Palais Rohan. Its permanent collection covers the main art movements from the Renaissance to World War II. Temporary exhibitions are held in the Galerie des Beaux-Arts opposite. Although relatively small, the museum's collection includes works by masters such as Titian, Van Dyck, Delacroix, Rubens and Matisse.

ÉGLISE NOTRE-DAME

⊞ 198 B3 • Place du Chapelet ☎ 05 56 81 01 37 ⏰ Mon–Sat 2.30–5

Once associated with the nearby Dominican convent, this imposing church was completed in 1707 by Pierre Michel, an architect already engaged to construct the nearby fortress. The elaborate decoration of the church contrasts with the simplicity of its construction. The central nave, flanked by a series of small side chapels, extends beyond two ornate gilded wrought-iron gates to a baroque altar. On the west wall, an elaborate bas-relief depicts St. Dominic's vision of the Virgin Mary handing him a rosary.

BASILIQUE ST-SEURIN

⊞ 198 off A2 • Place des Martyrs de la Résistance ⏰ Daily 8–11.30, 2–5.30 📷 Guided tours Sat 2.30–5.30

St-Seurin church was granted the title of basilica by the Pope in 1873, because of its significance to the Christian faith. It is also a UNESCO World Heritage Site, with origins dating back to Gallo-Roman times. You'll find an eclectic collection of styles and forms from the 11th to the 18th centuries, with both austere and lavish types of decoration. Excavations in 1910 revealed a huge Christian burial ground dating from the fourth century.

BACKGROUND

Bordeaux is one of France's oldest trading ports, with its wealth built on wine. The Romans were among those who took advantage of the city's coastal position and proximity to plentiful vineyards. When the marriage of Eleanor of Aquitaine and the future Henry II brought the western half of France under English rule in the 12th century, the city enjoyed a vast upsurge in revenue. Many wine merchants became wealthy and their legacy lives on in the elegant mansions and palaces they built.

The 18th century, in particular, sealed the city's reputation, and many of the great monuments date from that time. Like Paris, only a century earlier, the city was rationalized with the creation of wide boulevards, public gardens and the colonnaded Grand Théâtre. During this time, wealth was also boosted from trade with the colonies in sugar, spices and coffee.

BASILIQUE ST-MICHEL

⊞ Off 198 C4 • Place Meynard ☎ 05 56 94 30 50 ⏰ Mon–Sat 8.30–6, Sun 8–noon

This triple-naved Flamboyant Gothic basilica, now a UNESCO-listed site, became a focal point for pilgrims throughout the Bordeaux area. Its freestanding bell tower gives a wonderful panorama of the city and river.

CAPC–MUSÉE D'ART CONTEMPORAIN

⊞ 198 C1 • 7 rue Ferrère ☎ 05 56 00 81 50 ⏰ Tue–Sun 11–6 (also Wed 6–8pm) 📷 Wed 12.30, Sat and Sun 4

A converted 19th-century warehouse is now a multimedia exhibition space, with cutting-edge exhibits and lively temporary exhibitions.

ÉGLISE SAINTE-CROIX

⊞ 198 C4 • Place Pierre Renaudel ☎ 05 56 94 30 50 ⏰ Daily 9–6

Outside, there are 12th-century sculptures above the main door. Inside, look for the baroque organ and an unusual collection of 17th-century religious paintings.

ESPLANADE DES QUINCONCES

⊞ 198 C2

This huge tree-lined space, on the site of the 15th-century Château de Trompette, is said to be the largest centrally located square of any city in Europe.

MUSÉE D'AQUITAINE

⊞ 198 B4 • 20 cours Pasteur ☎ 05 56 01 51 02 ⏰ Tue–Sun 11–6

The history of Bordeaux from prehistoric times to today is covered in this museum, on the site of a convent. Objects from foreign cultures underline the city's role in exploration and trade.

PLACE DE LA BOURSE

⊞ 198 C3

A sculpture of Neptune symbolically opening the road to trade stands in front of this elegant semicircular sweep of golden buildings looking out over the quayside.

THE SIGHTS

Flowers outside a building in Collonges-la-Rouge

Musée Nationale de la Préhistoire, at Les Eyzies

The wacky Futuroscope

COLLONGES-LA-ROUGE

🔲 435 H11 🛈 Avenue de l'Auvitrie, Meyssac, 19500, tel 05 55 25 32 25; Tue–Sat 9–12.30, 2–6.30 www.pays.de.collonges.la.rouge. wanadoo.fr

Collonges-la-Rouge is grouped with a dozen nearby villages with the title *Le Pays de Collonges-la-Rouge*. It is full of delightful buildings made from red sandstone. The Maison de la Sirène bears the figure of a mermaid, there are whimsical turrets on the Hôtel de la Ramade de Friac, and the Castel de Vassinhac has mullions, watch-towers and loopholes for firing missiles. Ask at the tourist office for a map showing the main buildings, with an itinerary in French. To the south, there is a 20-minute circular walk through countryside, giving good views of the village.

DOMME

🔲 429 H11 🛈 Place de la Halle, 24250, tel 05 53 31 71 00; daily 10–7 Jul, Aug; 10–noon, 2–6, rest of year www.domme-tourisme.com

Clinging to a clifftop, Domme is a neat *bastide* (fortified village), with narrow, flower-filled streets and beautiful stone buildings. Views from the terrace on the Belvédère de la Barre are exceptional, with the Dordogne river weaving through the landscape far below.

Domme is clustered around its old market hall and the handsome Maison du Gouverneur built, like the rest of the village, from stone that glows gold in sunlight. Below the village lies the largest stalactite-filled cave in Périgord Noir *(tours daily Feb to mid-Nov)*. Domme's population often took shelter here during wars. In 1307, an assembly of Knights Templar, falsely accused of heresy, were imprisoned in the Porte des Tours, part of

Domme's still-visible defences. The graffiti they scratched into the stonework of the Prison des Templiers, including Christ in Majesty and scenes of paradise or crucifixion, are a moving testimony to their faith. On place de la Halle, the small Musée d'Arts et de Tradition Populaire uses everyday objects and scenes to tell the story of local customs and culture *(daily, Mar–end Sep; times vary)*.

LES EYZIES

🔲 434 G11 🛈 19 avenue de la Préhistoire, 24620, tel 05 53 06 97 05; Mon–Sat 9–7, Sun 10–noon, 2–5, Jun–end Sep; Mon–Sat 9–noon, 2–6, Sun 10–noon, 2–5, Apr, May, Oct; Mon–Sat, 9–noon, 2–6, rest of year ❓ You must reserve ahead for Grotte de Font de Gaume, Grotte des Combarelles and Abri du Poisson 🚇 Les Eyzies-de-Tayac www.leseyzies.com

Caves in the limestone cliffs surrounding the village of Les Eyzies-de-Tayac-Sireuil provided shelter for humans as far back as 400,000BC. The cave-dwelling people who settled here were resourceful, intelligent and exceptional craftsmen, decorating their caves with paintings and carvings of great artistry. Buffalo, deer, horses and cattle gallop across the stone surfaces. Les Eyzies (now with UNESCO World Heritage status) is one of the densest concentrations of such sites anywhere in the world and hundreds of thousands of people visit each year (it can get very crowded in summer).

The best place to start is the Musée National de Préhistoire *(Wed–Mon 9.30–12.30, 2–5.30 Sep–end Jun; daily 9.30–6.30 Jul, Aug)*. In an old chateau, built under the cliff face, this remarkable museum exhibits flint axes, bone carvings, body ornaments, hunting weapons and domestic tools.

Of the various caves, Abri du Poisson offers a rarity—the first conclusive proof that Cro-Magnon people were adept at fishing—a superb, life-sized fish engraved in the ceiling vault. The Grotte des Combarelles, dating from around 13000BC, has over 600 wall engravings depicting ibex, mammoth, reindeer and cattle, as well as enigmatic symbols and human figures, while the Grotte de Font de Gaume contains polychrome paintings ranked among the true masterpieces of prehistoric art.

FUTUROSCOPE

🔲 434 G8 • Parc Futuroscope, BP 2000, 86130 Jaunay-Clan ☎ 05 49 49 11 12 ⏰ Daily 10–dusk, Apr–end Aug; 10–6, Sep to mid-Nov (hours may vary) 💶 Adult 1-day ticket: €21–€30, child (5–12) €16–€22, under 5 free; adult 2-day ticket: €40–€57, child (5–12) €29–€40, under 5 free. Prices depend on season 🚌 From Poitiers station (routes 9 and E) 🚉 On-site station served by TGVs from Paris 🏧 📷 🍴 www.futuroscope.com

Constantly evolving, this leisure park, 11km (7 miles) north of Poitiers, now offers 22 different attractions based on the moving image and high-tech visual effects.

The architecture shouts for attention, with forms ranging from the weird to the wonderful, or just plain wacky: Soaring organ pipes; mirrored, interlocked crystals; a giant sphere hovering above angled sheets of glass; and even, in the Pavillon de la Créativité, what looks like a giant dollop of whipped cream. These extraordinary structures house attractions such as huge semicircular 3-D screens, seats moving in synchronization with the images, or 360° panoramas. The park also has interactive water fountains, children's play areas and a lake which children

THE SIGHTS

Playing boules on the Île de Ré

can ride across on tricycles. In summer, the lake is lit to form a backdrop to various spectacles and shows.

ÎLE DE RÉ

🔖 433 E9 ℹ️ Île de Ré Tourisme, BP 28, 17580 Le Bois-Plage-en-Ré (also tourist offices in each of the main villages), tel 05 46 09 00 55 🚉 La Rochelle on mainland (approximately 14km/9 miles east of Rivedoux-Plage). Regular bus service from La Rochelle train station to Île de Ré 🚌 Various guided tours—contact the tourist office for details
www.iledere.fr

Long, narrow Île de Ré extends 30km (19 miles) into the Atlantic and is linked to the mainland by an elegantly curved bridge. The south side is a succession of long beaches; the north, sheltered from direct ocean winds, provides safe berths for yachts in several small ports. A gentle climate and the Île de Ré gastronomy—potatoes and wine from the land, fish and oysters from the sea—are two of the attractions of this pretty and much-loved island.

Even in summer, when the main roads can be busy, it is possible to find a quiet spot, though you may have to seek it on foot or by bicycle—there are more than 100km (60 miles) of official bicycle tracks to explore.

Each of the villages has its unique character. Watch yachts riding quietly at anchor in front of whitewashed houses on the quayside at La Flotte, or visit its superb medieval market hall. Ars, one of the prettiest villages in France, hosts a wonderful market with a range of high-quality produce.
Don't miss There are exceptional views from the church tower in St-Martin-de-Ré *(for opening times contact the local tourist office, tel 05 46 09 20 06)*.

A cave painting of a horse at Lascaux II

LASCAUX

Venture back to pre-historic times and see replicas of cave paintings around 17,000 years old.

The original Lascaux cave system was discovered in 1940 by local schoolboys after their dog disappeared down a pothole. What they encountered underground was one of the world's most significant Palaeolithic sites, its walls alive with uniquely vibrant cave paintings.

The magnificent original cavern, a short distance southeast of the town of Montignac, is sadly no longer open to the public. The carbon dioxide-laden breath of countless visitors was destroying the paintings and a film of greenish micro-organisms was creeping steadily across the walls. Using sophisticated 3-D plotting techniques, and new advances in resin and ferro-cement technology, experts created a perfect replica some 200m (220yds) away, and Lascaux II is what today's visitors experience.

RATINGS	
Historic interest	●●●●●
Special interest (prehistory)	●●●●

BASICS

🔖 435 H11 • Lascaux II, Montignac (enquiries via Semitour Périgord, BP 1024, 24001, Périgueux)
☎ 05 53 51 95 03
🕐 Daily 9–7, Jul, Aug; 9–6 Apr–end Jun, Sep; 10–12.30, 2–5.30, rest of year; closed Jan
💶 Adult €8, child (6–12) €4.50, under 6 free
🚉 Le Lardin (12km/8 miles north) or Sarlat-la-Canéda (25km/15 miles south)
🚌 Guided visits approximately every hour, depending on the number of people waiting. Tours are mainly in French, but English is possible Jul and Aug
❓ Pushchairs and mobile phones are not permitted. It is advisable to wear a light sweater when venturing underground
🎁 Gift shop
www.perigord.tm.fr

During your visit you can learn more about the techniques used by the original artists as they worked by the light from fat burning on stone lamps. They mixed mineral pigments such as haematite and kaolin to achieve the desired shades and often allowed the natural contours of the rockface to accentuate the forms of the animals depicted. Speckled effects were achieved by blowing diluted pigment through plant stems to create gradations of tone.

Even if the original intent behind the pictures remains a mystery, the overall effect is superb. Horses, antelope and bulls—many of them life-size—swirl around the walls and roof of the caves with undiminished exuberance. The whole re-created cave structure looks, and even feels, authentic. It is no surprise that Lascaux has been called 'The Sistine Chapel of Prehistory'.

The Gothic Cathédrale St-Étienne, in Limoges

Religious souvenirs for sale in Lourdes

Tour de France sculpture by Jean Bernard Metais, in Pau

LIMOGES

🗺 435 H9 🛈 12 Boulevard de Fleurus, 87000, tel 05 55 34 46 87; Mon–Sat 9–7, Sun and public hols 10–6, mid-Jun to mid-Sep; Mon–Sat 9–7, Apr to mid-Jun and mid-Sep to early Oct; Mon–Sat 9–noon, 2–7, rest of year 🚇 Limoges 🚌 The tourist office arranges a variety of guided tours on subjects of general and specific interest
www.ville-limoges.fr
www.tourismelimoges.com

The name Limoges is inextricably linked with fine porcelain. The city was originally renowned for exquisite *champlevé* enamels, and it was only in 1768, with the discovery of kaolin deposits nearby, and new firing techniques, that porcelain manufacture took off. The so-called 'arts of fire' still flourish. The tourist office has details of manufacturers and retail outlets.

Behind this artistic heritage lies a modern, lively university city with gardens and paths alongside the river Vienne.

In the Middle Ages, Limoges was made up of two adjoining settlements—the old Cité, on a mound around the cathedral and bishop's residence, and the administrative and commercial hub, to this day known as *Le Château*. At the heart of the historic quarter, the Gothic Cathédrale St-Étienne *(daily 10–6 in summer; 10–5 in winter)*, on place St-Étienne, looks out over a distinct medieval village, once domain of the bishops.

Exhibits at the Musée Municipal de l'Évêché, in place de la Cathédrale, *(daily 10–11.45, 2–6, Jul–end Sep; Wed–Mon 10–11.45, 2–5, rest of year)* include a priceless display of enamels and several Impressionist paintings, including works by Renoir, who was born in Limoges in 1841.

For a thought-provoking account of World War II experiences, head to the Musée de la Résistance et de la Déportation *(daily 10–11.45, 2–6, Jun to mid-Sep; Wed–Sun 2–5, mid-Sep to end May)*.

LOURDES

🗺 428 F14 🛈 Place Peyramale, 65101, tel 05 62 42 77 40; Mon–Sat 9–6.30, Sun 10–noon, May, Jun, Sep; Mon–Sat 9–7, Sun 10–6, Jul, Aug; Mon–Sat 9–noon, 2–5.30, Nov–end Feb; Mon–Sat 9–noon, 2–6, Feb–end Apr, Oct 🚇 Les Sanctuaires Notre-Dame de Lourdes: tel 05 62 42 78 78
www.lourdes-france.com

Lourdes is famous worldwide as a place where people seek healing. It all began when a young country girl, Bernadette Soubirous, saw the Virgin Mary here on 11 February 1858, and on 17 subsequent occasions.

Today, Lourdes attracts more than 5 million visitors each year, including around 100,000 volunteers who help people with illnesses and disabilities during their stay. The town's many places of worship are known collectively as Les Sanctuaires Notre-Dame de Lourdes. They vary from the small and intimate to a cavernous underground basilica that can accommodate more than 20,000 people.

The information office issues a useful map that lists times and dates of Masses, blessings of the sick and torchlight processions. The guided tour 'In the footsteps of Bernadette' includes the Museum of St. Bernadette *(10–noon, 2–5 Whitsun–end Oct)*, a free video show at the information office on the story of her life, her birthplace *(daily 9–noon, 2–7)*, the house where she lived at the time of the visions *(daily 9–12.15, 2.15–7)*, the Church of the Sacred Heart *(daily 8.30–7)*, and the Hospice of St. Bernadette *(daily 9–noon, 2–7 in summer; 3–5 in winter)*.

PAU

🗺 428 F13 🛈 Place Royale, 64000, tel 05 59 27 27 08; Mon–Sat 9–6, Sun 9.30–1 🚇 Pau
www.pau.fr

Pau was the birthplace of the popular King Henri IV in 1553, and became a cosmopolitan resort in the 19th century thanks to its mild winters. Development into a high-class spa and casino town soon followed. But Pau has managed to retain plenty of green space. Just about everything grows well, including bamboo, American sequoias, Lebanese cedars and Mexican cacti.

Pau has been called 'the town of a thousand palm trees', many of which can be seen from the Boulevard des Pyrénées, which runs along the southern edge of the town between the chateau and Parc Beaumont. The terrace here overlooks the Gave de Pau and provides a memorable view of the snow-capped Pyrenees to the south. A free funicular railway goes between the terrace and the lower level, where both the railway and river run.

Don't miss The Musée National du Château de Pau has a rich collection of Gobelin tapestries *(daily 9.30–12.15, 1.30–5.45, mid-Jun to mid-Sep; 9.30–11.45, 2–5, Apr to mid-Jun and mid-Sep to end Oct; 9.30–11.45, 2–4.15, rest of year)*.

PÉRIGUEUX

🗺 434 G10 🛈 26 place Francheville, 24070, tel 05 53 53 10 63; Mon–Sat 9–1, 2–6; public hols 10–1, 2–6 🚇 Perigueux
www.ville-perigueux.fr

Truffles, foie gras, walnuts, charcuterie and Perigord pâtés epitomize the cuisine of

Dinner with a musical accompaniment in the old part of Périgueux

Rochefort was once a hub of rope-making

Périgueux, and you can find them all in the town's legendary markets. The biggest in the area, they fill the ancient streets and squares of what was once *Vesunna*, a Gallo-Roman settlement astride the river Isle.

In the old quarter, the town's medieval history is tangible in place de la Clautre, place du Coderq and rue Limogeanne. To find traces of the town's earlier history, you can follow rue des Gladiateurs to the Roman arena, where there are vestiges of an early settlement dating from the 1st and 2nd centuries AD, or examine the prehistoric items in the Musée du Périgord, on cours Tourny *(Mon, Wed–Fri 10.30–5.30, Sat, Sun 1–6, Apr–end Sep; Mon, Wed–Fri 10.30–5, Sat, Sun 1–6 rest of year)*.

As you wander around the town, admire the half-timbered medieval houses, redeveloped waterfront, finely ornamented Renaissance *hôtels* and *belles demeures*, and—on place de la Clautre—the strangely Levantine Cathédrale St-Front. This is a UNESCO World Heritage Site, with Byzantine domes and spiky finials *(daily 8–12.30, 2.30–7)*.

The town hosts various fêtes and festivals, celebrating everything from mime to mushrooms.

POITIERS

🏛 434 G8 🛈 45 place Charles de Gaulle, BP377, 86009, tel 05 49 41 21 24; Mon–Sat 9.30am–11pm, Sun and public hols 10–6, 7.30–11, 21 Jun–21 Sep; Mon–Sat 10–6, closed Sun, rest of year 🚉 Poitiers
www.mairie-poitiers.fr

Perched on a plateau between the rivers Clain and Boivre, Poitiers has a rich artistic and historical heritage and is home to one of the oldest universities in France. It is a lively town, with an attractive mixture of culture, business, science, academic research and tourism. It is also the administrative capital of Poitou-Charentes.

Often acclaimed as 'the town with 100 bell towers', Poitiers has more than 70 classified monuments around its inner maze of narrow streets. Romanesque sights include the Église Notre-Dame-la-Grande *(daily 8.30–7)*, on place Charles de Gaulle. It has a barrel-vaulted nave and superb 12th-century frescoes over the choir.

Poitiers has had a Christian presence since the fourth century, notably in the tiny jewel of the Baptistère St-Jean, on rue Jean-Jaurès *(daily 10–12.30, 2.30–6, Jul, Aug; 10.30–12.30, 3–6, Apr–end Jun and Sep, Oct; Wed–Mon 2.30–4.30, rest of year)*. Rebuilt in Carolingian and Romanesque times, it retains several ancient sarcophagi and a superb collection of frescoes.

Other buildings to look out for in the old town include half-timbered merchant properties, Renaissance town houses, medieval artisan dwellings and graceful 18th-century mansions. Modern additions, like the multi-function Espace Mendès-France and the state-of-the-art Médiathèque François Mitterrand, strike a distinctive, new note, but contrast rather than conflict with the heritage of the town.

Don't miss In summer, short but spectacular *Polychromies* shows bathe the western façade of the Église Notre-Dame-la-Grande in light, reproducing the church's appearance in the Middle Ages and highlighting the artistry of the stonemasons *(Jul, Aug from 10.30pm; Sep from 9.30pm)*.

ROCHEFORT

🏛 433 E9 🛈 Avenue Sadi-Carnot, 17300, tel 05 46 99 08 60; Mon–Sat 9.30–7, Jul, Aug; 9.30–12.30, 2–6.30, Apr–end Jun, Sep; 9.30–12.30, 2–6, rest of year. Closed Sun and public hols 🚉 Rochefort 🛈 An additional tourist office is at the Porte d'Arsenal
www.tourisme.fr/rochefort
www.ville-rochefort.fr

Louis XIV commissioned Colbert, minister of finance and the navy, to create a fine naval arsenal here, assembling in one place every craft and trade required to build, arm and fit out a huge succession of warships. Today the superbly restored dockyard still evokes the spirit of distant discovery.

You can visit the beautifully preserved Corderie Royale, at the Centre International de la Mer *(daily 9–7, Apr–end Sep; 10–6, rest of year)*. Once Europe's longest factory, it produced the vast quantities of rope and sail needed by France's navy. The 65m (212ft) frigate *L'Hermione*, at the Arsenal Maritime, has been re-created using 18th-century techniques *(daily 9–7, Apr–end Sep; 10–6, rest of year)*.

On rue Pierre Loti, behind the plain façade of the town house where naval officer and writer Pierre Loti (1850–1923) lived, you can see rooms furnished with exotic mementos of his travels *(Wed–Mon Feb, to mid-Dec; daily Jul to mid-Sep, times vary; guided tours only—reserve at the tourist office)*.

The elegant Hôtel de Cheusses, on place de la Galissonnière, is home to the Musée National de la Marine *(daily 10–6.30, Apr to mid-Sep; 10–noon, 2–6, rest of year)*. It contains a wonderful collection of naval items, including superbly crafted model ships, gilded figureheads and navigation instruments.

Don't miss The Jardin des Retours, alongside the river Charente, is ideal for a relaxing walk.

ROCAMADOUR

See pages 332–333.

The sheer rock face of La Roque-Gageac

LA ROCHELLE

The seaport of La Rochelle is sophisticated, lively and modern, but retains reminders of its long history.

A stroll around La Rochelle's quiet, arcaded walkways reveals evidence of a past based on fishing and shipbuilding. Medieval half-timbered houses, ornamented Renaissance *hôtels* and graceful 18th-century mansions sit in harmony around an attractive harbour.

Around 1,000 years ago, Rochela was a fishing village. It became wealthy and influential in the 12th century, under the patronage of Eleanor of Aquitaine, and was renamed La Rochelle.

Today, the Port des Minimes marina, where vast numbers of sailing craft tie up, is the largest on the Atlantic seaboard and is boosted by international sailing races and boat shows.

At the heart of La Rochelle, the Vieux Port is constantly busy and a great place to watch boats come and go. The Aquarium (*daily 9–11, Jul–end Aug; 9–8, Apr–end Jun, Sep; 10–8, rest of year*), south of Le Gabut, at the Bassin des Grands Yachts, brings you face to face with the flora and fauna of the ocean.

Don't miss There are good views from the towers flanking the Vieux Port.

RATINGS		
Good for kids	● ● ●
Historic interest	● ● ●
Photo stops	● ● ●

BASICS
✚ 433 E9 ▐ Le Gabut, 17025, tel 05 46 41 14 68; Mon–Sat 9–8, Sun and public hols 11–5, Jul, Aug; Mon–Sat 9–7, Sun 10–1, Jun, Sep; Mon–Sat 9–6, Sun and public hols 10–1, rest of year ▐ La Rochelle www.ville-larochelle.fr www.tourisme-larochelle.com

TIPS
● To get around La Rochelle quickly and inexpensively, try one of the town's yellow bicycles, reserved for visitors. It's free for the first two hours, and around €1 per hour after that. Contact Autoplus (tel 05 46 34 02 22), on place de Verdun.
● Getting across the Vieux Port or to the yacht marina is easy with *Le Passeur Autoplus* or the *Bus de Mer*, a fast service from Vieux Port landing stage to the Port des Minimes. Both are ideal for the Aquarium.

LA ROQUE-GAGEAC

✚ 435 H11 ▐ Rue Tourny, BP 114, 24203 Sarlat, tel 05 53 31 45 45; Mon–Sat 9–7, Sun and public hols 10–noon, 2–6, Apr–end Oct; Mon–Sat 9–noon, 2–6, rest of year www.la-roque-gageac.com

This pretty village has been inhabited since prehistoric times and occupies a dramatic position beside the Dordogne river. The Hundred Years War and the 16th-century Wars of Religion turned the village's troglodytic fortress into an impregnable stronghold (*daily 10.30–1, 2–6, April to mid-Nov*). First created in the 12th century, the fortress incorporated a number of ingenious devices, using caves in the limestone, to defy hostile attempts to scale the rockface.

The village's position between the cliffs and the river gives it almost Mediterranean weather patterns, and vegetation thrives. Alongside the small church, perched high up, you'll find the Jardin Exotique (*open all year*), home to exotic plants, trees and shrubs. Another garden worth a visit is the Jardin de la Ferme Fleurie (*daily 2–5, mid-May to mid-Sep*).

ST-CIRQ-LAPOPIE

✚ 429 H12 ▐ Hôtel de Ville, 46330, tel 05 65 31 29 06; daily 10–1, 2–7, Jun, Sep; 10–1, 2–7.30, Jul, Aug; Wed–Sat 10–1, 2–6, Sun 2–6, rest of year¶

This golden-stone village, huddled on wooded limestone cliffs 80m (262ft) above the river Lot, has medieval houses with half-timbered walls and brown roof tiles, packed tightly together in narrow lanes. There is no vehicular access for visitors. The narrow road (CD8) from the Lot valley up to St-Cirq hugs the rockface on the left, passes the bulk of the village on the right, and continues up to a

Narrow, steep lanes in St-Cirq-Lapopie

designated parking area, from where there's a rather steep walk back to the village.

For good views, climb the castle ruins. Next to the ruins, the Gothic Église de St-Cirq juts out from the rock face to survey a dizzying sweep of the Lot and Cère valley.

The village was once a wood turners' colony and you can still buy various wooden items here.

SAINTES

⊞ 434 F10 ⓘ Villa Musso, 62 cours National BP96, 17103, tel 05 46 74 23 82; Mon–Sat 9–1, 2–6, Jun to mid-Sep (also 6–7pm, Jul, Aug), Sun 10–1, 2–6, Jul to mid-Sep; Mon–Sat 9.30–12.30, 2.15–6, mid-Sep to end May ⓡ Saintes www.ot-saintes.fr

Saintes, a historic port on the Charente, is the tourist hub of Saintonge. The town was capital of Aquitania under Roman rule and became an early convert to Christianity. Today, visitors come to enjoy its Roman and religious monuments, shopping streets and riverside.

The old town is set back, below and behind the main boulevards. On the riverbank is the Arch of Germanicus, erected in AD19, while the fascinating Musée Archaeologique, in esplanade André Malraux, offers an insight into the life of the town in Gallo-Roman times *(daily)*. A first-century chariot is among the exhibits. There is more classical heritage in the Amphitheatre in rue Lacurie *(daily)*, built in AD40.

Churches worth a look include St-Eutrope, in rue St-Eutrope *(daily 9–7)*. Compare the Romanesque delicacy of the bell tower on the Abbaye-aux-Dames *(daily 10–12.30, 2–7 Apr–end Sep; Tue–Sun 2–6, also Wed, Sat 10–noon, rest of year)* with the heavy-handed Gothic treatment of the roof of the Cathédrale St-Pierre *(daily 9–7)*.

SARLAT-LA-CANÉDA

This beautifully restored golden-stone town is now one of the most popular places in the Dordogne.

Sarlat, in the heart of the Périgord Noir area, is renowned for its gastronomy, and devotees of foie gras and other delicacies make regular pilgrimages to the town's specialist suppliers and restaurants. But the town itself is also an attraction. Apart from the nondescript rue de la République, Sarlat looks much as it must have done in its Renaissance heyday, with narrow winding alleys and passages wriggling between well-preserved town houses.

La Maison d'Étienne de La Boétie, birthplace in 1530 of the eponymous philosopher and poet, is one of the most photographed buildings in Sarlat, with its Renaissance mullions and gables.

At the end of the Hundred Years War Sarlat was eventually returned from English to French rule, and was granted special privileges to reward its loyalty to the king. It entered a golden age, as a new merchant class brought wealth to the area and created many of the fine stone houses that survive today. Sarlat became a pearl of the French Renaissance. It fell on harder times at the end of the 18th century but this was a blessing in disguise, as it meant the town escaped wholesale redevelopment. The *Loi Malraux*, passed in 1962 to help preserve France's older towns, ensured it remained that way.

RATINGS				
Good for food	●	●	●	●
Historic interest	●	●	●	
Specialist shopping (food)	●	●	●	

BASICS

⊞ 435 H11 ⓘ Rue Tourny, BP 114, 24203, tel 05 53 31 45 45; Mon–Sat 9–7, Sun and public hols 10–noon, 2–6, Apr–end Oct; Mon–Sat 9–noon, 2–6, rest of year

ⓡ Sarlat-La-Canéda www.ot-sarlat-perigord.fr

TIPS

● If you can't decide which delicacies to buy, visit the Halle Paysanne des Produits Fins du Terroir, on rue de Cahors, and see them all—*foie gras*, chestnuts, mushrooms, walnuts, truffles—under one roof.

● Sarlat's Saturday market *(8.30–6)* is one of the most varied and best known in France. There is also a food market in place de la Liberté on Wednesday mornings *(8.30–1)*.

● Parking can be very difficult so it is best to use the parking areas around the edge.

Toulouse

Toulouse is capital of the Midi-Pyrénées and one of France's great cities, with both a historic university and a state-of-the-art space museum.

SEEING TOULOUSE

Toulouse lies on the river Garonne and the Canal du Midi and is often referred to as the 'pink city' because of the local brick and marble. Visitors come for its history, art, music and shopping. It's also a place with a passion for dancing (especially the tango) and for rugby football. The central area can be explored reasonably easily on foot. The old quarter has narrow, mainly traffic-free lanes, crammed with small boutiques. The first of two new Métro lines is due to be in full service by spring 2004 and a second line is currently under construction. These should help alleviate the city's traffic problems.

RATINGS

Cultural interest	●●●○
Shopping	●●●○
Special interest (space travel)	●●●○

BASICS

✚ 429 H13 🛈 Donjon du Capitole, 31080, tel 05 61 11 02 22; Mon–Sat 9–7, Sun 9–1, 2–5.30, May–end Sep; Mon–Fri 9–6, Sat 9–12.30, 2–6, Sun 10–12.30, 2–5, rest of year
🚆 Toulouse
www.ot-toulouse.fr (in English, Spanish and French)

TIPS

● If you've come to shop, the narrow lanes between place du Capitole and rue de Metz have bijou boutiques, while larger shops can be found along the rue d'Alsace.
● Shaded by trees, the UNESCO-listed Canal du Midi is the perfect place for a walk, jog, boat trip or meal on a barge restaurant.
● Get free entry to certain museums and discounts on other attractions with the *Toulouse en Liberté* pass, which you can buy at the tourist office.

The striking Capitole (above)

Learn about space travel at the Cité de l'Espace (above right)

HIGHLIGHTS

PLACE DU CAPITOLE

This fine square, lined by bars and restaurants, is the city's heart. Its east side is dominated by the imposing façade of the Capitole (town hall). Inside, the Capitole has fine staircases and 19th- and 20th-century paintings *(Mon–Fri 8.30–5; Sat am only)*.

ART

The art collections of the Musée des Augustins-Musée des Beaux-Arts de Toulouse *(Wed–Mon 10–6, also Wed 6–9pm)* are in buildings of a former monastery on rue de Metz. Devotees of modern art should head for the Espace d'Art Moderne et Contemporain *(Tue–Sun 11–7)* in the old abattoir buildings on allées Charles-de-Fitte. At the southern end of the Pont Neuf, the city's oldest bridge, is a photography gallery, Le Château d'Eau *(Tue–Sun 1–7)*, housed in the old water tower.

CHURCHES

The Basilique St-Sernin, on place St-Sernin, is the largest Romanesque church in France and is dedicated to a saint martyred by bulls in AD250. Built to welcome pilgrims on their way to Santiago de Compostela, it has an amazingly light interior. There's a morning market outside the basilica during the week, and a flea market on Sunday mornings. Farther south is Cathédrale St-Étienne, constructed over several centuries. With its asymmetrical structure, it is the antithesis of the all-of-a-piece Basilique St-Sernin. West of place du Capitole, the Église des Jacobins is a severe Gothic church with an unexpectedly flamboyant interior.

CITÉ DE L'ESPACE

✚ Off 207 C2 • Avenue Jean Gonord, 31506 ☎ 05 62 71 48 71 🕐 Daily 9–7
🎫 Adult €12, child (6–12) €9
www.cite-espace.com
On the northern perimeter of the city is the Cité de l'Espace, an educational adventure park dedicated to space exploration. Attractions

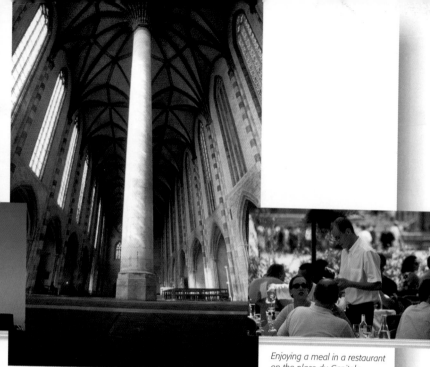

Enjoying a meal in a restaurant on the place du Capitole *(above)*

Inside the Église des Jacobins *(above left)*

include a life-size Ariane rocket, a planetarium and an audio-visual presentation charting life on Earth. You can also see the Mir space station.

BACKGROUND

Toulouse was a key city of learning and culture in the Middle Ages, but its focus is now high-tech industry. It has become France's hub for aeronautics—Airbus Industrie is the largest aeronautical site in Europe. (You can visit the site, by reservation only; tel 05 61 18 06 01.)

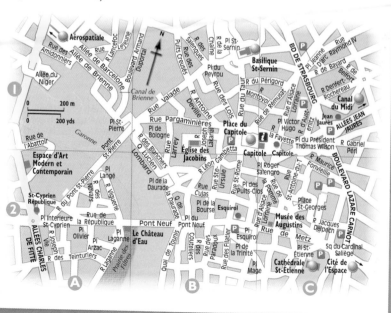

Small boats on a waterway in the Marais Poitevin

ST-ÉMILION

A UNESCO World Heritage Site, St-Émilion has mellow golden stonework and is home to some celebrated wines.

St-Émilion, clinging to a rocky outcrop, is effectively an open-air museum, with its preserved ramparts, seven medieval town gates and winding, narrow streets. The steepest, called *escalettes*, run from west to east, following the hillside's contours. And wine runs through the town's veins. Vineyards stretch to every horizon, shops sell wine and every accessory for its enjoyment, and the legendary, wallet-denting vintages await in dark, cool cellars.

The Romans planted vines here, but it wasn't until after the French Revolution that St-Émilion and the surrounding villages began to develop their disciplined wine monoculture.

The town has three underground sights, all near place des Crénaux: the Église Monolithe, the Catacombs and the 8th-century Hermitage *(daily 10–6)*. Above ground, visit the 13th-century Chapelle de la Trinité *(daily 10–6)* and the Église Collégiale *(accessible behind the tourist office; daily 10–6, winter; an hour longer in summer)*, founded in the 11th century.

Don't miss You'll get some wonderful views from the Tour du Roy, between rue Sainte-Marie and rue du Couvent.

RATINGS

Good for wine	●●●●
Historic interest	●●●●
Photo stops	●●●●

BASICS

🔒 434 F11 🚹 Place des Crénaux, 33330, tel 05 57 55 28 28; 9.30–8 Jul, Aug; 9.30–7, mid to end Jun and early to mid-Sep; 9.30–12.30, 1.45–6.30, Apr to mid-Jun and mid-Sep to Oct; 9.30–12.30, 1.45–6, Nov–end Mar 🚉 St-Émilion 🎫 Various guided tours—contact the tourist office for details www.saint-emilion-tourisme.com

TIPS

● Parking is notoriously difficult, and negotiating the narrow main street, rue Gaudet, can be hazardous. It is better to park at one of the parking areas just outside the town walls.
● High heels are impractical for the steep streets, many of them cobbled. And remember to take a light sweater when visiting cellars, as even in summer below-ground temperatures remain low.
● In high season, reserve ahead for guided visits.

🔒 433 E9 🚹 18 place de l'Église, 79510 Coulon, tel 05 49 35 99 29; daily 10–noon, 2–7, Apr–end Jun and Sep; daily 10–7, Jul, Aug; Tue–Sat 10–noon, 2–5.30, Oct–end Mar www.ville-coulon.fr

When Henri de Navarre, the future king Henri IV, rode through this marshland, he described it as 'a great, green, natural Venice'. The name stuck, and La Venise Verte (the Marais Poitevin) continues to attract visitors seeking peace and quiet.

Here, where the car is replaced by the boat and there are endless stretches of narrow waterways lined with irises and cowslips, life takes on a much slower pace.

The Marais Poitevin is a paradise, but a man-made one. Hundreds of years ago local inhabitants—mainly fishermen, farmers and Benedictine monks from the nearby abbey of Maillezais—began to drain and reclaim the land, and Dutch engineers in the 16th century continued the process.

Today there are two distinct landscapes. Nearer the Vendée coast, the 'dry marshes', the *Marais Desséchés*, peter out in a wind-scoured canvas of huge skies, fields of wheat and bleached salt pans, home to purple herons and black kites. Inland, enclosed and inaccessible without a boat, lie the *Marais Mouillés*, the secretive wetland area criss-crossed by narrow channels leading to tiny, poplar-lined fields and low, whitewashed houses. This is where the area's tourist industry has developed and it is great for walking, bicycling, fishing, canoeing and punting. In Coulon you can hire a punt *(une plate)* and oar *(la pigouille)*, with or without a boatman to guide you.

CORSICA

Corsica has a distinct Italian accent, with Genoese citadels in Calvi and Bonifacio, and Pisan churches and Genoese watchtowers across the island. Finds at Filitosa reveal a prehistoric past and Ajaccio is the birthplace of Napoleon. For peace and quiet, head to the Scandola nature reserve or the fishing villages of Cap Corse.

MAJOR SIGHTS

THE SIGHTS

The fishing port, surrounded by pastel-shaded buildings

RATINGS

Cultural interest	●●●○
Historic interest	●●●○
Photo stops	●●●○

BASICS

432 Q15 ℹ 3 boulevard du Roi Jérôme, 20181, tel 04 95 51 53 03; Mon–Sat 2–8.30, Sun 9–1, 4–7, Apr–end Sep; Mon–Sat 8–6, rest of year
🚉 Ajaccio
www.tourisme.fr/ajaccio

TIPS

● For one of the best sights in Corsica, take a 2-hour boat trip *(mid-Apr to end Oct)* to see the Îles Sanguinaires, deserted islands which turn a deep red as the sun sets.
● Every morning a farmers' market in square Campinchi, sells fresh produce from around the island.
● For a break from sightseeing, shop on rue Cardinal Fesch, then head to boulevard Lantivy and boulevard Pascal Rossini which are behind the beach, around from the Citadelle. They have magical sea views and are lined with bars and restaurants.

AJACCIO

The attractive capital of south Corsica is the birthplace of Napoleon Bonaparte.

Ajaccio is a scenic port on the west coast of the island, framed by mountains. The streets are great for strolling, with plenty of bars, restaurants and shops, while the pastel shades of the old town are easy on the eye. The main street, cours Napoléon, runs north of place du Général de Gaulle for almost 2km (about a mile) alongside the Golfe d'Ajaccio. Place du Général de Gaulle is the heart of the new town, a large, undistinguished square. In contrast, place Foch, in the middle of the old town, is green with palm trees and lined with shops and cafés.

NAPOLEON

Ajaccio delights in its links with Napoleon, who was born here in 1769. Statues, plaques and monuments dedicated to the Bonaparte family can be seen at every turn. South of place Foch, in rue St-Charles, is Maison Bonaparte, the house where Napoleon was born and lived until he was nine *(Mon 2–6, Tue–Sat 9–noon, 2–6, Sun 9–noon, May–end Sep; Mon 2–6, Tue–Sat 10–noon, 2–5, Sun 10–noon, rest of year)*. On the first floor is the sofa where he was born and at the end of the long gallery is the Trapdoor room, where his mother Letizia and her children escaped from the forces of Pascal Paoli (leader of the island's independence movement) in 1793. The Musée Napoléonien, in the town hall on place Foch *(Mon–Fri 9–11.45, 2–5.30, mid-Jun to mid-Sep; Mon–Fri 9–11.45, 2–4.45 mid-Sep to mid-Jun)* has a copy of Napoleon's death mask. The Chapelle Impériale, next to the Palais Fesch, contains the bodies of several members of the Bonaparte family. Napoleon himself is buried in Les Invalides in Paris (see page 77). In June there's a festival dedicated to the emperor.

ART

Joseph Fesch, Cardinal of Lyon and Napoleon's uncle, used his wealth to amass an extraordinary collection of paintings. See them in the Musée Palais Fesch *(Mon 1.30–6, Tue–Sun 9–6.30, Apr–end Sep; Mon 2.15–5.15, Tue–Sat 9.15–12.15, 2.15–5.15, rest of year)*, in rue Cardinal Fesch. Works include *Portrait of a Gloved Man* by Titian, *Leda and the Swan* by Veronese, and a *Virgin and Child* by Botticelli.

The port and citadel at Bonifacio

BONIFACIO

📍 432 Q15 ℹ️ 2 rue Fred Scamaroni, 20169, tel 04 95 73 11 88; daily 9–8 May to mid-Oct; Mon–Fri 9–noon, 2–6, rest of year
www.bonifacio.fr

On Corsica's southern tip, Bonifacio offers wonderful views of Sardinia over the turquoise water of the Mediterranean. The town has a spectacular citadel, built by the Genoese and perched on sculpted limestone cliffs 70m (230ft) above the sea.

The old town, enclosed within the ramparts, is one of the island's best sites and gets very crowded in high season. Look out for the high houses, once only accessible by retractable ladders, and the flying buttresses used for collecting rainwater.

The steps of Montée Rastello are quite a climb, but worth it for the view from the old town. At the top, cross avenue de Gaulle to Montée St-Roch for the spectacular view of the limestone cliffs and the Grain de Sable, an enormous piece of cliff face that plunged into the sea 800 years ago.

In rue du Palais de Garde is the 14th-century church of Sainte-Marie Majeure, modified in the 18th century. This contains a relic of the True Cross rescued from a shipwreck. The relics of St-Boniface are kept in the church in an ivory casket.

If you want to take to the water, several companies offer boat trips around the coast and to the Lavezzi islands, and the area also has some excellent diving.

Bonifacio is a place of legends, reputedly the setting for Ulysses' encounter with the Lestrygon giants in the *Odyssey,* and home to the 'Staircase of the King of Aragon', supposedly built in one night by Aragonese soldiers in a siege in 1420.

BASTIA

Corsica's largest town, with an unspoiled old quarter, is the ideal starting point for exploring mountainous Cap Corse.

Bastia is at the southern end of Cap Corse (see page 212), Corsica's vast mountainous peninsula in the north. The Genoese made it the island's base of government in the 15th century and built the *bastiglia* (fortress) that gave the town its name. They exported wine to Italy from here, bringing prosperity.

Bastia is still Corsica's commercial heart, although the original town, the Terra Vecchia, is untouched by modern business. This old quarter exudes charm, with winding streets and beautiful baroque churches.

Place St-Nicolas, an immense square more than 300m (300 yards) long, with a statue of Napoleon, is the perfect point to start a tour of Bastia. Boulevard Paoli and rue César Campinchi run parallel to the square and are great for shopping. The Terra Vecchia, with the best of Bastia's historic sights, lies to the south of place St-Nicolas. Farther south along the quai du Sud is the citadel, Terra Nova.

On rue Napoléon, you'll find the Oratoire de l'Immaculée Conception, with a sumptuous interior of crimson velvet, gilt and glittering chandeliers. In the Terra Nova, by place du Donjon, is the Moorish-looking 14th-century Palais des Gouverneurs, built at the height of Genoese power. This contains the Musée d'Ethnographie Corse, which will focus on the history of Corsica from prehistoric times onwards when it reopens after renovation work.

In the baroque interior of the Oratoire Sainte-Croix, in rue de l'Évêché, is a holy relic, the Christ des Miracles—a crucifix found in 1428 floating in the sea bathed in a mysterious glow.

RATINGS			
Historic interest	●	●	● ●
Photo stops	●	●	●
Shopping	●	●	●

BASICS
📍 432 Q14 ℹ️ Place St-Nicolas, 20200, tel 04 95 54 20 40; daily 8–8, Jun to mid-Sep; Mon–Sat 8–6, Sun 8–1, rest of year
🚂 Bastia
www.bastia-tourisme.com

TIPS
● There is a farmers' market *(Tue–Sun)* in place de l'Hôtel de Ville.
● Head south of town for sandy beaches and the bird reserve at l'Étang de Biguglia.

The Genoese citadel dominates Calvi

CALVI

⊞ 432 Q14 🛈 Port de Plaisance, 20260, tel 04 95 65 16 67; daily 9–1.30, 2.30–7, Jun–end Oct; Mon–Fri 9–noon, rest of year 🚊 Calvi
www.tourisme.fr/calvi

Calvi, on the northwest coast of the island, is dominated by a Genoese citadel on a rocky promontory. Inside its walls, the pretty baroque church of St-Jean Baptiste contains the *Christ des Miracles*, an ebony statue said by locals to have deterred the Turks besieging the town in 1553, when it was carried through the streets. Also inside the citadel is the St-Antoine oratory, which has frescoes from the 15th and 16th centuries, and the Musée d'Art Religieux et d'Archéologie.

South of the citadel, in the lower town, is the baroque church of Sainte-Marie-Majeure, with its pink door. Farther south is a beautiful bay, with a sandy beach that is 4km (2.5 miles) long and backed by pines.

There is plenty to do in and around Calvi, including water sports such as sailing and diving, or boat trips to the Scandola coast (see page 214). You can drive or take the train to the sea-side resort of l'île Rousse to the north. This is a pleasant place to spend an afternoon and browse in the excellent covered market in a 19th-century building.

West of Calvi, the Revellata peninsula has a sandy beach and beautifully clear water.

Calvi beach

CAP CORSE

This island within an island has mountains, tiny fishing villages, Romanesque churches, vineyards and sandy coves.

Cap Corse is a mountainous peninsula with a central ridge more than 1,000m (3,300ft) high. At Corsica's northeastern extremity, it points like a finger, 40km (25 miles) long and 15km (9 miles) wide, towards Italy's Ligurian coast.

On the *Cap's* western coast, white villages and Genoese watchtowers cling to the top of rugged cliffs. On the east side, smoothed by the lava from ancient volcanoes, there are sandy coves and little ports.

Cap Corse was once intensively cultivated but is now covered in *maquis*, the scrubland vegetation typical of Corsica. The *capcorsins* (residents of Cap Corse) traditionally ventured further than people from other parts of the island. They became skilful sailors and merchants, going to Italian, French and African ports to trade wine, oil, cork and fish.

On the west coast, the ancient settlement of Nonza clings to the cliffs 150m (500ft) above a distinctive black beach and is topped by the remains of a Genoese watchtower. Its fine 16th-century church is dedicated to St. Julie and has an impressive marble altar. On the east coast, Macinaggio has beautiful white beaches, and just north is the Réserve Naturelle des Îles Finocchiarola, a nature reserve of little islands.

Farther south, towards Bastia, is the village of Erbalunga, with its small port. It was once popular with French artists. Many people from Cap Corse who emigrated to South America returned to this area and built spectacular houses with the money that they made abroad. You can still see some of these *palazzi americani*—Renaissance-style palaces and Colonial mansions—in the small villages of Sisco and Cannelle.

RATINGS			
Historic interest	●	●	●
Photo stops	●	●	●	●

BASICS

⊞ 432 Q14 🛈 Port de Plaisance, 20248 Macinaggio, tel 04 95 35 40 34; Mon–Fri 9–noon, 2–6, Sat, Sun 9–noon, Jun; Mon–Sat 9–noon, 3–7.30, Sun 9–noon, Jul, Aug; Mon–Sat 9–noon, 3–6, Sun 9–noon, Sep; Mon–Fri 9–noon, 2–5, rest of year
www.corsica.net

TIP

● Cap Corse produces some of the best wines in Corsica. Try the Muscat du Cap Corse or the rich reds from Patimonio.

Buildings and conifers cling to the hillsides in Corte

Porto's sheltered sandy beach

CORTE

432 Q14 Citadelle de Corte, 20250, tel 04 95 46 26 70; daily 9–8 Jul, Aug; Mon–Sat 9–6, Jun, Sep; Mon–Fri 9–noon, 2–6, Oct–end May
Corte
www.corsica.net

Corte is surrounded by the mountains of the Parc Naturel Régional de Corse and is home to the island's only university, with around 4,000 students. The town is built on a rocky outcrop, and, like many other Corsican towns, has a 15th-century citadel standing high above. Inside is the Musée de la Corse, which focuses on Corsican society and culture.

For panoramic views of the Restonica and Tavignano valleys, climb up to the Belvédère viewing platform.

This region is excellent for walking and Corte is a popular stop-off with walkers. To get to the Niolo region—a plateau surrounded by the island's highest peaks—take the Scala di Santa Regina, a stunning mountain pass northwest of town.

FILITOSA

432 Q15 • On the D57 north of Propriano 04 95 74 00 91
8–dusk, May–end Sep Adult €5

Filitosa, an easy day trip from Propriano, is a prehistoric site inhabited from the Neolithic period to Roman times. Finds reveal that people lived in the caves here as early as 5,000 years ago. The most impressive part of the site is the megalithic standing stones (or menhirs) with their carved faces. It is not known why they were put here.

There is also a small museum, and the location in the Tavaro Valley makes this an ideal spot for a picnic.

LA PORTA

432 Q14

This small village is notable for some fine Corsican baroque religious architecture and is set among chestnut groves and rolling hills in the heart of the Castagniccia area, nearly 40km (25 miles) northeast of Corte. The region is named after the Corsican word for chestnut, *castagnu*. The nuts that were harvested here formed part of the staple diet of many Corsicans.

In previous centuries, La Porta saw battles against the Romans, the Vandals, the Arabs, the Genoese and the French. Today it is a peaceful village of narrow streets, with tall buildings with painted shutters.

La Porta is a good place for walks, as many paths lead from here into the hills and mountains of La Castagniccia.

In Piazza di u Piano locals sit on the benches chatting and watching visitors who come to see the Église St-Jean-Baptiste, an ochre-and-white 17th-century church. Its façade is ornately decorated with pinnacles and scrolls, and its 18th-century campanile is thought to be the finest

Boats at Porto

baroque bell tower on the island. Inside, the church has a magnificent Italian organ, built by a monk in 1780, a fine painted ceiling and a 17th-century figure of Christ painted on wood.

PORTO

432 Q14 Place de la Marine, 20150, tel 04 95 26 10 55; Mon–Sat 6–6, mid-Apr to end Jun; daily 9–7, Jul, Aug; Mon–Fri 9–noon, 2–5 rest of year
www.porto-tourisme.com

The Gulf of Porto, on Corsica's west coast, is a UNESCO World Heritage Site, while the town of Porto is a popular seaside resort, especially busy in summer. The focal point is the Genoese tower (daily 11–7, Apr–end May, Sep, Oct; 9.30–9.30, Jun–end Aug), which stands at the front of the port and is a perfect viewing point for the beautiful sunsets for which the town is famous. Built in the second half of the 16th century, it is unusual in being square rather than round like most of the other Genose towers on the island. Inside, there is a museum with a permanent exhibition on the various towers on the island.

In the summer, you can take a boat trip to see the flora and fauna in the nearby Réserve Naturelle de Scandola (see page 214), or to *les calanches de Piana,* rocky inlets with sides hundreds of metres high.

The aquarium at the marina (daily 8–10, Jun–end Aug; 8–9, Sep; 8–5, rest of year) is in a former Genoese warehouse and has various Mediterranean species that can be found in the Gulf and in the Scandola nature reserve. Expect to find grouper, moray eels and octopus. For those who prefer their marine life in the sea, experience the superb diving in the Golfe de Porto, where you may see coral, tuna, lobster and even barracuda.

THE SIGHTS

The beautiful Réserve Naturelle de Scandola

Sartène, in the southwest of Corsica, is proud of its long history

RÉSERVE NATURELLE DE SCANDOLA

✚ 432 P14

This nature reserve was created in 1975 and is part of the Parc Naturel Régional de Corse. The site covers 1,900 hectares (4,700 acres), of which 900 hectares (2,200 acres) are land and 1,000 hectares (2,500 acres) are sea. The whole area is a UNESCO World Heritage Site. There are no paths to the reserve, so the only way to get there is by boat—companies in Calvi, Porto, Cargèse and Ajaccio run boat tours.

The reserve is popular with scientists and visitors because of the varying geology, flora and fauna, and there are even some Roman remains. There are jagged and sheer cliffs (some of the distinctive red cliffs are up to 900m/3,000ft high), with caves and grottos and stacks left by wave erosion. Animal and bird spotters will have a great time, as the reserve is home to peregrine falcon, osprey, puffins, bearded vultures, Audouin gulls and dolphins. Unfortunately the seal colony is no more and commercial fishing has reduced the number of spiny lobster dramatically. With such a rich variety of wildlife and marine life, activities such as fishing, diving and camping are prohibited.

Nearby Girolata (not part of the reserve although part of the UNESCO site) can be reached only by foot or boat, and is worth a visit for its Genoese fortress.

ST-FLORENT

✚ 432 Q14 🅸 Centre Administratif, 20217, tel 04 95 37 06 04; Mon–Fri 9–noon, 2–5, Sat 9–noon, summer only www.corsica.net

St-Florent, a pretty port in the Nebbio region in the northeast, is a popular holiday spot because of its beaches and Moorish-style Genoese citadel, which overlooks the harbour. At its heart is place des Portes, a good place to sit with a drink and watch the local action.

The main sight here is the 12th-century Pisan Cathédrale de Nebbio, to the east, on the site of the old Roman city. St-Florent's main beach, Plage de la Roya, is in the south.

For the energetic, a path goes west along the Agriates coast, past the beautiful beaches of Lodo and Saleccia and the protected Désert des Agriates. For those who prefer to take things easy, boats leave for the beaches from the marina in town.

Patrimonio, 6km (4 miles) northeast of St-Florent, is surrounded by vineyards and produces red, white, rosé and dessert wines. The area has long been recognized as a producer of some of the best wines in Corsica. Patrimonio exported wine to Italy during the Middle Ages, and it is known that Cap Corse muscat was drunk at papal tables during the Renaissance.

SARTÈNE

✚ 432 Q15 🅸 6 rue Borgo, 20100, tel 04 95 77 15 40; daily 9–2, 3–7, Jun–end Aug; Mon–Fri 9–1, 2.30–6.30, Sat 9–1, rest of year www.corsica.net

Sartène, in the southwest of the island, is proud of its traditions, dating back to the Middle Ages. On Good Friday, the *Catenacciu* procession takes place, during which a penitential citizen in a red, hooded robe, his feet wrapped in chains, carries a heavy cross through the town. The rest of the year, the cross and chains can be seen in the Église Sainte-Marie in the old town, a maze of very narrow streets. The Santa Anna quarter, with its cobbled streets, is worth exploring.

The Musée Départemental de la Préhistoire Corse, in a former prison, displays items from prehistoric sites in Corsica *(closed for renovations—due to reopen in 2004)*.

There are interesting prehistoric sites with menhirs (standing stones) to the south of Sartène, reached via quiet roads that take you into the countryside. Once you have parked your car, there is usually a walk to the stones.

About 15km (9 miles) south are the menhirs at Cauria and the Fontanaccia dolmen. Off the D48 are the Palaggio menhirs, one of the best collections of megalithic standing stones in the Mediterranean.

Punta Palazzu, in the Réserve Naturelle de Scandola

This chapter provides information on things to do in France other than sightseeing. In Paris and the Île de France entries are ordered by theme. The rest of the regions are sub-divided by area. Shops, arts venues, nightlife, sports and activities are listed alphabetically by town within these areas. Festivals and events are listed in date order at the end of each section.

What to Do

SHOPPING

Shopping is one of the joys of a visit to France. The French are demanding and discerning consumers, whether shopping for their daily bread or for haute couture. France is renowned for food, wine, porcelain and crystal. Prices are often as high as at home, but in one category—wines and spirits—British visitors can take advantage of the lower levels of duty. Non-EU visitors can reclaim VAT on certain purchases.

FOOD

It's not surprising that in the country that gave us foie gras, champagne and haute cuisine, food has always been taken very seriously, with quality and freshness high on every shopper's list of priorities. Food stores (other than supermarkets) are specialists, usually selling only one type of product. The ones you are most likely to see are the *boulangerie* (bakery), *pâtisserie* (pastry/cake shop), *fromagerie* (cheese shop), *boucherie* (butcher's shop), *charcuterie* (originally a pork butcher, today a delicatessen), *poissonnerie* (fishmonger's) and *caviste* (wine shop).

INDIVIDUAL BOUTIQUES

The predominance of the specialist shop also carries through to the non-food sector. France has seen less of an ingress of high street names than other countries, so there are smaller, individual boutiques selling fashion (*prêt-à-porter*), lingerie, shoes and items such as china and kitchenware. In larger cities the department store (*grand magasin*) brings all these specialists under one roof.

MARKETS

The *marché* (market) is a French institution. Large cities hold at least one daily market, and smaller towns have a weekly market. They start around 7am and finish at noon. This is where to find the freshest seasonal produce,

CHAIN STORES

NAME	Menswear	Womenswear	For children	Shoes	Cosmetics and toiletries	Sports equipment and clothing	Accessories	Household items	Books, music and DVDs	Perfume	CONTACT NUMBER
Alain Manoukian	✔	✔		✔			✔				04 75 07 50 50
André			✔	✔			✔				01 53 26 28 28
Bata			✔	✔			✔				01 47 76 40 04
The Body Shop					✔		✔			✔	01 53 05 51 51
Caroll		✔		✔			✔				04 75 07 50 50
Celio	✔						✔				01 49 48 13 00
Courir			✔	✔			✔				01 46 15 55 00
Du Pareil au Même			✔	✔			✔				01 69 81 46 46
Etam		✔					✔				01 44 76 73 73
FNAC									✔		01 53 53 64 64
Foot Locker			✔	✔		✔	✔				01 70 20 00 57
Gap	✔	✔	✔	✔			✔			✔	01 44 88 28 28
Go Sport	✔	✔	✔	✔		✔	✔				04 76 28 20 20
H&M	✔	✔	✔				✔				01 53 20 71 11
Kookaï		✔					✔				01 43 52 52 52
Mango		✔		✔			✔				+34 93 860 24 2
Marionnaud										✔	01 48 08 69 69
Minelli				✔			✔				01 53 35 86 10
Monoprix	✔	✔	✔	✔	✔		✔	✔		✔	01 55 20 74 42
Morgan		✔					✔				01 49 34 06 95
Naf Naf	✔	✔	✔	✔			✔				01 48 13 88 88
Pimkie		✔	✔	✔			✔				03 20 81 48 48
Promod		✔		✔			✔				03 20 01 10 00
Virgin Megastore									✔		01 49 53 50 00
Zara	✔	✔		✔			✔				+34 981 185 40(

including fruit, vegetables, regional foodstuffs and cheeses, and other products from basketware to pottery. Other forms of market are advertised in the local press or by flyers attached to posts in the area. *Foires artisanales* bring together potters, sculptors and other artists, and are held once or twice a year at historical locations such as medieval villages or chateaux. *Marchés aux puces* (flea markets) can be found in some of the larger cities in France. *Brocante* is the collective term for items that fall into a category between genuine antiques and flea market goods—anything from furniture to china. *Vide grenier* is the French equivalent of a British car boot sale.

MODERN STORES

France has not totally missed out on the shopping revolution of the last 30 years. On the outskirts of every big town or city, supermarkets and hyper-markets *(hypermarchés* or *grandes-surface)* have sprung up; the main names include Carrefour, Auchan, Champion and E. Leclerc. Here you will find the specialist *boulangerie, boucherie* and *charcuterie* under one roof. Often the *hypermarchés* are surrounded by other stores, for example DIY and sports stores, in a *centre commercial*.

CHIC SHOPPING

Paris is of course the hub of *la mode française*, but away from the capital, French style at its best can be found in any of the chic resorts, such as Nice or Cannes in the southeast, Biarritz in the southwest, La Baule in the north and Chamonix in the Alps.

WINES AND SPIRITS

Hypermarchés sell an excellent range of French wines and spirits but it is more fun to buy from the vineyards *(domaines)* themselves. You can taste the youngest bottled wine of the finest producers in Bordeaux, Burgundy or Champagne but you will be expected to buy at least one bottle in return. If you are not sure your budget will stretch to fine wines then many areas have cooperatives where you can sample local AOC *(Appellation Contrôlée)* wines or *vins de pays* (country wines) for fewer euros.

WHAT TO DO

In addition to countless individual boutiques and specialist shops, France, like most other European countries, has some chain stores including well-known American, Spanish and British names. You will find branches of the stores listed in the chart below in shopping areas and malls throughout the country.

NUMBER OF SHOPS	DESCRIPTION	WEBSITE
115	Stylish clothes and accessories for women and men	www.alain-manoukian.com
200	Footwear for men, women and children	www.vivarte.fr
251	Smart and sporty shoes and boots for men, women and children	www.bata.com
29	Make-up and skin and body products for men and women	www.thebodyshop.com
164	Elegant clothes and accessories for women	www.caroll.com
142	Popular clothing and accessories for men	www.celio.com
176	Sports footwear and accessories (watches and bags) for the whole family	www.courir.com
118	Clothes, toys, pushchairs (strollers) and equipment for babies/children	www.dpam.com
223	Inexpensive fashion, lingerie and accessories for women	www.etam.com
64	Books, music, DVDs, computer equipment and concert tickets	www.fnac.com
58	Sports shoes and sporty accessories such as sunglasses, watches and bags	www.footlocker.com
12	Everyday clothes and accessories for the whole family	www.gap.com
116	Sports clothing, shoes, equipment and accessories for all	www.gosport.fr
41	A must for fashion lovers on a budget. High fashion at rock-bottom prices	www.hm.com
56	Fashion and accessories for women	www.kookai.com
44	Fashion and accessories for women	www.mango.es
552	Perfume stores	www.marionnaud.com
133	Funky shoes and boots	www.vivarte.fr
243	Department store selling food, household items, clothes and cosmetics	www.monoprix.fr
86	Fashions for women	www.morgandetoi.com
138	Clothes for women and children (Naf Naf) and men (Chevignon)	www.nafnaf.com
255	Clothes and accessories at rock-bottom prices for women and girls	www.pimkie.fr
135	Reasonably priced clothes for women	www.promod.com
28	DVDs, videos, books, CDs, posters, computer games and concert tickets	www.virgin.com
60	Smart clothes and accessories for men and women	www.zara.es

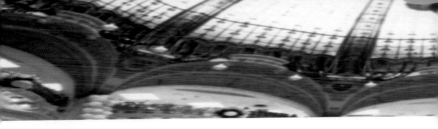

Regional Shopping

Modern transportation and commerce mean that the best-known products of the different regions, for long a trademark of France and once obtainable only from their source, can now usually be bought all across the country. However, there is a particular pleasure in buying your souvenirs from their place of origin, or seeking out local producers for food and wine to take home as a taste of France.

NORTHWEST FRANCE AND THE LOIRE

Brittany has long been known for its lace, but the handmade variety is now rare and expensive. Pottery is much more common. The best is from the town of Quimper, although imitations crowd souvenir shops around the region. Local food items are farm-produced Camembert cheese, honey or salt from the coastal flats at Guérande. Drinks include excellent cider, Calvados (apple brandy) and crisp Muscadet wine, the best of which is produced *sur lie*—where the newly fermented wine remains in contact with the lees (sediment).
The towns of Auray and Honfleur are artists' enclaves.

NORTH AND NORTHEAST FRANCE AND ÎLE DE FRANCE

The north's principal lure is the champagne produced around Reims, but Alsace-Lorraine has interesting white wines in Riesling and Gewürztraminer. Head north for beer too. Soft, creamy Brie is the principal

cheese of the region, produced in the Île de France, east of Paris. Mustard from Meaux is another excellent buy.

CENTRAL FRANCE AND THE ALPS

Natural products made by hand from the raw materials of the area are very much in vogue today: Bone-bladed knives, wooden walking sticks, items made of slate, even fur—all items that have been produced here for centuries. Coming up to date, look for winter and summer sportswear and adventure equipment from snowboards to mountain bikes.

Preserved foods such as *charcuterie* (dried and prepared meats) and jams also make excellent purchases.

Burgundy equals Bordeaux in its reputation for wine, with sublime reds and whites, the best of which are produced along the Côte d'Or near Beaune. *Eau-de-vie* (a clear spirit) and *marc* (local brandy), made from distilled grape skins, are the main after-dinner drinks. Dijon is synonymous with mustard.

Moving down the Saône valley through the Beaujolais vineyards brings you to Lyon with its centuries of experience in silk production. Today you can still buy hand-produced silk items. South of Lyon you will find the Rhône valley, with its world-famous wines.

Thiers has been France's main producer of cutlery for several centuries and some is still made by hand here.

SOUTHWEST FRANCE

In the southwest food should be top of your shopping list. Truffles, *cèpes* (ceps) and foie gras (goose or duck liver) are all at their best here.

Bordeaux needs no introduction as a wine-producing area and some of the finest names in the business have chateaux in the region, including Margaux and Pomerol. You can taste and buy fine French brandies around Cognac.

Porcelain from Limoges has long been renowned around the world, while the town of Aubusson has supplied the chateaux of France with tapestries since the Middle Ages.

SOUTHEAST FRANCE AND CORSICA

Several staple foodstuffs grown in the southeast will enhance your larder, including dried wild herbs, virgin olive oil (best around Nyons) and strings of garlic. Head to

Castelnaudary for authentic cassoulet, the slow-cooked dish of sausage and duck or goose with beans, which you can take home in tins.

In addition to the aroma of wild herbs, the air in the south is heavy with the scent of flowers, particularly around Grasse, famous for its perfumes. *Savon* (soap) *de Marseille* is known for its quality, and soap is available throughout the region, often made with a base of olive oil. Nothing of the olive tree is wasted: The wood is carved into items, from salad bowls to coasters. Terracotta pottery is also widespread.

In Corsica, pick up local cheeses and wines, ceramics and hand-carved wood items.

PERFORMANCE

France has a rich cultural heritage in the performing arts, ranging from acknowledged classics to the most avant-garde productions, and venues from small smoky clubs to 50,000-seat stadiums. Paris has the richest selection, but more than 300 music festivals are held around the country each year, plus an abundance of live performances at Maisons de la Culture or Maisons d'Animation Culturelle in the provinces. Listings magazines are the best source of information.

THEATRE

The founding of Paris's Comédie Française (*www.comedie-francaise.fr*) in 1680 kick-started a national love of the theatre. Paris continues to stage a wealth of classical, avant-garde and foreign-language plays. The Comédie, which performs mainly at the Palais Royal in Paris, still concentrates on the classics, and the great French dramatists (Molière, Racine, Victor Hugo) are revisited each season.

Every major French city has a theatre. Almost all productions are in French, but with some knowledge of the language, a visit to the theatre can still be enjoyed. In most auditoriums smoking is not permitted.

BALLET AND CONTEMPORARY DANCE

The Opéra de Paris Ballet (*Théâtre de l'Opéra, 8 rue Scribe, 75009, Paris; tel 01 47 42 53 71; www.balletdelopera.com*) is more than 300 years old; its reputation reached its zenith under the direction of the Russian dancer Rudolf Nureyev in the late 1980s. Several other major cities have ballet companies including Lyon (*www. opera-lyon.org*), Biarritz (*www.balletbiarritz.com*) and Monte Carlo (*www. balletsdemontecarlo.com*). Modern and contemporary dance are popular. In Paris, the Centre Georges Pompidou (*www.centrepompidou.fr*) leads the way with performances by French and

international companies. Montpellier's Centre Chorégraphique National (*www.ville-montpellier.fr*) is regarded as a focus of excellence for contemporary dance.

OPERA

One of the capital's finest examples of modern architecture, the Opéra Bastille, opened in 1989 (*www.opera-de-paris.fr*) and has a regular schedule of performances. There are 12 regional opera companies around the country including those in Lyon (*www.opera-lyon.org*) and Toulouse (*www.theatre-du-capitole.org*).

CLASSICAL MUSIC

Paris has no world-renowned orchestra, and live classical music has a lower profile here than in some European capitals. However, several ensembles, such as the Orchestre de Paris (*www. orchestredeparis.com*), have an annual schedule and autumn is the main classical music season.

Classical recital seasons held in important historical venues are a popular addition to arts calendars across France. Two of these are the Grandes Eaux Musicales at Versailles and the International Organ Festival at Chartres cathedral.

JAZZ

Paris is one of Europe's leading jazz venues, with a plethora of small clubs including Le New Morning (see page 229) catering to an army of

aficionados. Jazz is also the focus for many festivals, including the autumn Festival du Jazz in the capital, festivals

in Nice, Antibes and at the Roman amphitheatre in Vienne in July, and the Grenoble festival in March.

BOOKING TICKETS

Most theatre box offices sell tickets for their own performances and will accept telephone bookings with payment by credit card. FNAC stores (*www.fnac.com*) are ticket agents; for rock, pop or jazz concerts try Virgin Megastore (*www.virginmega. fr*), or for multi-venue arts festivals try the tourist office.

Matinée performances are often less expensive than evening shows, and same-day tickets (if available) are also sold at a price reduction. In Paris, the Kiosque Théâtre sells reduced-price tickets for the day of the performance for most Paris theatres. There are outlets at 15 place de la Madeleine and at Gare Montparnasse.

DRESS CODES

Evening orchestral, operatic and theatre performances require smart but not necessarily formal clothing, although you can dress up without feeling overdressed. For other types of performance, casual clothing is perfectly acceptable.

NIGHTLIFE

There are great contrasts in nightlife throughout France. Large swathes of countryside might as well be desert for those seeking nightlife, other than an alfresco dinner followed by a few pages of your summer reading.

The major cities, of course, are a different matter. Paris leads the way, with a worldwide reputation as a party city. Lyon, Marseille, Nantes, Toulouse, Montpellier and others have a thriving nightlife and the youth base of many university towns drives a vibrant club scene.

In addition to the geographical divide, there is the seasonal schism. The resorts of the Alps are buzzing during the ski season, but close down in the summer. This is the time of year when there's a mass exodus from the cities to the coast. It is then that Côte d'Azur clubs come alive.

substantial amount of flesh.

The Moulin Rouge (see page 227) is the Grand Dame of the genre, and its 100-artiste costumed spectacles continue to enthuse new audiences, particularly since the eponymous movie blockbuster in 2001. For a more intimate, and perhaps more titillating performance, try Crazy Horse (see page 227).

CLUBS

All major urban areas have a lively club scene, particularly in the university towns. Flyers at tourist offices, record stores or fashionable cafés will point you in the right direction. Clubs open around 9pm but don't really get started until around 11pm, then partying continues until the early hours.

CASINOS

Not necessarily just for James Bond types, a night at a casino is part entertainment, part spectator sport, and provided you don't go totally over the top and lose your shirt, a great place to mix with European high rollers.

You'll find casinos in all the grand Belle-Époque resorts or spas, although the doyenne has to be Monte Carlo (www.casino-monte-carlo. com). Grands Casinos are the epitome of elegance, and you should be too if you want to get past the doormen. The tables open around 10pm and close around 4am.

THE CAFÉ-BAR

The inextricably linked café-bar is the lifeblood of French nightlife. Even the most humble village will have at least one place to hang out over a few drinks. In country areas French bars have multiple personalities—they are a place for teenagers to hang out around the slot machine or over a game of pool, and somewhere for farmers to meet to discuss the latest subsidy controversy. In the cities, and especially in the resorts, bars are more sophisticated—diners drop in for an aperitif before dinner or a coffee and *digestif* afterwards. Every bar worth its salt will have tables outside during the summer, and the most popular are those where the clientele can watch the world go by as evening turns to night.

A PMU bar is a branch of the French tote system where you

can bet on horse races and often watch meetings live on TV. However, these venues can be smoky and are not always used to welcoming visitors.

In cities, bars open as early as 7am to serve breakfast and stay open until the early hours of the morning. There are no set licensing hours though a late-night permit is needed to serve drinks after midnight. Out of season and out of the cities, bars may close as early as 9pm.

Unaccompanied children under 16 are not allowed into bars and the legal age for drinking is 16, although children aged 14–16 may drink wine or beer if accompanied by an adult.

CABARET

Revues are a peculiarly Parisian form of entertainment, and although Toulouse-Lautrec might be disappointed, today's leg-shows still display a

GAY AND LESBIAN SCENE

Paris is an excellent destination, particularly the Marais district, which has a wealth of gay hotels, bars, clubs and businesses. Other hotspots are in the south around St-Tropez and along the Côte d'Azur.

To find out more see regional listings magazines.

SPORTS AND ACTIVITIES

Spectator Sports

Whatever the season there's a full schedule of sporting action in France, and, surprisingly, many of the premier events don't cost a cent to watch unless you want to cosy up to the glitterati in the VIP box.

BICYCLING

The Tour de France is arguably the most important sporting event in France. The three-week-long event crosses the country in July, with the last stage and dramatic climax in Paris when the competitors push for the line at the end of the Champs-Élysées.

You don't need a ticket to be a spectator of the Tour de France. Simply find a suitable spot along the route on any stage. You'll need to arrive early as the roads are closed at least a couple of hours before the race is due to pass by. www.letour.fr

DOWNHILL SKIING

The European ski season kicks off each year with the Premier Neige men's downhill race on the first Sunday in December at Val d'Isère, in the Alps.

Large crowds gather in the finish area at La Daille to cheer on their preferred skier and drink mulled wine (vin chaud). You don't even need a ticket for this event.

The Val d'Isère tourist office has details of the race dates: B.P. 228, 773115 Val d'Isère (tel 04 79 06 06 60; www.valdisere.com).

FRENCH OPEN TENNIS

The first European Grand Slam tournament of the tennis season is on the clay courts of Roland-Garros Stadium in Paris at the end of May/beginning of June.

You'll need to apply for tickets for set dates by the end of February. For a booking form contact: FFT, Service Réservation, B.P. 33316, 75767 Paris Cedex 16 (www.rolandgarros.com).

Any unsold tickets go on sale at the stadium a few days before the tournament begins. Ticket prices range from €9 to €57.

HORSE-RACING

Horse-racing is a popular sport in France, and the most popular flat race for owners and betters takes place in October at Longchamps in the Bois de Boulogne, outside Paris. The Prix de l'Arc de Triomphe is an opportunity for ladies to don their hats, drink champagne and cheer on their horse. Hippodrome de Longchamps: Route du Tribune, Bois du Boulogne, 75116 Paris (tel 01 44 30 75 00).

MOTOR SPORTS

The most important highlight of the four-wheel racing calendar in France is a close-run thing. First contender is the Le Mans 24-hour rally, where the cars test their endurance around this part racing circuit, part road track. General entry tickets range from €40 to €50 and a pit walk is €450. Order from the Ticket Office (Billetterie), Circuit des 24 Heures du Mans, 72019

Le Mans Cedex 2 (tel 02 43 40 24 75; www.lemans.org).

There are two possibilities for Formula One fans. The most glamorous race is at Monte-Carlo in Monaco, where the cars twist and turn through the narrow streets. The presence of the jet set turns Monaco into much more than a Grand Prix, but if you simply want to watch the racing, prices for hillside viewing start at €115, with stand seats costing from €250 to €800 (www.monte-carlo.mc).

The French Grand Prix proper is held at Magny Cours circuit, with general entry starting at €115 and stand prices at €250 (www.magnyf1.com).

RUGBY

There is a strong rugby following in France and the season (Sep–end May) culminates in the international Six Nations Tournament when France takes on England, Scotland, Wales, Ireland and Italy in a bid to be the best in Europe. Teams scrum down at the Stade de France: ZAC du Cornillon Nord, 93216 St-Denis La Plaine Cedex (tel 01 55 93 00 00; ticketline 0892 700 900; www.stadefrance.fr).

SOCCER

Soccer is one of the premier sports in France. Olympique Lyonnais and A.S. Monaco were top of the league in 2003, but tickets for matches (season Aug–end May) are like gold dust.

Olympique Lyonnais: Siège de l'Olympique Lyonnais, 350 avenue Jean Jaurès, 69007, Lyon (ticketline 04 72 76 76 13; www.olympiquelyonnais.com).

A.S. Monaco: Stade Louis II, B.P. 698, 9814 Monaco (tel 00 377 92 05 40 00; www.asm-foot.mc).

Activities

With its magnificent landscapes—snow-covered alpine peaks, hillsides festooned with wild flowers, magnificent rivers and Atlantic, Channel and Mediterranean coastlines—it would be surprising if the French did not enjoy outdoor activities. But enjoy is perhaps too bland a word: They have a great enthusiasm for sporting activities, and indeed have had a pivotal influence on several modern technical sports. Think of the Montgolfier brothers for ballooning, the Blériots for flying or Jacques Cousteau for scuba-diving. If you can climb it, jump from it, ski down it, sail on it, swim under it, ride on it or slither through it, the French do it—and there will be an association to organize and publicize the activity.

GENERAL INFORMATION

Each district in France has some form of sporting facility, be it a simple *boules* (bowls) pitch, sports hall, swimming pool (*piscine*), tennis court or golf course. Information about these facilities appears in locally and regionally produced tourist information publications under *loisirs* (leisure). Most regional tourist organizations publish separate booklets specifically relating to their leisure facilities.

The various associations on this page and page 223 can provide extra information about their particular sports. However, the French Government Tourist Office (FGTO) also produces some excellent brochures on leisure and sporting activities throughout the country, which may be a better starting point.

AIR SPORTS

Most regions in France have at least one airfield where a

variety of clubs meet to practise flying *(vol)*, gliding *(vol*

à voile) or launching themselves out of aeroplanes *(parachutisme)*. These are privately run members' clubs which generally welcome foreign members (although the price, at around €200, may be prohibitive for short-term holiday benefit). They also offer introductions *(baptêmes)* to the sport for beginners, with prices of around €75 for a flight, €400 for parachute training and €230 for a tandem parachute jump.
Fédération Française de vol libre: www.ffvl.com
Fédération Française de vol à voile: www.ffvv.com

BICYCLING/ MOUNTAIN BIKING

Cycling *(cyclisme)*, either off or on road, is a popular pastime, as well as a serious sport. It is easy to rent bicycles in towns and at more than 200 railway stations (around €10 per day). For beginners, the flat areas of the Landes in Aquitaine are ideal. Experienced riders with mountain bikes *(vélo toutes terrain—VTT)* could head for the Alps or the Massif Central. Fédération Française de Cyclisme: www.ffc.fr

CLIMBING

The Alps have some of the most challenging climbs in the world and Mont Blanc is Europe's highest mountain. It's also possible to climb in the Pyrenees and the Massif Central.

The Club Alpin de Français *(www.clubalpin.com)* has information about climbing schools and lessons, or equipment rental for experienced climbers. Prices for guides are around €300 per day, or €300 per person for a two-day group climb.

FISHING

France's 240,000km (150,000 miles) of rivers, 120,000 ha (300,000 acres) of lakes and 4,800km (3,000-mile) coastline are perfect for a spot of fishing. However, on rivers and lakes, some of which are private, you will require a licence (available from fishing shops) to cast your line.

GOLF

Although France was somewhat left behind as golf mania swept through the UK and North America, it has been catching up fast, with hectares of new greens springing up. Some of the best courses are linked to venerable French resorts—Dinan, Nice and Vichy to name just three—where the golf course is seen as an extension of the experience of spa and casino. You can take to the course for around €40 per round. Fédération Française de Golf: www.ffg.org

HORSE-RIDING

Horse-riding *(équitation/ randonée equéstre)*, or perhaps a little gymkhana practice, is available throughout France but is more concentrated in holiday areas during the summer months. Some of the most spectacular yet undemanding routes are on the flat marshes of the Camargue in the southeast, the Marais Salants in the northwest, or the dry pine forests of the Landes in the southwest. A day-long guided ride with picnic costs around €55. One hour is around €20. Fédération Française d'Équitation: www.ffe.com

KARTING

Even if you can't drive at Le Mans, you can still take to the track at specially built karting venues across the country. All

the equipment is provided, plus an introduction to the karts if required. Prices start at €10 for 10 minutes of track time. During peak times track time is limited.

KAYAKING

Many of France's waterways offer excellent opportunities for kayaking, including the Gorges de l'Ardèche or the Lot or Dordogne rivers. You can rent equipment on site by the hour, the day or longer, or you can take a day group kayak ride for around €25.
Fédération Française de Canöe-Kayak: www.ffck.org

PARAPENTE

The *parapente* is a little like a parachute but more controllable, and you don't need to take an aeroplane ride—a running jump from any high point launches you into the air. Pioneered in France, it is a popular sport. Obviously mountainous areas—the Alps, the Massif Central and the Pyrenees—are the best places to try it. Parapente training courses cost around €400, or try a tandem flight for €70.
Fédération Française de Vol Libre: www.ffvl.com

SKIING/SNOWBOARDING

These are the principal sports of the winter season, with as many resorts as there are

snowy days of the year, each offering different options for the beginner, intermediate or expert. Val d'Isère is popular, but you can mix with the European glitterati at chic Courcheval or Chamonix, or go for off-piste action at Argentière.

The Pyrenees offer excellent skiing but fewer resorts than the Alps. There's also good skiing in the Massif Central at Le Mont-Dore.

You will need to buy a ski pass, which cost up to €36.50 per day in Val d'Isère. If you don't have your own equipment you can rent it for around €100 per week. Lessons conducted in English are available in a group (€196 for three three-hour lessons) or as an individual (€34 per hour). Contact the École du Ski Français: www.esf.net or Club Alpin Français: www.clubalpin.com

WALKING AND HIKING

France has over 30,000km (18,600 miles) of footpaths, with a series of Grandes Randonées (long distance footpaths) and Petites Randonées that are included on maps published by Institut Géographique National *(IGN, Éspace IGN rue La Boétie, 75008 Paris; www.ign.fr)*. The premier Grandes Randonées routes are GR34 around the coast of Brittany and GR20 across the rugged interior of Corsica. These take at least two weeks to complete in full, but you can walk sections.

To supplement this network, every *département* (region) and even local *communes* (districts) have shorter walks, including footpaths signposted around lakes, along river banks or linking historical monuments. Most tourist offices in France have plenty of information about footpaths and walks in their area, and town halls usually have free maps of local walks.

WINDSURFING

There are usually perfect conditions for windsurfing along the southwest coast from Biarritz up past Arcachon in the Landes and north into the Loire Atlantique. However, windsurfing schools and board rental can be found all around the French coastline and on the major lakes. Renting a board costs from €20 an hour.

Health and Beauty

What the rest of the world has discovered in the last 10 years the French have known for centuries—that a little pampering is good for everyone.

SPAS

France is dotted with natural water sources, which over time developed into therapeutic spas. In the 18th century spas became places for pleasure as well as health, with Vichy leading the way. During the latter part of the 19th century, grand coastal resorts such as Dinard and Biarritz joined the pampering business.

Today France's spas are some of the finest in the world, with high standards of training and cleanliness, plus a genteel clientele. Spa towns usually also offer high-class shopping and dining for a total package of enjoyment.

THALASSOTHERAPY

The French invented thalassotherapy—the use of seawater in a variety of therapies. Thalassotherapy venues, often linked with spas, are dotted along France's coastline—almost equally distributed between the Mediterranean, Atlantic and northern coasts. Treatments are also available in spas across the country—locations include Paris and Aix-les-Bains.

CHILDREN

At first glance it may appear that France—with its abundance of museums, chateaux and art galleries—offers little for children. But although the Louvre in Paris or Chartres cathedral may not make all kids jump up and down with excitement, France has a different set of attractions for the young.

BEACHES
There is an excellent range of beaches along France's 4,800km (3,000 miles) of coastline, from the wide sandy bays of La Baule to the rock pools of Finistère and river beaches in the Ardèche. These have areas where children can play or explore for hours.

FESTIVALS AND FAIRS
These are held throughout France in the summer and are perfect for children. There are marching bands, merry-go-rounds, costumed minstrels, clowns and face painting.

SPORTS
France has a comprehensive range of sports. The level of training and supervision is usually very high, so children can try a new sport or simply enjoy one in which they are already proficient—from horse-riding to bicycling or windsurfing to snowboarding.

THEME PARKS
France's premier theme park, Disneyland Resort Paris, needs little introduction but it is not the only attraction of this type. Parc Astérix, 30km (19 miles) north of Paris, re-creates the

cartoon world of Asterix the Gaul. Planète Sauvage safari park (see page 245), just south of Nantes, brings Africa

to France. There are three Walibi adventure parks (www.walibi.be), while Futuroscope (see page 200) has attractions based on the moving image and high-tech visual effects.

FESTIVALS AND EVENTS

Whenever and wherever France celebrates, one thing is certain—you are unlikely to go hungry or thirsty. Even in cities the atmosphere is more family party than public event. Whatever the theme, glasses and plates are filled and refilled, and visitors get to see the true identity of a town or village, reflecting as much the history and traditions of the region as of France itself. For France's national holidays see page 414.

RELIGIOUS
In the east, St. Nicolas parades through town on 6 December, offering children sweets and gingerbread. Provence focuses on nativity scenes: Craftsmen make santon figurines and shepherds lead their flocks to church on Christmas Eve. Easter sees Corsican processions of penitents. Saints' day festivities range from Burgundy's bacchanalia to celebrate St. Vincent, patron of the vine, to Brittany's portside blessings.

ARTS
The Cannes Film Festival in May has the highest profile,

but summer nights are filled with the sound of dying sopranos as countless Mimis and Violettas warble their last in open-air operas across Provence. These are big money events, whereas Avignon has a lively fringe where you can enjoy the off-beat on a budget. Cultural serendipity is served best at events such as classical concerts in churches. Jazz is France's adopted art form with top artists appearing in unlikely settings, such as Normandy's apple orchards.

FOOD AND DRINK
In October, France celebrates a week of food festivals, street

fairs and cookery contests. However the eating continues year-round. Wine country produces some excellent combination festivals, with chestnuts, roasted, puréed and baked, served alongside local wines in Rhône, and figs, olives and goats cheeses served at November's Primeur wine launches in Languedoc. Delicacies in the north include cider, crêpes and apple tarts.

TRADITIONAL
Traditional is sometimes a euphemism for off-beat. With origins lost in the mists of time, events such as the Soufflaculs parade in Nontron, Aquitaine, have to be seen to be disbelieved. Here, villagers walk through town in their nightshirts, pumping bellows to ward off evil spirits. Many villages still celebrate the Day of the Donkey in lieu of Bastille celebrations on 14 July.

WHAT TO DO

PARIS AND THE ÎLE DE FRANCE

There is much more to the area around the capital than the city and its suburbs. For a start there are the chateaux. Versailles may be the one that pulls in the busloads, but at least half a dozen royal residences encircle Paris. The Château de Vincennes is even served by the Métro, just minutes from the heart of town.

Outside the city limits, the area's profile has been raised by theme parks such as Disneyland Resort Paris (see page 73), with its self-contained culture. The Île de France was the landscape of 19th-century artists, and in springtime, steam trains leave the capital for the Impressionist town of Auvers-sur-Oise where Van Gogh and his contemporaries worked. Canny shoppers head out of town for bargains at the factory outlet fashion stores near Disneyland Resort Paris, and the regional produce markets half an hour from the capital.

The area is not renowned for its food and wine—the best-known vineyard is tucked away behind the Moulin Rouge in Montmartre—but the unassuming country farms are worth a detour, for this is the country of arguably France's most popular cheese—Brie.

Shopping

FOOD AND DRINK
BARTHÉLÉMY (STÉ)
51 rue de Grenelle, 75007
Tel 01 42 22 82 24
Established in 1904, this is a cheese-lover's paradise: Brie, Mont d'Or (from Jura), Roquefort and much more. The old-fashioned shop supplies both the Élysée Palace and Matignon, home to France's president and prime minister respectively.
Ⓣ Tue–Sat 8–1, 4–7.30 Ⓜ Rue du Bac

BOULANGERIE POILÂNE
8 rue du Cherche-Midi, 75006
Tel 01 45 48 42 59
www.poilane.fr

The legacy of artist bread-maker Lionel Poilâne lives on

in what is often regarded as the best French bread, baked here from secret family recipes. The country nut-and-raisin bread is a must, but other delicacies include the traditional baguette, croissant and rye loaf.
Ⓣ Mon–Sat 7.15am–8.15pm
Ⓜ Sèvres-Babylone, St-Sulpice

FAUCHON
26 place de la Madeleine, 75008
Tel 01 47 42 60 11
The tastiest and probably the most expensive delicatessen in Paris. The best of French cuisine, including foie gras, fine condiments and great wines, has been sold here since 1886. And not only

French: You can find Beluga caviar, the best vintages of the

finest spirits from all over the world, and many more exotic delicacies. There's also a tea room here.
Ⓣ Mon–Sat 9.30–7 Ⓜ Madeleine

PIERRE HERMÉ
72 rue Bonaparte, 75006
Tel 01 43 54 47 77
Couture pastries? Chef Pierre Hermé works in association with a designer so his creations are as visually exciting as they are tasty. His gold-leaf ornamented chocolate cake is almost legendary. Be prepared for a wait at his small boutique, more like a jeweller's shop than a patisserie, but remember, satisfaction is at the other end of the line.
Ⓣ Tue–Sun 9–7 Ⓜ St-Sulpice, Mabillon

FASHION
AGNÈS B
6 rue du Jour, 75001
Tel 01 45 08 56 56
www.agnesb.fr
Sober yet trendy, Agnès B's fashion is the epitome of young Parisian chic. Sharply cut clothes with original details are her signature, and her little waistcoat with press studs is a classic. Also worth celebrating for her artistic engagement—she sponsors many budding designers.
Ⓣ Mon–Sat 10–7, Sun 9–2, 3–6
Ⓜ Les Halles

BILL TORNADE
44 rue Étienne-Marcel, 75002
Tel 01 42 33 66 47
www.billtornade.com
Bill Tornade's modern and classy range caters to the urban dandy, with beautiful fabrics, 60s-style jackets, pin-striped suits, and Italian leather shoes. For a more exclusive touch, some outfits are part of a limited edition.
Ⓣ Mon–Sat 11–7.30
Ⓜ Étienne Marcel

WHAT TO DO

CHANEL
31 rue Cambon, 75001
Tel 01 42 86 28 00
www.chanel.com
The tweed suit and the little black dress, Coco Chanel's signature outfits, keep on

being reinvented by Karl Lagerfeld, head of this fashion house since 1984. Classic, sexy, feminine and chic, Chanel's designs embody Parisian elegance.
🕐 Mon–Sat 10–7 🚇 Madeleine

COLETTE
213 rue St-Honoré, 75001
Tel 01 55 35 33 90
www.colette.fr
Paris's fashion heaven offers exclusive shopping par excellence. Come here for cutting-edge design from one of the industry's rising names, or for imported beauty products that are difficult to find elsewhere. A glance at the press box will ensure you keep abreast of the trends. The water bar downstairs offers more than a hundred different brands of bottled water.
🕐 Mon–Sat 10.30–7.30 🚇 Tuileries, Pyramides

COMME DES GARÇONS
54 rue du Faubourg St-Honoré, 75008
Tel 01 53 30 27 27
Japanese designer Rei Kawakubo's approach to fashion is almost architectural. Her asymmetrical cuts produce sleek lines and one of her outfits can remodel a body. The collection caters to those looking for something unique, modern and with a couture

accent. Comme des Garçons' perfume is also sold here.
🕐 Mon–Sat 11–7 🚇 Madeleine, Concorde

ISABEL MARANT
16 rue de Charonne, 75011
Tel 01 49 29 71 55
With her fashions regularly on the catwalk, Isabel Marant has updated Parisian elegance with a bit of a bohemian bourgeois twist. Silk paisley shirts, big woollen wrap-over tops: This is casual chic at its best.
🕐 Mon–Sat 10.30–7.30 🚇 Bastille

XULY BËT
1 rue Pierre-Lescot, 75001
Tel 01 42 33 50 40
Malian designer Lamine Kouyate adds an ethnic twist to elegance. His creations show the influence of his native Africa (distinctive, patterned fabrics), but the sexy cuts are more reminiscent of a daring couture designer such as Versace, with some beautiful tight-fitting dresses, often with red stitching. Alongside the clothes, there is a collection of objects for the home, handmade in Africa.
🕐 Daily 11–2, 3–7 🚇 Chemin Vert

ACCESSORIES

LOLLIPOPS
40 rue du Dragon, 75006
Tel 01 42 22 09 29
www.lollipops.fr
Bags, scarves, hats and some jewellery, form a collection that is both chic and playful with interesting use of materials such as wool, suede and velvet. The range of products is displayed by colour, so it is easy to find matching pieces.
🕐 Mon noon–7, Tue 11–7, Wed–Fri 10.30–7, Sat 10.30–7.30
🚇 St-Sulpice

LOUIS VUITTON
101 avenue des Champs-Élysées, 75008
Tel 01 53 57 24 00
www.vuitton.com
The beige and brown chequered pattern, and the interlaced LV initials are the

house's signature and a symbol of designer chic. There's a wide range of co-ordinated leather goods, including suitcases, key rings,

wallets, purses and shoes. There are also some high quality clothes with prices to match.
🕐 Mon–Sat 10–8 🚇 George V

DEPARTMENT STORES

LE BON MARCHÉ
24 rue de Sèvres, 75007
Tel 01 44 39 80 00
www.lebonmarche.fr
The classiest brands and goods can be found at this department store. The modernist interior design adds to the atmosphere. Don't miss the beauty parlour on the ground floor and the food hall, which stocks delicacies from around the world, in a nearby building.
🕐 Mon–Wed, Fri 9.30–7, Thu 10–9, Sat 9.30–8 🚇 Sèvres-Babylone, Vaneau

GALERIES LAFAYETTE
40 boulevard Haussmann, 75009
Tel 01 42 82 34 56
www.galerieslafayette.com

Opened in 1912, the main building of this grand old department store has an impressive stained-glass dome, balconies, and gilded balustrades. It's a luxurious setting for the hundreds of brands and goods that are stocked here, including fashion and beauty items, accessories, home goods and fine foods.
🕐 Mon–Wed, Fri–Sat 9.30–7.30, Thu 9.30–9 🚇 Chaussée d'Antin

PRINTEMPS
64 boulevard Haussmann, 75009
Tel 01 42 82 50 00
www.printemps.com
Since 1865 it has been this store's ambition to be the most modern of its time. Under its main building's impressive stained-glass cupola, there are six floors dedicated to women's fashion, and Europe's largest perfume department. There is also a men's store, and a department dedicated to home decoration.
🕐 Mon–Wed, Fri–Sat 9.15–7, Thu 9.15am–10pm 🚇 Havre-Caumartin

LA SAMARITAINE
19 rue de la Monnaie, 75001
Tel 01 40 41 20 20
www.lasamaritaine.com
Brands and goods galore on the banks of the Seine. You name it, this place probably has it: home goods, furniture, clothes, and a great deal more. Don't miss the panorama from the rooftop on the 10th floor of this art deco building—it is one of the best in Paris, and it's free (open Apr–end Oct). There's also a café and a restaurant.
🕐 Mon–Wed, Fri 9.30–7, Thu 9.30–9, Sat 9.30–8 🚇 Pont Neuf

MARKETS
MARCHÉ D'ALIGRE
Place d'Aligre, 75012
This is one of Paris's liveliest markets—many restaurants send staff here to shop for fresh fruit and vegetables, fish and meat. Some merchants sell by auction, and everyone joyfully jostles everybody else—a truly Parisian experience.
🕐 Tue–Sun 6.30am–1pm 🚇 Ledru-Rollin, Faidherbe Chaligny

MARCHÉ DU BOULEVARD RASPAIL
Boulevard Raspail, 75006
The fruit and vegetables sold at this strictly organic market have been grown without pesticides, so they may not always look as good as at the local supermarket, but they certainly have more taste. You will also find organic honey, bread and wine. Another organic market is held on boulevard des Batignolles on Saturday mornings.
🕐 Tue, Fri and Sun 9–1 🚇 Rennes

MARCHÉ AUX FLEURS
Place Louis Lépine, Île de la Cité, 75004
This market has a lovely setting on an island in the Seine, close to Notre-Dame. There's a wide selection of plants and flowers, displayed on the banks of the river or in greenhouses, with a couple of specialist stands (orchids and herb gardens).
🕐 Mon–Sat 8–7 🚇 Cité

Performance

CABARET
CRAZY HORSE
12 avenue George V, 75008
Tel 01 47 23 32 32
www.crazy-horse.fr
This Parisian institution was established in 1951. Its high-class 'Teasing' show presents dancers who, thanks to some clever lighting effects, appear to be almost nude. Dinner is served during the show.
🕐 Shows: Tue–Sun 8.30pm, 11pm
🍽 Show and dinner: €125 🚇 Alma-Marceau, George V

FOLIES-BERGÈRE
32 rue Richer, 75009
Tel 01 44 79 98 70
A legendary venue, the Folies-Bergère has been in operation since 1869. Formerly famous for its risqué performances, it is now home to Broadway-style musicals. Dinner is served by uniformed waiters before or after the show.

🕐 Show: Tue–Sun 7pm 🍽 Show and dinner: €127–132 🚇 Cadet, Grands Boulevards

MOULIN ROUGE
82 boulevard de Clichy, 75018
Tel 01 53 09 82 82
www.moulin-rouge.fr
Established in 1889, and even more of an institution since the eponymous Hollywood movie. Magnificent interior within an almost authentic red windmill, where fine food is served while you enjoy the titillating 'Féerie' show.
🕐 Shows: daily 9pm, 11pm
🍽 Show: €82–92. Show and dinner: €130–160 🚇 Blanche

CINEMAS
CINOCHE
1 rue de Condé, 75006
Tel 01 46 33 10 82
The schedule features relatively recent movies, but they are those that one day may be considered classic, with most shown in their original language. On Wednesday, Saturday and Sunday there are plenty of children's movies.
🕐 Daily 2–9.30pm 🍽 Adult €6.10, child €4.50 🚇 Odéon

LA GÉODE
26 avenue Corentin-Cariou, 75019
Tel 0892 684 540
www.cite-sciences.fr
A gigantic hemispheric-screen cinema with digital stereo sound in the auditorium. You

really are taken into the movie. No recent releases, as only films specially adapted to this technology can be shown.

⏱ Daily 10.30–8.30 💶 Adult €8.75, child €6.75 🚇 Porte de la Villette

UGC CINÉ CITÉ LES HALLES
7 place de la Rotonde, 75001
0892 700 000
www.ugc.fr
This 19-screen complex offers a large choice of films, all shown in their original language. Fantastic jumbo-sized pictures of film stars are exhibited in the hall.
⏱ Daily 9am–10.30pm 💶 Adult €8.90, child €5.50 🚇 Châtelet-Les Halles

WHAT TO DO

CLASSICAL MUSIC, DANCE AND OPERA

AUDITORIUM DU LOUVRE
Le Louvre, 75001 (entrance by the Pyramid)
Tel 01 40 20 55 00
www.louvre.fr
The impressive setting of this 420-seat auditorium, right beneath I. M. Pei's Louvre Pyramid, is matched by an excellent and varied schedule, including church music, film themes and recitals.
⏱ Concerts: Wed 8pm, Thu 12.30pm 💶 €23 (8pm concert), €10 (12.30pm concert) 🚇 Louvre-Rivoli

MAISON DE RADIO FRANCE
116 avenue du Président-Kennedy, 75016
Tel 01 56 40 15 16
www.radio-france.fr
Top-notch symphony orchestras, jazz concerts and operas are all presented

here, either as live broadcasts or pre-recorded for subsequent broadcasting.
⏱ Varies 💶 Free (or small charge) 🚇 Kennedy Radio France

MÉNAGERIE DE VERRE
12 rue Léchevin, 75011
Tel 01 43 38 33 44
A glass roof and concrete walls distinguish this former printing house. Expect modern dance performances and some multi-disciplinary festivals: video, dance and visual arts. Credit cards are not accepted.
⏱ Performance: daily 8.30pm 💶 Varies 🚇 Parmentier

OPÉRA BASTILLE
120 rue de Lyon, 75012
Tel 0892 899 090
www.opera-de-paris.fr
This massive modern auditorium, with its 2,700 seats, was inaugurated in 1989, amid much controversy. However, operas and

symphony orchestras continue to benefit from the exceptional acoustics. There is also some ballet.
⏱ Varies 💶 €10–110 🚇 Bastille

OPÉRA DU CHÂTEAU DE VERSAILLES – OPÉRA ROYAL
Château de Versailles, RP 834, 78008
Tel 01 30 83 78 98
www.chateauversailles.fr
The auditorium at the Château de Versailles was originally built for Louis XVI's wedding, and inaugurated in 1770. Ballet, opera and drama are all performed here, in an impressive setting, surrounded by statues, trompe l'œil

marble and a painted ceiling.
⏱ Varies 💶 Varies 🚇 Versailles Rive Droite, Versailles Rive Gauche, Versailles Chantier

OPÉRA PALAIS GARNIER
Place de l'Opéra, 75009
Tel 0892 899 090
www.opera-de-paris.fr
An architectural masterpiece, built during the 19th century by Charles Garnier, this venue offers a lavish and prestigious setting for visiting ballet and opera companies, as well as symphony orchestras.
⏱ Varies 💶 €10–110 🚇 Opéra

THÉÂTRE DES CHAMPS-ÉLYSÉES
15 avenue Montaigne, 75008
Tel 01 49 52 50 50
www.theatrechampselysees.fr
This grand auditorium, with red velvet seats and balconies, hosts performances of opera, ballet, classical and chamber music, as well as some jazz and solo variety singers.
⏱ Performances: almost daily at around 8–8.30pm 💶 Varies 🚇 Franklin D. Roosevelt, Alma-Marceau

COMEDY CLUB

POINT-VIRGULE
7 rue Sainte-Croix de la Bretonnerie, 75004
Tel 01 42 78 67 03
The varied schedule stages all sorts of comedy acts, including improvisation, one-man shows and sketches. It's renowned for its comedy festival held every year in September. Credit cards are not accepted.
⏱ Shows: daily 8pm, 9.15pm, 10.15pm 💶 €15 🚫 🚇 Hôtel de Ville

CONTEMPORARY LIVE MUSIC

LA DANSE
5 passage Louis-Philippe, 75011
Tel 01 47 00 57 59
www.chez.com/cafedeladanse
There's an intimate feel to this auditorium, with its small platform and exposed brick walls, with room for up to 500 people. Pop, rock and world

music dominate the bill, with some theatre and dance performances. Small bar on the premises. Credit cards are not accepted.
🎭 Performance: daily around 8.30pm 💶 Around €20, but varies 🚇 🚇 Bastille

DUC DES LOMBARDS
42 rue des Lombards, 75001
Tel 01 42 33 22 88
This Parisian institution is where the most prestigious jazz musicians regularly warm the club's intimate atmosphere, their performances culminating in memorable jam sessions.
🎭 Performance: Mon–Sat 9.15pm 💶 €19 🚇 Châtelet

ÉLYSÉE MONTMARTRE
72 boulevard Rochechouart, 75018
Tel 01 44 92 45 36
www.elysee-montmartre.com
Over a century old, this establishment has retained its original retro-style interior and is now host to some of the best pop-rock concerts. It's also famous for its ball and techno nights.
🎭 Varies 💶 About €23 (depending on performance) 🚇 Anvers

LE NEW MORNING
7–9 rue des Petites-Écuries, 75010
Tel 01 45 23 51 41
Heaven for jazz fans, this famous club has welcomed the world's most prestigious musicians over the years. Bossa nova and salsa are also played here.
🎭 Concert: 9pm (days vary) 💶 Varies 🚇 Château d'Eau

SATELLIT CAFÉ
44 rue de la Folie-Méricourt, 75011
Tel 01 47 00 48 87
www.satellit-cafe.com
This self-proclaimed Parisian ambassador of world music can hold up to 250 people. The varied schedule includes Latino, blues, African, Balkan and Mediterranean music.
🎭 Concert: daily 8.30pm 💶 Around €10 🚇 Oberkampf

COMÉDIE FRANÇAISE/SALLE RICHELIEU
2 rue de Richelieu, 75001
Tel 01 44 58 15 15
www.comedie-francaise.fr
Don't expect comedy at the Comédie Française, which was established in 1680 by playwright Molière. It's home to France's most prestigious troupe of actors. Classics make

up the repertoire, including works by Shakespeare and, of course, Molière.
🎭 Performance: daily 8.30pm 💶 €11–30 🚇 Palais Royal-Musée du Louvre

THÉÂTRE NATIONAL DE CHAILLOT
1 place du Trocadéro, 75016
Tel 01 53 65 30 00
www.theatre-chaillot.fr
This theatre is housed in the imposing neoclassical Palais de Chaillot, built for the 1937 Universal Exhibition. The largest auditorium can accommodate productions of all kinds, including top-quality contemporary works, as well as classics.
🎭 Performances: Tue–Sat 8.30pm, Sun 3pm 💶 €18–30 🚇 Trocadéro

THÉÂTRE DU PALAIS ROYAL
38 rue Montpensier, 75001
Tel 01 42 97 59 81
www.theatrepalaisroyal.com
A prestigious setting—within the gardens of the Palais Royal—for this elegant theatre (red velvet seats, gilded panels) built in 1783. Plays and comedy acts dominate the schedule but there are also

---

some classical music concerts.
🎭 Performances: Mon–Sat 9pm, Sun 4.30pm 💶 Varies 🚇 Bourse, Palais Royal-Musée du Louvre

Nightlife

BUBBLES
6 rue Edouard VII, 75009
Tel 01 47 42 77 95
www.bubbles-paris.com
This modern and bright bar is entirely dedicated to champagne. Over one hundred vintages are on offer—you can even buy and take out. There is also a restaurant upstairs.
🎭 Tue–Sat noon–2am 🚇 Madeleine, Opéra

CAFÉ RUC
159 rue St-Honoré, 75001
Tel 01 42 60 97 54
A smart interior—red velvet, columns and indirect lighting—coupled with a prestigious address on a street famous for its couture shops, make this bar a hit with the fashion crowd.
🎭 Daily 8am–2.30am 🚇 Palais Royal-Musée du Louvre

CHINA CLUB
50 rue de Charenton, 75012
Tel 01 43 43 82 02
www.chinaclub.cc
A mixture of art deco and colonial influences make this a thoroughly chic venue. The large bar with some comfortable Chesterfield sofas makes it the perfect place to sip cocktails. There's a restaurant that serves Chinese cuisine and a smoking room upstairs.
🎭 Sun–Thu 7pm–2am, Fri–Sat 7pm–3am 🚇 Bastille, Ledru-Rollin

L'ENDROIT
67 place du Docteur-Félix-Lobligeois, 75017
Tel 01 42 29 50 00
The stylish modern interior has long, black leather wall-seats, indirect lighting and a massive semi-circular bar in the middle of the room.

Expect a young, fashionable crowd and ambient techno and trip hop.

🕐 Daily noon–2am 🚇 Rome

WEB BAR
32 rue de Picardie, 75003
Tel 01 42 72 66 55
www.webbar.fr

This lofty establishment, with its mezzanine and glass roof, used to be a silversmith's workshop. It is now an Internet café, and more with concerts, video projections and exhibitions.

🕐 Mon–Fri 8.30am–2am, Sat 11am–2am, Sun 11am–midnight
🚇 Temple

BAZOOKA CAFÉ
9 rue Nicolas Flamel, 75004
Tel 01 42 74 45 82

Formerly named Onix café, this chic, trendy spot is near the Centre George Pompidou and close to Paris's gay district. There's a good atmosphere here in the evening.

🕐 Daily 3pm–2am
🚇 Châtelet

CAFÉ DE L'ATELIER
95 boulevard du Montparnasse, 75014
Tel 01 45 44 98 81

This café welcomes you round the clock for a drink or a snack, inside or on its terrace (heated when necessary). It's quite a young and trendy spot in this district, otherwise home to timeless eateries such as Brasserie La Coupole.

🕐 Daily 24 hours 🚇 Vavin

CAFÉ DE FLORE
172 boulevard St-Germain, 75006
Tel 01 45 48 55 26

Once the haunt of celebrated writers and philosophers (Jean-Paul Sartre used to be a regular), this café welcomes customers all day long, for a snack or a drink, in an elegant atmosphere.

🕐 Daily 7.30am–1.30am
🚇 St-Germain-des-Prés

CLUBS

L'ÉTOILE
12 rue de Presbourg, 75016
Tel 01 45 00 78 70
www.letoileparis.com

Dressing smartly should grant you entry into this temple of chic Parisian nightlife. Disco, dance and techno are played and the setting is beautiful with a superb view of the Arc de Triomphe from the terrace.

🕐 Wed–Sun 11pm–5am 🎫 Free
🚇 Charles de Gaulle-Étoile

LE NOUVEAU CASINO
109 rue Oberkampf, 75011
Tel 01 43 57 57 40
www.nouveaucasino.net

Opened in 2001, it didn't take long for this club to develop a regular clientele. Excellent DJs, a beautiful

interior, and a great location in a very busy district, are the keys to its success.

🕐 11pm–5am (days vary according to schedule) 🎫 Around €10
🚇 Parmentier, Ménilmontant, Rue St-Maur

WAGG
62 rue Mazarine, 75006
Tel 01 55 42 22 00

A small dance floor (up to 350 people) gives this venue its welcoming atmosphere. The house and dance music draws a trendy mid-20s to mid-30s crowd here, in the heart of St-Germain-des-Prés.

🕐 Wed–Sun 11.30pm–5am
🎫 Fri–Sat €12; Thu, Sun €10; Wed free
🚇 St-Germain-des-Prés, Odéon

GAY AND LESBIAN

BANANA CAFÉ
13–15 rue de la Ferronnerie, 75001
Tel 01 42 33 35 31
www.bananacafeparis.com

A strictly gay clientele enjoys the house and techno music at this club. The themed interior changes every week (oriental, Latino, etc). There is also a piano-bar downstairs.

🕐 Daily 6pm–6am 🎫 €9 Fri and Sat, free rest of the week 🚇 Châtelet

PULP
25 boulevard Poissonnière, 75002
Tel 01 40 26 01 93

This is the only lesbian club in Paris, with house and techno played by mainly female DJs. Some parties are open to gay men, and everyone is welcome on Wednesday and Thursday nights.

🕐 Wed–Sat midnight–6am
🎫 around €10 🚇 Grands Boulevards

QUEEN
102 avenue des Champs-Élysées, 75008
Tel 01 53 89 08 90
www.queen.fr

A prestigious address for this gay club, which is also the haunt of a trendy straight crowd. House and garage music are mixed by interna-tional DJs, with themes and atmospheres changing each night of the week.

🕐 Daily midnight–7am 🎫 Mon €12; Tue–Thu, Sun €10; Fri–Sat €20
🚇 George V

Sports and Activities

SPECTATOR SPORTS

SOCCER

PARC DES PRINCES
24 rue du Commandant-Guilbaud, 75016
Tel 0825 075 078 (closed Sun and public hols)
www.psg.fr

Inaugurated in 1972, the park has been home to Paris-St-Germain (PSG) soccer club since 1990. Within its

boundaries you'll also find the Musée National du Sport (National Sport Museum), a shop and a restaurant.
💷 €18–€70 🚇 Porte d'Auteuil, Porte de St-Cloud

STADIUM
STADE PIERRE DE COUBERTIN
82 avenue Georges-Lafont, 75016
Tel 01 45 27 79 12
Built for the 1937 International Exhibition, destroyed during World War II and rebuilt in 1946, this 4,500-seat stadium hosts sporting competitions including handball, dance, boxing and fencing.
💷 Varies 🚇 Porte de St-Cloud

ACTIVITIES

AQUAPARK
AQUABOULEVARD
4–6 rue Louis Armand, 75015
Tel 01 40 60 10 00
www.aquaboulevard.com
Alongside the aquapark, which has waterslides and a wave machine, there are squash courts, tennis courts, a putting range, restaurants and shops.
🕐 Mon–Thu 9am–11pm, Fri 9am–midnight, Sat 8am–midnight, Sun 8am–11pm 💷 Aquapark: adult €20, child €10 🚇 Balard, Porte de Versailles

BOWLING
BOWLING DE MONTPARNASSE
25 rue du Commandant-Mouchotte, 75014
Tel 01 43 21 61 32
Sixteen bowling lanes, pool, billiards, and some video games. Every Friday and Saturday night you can bowl in the dark, with the lanes illuminated by fluorescent lighting.
🕐 Sun–Thu 10am–2am, Fri 10am–4am, Sat 10am–5am 💷 €4.30–5.80 per game per person 🚇 Montparnasse-Bienvenüe

GOLF
GOLF DU BOIS DE BOULOGNE
Hippodome d'Auteuil, 75016
Tel 01 44 30 70 00
www.golfduboisdeboulogne.com
Paris's largest golf course, in the middle of a race track, includes a course where you can practise your swing, a putting green and a crazy-golf area for practising shots, which has small greens with bunkers and watercourses.
🕐 Daily 8–8 (closed on race days) 💷 €4 per bucket of balls, €4 per half-hour of crazy golf 🚇 Porte d'Auteuil

HELICOPTER TOURS
PARIS HÉLICOPTÈRES
Zone Aviation Affaires, Aéroport, 93350 Le Bourget
Tel 01 48 35 90 44
www.paris-helicoptere.com
Want to see everything in less than 30 minutes? Take a tour and monument-spot across Paris. Longer tours are also available, for a bird's-eye view of the Château de Versailles and farther afield.
🕐 Sun afternoon, advance booking necesary 💷 €122 for a 25-minute tour 🚇 Le Bourget 🚌 Number 152, stop Musée de l'Air

HOT-AIR BALLOON TOURS
FRANCE MONTGOLFIÈRES
63 boulevard de Ménilmontant, 75011
Tel 01 47 00 66 44
www.franceballoons.com
These hot-air balloon tours let you discover Paris's surround-ings, soaring above villages, chateaux, rivers and forests. You can also go as far as Burgundy and the Loire. Some trips include hotels.
🕐 Tours from mid-Mar to end Nov, on booking 💷 From €165 for 3.5-hour tour 🚇 Père Lachaise

ROLLERBLADING
RANDONNÉE EN ROLLERS
Meet in front of Nomades: 37 boulevard Bourdon, 75004
Tel 01 44 54 07 44
www.rollers-coquillages.org
In partnership with Nomades sports store, the Rollers and Coquillages Society organizes rollerblading through Paris every Sunday. The three-hour circuit changes regularly.
🕐 Sun 2.30pm 💷 Free 🚇 Bastille

TENNIS
TENNIS DU LUXEMBOURG
Jardin du Luxembourg., 75006
Tel 01 43 25 79 18
The heart of the Luxembourg Garden is a prestigious and pleasant setting for these six tennis courts, although no membership and competitive rates mean it can be difficult to reserve a court.
🕐 Daily 8.30–4.30, until 9.30 summer 💷 €3 for 30 mins, €6 per hour 🚇 Luxembourg

HEALTH AND BEAUTY

LE AMAK
45 avenue George-V, 75008
Tel 01 40 73 40 73
This smart venue, near the Champs-Élysées, is one of the few institutes in Paris to use Botox (in powder form only). Launched in summer 2002, the Botomax facial aims to help facial lines disappear. Amak also offers fitness classes and anti-stress treatments such as massages.
🕐 Daily 10–8 (Thu and Sun till 9pm) 💷 Botomax €160, 90-minute Indian massage €100 🚇 George V

AQUAMASSAGE AT PRINTEMPS
64 boulevard Haussmann, 75009
Tel 01 42 82 50 00
www.aquamassage.co.uk
Department store Printemps was the first in Paris to offer this revolutionary technique: An aquamassage that doesn't

get you wet. A machine which looks like a sunlamp surrounds your body with a completely waterproof envelope while

WHAT TO DO

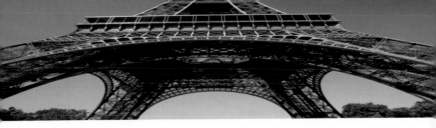

36 high-powered water jets give you a massage. There are seven different massages.
🕐 Mon–Sat 9.30–7 (Thu till 10pm)
💶 €15 for 10 minutes 🚇 Havre-Caumartin

SENSO PIU
71 avenue Raymond-Poincaré, 75016
Tel 01 45 53 29 23
A variety of treatments, inspired by the Orient, are on offer here, such as Ayurvedic Indian massages with warm oils and biokinergy (reaching mind and body balance by working on certain muscles). The tchong-mo massage (a therapeutic stimulation of energy meridians) was created here and remains exclusive to the institute.
🕐 Mon–Fri 10.30–7, Sat 10.30–1
💶 60-minute tchong-mo massage €61
🚇 Victor Hugo, Trocadéro

VILLA THALGO
218–220 rue du Faubourg St-Honoré, 75008
Tel 01 45 62 00 20
www.thalgo.fr
This high-class institute brings thalassotherapy to the heart of Paris. The seven-hour session includes bodyscrub, seaweed wrap, balneotherapy, aquagym, jet shower and massages. There are also one-hour and half-day treatments
🕐 Mon, Tue, Thu 8.30–8.30, Wed, Fri 8.30–7, Sat 9–7 💶 One-hour treatment €60 🚇 Ternes, Charles de Gaulle-Étoile

Children

AQUABOULEVARD
See page 231.

CITÉ DES SCIENCES ET DE L'INDUSTRIE
See page 89.

DISNEYLAND RESORT PARIS
See page 73.

JARDIN D'ACCLIMATATION
Main entry: boulevard des Sablons, Bois de Boulogne, 75016
Tel 01 40 67 90 82

With its ponds and tree-lined alleys, this 'garden within a wood' is a walker's paradise. There are many activities for children including minigolf, playgrounds, bowling, wildlife discovery, theatre and sports. A trip on the little train is a good way to discover the area.
🕐 Daily 10–7 (closes 6pm winter)
💶 Adult €2.50, child €1.50, under 3 free 🚇 Les Sablons

THÉÂTRE DE LA MAINATE
36 rue Bichat, 75010
Tel 01 42 08 83 33
www.lamainate.com
This venue caters to very young children, from two to eight years old. There are puppet shows, fairytale readings, and kids cabaret with a clown and magic tricks on Sundays. Credit cards are not accepted.
🕐 Performances: Wed (and French school holidays) 10.30am, 2.30pm, 4pm, Sat 4pm, Sun 3.30pm, Sep–end May 💶 €9 🚇 République, Goncourt

Festivals and Events

MARATHON INTERNATIONAL DE PARIS
First Sunday in April
Tel 01 41 33 15 68
www.parismarathon.com
The marathon attracts more than 30,000 runners. It starts at the Champs-Élysées and finishes in avenue Foch, behind the Arc de Triomphe.
🚇 Charles de Gaulle-Étoile (finish line)

ROLAND-GARROS
May–June
Stade Roland Garros, 2 avenue Gordon-Bennett, 75016

Tel 01 47 43 48 00
www.rolandgarros.com
The prestigious French Tennis Open takes place over a two-week period.
🚇 Porte d'Auteuil

FÊTE DE LA MUSIQUE
21 June
Tel 01 40 03 94 70
www.fetedelamusique.culture.fr
Free concerts are held all over the city, with everything from jazz and classical to techno and rap.

PARIS JAZZ
June–July
Parc Floral, Route de la Pyramide, Bois de Vincennes, 75012
Tel 01 73 04 75 75
www.parcfloraldeparis.com
The sound of jazz fills the Parc Floral, courtesy of musicians from Europe and America.
🚇 Château de Vincennes

BASTILLE DAY
14 July
Celebrations include fireworks and fire station balls on 13 July, followed by the annual military parade down the Champs-Élysées on 14 July.

TOUR DE FRANCE
July
Tel 01 41 33 15 00
www.letour.fr
The participants of this wildly popular bicycle race cross the finish line on the Champs-Élysées.

FESTIVAL DE CINÉMA EN PLEIN AIR
July–August
Parc de la Villette, 75019
Tel 01 40 03 75 75
www.villette.com
Open-air film festival.
🚇 Porte de la Villette, Porte de Pantin

NUIT BLANCHE
One night in October
Tel 0820 00 75 75
www.paris.fr
Concerts and other events take place in unusual venues across the city, through the night.

NORTHWEST FRANCE

Dramatic coastlines, from the high cliffs of Normandy to the quaint coves of Brittany, provide the most enduring distractions for visitors. Messing around in boats and exploring islands and caves are among the simple family pleasures here. Hiking and golf, and horse-riding especially, take outdoor types from the seashore to the hinterland. For the less active, the hedgerows and countryside make for diverting drives.

Normandy's formal gardens attract thousands of visitors each week. There are countless artists' trails to follow through the villages that nurtured the talents of the late 19th and early 20th centuries—from Paul Gauguin and the Pont-Aven School of modernists in Brittany, to Impressionists such as Claude Monet, who were inspired by the scenery of Normandy. Spiritual themes range from the Celtic ruins and landscapes in Brittany to the Gothic churches and abbeys of Normandy.

The saints' day *pardons* and waterside blessings in fishing ports are living evocations of the spirit of Brittany past, and the *Fest Noz* late-night parties are a chance to mingle with the locals. In Normandy, a season of music festivals kicks off with the springtime *Jazz Sous les Pommiers* in Coutances.

Traditional resorts such as St-Malo are fun for families, whereas young people prefer the bar and club scene in Rennes. The jet set head to the racecourse, blackjack tables and film festival parties of Deauville.

In the shops, look out for Breton lace, pottery in Quimper and in Rouen hunt down the tableware named after the city.

Bretagne

ARRADON
BELLE PLAISANCE
Nicolas Bourdy, 24 chemin de Gravellic, 56610 Arradon
Tel 02 97 44 80 91
www.belleplaisance.com
On the Golfe du Morbihan you can rent old-fashioned and beautifully restored sailing boats with a professional sailor to navigate and give instruction. Decide where you want to go and for how long, or leave it to the experts. Book at least one week in advance and note that credit cards are not accepted.
🕐 Mar–end Oct, by appointment
💶 €300 for 1 day/5 people in the Golfe du Morbihan

BREST
LE QUARTZ
2/4, avenue Georges Clémenceau, 29200 Brest
Tel 02 98 33 70 70
www.lequartz.com
Inject a shot of culture into your visit to Brest. There are two performance halls, one which seats 2,500, the other 400. This venue (take the bus to place de la Liberté) hosts, at various times of the year, plays, ballet and dance, classical music, jazz, world music, opera, operetta and even films. There is no bar.
🕐 Performances: Tue–Sat 5pm, 8.30pm, 10pm (depending on schedule), Sep–end Jun 💶 €5–€37

PATINOIRE DE BREST RÏNKLA STADIUM
Place Napoleon III, 29200 Brest
Tel 02 98 03 01 30
This ice rink is home to the Albatross professional ice hockey team. Watch a live game or highlights on one of two huge TV screens, or go skating yourself. There is a restaurant and snack bar on site. You can take bus line 5 or 6 to Belle-vue or Patinoire.
🕐 Public skating Tue, Thu 2.30–4.30pm, 8.30pm–11.30pm, Wed, Sat 2.30–5.30pm, Fri 8.30pm–11.15pm, Sun 10.30am–1pm, 2.30–5.30pm
💶 Adult €5, skate rental €7

CAP FRÉHEL
PÂTISSIER-CHOCOLATIER R. JOUAULT
Place de Chamblis, 22240 Fréhel
Tel 02 96 41 41 31
In this cottage-style building you can buy Breton pastries such as *far* and *élisa*. The bakery has won the European Lauriers d'Or trophy for its superb *kouignamann* (cake made with sugar, butter and almonds). Their special is *palet de Fréhel* (nougatine, almond and chocolate) with a depiction of Cap Fréhel.
🕐 Daily 8–8, Jun–end Sep; 8–1, 3–6.30, rest of year; Closed mid-Sep to mid-Oct

CARNAC

LES NINICHES

7 avenue du Parc, 56340 Carnac
Tel 02 97 52 73 51
www.maison-armorine.com
This sweetshop (candy store)
sells 49 different varieties of
niniche, a long, thin lollypop,
well known to Breton children.
There are other sweets, including toffee made with salted
butter, another local treat.
🕐 Mon–Sun 9.30–12.30, 2.30–7,
Apr–end Sep

DINAN

**CLUB CANOË KAYAK DE
LA RANCE**

18 quai Tallard, 22100 Lanvallay
Tel 02 96 39 01 50
At Lanvallay, just east of Dinan,
this club rents out canoes and
kayaks for trips on the Rance
river lasting from one hour to
one day. Take the bus to Le
Port. Credit cards are not
accepted.
🕐 Daily 9–7, Jul–end Aug; by
appointment only, rest of year 💶 €13
for 3 hours

LA BOURBANSAIS

Domaine de la Bourbansais, 35720
Pleugueneuc
Tel 02 99 69 40 07
www.labourbansais.com
You'll find this zoo, with many
protected species, in the
grounds of the impressive
Château de Bourbansais
(which is worth a visit in its
own right) east of Dinan.
There is a playground with a
bouncy castle for children,
a snack bar, a tea room and a
gift shop. Credit cards are
not accepted.
🕐 Daily 10–7, Apr–end Sep; 2–6,
Oct–end Mar 💶 Zoo: Adult €11; Zoo
and chateau: Adult €13

DINARD

**CASINO BARRIÈRE DE
DINARD**

4 boulevard Wilson, 35802 Dinard
Tel 02 99 16 30 30
www.lucienbarriere.com
Here you'll find roulette, blackjack, stud poker, more than
100 one-armed bandits and

other gambling temptations.
The cocktail bar has a great
view of the beach and there is

a restaurant. Food is served all
day and there's also live music.
🕐 Sun–Thu 10am–3am, Fri–Sat
10am–4am 💶 €11 (over-18s only)

PISCINE MUNICIPAL

2 boulevard Wilson, 35800 Dinard
Tel 02 99 88 10 67
This Olympic-sized pool,
50m by 25m (164ft by 82ft),
is filled with heated seawater.
There is also a beach with
activities for children. It's on
bus circuit 3; ask for Piscine.
🕐 Mon 3–6.30, Tue 5–8, Wed 2–6.30,
Thu 5–7.30, Fri 5–8.30, Sat 2–6.30, Sun
9–12.30 💶 Mon–Fri €3, Sat–Sun €4

DOUARNENEZ

CHAR À VOILE

Pentrez Plage, 29550 St-Nic
Tel 06 11 80 09 79
Try sand yachting and kite
surfing on this beach north of
Douarnenez which, at low
tide, is 3km (1.9 miles) long
and 5km (3.1 miles) wide,
giving you plenty of space.
The minimum age for these
activities is seven and it's a
good idea to reserve. Credit
cards are not accepted.
🕐 Daily 9–noon, 1.30–6 in summer;
Fri–Sun 1.30–6, most of rest of year
💶 €11 per hour

ÎLE D'OUESSANT

TY CRENN ÉQUITATION

Stang Ar Glann, 29242 Ouessant
Tel 02 98 48 83 58
Discover this island, France's
westernmost point, on a
horse or Shetland pony. There
are several different routes

passing many beautiful spots
and trek lengths vary from an
hour to three days. Call ahead
to book your place and note
that credit cards are not
accepted.
🕐 Daily 9–6 💶 1 hour €16, 2 hours
€31, half-day €45

LAMBALLE

GP CIRCUIT

Zone Sports-Méchanique, 22400
Lamballe
Tel 02 96 50 09 09
www.gp-circuit.com
This is an excellent karting
track of 800m (2,600ft), with
70 karts in a range of engine
sizes. You can have lessons if
you wish or simply rent a kart
in blocks of ten minutes. The
bar, snack bar and terrace all
have great views.
🕐 Wed, Sat 2–dusk, Sun 10am–dusk;
other times by appointment only
💶 €10 for 10 minutes

MORLAIX

**LE THÉÂTRE DU PAYS DE
MORLAIX**

20 rue Gambetta, 29600 Morlaix
Tel 02 98 15 22 77
www.ville.morlaix.fr
After six years of extensive
renovations, this theatre finally
reopened in 2002 and it is a
superb location for plays, local
and world music, films and
ballet. There are street performances every Wednesday
from mid-July to mid-August.
🕐 Performances daily 8pm (ticket
office open daily 1.30–5pm) 💶 Adult
€15, child (under 12) €4

PAIMPOL

LES VINS DE BORDEAUX

5 rue des Huit Patriotes, 22500 Paimpol
Tel 02 96 55 04 45
This wine shop in the middle
of town is the sales outlet of a
chateau in the Côtes de Blaye.
You can buy per bottle, per 5
or 10 litres (1.1 or 2.2 gallons),
or bring your own container
and fill it up.
🕐 Mon–Tue 9–noon, 3–7.30, Thu–Sat
9–noon, 3–7.30, Sun 10–1

WHAT TO DO

LE PUB

rue des Islandais, 22500 Paimpol
Tel 02 96 20 82 31
At this piano bar and pub,
there's a bar on the ground
floor and a dance floor upstairs.
There is music to please all as
the clientele is aged from 18 to
50. You can order bar food.
⊙ Thu–Sun 9pm–5am, Mon–Wed
9.30pm–4am

PERROS-GUIREC

GALLERIE DE KER-ILIZ

rue du Général de Gaulle, 22700
Perros-Guirec
Tel 02 96 91 01 62
This large mall, formerly the
home of architect James Boullié,
sells products made or crafted
in Brittany, such as Quimper
porcelain, Celtic jewellery,
music, pottery, wooden items,
biscuits and nautical clothing.
⊙ Daily 10–noon, 2.30–7 Apr–end Sep;
closed Sun afternoon and Mon morning
rest of year

PONT-AVEN

PHILIP PLISSON

4 place Gauguin, 29930 Pont-Aven
Tel 02 98 09 11 12
www.plisson.com
Philip Plisson is France's official
painter of seascapes, and his
photographs of the sea are also
well known. Take home an
original or a less expensive
mass-produced print. Subjects
include deserted lighthouses
battered by the surf.
⊙ Daily 10–12.30, 2–7, Apr–end Sep;
Tue–Sun 10–12.30, 2–7, rest of year

PORT-LOUIS

LE TEMPS D'UNE ESCALE

11 rue de la Marine, 56290 Port-Louis
Tel 02 97 82 41 13
Here you'll find decorative
objects, art and sculptures
made from wood, clay and
other materials in the form of
animals and ships. There are
also ceramic vases and lamps.
Everything is made locally.
Credit cards are not accepted.
⊙ Daily 9–noon, 2–7, May–end Sep;
Mon–Wed, Fri, Sat 9–noon, 2–7, Thu and
Sun 9–noon, rest of year; Closed 2 weeks
in Sep 🚢 Taxi boat from Lorient

QUIBERON

BAR LE NELSON

20 place Hoche, 56170 Quiberon
Tel 02 97 50 31 37
www.lenelson.com
This fun bar/pub is not to be
missed. It's basically a rum bar
with 54 different types of rum
and plays music from the
1960s to the 90s.
⊙ Mon–Sun 2pm–2am, Apr–end Sep;
Mon–Sat 2pm–2am, rest of year; closed
15 Jan–1 Feb

QUIMPER

ARMOR LUX

60 bis rue Guy Autret, 29000 Quimper
Tel 02 98 90 05 29
www.armor-lux.com
This store specializes in marine
clothing and has been making
the classic Breton striped
sweaters here for more than
60 years. Reserve ahead to
tour the factory. In the shop,
you'll find the latest designs as
well as discontinued lines.
⊙ Mon–Fri 9.30–11.30, 2–4

RENNES

CAP-COD

1 rue St-Georges, 35000 Rennes
Tel 02 99 79 10 76
This unusual shop is furnished
as an ordinary house, but
everything you see is for sale.
Each month the theme of the
interior design changes to a
different country. Items for sale
are hand-picked objects and
antiques from across the
world. The shop is near the
République Métro stop.
⊙ Tue–Sat 10–noon, 1.30–7

PÉNICHE SPECTACLE

30 quai St-Cyr, 35000 Rennes
Tel 02 99 59 35 38
www.guideinfo.com/Prog-Cultu/
peniche.htm
Two barges—*L'Arbre d'Eau* and
La Dame Blanche—have been
transformed into theatres
presenting a varied selection of
world music, jazz, cabaret,
workshops, readings and
exhibitions. There are also
performances for children.
⊙ Performances: Thu–Sun 8.30pm
💶 Adult €13 concert, €8 cabaret

THÉÂTRE NATIONAL DE BRETAGNE (TNB)

1 rue St-Hélier, 35000 Rennes
Tel 02 99 31 12 31
www.t-n-b.fr
This theatre, at Gare on the
Métro, has three separate
performance halls for drama,
dance, jazz and classical music.
There's also a cinema screening independent and
experimental films in their
original language. You can
have lunch or dinner in the
restaurant and bar.
⊙ Tue–Fri noon–11, Sat 2–11
💶 Theatre tickets start at €20

ST-CAST-LE-GUILDO

LA FERME DES LANDES

Notre Dame du Guildo, 22380 St-Cast-
le-Guildo
Tel 02 96 41 12 48 and 06 83 22 00 09
A cider lover's heaven with
cider from different apple
varieties, plus cider vinegar
and apple juice, all home-
brewed by the passionate
owner. Taste, buy and tour the
farm (by appointment only).
Every Friday afternoon in summer, there's a market where
other local farmers sell their
produce. If you are arriving by
car, take the D786 and this
place is just before Notre-
Dame-du-Guildo coming
from the direction of St-Cast-
le-Guildo.
⊙ Daily 10–8, Jun–end Aug; Mon–Sat
2–7, Apr–end May, Sep; Fri–Sat
10–noon, 2–6, rest of year

CENTRE NAUTIQUE DE ST-CAST

Le Port, 22380 St-Cast-le-Guildo
Tel 02 96 41 86 42 and 02 96 41 71 71
www.cnautique-saintcast.com
At this water sports venue you
can rent all kinds of sailing
boats, windsurfers and kayaks,
although for larger boats you'll
need a permit. You can also
have individual sailing lessons
from one of the instructors.
Boat rental stops in November
and restarts in April.
⊙ Daily 9–8, Jul, Aug; 9–6, rest of year;
closed 15 Dec–7 Jan 🎫 Membership
€12, dinghy rental €22 per hour

GOLF CLUB DE PEN-GUEN

Route du Golfe, 22380 St-Cast-le-Guildo

Tel 02 96 41 91 20

www.ot-st-cast-le-guildo.fr

This superbly situated 18-hole golf course is 0.8km (0.5 miles) east of the town, and has access to the beach. There's also a driving range and putting green to keep the keenest golfer busy. Facilities include a changing room with showers and a bar. Call ahead to reserve in summer.

🕐 Daily 7.30am–8pm, Apr–end Sep; 10–5.30, rest of year 💶 €45 in summer, €27 rest of year, trolley €4, cart €19, clubs €8

ST-GILDAS-DE-RHUYS

GOLF DE KERVERT

La Ferme de Kervert, 56730 St-Gildas-de-Rhuys

Tel 02 97 45 30 09

www.formule-golf.com

Standard 18-hole, par-72 golf course, also with 30 practice holes and a putting green at the heart of a bird sanctuary on the Golfe du Morbihan.

🕐 Daily 8am–8pm, Jul–end Aug; daily 9–6.30 rest of year 💶 €45 Apr–end Sep, €31 rest of year

ST-MALO

THÉÂTRE ST-MALO

6 place Bouvet, 35400 St-Malo

Tel 02 99 40 18 30

www.theatresaintmalo.com

The leading theatre in the region hosts major touring productions, concerts, opera, big band, theatre, musicals, one-man shows and children's performances. The bar is open pre-show and in the interval and there is good access for visitors with disabilities.

🕐 Tue–Sat 8.30pm, Sun 4pm; children's shows once a month on Wed at 3pm 💶 Adult €22–€29, child (under 18) €8

TRÉGASTEL

ÉCOLE D'ÉQUITATION FOSSEY

13 rue du Calvaire, 22730 Trégastel

Tel 02 96 23 86 14

Go horse-riding through the Breton countryside, in a forest or along the seashore of the Côtes-d'Armor region. You can also take lessons at the school to improve your riding skills. Telephone in advance to reserve your place.

🕐 Tue–Sat 9–7, Sun–Mon 9–noon; Closed 2 weeks in Sep 💶 Adult €18.50 per hour

VANNES

PALAIS DES ARTS

Place de Bretagne, 56000 Vannes

Tel 02 97 01 62 00

www.mairie-vannes.fr/palaisdesarts

This large theatre with varied productions has something to please everyone, with plays, circus acts, ballet, dance, jazz, *chansons*, classical music and opera.

🕐 Mon–Fri 8.30pm 💶 Adult €4–€20, child €4–€12

Basse-Normandie

BLONVILLE-SUR-MER

LES PLANCHES

Les Longs Champs, 14910 Blonville-sur-Mer

Tel 02 31 87 58 09

www.lesplanches.com

This nightclub has maritime-themed decorations and an outdoor pool. There are two dance floors and one is dedicated to retro tunes from the 1960s to the 90s.

🕐 Daily 10pm–4am, Jul–end Aug; Fri–Sat 10pm–4am, rest of year 💶 €15

LE BREUIL-EN-AUGE

CALVADOS CHÂTEAU DU BREUIL

Les Jourdains, 14130 Le Breuil-en-Auge

Tel 02 31 65 60 00

www.chateau-breuil.fr

Not many distilleries have such an elegant setting. This one is in an elegant 17th-century chateau, where locally grown apples are turned into one of the region's most famous

exports, the apple brandy, Calvados. Take a guided tour then choose from different vintages of Calvados or opt for derivatives such as *pommeau* (a mix of Calvados and apple juice) or *Cœur du Breuil* (a Calvados-based liqueur).

🕐 Daily 9–noon, 2–6 (sometimes closed Sun in winter)

CAEN

ZÉNITH DE CAEN

Rue Joseph Philippon, 14000 Caen

Tel 02 31 73 74 75

www.zenith-caen.fr

The auditorium can hold audiences of up to 7,000 for comedy, ballet, classical music concerts and more.

🕐 Performances usually start at 8.30pm

CHERBOURG

L'ANTIDOTE

41 rue du Blé, 50100 Cherbourg

Tel 02 33 78 01 28

You can try wine by the glass from one of this bistro's hundreds of vintages. The bright interior is designer wood and brass and there's a pleasant terrace, open in fine weather.

🕐 Tue–Sat 8–midnight, summer; Tue, Wed, Thu 8–midnight, rest of year

WHAT TO DO

DEAUVILLE

CASINO DE DEAUVILLE

Rue Edmond Blanc, BP 32400, 14802 Deauville

Tel 02 31 14 31 14

www.lucienbarriere.com

This casino and club is in a beautiful Belle-Époque building on the seafront. There are slot machines, gaming tables, two bars, three

restaurants and a nightclub and the dress code is formal.

⊙ Mon–Thu 10am–2am, Fri 11am–3am, Sat 11am–4am, Sun 10am–3am 🗲 €11 cover charge for the game room

GOLF BARRIÈRE DE DEAUVILLE

Mont Canisy St-Arnoult, BP 63500, 14803 Deauville

Tel 02 31 14 24 24

www.lucienbarriere.com

You'll get beautiful views of the sea and the countryside from this 18-hole golf course on top

of Mont Canisy, which offers fast greens and tough rough. After your round of golf, have a drink in the clubhouse or browse in the shop.

⊙ Daily 9–6 🗲 €28–€39 green fee

DOUVRES-LA-DÉLIVRANDE

PÂTISSERIE DE LA BASILIQUE

3 place de la Basilique, 14440 Douvres-la-Délivrande

Tel 02 31 37 29 74

You'll find this small village a stone's throw from the local beaches north of Caen. The patisserie itself is in a pretty half-timbered house. For three generations, the Jung family have been making Normandy specials such as *brasillés* (bread made with the local salted butter) and biscuits similar to Scottish shortbread.

⊙ Wed–Sat 7.45–12.45, 2.15–7.45, Sun 7.45–7.45

ESSAY

KARTING 61

Circuit du Pays d'Essay, La Barre, 61500 Essay

Tel 02 33 81 97 85

www.karting61.com

A 1.6km (1-mile) karting track with a self-draining surface that guarantees road-hugging performance even in rain.

⊙ Tue–Sun 2–6 🗲 €15 for 15 mins

GRANVILLE

STATION DE VOILE DE GRANVILLE

260 boulevard des Amiraux, 50400 Granville

Tel 02 33 91 83 72

www.station-nautique-granville.com

The water and beach sports on offer here include windsurfing, catamaran sailing, sea kayaking and sand yachting. The bay of Granville has some of Europe's strongest tides.

⊙ Reserve ahead 🗲 €16–€19 per session of catamaran sailing, windsurfing or kayaking

HONFLEUR

MARCHÉ TRADITIONNEL

Place de l'Église Sainte-Catherine, 14600 Honfleur

This traditional market takes place on a charming square presided over by a 15th-century church and lined with cafés in half-timbered houses. Treat yourself to the locally caught fish and farm produce on sale here such as fruit, vegetables and dairy products including the Normandy cheeses Camembert and Livarot.

⊙ Sat 9.30–12.30

ISIGNY-SUR-MER

COOPÉRATIVE LAITIÈRE D'ISIGNY STE-MÈRE

2 rue du Docteur Boutrois, 14230 Isigny-sur-Mer

Tel 02 31 51 33 88

www.isigny-ste-mere.com

The produce from this dairy cooperative is famous the world over and since 1986, use of the name has been controlled, just as with champagne. The dairy is known for its crème fraiche, but it also produces a butter with a particularly distinctive taste, and cheeses (Camembert, Mimolette, Pont l'Évêque), some of which are made from unpasteurized milk. Reserve in advance if you want to take a guided tour.

⊙ Mon–Sat 9–noon, Oct–end May; Mon–Fri 9–noon, 2.30–5, Jun–end Sep

ST-LÔ

LE DRAKKAR

29 rue Alsace-Lorraine, 50000 St-Lô

Tel 02 33 05 16 50

This cinema has four screens showing the latest releases, mainly Hollywood blockbusters, but occasionally independent films shown in their original language. Movies for children are shown on Wednesdays.

⊙ Thu–Tue 6–10; all day Wed 🗲 Adult €7

WHAT TO DO

BRETAGNE, BASSE-NORMANDIE 237

VILLEDIEU-LES-POÊLES

GENEVIÈVE PERRUT

39 rue du Docteur Havard, 50800
Villedieu-les-Poêles
Tel 06 88 31 30 46
www.gene-perrut.com
Geneviève Perrut creates truly
original jewellery made of
glass and paper and protected
by a clear resin. Her wonderful
pieces are almost weightless
but hard-wearing and come in
classic and distinctive designs.
🕐 Daily 10–7, mid-May to end Sep

VILLERVILLE

MA POMME

Rue du Général Leclerc, 14113 Villerville
Tel 02 31 98 11 42
www.adeauville.com/siteclient/mapom
me/accueil.htm
Ma Pomme stocks a range of
products all derived from
locally grown apples including
cider, Calvados and sparkling
pommeau (a mix of Calvados
and apple juice). Other local
specials on offer include
caramels, preserved meat
and marmalade. You can also
sample the produce for free.
🕐 Daily 9–1, 3–7 (sometimes closed
Tue–Wed)

Haute-Normandie

LE BEC-HELLOUIN

**ABBAYE NOTRE-DAME
DU BEC**

Abbaye Notre-Dame du Bec, 27800
Le Bec-Hellouin
Tel 02 32 43 72 60
Established in 1034, this
abbey has been home to a
community of Benedictine
monks since 1948 (see
page 97). The brothers run a
workshop manufacturing fine
ceramics (tableware, dishes,
vases and candlesticks),
some of which use antique
designs, and which make
original souvenirs.
🕐 Daily 11–11.45, 2.45–5.45

DIEPPE

DIEPPE SCÈNE NATIONALE

Quai Bérigny, 76374 Dieppe
Tel 02 35 82 04 43
www.dsn.asso.fr
This modern auditorium hosts
to all sorts of performances,
including plays and concerts,
and has a cinema showing
independent films and classics.
🕐 Daily 2–10 🎬 Films €5, live
performances €12

ÉTRETAT

**VILLAGE ÉQUESTRE
D'ÉTRETAT**

248–250, rue de la Sauvagère, 76790
Le Tilleul
Tel 02 35 27 04 22
www.village-equestre.cjb.net
This equestrian venue, which
welcomes beginners, is in a
seaside resort. It offers guided
rides through beautiful countryside and forest and on the
cliffs of Étretat. There's a
maximum of eight per group.
🕐 Fri–Wed, all year 💶 €23 per hour

LE HAVRE

L'AGORA

Éspace Oscar Niemeyer, 76600
Le Havre
Tel 02 32 74 09 70
www.infoceane.com/agora
Expect hip hop and jazz
among other types of music
at this venue. The bar plays
extracts of the music to be
performed on stage to get
you in the mood.
🕐 Sep–Jun (performance times vary)
💶 From €9

LE LASCAUX

81 rue Guillemard, 76600 Le Havre
Tel 02 35 42 57 15
There's a grotto theme at this
bar, close to the beach, which
is decorated with primitive
rock paintings. Musically,
expect soul, R&B and
electronica.
🕐 Mon–Sat 7pm–2am

ROUEN

GLOBO LOCO CLUB

19 rue Jeanne d'Arc, 76000 Rouen
Tel 02 35 15 00 58
Not a club, but a shop that is a
major meeting point for Rouen
youth. They pick up the coolest
streetwear here (such as the
Comète label), as well as
accessories and skateboards.
🕐 Mon 10–noon, Tue–Sat 10–noon,
2–7pm

LE LUTIN BRASSEUR

62 rue Ganterie, 76000 Rouen
Tel 02 35 89 36 82
This is *the* beer specialist in
Rouen, with hundreds of types.
The owners have a fondness
for the Belgian *blanches*
(white beers) such as Leffe
and Hoegaarden, but are also
fans of French beers that have
been traditionally brewed.
🕐 Tue–Sat 10–12.30, 2–9

PÂTISSERIE DU PALAIS

35 bis rue Jeanne d'Arc, 76000 Rouen
Tel 02 35 71 02 98
www.cirette-traiteur.com
This patisserie makes
Calvados-filled chocolates and
caramels made from Isigny
butter. The lovely cakes are
well worth trying. For a great
souvenir, get an assortment
of sweets packed in a Rouen
earthenware box.
🕐 Mon–Sat 9–7

Festivals and Events

JAZZ SOUS LES POMMIERS

May
Coutances
Tel 02 33 19 08 10 (tourist office)
www.jazzsouslespommiers.com

The musical year starts here with Maytime jazz sessions in cider country. Most concerts have a modest admission fee, but a festival pass gives free admission to many events.

FESTIMUSICALES
June–September
Tel 02 98 53 04 05 (tourist office)
Centre Culturel, 10 boulevard Bougainville, 29900 Concarneau
Tel 02 98 50 38 85
Free concerts and performances all summer long in a 500-seat amphitheatre. Expect jazz, African, reggae and Celtic music, folk dancing and street theatre.
🕐 Tue and Thu 9pm

FÊTES HISTORIQUES
First two weeks in July
Service d'Animation Culturelle, 31 rue Thiers, 56000 Vannes
Tel 02 97 01 62 40
www.mairie-vannes.fr
Every year at the beginning of July, the citizens of Vannes go back in time for one week. The theme changes annually and could be anything from the Vikings to the early 1800s, with street performances, parades in original costumes and fireworks. The theme in 2004 is the Napoleonic era.

TOMBÉES DE LA NUIT
July
Rennes
Tel 02 99 67 11 11 (tourist office)
www.ville-rennes.fr
As dusk descends on Rennes, discover light shows and concerts as the city gets a magical makeover each July. And its all free!

FESTIVAL DES VIEILLES CHARRUES
Third weekend in July
Association Ti ar Vro, 6 place des Droits de l'Homme, 29834 Carhaix
Tel 02 98 99 25 45
www.vieillescharrues.asso.fr
One of France's biggest music festivals welcomes 150,000 music fans to watch bands

which cover the musical spectrum from techno to rock and folk on four separate stages. The three-day festival has a free campsite. To be sure of getting your ticket, buy it at least one month in advance.
🚌 Shuttle buses from railway stations in Loudeac, Morlaix, Brest, Quimper, Crozon and Chateauneuf

FÊTE DES REMPARTS
Last weekend in July
Office du Tourisme, rue du Château 22100, Dinan
Tel 02 96 87 94 94 or 02 96 87 69 76
One of the largest medieval festivals in Europe is held once every two years. During the last weekend of July the city is literally invaded by 800 actors and 3,000 extras in costume.
🕐 Every two years, next one in 2004

FESTIVAL DU JAZZ
End of July
Service Animation Culturelle, 31 rue Thiers, 56000 Vannes
Tel 02 97 01 62 44
www.mairie-vannes.fr/jazzavannes
Six days of evening jazz concerts begin with a free concert in front of the city hall. Three bands play per evening with some playing in the garden of Limur, and in the afternoons, amateur musicians play throughout the town. Bars offer special jazz buffets.

FESTIVAL INTERCELTIQUE
First ten days in August
2 rue Paul Bert, 56100 Lorient
Tel 02 97 64 03 20
www.festival-interceltique.com
For ten days in August, Lorient is the scene of a large Celtic

festival, with bagpipe and other traditional musical instrument contests, folk dancing demonstrations, Breton parties (fest-noz), cabaret, concerts across the city and street stands selling Celtic crafts.

LA ROUTE DU ROCK
Mid-August
Fort St-Père or Office de tourisme de St-Malo, esplanade St-Vincent, 35400 St-Malo
Tel 02 99 53 50 30 (Fort St-Père) or 02 99 56 64 48 (tourist office)
www.laroutedurock.com
This three-day popular music festival covers music from rock to techno. There's free camping in the moat around the castle, free parking, a restaurant and bar, a left-luggage office, a supermarket and free shuttle from St-Malo railway station.

FESTIVAL DE MUSIQUE CLASSIQUE DE DINARD - CÔTE D'EMERAUDE
Three weeks in August
Dinard tourist office, 2 boulevard, Féart, Dinard
Tel 02 99 46 94 12
www.festival-music-dinard.com
Dinard's three-week festival has exquisite classical music with many different styles on offer, from Beethoven to Gershwin to contemporary composers, performed by well-known musicians and young talents. There's also a concert for children and the closing concert is always free.
🕐 4–23 Aug 🎟 Adult €24, child €12

TRANSMUSICALES ROCK FESTIVAL
December
Rennes
Tel 02 99 31 12 10
www.transmusicales.com
Local bands play alongside international music legends at Brittany's music festival. Some concerts are free, while others have a small admission charge.

NORTH AND NORTHEAST FRANCE

This vast sweep of France is a mosaic of contrasting images. Art lovers can admire the Gothic churches of Picardie and seek out the pioneers of French art nouveau in Lorraine. Nancy has long been a hub of glass-making, and the workshops of Baccarat and Gallé still draw visitors. Charleville-Mézières in the Ardennes is the world capital of marionettes; it has France's college of puppetry, and a remarkable triennial festival (next scheduled for 2006).

Shoppers can seriously damage their plastic, since the area is the heart of the French mail order industry and has huge outlet stores selling designer clothes, discounted up to 70 per cent at Roubaix and Troyes. The big event for serious bargain hunters is the 24-hour Braderie de Lille—France's largest second-hand goods rummage sale (see page 243).

The Parc Astérix theme park (see page 242), north of Paris, is witty, European and essentially French, with animated displays and attractions evoking the culture of medieval *chansons*.

Christmas time sees the famous Yuletide markets across the north and east: Hundreds of wooden chalets sell candles, carved ornaments and handicrafts, with warm gingerbread and mulled wine served in the streets. St. Nicolas is bigger than his namesake Santa Claus here and the festivities focus around the saint's day on 6 December.

In summer, Lille's annual *fêtes* combine local festivities with Gay Pride events in a city-wide weekend of parties, while in Reims the Flaneries provide weeks of free concerts. Year round, Strasbourg defies its suits and red tape image, with a lively bar and club scene along the quayside student district.

WHAT TO DO

Nord-Pas-de-Calais

ARRAS
OULD SHEBEEN
6 boulevard Faidherbe, 62000 Arras
Tel 03 21 71 87 97
www.ouldshebeen.com

This little corner of Ireland in France is decorated in green and white, and would stand proudly on any street in Dublin.
🕐 Tue–Thu 4pm–1am, Fri–Sat 4pm–2am, Sun 6pm–1am

BERCK-SUR-MER
CLUB NAUTIQUE BERCKOIS
Chemin au Raisins, BP 124, 62600 Berck-sur-Mer
Tel 03 21 84 80 53
www.site.voila.fr/clubnautiqueberckois
Choose from a range of sea activities in the beautiful bay of Authie, including motorboats, jet-skiing, waterskiing, wakeboarding, windsurfing and catamaran sailing. You can rent all equipment including a wetsuit.
🕐 Daily on reservation, Jun–end Sep; Sat–Sun, Apr, May, Oct 💶 Jet skiing €25 for 15 min

BOULOGNE-SUR-MER
CHAR À VOILE CLUB DE LA CÔTE D'OPALE
272 boulevard Sainte-Beuve, 62200 Boulogne-sur-Mer
Tel 03 21 83 25 48
www.cvcco.com
Northern France's long, windy and sandy beaches are ideal for sand yachting (riding a three-wheeled cycle with a sail and propelled by the wind). This club offers sand yacht rental and instruction. Credit cards are not accepted.
🕐 Throughout the year depending on reservations 💶 3-hour session with an instructor, one yacht per person: €35

CALAIS
CALAIS VINS
Rue Gutenberg, 62100 Calais
Tel 03 21 36 40 40
www.calaisvins.com
One thousand wine vintages line the walls of this shop, plus 60 English beers, *plus* whiskies and ports. Some regional products complete the selection. Best of all, you can try before you buy.
🕐 Mon–Sat 9–7, Sun 10–7

CITÉ EUROPE
1001 boulevard du Kent, 62902 Coquelles Cedex
Tel 03 21 46 47 48
www.cite-europe.com
Since opening in 1995, this shopping mall 4km (2.5 miles) from Calais has been popular with English shoppers. There's a huge hypermarket, wine merchants, clothes and shoe shops and lots of different restaurants for a mid-shop break, selling everything from pizza to *moules frites*.
🕐 Mon–Thu 10–8, Fri 10–9, Sat 9–8

LES PIRATES
130 boulevard Jacquard, 62100 Calais
Tel 03 21 97 93 39
Though landlocked in the heart of the city, this bar transports you straight to the sea. Claim a seat on a barrel in the pirate-ship interior, or venture out onto the ship's deck— otherwise known as the terrace.
🕐 Fri–Sat 11am–2am, Sun–Thu 11am–1am

JENLAIN

BRASSERIE DUYCK
BP6, 59144 Jenlain
Tel 03 27 49 70 03
www.duyck.com
Since 1922, this family business has been brewing Jenlain, a beer named after the little village near Valenciennes where the beer is brewed, and it has become an unofficial emblem of Flanders. The brewery also produces *Bière de Noël* (Christmas beer) and *Bière de Printemps* (Spring beer) and sells special beer glasses.
🕐 Mon–Fri 7.30–noon, 1–4.30

LILLE

LE CÈDRE ROUGE
Parvis de La Treille, 3 place Gilleson, 59000 Lille
Tel 03 20 51 96 96
www.lecedrerouge.com
An institution in Lille, this shop gathers together high-quality handicrafts and furnishings from all over the world to complement the house and garden. Among its offerings are terracotta from Tuscany, teak from Indonesia and high-quality porcelain from France.
🕐 Mon 2–7, Tue–Sat 10.30–7

CHARLES ET CHARLUS
4 rue Basse, 59800 Lille
Tel 03 20 51 01 01
Sells contemporary bags and other leather goods made using traditional methods. There is a choice of leathers and a wide range of shades.
🕐 Mon 2.30–7, Tue–Sat 10.30–7

MARCHÉ AUX LIVRES ET AUX FLEURS
Cloîtres de Vielle Bourse, 59800 Lille
These small markets, selling books and flowers, are held inside the courtyard of the old stock exchange building, a marvel of 17th-century Flemish architecture. It's worth stopping here just to admire the surroundings, but the goods are tempting too. Credit cards are not accepted.
🕐 Tue–Sun 1–7 🚇 Rihour

MARCHÉ DE WAZEMMES
Place de la Nouvelle-Aventure, 59000 Lille
This interesting market is popular with locals who like to shop here on their Sunday stroll. Most of the stalls are set around Wazemmes church, but there is also a covered section. It's the place to buy cheap vegetables and some North African products, and there's also a small antiques section.
🕐 Sun, Tue and Thu 7am–2pm 🚇 Wazemmes

N DE B HAUTE MODE
6 rue Jean-Jacques Rousseau, 59800 Lille
Tel 03 20 42 19 79
This tiny shop on a picturesque street sells unique hats, bags, gloves and hair accessories to discerning but budget conscious customers. The designs and quality are as good as haute couture, but the prices remain affordable. There's a tailor-made service available.
🕐 Tue 2–7, Wed–Sat 10.30–noon, 2–7

LE METROPOLE
26 rue des Ponts de Comines, 59000 Lille
Tel 0892 680 073 or 0892 680 303
This modern building with a glass façade has a repertory cinema. A variety of retrospectives are screened, with debates following the films, al of which are shown in their original language.
🕐 Daily 11am–10pm 🎟 Adult €7 🚉 Gare Lille Flandres

LE KREMLIN
51 rue Jean-Jacques Rousseau, 59800 Lille
Tel 03 20 51 85 79
There's a Russian theme to this bar, with an imposing bust of Lenin presiding over an interior where inscriptions in Russian announce revolution and they have 40 varieties of vodka.
🕐 Mon–Sat 6pm–1am

MAROILLES

DEFROIDMONT
159 Grand'Rue, BP 1, 59550 Maroilles
Tel 03 27 84 65 65
www.defroidmont.fr
This family has been making regional foods since 1960 and is famed for its *flamiche au Maroilles* (made with the cheese named after the village where it is produced). Also look for the *crottin d'Avenois* (nuggets of brioche filled with Maroilles cheese) and *tarte Vergeoise* (soft dough topped with brown sugar).
🕐 Mon–Fri 9–noon, 2–6, Sat 9–noon

LE TOUQUET

GOLF DU TOUQUET
Avenue du Golf, BP 41, 62520 Le Touquet
Tel 03 21 06 28 00
www.opengolfclub.com/ltq

This is one of the most famous golf clubs in France. There are two 18-hole courses: The first winds through a pine grove; the second has sand hills typical of the region. Facilities include a restaurant and hotel on site.
🕐 10am–6pm; closed Jan to mid-Feb 🎟 €22–€55 for round on the 18-hole course

Picardie

AMIENS

LA MÈRE L'OIE
33 quai Belu, 80000 Amiens
Tel 03 22 22 00 00
www.la-mere-loie.com
A restaurant that offers various canned delights to take away. Alongside the goose delicacies, such as foie gras, you'll find duck foie gras, duck and cep pâté, and other meaty delights from elsewhere in France such as pâté from Périgord.
🕓 Thu–Tue 9–3, 6–midnight

COULEUR CAFÉ
8 rue des Bondes, 80000 Amiens
Tel 03 22 91 40 14
Come to this exotic bar for rum cocktails. There's live music and a DJ (usually Thursday, Friday and Saturday) who plays ethnic and techno music.
🕓 Tue–Sat 4pm–3am, Sun–Mon 4pm–1am

LA LUNE DES PIRATES
17 Quai Bélu, 80000 Amiens
Tel 03 22 97 88 01/03 22 22 14 05
www.lalune.net
This rock music venue on the bank of the Somme has an auditorium attached to the bar, which can hold 170 people. It's a springboard for local talent but also welcomes established musicians like Mano Solo.
🕓 8.30pm–1am 💶 €4–€14

AÉROCLUB DE PICARDIE AMIENS-MÉTROPOLE
Aérodrome d'Amiens-Glisy, route de St-Quentin, 80440 Glisy
Tel 03 22 38 10 70
www.aeroclub-picardie-amiens.com
Established in 1909, this flying club lets you discover the region of Picardie from a microlight and other small, motorized planes. There are also night flights and aerobatics sessions for the strong of stomach. Credit cards are not accepted.
🕓 Throughout the year depending on the weather and reservation 💶 First flight: €50 for one person, €70 for two

DURY

FARMER'S MARKET
Facing IME, Route de Paris, 80480 Dury
Dury's farmer's market is a delight for the palate, as it sells a range of home-made foodstuffs, including foie gras, jams, preserves and honey as well as organic vegetables. A section with plants and flowers adds a touch of brightness.
🕓 Fri 8.30am–1.30pm

PLAILLY

PARC ASTÉRIX
A1 Paris–Lille Highway, 60128 Plailly
Tel 03 44 62 30 30
www.parcasterix.fr
Parc Astérix theme park is based on the characters from the famous cartoon books featuring the Gaulish heroes Astérix and Obélix. There are plenty of rides, shows and attractions and at the Gauls' village a scale model depicts Paris through the centuries. Hotel accommodation is available. Car drivers should take the A1 Paris to Lille autoroute.
🕓 Apr to end-Oct; days and times vary 💶 Adult €31, child (3–11) €23, children under 3 free 🚇 Roissy-Pôle

Champagne-Ardenne

REIMS

LE TIGRE
2 bis avenue Georges Clemenceau, 51100 Reims
Tel 03 26 82 64 00
This rock music venue is first and foremost a concert hall, but it also has a dance floor. The great interior includes a collection of guitars hanging on the walls.
🕓 Daily 5pm–5am
💶 Varies according to performance

L'ESCALE
132 rue de Vesle, 51100 Reims
Tel 03 26 88 17 85
L'Escale is a beer-drinker's paradise, with more than 200 kinds of beer available including a dozen on tap. The interior is in the pub style, with a long bar and lots of wood.
🕓 Fri–Sat 4pm–1.15am, Sun–Thu 4pm–midnight

CHAMPAGNE TAITTINGER
9 place St-Nicaise, 51100 Reims
Tel 03 26 85 84 33
www.taittinger.com
Start with a tour of this impressive champagne cellar. The vaulted basement runs for miles and you can still see the vestiges of a 13th-century chapel. The guided tour includes a tasting session, to help you choose before you buy.
🕓 Mon–Fri 9.30–noon, 2–4.30, Sat–Sun 9–11, 2–5, Mar–end Nov; phone to reserve at other times
💶 Adult €6

MAXIM'S
17 rue des Crénaux, 51100 Reims
Tel 03 26 82 70 67
www.champagnemartel.com
A visit to this cellar will enable you to learn about the production process of champagne. At the end of the tour, you can buy Maxim's vintage, a Brut rosé.
🕓 Daily 10–7

PATINOIRE BOCQUAINE
41 chaussée Bocquaine, 51100 Reims
Tel 03 26 82 60 00
www.reims.fr
Get your skates on at this popular ice rink, framed by terraces and with a light and sound system. The rink also has theme nights and parties such as a 1980s night and Valentine's Day party.
🕓 Tue and Thu 9.45–5.30, 8.30–10.45, Wed and Fri 9.45–11.45, 2.30–5.30, 8.30–10.45, Sat 2.30–5.30, 8.30–10.45, Sun 9.30–noon, 2.30–5.30, Mon 2.30–5.30 💶 Entry €4, skate rental €3

orraine

METZ

EN CAFÉ
1 en Fournirue, 57000 Metz
el 03 87 36 56 75
Paintings inspired by Manga
(Japanese cartoon books)
decorate the back room of
this bar, where you'll also
and a pool table. A DJ gets
the crowd dancing to house
music at the weekend.
🕐 Mon–Sat 8pm–2am, Sun 3–8pm

NANCY

PIERRE KOENIG
2 rue des Dominicains, 54000 Nancy
Tel 03 83 35 18 36
www.chocolats-koenig.com
Pierre Koenig uses the best
ingredients (Normandy butter,
Forastero chocolate beans and
Italian hazelnuts) to make his
chocolate. Among his creative
offerings are the connoisseur's
stick and a chocolate 'sausage'
incorporating pistachios and
sugared almonds.
🕐 Mon 2–7, Tue–Sat 9.30–12.30, 2–7

VELAINE-EN-HAYE

TENNIS CLUB NANCY FORÊT DE HAYE
Zone de Loisirs, 54840 Velaine-en-Haye
Tel 03 83 23 28 87
www.club.fft.fr/tcnfh/
At the heart of the Haye forest,
these 26 tennis courts (some
indoor, some outdoor) have a
beautiful setting. There's also
a bar, restaurant, swimming
pool, fitness room and shop.
🕐 Daily on reservation 🎫 €16
per hour

Alsace

STRASBOURG

MARCHÉ DES PRODUCTEURS
Place du Marché-aux-Poissons, 67000
Strasbourg
Vegetable growers and other
food producers (including
some organic) come from all
over Alsace to display their
produce at this market. The
closest tram stop is Langstross
Grand'Rue.
🕐 Sat 7–1

PÂTISSERIE CONFISERIE KUBLER
29 avenue des Vosges, 67000
Strasbourg
Tel 03 88 35 22 27
www.kubler.fr
A winner of the prestigious
confectioners' competition
Meilleur Ouvrier de France,
Antoine Hepp's delights

include *Verger d'Alsaces*
(Alsatian orchards), a cake that
contains an apple and cinna-
mon mousse. Other specials
include chocolate-coated
gingerbread and crystallized
orange slices dipped in white
and bitter chocolate. Take the
tram to République.
🕐 Tue–Sun 7.30–7

LA LAITERIE
13 rue Hohwald, 67000 Strasbourg
Tel 03 88 23 72 37
Once a dairy, this building, not
far from the Laiterie tram stop,
is now home to underground
culture, with a bar, an exhibition hall, a theatre, and a main
hall where live music from
reggae to rock is performed.
🕐 7.30pm–11.30pm Tue–Sat

IRISH TIMES
19 rue Sainte-Barbe, 67000 Strasbourg
Tel 03 88 32 04 02
Quiz nights on Wednesdays
and live music give this little
piece of the Emerald Isle an
animated and convivial atmosphere. Lots of wood, a lovely
long bar and a fireplace
complete the atmosphere.
The tram stops at Langstross
Grand'Rue.
🕐 Daily 2pm–midnight (slightly later at
the weekend)

Festivals and Events

SUMMER FÊTES
June
Lille
Tel 03 20 21 94 21 (tourist office)
www.lilletourism.com
There's partying in Grand'
Place and free fun in the
streets every June with
National Music Day, Gay Pride
and the parade of giants.

LES FLÂNERIES MUSICALES D'ÉTÉ
July–August
Reims
Tel 03 26 77 45 25 (tourist office)
www.ville-reims.fr
Yehudi Menuhin founded this
summer season of 100 (mostly
free) classical and blues
concerts during July and
August. Many concert-hall
legends take part.

BRADERIE DE LILLE
September
Lille
Tel 03 20 21 94 21 (Tourist information)
Bargain hunters should head
for the 24-hour Braderie de
Lille in the first weekend of
September. Nearly 200km
(125 miles) of walkways are
covered with bric-a-brac as the
entire city sells off its second-
hand goods in France's biggest
yard sale.

CHRISTMAS MARKETS
December
Strasbourg
Tel 03 88 52 28 28 (Tourist information)
www.ot-strasbourg.fr
Throughout December, the
city is transformed into a
Christmas wonderland of
quaint wooden chalets selling
homemade toys, gingerbread,
gifts and mulled wine, from
the Cathedral to the Christmas
tree on place Kléber.

THE LOIRE

The chateaux of the Loire inevitably dominate the visitor's agenda in this region. Daytimes can be spent exploring the homes of the countesses and duchesses of past times (invariably it is the women who provide the most entertaining histories), while *son et lumière* entertainments in the grounds provide evening entertainment. Most such shows recount the history of the building, but one in particular—at Puy du Fou—is a lavish blockbuster re-enactment with a cast of hundreds. The same site during the day provides a fascinating park, with reconstructions of village life in centuries past.

For active visitors, there's golfing, bicycling along dedicated paths besides the Loire, or taking to the water in a kayak. For the more sedentary, there's fishing or indulging in a little wine tasting. The Cadre Noir equestrian facility at Saumur provides great diversion for families, as do the dockyard museums at St-Nazaire. The troglodyte villages at Doué la Fontaine and Rochecorbon offer fascinating glimpses into the subterranean communities of the recent past.

The waterside districts of Nantes are popular with those searching for cultural nightlife, with some bar-hopping too.

Pays de la Loire

ANGERS

GAUMONT ANGERS MULTIPLEXE
Avenue des Droits de l'Homme, 49100 Angers
Tel 0892 696 696 (€0.34/min)
www.gaumont.fr
This large multiplex cinema in the St-Serge district, near the university, offers first-run films with at least half of them in English.
🕑 Films start from 2pm 💶 Adult €7

BEAULIEU-SUR-LAYON
LE METRO
49790 Beaulieu-sur-Layon
Tel 02 41 78 30 97

The largest disco in the Loire offers a mix of dance music in a huge 3,000-capacity venue. Follow the lasers lighting up the sky, visible from more than 10km (6 miles) away. Drivers should head south from Angers on the N160 and pick up the D125.
🕑 11pm–dawn Thu–Sat 💶 Cover charge €7

CHOLET
CYBERPUB DU CADRAN
105 Route Nationale, 49300 Cholet
Tel 02 41 62 00 78
www.cadran.net
An eclectic mix of cybercafé, dance club and restaurant (offering everything from espresso to Tex-Mex cooking and Cuban mixed drinks), with theme nights and a lively atmosphere.
🕑 Mon–Sat 11am–2am 💶 Cover charge some theme nights

LE MANS
LA PÉNICHE EXCELSIOR
Z.A. La Raterie, 72000 Le Mans
Tel 02 43 80 35 06
An intimate club south of the city heart on an old barge moored to a quay on the river Sarthe. There are events almost daily, from raves to concerts—mainly techno, ethnic and house.
🕑 Varies according to event, usually 10pm onwards 💶 Average €15–€30

LE ST-FLACEAU
9 rue St-Flaceau, 72000 Le Mans
Tel 02 43 23 24 93
This bar has a terrace perched on the old Roman town wall, or you can claim a comfortable armchair in the parquet-floored 18th-century apartment, and enjoy a reasonably priced drink from the huge range on offer.
🕑 Daily 4pm–1am

24-HOUR CIRCUIT, LE MANS
Circuit des 24 heures, 72019 Le Mans
Tel 02 43 40 24 75
www.lemans.org

Home to much more than the famous Le Mans race, this legendary circuit offers plenty of other high-speed racing events. In summer motorsport fans flock here to watch the

WHAT TO DO

renowned 24-hour race. The circuit is 5km (3 miles) outside Le Mans on the D147.
🕐 24-hour race mid-Jun
💶 Approximately €40

MISSILLAC
COSMOPOLIS
La Galina, 44780 Missillac
Tel 02 40 66 96 01
Cosmopolis, half-way between Vannes and Nantes, is a night-club which has different music depending on the night of the week. Once a month there's a special event with, for example, live music or a theme party. If you plan on coming here several times, ask for the Cosmopass.
🕐 Fri–Sun 10.30pm–4.45am summer; Fri–Sat 10.30pm–4.45am, rest of year
💶 Fri, Sun €8, Sat €10 (1 drink included)

NANTES
BIJOUX LA JALURA
21 rue Mercoeur, 44000 Nantes
Tel 02 40 35 60 84
Antique and second-hand jewellery from a variety of eras and locations, with fine pieces from all parts of Europe, and occasionally some from Asia. The staff are patient and knowledgeable and it's best to call in advance, as the owner is sometimes away on buying trips.
🕐 Tue–Sat 10–12.30, 2.30–7

RUE CREBILLON/PASSAGE POMMERAYE
44000 Nantes

Rue Crebillon is Nantes's main shopping street, and window-shopping at the top-range

stores is a popular activity. The nearby boutiques that crowd passage Pommeraye, built in 1843, are on three levels, joined by wooden stairs, with wrought-iron balconies topped by statues.

LE LIEU UNIQUE
Quai Ferdinand Favre, 44000 Nantes
Tel 02 40 12 14 34
www.lelieuunique.com
This cutting-edge theatre on canal St-Félix offers all kinds of productions, from Shakespeare (at least once a year in English) to modern plays.

There's a bar and restaurant open for a pre- or post-show drink or meal.
🕐 Open all year 💶 Adult from €15

PORT ST-PÈRE
PLANÈTE SAUVAGE
44170 Port St-Père
Tel 02 40 04 82 82
www.planetesauvage.com
One of the best safari parks in France, with more than 10km (6 miles) of roads winding through thirteen separate environments. The safari village offers activities, food, drink and shopping, and if you can't get enough wildlife, there's a serpent house in the village. From the D65, take the D11 in the direction of St-Mars de Coutaism and then follow the signs.
🕐 Daily 10–5, Apr to early Nov; closed mid-Nov to end Mar 💶 Adult €14.50; child €9.15

ST-BARTHÉLEMY-D'ANJOU
LA DISTILLERIE COINTREAU
Rue Croix Blanche, 49124
St-Barthélemy d'Anjou
Tel 02 41 31 50 50
Visit the home of the liqueur that scents many mixed drinks. In the museum, the knowledgeable staff can help you learn about the distillation process and will let you sample before you buy at this distillery just east of Angers.
🕐 Daily 10–6, Jul–end Aug; 10–12.30, 1.30–6, Feb–end Jun; closed Jan

Centre

AZAY-LE-RIDEAU
COOPERATIVE DE LA VANNERIE
1 rue de la Cheneillère, 37190
Azay-le-Rideau
Tel 02 47 45 43 03
This is a cooperative of local artisans who produce a variety of goods, from small baskets to large outdoor benches.
🕐 Mon–Sat 9–12.30, 2–7, Sun 2–7

TOURAINE JUS DE POMMES
ZA la Loge, 37190 Azay-le-Rideau
Tel 02 47 45 98 98
www.tourainejusdepommes.fr
Monsieur Robert and his staff transform the apples from their varied orchards into delicious fresh fruit juices, and barley from the fields into a fabulous small-batch beer. You can enjoy samples here (near the middle of the village), then buy larger quantities in the boutique if you're impressed.
🕐 Mon–Fri 8.30–12.30, 2–6

BLOIS
AIR MAGIC LOIRE VALLEY
1 boulevard Leo Lagrange, 37510
Ballan Mire
Tel 06 11 48 78 43
www.air-magic.com
Float into the clouds in a hot-air balloon for a breathtaking 60- or 90-minute adventure over the Loire Valley. Take-off points vary, but choices include the vineyards of Amboise, Villandry or Azay-le-Rideau.
🕐 Flights all year 💶 €160 per person

WHAT TO DO

ANTEBELLUM
12 rue St-Lubin, 41000 Blois
Tel 02 54 78 38 78
This antique jewellery shop in the rue St-Martin and rue du Commerce shopping area is worth a special visit for its superb selection of pieces from different periods. Browse the range of precious and semi-precious stones and fine gold and silver work.
🕐 Tue–Sat 10–12, 2–7

LE PARADIS DES ENFANTS
2 rue des Trois-Clefs, 41000 Blois
Tel 02 54 78 09 68
For something out of the ordinary for children (and their parents), this restored 15th-century house offers both modern and antique toys of every possible make and kind. It's in the easy-to-find rue St-Martin and rue du Commerce shopping area and is a great stop for a birthday or just an en-route diversion.
🕐 Tue–Sat 9.30–noon, 2–7

TAPISSERIE LANGLOIS
Route du Château, 41000 Blois
Tel 02 54 78 04 43
Anyone inspired by the tapestries seen in the Loire chateaux can pick up a historically accurate copy here. You'll find tapestries from many of the area's most famous chateaux with prices from €180 to €3,000 depending on the size and the amount of detail.
🕐 Mon–Sat 9.30–noon, 2–7, Sun 9.30–noon

MAISON DE LA CULTURE
Place André Malraux, 18005 Bourges
Tel 02 48 67 74 70
www.mcbourges.com
Modern facility staging dance, classical music concerts and theatre, with children's shows on the bill during summer.
🕐 Shows usually start at 7.30pm except for Sundays 🎫 Adult from €24

CHEVERNY GIFT SHOP
41700 Cour-Cheverny
Tel 02 54 79 96 29
There are many chateau gift shops in the Loire Valley, but this is possibly the best of all. Two large showrooms have all of the usual souvenirs, as well as art, comic books, suits of armour, beautiful collectable swords and fine glassware.
🕐 Daily 9.15–6.45, Jul–end Sep; 9.30–noon, 2.15–5.30, Oct and Feb–end Mar; 9.30–noon, 2.15–5, Dec; 9.15–6.15, Apr–end Jun; Closed Nov, Jan–end Feb

CHRISTIAN DUMARTIN
Manoir de Beauvais, 37500 Ligre
Tel 02 47 98 36 63
Antiques aficionados come to the elegant Manoir de Beauvais, southeast of Chinon, for fine quality. The 17th- and 18th-century pieces of art are stunning, matched only by the many small treasures among the collection covering the 19th-century Louis-Philippe and Napoleon III era. The owner, Monsieur Dumartin, and his staff are welcoming and willing to share their considerable knowledge.
🕐 Tue–Fri 9–noon, 2–7; Call ahead to check if open if making a special journey

MUSÉE DE LA FAÏENCERIE
78 place de la Victoire, 45500 Gien
Tel 02 38 67 00 05
There's a long tradition of faience (glazed earthenware) in the village of Gien, with a style noted for its midnight-

blue glaze and golden highlights. You can see examples at this museum, tour the factory (by prior arrangement) to see how it's made, then buy your own piece in the shop.
🕐 Tue–Sat 9–noon, 2–7

LA CHOCOLATERIE ROYALE
53 rue Royale, 45000 Orléans
Tel 02 38 53 93 43
This *chocolaterie*'s specialty is *cotignac*, a jam made from quince, but the range of other regional and traditional delicacies is vast—from bonbons to large seasonal pieces that are more art than chocolate. They do especially beautiful gift-wrapping.
🕐 Mon 2–7.15, Tue–Sat 9–12.30, 2–7.15

MARCHÉ DE L'ORLÉANS
Known across France as one of the best in the region, this open market sells the varied produce of the surrounding regions. The appeal lies in its bustling settings; it rotates, with a different small area of the city transformed into a village on market day.
🕐 Blossière Tue 7–2; Dauphine Tue 7–noon; Place Dunois Thu 3–7.30; Charpenterie Quai de Roi Sat 6–12.30

G. MARTIN POURET
236 Faubourg-Bannier, 45400 Fleury les Aubrais
Tel 02 38 88 78 49
Wine vinegar has been made here by the traditional Orléans method since 1797, and it is one of the only places in the region where this is still done. The result is unique vinegar that adds a special touch to any recipe. Learn about the process and buy some in the shop.
🕐 Mon–Fri 8–noon, 1–5.30

MIREILLE BESNARD
92 rue Bannier, 45000 Orléans
Tel 02 38 53 18 02
Come here if you are interested in 19th-century decorative arts. Items range from small ornaments for

the mantelpiece or side table to large paintings. There's also a fine range of 17th- and 18th-century furniture and art, although most pieces are probably too large to take home. The staff are particularly helpful.

🕐 Tue–Sat 10–noon, 2–7

LES MUSARDISES
38 rue de Republique, 45000 Orléans
Tel 02 38 53 30 98

Jacques Desbois is the proprietor of this house devoted to blending the arts of pastry chef and *chocolatier*. Try the aptly named *paradis,* a blend of *crème d'orange* and a delicate chocolate mousse on an airy foundation of meringue. There are dozens more varieties to sample.

🕐 Tue–Sat 8–7.30

PAXTON'S HEAD
264 rue de Bourgogne, 45000 Orléans
Tel 02 38 81 23 29

Paxton's Head is a jazz club with an English pub feel and is one of the best venues in the area for touring jazz.

🕐 Daily 3pm–3am 💰 Cover charge on show nights averages €10

ZÉNITH
1 rue du Président Robert Schuman, 45074 Orléans
Tel 02 38 25 04 29
www.orleans-gestion.fr/zenith/

A sleek tower of glass, the Zénith is Orléans's venue for most large cultural activities. There are pop concerts from rap to rock, as well as shows for children.

🕐 Concerts 7.30pm, shows for children in the afternoon 💰 €18–€30

ST-CHRISTOPHE-SUR-LE-NAIS

ST-CHRISTOPHE-SUR-LE-NAIS ANGLING
7 rue St Gilles, 37370 St-Christophe-sur-le-Nais
Tel 02 47 29 39 04
www.touraine-fishing.com

Professional fishing guide Philippe Pagnoux leads day trips (and longer trips) on

nearby Lac Guerlédan and the Loire. Lessons for children or adults can be arranged.

🕐 May, Jun, Oct–end Jan 💰 €130 per day

TOURS

CENTRE CHORÉGRAPHIQUE NATIONAL DE TOURS
47 rue du Sergent Leclerc, 37000 Tours
Tel 02 47 36 46 00
www.cntours.com

Daniel Larrieu here directs his company in a wide range of dance. The emphasis is on modern dance, but you can sometimes catch a ballet here.

🕐 Check the schedule for the latest performance times 💰 €15

LE CORSAIRE
187 avenue de Grammont, Tours 37000
Tel 02 47 05 20 00

Come aboard this centrally located, amusingly nautical-themed bar. The owners pride themselves on offering more than 400 cocktails, to be enjoyed amid the portholes and hanging lanterns.

🕐 Mon–Sat 6pm–4am

MARCHÉ
Place des Halles, 37000 Tours

Although the market, in the heart of the city, is lively at all times, Sundays are busiest. The *charcuterie* is particularly good, with a bewildering selection of fresh meats and dozens of types of sausages. Produce is abundant and fresh and the hand-crafted goods are well made.

🕐 Daily 7–2

MARCHÉ DE PUCE
Place de la Victoire, 37000 Tours

For those in search of value for money, the open-air flea market at place de la Victoire is the market of choice. Be prepared to have to hunt for the pearls, and it's a case of 'buyer beware', especially when bargaining in a language that's not your own.

🕐 Wed and Sat 7–5

PHILIPPE BRUNEAU
62 rue de la Scellerie, 37000 Tours
Tel 02 47 05 25 87

A rare and beautiful collection of antique gilded wood and bronze pieces—most notably from the 17th and 18th centuries—is on offer in this quaint shop in central Tours. There's also an excellent selection of period clocks and watches.

🕐 Tue–Sat 10–noon, 2–6.30 (Call ahead to check)

LE PYMS
170 avenue de Grammont, Tours 37000
Tel 02 47 66 22 22

A club with a crowd ranging from young to youthful, in a lively quarter of Tours. The strong selection of up-to-the-minute music makes it a regional draw, and it's usually packed.

🕐 Tue–Sun 10.30pm–4am or later

PALAIS DES SPORTS
1 boulevard Laittre de Tassigny, 37042 Tours
Tel 02 47 70 86 80

This is a large leisure complex with a sports hall, two swimming pools (one of

WHAT TO DO

which is Olympic-sized) and an ice rink. Credit cards are not accepted.

🕐 Varies, based on holiday schedule, call for details 💶 Swimming session €3

RUE DE BORDEAUX/RUE NATIONALE
37000 Tours

The largest concentration of major shops and department stores in the region stretches from the dignified 19th-century train station towards rue Nationale. On rue Nationale towards the river there are expensive boutiques and many small chain stores. Not all of the shops accept credit cards.

TOURS AERO CLUB
Aéroport Tours Val de Loire, 37100 Tours
Tel 02 47 51 25 68
perso.wanadoo.fr/toursaeroclub
Take an introductory or guided flight over the Loire Valley in a training plane. Flights leave from the Tours-Val de Loire Airport on the N152, just outside Tours.

🕐 Open all year 💶 €55 for first flight

VEIGNÉ

VAL D'INDRE CANOË-KAYAK
Moulin de Veigné-Mairie, 37250 Veigné
Tel 02 47 73 13 19
www.ifrance.com/Veigne-Infor/Asso/Kayak
Explore the quiet Indre river by kayak. Take a short course or a tour with a guide, or rent a kayak and go on your own. All guided trips are led by certified instructors.

🕐 Daily Jul–end Aug; Sat–Sun Apr to end-Jun 💶 Kayak rental €65, guided tour €130

VILLANDRY

CHÂTEAU DE VILLANDRY GIFT STORE
Château de Villandry, 37510 Villandry
Tel 02 47 50 02 09
This gift store reflects the chateau (see page 150) in specializing in garden products. Shelves are stocked with a variety of seeds, solidly crafted garden tools and

books about the garden itself, with some in English. The store occasionally closes at

lunchtime, so phone to check. Villandry is 10km (6 miles) from Tours on the D7 and it is clearly signed.

🕐 Daily 9–7.30, May to mid-Sep; 9–7 Mar–end Apr and mid-Sep to mid-Oct; 9–5.30, mid-Oct to Feb

Festivals and Events

CINÉSCÉNIE
May–September
Château du Puy du Fou, 44190 Clisson
Tel 02 51 64 11 11
www.puydufou.com
A spectacular sound and light show lasting nearly two hours, with pyrotechnics and lasers, armies of dancers, 50 mounted knights and a chateau backdrop, make this well worth a summer visit. Reservations are recommended.

🕐 Fri–Sat 10.30pm, Jun to end Jul; Fri–Sat 10pm, Aug; first Fri, first and second Sat in Sep 10pm
💶 Adult €22.50, child €12

LE MANS 24 HOUR RACE
Mid-June
See page 244.

ILLUMINATIONS AT VILLANDRY (LES NUITS DES MILLE FEUX)
July
Château de Villandry, 37510
Tel 02 47 50 02 09
www.chateauvillandry.com
In early July, 2,000 candles illuminate the gardens of the chateau from sunset as baroque musicians stroll through the grounds. (See shop entry on this page and also page 150.)

💶 Admission to the gardens €5

CHARTRES INTERNATIONAL ORGAN FESTIVAL
July–August
Place de la Cathédrale, 28005 Chartres
Tel 02 37 18 26 26
orgues.chartres.free.fr
www.ville-chartres.fr

Throughout the summer enjoy great organ music at one of France's finest cathedrals, Notre-Dame de Chartres (see page 146), famous for its mismatched spires.

THREE CONTINENTS FESTIVAL
From Late November
Nantes
Tel 02 40 69 74 14
www.3continents.com
Forget Hollywood-sur-Med at the Cannes Film Festival in May. This film festival highlights the work of directors from Asia, Latin America and Africa and ticket prices are inexpensive.

WHAT TO DO

CENTRAL FRANCE AND THE ALPS

Burgundy has its fine wines, summer baroque concerts in the old city of Beaune and, for motor-sport lovers, the French Grand Prix; the Alps draw thousands to their Olympic ski resorts; and Lyon is a gastronome's heaven. But the rest of central France retains its discreet pleasures away from the glare of publicity. Escape to the gentle grandeur of the Auvergne, where once-violent volcanoes now wear a velvet coat of greenery, providing a lush backdrop to winter sports and summer sky-riding and windsurfing. Take to the fast-moving waters of the Ardèche Gorges or imbibe the curative waters of the many spa resorts, famous today for the names of mineral waters sold worldwide.

In Loire-Forez, summer festivals make the most of the glorious landscapes around the Batie d'Urfé. Lyon, like Grenoble, has a pulsating party scene, with events posted and screened online at www.nuit-lyonnaise.com, and a remarkable cultural calendar with biennial celebrations of modern dance and art. Nearby St-Étienne hosts well-known festivals of design and contemporary classical music. The dark stone city of Clermont-Ferrand has busy bars and a surprising literary scene and book market.

Franche-Comté, one of France's least-known regions for tourism, is well-established on the popular music map. Each July, in the shadow of the Belfort Lion, there is the Eurockéennes rock festival.

As for shopping, buy silk in Lyon, olive products in the Drôme and tins of *marrons* (chestnuts) from Ardèche.

Auvergne

GALERIE DE L'OPÉRA

6 rue Casino and 13 passage Noyer, 03200 Vichy
Tel 04 70 31 90 27
http://perso.wanadoo.fr/galerie.opera.vichy
Antiques and ornamental decorative objects are for sale here close to the Grand Casino. Goods include stone and ivory figurines, furniture, lighting and contemporary and religious art.
◉ Daily 2.30–7.30

LE MARCHÉ COUVERT

Place Leger, 03200 Vichy
Tel 04 70 30 55 08
Flowers, fresh and dried meats, cheeses, bread and cakes fill the stands of this covered market in the heart of the town. Look in particular for the fishmonger, wine outlet, Spanish stand, and a regional specialist selling cheeses and sausages from the Bourbonnais mountains.
◉ Tue–Sun 7am–1pm

L'OPÉRA

rue du Parc, 03200 Vichy
Tel 04 70 30 50 30 or 04 70 30 50 56
www.ville-vichy.com
Constructed in 1901 and entirely renovated in 1995, the opera house hosts concerts, plays and ballet as well as opera. The interior is Italian art nouveau in style and there's a bar which serves drinks but no food.
◉ Open all year; box office Tue–Sat 1.30–6.30 ▥ Plays €29–€37, opera €27–€59

LE CENTRE THERMAL DES DÔMES

132 boulevard des États-Unis, 03200 Vichy
Tel 04 70 97 39 59
www.vichy-thermes.tm.fr
Beautiful thermal spa complex offering set or 'à la carte'

treatments. Choose from the thermal pool, gym, sauna, hammam (Turkish bath), Jacuzzis, Vichy showers and massage cabins. Robes and towels are supplied, but you buy special sandals to wear around the spa. Children under 16 are not admitted
🕐 Mon–Sat 8–noon, 2.30–6; closed Dec to mid Feb 💶 From €53 per day

L'HIPPODROME
2 route de Charmeil, 03700 Bellerive
Tel 04 70 32 03 77
www.courses-de-vichy.fr
Horse-racing began here at Bellerive, on the opposite side of the river from Vichy, in 1875. There are both afternoon and evening meetings of flat racing and trotting. The Grand Prix de Vichy takes place in July.
🕐 Varies according to races 💶 From €6 🚌 Shuttle bus service (TPN) takes about 20 min from La Poste; various stops en route include railway station and covered market
🚤 Free shuttle service by boat departs from La Rotunde du Lac

Bourgogne

ATHENAEUM DE LA VIGNE ET DU VIN
5 rue de l'Hôtel-Dieu, 21200 Beaune
Tel 03 80 25 08 30
The art of the table is the theme of this shop directly opposite the famed Hospices de Beaune. The shop sells fine tableware, wine, books about wine and local food and drink such as Dijon mustard, crème de cassis and *pain d'épices*.
🕐 Daily 10–7

BEAUNE CHOSES
10 place Carnot, 21200 Beaune
Tel 03 80 22 11 56
www.beaune-choses.com
Devoted to beautiful tableware, this shop sells china, crystal and pewter by famous makers like Lalique, Baccarat and Daum. There's tax-free shopping and they can ship your purchases abroad.
🕐 Tue–Sun 9–12.30, 2–7.30

MAISON DENIS PERRET
Place Carnot, 21200 Beaune
Tel 03 80 22 35 47
www.denisperret.fr
Maison Denis Perret has been here since 1973 (the Denis Perret grocery shop preceded it). Today you can find the most complete range of Burgundy wines with more than 300 labels.
🕐 Mon–Sat 9–7, Apr–end Nov; Mon–Sat 9–noon, 2–7, rest of year

LE TAST'FROMAGES
23 rue Carnot, 21200 Beaune
Tel 03 80 24 73 51
This cheese shop sells about 120 different types including *Délice de Pommard* made from a ball of Brillat-Savarin (the creamy cheese from Normandy) matured in mustard seeds or blackcurrant buds. Burgundy specials include *Époisses au Marc de Bourgogne* and *Amour de Nuits-St-Georges*.
🕐 Mon–Sat 8.30–12.30, 2.30–7.30, Sun 8.30–12.30

L'OPERA NIGHT
Rue de Beaumarche, Palais des Congrès, 21200 Beaune
Tel 03 80 24 10 11
www.operanight.fr
One thing you won't find here is opera, despite the name. This nightclub complex has three different rooms: L'Opera has the largest dance floor, Le Kiss plays music from the 1980s and 90s, and L'Armstrong attracts a well-dressed crowd. There's also a cocktail bar, Le Viva Café.
🕐 Fri–Sun 10.30pm–5am 💶 Fri–Sat €5; Sun free 🚉 Gare SNCF

LA MOUTARDERIE FALLOT
31 faubourg Bretonnerie, 21200 Beaune
Tel 03 80 26 21 34 (tourist info office)
www.fallot.com
The Fallot mustard mill, five minutes on foot from the heart of the historic town, is Burgundy's last independent mustard business. The one-hour interactive tour using infrared lighting and 3-D

animation shows both modern and traditional manufacturing methods.
🕐 Mon–Sat tours at 9.30am and 11am; Closed mid Nov to end Feb 💶 €10

Franche-Comté

DOMAINE ROLET PÈRE ET FILS
Montigny, 39600 Arbois
Tel 03 84 66 00 05
www.rolet-arbois.com
One of the most renowned producers of Jura wines including award-winning Arbois reds, *vin jaune* and *vin de paille*. Taste and buy direct from the domaine.
🕐 Mon–Sat 10–12, 2.30–6, Jul–end Aug; Mon–Fri 10–12, 2.30–6, rest of year

L'OPÉRA-THÉÂTRE BESANÇON
Place du Théâtre, 25000 Besançon
Tel 03 81 87 81 97
www.opera-besancon.com
Franche-Comté's leading classical performing-arts venue has a varied schedule of opera, operetta, ballet and classical recitals.
🕐 Evening performances from 7.30pm
💶 Adult €10–39

YVES FAILLENET
La Louve du Val d'Amour
Impasse du rang
39600, Champagne-sur-Loue
Tel 03 84 37 70 17
jura.peche.free.fr/formules
Professional fly fishing tuition with one- to five-day courses

WHAT TO DO

on the river-banks of the Jura.
🕐 Fishing season runs from May–Dec (for various species) 📅 1-day course €120 per person or €100 per person for 3 people

LE FRASNOIS
ECURIE DES 4 LACS
Didier Méjard, 39130 Le Frasnois
Tel 03 84 25 50 20
www.ecuriedes4lacs.com
Go on a horse-riding holiday in the Jura with accommodation and meals included or simply go riding for half a day or a full day on a cross-country trail (for beginners and experienced riders). Maximum group size is ten people.
🕐 Mid-Jan–end Nov 📅 2 day, 1 night packages from €210 per person

Rhône-Alpes

ANNECY

COURRIER
65 rue Carnot, 74000 Annecy
Tel 04 50 46 46 76
This is a contemporary indoor, air-conditioned shopping mall. It has about 40 boutiques selling house-hold goods, clothes, beauty products, perfume and gifts, and there's a large supermarket. Relax in a comfortable leather armchair in the brasserie with a post-shopping drink.
🕐 Mon–Sat 9.30–7.30; supermarket 9am–9pm; brasserie 8am–11pm

MARKETS
Tel 04 50 45 00 33 (tourist information)
A weekly food market lines rue de la République, rue St-Claire, Pont Morens and quai

l'Évêché, while clothes, books and leather goods are sold on place Romains. A monthly art and antiques market is held in rue St-Claire, place St-Claire, quai l'Évêché, Pont Morens, rue de la République and rue de l'Isle.
🕐 Food market: Tue 8–noon; miscella-neous goods: Tue 8–7; antiques: last Sat of month 8–7

BATEAUX DUPRAZ
Quai Napoléon 111, 74000 Annecy
Tel 04 50 51 52 15 or 04 50 52 42 99
www.bateauxdupraz.com
Take a boat trip on Lac d'Annecy in a 30-seater boat, L'Arc en Ciel ('The Rainbow'). The lake tour, lasting 30 or 50 minutes, has commentary in English and French. Board at Jardins de l'Europe opposite L'Île des Cygnes.
🕐 Tours at 11, 2.15, 3, 4.15 and 5.15 (also 12.30 and 6.30, Jul–Aug). Closed mid-Nov to mid-Feb 📅 Adult €10.50

BICYCLING
Office de Tourisme, 1 rue Jean Jaurès, 74000 Annecy
Tel 04 50 45 00 33
www.lac-annecy.com
A bicycle track from Annecy to Giez skirts Lac d'Annecy, with superb views of surrounding mountains. You can rent bicycles from various places, including Little Big Shop (80 rue Carnot, 74000 Annecy, tel 04 50 67 42 13).

CHAMBÉRY
L'ÉCOLE DE PARACHUTISME DE SAVOIE
Aéroport de Chambéry, 73420 Viviers du Lac
Tel 04 79 54 42 93 or 06 13 09 61 56
www.veloce-skydive.com/chambery
This parachute school runs jumps for beginners and expe-rienced skydivers. Beginners can do a tandem jump with an instructor over Lake Bourget, providing wonderful views of Mont Blanc and the Alps. Those arriving by car should take the A43 from Lyon or the A41, then follow signs for the airport. EPS offices are next to

the airport building but the activity area is next to Savoie Technolac. If you arrive at Chambéry's SNCF railway station you can be collected if you give advance notice.
🕐 Daily 8am–9pm; closed Jan, Feb 📅 First tandem jump €220

CHAMONIX
CHERVERNY
126 rue Paccard, 74400 Chamonix
Tel 04 50 53 03 74
www.savoie-specialite.com
Established more than 30 years ago, Cherverny stocks high-quality kitchen gifts. You can buy items relating to Alpine cuisine, such as fondue sets, as well as Limoges porcelain, Lalique and Baccarat crystal, kitchen utensils and more everyday glassware.
🕐 Mon–Sat 9–noon, 2.30–7, Sun 10–noon, 3.30–7

REFUGE PAYOT
166 rue Vallot, 74400 Chamonix
Tel 04 50 53 18 71
www.refugepayot.com
This fine food store sells local and gourmet cheeses, cold meats, wines and spirits, chocolate, honey and preserved fruit.
🕐 Daily 8.15am–7.45pm

VOX
Cours de Bartavel, 74400 Chamonix
Tel 04 50 55 89 98 or 04 50 53 03 39 (recorded film times and info in French)
This cinema has three screens, one with Dolby surround sound. There are several screenings per day and additional shows in bad weather to entertain grounded skiers and snowboarders. Films are often in English with French subtitles.
📅 Adult €7, child (under 12) €4.80, €5.80 per person for groups

CASINO DE CHAMONIX
12 place de Saussure, 74400 Chamonix
Tel 04 50 53 07 65
www.casinodefranceonline.com
You'll need your passport to get into this casino which has French and English roulette,

WHAT TO DO

two blackjack tables, stud poker and slot machines. If you're hungry there's a restaurant serving Italian dishes, and there's a karaoke bar.

🕐 Daily 9pm–3am; slot machines from noon 💶 Entry to tables €13

CENTRE SPORTIF
214 avenue de la Plage, 74400 Chamonix
Tel 04 50 53 09 07
www.sports.chamonix.com
Facilities include a swimming pool (with a slide and paddling pool), a Jacuzzi, saunas, steam rooms, a weights room, an ice rink, a climbing wall and tennis and squash courts. The restaurant and bar are next to the ice rink.

🕐 Pool, weights room, sauna, sunbeds and climbing wall: daily 10–7, closed May, 15 Sep–end Oct; tennis and squash: daily 9–noon, 3–7.30; ice rink: Thu–Tue 3–6, Wed 3–9 💶 Pool or ice rink €4.10, squash/tennis €6.70, weights room €8.10, sauna plus pool €10.30

CHAM'SKI
35 place de la Mer de Glace, 74400 Chamonix
Tel 04 50 53 22 75
www.compagniedumontblanc.fr
This company arranges summer and winter sports including skiing, snowboarding and walking. It sells ski passes valid for all ski areas in Chamonix valley except Les Houches. A photo is essential for passes of four or more days. Cham'first (€220) is a six-day pass for beginners with a day of instruction which you can buy at the tourist information office or cash desks of Compagnie du Mont Blanc.

🕐 Open according to season and weather conditions 💶 One-day pass from €40, 13 days €360

GRENOBLE

GALERIES LAFAYETTE
12 place Grenette, 38000 Grenoble
Tel 04 76 47 28 54
www.galerieslafayette.com
This major French department store sells men's, women's and children's clothes (major

brand names and designer labels) as well as household goods, beauty products and perfume. Tax-free shopping is available for visitors from outside the EU. Remember to ask for your purchases to be gift-wrapped free of charge.

🕐 Mon–Sat 9.30–7.30

GRAND'PLACE
55 Grand'place, 38100 Grenoble
Tel 04 76 09 55 45
www.grandplace.fr
With about 140 shops and some restaurants, this large, purpose-built shopping mall on the edge of Grenoble and Echirolles offers a wide range of goods such as fashion, shoes, leather and sports equipment, and a Carrefour supermarket. To get here, take cours Jean Jaurès south. It becomes cours de la Libération et du General de Gaulle. Turn left onto avenue Paul Verlain and at roundabout Pierre et Marie Curie, go straight on to avenue Edmond Esmonin, then avenue de l'Europe. Grand'place is on the right.

🕐 Mon–Sat 9.30–8

MARKETS
Hôtel de Ville, 11 boulevard Jean Pain, 38000 Grenoble
Tel 04 76 76 36 36

Grenoble has several markets—you can get a complete list from the Tourist Office. Some of the best are Marché place aux Herbes for food, Marché Victor Hugo on place Victor Hugo for manufactured goods and Marché de l'Abbaye on

place de la Commune for food and crafts.

🕐 Marché place aux Herbes: Tue–Sun 6–1; Marché Victor Hugo: Mon–Sat 10–8; Marché de l'Abbaye: Tue–Sun 6–1

LE CLUB
9 bis rue de Phalonstère, 38000 Grenoble
Tel 04 76 46 13 38 (recorded info)
www.cinemaleclub.com
Six-screen cinema which often shows films in their original language.

💶 Adult €5.80

LA SOUPE AUX CHOUX
7 route de Lyon, 38000 Grenoble
Tel 04 76 87 05 67
www.jazzclub.grenoble.free.fr
On the north side of the river, La Soupe aux Choux is home to the Grenoble Jazz Club. Concerts feature all types of jazz, including modern, swing, blues and New Orleans. The number 33 bus stops outside the club.

🕐 Tue–Sat 8.30pm–1am; closed Aug
💶 Tue–Thu €5; Fri–Sat €7

TÉLÉPHÉRIQUE DE GRENOBLE-BASTILLE
Quai Stéphane Jay, 38000 Grenoble
Tel 04 76 44 33 65
www.telepherique-grenoble.com
The first aerial cable car in

France, built in 1934, is a relaxing way of reaching the Bastille Fort. At the top are restaurants, a souvenir shop and views.

🕐 Daily 9.15am–11.45pm, Jun–end Aug; 10.45–6.30, rest of year; closed 6–31 Jan 💶 Adult return €5.50, child (5–18) return €3.50

LYON

BERNACHON
42 cours Franklin Roosevelt, 69006 Lyon
Tel 04 78 24 37 98
Chocolate shop and tea room in the 6th *arrondissement* (take Métro line A to Foch). This chocolate heaven is filled with a variety of beautifully packaged sweets (candies). Prices are high, but the quality is worth it. The tea room serves refreshments and lunch. Try the superb hot chocolate.
🕐 Shop: Mon–Fri 9–7, Sat 8.30–7, Sun 8.30–5; tea room: Tue–Sat 9–6.30

DECITRE
6 place Bellecour, 69002 Lyon
Tel 04 26 68 00 10
A bookworm's paradise in the heart of the city, opposite place Bellecour. Subjects include travel, cookery, language and educational material as well as maps and calendars. There is a huge section of paperback fiction in English at the shop entrance and English is spoken here. (A second Decitre shop is on the opposite, southern side of Bellecour.)
🕐 Mon–Sat 9.30–7
🚇 Lines A and D: Bellecour

LES HALLES DE LYON
102 cours Lafayette, 69003 Lyon
Tel 04 78 62 39 32
www.lyon.fr
This covered market with stands, cafés and small shops offers superb food and flowers. Don't miss Bahoudrian, a shop full of Asian and North African spices and foodstuffs. And look for 'Saint Marcellin affinée par la Mère Richard', the only cheesemaker whose name appears on local restaurant menus. You can take Métro line B, or tram T1 to Part-Dieu.
🕐 Mon–Thu 7.30–noon, 3–7, Fri–Sat 7.30–7, Sun 7.30–noon

MARCHÉ DE LA CROIX ROUSSE
Boulevard de la Croix Rousse, 69001 and 69004 Lyon
Tel 08 25 08 15 15
www.lyon.fr
Covering almost the entire length of boulevard de la Croix Rousse, the Tuesday morning street market sells fruit, flowers and vegetables, household goods, clothes, shoes, pottery, fabric, baskets and beds. From Wednesday to Sunday the market only has food and on Saturday morning there is also organic food. Arrive early to avoid the crowds. Buses 13 and 18 will get you here.
🕐 Tue–Sun 7–1

MARÉCHAL
17 rue Lanterne, 69001 Lyon
Tel 04 72 98 24 00
Wonderful aromas emanate from the ornate displays of fresh fruit and vegetables in this classy supermarket. French meats and cheeses are on offer alongside the more usual groceries (and even occasionally, baked beans, Cheddar cheese and other items). The superb wine section has a vast choice to suit every taste and budget. The closest Métro stop is Hôtel de Ville.
🕐 Mon–Fri 8.30–12.30, 3–8.30, Sat 8.30am–8.30pm

PART DIEU SHOPPING CENTRE
17 rue de Dr Bouchut, 69003 Lyon
Tel 04 72 60 60 62
A huge water feature dominates this indoor shopping mall with banks, a cinema, restaurants, tea rooms, bars, the Galeries Lafayette department store and Carrefour supermarket.
🕐 Mon–Sat 9.30–7.30

NUITS DE FOURVIÈRE
6 rue de la Antiquaille, 69005 Lyon
Tel 04 72 57 15 40 and 04 72 32 00 00 (concert info and tickets)
www.nuits-de-fourviere.org
The remains of Lyon's Roman amphitheatre are transformed into a spectacular concert venue each year with theatre, opera, dance, cinema and music. You sit on the stone seats of the amphitheatre as the Romans did, so take a cushion. To get here, take the

Métro to Vieux-Lyon station and then take the funicular in the direction of St-Just. Alight at Minimes-Théâtres Romains.
🕐 Mid Jun–mid Aug 🎫 Adult €10–€45

L'OPÉRA NATIONALE DE LYON
Place de la Comédie, 69001 Lyon
Tel 04 72 00 45 45 (recorded info)
www.opera-lyon.org
Built in 1831, the opera building was altered in 1993 by Jean Nouvel, who created a

profoundly different building surrounding the old theatre. Inside, the Italianate auditorium has retained its character. There is a restaurant on site. Take Métro lines B and C to Hôtel de Ville.
🕐 Box office: Mon–Sat 11–7 🎫 Opera €14–€80, concerts and ballet up to €42

UGC ASTORIA

31 cours Vitton, 69006 Lyon
Tel 0892 70 00 00 (recorded info)
www.ugc.fr
This small cinema, near
Masséna Métro stop, often
shows films in their original
language (indicated by VO
after the title). There is no café
but you can get drinks from
the vending machine.
🎫 Adult €6.90, child (under 12) €5.50

UGC COMOÉDIA

13 avenue Berthelot, 69007 Lyon
Tel 0892 70 00 00 (recorded info)
www.ugc.fr
This multi-screen cinema (take
the Métro to place Jean Mace)
shows many films in their
original language. You can get
drinks and snacks in the lobby
and the auditorium.
🎫 Adult €6.90, child (under 12) €5.50

THE ALBION

12 rue Sainte-Catherine, 69001 Lyon
Tel 04 78 28 33 00
The oldest English pub in Lyon
has a big-screen TV for major
soccer matches and a dart-
board for traditional English
entertainment. Enjoy Irish,
Danish and French beers and
live music once a month. The
nearest Métro is Hôtel de Ville.
🎫 Daily 5pm–1am (later when there's
live music)

PARC DE LA TÊTE D'OR

69006 Lyon
Tel 04 72 69 47 60
www.lyon.fr
Dating from 1856, this fabulous park includes botanic
gardens, a zoo, a rose garden,
a boating lake, children's play
areas and a café/restaurant.
You can walk, jog or
rollerblade in the park, or rent
a bicycle. Arrive by buses 4 or
47 or Métro to Masséna.
🎫 Park daily 6am–11pm summer, daily
6am–9pm winter; botanical gardens
9–11.30, 1.30–3.45; zoo 9–5 🎫 Free
entry to the park

STADE DE GERLAND

350 avenue Jean Jaurès, 69361 Lyon
Tel 04 72 76 76 13
www.olympiquelyonnais.com
Olympique Lyonnais, part of
the French premier football
league, plays home games at
this stadium. Renovated for
the World Cup in 1998, it has
a capacity of 41,000. Buy
tickets for a match night and
enjoy the atmosphere.
🎫 Ticket office: Mon–Sat 9–12.30, 2–6
🎫 €10–€40

MARCHÉ AUX PUCES DU CANAL

1 rue du Canal, 69100 Villeurbanne
Second-hand and new furniture, paintings, ornaments,
tools and bric-a-brac fill this
huge antiques and flea market.
Be prepared to barter and look
closely at what you're buying.
If you're after a bargain get
there early, otherwise just
wander and soak up the
atmosphere.
🎫 Thu, Sat, Sun 8–1

ASTROBALLE

40-44 avenue Marcel Cerdrun, 69100
Villeurbanne
Tel 04 72 14 17 17
www.asvel.com
This is home to ASVEL,
Villeurbanne's basketball team.
The team plays in the Pro A
league and the Euro league.
Get tickets from Astroballe or
Virgin Megastore *(41 rue
Eduard Herriot, 69002, Lyon)*.
🎫 Adult €12–€30, child €10–€18

Festivals and Events

JAZZ À VIENNE

June or July
21 rue des Célestes, 38200 Vienne
Tel 04 74 78 87 87 or 0892 702 007
(Théâtre Antique info line)
www.jazzavienne.com
Vienne's annual two-week
summer jazz festival, attracting
international performers and
almost 95,000 people, is held
in the Roman amphitheatre.
Take a cushion and a torch as

the amphitheatre is steep and
dark. There are free concerts
in public squares and gardens.
Bars and restaurants have
live music.

EUROCKÉENNES

First weekend in July
Tel 03 84 22 46 58
Belfort
www.eurockeennes.fr
The ultimate European rock
festival—Eurockéennes—is
held in Belfort each summer.
This festival plays host to
muddy fans enjoying the
moment by the waterlogged,
waterside venues.

FÊTE DU LAC

First Saturday in August
Office de Tourisme, 1 rue Jean Jaurès,
74000 Annecy
Tel 04 50 45 00 33 (tourist office)
Tel 04 50 45 01 42 (for 2 weeks
before festival)
www.lac-annecy.com
This annual lake festival dates
back to 1860 and attracts
thousands of spectators.
There's a different theme each
year, but attractions usually
include a water pageant and
music and fireworks at sunset.

FOLK AND WINE FESTIVAL

August
Dijon
Tel 03 80 30 37 95
www.folkloriades.org

Burgundy's wine flows as folk
musicians from around the
world perform across the city,
with many events free of
charge. The festival ends with
a parade through the streets.

SOUTHEAST FRANCE

The Riviera comes into its own in the summer. From the Cannes Film Festival in May, through to the summer Jazzfests in Nice and Antibes, elegance and glitz set the agenda.

In winter and early spring however, the Côte d'Azur belongs to the locals, who celebrate the early sunshine with Mardi Gras parades and parties well into the night. At Christmas there are wonderful Yuletide markets across the region selling the famous *santons*, crib figurines, often based on local and well-known characters. In Aubagne, home town of writer and film-maker Marcel Pagnol, look out for *santons* of movie stars who appeared in his films.

There's year-round shopping in the main market in the heart of Aix-en-Provence: good buys are Provençal herbs, Marseille soap, linens and ceramics.

In summer visit the Avignon festival to catch major theatrical productions before they reach Paris, and see epic opera in the stunning setting of Orange's Roman theatre. Languedoc also has amazing Roman remains, more than anywhere else outside Rome itself. They include the mosaic floors of a villa found under a vineyard in Loupian, the Pont du Gard aqueduct and, in nearby Nîmes, the wonderfully preserved amphitheatre, where events range from concerts to a celebration of the town's most famous export, denim (named after Serge de Nîmes). Visit the atmospheric *étangs*, inland saltwater lakes, behind the coastline between the Camargue and Spain, and enjoy tiny museums devoted to local heroes— the singer Charles Trenet in Narbonne, Nostradamus in St-Rémy—and art trails tracking Van Gogh and his contemporaries.

Places for the image-conscious to be seen are the Croisette in Cannes, cours Mirabeau in Aix and the place de la Comédie in Montpellier. St-Tropez has a reputation for topless bathing on the beach, but wearing swimwear in the street is frowned upon in many chic resorts, where those who don't cover up face a fine. Those seeking an all-over tan head to the world's largest naturist 'city' at Cap d'Agde.

Languedoc-Roussillon

AGDE

CENTRE INTERNATIONAL DE TENNIS
Avenue de la Vigne, 34300 Cap d'Agde
Tel 04 67 01 03 60
Pine trees surround this internationally renowned tennis club with 33 outdoor courts and 8 indoor courts. Other facilities include badminton and squash courts, beach volleyball, a sauna, a gym and a small swimming pool. There's also a café and salad bar. By car, the club is just five minutes from the A9.
🕐 €20 per hour for group tuition

BÉZIERS

CHARME D'INTERIEUR
Voie Domitienne, 34500 Béziers
Tel 04 67 31 01 12
Crammed with all the knick-knacks that make a house a home, this interior design shop on the edge of town, near Rond Point Vincent Bach, has plenty of small, lightweight items, such as textiles, lighting and ornaments, that can be easily packed and taken home as souvenirs. Styles range from traditional Mediterranean to contemporary.
🕐 Mon–Sat 8–7

MÈZE

FIL D'AIR–ÉCOLE DE KITEBOARD
BP 72, 34140 Mèze
Tel 06 10 25 22 58
www.fildair.com
The vast salt lake of the Bassin de Thau is a great place to do the exciting sport of kiteboarding. Fil d'Air has classes for all levels, from an hour-long introductory lesson to a seven-day schedule. Take bus 21 or 24 out here.
🕐 Closed Nov–end Mar 🕐 One-day lesson €115

MONTPELLIER

AUX GOURMETS
2 rue Clos René, 34000 Montpellier
Tel 04 67 58 57 04
This is one of the few patisseries open on a Sunday in Montpellier. It's the place to find top-quality home-made ice cream, chocolate and a wide selection of traditional pastries and cakes including the popular *pain au chocolat* (pastry filled with chocolate).
🕐 Mon–Sat 7–5, Sun 7–noon

L'OPÉRA COMÉDIE
11 boulevard Victor Hugo, 34000 Montpellier
Tel 04 67 60 19 99
This grandiose 19th-century opera house takes pride of place in the heart of town. It plays host to some of the biggest stars, particularly in the summer.

🕐 Open all year 🕐 Adult from €15

CAFÉ JOSEPH
3 place Jean Jaurès, 34000 Montpellier
Tel 04 67 66 31 95
The ideal bar in which to get a real taste of what Montpellier's livelier side is all about. Waiters with attitude, fashion-conscious youth and just the right amount of chic. Take the tram to place de la Comédie.
🕐 Mon–Sat 11am–2am

NÎMES
LES ARÈNES
Les Arènes, 30000 Nîmes
Tel 04 66 76 72 77
Major events from bullfights to the biggest pop concerts are held in Nîmes's stunning 24,000-seat Roman amphitheatre, which is open

to the public during the day (see page 189).
🕐 Open all year but check for concerts and events 💶 Adult €4.50

LA MOVIDA
2 place la Placette, 30000 Nîmes
Tel 04 66 67 80 90
This intriguing little café, which serves tapas, is worth a visit for its live flamenco music. The former stomping ground of the famous Gypsy Kings group, the place gets livelier as the night gets longer.
🕐 Mon–Sat 7pm–2am; Closed 3 weeks Aug

PAULHAN
MIEL ROUQUETTE
43 rue des Lavandes, 34230 Paulhan
Tel 04 62 04 40

Honey lovers should definitely pay this place a visit. The shop is part of a working bee farm between Agde and Lodève. As well as selling an extensive range of honey, it has a host of honey-based products, including nougat and honey vinegar. Sample the honey, visit the hives or go on the free 90-minute tour.
🕐 Mon–Sat

PERPIGNAN
HEURES ET MONTRES 66
9 rue de la Loge, 11000 Perpignan
Tel 04 68 34 00 33
This watch shop stocks 400 different types of watch and carries some of the best names in the business—a great place to find a classic timepiece. The shop itself is a modern chrome and glass affair and the staff know their watches and are helpful.
🕐 Mon–Sat 9.30–noon, 2–7

ST-VICTOR-LA-COSTE
DOMAINE PÉLAQUIÉ
7 rue Vernet, 30290 St-Victor-la-Coste
Tel 04 66 50 06 04
www.domaine-pelaquie.com
Stock up on quality wine and find out what goes into making it at this winery, 30km (19 miles) northeast of Nîmes, which is one of the finest in the region. As well as its Pélaquié, the domaine is renowned for its Côtes du Rhône, Tavel and Lirac wines.
🕐 Mon–Sat 9–noon, 2–6

SÈTE
THÉÂTRE DE LA MER
Route de Corniche, 34200 Sète
Tel 04 67 74 98 86
An old fort on the coast road, about 2km (just over a mile) outside Séte, has been converted into an open-air theatre and is the perfect place for enjoying a performance with the sun setting in the background. Performers are mainly French and international fringe artists.
💶 Adult from €15

Provence-Alpes-Côte-d'Azur

AIGLUN
CLUB 4X4 AIGLUN WHEEL DRIVE
USCA Mairie d'Aiglun, 04510 Aiglun
Tel 04 92 34 70 09
www.aiglunwheeldrive.com
This four-wheel-drive society organizes monthly drives through the gorges of Verdon for a maximum of 10 vehicles. You stop at viewpoints along the way and have a picnic.
🕐 All year, once a month on reservation 💶 €20 per vehicle per day plus €10 per person

AIX-EN-PROVENCE
CONFISERIE ENTRECASTEAUX
2 rue Entrecasteaux, 13100 Aix-en-Provence
Tel 04 42 27 15 02
The place to buy *calissons* (marzipan, almond and glacé fruit), an Aix special. Made according to a family recipe for four generations, they come in a distinctive diamond-shaped box, reproducing the original shape of the *calisson*. Other treats on offer include glacé fruit, nougat and chocolate.
🕐 Mon–Sat 8–noon, 2–7

CINÉMA LE RENOIR
24 cours Mirabeau, 13100 Aix-en-Provence
Tel 08 36 68 72 70
www.lecezanne.com
This cinema has three auditoriums, one with a giant

screen and THX sound. Most films shown are art house, but there are also some box office hits. All films are shown in their original language.
◉ Daily 2–10 🎟 Adult €8

BISTROT AIXOIS
37 cours Sextius, 13100 Aix-en-Provence
Tel 04 42 27 50 10
The place to see and be seen for Aix's beautiful young people. It's so packed at weekends that it can be difficult to find dancing space. Luckily, there's more room—and air—upstairs.
◉ Mon–Sat 7pm–2am

HAPPY DAYS
Place Richelme, 13100 Aix-en-Provence
Tel 04 42 21 02 35
On the liveliest square in town, this bar is popular with the fashionable crowd. The interior is funky with yellow and burgundy walls and furniture.
◉ Mon–Sat 8am–2am

ANTIBES
LA SIESTA
Route du Bord de Mer, 06600 Antibes-Juan-les-Pins
Tel 04 93 33 31 31
On the seafront road, this club is packed all summer thanks to a great variety of entertainment, including several dance floors, a swimming pool, restaurant, casino and access to the beach.
◉ Daily 11pm–5am, mid-Jun to mid-Sep, Fri–Sat, rest of year 🎟 €15–€20

ARLES
BIJOUX DUMONT
3 rue du Palais, 13200 Arles
Tel 04 90 96 05 66

This family business has been making reproductions of original Provençal jewellery since 1967. Most are made using 18-carat gold, silver or semi-precious stones and they incorporate emblems of the region. Choose from cicada brooches, Provençal crosses or Saintes-Maries-de-la-Mer cross pendants.
◉ Tue–Sat 9–noon, 2.30–7

LA CABANO DIS EGO
Le Sambuc, 13200 Arles
Tel 04 90 97 20 62
www.cabano-dis-ego.com
Horses and bulls are bred here and the owners organize activities including traditional horse-riding, French cowboy games and even hot air balloon flights.
◉ Open all year 🎟 Varies according to activity

EUROPBIKE PROVENCE
1 rue Philippe Lebon, 13200 Arles
Tel 04 90 49 54 69
www.europbike-provence.com
Explore the area around Arles on two wheels. Europbike has been renting out bicycles since 1978, and they can offer you a number of suggested circuits. They also rent out in-line skates.
◉ Open all year 🎟 Bicycle rental €16 for one day, €58 for one week

AVIGNON
CHAPELIER MOURET
20 rue des Marchands, 84000 Avignon
Tel 04 90 85 39 38

This hat shop is worth visiting for the interior alone. The same family has been making

hats here since 1860, following methods passed from father to son. There's a great collection of panamas and *capelines* (wide-brimmed hats typical of the region).
◉ Tue–Sat 10–12.30, 2–7

BIG BANG THÉÂTRE
18 rue Guillaume-Puy, 84000 Avignon
Tel 04 90 27 12 71
This popular little theatre likes to experiment. The schedule is eclectic, including dance, musical productions and drama by local and national groups. It also stages more daring, offbeat productions.
◉ Open all year round
🎟 Adult from €13

LE ROUGE GORGE
10 bis rue Peyrollie, 84000 Avignon
Tel 04 90 14 02 54
www.lerougegorge.fr
On Fridays and Saturdays this former printing works hosts dinner theatre in the cabaret tradition, with elaborately dressed dancers and fine food. The rest of the week sees jazz, rock, samba and flamenco.
◉ Fri–Sat (and other show nights) 8pm–3am; closed Aug
🎟 Dinner/cabaret €40–45, concert €5–€15

LE BLUES
25 rue Carnot, 84000 Avignon
Tel 04 90 85 79 71
Come here for live rock, jazz and blues, karaoke nights and disco parties.
◉ Daily 11pm–5am

CUBANITO'S CAFÉ
51 rue Carnot, 84000 Avignon
Tel 04 90 27 90 59
Che Guevara posters adorn the walls at this Cuban den where you can enjoy a rum cocktail. Try a free salsa class any evening at 9pm.
◉ Tue–Fri 8am–1am, Sat 10am–1am

WHAT TO DO

RED ZONE BAR
25 rue Carnot, 84000 Avignon
Tel 04 90 27 02 44
www.redzonebar.com
Here you'll find salsa on Tuesday night, live music on Wednesday, student night on Thursday and dancing on Friday and Saturday. The crowd is eclectic but always fashionable.
🕐 Daily 9pm–3am

DISTILLERIE MANGUIN
Île de la Barthelasse, 84000 Avignon
Tel 04 90 82 62 29
www.manguin.com

This distillery produces *eaux de vie* according to traditional methods. The fruit, grown on the distillery's own land, is saturated with sugar before it is marinated in alcohol.
🕐 Mon–Sat 9–noon, 2–6

CANNES

JACQUES LOUP
21 rue d'Antibes, 06400 Cannes
Tel 04 93 39 28 35
www.jacques-loup.com

In addition to its own collection, this shoe shop carries the hottest designs from international shoemakers such as Bottega Veneta, Rossi, Church's and Tod's. It also stocks clothes from Prada, Marni and Miu Miu. An institution for every fashionista in Cannes.
🕐 Mon–Sat 9.30–8

ALEXANDRE III
19 boulevard Alexandre, 06400 Cannes
Tel 04 93 94 33 44
Old cinema turned theatre which has kept its retro interior and stages plays, including the classics as well as modern interpretations.
🕐 Open all year

ÉGLISE RÉFORMÉE DE FRANCE
7 rue Notre-Dame, 06400 Cannes
Tel 04 93 39 35 55
With excellent acoustics, this Protestant church, built in 1874, regularly hosts choral, classical and chamber music concerts and organ recitals.
🕐 Usually Sat or Sun at 5pm
💶 Donation

PALAIS DES FESTIVALS ET DES CONGRÈS
1 boulevard La Croisette, 06400 Cannes
Tel 04 93 39 01 01
www.cannes.fr
This modern venue, built in 1982, hosts the Festival du Film every year. At other times, it welcomes international exhibitions, various perform-ances in its 2,300-seat Lumière auditorium and plays, ballets and concerts in the 1,000-seat Théâtre Debussy.
🕐 Varies according to performance

CASINO CROISETTE
1 Esplanade Lucien Barrière, BP284, 06406 Cannes
Tel 04 92 98 78 00
www.lucienbarriere.com
If you have money left to burn after your visit to Cannes, blow it (or win some more) at this casino which has nearly 300 slot machines as well as roulette and blackjack.
🕐 Daily 10am–5am, 8pm for the games room 💶 Games room €10

LE FESTIVAL
52 La Croisette, 06400 Cannes
Tel 04 93 38 04 81
www.lefestival.fr
Between two luxury hotels and facing the sea, the bar's terrace, which is open all year round, is a popular place for people-watching and admiring the beautiful expanse of blue to the horizon.
🕐 Daily 9am–midnight

AÉROCLUB D'ANTIBES
Aérodrome de Cannes Mandelieu, avenue Francis Tonner, 06150 La Bocca, Cannes
Tel 04 93 47 64 43
www.aeroclub-antibes.com
This flying club, just west of Cannes, organizes tours that fly over a variety of landscapes including the bay of St-Tropez, the Alps and the cliffs of Bonifacio in the south of Corsica.
🕐 On reservation 💶 €45 for a first flight of 20 minutes

CASTELLANE

ABOARD RAFTING
8 place de l'Église, 04120 Castellane
Tel 04 92 83 76 11
www.aboard-rafting.com
Experience the thrill of white

water rafting through the gorges of Verdon, or if you prefer, see the waterfalls and natural pools by canoe. Alternatively, avoid getting wet altogether by renting a mountain bike and seeing the area on two wheels.
🕐 Daily 9–7, Apr to mid-Oct 💶 Half a day's rafting €55, guided 90-min airboat trip €30

WHAT TO DO

CAVAILLON
LE GRENIER À SONS
157 avenue du Général-de-Gaulle,
84301 Cavaillon
Tel 04 90 06 44 20
www.grenier-a-sons.org
This dynamic 350-seat
concert hall stages jazz, rock,
blues, reggae and more, by
established musicians and
budding talents. There's also
a bar and gallery.
🕐 Daily 9–noon, 2–7pm (or midnight
when there is a concert); closed Aug
💶 Approximately €10

CHÂTEAU ARNOUX ST-AUBAN
LE CINÉMATOGRAPHE
Centre Culturel Simone Signoret, Route
de Manosque, 04160 Château Arnoux
St-Auban
Tel 04 92 64 41 24
This cultural complex has two
cinema auditoriums, a library
and an exhibition space. The
cinema shows box office hits,
films for children and some
art house offerings all
screened in their original
language. There's also parking
and a café/restaurant.
🕐 Films every evening and Wed, Sat,
Sun afternoons 💶 Adult €6

COUSTELLET
GARE DE COUSTELLET
Quai Entreprises, 84660 Coustellet
Tel 04 90 76 84 38
avec.lagare.free.fr
Formerly a railway station, this
is now a 280-seat venue with
a bar hosting gigs by local and
national groups performing
anything from jazz to hard
rock. Painting and photography exhibitions are held in
what was previously the
concourse. Credit cards are
not accepted.
🕐 Fri–Sat 9pm–2am 💶 Concerts
€5–€15

DIGNE-LES-BAINS
TRAIN DES PIGNES
1 avenue Pierre Sémard, 04000
Digne-les-Bains
Tel 04 92 31 01 58
www.trainprovence.com
Since 1891, a single steam-
powered carriage has chugged

along a track linking the Alps
to Provence. The train with
old-fashioned wooden
benches is a stylish way to see
Provence's mountain scenery.
🕐 Daily from 7am, May–end Oct
🚂 From €13 (a return to Nice is
€35.30)

ÈZE
VERRERIE D'ART
Place du Général-de-Gaulle, 06360 Èze
Tel 04 93 41 16 74
At the heart of the picturesque
village of Èze, this glass
workshop produces beautiful
pieces from small figurines to
imposing sculptures. You can
watch the craftsmen who use
traditional methods to heat the
glass before they shape it.
🕐 Daily 9–7

FORCALQUIER
PIANO BAR LE SAXO
13 boulevard Latourette, 04300
Forcalquier
Tel 04 92 75 00 30
Three rooms accommodate a
piano bar, a bar and a restaurant with a rustic wood interior
throughout. In winter there's
live music and pizza, in
summer themed party nights.
🕐 Daily 9pm–2am, Apr–end Oct;
Fri–Sat, 8pm–2am, rest of year

LE PAYS DE FORCALQUIER
ET LA MONTAGNE DE LURE
EN VÉLO
Office de tourisme du Pays de
Forcalquier, 13 place du Bourguet,
04300 Forcalquier
Tel 04 92 75 10 02
www.velopaysforcalquier.com
This 60km (37-mile) bicycling
route winds through the

villages surrounding
Forcalquier and the Montagne
de Lure. You can stay at guest-
houses and eat at roadside
restaurants en route.

GORGES DU VERDON
AVENTURES ET NATURE
04120 La Palud sur Verdon
Tel 04 92 77 30 43
www.aventuresetnature.com
Pascal Faudou, a certified
hiking instructor, leads various
activities which you can do in
the Verdon gorges. Try canyoning, hiking or 'aqua rando' (a
mix of walking and swim-
ming). He also runs five-day
intensive training sessions.
Credit cards are not accepted.
🕐 Mar–end Nov on reservation
💶 Half a day's canyoning €44

GRASSE
FRAGONARD
20 boulevard Fragonard, 06130 Grasse
Tel 04 93 36 44 65
www.fragonard.com

World-renowned as the
perfume capital, Grasse is
home to many perfumeries, of
which Fragonard, dating back
to the 18th century, is one of
the oldest. It is also the most
prestigious. Visit the perfume
museum before shopping for
home fragrances, perfumed
soaps and fragrances for men
and women.
🕐 Factory daily 9–6.30, shop 9–6

GRÉOLIÈRES

GRÉOLIÈRES LES NEIGES
06620 Gréolières les Neiges
Tel 04 93 59 70 12 (snow report)
www.greolieres.com
The ski resort at Gréolières is a mere hour's drive from Cannes at an altitude of 1,400m–1,800m (4,600ft–5900ft) with 21 slopes and 14 ski lifts in winter. In summer, skiing is replaced by hiking, mountain biking and horse-riding.
🅖 Ski resort: Christmas to mid-Mar
💶 Ski pass €15 per day

L'ISLE SUR SORGUE

L'OCCITANE
30 rue République, 84800 L'Isle sur Sorgue
Tel 04 90 20 71 47
www.loccitane.com
Famous all over the world, L'Occitane purveys the smells and tastes of Provence. There's a host of products to pamper the body and face, including lavender-scented creams and soaps from Marseille enriched with honey, and incense to make your home smell nice.
🅖 Daily 10–7.30 summer, Tue–Sat 10–1, 2–7, Sun 10–2, 3–6 rest of year

ISOLA

ISOLA 2000
Tourist Office, Résidence Travels, 06420 Isola
Tel 04 93 23 15 15
At an altitude of 2,000m (6,500ft), this ski resort offers 50 tracks and one snow park with heli-skiing, snow scooters and an ice rink. In summer the outdoor activities continue with hiking and horse-riding.
🅖 Ski resort: Dec–Apr, depending on snowfall 💶 Ski pass €20–€23 per day

JUAN-LES-PINS

HYDRO ULM JUAN-LES-PINS
Ponton Hollywood, 06160 Juan-les-Pins
Tel 04 93 67 05 11
www.hydro-ulm.com
Touring the Rade du Golfe on a hybrid of a super-light plane and a boat provides a unique experience and a bird's-eye view of islands and lighthouses.

Juan-les-Pins is on the Golfe Juan, west of Antibes.
🅖 Daily by appointment; closed Jan
💶 €60 for a 25-min flight

LAURIS

CAP RANDO
Mas de Recaute, 84360 Lauris
Tel 04 90 08 41 44
www.caprando.com

Discover Provence on horseback with this equestrian facility. There are different trails to follow including the Parc Naturel Régional du Lubéron trail, a lavender route from Lubéron to Verdon and on to Nice, and one crossing the Provençal Alps. The venue also offers carriage tours.
🅖 All year by appointment
💶 €800–€1,000 per week, including all meals and accommodation

MANOSQUE

LE LIDO
2 avenue St-Lazare, 04100 Manosque
Tel 04 92 72 00 85
www.cinemovida.com
This cinema shows the latest blockbusters, dubbed in French, on its four screens.
🅖 Daily 2–9 💶 Adult €7

CANTINA TEX MEX
8 place de l'Hôtel de Ville, 04100 Manosque
Tel 04 92 72 13 94
The ambience changes on each of the three floors here. There's a pub atmosphere in the basement, an exotic touch with teak furniture and lush plants in the ground floor bar and a bright Mexican restaurant upstairs.
🅖 Tue–Sat, times vary

MARSEILLE

LA BALEINE QUI DIT VAGUES
48 rue Barbaroux, 13001 Marseille
Tel 04 91 48 95 60
www.labaleinequiditvagues.com
The name of this venue, near the Réformes Métro stop, means 'the whale who says waves', in reference to the native American traditional tale in which a whale symbolizes the memory of the world. It hosts storytelling performances, many for children.
🅖 Fri–Sat 8pm, Wed 2.30pm, children's performances Oct–end Jun

LE PELLE-MÊLE
8 place aux Huiles, 13100 Marseille
Tel 04 91 54 85 26
France's greatest jazz musicians have played here on the small stage. The leather and wood interior creates a warm atmosphere and an intimate setting for gigs.
🅖 Tue–Sat 6pm–3am 💶 Varies according to performance

LES TROIS PALMES
2 boulevard Léon-Bancal, 13011 Marseille
Tel 04 91 87 91 87
www.les3palmes.com
Named after the three palm trees at its entrance, this cinema complex has 11 superbly equipped auditoriums as well as a bar. It shows major box office hits.
🅖 Daily 1.30–10 💶 Adult €8.20, child (under 12) €5.90

BAR DE LA MARINE
15 quai de Rive-Neuve, 13007 Marseille
Tel 04 91 54 95 42
Facing the old harbour, this authentic local bar is evocative of scenes described by Provençal author Marcel Pagnol. It's a fashionable place with a cool atmosphere and a soundtrack of acid jazz.
🅖 Daily 7am–2am

BAR DE LA SAMARITAINE
2 quai du Port, 13002 Marseille
Tel 04 91 90 31 41
Remaining true to its quintessential 1930s character, this bar is a local institution. Its terrace, facing the picturesque old harbour, becomes a piano bar from Thursday to Saturday.
🕐 Daily 6am–10pm (also 10pm–2am, Jul–end Aug)

CENTRE DE LOISIRS DES GOUDES
2 boulevard Alexandre Delabre, 13008 Marseille
Tel 04 91 25 13 16
www.goudes-plongee.com
This company will take you diving in the bay of Marseille, around the Rioux archipelago, where caves and old wrecks are host to extraordinary flora and fauna. Some packages include all meals, use of kayaks and mountain bikes for a weekend or longer. You can get to Les Goudes on a 19 bus.
🕐 Daily 8am–10pm summer only
💶 €41 for first dive, €167 for a weekend

STADE VÉLODROME
3 boulevard Michelet, 13008 Marseille
Tel 04 91 76 91 76
www.olympiquedemarseille.com
This 60,000-seat stadium is home to Olympique de Marseille, the city's soccer team. The locals are passionate about the sport and every game is a big event.
🕐 8–11pm on match nights 💶 Adult approximately €30 per ticket

MOUGINS

BUGGY CROSS
909 chemin Font-de-Currault, 06250 Mougins
Tel 04 93 69 02 74
www.multimania.com/azurquad
Next to the Automobile Museum, you can experience the thrill of speed on one of three tracks in a quad, kart or mini-motorcycle. There are also vehicles for children aged four and over.
🕐 Wed, Sat, Sun 11–8 summer; Wed, Sat, Sun 11–6 rest of year 💶 Adult €14.50 for 10 min, child €7 for 10 min

MOUSTIERS-SAINTE-MARIE

ATELIER ST-MICHEL
Moustiers-Sainte-Marie 04360
Tel 04 92 74 67 73
http://perso.wanadoo.fr/ateliersaint-michel/
Moustiers-Sainte-Marie is famous for its faience and has many makers of fine ceramics. Particularly striking are the Martial and François Baudey reproductions of pieces from the city's faience museum. These include beautiful 18th-century rectangular plates, pot-holders and bowls with painted birds, flowers and country life scenes. You can also order personalized china.

🕐 Daily 9.30–6 summer; 9.30–noon, 2–6 winter

NICE

JEAN-LOUIS MARTINETTI
17 rue de la Préfecture, 06300 Nice
Tel 04 93 85 61 30
www.webstore.fr/couleurs-de-nice/
Jean-Louis Martinetti's photography is an ode to Nice. Simple

compositions (for example, a palm tree framed by the sea) in bold tones give his pictures a contemporary, local identity.
🕐 Tue–Sat 10–12.30, 3–7

MARCHÉ SALEYA D'ARTISANAT D'ART
Cours Saleya, 06300 Nice
Take a stroll through Nice's evening arts and crafts market after a drink at a nearby bar. You'll find Provençal handicrafts (pottery, glasswork, olive wood kitchenware), plus crafts from other regions of the world.
🕐 Tue–Sun 6pm–midnight, Jun–end Sep

MOULIN À HUILE ALZIARI
4 rue St-François-de-Paule, 06300 Nice
Tel 04 93 85 76 92

The olive oil on sale in this shop comes from a mill in Nice's northwest corner which you can visit by appointment. As well as bottles of the oil, you can buy products containing olive oil, such as soap or olive spread.
🕐 Tue–Sat 8.30–12.30, 2.15–7

AUDITORIUM DU CONSERVATOIRE NATIONAL DE RÉGION
24 boulevard de Cimiez, 06100 Nice
Tel 04 92 26 72 20
Under the name *Les Lundis Kosmas*, the students at the Regional Academy of Music open their rehearsals every Monday. Established over 20 years ago in honour of the composer Kosma, the event is an institution in Nice.
🕐 Mon 6pm but closed during school holidays. Call to check schedule
💶 Free

WHAT TO DO

CASA DEL SOL
69 quai des États-Unis, 06300 Nice
Tel 04 93 62 87 28
Latin America and Morocco
inspire the interior of this tapas
bar, which has wrought-iron
decorations, warm hues and
table-top mosaics. There's
lounge music during dinner
and a disco after midnight.
🕐 Tue–Sat 6pm–2.30am

L'F
6 place Charles-Félix, 06300 Nice
Tel 04 93 85 74 10
www.l-f2000.com
On the liveliest street in town,
this café has one of Nice's best
terraces–and it's even heated
during colder spells. Inside is a
1930s and 1940s interior with
banquette seating and a black-
and-white chequered floor.
🕐 Daily 8am–2.30am

LE GHOST
3 rue Barillerie, 06300 Nice
Tel 04 93 92 93 37
This fashionable bar has
comfortable sofas, gleaming
mirrors and a well-stocked
library. The place packs out
when the resident DJ plays
techno, hip hop or soul on
theme nights.
🕐 Daily 7pm–2.30am

GRAND CAFÉ DE LYON
33 avenue Jean Médecin, 06000 Nice
Tel 04 93 88 13 17
www.cafedelyon.fr
This art nouveau-style bistro,
established in 1900, is an
institution in Nice. It's a
brasserie at lunchtime, a tea
room in the afternoon and
later, a good place for a drink.
🕐 Daily 7am–midnight

THÉÂTRE ANTIQUE
Place des Frères-Mounet, 84100 Orange
Tel 04 90 51 17 60
www.culture-espaces.com
Probably the best maintained
ancient Roman theatre anywhere, and home since 1869
to the annual Chorègies, a
world-famous opera and
classical music festival. The

rest of the year it sees a varied
schedule of circus, dance
and concerts.

🕐 Daily 9–8, Jun–end Aug; 9–7,
Apr–end May, Sep; 9–6, Mar, Oct; 9–5,
Nov–end Feb 💶 Adult €7.50

PORQUEROLLES
PORQUEROLLES PLONGÉE
Zone Artisanale 7, 83400 Porquerolles
Tel 04 98 04 62 22
www.porquerolles-plongee.com
One of the three îles d'Hyères,
Porquerolles has rocky bays
which host an extraordinary
array of sea flora and fauna.
Some dives are on to wrecks,
including cargo ships and even
a submarine.
🕐 Daily dawn–dusk, Apr to mid-Nov;
by appointment rest of year 💶 €43 for
the first dive

ROUSSILLON
SENTIER DES OCRES
Village de Roussillon, 84220 Roussillon
Tel 04 90 05 60 25 (tourist office)

Former ochre quarries have
created a site of breathtaking
beauty, known as Provence's
little canyon, the setting for a
45-minute hike.
🕐 Daily 10–5.30, Mar–end Nov
💶 Entry €2

ST-ÉTIENNE DE TINÉE
AURON ST-ÉTIENNE DE TINÉE
Tourist Office: 1 rue Communes de
France, 06660 St-Étienne de Tinée
Tel 04 93 02 41 96
This ski resort in the Alpes
Maritimes, at an altitude
between 1,600m (5,250ft)
and 2,400m (7,900ft), has 39
tracks and 27 ski lifts. Ski,
snowboard or choose from
hang-gliding, sledge tours,
ice-skating, quads and snow
scooters. From Nice take the
A8 exit at St-Isidore, then the
RN 202 towards Digne/
Grenoble.
🕐 Ski resort open Dec–end Apr 💶 Ski
pass €20–€23 per day

**ST-MARTIN-DE-
CASTILLON**
LOU CALEU
Madame et Monsieur Rondard, RN100,
84750 St-Martin-de-Castillon
Tel 04 90 75 28 88
www.loucaleu.com
The owners of this hotel and
restaurant also run stables. Go
on a short ride or a trekking
adventure of several days. The
circuits showcase the beautiful
area of the Lubéron with plains
and peaks reminiscent of
Colorado.
🕐 Phone to reserve 💶 1-hour ride
€17, full day (including meal) €77

ST-TROPEZ
RONDINI
16 rue Clémenceau, 83990 St-Tropez
Tel 04 94 97 19 55
www.nova.fr/rondini
Since 1927, this family
business has been making
Tropézienne, a Roman-style
sandal worn by many
celebrities including Picasso.
The sandals are still handmade
today and now come
in various styles.
🕐 Daily 9.30–noon, 3–7

LA TARTE TROPÉZIENNE
36 rue Georges Clémenceau, 83990
St-Tropez
Tel 04 94 97 71 42
www.tarte-tropezienne.com
It was in 1955, while he was
catering for the actors and

WHAT TO DO

crew of the film *And God Created Woman,* that confectioner Alexandre Micka created the cake filled with butter cream which gives this shop its name. It was a great success, and one of the stars, Brigitte Bardot, christened it *tarte tropézienne.*

🕐 Daily 10–8; closed Nov–end Jan

SAINTES-MARIES-DE-LA-MER
PROMENADE DES RIÈGES
Route de Cacharel, 13460 Saintes-Maries-de-la-Mer
Tel 04 90 97 91 38
www.promenadedesrieges.com
These horse-riding excursions let you discover the magical scenery of the Camargue's inland waters, beaches and wildlife (including flamingos). The stables have the unique white horses for which the Camargue is known, and use locally made saddles. Credit cards are not accepted.
🕐 All year by appointment ⏱ 2-hour excursion €27, day-long excursion from €61

LA TURBIE
GOLF CLUB DE MONTE-CARLO
Route du Mont Agel, O6320 La Turbie
Tel 04 93 41 09 11
www.montecarloresort.com
At an altitude of 900m (3,000ft), this 18-hole golf course has great views of the French and Italian mountains and the sandy coastline.
🕐 Tue–Sun 8–6, Mon 8–5 ⏱ Round of golf €85–€100

Monaco

OPÉRA DE MONTE-CARLO
Place du Casino, 98000 Monaco
377 92 16 22 99
www.opera.mc
Since its inauguration by actress Sarah Bernhardt in 1879, this impressive Belle-Époque opera house has welcomed the world's greatest voices. The architect, Charles Garnier, also designed the Opéra Garnier in Paris.
🕐 Varies according to performance
⏱ Varies according to performance

LE SPORTING D'ÉTÉ
Avenue Princesse Grace, 98000 Monaco
377 92 16 36 36
www.sportingmontecarlo.com
With a sunroof and large windows facing the sea, this concert hall has a majestic setting. It welcomes the biggest international stars to the complex, which also includes a casino and a club.
🕐 Daily show 11pm, end Jun–beginning Sep ⏱ Varies

CASINO DE MONTE-CARLO
Place du Casino, 98000 Monaco
377 92 16 20 00
www.casino-monte-carlo.com
The rich and famous flock to this grand Belle-Époque

gambling temple decorated with frescoes and paintings and featured in several movies, including James Bond films. The dress code is smart and you must be over 21.
🕐 Café de Paris (slot machines) opens at 10am ⏱ Entry €8 and a further €8 to enter games room

Festivals and Events

NICE CARNIVAL
February
Nice
Tel 04 92 14 46 46 (tourist office)
www.nicecarnaval.com
The Riviera celebrates Mardi Gras with two weeks of parades. Huge papier mâché floats proceed through the town to be set alight at sea on the final night. Pay to sit in the stands or look out of your hotel window for free.

FILM FESTIVAL
May
Cannes
Tel 01 53 59 61 00
www.festival-cannes.fr/
May means Hollywood comes to the Riviera as starlets are photographed along the Croisette and the steps of the Palais des Festivals. All the biggest screenings and parties are invitation only, but there are some public screenings.

GRAND PRIX
May
Monaco
Tel 377 92 166 116 (tourist office)
www.monaco-tourism.com
Monte Carlo's annual weekend in the spotlight, when the city becomes a race track, with Formula One cars screeching through the streets around the casino.

AVIGNON FESTIVAL
July
Avignon
Tel 04 90 14 14 14
www.festival-avignon.com
Provence becomes the world capital of culture in July when the biggest names in theatre, dance and music flock to the walled city for a season of spectacular performances against a stunning backdrop. There's also plenty of free street entertainment.

WHAT TO DO

SOUTHWEST FRANCE

The bold curve of the Atlantic from the Loire down to the Pyrenees is just the veneer on a lush and varied region. On the coast are the fashion-conscious resorts of Biarritz and La Rochelle, with countless water sports and attractions. Biarritz manages to juggle two reputations—a royal playground and a top surfing destination. The July surf-fest is the biggest in Europe.

Bordeaux, at the heart of possibly the most expensive wine region in France, is a fascinating city to explore; use its popular talking bicycles which give a perfect English commentary to the sites as you pedal past.

For culture, you can see prehistoric cave paintings, indulge yourself at the Périgord music festivals, and visit the region's art collections. To keep cool in this lush, green corner of France, go boating on the majestic Gironde and Dordogne rivers, canoe the fast waters of Limousin, or take a barge along the tranquil Canal du Midi. For the children, there's the Futuroscope theme park north of Poitiers.

In Basque country, watch local sports and nibble cross-border tapas snacks. In Toulouse, the heart of Europe's aerospace industry, visit the space museum, take in a summer concert or two, or hit the clubs.

Shop for food: The duck and goose industry is huge here, and jars of pâté rival bottles of wine and Limoges china as the most appreciated presents.

Aquitaine

ARCACHON

POISSONNERIE DE L'AIGUILLON
51 boulevard de Mestrezat, 33120 Arcachon
Tel 05 56 83 70 53
This family-run shop sells a mouth-watering selection of fish and seafood, including mussels, scampi, prawns, whelks and oysters. Pick up a fish or shellfish platter for a picnic meal.
🕐 Mon–Sat 8–1, 3.30–7.30, Sun 8–1

CERCLE DE LA VOILE DE LAC DE CAZAUX
Port de Cazaux, 33630 Cazaux, Arcachon
Tel 05 56 22 91 00
This school offers a variety of nautical activities. The Lac de Cazaux, France's second largest lake, offers safe sailing in most weathers. You can rent and receive instruction on how to use catamarans, sailing boats and windsurfing boards.
🕐 Daily 10–6, May–end Sep
💶 2-hour catamaran rental €31, 1-hour windsurfer rental €12

HIPPODROME DU BEQUET
Route de Cazaux, La Teste-de-Buch, 33260 Arcachon
Tel 05 56 54 19 90 or 05 56 54 74 26
The racecourse at La Teste-de-Buch, southeast of Arcachon, past the Dune du Pilat, makes for a fun day out. Bet on a horse, watch a race or hang out in one of the many bars and restaurants on site.
🕐 Various race days May–end Sep, call ahead to check 💶 Varies according to meeting

IN-LINE SKATING
For a fun and healthy way to do a spot of sightseeing, join the regular in-line skating night along the promenade and beach front at Arcachon, with a view over to the Île aux Oiseaux.
🕐 Last Sun of month 💶 Free

VOL LIBRE DU PYLA
1 rue Aurélian Dasson, Gujan-Mestras, 33120 Arcachon
Tel 05 56 22 15 02
Among the adrenalin sports you can do off the Dune du Pilat near Arcachon are delta-planing, hang-gliding and

parapenting (a cross between hang-gliding and parachuting). You'll need to reserve in advance and bring some identification with you. Training is provided. You get here by taking a train to Arcachon (from Bordeaux). There are several Citram buses from from Bordeaux each day.
🕐 Daily 10–6, mid-Jun to mid-Sep
💶 €10 for 30 min

VSM ÉCOLE DE PLONGÉE

1 quai Capit Allègre, 33120 Arcachon
Tel 05 56 83 98 95
www.vsmplongee.free.fr/
This well-known diving school
along the A660 from
Bordeaux, (there's another
another dive school at Cazaux)
gives one-to-one tuition or
group lessons.
🕓 Various dive times (call ahead),
Jun–end Aug 💶 €20; accreditation
€250

BERGERAC

LES ABBAIES BERGERA-COISES

Place Pelissière, 24100 Bergerac
Tel 05 53 57 03 11 (tourist information)
One evening a week in
summer (often Tuesday),
traditional folk dancers
perform through the streets
of Bergerac's old town. They
start from the square in front
of the church of St-Jacques.
🕓 1 day a week at 9pm, Jul–end Aug

BIARRITZ

BALLET BIARRITZ

Gare du Midi, 23 avenue Foch, 64200
Biarritz
Tel 05 59 24 67 19
www.ville-biarritz.fr
www.balletbiarritz.com
This dance venue run by
choreographer Thierry
Malandain, has creative, touring and educational activities
and is home to Ballet Biarritz.
🕓 Performances all year 💶 From €10

BORDEAUX

BAILLARDRAN

Baillardran, Galerie des Grands
Hommes, 33000 Bordeaux
Tel 05 56 79 05 89
Come here to try *canelé*, a
small cake still produced
according to an old, not-so-
secret recipe. It has a creamy
inside hidden beneath a
caramelized outer crêpe-like
layer infused with rum,
orange-flower water and
vanilla. You can watch the
pastry chef working through
the glass partition then try
some of this delicious cake.
🕓 Mon–Sat 10–7.30

BRADLEY'S BOOKSHOP

8 cours d'Albret, 33000 Bordeaux
Tel 05 56 52 10 57
www.bradleys-bookshop.com

This is the place to come for
English-language books in
Bordeaux. It has the full range
of guidebooks, phrasebooks
and holiday reading, plus a
large selection of original
language videos and DVDs.
The helpful staff will also order
things for you that they don't
have in stock.
🕓 Mon 2–7, Tue–Sat 9.30–12.30, 2–7

GALERIE DES REMPARTS

63 rue des Remparts, 33000 Bordeaux
Tel 05 56 52 22 25
www.galeriedesremparts.com
The gallery and art shop are
dedicated to the promotion of
a wide selection of international painters, such as Loilier
and Dubuc, with a focus on
contemporary artists. The
gallery holds regular
exhibitions and offers a
good service for resale and
valuation. Exhibitions often
travel the globe, and the staff
are highly knowledgeable.
🕓 Mon–Sat 10–6

L'INTENDANT

2 allées de Tourny, 33000 Bordeaux
Tel 05 56 48 01 29
This extraordinary wine shop,
opposite the Grand Théâtre, is
owned by the Duclot group.
The building is a circular
tower, climate-controlled to
protect the 15,000 bottles of
wine lining the walls, with the
top floor reserved for the
oldest vintages.
🕓 Mon–Sat 10–7.30

MARCHÉ BIOLOGIQUE

Opposite place des Quinconces, 33000
Bordeaux
Tel 05 56 00 66 00 (tourist information)
This organic market is a recent
addition to Bordeaux's market
scene and one not to be
missed. It is held opposite
warehouse 5 on the quay.
🕓 Thu 5am–1pm

MARCHÉ CAMPAGNARD

Quai Chartron, 33000 Bordeaux
Tel 05 56 00 66 00 (tourist information)
Bordeaux's most atmospheric
market is the beautifully
located Marché Campagnard,
which springs up on the banks
of the Garonne on Sunday
mornings. Local producers
and artisans sell everything
from home-made jam and
bread to paintings.
🕓 Sun 9–noon

MARCHÉ CAPUÇINS

Cours de la Marne, 33080 Bordeaux
Tel 05 56 00 66 00 (tourist information)
This is one of Bordeaux's most
typical markets. Find fresh
flowers and local delicacies
such as foie gras, caviar,
cheeses and the locally made
cake called *canelé*. Recently
restored to meet European
Union standards, the market
also frequently hosts cultural
events and shows.
🕓 Tue–Sun 9am–1pm

MARCHÉ ST-MICHEL

Place St-Michel, 33000 Bordeaux
Tel 05 56 00 66 00 (tourist information)
The St-Michel flea market is a
busy Sunday morning market,
with goods ranging from
furniture to crockery, paintings,
dolls, bicycles and retro
clothes. On the second Sunday
of March, June, September
and December the market
swells to become the Grande
Déballage de Brocante—a
giant bric-a-brac market.
🕓 Sun 9–noon

PAIN MAÎTRE
25 rue Camille-Sauvageau, 33000 Bordeaux
Tel 05 56 92 28 64
This bread emporium is dedicated to all shapes and sizes of the French art of baking. Here whole wheat, unrefined sea salt, natural yeast, wood-fired ovens and innumerable little secrets combine to produce incredible bread. Varieties include *fougasse* with olives and anchovies and rye bread with hazelnuts. Arrive early for the best choice.
🕐 Mon–Sat 10–6

VILLAGE NOTRE-DAME
61–67 rue Notre-Dame, 33000 Bordeaux
Tel 05 56 52 66 13
An enormous two-floor building in the Chatrons district, houses about 30 antique dealers selling furniture in all styles and from all periods. There is also a maintenance and restoration specialist. This is a great place to find out about smaller regional antique fairs and exhibitions.
🕐 Mon–Sat 10–12.20, 2–7, Sun 2–7, Oct–end Apr

ESPACE CULTUREL DU PIN GALANT
34 avenue du Maréchal de Lattre de Tassigny, 33698 Mérignac
Tel 05 56 97 82 82
www.lepingalant.com
You'll find this sleek, modern cultural venue near Bordeaux's Mérignac airport, west of the city. There's an extensive and international schedule, with events ranging from opera, musicals, classical and modern concerts, to jazz, dance and theatre. Reserve your seats in advance.
🕐 Performance times vary 💶 Varies

LE GRAND THÉÂTRE
Place de la Comédie, 33000 Bordeaux
Tel 05 56 00 85 95
www.opera-bordeaux.com
This magnificent neoclassical building, home to the National

Opera of Bordeaux, is worth a visit for the architecture alone. There are guided tours when rehearsals and performances allow. Performances take place most days, with matinées on Saturdays. (See page 196.)
🕐 Open all year 💶 Tour and performance from €11.40

UGC CINÉ CITÉ
15 rue Georges Bonnac, 33000 Bordeaux
Tel 0892 70 00 00
One of two original-language cinemas in Bordeaux, this ten-screen UGC shows all the latest blockbusters as well as art house productions. Film times vary—call or check local papers for details.
🕐 Daily, first showing approximately 1pm, last 9.30pm 💶 Adult €7.50

HERALD'S PUB
5 rue du Parlément Sainte-Catherine, 33000 Bordeaux
Tel 05 56 81 37 37
You'll find this relaxed bar, where jazz plays in the backround, in a building under stone arches off place du Parlément. Order whisky or champagne at the beautiful bar inlaid with brass.
🕐 Daily 7.30pm–1am

LE SHADOW LOUNGE
5 rue Cabanac, 33000 Bordeaux
Tel 05 56 49 36 93
www.leshadow.com
This elegant cocktail bar on the bank of the river has a delicately baroque interior with drapes, crystal chandeliers and book-filled shelves.
🕐 Wed–Sun noon–5am

GOLF DE BORDEAUX-LAC
Avenue de Pernon, 33000 Bordeaux-Lac
Tel 05 56 50 92 72
Close to flower gardens and the Bordeaux woods are two 18-hole golf courses and a covered driving range with 25 posts. Group lessons and courses are available and there's a golf shop. Credit cards are not accepted.
🕐 Daily 8–6 💶 Entry free, but call ahead to book a time slot

IN-LINE SKATING
www.bordeaux-roller.com
Downtown Bordeaux is a pedestrian-only zone and attracts large numbers of bicyclists, walkers and in-line skaters. There is a regular in-line skating night when more than 500 bladers take over the heart of the city.
🕐 First Sun of the month in Bordeaux, times vary 💶 Free

FRONSAC
CENTRE HIPPIQUE LIBOURNAIS
Chemin de l'Isle, 33126 Fronsac
Tel 05 57 51 41 46
This riding school, west of the town of Libourne, offers a range of lessons from beginner to advanced. Children aged four to seven can ride small ponies, while larger ones are available for children aged eight to fifteen. Credit cards are not accepted.
🕐 Tue–Sun 9–noon, 2–8 💶 Adult €17.50, child €14.50 (for one hour)

GRADIGNAN
THÉÂTRE DES QUATRE SAISONS
Parc de Mandavit, 33170 Gradignan
Tel 05 56 89 03 23
www.t4saisons.com
With reasonably priced family theatre, dance and musical events, from classical concerts to acrobatic circus displays, this refurbished space is a great addition to live events in the Gironde.
🕐 Performances daily all year
💶 Family events from €4

LACANAU-OCÉAN

LACANAU SURF CLUB

Maison de la Glisse, 17 boulevard de la
Plage, 33680 Lacanau-Océan
Tel 05 56 26 38 84
www.lacanausurf.com
The area has long been a
popular weekend retreat for
the Bordelais, but it is now
frequented by visitors who
come for the surfing. This
club runs courses for novices
through to advanced surfers.
If you're here in August, you
can watch Europe's surfing
championships. Ouest
Aquitaine buses run from
Bordeaux and if you are
driving, follow signs to
Lacanau-Océan, Côte d'Argent.
Ⓒ Daily 10–6, Mar–end Jun; 10–8
Jul–end Aug 🅿 1-hour instruction €27,
5-day course €214

MARTILLAC

LES SOURCES DE CAUDALIE

4 chemin de Bourran, 33650 Martillac
Tel 05 57 83 83 82
www.caudalie.com
This unique spa, a 15-minute
drive south of Bordeaux, offers
vinotherapy, where wine and
wine by-products form the
basis for a range of treatments.
They include Sauvignon
massages, Merlot wraps,
crushed Cabernet scrubs
and the Premier Grand
Cru facial.
Ⓒ Daily 10–7 🅿 €49 for 30-minute
facial, €80 for a 1-hour facial

PÉRIGUEUX

MARKETS

Place du Coderc and place de la
Clautre, 24000 Périgueux
Tel 05 53 53 10 63 (tourist information)

Périgueux's markets are a
rich source of the region's
delicacies. Stock up on foie
gras and other foods produced
from fattened geese and ducks
(confit, gizzards, terrines,
breast fillets), and truffles.
Outside the truffle season
(November to March), you
can buy the precious fungus
preserved in small jars. Drivers
can take either the N21 or
D939 to get here.
Ⓒ Wed, Sat 9–noon

PRÉCHAC

BASSE NAUTIQUE

La Trave, 33730 Préchac
Tel 05 56 65 27 16
Basse Nautique belongs to the
French Federation of Canoeing
and Kayaking and leads guided
trips and a number of different
descents on the Ciron. This
tributary of the Garonne is
particularly beautiful here.
Ⓒ Daily 9–12.30, 1.30–6.30 🅿 Adult
prices start from €8

RIBÉRAC

MARKETS

Place du Marché, 24600 Ribérac
Tel 05 53 90 03 10 (tourist information)
Cheese-makers, bakers and
florists gather in Ribérac's
market square on Friday
mornings. You can pick up
great picnic food, pottery or
even local paintings. On
Fridays in October and
November there's a walnut
market and there are night
markets at the height of the
tourist season in July and
August (days vary, call ahead
for information).
Ⓒ Fri 9–noon

ST-CHRISTOPHE-DE-DOUBLE

AIRE NAUTIQUE ET DE LOISIRS

33230 St-Christophe-de-Double
Tel 05 57 69 51 11
At this leisure complex on the
edge of the Double forest, east
of Coutras, there are 80km (50
miles) of tracks and trails for
walking, bicycling and riding.
Activities include swimming,
fishing, windsurfing and games
such as pétanque and croquet.
There's also a restaurant and a
two-star campsite. Credit cards
are not accepted.
Ⓒ Daily 10–9; campsite Jun–end Sep
🅿 €3 Jul–end Aug; free entry rest
of year

ST-ÉMILION

CVS

1 place Marché, 33330 St-Émilion
Tel 05 57 24 63 00
St-Émilion is not short of wine
shops, with most of them
displaying a vast selection of
Bordeaux wines. This shop,
which is right on the town's
main square, is a good choice
for tasting before deciding
what you want to buy.
Ⓒ Mon–Sat 10–1, 2–6

ST-MÉDARD-EN-JALLES

JENNY FLEURS

51 avenue Anatole France, 33160
St-Médard-en-Jalles
Tel 05 56 05 60 37
www.jennyfleurs.com
Jenny offers cut flowers, plants
and elaborate floral designs.
Simple bouquets cost about
€20 and fresh flowers from
€7.60.
Ⓒ Tue–Sat 9–12.30, 3–7.30, Sun
9–12.30

SARLAT-LA-CANÉDA

MARKETS

Tel 05 53 31 45 45 (tourist information)
The Saturday market in the
heart of the town has local
products with an emphasis on
fresh fruit and vegetables.
Wednesday sees a smaller
fresh produce market in place
de la Liberté, and there are
covered markets every day
except Monday at the

WHAT TO DO

Ancienne Église Sainte-Marie from May to October. Sales of foie gras are held in place

Boissarie on Saturday mornings, and of truffles in the same place on Saturday mornings during December, January and February.

WHAT TO DO

📅 Main market Sat 8.30–6, Wed market 8.30–1

ROUGIÉ SARLAT
5 rue des Consuls, 24200 Sarlat-la-Canéda
Tel 05 53 31 72 00
Rougié has been producing and selling foie gras and other local delicacies since 1875. This traditional delicatessen is popular with locals and is an easy way to discover and appreciate the best of the local goose and duck produce. Because most products are canned, they make easily transportable gifts.
📅 Mon–Sat 10–1, 2–6

Poitou-Charentes

ANGOULÊME

CHOCOLATERIE LETUFFE
10 place Francis-Louvel, 16000 Angoulême
Tel 05 45 95 00 54
This chocoholics heaven is known throughout France and beyond for its chocolate artistry, from the humblest nougat to delights such as *guinettes* (cherry and cognac) and *marguerites d'Angoulême* (chocolate and orange). Whether you love chocolate or are just looking for a gift, Letuffe is worth a detour.
📅 Mon–Sat 10–1noon, 2–7

MONTBRON

MAISON DU CANOE LA BOULOGNE
A.P.A.L.M Canoë Kayak, route Rochefoucauld, 16220 Montbron
Tel 05 45 23 93 58
The Tordaire river winds its way around Angoulême and through the gorges of Chambon. Maison de Canoe, just 30km (19 miles) from Anguleme, off the D939, offers guided canoe trips and canoe rental for a water-level view. The gorges take a full day or you can do a shorter trip. Credit cards are not accepted.
📅 By prior arrangement May–end Jun; daily Jul–end Aug; limited hours Sep; closed Oct–end Apr 💶 From €35 half-day unguided

LA ROCHELLE

MARCHÉ
Place du Marché, 17000 La Rochelle
Between rue Theirs, rue Gambetta and rue St-Yon
The market is frequented by Rochelais and residents from miles around, and sells fresh seafood and other products ranging from glassware to electronics, all in a charming, lively setting. Come early on Sunday for the best atmosphere.
📅 Daily 7–1

CINÉMA MÉGA CGR
Avenue Becquerel, 17000 La Rochelle
Tel 0892 680 445
www.cgrcinemas.fr
You'll find this huge 15-screen cinema complex near the university, with at least half of the films in English. The first screening is mid- to late morning, depending on the time of year. Holiday schedules differ.
📅 Open year round 💶 Adult €7.60, child €4.60

LA ROCHELLE AQUARIUM
Bassin des Grand Yachts, 17000 La Rochelle
Tel 05 46 34 00 00
www.aquarium-larochelle.com
A large, well-run aquarium with a global cross-section of ocean environments. Café

Tropical offers the chance for a post- or mid-visit snack.
📅 Daily 9–8, Apr–end Jun, Sep; 9–11, Jul to end Aug; 10–8, rest of year
💶 Adults €12, child (3–17) €9, under 3 free

ROIFFÉ

DOMAINE ST-HILAIRE
Domaine St-Hilaire, 86120 Roiffé
Tel 05 49 98 78 06
This is an internationally known 18-hole golf course which also has a practice putting green with bunker and a covered driving range.
📅 Open all year 💶 €23–€31 per round

Limousin

LIMOGES

LA MAISON DE LIMOGES
3 boulevard Victor-Hugo 87000 Limoges
Tel 05 55 77 31 61
This store stocks all the major Limoges pottery names, so you can compare the differing patterns and prices under one roof. Other objets d'art for the home are also available.
📅 Mon 2–6, Tue–Sat 9–12, 2–7

GRAND THÉÂTRE MUNICIPAL
48 rue Jean-Jaurès, 87000 Limoges
Tel 05 55 34 12 12
Home to the Limoges Regional Symphony Orchestra and with its own theatre company, this theatre offers a rich selection of productions, plus a season of ballet and opera.
📅 Evening performances from 7.30pm
💶 €12–€40

ST-GEORGES-LES-LANDES

LE COCHON FIDÈLE
Croix de la Chaudière St-Georges-les-Landes
Tel 05 55 76 74 97
The 'Loyal Pig' is a family-owned bar with a list of 280 specialist beers from around the globe, plus delicious home-made ice cream and sorbet. Cold meat platters are available at all times, but you'll need to reserve for a full meal.
📅 Thu–Mon noon–11, Tue noon–2

Midi-Pyrénées

ALBI

L'ARTISAN CHOCOLATIER
4 rue du Docteur Camboulives, 81000 Albi

Tel 05 63 54 18 46

Owner Michel Belin has been judged among the ten best chocolate-makers in France–he even has a chocolate creation meant to smell of Havana cigars. In addition to chocolate, he also makes delicious cakes and pastries. Credit cards are accepted for purchases over €15.

Tue–Sat 9–12.30, 2.30–7.30, Mon 2.30–7, Sun 9–12.30

SHAMROCK PUB
57 avenue Charles de Gaulle, 81000 Albi

Tel 05 63 43 08 50

You can expect all the usual Irish pub paraphernalia, but also concerts, darts matches and open-mike events most nights of the week at the Shamrock. The pub attracts all ages and types and there's a pleasant inner courtyard.

Mon–Sat 2pm–2am

BUZET-SUR-TARN

GOLF DE TOULOUSE PALMOLA
Route d'Albi, 31660 Buzet-sur-Tarn

Tel 05 61 84 20 50

This 18-hole course in Buzet-sur-Tarn, 20 km (12 miles) north of Toulouse, is one of France's best. It was designed in 1974 by an English architect and covers 70 hectares (173 acres).

Wed–Mon 9–7 €66 at weekends and holidays, €48 during the week

CAHORS

LIBRAIRIE CALLIGRAMME
75 rue Joffre, 46000 Cahors

Tel 05 65 35 66 44

Bookshop with an English-language section. It also sells classical CDs, and there are art exhibitions in the basement gallery.

Tue–Fri 9.30–7, Sat 9.30–6.30

MARCHÉ TRADITIONNEL
Place de la Cathédrale, 46000 Cahors

Tel 05 65 53 20 65 (tourist information)

Classed as one of the 100 most beautiful markets in France, this open-air market has real character. The classification comes from its generous supply of gastronomic ingredients, from goat's cheese to foie gras and tasty breads to fresh seasonal vegetables. At certain times of the year you can also get local wines.

Wed and Sat mornings, 7.30–12.30

CAUTERETS

CONFISERIE AUX DELICES
Place de la Mairie, 65110 Cauterets

Tel 05 62 92 07 08

www.berlingots.com

Eric Lestable still follows his grandmother's recipe for *berlingots* (boiled candy), a centuries-old tradition in Cauterets. Watch them being made by hand in this old village shop, then have a free taste.

Daily 9–12.30, 2–7.30

ESPACE CAUTERETS
Place Foch, 65100 Cauterets

Tel 05 62 92 13 00

www.cauterets.com

The Cirque du Lys region has more than two dozen runs for downhill and cross-country skiing. There's also a snow park, ice rink and thermal baths. In summer when the snow has gone, you can hike in the mountains.

Skiing Nov–15 Apr 1-day ski pass €17–€21

FOIX

ÉCOLE DE PARAPENTE GYPAÈTES
BP05, 09001 Foix

Tel 05 34 09 86 08 or 06 78 55 39 26

www.gypaetes.com

This hang-gliding school offers flights with instructors for beginners, equipment rental for experienced gliders and courses of up to five days. Flights go over the Pyrenees and in winter, they leave from ski resorts. Make sure you reserve at least a week ahead in summer and note that credit cards are not accepted.

Open all year €55 for a flight of 15–20 min with an instructor, €107 for a one-day course

LOURDES

MAYFLOWER CAFÉ
6 rue de l'Égalite, 65104 Lourdes

Tel 05 62 94 01 56

Popular with seasonal workers, this pub with a lovely terrace is right on the tourist trail but without the high prices to match. Expect rock and Celtic music and a mixed clientele.

Sun–Thu 2pm–2am, Fri–Sat 2pm–3am, Apr–end Oct; Fri–Sat 6pm–2am, rest of year

MADIRAN

MAISON DES VINS DU MADIRAN & DU PACHERENC
Rue de l'Église, 65700 Madiran

Tel 05 62 31 90 67

www.vins-du-sud-ouest.com

This organization is in an old monastery about 20km (12 miles) from Tarbes. It offers advice and information on the appellations and vineyards of more than 50 producers of the well-respected local Madiran wines. You can taste and buy a selection of the best here.

Daily 8.30–5.30, Jun–end Sep; Mon–Fri 8.30–5.30, Sat 2–6, rest of year

MARTRES TOLOSANE

RENAISSANCE ARTISANALE
8 bis Grande Rue de L'Église, 31220 Martres Tolosane

Tel 05 61 98 89 31

Just below the church, this shop is one of many faience (earthenware glazed with opaque colours) producers in the village. Browse and buy lamps, vases, dinner services and decorative items. Call in advance to arrange a tour of the workshop, which is about 70km (43 miles) from Toulouse off the A64.

Tue–Sun 10–noon, 3–6

MILLAU

ATELIER DU GANTIER
21 rue Droite, 12100 Millau
Tel 05 65 60 81 50
Monsieur and Madame
Canillac produce handmade
gloves in the Millau tradition
for €40 a pair (€60 for a silk-
lined pair). Call in advance to
arrange a tour of the workshop
or provide measurements for
custom-made gloves.
🕐 Mon–Sat 9–noon, 2–7

LA LOCOMOTIVE
33 avenue Gambetta, 12100 Millau
Tel 05 65 61 19 93
Well-known for its eclectic mix
of music, this venue hosts
concerts of anything from
Celtic to gypsy music.
Photographs of local bands
cover the old baroque interior
and you can also have
food here (the lunch special
costs €8).
🕐 Mon–Sat 9am–1am. Concerts every
Fri (also Wed, Jul–end Aug). Closed 28
Dec–13 Jan 🎫 Free entry

MONTSÉGUR

LE MONTSÉGURIEN
115 rue Principale, 09300 Montségur
Tel 05 61 01 54 46
Stop at this delicatessen for its
wild boar pâté. Many of its
meat products (dried sausage,
salami, pâtés and cured ham)
are made on the premises.
🕐 Tue–Sat 9–noon, 3–7, Sun 9–noon

RABAT-LES-TROIS-SEIGNEURS

L'ÉCOLE BUISSONIERE
Le Barry, 09400 Rabat-les-Trois-
Seigneurs
Tel 05 61 05 19 37
www.ecolebuissonniere.info
The team here offers courses
on canyoning, climbing and
potholing, and they can take
you hiking in the mountains.
For children under the age of
six, there's an adventure park.
Take the N20 south from Foix.
🕐 Daily 9–7 💶 €28–€37 half-day
activity, €14 guided hike

ROQUEFORT-SUR-SOULZON

FROMAGERIES PAPILLON
8 bis avenue de Lauras, 12250
Roquefort-sur-Soulzon
Tel 05 65 58 50 08
www.roquefort-papillon.com
The Papillon cheese-maker is
one of the smaller producers
of Roquefort but their tour is
free. You watch a short film
about production, take the
guided tour through the cellars
taste the finished product and,
if you like it, buy some for your
next picnic lunch.
🕐 Daily 9.30–11.30, 1.30–4.30,
Oct–end Mar; 9.30–11.30, 1.30–5.30,
Apr–end Jun and Sep; 9.30–6.30,
Jul–end Aug.

SOUILLAC

AQUARÈVE
Rue Morlet, 46200 Souillac
Tel 05 65 32 79 43
Spoil yourself here at 'Aqua
Dream' with the heated
indoor swimming pool, gym,
hammam (Turkish bath),
massage and sauna. Daily
passes are available for the
pool, but it's best to reserve
ahead for a massage.
🕐 Daily 2pm–6pm 💶 €4 entry to
pool, €10 for 30-minute hammam

TARBES

FERME ÉQUESTRE DU BOSC CLAR
8 Cami Deu Bosc Clar, 65800 Chis
Tel 05 62 36 27 36
These relaxed, family-run
stables in Chis, a village north
of Tarbes, arrange two-day
treks in summer, through
forests and mountains with
camping overnight. They also
organize lessons, competitions
and special rides for children.
Credit cards are not accepted.
🕐 Tue–Sun 9–7 💶 Adult €13, child
(under 10) €10 for 1-hour lesson, €45
day trek

TOULOUSE

DÉLICES DE TUNIS
22 bis rue des Tourneurs, 31000
Toulouse
Tel 05 61 53 31 20
More than 60 kinds of Tunisian
cakes are on offer here. Try the
baklava, *cornes de gazelles*
(horn-shaped almond pastries)
or Turkish delight. To taste the
goodies, you can have a seat
and drink mint tea or lemon-
ade with your pastry.
🕐 Mon–Sat 9–7.45

ESPACE STADE TOULOUSAIN
75 rue Alsace Lorraine, 31000 Toulouse
Tel 08 20 31 15 15
www.stadetoulousain.fr
Pick up tickets for a rugby
match, the official Toulouse
rugby jersey (€86) or branded
sports clothes. There's even a
range of team paraphernalia
for babies.
🕐 Mon 2–7, Tue–Sat 10–7

MARCHÉ VICTOR HUGO
Place Victor Hugo, 31000 Toulouse
Tel 05 61 11 02 22 (tourist information)
The biggest covered market in
Toulouse is on the ground
floor of a car park. The high-
quality fresh produce includes
excellent duck, cold meat, fish
and cheese. The restaurants on
the upper level maintain the
lively atmosphere.
🕐 Tue–Sun 8–1

LE MONDE DU VIN
7 Esplanade Compans Caffarelli, 31000
Toulouse
Tel 05 61 22 60 62
An extensive range of wines
from all over France and, of
course, several Fronton wines

are sold here beside the Hôtel Mercure. Try the Armagnac, the pastis or the violet liqueur. They also sell produce such as foie gras and cassoulet.
🕐 Tue–Sat 9–7.30, Mon 3–7.30

NOUVELLES GALERIES
4–8 rue Lapeyrouse, 31000 Toulouse
Tel 05 34 45 98 98
www.galerieslafayette.com
Part of a nationwide chain, this five-floor department store is a good stop for almost anything from designer clothes to household goods—but be aware that prices are rather high. The basement super-market is a great place to stock up on culinary souvenirs. The top-floor restaurant (open 11–6) serves local dishes.
🕐 Supermarket Mon–Sat 8.30–8, main store 9–8

PILLON
23 rue du Languedoc, 31000 Toulouse
Tel 05 61 55 03 08
www.maison-pillon.fr
With its traditional shop front, this is one of the most popular confectioners and bakeries in the city, valued for the superior quality of its chocolates. Pillon have four shops in total, two selling chocolates, the others selling pastries. Here you can watch chocolates being made and buy the house special, *le pavé du Capitole* (orange-scented chocolate).
🕐 Mon–Sat 9–7.30, Sun 9–1

ST-SERNIN SUNDAY MARKET
Around Basilique St-Sernin, 31000 Toulouse
Tel 05 61 11 02 22
A popular Sunday morning event with locals and visitors, this flea market is diverse. The location provides a stunning backdrop to browsing. Goods range from the exotic—African jewellery, dyed fabrics, Spanish leather—to the ordinary and practical, such as stockings, thread and pottery. The rest of the week (Tue–Sat 8–1) there is a normal market here.
🕐 Sun 8–1

VIOLETTES & PASTELS
10 rue St-Pantaléon, 31000 Toulouse
Tel 05 61 22 14 22
Part of this shop is devoted entirely to the famous *violette* (violet) and you will be surprised how many things can be transformed with the ancient dye. There's even tea and violet-scented jam alongside bath salts and oils, dried flowers, linen, candles and china. The perfect gift stop, it's known for its beautiful gift boxes.
🕐 Tue–Sat 10–7 🚇 Capitole

XAVIER
6 place Victor Hugo, 31000 Toulouse
Tel 05 34 45 59 45
Experts in traditional cheeses, this shop deals with small local farmers and dairy farmers producing cheeses made from unpasteurized milk. Try the various goat's cheeses. The shop also offers foreign cheeses, and some extras to make the cheese taste special, such as truffles and home-made bread.
🕐 Mon 3–7.30, Tue–Fri 9–1, 3–7.30, Sat 9–1.30, 2.30–7.30

CINÉMATHÈQUE DE TOULOUSE
69 rue Taur, 31000 Toulouse
Tel 05 62 30 30 10
www.lacinemathequedetoulouse.com
Part of the Paris Film Association, this cinema shows art house and foreign-language films. A rotating exhibition of photographs from its collection and a film library are open to the public.
🕐 Screenings Mon–Sat 6.30, 8.30 (also Wed 2.30, 4.30), Sun 2.30, 4.30; Library open Tue–Sat 2–11, Sun 2–7 🎟 Adult €4.30, child €3.80, library €2.30

HALLE AUX GRAINS
Place Dupuy, 31000 Toulouse
Tel 05 61 62 02 70 or 05 61 63 13 13
www.onct.mairie-toulouse.fr
Once a wheat and cereal market, this smart concert hall is home to the highly praised musicians of the Toulouse National Orchestra.

International singers and comedians also perform here.
🕐 Box office 9.45–12.45, 1–5.30 Oct–end Jun 🎟 Varies according to performance

THÉÂTRE DU CAPITOLE
1 place du Capitole, 31000 Toulouse
Tel 05 61 22 31 31 or 05 61 63 13 13
www.theatre-du-capitole.org
Part of Toulouse's impressive central square, this internation-ally known theatre with a grand interior, hosts operas, ballet, recitals and classical music. The bar is open on performance nights.
🕐 Tue–Sun, all year 🎟 Varies accord-ing to performance

BAR ONE
27 boulevard de Strasbourg, 31000 Toulouse
Tel 05 61 22 9499
Low tables, candles and soft lighting create a soothing atmosphere for the youthful clientele. From 6.30pm to 8.30pm, drinks are two for the price of one and you can sit outside in summer.
🕐 Mon–Fri 6pm–2am, Sat 6pm–4am

LE PÈRE LOUIS
45 rue des Tourneurs, 31000 Toulouse
Tel 05 61 21 33 45
For a real sense of Toulouse history, visit the oldest wine bar in town. It has an extensive wine list, exotic aperitifs and serve traditional bistro food from noon.
🕐 Mon–Sat 8.30–2.30, 5–10

VISITE ROLLERS
10 rue Jardins, 31000 Toulouse
Tel 05 61 62 95 22
On the first Sunday of every month you can explore the town on in-line skates with a French-language, two-hour tour arranged by the Association Patrimoine Histoire de l'Art, with a different theme each time. Meet outside Aracades jewellers on place du Capitole.
🕐 Tours Sun 3pm, no tours Dec–end Feb 🎟 Adult €6, child (12–18) €4, under 12 free

Festivals and Events

BORDEAUX INTERNATIONAL FAIR
Mid-May
Parc des Expositions, Bordeaux-Lac, 33300 Bordeaux
Tel 05 11 99 00
www.foiredebordeaux.com
A 10-day annual event established more than 80 years ago, with cultural events alongside main exhibitions dedicated to interior design, the environment and agriculture. It is the largest such fair in France, with exhibitors from more than 50 countries. It's about a 15-minute bus ride from places Quinconces, or follow signs to *Bordeaux lac* (there is free parking).
🕐 Daily 9–5, for 10 days from mid-May
🎟 Adult €6, child €4.50

BORDEAUX PRIDE
Mid-June
www.lgpbordeaux.com
Bordeaux's annual gay and lesbian festival offers a range of intellectual events (lectures, discussions), as well as a parade through the city followed by a legendary party.
🕐 2pm–dawn, mid-Jun 🎟 Free

BIARRITZ SURF FESTIVAL
Mid-July
64200 Côte des Basques
Tel 05 59 23 56 75 (Surfing Association)

For a week in summer, Biarritz is transformed into a California-style beach party as some of the world's top surfers and thousands of holiday-makers descend on the Côte des Basques. Competitions are interspersed with demonstrations of tandem surfing, paddle-board racing and Tahitian canoes. There's also the chance for novices to try surfing.

BLUES PASSIONS FESTIVAL
End of July
Associations Blues Passions, 14 rue Louise de Savoie 16100, Cognac
Tel 05 45 36 11 81
This four-day festival's combination of world-class blues and the rich visual and culinary offerings of Cognac, (including the drink itself) make this a festival worth attending.

MIMOS INTERNATIONAL FESTIVAL OF MIME
First week in August
Nouveau Théâtre de Périgueux, 1 avenue d'Aquitaine, 24000 Périgueux
Tel 05 53 53 18 71
www.ville-perigueux.fr/mimos/p1.htm
This is the only major international festival in the world dedicated to the art of mime. Performances run during the first week in August, with many artists performing in the street.

WHITE WINE AND OYSTER FESTIVAL
15th August
24500 Eymet
Tel 05 53 23 74 95 (tourist office)
This is the highlight of the summer in the Dordogne town of Eymet, south of Bergerac. Proceedings begin in the town square soon after dawn, when oyster and wine producers from all over the region set up their stalls. Wine sampling gets going early–people start at 6am. It makes sense to arrive early as after mid-morning supplies of some of the finer products can run low.

ST-ÉMILION FÊTES DES VENDAGES
Third Sunday in September
Place Pierre Meyrat, 33330 St-Émilion
Tel 05 57 55 50 50 (Syndicat Viticole)
Tel 05 57 55 50 55 (Maison de Vin)
Every September, St-Émilion celebrates the start of the all-important grape harvest with spectacular ceremonies in the town's Collegiate Church of the Cordeliers. The day culminates in the announcement of the start of the harvest, which is made to the crowds from the top of the Tour du Roy.

CHRISTMAS REGATTA
December
17000 La Rochelle
Tel 05 46 41 14 68 (tourist information)
www.ville-larochelle.fr
Just before Christmas, boats set sail from Port des Minimes in La Rochelle for a winter's race on the high seas. Get a free view of the race from the quayside and toast the victor in the town's bars.

CORSICA

Corsica's topography marks out the island as a destination for lovers of strenuous outdoor activities. Of course you can explore on four wheels, but take advice from locals, since dramatic changes in weather conditions can lead to the closure of even principal roads. The variation in the weather means that, from December to April, tracts of the island can be discovered by cross-country skiers, while in the heat of the summer sun, hardy hikers can take two weeks or more to walk the gruelling Fra I Monti mountain path linking Calenzana and Porto Vecchio. Throughout the year, activities such as white-water rafting and hang-gliding attract adventurous spirits.

For the less energetic, there's Corsica's rich cultural past, which embraces all of the major and several minor European civilizations. Military and religious history is served by local museums in every town.

Holy Week is the highlight of the Corsican calendar, with parades of penitents and vivid processions across the island. The rest of the year brings an abundance of festivals, with jazz in June, guitar recitals in July and a celebration of Napoleon, Corsica's most famous son, in August.

Woodcarvings created by local artists and shepherds make good buys. The best time to shop in Ajaccio, away from the heat of the Mediterranean sun, is between 8pm and midnight on summer Fridays, when shops and markets stay open and musicians mingle with shoppers.

AJACCIO

BELLINI-CAGGIARI
Port Charles Ornano, route Amirauté, 20090 Ajaccio
Tel 04 95 10 16 52
These two artisans work in partnership to produce high quality traditional Corsican knives and exquisite cutlery. They will produce customized items including full canteens (sets of cutlery), but also keep a good range in store.
🕐 Daily 10–12.30, 2–7, Jul–end Aug; Tue–Sat 10–12.30, 3–6, rest of year

MARCHÉ DE BROCANTE
Rue Pascal Rossini, Ajaccio
The major *brocante* (second-hand goods) and antiques market of southern Corsica is a great place to browse for a souvenir of the island, with old photographs, books, ceramics and textiles the most popular items on sale. There are food and drink stands. Credit cards are not always accepted.
🕐 Sun 8–12.30

CORSICA 2001
Port Charles Omano, 20090 Ajaccio
Tel 04 95 10 13 89
www.corsica2001.com
Yachting is an excellent way to explore picturesque ports and more remote sections of the Corsican coastline. This small yacht charter company has yachts (with or without crew) for rent in Ajaccio, Propriano and Bonifacio.
🕐 Daily 9–noon, 3–7, Jul–end Aug; 10–12.30, May–end Jun and Sep; other times by appointment 🚤 1 week's rental of a cabin boat without crew in peak season (Aug) €1,250

BASTIA

LA ROUTE DU SUD OCCITANE
3 rue J. Casale, 20200 Bastia
Tel 04 95 32 79 83
This showroom is full of furniture and objets d'art from Morocco, Tunisia and Spain. They can ship bulky items like furniture, but smaller items such as candle-holders and other home accessories make more portable souvenirs.

🕐 Daily 9.30–12.30, 3.30–7.30 summer; Mon 2.30–7, Tue–Sat 9.30–noon, 2.30–7, rest of year

BONIFACIO

BONIFACIO WINDSURF
Hameau de Pianterella, 20169 Bonifacio
Tel 04 94 73 52 04
www.bonifacio-windsurf.com
Bonifacio Windsurf is a school offering various courses in windsurfing and kite surfing, from introductory sessions and courses for beginners to expert and specialist techniques. You can also rent equipment by the hour, the day or longer.
🕐 Daily 9–8, May–end Sep 🚤 3-stage windsurfing course €90 per stage; kite surfing 5 sessions of 3 hours €320; kite surf initiation of 2 hours €50; windsurf rental for 3 hours €25

CALVI

ÉCOLE DE PLONGÉE INTERNATIONALE CALVI
Port de Plaisance, 20260 Calvi
Tel 04 95 65 43 90
www.epic-corse.com
This diving school offers introductory sessions and a range of courses leading to initial or higher level qualifications. For qualified divers the school organizes guided dives to various locations on the east coast of the island.
🕐 Daily 9–noon, 2–7, May–end Sep (dives take place throughout the day) 🚤 Introduction to diving €38, PADI open water qualification course €350

CORTE

ÉPICERIE DU VIEUX MARCHÉ
9 rue du Vieux Marché, Haute Ville, 20250 Corte
Tel 04 95 46 17 30
This is a little cornucopia for all Corsican foodstuffs such as honey, cheese, wines, liqueurs and the Corsican pork dishes *coppa* and *lonzu*. It's a great place to stock up on provisions for a picnic.
🕐 Mon–Sat 9–12.30, 2–7, Sun 9–12.30

GHISONACCIA

CAVE SAINT ANTOINE
20240 Ghisonaccia
Tel 04 95 56 61 00
www.cavesaintantoine.com
The vineyard produces a range of labels mixing local Niellucciu, Vermentinu and Sciaccarellu grape varieties with the standard varieties used in mainland wines. You can view the maturing wines, enjoy a tasting and, if you're impressed, buy.
🕐 Mon–Fri 8–noon, 2–5

OLMETO

LE VOYAGE À CHEVAL
Route de Baracci, B.P 65, 20113, Olmeto
Tel 04 95 76 08 02
www.corse-equitation.com
This company offers excellent and well-planned tours of Corsica on horseback. Choose from mountain or coastline itineraries, or take a fully comprehensive island tour. Tours include a picnic lunch, evening meal and simple lodgings.
🕐 Apr–end Oct 🎫 8-day tour €640

PATRIMONIO

CORSICA CERAMICA
20253 Patrimonio
Tel 04 95 37 11 62
You can watch pottery being made at this ceramicist,

which produces excellent public and private commissions as well as smaller items like jugs, mugs and lamp bases. You can take a bus from Bastia and St-Florent.
🕐 Daily 8–8

PIETRABUGNO

ALBO
39 rue du Cap, 20200 Pietrabugno
Tel 04 95 31 93 41
www.albo.com
Sculptor and jeweller Albo creates unique pieces using semi-precious stones and local Corsica stone in his work. He also customizes Corsican knives (a traditional Corsican artisanal industry) with semi-precious handles.
🕐 Daily 10–8 (phone to check)

PIGNA

CASA MUSICALE
20220 Pigna
Tel 04 95 61 76 57
www.casa-musicale.org
Pigna village is an artistic and musical commune keeping traditional Corsican art forms alive. Casa Musicale is the central point for information about lectures, artists' workshops, concerts and other activities, as well as being a hotel and restaurant.
🕐 Reception 8am–10pm
🎫 Workshops from €60 per day; concert tickets start at €8

PORTICCIO

INSTITUTE OF THALASSOTHERAPY
Hotel Sofitel, Domaine de la Pointe, Golfe d'Ajaccio, 20166 Porticcio
Tel 04 95 29 40 40
www.sofitel.com
The most prestigious spa on the island has a range of treatments including massage, hydrotherapy, aromatherapy, algae baths and facials. Packages are available that include a room at the hotel.
🕐 Daily 8am–10pm 🎫 Treatments from €49

PORTO VECCHIO

CASA DI L'ARTE
10 rue Jean Jaurès, 20137 Porto Vecchio
Tel 04 95 70 12 58
You'll find an excellent range of local art and ceramics here, making it easy to compare different styles and prices. The shop specializes in products such as Terraghia

pottery, paintings and wooden objects.
🕐 Mon–Sat 9.30–12.30, 2.30–7, also summer Sun 9.30–12.30, 2–5

CORSICA MOUNTAIN QUAD
L'Ospedale–direction Zonza, 20137 Porto Vecchio
Tel 04 95 78 68 08
Enjoy the countryside quad-riding on day-long exploration routes with a guide, or simply book half an hour of fun.
🕐 Daily 10–6 🎫 €20 for 30 mins, €38 for 1 hour, €150 for 5 hours including picnic lunch

QUENZA

CORSE ODYSSÉE
Quartier Pantenella, 20122 Quenza
Tel 04 95 78 64 05
www.corseodyssee.com
This company offers a range of guided outdoor activities for a day or longer, including hiking excursions, climbing and canyoning.
🕐 Daily mid-Apr to end Sep for pre-booked activities 🎫 1 day canyoning €55, guided hike €31

ST-FLORENT

OSHADI
Quai de l'Aliso, 20217 St-Florent
Tel 04 95 37 00 21
The shop attached to this hammam/beauty centre sells an excellent range of natural cosmetics, essential oils, beauty products as well as organic food. Enjoy a relaxing treatment before you shop then have a drink in the tea room or juice bar.
🕐 Mon–Sat 9–12.30, 3–7

Festival

CALVI JAZZ FESTIVAL
June
Tel 04 95 65 16 67 (tourist office)
www.calvi-jazz-festival.com
The main jazz festival in June has ticketed and free concerts in the port, and around 100 other unofficial events and performances in bars and cafés around the town.

Go out and about in France with these 16 driving tours, a bicycle ride and 15 walks. They explore France's varied scenery, from a city walk in Paris to a drive through the heart of Provence. The locations of the walks and tours are marked on the map on page 276. Tours are also plotted on individual maps. Walks have their own locator maps unless the walk starts from a point on a tour, when it is marked by a red star on the tour map. For both walks and tours, it is advisable to buy a detailed map of the area before you set out.

Out and About

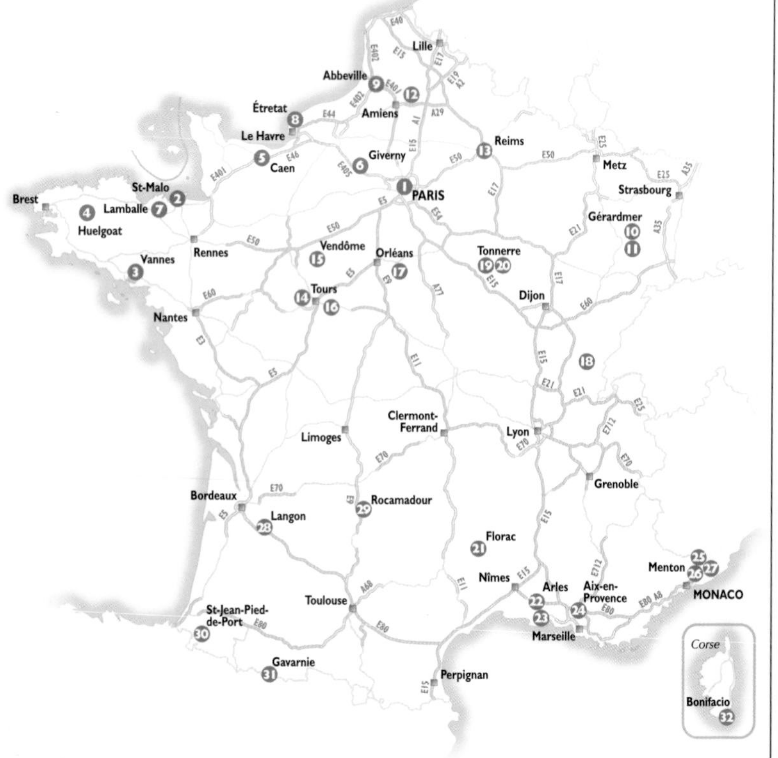

1. WALK

MONTMARTRE

There is so much more to Montmartre than the towering Sacré-Cœur basilica, impressive though this is. This walk shows you the lesser-known side of Paris's historic hilltop village, with its picturesque cottages, cobbled streets and panoramic views.

THE WALK

Length: 3km (2 miles)	
Allow: 2 hours	
Start: place Blanche	
End: place des Abbesses	

HOW TO GET THERE

🚇 Blanche 🚌 30, 54, 68, 74

Starting from place Blanche, walk west along boulevard de Clichy,

past the Moulin Rouge ❶ on your right.

When the Moulin Rouge opened its doors in 1889, its vivacious cancan dancers were an immediate hit. The venue still stages cabaret shows.

Turn right into avenue Rachel and carry on to the entrance of

Cimetière de Montmartre ❷.

Here you can seek out the tombs of the writer Stendhal, composer Hector Berlioz and saxophone inventor Adolphe Sax.

Leave the cemetery at avenue Rachel and go up the steps on the right to rue Caulaincourt (a flyover). Turn right onto this road and walk to the intersection. Turn right along rue Joseph de Maistre. After a few minutes, turn very sharp left up rue Lepic. Van Gogh lived at No. 54 of this winding road from 1886 to 1888. Follow the curve until you come to the intersection with rue Tholozé. Look up to the left, past the green arch, to the Moulin de la Galette ❸.

The Moulin de la Galette became a dance hall in the 19th century and was the inspiration behind Renoir's painting *Le Bal du Moulin de la Galette*.

Turn left into rue Girardon, cross avenue Junot and enter the pleasant square Suzanne-Buisson ❹, on the left.

The square is named after a World War II heroine. The macabre statue is of the 3rd-century bishop St. Denis, who was beheaded by the Romans. Legend has it that he picked up his head and washed off the blood in a fountain here.

Facing the statue, turn right and leave the square into place Casadesus, in rue Simon Dereure. Turn right into the allée des Brouillards. Pierre-Auguste Renoir lived in one of the houses on the left in the 1890s.

Continue to place Dalida then walk up cobbled rue de l'Abreuvoir.

Formerly a country lane, the road takes its name from the watering trough (*l'abreuvoir*) that stood at No. 15. Number 14 attracted many of the area's artists when it was the Café de l'Abreuvoir, while No. 12 was home to artist Camille Pissarro from 1888 to 1892. If you're feeling hungry, stop for lunch at La Maison Rose.

Turn left after La Maison Rose and walk down the steep, cobbled rue des Saules to the legendary cabaret spot Au Lapin Agile. Turn right (east) along rue St-Vincent, past Montmartre's vineyard on your right. Cross rue du Mont Cenis, once home to Hector Berlioz (No. 22), and walk uphill to rue de la Bonne. This leads into the secluded Parc de la Turlure ❺.

This tranquil park, well off the tourist trail, gives you magnificent views over Paris, as well as an unusual perspective on Sacré-Cœur.

Wander up through the park, then exit onto rue du Chevalier de la Barre. Continue along rue du Cardinal Guibert to the entrance to Sacré-Cœur ❻, on place du Parvis du Sacré-Cœur.

The neo-Byzantine basilica of Sacré-Cœur (see page 91) was commissioned as atonement for the 58,000 victims of the Franco-Prussian war (1870–1871). Building work took nearly 45 years.

Leave Sacré-Cœur and turn right along rue Azaïs, with its wonderful views over the city. Turn right up rue St-Eleuthère to the church of St-Pierre-de-Montmartre ❼.

Humbler than its grand companion, St-Pierre has a peaceful atmosphere. The church was originally part of the 12th-century abbey of Montmartre.

Enter touristy place du Tertre and leave by rue Norvins, packed with gift shops. Turn second left, through place Jean-Baptiste Clément. Then turn right into rue Ravignan, and continue round to the left into the tree-shaded place Émile Goudeau ❽.

On the right of this square, look for the Bateau-Lavoir, where Picasso, Juan Gris and Braque had studios and where Cubism was born. The original building burned down in1970.

Leave the square down a small flight of steps and walk down rue Ravignan until you reach rue des Abbesses. Turn left here to place des Abbesses ❾.

Before stopping for a drink, take a look at the magnificent art nouveau Métro entrance and the unusual façade of the church of St-Jean-l'Évangéliste (1904), nicknamed St-Jean-des-Briques for its profusion of red bricks.

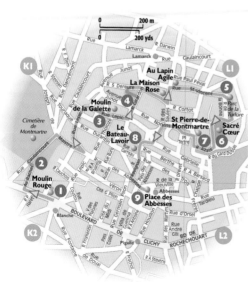

WHEN TO GO

This walk is best during the day, as parts of Montmartre can be seedy at night.

TIP

For a stunning view of Sacré-Cœur, head down rue Yvonne Le Tac to the base of the funicular.

WHERE TO EAT

Try La Maison Rose, or one of the cafés around place des Abbesses.

OUT AND ABOUT

ST-MALO AND DINAN

No visitor to Brittany should miss the two north-coast towns of St-Malo and Dinan. Although very different in character—St-Malo is a busy port and Dinan a splendidly preserved medieval town—both are beautiful. The river Rance flows past Dinan and out to sea at St-Malo, and is barred on the way by a great tidal dam.

THE DRIVE

Length: 90km (56 miles)

Allow: 1 day

Start/End: St-Malo

St-Malo ❶ (see page 121) is a ferry port, yachting base and commercial port, with a walled citadel well worth exploring. Walk the ramparts for views of the town, the sea and nearby islands.

Follow signs for Rennes through the suburb of St-Servan-sur-Mer and, keeping the estuary of the Rance on your right, carry on past Tour Solidor ❷.

Medieval Tour Solidor, in the St-Servan district of St-Malo, was built in the late 14th-century to protect shipping in the Rance from English pirates and Malouin corsairs. It was once the town jail and is now a museum with model ships and information about St-Malo's seafaring tradition.

Follow signs for Dinard ❸, crossing the top of a huge dam, the Barrage de Rance, which generates electricity by harnessing the tidal current. Turn right onto the D266 into Dinard.

Dinard is a fashionable seaside town, a resort of the smart set since the turn of the 19th century, when the Prince of Wales used to holiday here. There are good views over a forest of yacht masts to the walls of St-Malo. From here you can go on a boat trip up the Rance to Dinan.

Return to the D266, following signs for Dinan and Pleurtuit. Pass the aerodrome on the right and stay on this road, which becomes the D766, all the way into the middle

of Dinan ❹. Although the town is often crowded, it's usually possible to park in the Champ-Clos near to all the sights.

With its half-timbered houses and the Jardin Anglais near St-Saveur, Dinan is a place to explore on foot. Walk down to the banks of the Rance by rue du Jerzual, a steep street lined with medieval houses, including a spectacular three-floor half-timbered building, the Maison du Gouverneur. The riverside is lined with restaurants, great for lunch or dinner.

From Dinan, follow signs to the suburb of Lanvallay, east of Dinan, and pick up the D2176. Fork left onto the D29 and head north past Pleudihen-sur-Rance. Continue north via the D74 and D76, following signs for Le Port as you come into Cancale ❺.

This oyster port and seaside resort is tucked into a corner of the Baie du Mont-St-Michel. You can see the Mont itself on

the far side of the bay. Oysters are bred out in the bay and are gathered from the flat-bottomed boats that you can see in the harbour. There are plenty of small restaurants along the wharf, where the first course on any menu should be Cancale oysters.

From Cancale harbour, follow signs for Pointe du Grouin or St-Malo par la Côte, onto the D201 for Pointe du Grouin ❻, 7km (4.5 miles) farther on.

Pointe du Grouin is a nature reserve and bird sanctuary, with marvellous views over the bay to Mont-St-Michel and, to the south, to Mont-Dol near Dol-de-Bretagne. From the parking place there is a footpath up to the tip of the Pointe and from there another footpath leads along the coast to St-Malo.

Continue along the picturesque coast road past the Baie du Guesclin and through the suburb of Rothéneuf ❼.

Rothéneuf is a pleasant suburb of St-Malo, next to a wide beach. Sights here include the coastal rocks carved by the Abbé Foure in the 19th century and the manor house lived in by the 16th-century explorer and discoverer of Canada, Jacques Cartier.

Pass through Paramé, and then along the waterfront and you reach the main gateway into St-Malo.

A path leads between tree-shaded lawns to a cross and beyond to a domed building near Cancale

OUT AND ABOUT

The dam across the Rance
estuary (above).
A cobbled street
in Dinan (right)

Dinan Castle (above)

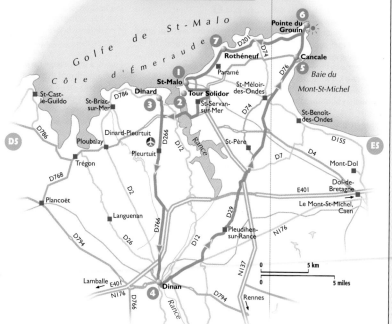

WHERE TO EAT

Chez La Mère Poucel
3 place des Merciers, Dinan
🍴 Lunch and dinner Mon–Sat, lunch
Sun; closed 4 weeks in Feb and Mar

BASICS

Maison du Gouverneur
Rue Petit Fort, Dinan
☎ 02 96 97 58 72
🕙 10–6.30, Jun–end Sep
🎫 Adult €1.60, child €0.80,
under 12 free

Cancale port (right)

VANNES TO THE LANDES DE LANVAUX

Morbihan is the most southerly *département* in Brittany, an area full of interesting towns, pretty villages and fine countryside. The region's most popular attraction is the Golfe du Morbihan and you can take a boat trip from Vannes to the small islands in the gulf. This drive heads inland, away from the gulf, to explore lesser-known places, slightly off the beaten track but well worth visiting.

THE DRIVE	
Length: 97km (60 miles)	
Allow: 1 day	
Start/End: Vannes	

Vannes ❶ is a medieval town still largely within its original fortified walls, which now overlook attractive public gardens. It is at the head of the Golfe du Morbihan and is the departure point for cruises and ferry boats visiting the islands out in the gulf, such as the picturesque Île-aux-Moines. The town was founded in the 9th century, but the walls were built much later. They completely surround the old quarter near the great Cathédrale St-Pierre, which contains the tomb of the mystic St. Vincent-Ferrier, who was born in Vannes and died there in 1419. One of the town's most popular sights is the Maison de Vannes with two grinning gargoyles known as 'Vannes and his wife'. If you're here on a Saturday, you can browse in the market in the heart of the town.

Leave Vannes on the main road east to join the dual carriageway (divided highway) ring road, the N165, before leaving it for the village of Theix ❷.

This pretty village has some interesting sights, including La Chapelle-de-la-Dame-Blanche, built in 1239 and one of the oldest chapels in the province. It has been restored several times. Nearby is the Château de Plessis-Josso, which dates from the 13th to the 18th centuries.

Pick up the D7, signed for le Gorvello and Questembert, and follow it to the market town of Questembert ❸.

A carved wooden figure on a building in Malestroit (right)

The great covered market hall here dates from the mid-16th century and is surrounded by a square with medieval houses.

From the middle of Questembert, follow the *Toutes Directions* signs onto the ring road, and then take the D777 for 10km (6 miles) to Rochefort-en-Terre ❹.

Pretty Rochefort-en-Terre is the capital of the moorlands of the Landes de Lanvaux. The town is on a ridge above the river Arz and most of it is medieval or dates from the 16th or 17th centuries. The church, Notre-Dame-de-la-Tronchaye, has an unusual gabled façade and a delicate three-tiered calvary standing outside. Aristocratic stone mansions, embellished with carvings and window boxes, line the main cobbled streets, and some have been turned into shops and restaurants catering for the village's many visitors.

From Rochefort-en-Terre stay on the D777 to St-Gravé, turning left 1km (0.6 miles) before the village of St-Gravé and head north to Malestroit ❺.

This small town stands between the winding river Oust and the moors of the Landes de Lanvaux. Its historic core is around place du Bouffay and the church of

St-Gilles. Look for the bizarre carvings on the houses here, such as a hare playing the bagpipes. A little to the west, in the village of St-Marcel, the Musée de la Résistance Bretonne tells the story of the Morbihan Maquis (French Resistance).

The road out of Malestroit, the D10, follows the river Oust for a short distance before veering off west towards Sérent ❻.

Sérent, a little village on the northern edge of the Landes de Lanvaux, has a number of fine houses and a church in the Flamboyant Gothic style. It's popular as a touring base for the moorlands and woods that lie to the south.

From Sérent take the D766 south to Elven ❼.

Elven has a church with a 16th-century choir, but the main attractions lie outside the town. To the north is the Château de Kerfily, in a park beside the Arz, while to the south is the Forteresse de Largoët.

After another 3km (2 miles), turn right to the Forteresse de Largoët ❽.

The castle, also called Tours d'Elven, is an impressive feudal ruin in extensive wooded parkland. In 1488 the castle was burned down by the king of France, Charles XIII, and now the ruins make an atmospheric setting for sound and light shows. With a height of 44m (145ft), the main tower, or *donjon,* of Largoët is the tallest medieval tower in France, with supporting walls 6–9m (20–30ft) thick.

Return to the main road, the N166, and continue back into Vannes.

Clothes and postcards outside shops in Vannes (above)

The Forteresse de Largoët (above)

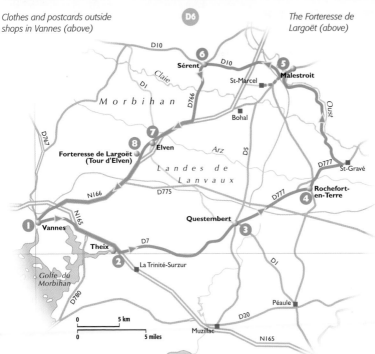

WHERE TO EAT

Le Canotier
Place du Docteur Queinnec, 56140 Malestroit
🕐 Lunch and dinner Tue–Sat Apr–end Aug; lunch only Tue–Sat, rest of year

Old houses in Vannes (left)

BASICS

Château de Plessis-Josso
☎ 02 97 43 16 16
🕐 2–6.30, mid-Jul to end Aug
🎟 Adult €5, child €3.50, under 7 free

Musée de la Résistance Bretonne
☎ 02 97 75 16 90
🕐 Daily 10–7 mid-Jun to mid-Sep; Wed–Mon 10–noon, 2–6, mid-Sep to end Mar
🎟 Adult €6, child (10–18) €4.30
www.resistance-bretonne.com

Tour du Connétable, Vannes (above)

OUT AND ABOUT

AROUND HUELGOAT

At the heart of inland Brittany, within the Parc Naturel Régional d'Armorique, Huelgoat is surrounded by magnificent countryside combining a lake, an unruly river and a forest scattered with rocks piled in curious formations. It is excellent hiking country and this walk takes you through many changes of scenery.

THE WALK

Length: 5km (3 miles)	
Allow: 2 hours	
Start: place Aristide Briand	
End: La Roche Cintrée	

HOW TO GET THERE

The village is 25km (15 miles) south of Morlaix and the N12 motorway, in the northwest corner of Brittany.

Huelgoat (meaning high forest) is beside a lake, and this position, together with the nearby wooded hills, makes it a popular summer resort and a base for activity holidays.

Start from place Aristide Briand ❶ at the heart of Huelgoat. Turn left at the northern end of the square, with the lake on your left. On the other side of the street, a well-marked path leads through the rocks.

The huge boulders are piled in a chaotic formation because of the consistency of the granite: Soft inclusions crumble, isolating harder minerals, which eventually collapse onto one another. A Breton legend has it that the inhabitants of two nearby villages, wanting to settle a quarrel, hurled the stones at each other.

Continue along the path.

Along the way you'll see the Chaos du Moulin and the Grotte du Diable ❷, where you can go down a ladder and watch the river foaming against the rocks. On the other side of the river, the Roche Tremblante ❸ is a single boulder, weighing an estimated 100 tonnes, which rocks slightly when pushed. A little farther on, the Ménage de la Vierge consists of several rocks looking vaguely like household utensils.

The pleasant allée Violette leads through the woods to the Pont Rouge and the D769A to Carhaix. Follow the road for approximately 100m (330ft) and turn right onto a path in the form of a horseshoe, called the Promenade du Fer à Cheval ❹. It dominates the Rivière d'Argent in a lovely setting before rejoining the road. Turn right and follow the road for another 300m (330 yards). A narrow staircase on the right goes down to Le Gouffre (the abyss) into which the river falls and disappears. Continue along the footpath past the Mare aux Fées (fairy pool), until you meet a gravel road where you should go right. Follow this road to the

old mine, where information plaques indicate that you've found the right place.

This is the site of an old silver mine ❺, although there's little to see other than an open clearing with a stream running through it.

Cross the stream and take the footpath up the hill following the signs *Huelgoat par la canal*. Halfway up the hill the route splits. Keep left and continue to the top where you'll find a small hydroelectric station at the head of the canal ❻.

The canal is more of a channel, at just 1m (3ft) wide. It was created to bring water to the silver mines, worked since Roman times but abandoned at the end of the 19th century.

The Promenade du Canal follows the canal back to town, about 3.5km (2 miles) away. Just before you arrive, on the left, a road leads to La Roche Cintrée ❼, with a good view of the town and the mountains.

Wild flowers by a forest track (below)

Walking through a towering rock formation (above)

Large boulders by the waterside (above)

A sign guides the way to Le Ménage de la Vierge (above)

WHERE TO EAT

Crêperie de l'Argoat
12 rue du Lac, 29690, Huelgoat
Wed–Sun 11–10, Mon 11–2 Apr–end Aug; Wed–Sun 11–8, Mon 11–2, rest of year

Walkers in Huelgoat forest (right)

THE SUISSE NORMANDE AND THE ORNE VALLEY

This tour takes in some of the high points of the Suisse Normande, a pretty, hilly region south of Caen and bounded by the river Orne. The river runs beside the road for much of your drive. The roads are narrow, single track in places, always winding and sometimes steep, so high speeds are not advisable. The route takes in attractive towns and villages and some good viewpoints.

THE DRIVE

Length: 110km (68 miles)
Allow: 1 day
Start/End at: Caen

Caen ❶ (see page 99) is the ancient capital of the Norman dukes and is full of interest. Sights include the castle, the Musée de la Paix and the two abbeys —the Abbaye-aux-Hommes, built by William the Conqueror and the Abbaye-aux-Dames, built by his wife Matilda.

Leave from below the castle, in the heart of town, and follow the *Toutes Directions* signs, then signs for Rennes-Granville as far as the racecourse at La Prairie. From there, pick up the D8, signed for Évrecy and Aunay-sur-Odon, and follow this road to Évrecy ❷, passing a small group of World War II memorials on the left.

The countryside around Caen is full of memorials to the bitter fighting of 1944. This one is dedicated to the men of the 43rd (Welsh) Division. There is a Churchill tank and a monument to Hill 112, declaring 'Whoever holds Hill 112 holds all of Normandy'.

Turn left at the church in Evrecy onto the D41. At Amayé-sur-Orne, turn right at the outskirts of the village onto the D212, signed for Thury-Harcourt. Turn left at the hamlet of Le Hom, crossing the river and an old railway track into the town of Thury-Harcourt ❸.

Thury-Harcourt is a market town and visitor base for the Suisse Normande and the Vallée de l'Orne. It is a pretty and prosperous town with a ruined moated chateau and a park. Two gatehouses, with strange beehive-shaped roofs, one wing and a bricked-up façade are all that can be seen of the chateau. A plaque on the park wall pays tribute to British forces.

Follow the D562 along the river for 13km (8 miles) then, at a large roadside cross, take the D133A down into the middle of Clécy ❹.

Clécy is set in one of the most attractive parts of the Orne Valley, at a point where the river is overlooked by high cliffs, and is popular as a base for walking and touring. It's a good place to stop for lunch and stroll around the town, admiring the fairy-tale architecture.

Parapenting in the Suisse Normande region

Follow signs to the Pont du Vey, passing Clécy's miniature railway museum. Don't cross the bridge, but admire the watermill on the other side.

There are fine views and walks along the Orne Valley ❺ from the Pont du Vey. The best way to see the river is from the footpath or the road that runs alongside it, overlooking the riverside hotels, the canoeists and the climbers who scramble on the cliffs by the old viaduct.

Follow the main road, signed for Le Lande, round past a little art gallery on your right and several riverside cafés and restaurants on your left. Drive through Le Bô and Cossesseville, with their charming churches. (These roads may be flooded in winter.) With the river on your right, continue along the D167 through Pont d'Ouilly. At Le Bateau take the D18E towards the parking and picnic area by the viaduct. At the end of the viaduct turn sharp right under the arches on the D18A, signed St-Philbert, continuing to the top of hill and the viewpoint ❻ at Roche d'Oëtre.

The viewpoint overlooks the river Rouvre. This 118m (387ft) precipice has no barrier, so observe the warning signs, be extra careful on wet or windy days, and keep control of small children.

Return the way you came, under the viaduct. Turn right back onto the D18 through Le Mesnil-Villemont. At the T-junction turn left onto the D511, then right onto the D43. It's then a left turn onto the D241 to Tréprel. Continue on the D241 through farming country north to Bonnoeil and Angoville, then left onto the D6 to Meslay. Turn right onto the D23 to Bretteville-sur-Laize. Cross the river Laize and turn left onto the D132, along the Laize Valley to the D562. Turn right here to return to Caen through small suburban towns.

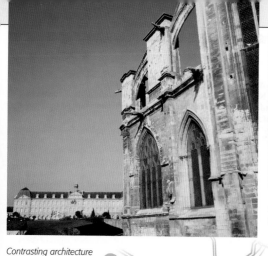

Contrasting architecture at Caen (above)

Rue du Vaugueux, in Caen's old town (above)

WHEN TO GO

Some roads on this tour may be flooded in winter.

WHERE TO EAT

Au Site Normand
1 rue des Châtelets, 14570, Clécy
☎ 02 31 69 71 05
🕐 Closed Nov–end Feb

Alternatively have a snack at one of the cafés by the Pont du Vey.

A scenic hillside in the Orne Valley (right)

Caen War Memorial (above)

GIVERNY

The delightful riverside village of Giverny (see page 106), spread across a hillside near Vernon, is the most visited place in Normandy. Crowds of art- and garden-lovers flock to see the home of Claude Monet and the world's most famous lily pond, immortalized in some of the artist's best known paintings.

THE WALK

Length: 9km (5.5 miles)
Allow: 2 hours 30 minutes
Start/end at: Fondation Claude Monet

HOW TO GET THERE

Giverny is near Vernon, off the D5, west of Paris (and possible as a day trip from the capital).

In 1883 Monet moved into a pastel-pink house with grass-green shutters in Giverny, where he had worked with Renoir, Sisley and Manet for a number of years. He designed the gardens himself and created his famous water garden with its lilies and Japanese bridge. The main garden, with its 12 resident gardeners, still keeps to Monet's design and is a palette of changing hues from spring to autumn. Near the house, Monet's enormous studio is filled with huge copies of his works. (For the real thing, visit the Musée Marmottan Monet in Paris, see page 84.)

Start outside the Fondation Claude Monet ❶, and head along rue Claude Monet, towards the Musée d'Art Américain. Take the lane to the right, called Chemin Blanche-Hoschéde, then go right again almost immediately up the narrow rue Hélène-Pillon, which curves left before becoming a dirt track. Follow this path along the backs of houses, running parallel to rue Claude Monet below, until you reach the end of the village. Turn left (signposted GR2 and marked with red-and-white paint markers) up a steep path, then turn right at the first intersection.

The path snakes across open meadowland towards the woods, with sweeping views over the Epte valley below.

At the next crossing of footpaths, go left and climb up through oak woods. At this point you leave the GR2 and the path is now marked in yellow. At the next crossroads, go right. At the edge of the woods, take the grassy path on the left, passing alongside pastureland then more woodland. As you reach the woods, turn right towards a small road.

Turn left onto the road, which runs steeply downhill. After 50m (55 yards), bear right, then right again along a track bordering the woods of La Réserve on the right, and flanked by fields on the left. When you come to a crossroads level with a small yellow house on the left, continue straight, then go left along the fringe of the Garenne woods.

Turn to the right in the woods (once again following the red-and-white signs of GR2). Soon you will come to a promontory marked by a large cross, with a magnificent view of the Seine.

Continue down a very steep, narrow path leading to the hamlet of Manitaux; it comes out on a small lane bordered by cottages. Turn left, following the course of a former railway track until you reach the edge of Giverny. Go along the grassy path behind the first houses in the village, until the path joins the Sente des Grosses Eaux and, soon afterwards, rue Claude Monet.

Back on the main street of the village, proceed past the church ❷, where Monet lies buried, and Hôtel Baudy ❸, the ancient boarding house and rendezvous of various painter friends of Monet, including Rodin, Sisley, Renoir, Cézanne, Pissarro and various visiting American artists. It was also the site of the first studio and the first art exhibitions in the village. Continue past the Musée d'Art Américain ❹, with its permanent collection of works by Monet's American contemporaries in France and many temporary exhibitions.

Continue along rue Claude Monet, filled with artists' workshops and galleries, before returning to Claude Monet's house and garden at the far end of the village.

Vivid flowers in Monet's garden (left)

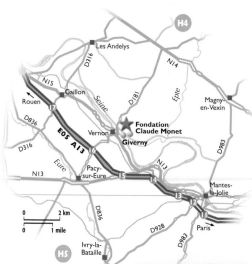

The Japanese bridge (above), immortalized in Monet's paintings

An arch of greenery in Monet's garden (below)

Monet's gardens are closed on Tuesdays and from November to the end of March.

Monet's house and gardens
See page 106.

Musée d'Art Américain
99 rue Claude Monet, 27620
☎ 02 32 51 94 65
🕒 Tue–Sun 10–6, Apr–end Oct
🎫 Adult €5.50, child (12–18) €3, under 12 free

THE EMERALD COAST

This drive takes in the fascinating Côte d'Émeraude, with its impressive cliffs, superb sandy beaches and the unforgettable Fort la Latte on a barren promontory. Inland, the Forêt de la Hunaudaye and the surrounding area provide an interesting contrast.

OUT AND ABOUT

THE DRIVE	
Distance: 92km (57 miles)	
Time: Half to a full day	
Start/end at: Lamballe	

❶ Lamballe, on a hillside beside a small river, is famous for its *haras national* (national stud farm), where you can take a guided tour. The Gothic Église Notre-Dame at the top of town has a finely carved rood screen and doorways.

Leave Lamballe eastwards by the D28, then bear right onto the D52A towards Plédéliac, 11km (7 miles) away. Turn left onto the D55 and drive for another 4km (2.5 miles), following the signs to Château de la Hunaudaye **❷**.

The Château de la Hunaudaye dates back to the 12th century. It was battered into its present ruins during the Revolution. The most impressive parts are the Tour de la Glacière, the Renaissance manor house and the 15th-century keep, with a remarkable spiral staircase.

Turn left and left again along the D28 and drive through the Forêt de la Hunaudaye to the hamlet of St-Aubin, 6km (4 miles). Follow the D52 and turn right. Follow the D13 and D43 for 24km (15 miles) through Hénanbihen and Pléboulle to the Baie de la Frénaye and Fort la Latte **❸**.

This medieval fortress perches on a rocky promontory and offers magnificent views of Cap Fréhel to the west and the Côte d'Émeraude to the east. Two drawbridges span the

deep cracks in the rock, filled by the sea at high tide. Inside, the oven heated cannonballs to set fire to enemy ships.

Drive round the Anse des Sévignés, 4km (2.5 miles), to Cap Fréhel (see page 100), then follow the D34 to Sables-d'Or-Les-Pins, 9km (5.5 miles). The scenic coast road winds through the wild Landes de Fréhel (Fréhel moors) to Pléhérel-Plage **❹**, with its beautiful beach.

Most people come to Sables-d'Or-les-Pins (see page 120) to walk on the long golden beach. Strong currents make it unsuitable for swimming.

Continue on the D34 and turn right onto the D786 towards Erquy **❺**, 8km (5 miles).

This resort and fishing port is sheltered by the cliffs of Cap d'Erquy, 3km (2 miles) to the north, and is worth the detour. There are impressive views of the wide bay of St-Brieuc as far as the Île de Bréhat.

Continue on the D786 towards Le Val-André for 5km (3 miles), past Château de Bienassis **❻** on your left.

This late-medieval castle was rebuilt in the 17th century and furnished in Louis XIV and Breton Renaissance styles.

Continue on the D786 for 6km (4 miles) to Le Val-André **❼**.

The beach at Le Val-André is one of Brittany's finest. A road running around the promontory has lovely views of the beach and of the Île du Verdelet, a bird sanctuary accessible at low tide.

Follow the D34 to Planguenoual, then the D59 back to Lamballe.

Lighthouse at Cap Fréhel

The view from Cap Fréhel
(above).
Erquy (right)

Fort la Latte (above)

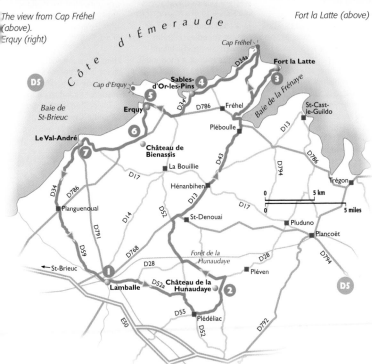

Côte d'Émeraude

Cap Fréhel

Fort la Latte

D5

Cap d'Erquy

Sables-
d'Or-les-Pins

4

3

Baie de la Frénaye

St-Cast-
le-Guildo

5

Erquy

D786

Fréhel

Baie de
St-Brieuc

6

Pléboulle

D13

St-Cast-
le-Guildo

Le Val-André

7

Château de
Bienassis

D43

D786

Trégon

D17

La Bouillie

D34

D786

Hénanbihen

D13

D794

D14

D52

St-Denoual

Pluduno

Plancoët

Planguenoual

D791

D768

Forêt de la
Hunaudaye

D28

Pléven

D794

D59

St-Brieuc

1

D28

0   5 km

Lamballe

D52a

Château de la
Hunaudaye

2

0   5 miles

D55

Plédéliac

D792

E50

D52

D5

OUT AND ABOUT

WHEN TO GO

The Château de la Hunaudaye
and Château de Bienassis are
open in peak season only (see
opening times, right).

WHERE TO EAT

Beauséjour
21 rue de la Corniche, Erquy
◉ Closed from Christmas to mid-Jan
and mid-Feb

BASICS

Château de la Hunaudaye
◉ Daily 11–6.30 (Sat pm only), Jul,
Aug

Château de Bienassis
◉ Daily 10.30–12.30, 2–6.30, mid-Jun
to mid-Sep

A stretch of sandy beach at
Sables-d'Or-les-Pins

ÉTRETAT WALK

The Côte d'Albâtre stretches 100km (60 miles) from Dieppe to Étretat and beyond. It is a formation of imposing white cliffs that seem to mirror the white cliffs of Dover across the Channel. At Étretat the seascape is at its most spectacular, with sheer cliffs pierced by massive arches and a solitary needle rock soaring to 70m (230ft) a little way offshore. This coastal walk can be rough in places (wear sturdy, non-slip shoes or walking boots), but the breathtaking panoramas make it worthwhile.

THE WALK

Length:	6.5km (4 miles)
Allow:	2 hours 30 minutes
Start/end at:	Étretat

HOW TO GET THERE

Étretat is on the Côte d'Albâtre, between Le Havre and Fécamp.

A modest fishing village for most of its history, Étretat **1** lay in obscurity until the mid-19th century when the writers Guy de Maupassant and Alexandre Dumas discovered the delights of the pebbled beach enveloped by the cliffs, and the great artists of the day began to paint the scene. Fashionable visitors began to arrive from Paris and elsewhere, lured by the views reproduced by Boudin, Delacroix and Monet. In town, visit place du Maréchal Foch, with its wooden covered market built in 1926 amid a cluster of charming 16th-century town houses. For golfers, the 18-hole clifftop course is France's highest golf links, with views guaranteed to put you off your stroke.

Start on the promenade. Walk to the eastern end, then turn right, up a flight of 83 brick steps that opens out onto a grassy clifftop pathway, past a children's theme park and up to the top of the Porte (or Falaise) d'Amont **2** and the Chapelle Notre-Dame-de-la-Garde.

Chapelle Notre-Dame-de-la-Garde

On the Falaise d'Amont, stop by the sailors' chapel and admire the views of the western Falaise d'Aval across the beach, with a 70m (230ft) rock stack known as the Aiguille (needle) d'Étretat standing alongside. Inland from the chapel, a monument commemorates the lost aviators Nungesser and Coli, whose plane *L'Oiseau Blanc* was last seen flying over these cliffs in 1927 on its ill-fated bid to fly from Paris to New York. The aviators were presumed drowned in the Atlantic and their bodies were never recovered.

Continue along the cliff edge, past the chapel and go down some steps leading to the arch of Amont. A steep, slippery and narrow pathway, cut into the chalky stack, offers wonderful views of the alabaster cliffs to the east. A wooden handrail and a ladder assist in the final descent to a small beach. Retrace your steps, past the chapel and back down the brick steps. Proceed along the promenade, an unbroken curve of café-lined concrete above the steep shingle beach. At the far end, another flight of steps, followed by a steep, well-trodden, flint-filled path, leads up beside a scenic golf course to Porte d'Aval. Bear right along the cliff edge, crossing a narrow bridge and onto the top of the cliff arch **3** —not for those with a fear of heights!

Here, there are spectacular views over Étretat's slate roofs and to the Porte d'Amont beyond. Legend has it that many centuries ago three beautiful sisters were imprisoned by an evil lord in a cave at the foot of these cliffs.

Continue along the windswept cliff edge, admiring the wild flowers, yellow gorse and purple sea cabbage, and on to a second arch, La Manne-Porte, with breathtaking views stretching as far as the port of Le Havre-Antifer. Just beyond the next headland, Pointe de la Courtine, follow a track inland (the GR21, marked with a red-and-white stripe), branching left, where two paths meet, to Valaine. At the next intersection, leave the GR21 and head straight on down a narrow country lane, through the attractive brick and stone farm buildings of Ferme le Valaine **4**.

On the left, the lovely old farmhouse sells delicious home-produced cider, Calvados and goat's cheese.

Follow the road as it winds gently downhill, past grazing goats, until you reach the D940. Turn left back into the middle of Étretat and left again back to the waterfront.

OUT AND ABOUT

The Falaise d'Aval chalk cliff (above).
A view from the cliff to Étretat (below)

A local brasserie (right)

WHEN TO GO

Check weather reports before starting the cliff walk, as the wind may be strong and the steps slippery. Hardy visitors might like to join the locals for the traditional New Year's Day swim!

WHERE TO EAT

Eat in Étretat or at the clifftop Dormy-House, at the end of the walk.

Dormy-House
Route du Havre
☎ 02 35 27 07 88
www.dormy-house.com

BASICS

Tourist information
place Maurice Guillard, 76790, Étretat
☎ 02 35 27 05 21
🕐 10–7, mid-Jun to mid-Sep; 10–noon, 2–6, mid-Mar to mid-Jun, mid-Sep to mid-Nov and French school hols; Fri–Sat 10–noon, 2–6, rest of year
www.etretat.net

ABBEVILLE AND LE TOUQUET

This tour explores the area between the rivers Somme and Canche, which includes the marshlands of the Bay of the Somme, the river valleys of the Authie and the Canche, undulating farmland pleasantly broken by woodland, and the natural forest of Crécy. It follows a route rich in history, from William the Conqueror to World War II, and along the way are great churches and abbeys, fortifications, seaports, resorts and villages.

THE DRIVE

Length: 150km (93 miles)

Allow: 1 day

Start/end at: Abbeville

In Abbeville ❶ the great 15th-century Cathédrale St-Vulfran, has a Flamboyant Gothic façade. Houses dating from the Middle Ages to the 18th century add character, and just outside town is the miniature Château de Bagatelle.

From the middle of town, follow the D925 towards Eu and Dieppe as far as Cambron. Turn right here onto the D3, a pretty, tree-lined road which winds its way alongside the canalized Somme. At a major roundabout (traffic circle) go straight on into St-Valéry-sur-Somme ❷.

This picturesque port is at the mouth of the River Somme. Fishing boats and yachts still fill the wharfs and fin-de-siècle villas overlook the beaches. The old town, with its narrow streets, is contained within ancient fortified walls.

Return along the D3, and at the roundabout turn left onto the D940. Cross the Somme and follow the road as it curves around the bay. To the right is Noyelles-sur-Mer. At a small roundabout take the third exit on the D144 into Le Crotoy ❸.

Le Crotoy is an old-fashioned fishing village and resort surrounded by acres of salt marsh populated by wild birds and *pré-salé* sheep. It's renowned for its seafood and its literary and artistic associations.

Leave by the same route, back on the D940, following signs to Rue and Berck. Turn right off the main road to enter Rue ❹.

In the Middle Ages, Rue was a seaport but it now lies well inland. It has the 15th- and 16th-century Chapelle du St-Esprit, a masterpiece of decorative Flamboyant Gothic architecture. Nearby are timber-framed buildings and the massive medieval bell tower.

To the left of the main road you'll see a turning to the Parc Ornithologique du Marquenterre ❺, on the D4.

The Bay of the Somme is one of the best sites in Europe for seabirds and migratory species, and a good place to spend a day birdwatching is the Parc Ornithologique du Marquenterre, a huge reserve with parking, a restaurant and places to picnic.

Continue along the D940 to Waben, then turn left towards Berck and Le Touquet, still on the D940. Follow this road past Berck, the Bagatelle Parc d'Attractions and various other resorts. At a roundabout (traffic circle) take the third exit onto the D144 into Le Touquet ❻.

Built by the English as a smart resort at the end of the 19th century, and a famous social venue between the world wars, Le Touquet still has plenty of period charm, with its streets of art nouveau seaside villas, grand church, covered market and smart restaurants.

Leave Le Touquet by the N39, cross the Canche and enter Étaples. (Turn left onto the D940 for the military cemetery). Turn right onto the N39 to follow the Canche towards Montreuil. At the junction with the N1, turn right for Montreuil ❼.

A half-timbered building at Le Crotoy

Montreuil is an inland, walled, hilltop town, which was a busy port in the Middle Ages. It has winding cobbled streets lined with 17th- and 18th-century houses, fine squares, an old citadel surrounded by ramparts and an abbey church.

From Montreuil, take the N39 Hesdin road along the southern side of the Canche valley and after 10km (6 miles) turn right onto a minor road towards Campagne-lès-Hesdin. Follow this past Campagne to Maintenay on the D130 and the D139. In the village turn right, pass the town hall, and then turn left at a roundabout (traffic circle). Cross the river Authie by a lovely mill, then turn left to Valloires ❽.

The Abbaye de Valloires stands in a beautiful wooded setting in the Authie valley. The 18th-century buildings, in soft-pastel stone, are surrounded by attractive gardens. Founded in the 11th century, the abbey was a burial place for many of the French knights killed at Crécy in the Hundred Years War.

From the abbey, follow the river valley on the D192 and the D224 to Argoules, Dominois, Estruval, Ponches-Estruval and Dompierre-sur-Authie. Turn right onto the D111 at Dompierre-sur-Authie towards Crécy-en-Ponthieu. Just before Crécy is the site of the battle. Go straight through Crécy, and then

*Abbaye de Valloires (above).
Cobbles in the Vieux Ville of
St-Valéry-sur-Somme
(above right)*

Château de Bagatelle (above)

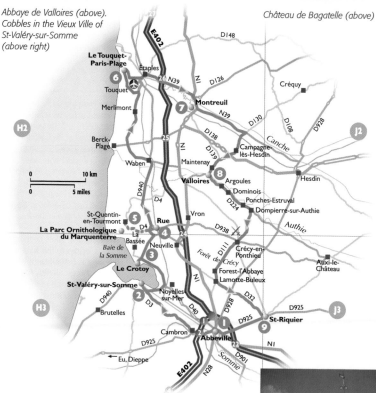

Clock at Abbeville station (right)

continue through the forest to
Forest-l'Abbaye. In Forest-
l'Abbaye bear left to Lamotte-
Buleux and then turn left onto
the D32 towards St-Riquier **9**.

On the side of a steep hill,
St-Riquier is an attractive small
town with a Benedictine abbey
at the end of a little square.

Follow the D925 back to
Abbeville.

WHERE TO EAT

There are plenty of restaurants
and cafés in Le Touquet.

BASICS

**Parc Ornithologique du
Marquenterre**
80120, St-Quentin-en-Tourmont
☎ 03 22 25 68 99
⏲ Daily 10–7.30, Apr to mid-Nov

Bagatelle Parc d'Attractions
62155, Merlimont
☎ 03 21 89 09 91
⏲ Daily 10–7, Jul, Aug; 10–6.30,
Mar–end Jun and Sep
www.bagatelle.fr
A theme park with 26 hectares
(64 acres) of attractions, mostly
white-knuckle rides.

Tourist information
1 place de l'Amiral Courbet, 80100
Abbeville
☎ 03 22 24 27 92
www.ville-abbeville.fr

FORÊT DE GÉRARDMER

Gérardmer, the pearl of the Vosges, has long attracted visitors to the shores of its magnificent lakes—Lac de Longemer, Lac de Retournemer and Lac de Blanchemer—framed by gently domed summits and pine forests crossed by numerous walking paths. This tour takes in a reminder of Charlemagne, an alpine garden, waterfalls, forests and a spectacular view of the highest mountain in the Vosges.

THE DRIVE

Length: 120km (75 miles)
Allow: 1 day
Start/end at: Gérardmer

The lakeside town of Gérardmer ❶, at an altitude of 660m (2,165ft), is in the heart of the massive Parc Naturel Régional des Ballons des Vosges (*ballons* being the rounded summits of the mountain ridge).

From Gérardmer follow the D417 towards Colmar. After only 2km (about a mile) you pass the Hôtel de la Pierre Charlemagne (Chez Dédé) on the right, and a parking area on the left signed La Cercenée, just before the roundabout (traffic circle) where the D8 from St-Dié joins the D417. Go all the way round the roundabout and back towards Gérardmer for 25m (27 yards) before swinging right into La Cercenée parking area (the entrance, at the roundabout end, and the exit, at the Gérardmer end, form a one-way system). Cross the D417 on the pedestrian crossing to find the Saut des Cuves ❷.

Here a footbridge gives you great views of the cascading waters through rocks and spruce trees. Children should be carefully watched as there are no safety barriers along the ravine edges.

Retrace your steps to the parking area, and follow the green rectangle signs on the GR533 footpath for five minutes to Charlemagne's Stone (the great

9th-century ruler hunted and fished in the area) and on to the Pont des Fées (10 minutes), an 18th-century bridge spanning the Vologne. The path carries on to the Îles Marie-Louise (15 minutes) and the Gorge des Poitelets (25 minutes). Information panels in the parking area give details of all the walks possible from here, including, for the determined, a 39-hour route to Sarrebourg. At the parking area exit, turn right towards Gérardmer and immediately left alongside the Hôtel de la Pierre Charlemagne onto the C12 Route du Saut des Cuves, towards Xonrupt-Longemer. Pass through the village, joining the D67A towards Longemer ❸.

Lac de Longemer and the smaller Lac de Retournemer, farther along the D67, are two beautiful lakes, relics from the Ice Age. They are surrounded by meadows and forests of firs and spruce trees and are dominated by the Schlucht and Hohneck mountains. There is a large caravan and camper park on the southern shore of Longemer. Just before the Lac de Retournemer comes into sight, a short but steep climb from a path on the left (nearly opposite the well-concealed Retournemer tunnel) up the Roche du Diable offers a wonderful view over the valley of the Vologne.

At the junction with the D34D, turn left to rejoin the D417 at the Col de la Schlucht, a pass linking the Vosges to nearby Alsace. Turn right off the D417 along the D430 towards the high altitude Jardin d'Altitude du Haut-Chitelet, which contains more than 2,500 plant species from mountain areas around the world (*open in high season only*). Follow the Route

des Crêtes (D430), a strategic road built during World War I to link Le Hohneck and Le Grand Ballon mountains.

Le Hohneck ❹, at 1,362m (4,467ft), is one of the most spectacular sights of this mountain ridge.

Continue along the D430 past the lovely Lac de Blanchemer to le Markstein, a winter sports resort. Here the D430 bears left towards the Lac de la Lauch and Lautenbach, and the starting point of the Lac du Ballon walk (see pages 296–297). After enjoying the two-hour walk, return to le Markstein to continue the tour along the Route des Crêtes, which now follows the D431 to Le Grand Ballon ❺, the highest mountain in the Vosges.

The view over lakes nestling in valleys, across to the Jura and the Alps, is magnificent on a clear day. Slightly below the summit of the road, the Diables Bleus (Blue Devils) monument indicates that this area saw fierce fighting during World War I. Farther along, Le Vieil Armand was another major battle front, where fighting cost 30,000 lives.

Continue to Cernay, then follow the N66 along the Thur Valley to Bussang ❻.

Bussang, one of the highest villages in the Vosges, is famed for the Théâtre du Peuple (People's Theatre), an experiment started in 1895 by Maurice Pottecher. His descendants have upheld the tradition, drawing crowds every summer to the theatre surrounded by forest.

Continue in the same direction on the N66 and at Le Thillot, a former mining area, take the D486 to return to Gérardmer.

OUT AND ABOUT

Enjoying a lakeside walk (above)

Mist over a forest in the Vosges (left)

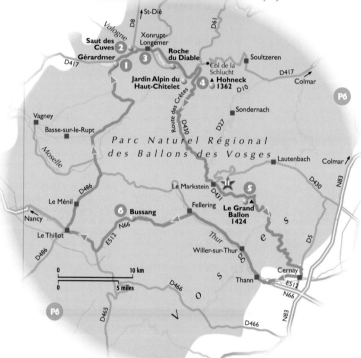

St-Dié

Vologne

D8

Xonrupt-Longemer

D61

Saut des Cuves ②

Gérardmer ③

Roche du Diable

D417

Jardin Alpin du Haut-Chitelet

Col de la Schlucht

Hohneck 1362 ④

D10

Soultzeren

D417

Colmar

P6

Vagney

Basse-sur-le-Rupt

Route des Crêtes

D430

D27

Sondernach

Moselle

Parc Naturel Régional des Ballons des Vosges

Lautenbach

Colmar

D430

N83

D486

Le Markstein

D431

Le Grand Ballon 1424 ⑤

Le Ménil

Bussang ⑥

Fellering

V o s g e s

D5

Nancy

E512

N66

Thur

Le Thillot

Willer-sur-Thur

Cernay

D486

0   10 km
0   5 miles

D465

D466

Thann

E512

N66

N83

P6

D466

OUT AND ABOUT

WHEN TO GO

This tour can be done at most times of year, although there is likely to be snow and ice on the Route des Crêtes in winter. The route is extremely popular, so expect heavy traffic between April and October.

WHERE TO EAT

There are innumerable picturesque places for a picnic, but finding solitude, even in these vast open spaces, can be difficult. The Route des Crêtes, with excellent views along most of its length, has eateries of all sizes, to suit all wallets, and parking is generally plentiful.

Yachts on a Vosges lake

FORÊT DE GÉRARDMER 295

LAC DU BALLON

This forest trail, rocky and wild but well marked, leads to a trout-filled lake beneath the summit of le Grand Ballon, at 1,424m (4,671ft) the highest peak in the Vosges.

THE WALK

Length: 7km (4 miles)

Allow: 2 hours

Start/end at: approximately 10km (6 miles) from le Markstein on the D430

HOW TO GET THERE

This walk is in the Vosges, close to the border with Germany. The directions below describe how to get to the start point by car, driving from Le Markstein, southeast of Gérardmer (see page 294).

From le Markstein, drive along the D430 towards Lautenbach—the road descends steeply through thickly wooded hills, passing the Lac de la Lauch on the right. After about 8km (5 miles), look for a circular road sign about 500m (550 yards) farther on the right, showing a white bicycle on a blue background and the words *Lautenbach 6.5 km*. Almost concealed behind this sign is a single-track road which double-backs below the D430 for several metres. As you turn right, two more signs become visible. One reads *La Rolle* and *Lac du Ballon*, the second, with white lettering on a brown background, indicates *Route Forestière Privée de la Rolle*.

Follow the minor road uphill for 5–7 minutes, watching for a right-hand bend which reveals an orange cross-country skiing sign on the right, with parking space also on the right. The ski sign indicates *Dauvillers 4.7km* (you'll return by this track). Across the road is a path sign with a red circle on a white background, and pinned to a tree is a small white rectangle with *64B* in black. Start the walk here, dropping below the level of the road.

In the Vosges ❶, expect to have to climb. The path is marked, although it is best to have a map with you.

Cross a stream soon and follow the arrow and the red-white-red marker pointing to the right, which indicates the way to the Cascades du Seebach and Lac du Ballon. It is uphill all the way to the lake from now on. Clear markers and directional arrows help along a very overgrown path, which could be slippery in wet weather. Continue up, and as you approach the falls, ensure you spot the correct path, which rises steeply in a zigzag on the

right. If you find yourself next to the falls, you have missed the path and should retrace your steps to find it. (If you don't, you will be faced with a hazardous climb among wet rocks up the right-hand side of the falls.)

The Cascades du Seebach ❷ are a slide of convoluted rocks, with little water in a dry season, but with a restraining metal barrier to stop the foolhardy risking their lives.

As the path continues, there is a wooden walkway which is now rotten. A short distance farther on, however, the log footbridge across the main watercourse is in excellent condition. Carry on along a path up to the right which leads through woods to a few rocks arranged as steps leading up onto a broad forestry road. Turn right where a sign indicates *Lac du Ballon*. Go up this broad forestry road and as you leave the forest there is a splendid view of Grand Ballon and its hotel ahead. Take the next

The monument to the Diables Bleus on Grand Ballon (below)

A wintry Lac du Ballon

There are plenty of waterfalls in this area

fork left, marked with a red-white-red sign, which leads to steps up on to the dam wall and Lac du Ballon ❸.

The lake lies in a small glacial hollow surrounded by pine forest. Every now and then, its mirror-like calm is ruffled by leaping trout breaking the surface. As they do so, they shatter the perfect image in the lake's waters of the wooded slopes of Le Grand Ballon looming above. A walk around the lake on the sandy shingle beach takes about 20 minutes.

Cross the dam wall, past a parking area, and turn sharp right, along a road signposted *Mordfeld* and *Lac de la Lauch*. The way is marked with both a red-white-red rectangle and a blue Latin cross on a white background. At the top of a rise, follow the Lac de la Lauch route ahead. At the next clearing, leave the blue-cross sign and double-back to the right, along a ski track marked with an orange sign and signposted *Lac de la Lauch 6km*. A stream chatters along beside you in the forest to your left. A short way down this slope, the path turns sharply back on itself to the left. Soon after, the path turns right and crosses the

stream. Follow a forestry road to continue gently downhill. At a T-junction, turn right along another forestry road, which leads straight back to the start.

WHEN TO GO

This walk is best tackled between late spring and early autumn, during a dry spell, as it can be fairly muddy and slippery after rain.

WHERE TO EAT

There are no refreshments available en route, so stock up before you go. On hot days make sure you take enough water with you. The shores of Lac du Ballon provide pleasant picnic spots.

A scenic stream (above) and the Vallée du Lacs (below)

ASPECTS OF THE SOMME

This walk explores the Somme—its landscape and architecture, and the memorials of World War I. It crosses rolling agricultural plains before descending into the wooded river valley. The field tracks can be muddy in wet weather so wear suitable shoes or walking boots.

THE WALK

Length: 8km (5 miles)

Allow: 2 hours

Start/end at: Fouilloy, near Corbie

HOW TO GET THERE

Fouilloy is on the Somme, just east of Amiens. Park in the middle of the town square.

The small town of Fouilloy is virtually a suburb of Corbie. In the middle is an unusual church built in 1958, which has a façade decorated with a series of modernist sculptures depicting the life of St. Martin.

Start from place de la République ❶, behind the church. Cross the main road and walk up rue Thiers, opposite the large Capsom concrete granary. Pass the school and at the end of the road turn right. At the main road, the D23, turn left. At the first fork after about 90m (100 yards), bear left, keeping a large garage and truck parking area on the right, and walk up the hill away from the town towards the tower of the Australian National War Memorial.

Abbaye St-Pierre, Corbie

The tall white tower of the Australian National War Memorial ❷ dominates the valley of the Somme for miles. The memorial is high above the Somme, where the Australians, at great cost, halted the German break-through of the spring of 1918. Designed by Sir Edwin Lutyens, the memorial incorporates many of his preferred motifs, such as classical entrance pavilions and furled flags in cut stone.

The road quickly becomes a track, which leads up the side of the hill to pass well to the left of the tower. Look back for fine views of the Somme valley and Corbie ❸.

A busy town beside the canalized Somme, Corbie is best known for its abbey. This was founded in 657 and housed 300 monks at the time of Charlemagne. It flourished until the Revolution, when much of it was destroyed. What remains is the 16th-century abbey church, an impressively solid building in the heart of town.

At the first intersection, turn right along a track that runs beside the memorial's boundary fence, and follow this until it meets the road. From the memorial, turn right along the road, the D23 again, and immediately turn left along a track that goes straight across the fields. There are good views back to the memorial and across to the church of Villers-Bretonneux.

Where the track meets a road (the D168e), turn left down the hill to the crossroads and then turn right. Take the first track on the left, clearly visible from the crossroads, and follow this until it meets another track. Turn right. This is something of a dog-leg, but it avoids the road. Keep on this track across the fields, dropping steadily down into the valley. Eventually the track joins the road. Bear left along the road, which is quite busy.

Cross the D1 to go straight into Aubigny, taking the pink gravel footpath, passing on the left a small military cemetery holding mostly Australian soldiers killed in the spring of 1918.

Continue to the middle of the village, where there are public lavatories and benches by a bus shelter. Turn right by a large crucifix, along rue de l'Abbaye. This leads down to the canalized Somme. Turn right along the towpath and follow it past the poplars back to Fouilloy. Stay beside the river until the path meets rue Émile Zola. This street is not signed where it meets the footpath, but can be recognized by a white house with a double garage. Turn right immediately before the house, or take the direction *Circuit du Bois l'Abbé (20m),* marked by a wooden post just before the turning. This leads back into place de la République.

OUT AND ABOUT

The Australian National War Memorial (above)

Graves at the Australian National Cemetery (right)

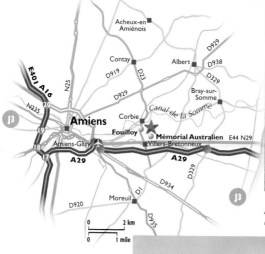

Aubigny countryside (above and below)

OUT AND ABOUT

WHERE TO EAT

There are no places to eat en route. The café-bar *Le Legend,* in place de la République, Fouilloy, serves drinks but no food.

BASICS

Tourist information
30 place de la République, 80800 Corbie
☎ 03 22 96 95 76
www.bocage3vallees.com

CHAMPAGNE

This tour, following the Champagne Route through the Montagne de Reims, takes you to scenic villages where you can learn about the art of champagne-making from local growers and merchants. It takes in a fantastic beech forest and includes a visit to the champagne capital, Reims (see pages 138–139).

THE DRIVE

Length: 119km (74 miles)	
Allow: Half a day	
Start/end at: Reims	

The chalky rock on which Reims stands is riddled with miles of caves that provide ideal conditions for the production and storage of champagne. Although it was known as a wine as early as Roman times, it took a 17th-century Benedictine monk, Dom Perignon of Hautvillers, to invent the process that gives champagne its unique sparkle. Cellars in Reims rank among the most impressive of the champagne producers, and you can visit *caves* of such famous names as Veuve-Cliquot, Pommery and Moët et Chandon for tastings.

From Reims, follow the D980 southwest and turn left onto the D26 at the turning for Jouy-lès-Reims towards Chamery ❶, a *premier cru* vineyard dominated by a 12th-century church.

This type of scenery is typical of the Montagne de Reims

Harvesting grapes

region, a plateau of forests and tidy vineyards planted with Chardonnay, Pinot Noir and Meunier grapes. The chalky soil acts as a natural regulator, providing the vines with the required amount of humidity and warmth.

Continue to Rilly-la-Montagne ❷, an attractive town on the edge of the forest.

Its church has beautiful 16th-century choir stalls carved with vine motifs. For a panoramic view over Reims and the surrounding vines, hamlets and Romanesque churches, climb to the top of Mont Joli (274m/900ft).

The D26 then winds along to Mailly-Champagne where, in 1931, 23 vine growers formed a co-operative to counteract the monopoly and power of wine merchants. Verzenay ❸, farther on, has more than 500 hectares (1,200 acres) of *premier cru* Pinot Noir grapes.

Le Phare de Verzenay lighthouse contains the Musée de la Vigne (see page 301). Nearby, Mont Sinaï, the highest point of the Montagne de Reims, (283m/928ft), offers another magnificent view over the vineyards. Farther along, the outskirts of Verzy ❹ are noted for a forest of strangely knotted beech trees, known as the Faux de Verzy, some of

which are more than 500 years old. Their contortions, once believed to stem from a divine curse, are now attributed to a genetic mutation.

The D26 continues through the picturesque village of Ambonnay. Take the D19 to Bouzy, which produces a light red wine, then the D34 to Louvois, where Louis XIV had a chateau built by his architect J. H. Mansart, with gardens by Le Nôtre. Take the D9 (the second exit at the roundabout) in the direction of Avenay-Val-d'Or. Go right on the D201 to Fontaine-sur-Ay, one of the prettiest villages in the region. Farther along is Ay, a town once surrounded by ramparts. Follow the road in the direction of Cumières, and turn right onto the D386 towards Hautvillers ❺, which overlooks the Marne river.

After walking up the steep, narrow streets of this picture-postcard village, with its wrought-iron signs illustrated with champagne motifs, you can visit the former Benedictine abbey. This was where Dom Perignon conducted his experiments with double fermentation and wine blending to obtain sparkling champagne. The property now belongs to a champagne house, which has reconstructed the cellar master's workshop.

Return to the D1, which runs along the Marne River to Damery and Châtillon-sur-Marne, the latter dominated by a colossal statue of Urban II, the 11th-century pope from Champagne who launched the First Crusade. The Marne also evokes an episode from World War I, when 4,000 troops were driven up to the front in 600 Parisian taxis in 1914 to stop the German advance. From Verneuil, follow the D980 back to Reims.

OUT AND ABOUT

A windmill at Verzenay (above). Countryside near Reims (above right)

Vineyards near Épernay, south of Reims

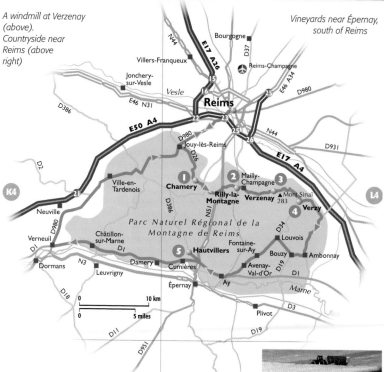

Working in a field (above)

Restaurant de l'Abbaye
Rue de l'Église, 51160, Hautvillers
☎ 03 26 59 44 79
⏰ Closed Mon, Tue, Sun dinner
The restaurant of Hautvillers Abbey serves local and regional cuisine and has an open-air terrace.

Tourist information
2 rue Guillaume de Machault, 51100 Reims
☎ 03 26 77 45 25
⏰ Mon–Sat 9–7, Sun 10–6, mid-Apr to mid-Oct; Mon–Sat 9–6, Sun 11–5, rest of year
www.tourisme.fr/reims

Musée de la Vigne
Le Phare de Verzenay, off D26 road
☎ 03 26 07 87 87
⏰ Mon–Fri 10–5.30, Sat, Sun and public hols 10–6, Apr to end-Oct; Tue–Sun 10–5.30, Nov, Dec and mid-Jan to Mar
💶 Adult €6, child (10–18) €3
www.lepharedeverzenay.com
Constructed in 1909 by wine-merchant Joseph Goulet for advertising purposes, the lighthouse now contains a museum of viticulture.

Countryside in the Montagne de Reims region (right)

LANGEAIS

This short walk is a pleasant tour of Langeais and the valley of the river Roumer. The route follows minor roads, tracks and footpaths and the going is easy, although there is some gentle hill climbing.

THE WALK

Length: 2.5km (1.5 miles)
Allow: 1 hour
Start/end at: Château de Langeais

HOW TO GET THERE

Langeais is a small town on the north bank of the Loire, about 22km (13.5 miles) west of Tours on the N152.

Best approached from the south, across the huge Gothic-style suspension bridge, Langeais ❶ is a compact town, which is undergoing renovation work to its roads, walkways and parking areas. The Château de Langeais ❷, right in the heart of town, has a rather severe appearance and, unusually for a Loire chateau, was built in just four years, at the end of the 15th century. It's on the site of an earlier fortress (the ruined keep is one of the oldest in France) and is where Charles VIII of France and Anne de Bretagne were married in 1491.

Start from the chateau. Cross the river Roumer and walk up rue Charles VIII to the church. Pass the church and climb a flight of steps. At the top, turn right and after 50m (55 yards) turn left up another flight, the Chemin du Paradis. At the top, carry straight on into the park, and turn left in the middle. There is no clear path—just head across the grass among the trees to the park's western perimeter. Turn left

and walk down towards the cemetery. At the cemetery gates, turn right along the road. At the crossroads, go straight on along a lane marked ominously *Mortvousêtes* ('You are dead'), which runs along the side of a hill.

There are troglodyte ❸ houses and pleasant views over the river valley, with its allotments and gardens and the church of St-Laurent.

Follow the lane as it drops down to the D57. Cross the main road, the D57, and follow a lane, the Chemin de la Raguenière, that runs parallel to the Roumer. At the first intersection, turn left along a sandy track. Cross the river and continue to the stone bridge. Turn left at the bridge along a lane and then take the first right, la Cueille aux Prêtres. This climbs steeply uphill towards the woods, running beside the stone wall that marks the boundary of the chateau park. Continue to the top, past a radio mast on the right, where there is an intersection backed by a screen of pine woods. Turn left and follow the path as it winds down through the woods, taking care not to slip if it is wet.

At the next intersection, there is a short detour to the right, down a steep path between stone walls. Here there is a fine view ❹ of the suspension bridge and the Loire.

The main path carries straight on, with more views of the Loire through the trees, and then ends at the top of some steps. Turn right down these, and follow the path as it winds down among the troglodyte houses to join the main road, rue Anne de Bretagne. Turn left to return to the Château de Langeais.

Waxwork figures at the Château de Langeais

OUT AND ABOUT

Café tables outside the Château de Langeais (above)

Formal gardens at the chateau (above)

A carved door to the Salle du Mariage, at the chateau (above)

If you've had enough of castles, go fishing on the Loire (below)

OUT AND ABOUT

WHEN TO GO

This walk can be done at any time of year. Autumn is good for the vibrant hue of the trees, but be careful of wet leaves, which may make paths slippery.

WHERE TO EAT

There are places to eat and drink in Langeais. The walk is not long, but consider taking a drink with you, particularly if it is hot.

BASICS

Château de Langeais
Fondation Jacques Siegfried, 37130
☎ 02 47 96 72 60
🕐 Daily 9.30–6.30, Apr to mid-Oct; 9.30–8, mid-Jul to mid-Aug; 10–5.30, rest of year
🎫 Adult €6.50, child (6–18) €4

VALLEY OF THE LOIR

The Loir is one of the least known yet most attractive of the Loire's tributaries. It winds its way through woods and quiet, undulating farmland, overlooked by ruined castles and picturesque towns and villages famous for their troglodyte houses carved out of the rocky cliffs. Leaving the Loir valley, with its associations with the poet Ronsard, the tour also explores the rich arable plains of the Gâtine Vendômois.

THE DRIVE

Length: 112km (70 miles)	
Allow: 1 day	
Start/end at: Vendôme	

Renowned for good food and wine, Vendôme ❶ is a delightful town, spread over the several branches of the Loir. Its streets have bridges, attractive vistas and old buildings, and high on a hill is the huge ruined chateau.

Start the tour at a small roundabout (traffic circle) on the north bank of the northernmost branch of the Loir, on the D957. With the river on your left, follow signs for Le Mans and Montoire. Follow the D957 along the river's north bank at first, then continue along the D5 as it swings away west towards Villiers-sur-Loir ❷.

Surrounded by fields and vineyards, Villiers is a pleasant little village whose main attraction is the nearby Château de Rochambeau.

Continue to Le Gué-du-Loir, which is surrounded by water-meadows and poplars. Then bear left on the D24 towards les Roches-l'Évêque, famous for its troglodyte houses. Carry on to Montoire-sur-le-Loir ❸.

This elegant town is full of decorative white stone buildings. The large central square leads to the river, which follows a flowery route, overlooked by the ruins of the medieval chateau. The Chapelle St-Gilles has remarkable wall paintings. It is locked, so ask for the key at the Mairie or at the Café de la Paix.

From Montoire, take the road west from the main square towards the chateau. Cross the river, turn left and drive through the woods of the Loir's south bank to Lavardin ❹.

Surrounded by woods, Lavardin is a classic medieval village, complete with winding streets of old houses, a Romanesque church with wall paintings and the spectacular ruins of a chateau. Just below the western edge of the church, by an entrance to the castle ruins, is a small parking area. A board here indicates a choice of three waymarked walk routes around Lavardin.

Leaving Lavardin, cross the river and return to Montoire along the more open north bank. Continue on this road, the D108, straight through Montoire, and follow the D917 to Trôo ❺.

Trôo is really two villages, the first a pleasant riverside settlement and the second something more extraordinary, on hills to the north. Here you'll find an old castle mound with good views over the Loir valley, a Romanesque church, the remains of fortifications and gateways and ancient stone houses. Linking the two villages is a precipitous staircase down the cliff and a mass of narrow, rocky passages connecting the houses of one of France's greatest troglodyte settlements.

The road up to the old hill town is clearly signposted soon after leaving Trôo's newer riverside quarter. From Trôo follow the same road, the D917, through Sougé, and at Pont-de-Braye proceed on the D305 towards Poncé-sur-le-Loir ❻.

Poncé-sur-le-Loir has a richly decorated Renaissance chateau with formal gardens. Between the railway and the river, an old paper mill houses potters and glass-blowers.

Return along the same road for 1.5km (1 mile), then turn right to cross the railway and the river on the D57 towards Couture-sur-Loir. This lovely stretch of road is flanked by steep, wooded hills.

Couture-sur-Loir ❼ is a pleasant farming village of quiet streets and old houses. A short detour outside town takes you to La Possonnière, an intimate Renaissance manor house in a pretty garden. It is the birthplace of the 16th-century poet Pierre Ronsard.

Leave Couture on the D10 and go through Artins. A short while after Artins, turn right at a crossroads onto the D8 towards Ternay. Ternay's unusual church, with its detached tower, sits in a flower-filled garden. Continue on the D8 to le Berloquet and then at an intersection turn right on the D116 to les Hermites. Follow this road and the D47 to la Ferrière. In the village turn right, then follow signs to St-Laurent-en-Gâtines ❽. At the intersection with the main road, turn left onto the D766, with St-Laurent's extraordinary church already in sight.

The remote village of St-Laurent-en-Gâtines is known for its church, which was formerly a huge 15th-century manor, brick-built in a commanding style. Unless you arrive during a service, you won't be able to see inside.

Continue along the D766 to Château-Renault ❾.

On a promontory overlooking the confluence of the Brenne and the Gault, Château-Renault is a pleasant town with a ruined medieval castle, riverside mills and shops.

Leaving Château-Renault, cross the railway and turn right along the main N10, which leads straight back to Vendôme across the Gâtine Vendômois.

OUT AND ABOUT

A glassblowing sign at Poncé-
sur-le-Loir

Troglodyte house in Trôo

A glassblowing demonstration at
Poncé-sur-le-Loir

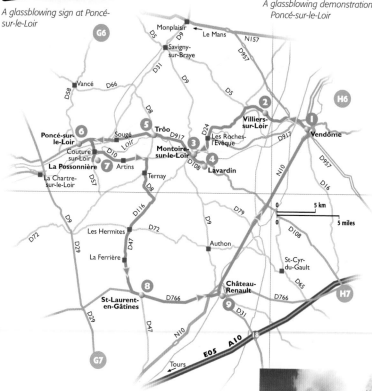

Castle ruins at Vendôme (right)

WHEN TO GO

This tour can be done at any
time of year, although during
rainy periods there may be local
flooding along the Loir valley, and
in low season the sights are likely
to be closed. May and June are
good months to go, when
Vendôme is at its most lovely,
with flowers and shrubs along
the banks of the river.

WHERE TO EAT

There are plenty of restaurants in
the towns and villages en route.

BASICS

Château de Poncé
72340, Poncé-sur-le-Loir
☎ 02 43 44 24 02 or 02 43 44 45 39
🕐 Mon–Sat 10–noon, 2–6, Apr–end
Sep
🎫 Adult €5.30

Manoir de la Possonnière
41800, Couture-sur-Loir
☎ 02 54 85 23 30
🕐 Daily 10–7 Jul, Aug; Fri–Mon 2–6,
Apr–end Jun; closed mid-Nov to
end Mar
🎫 Adult €6, child (12–18) €4.50

OUT AND ABOUT

VALLEY OF THE LOIR 305

CHATEAUX OF THE LOIRE

To visit the chateaux of the Loire is to take a step back in time to past centuries of French aristocratic life. No other stretch of river has so many noble residences, with more than 120 fairytale castles and mansions along the banks. This tour takes in three of the Loire's most famous chateaux (Chenonceau, Cheverny and Chambord) and passes many others en route.

THE DRIVE

Length: 128km (80 miles)
Allow: 1 day
Start/end at: Bléré

The Loire, the longest river in France, flows lazily for 1,020km (630 miles) from its source in the Massif Central to the Atlantic at St-Nazaire. The drive starts from Bléré ❶, just over 20km (12 miles) east of Tours.

From Bléré follow signs to La Croix-en-Touraine, Civray-de-Touraine and Chenonceaux. Cross the Cher and turn right in Civray-de-Touraine on the D40 to the Château de Chenonceau ❷.

Château de Chenonceau (see page 148) is the Loire's most photographed castle. Author Gustave Flaubert said it 'floats on air and water', because of its magnificent gallery which spans the river.

Continue on the D40 along the Cher valley, passing Chissay-en-Touraine, with its late Renaissance chateau, now a hotel, and the crumbling medieval keep at Montrichard. From here, turn left onto the D764 in the direction of Pontlevoy. Go as far as Sambin, then fork right onto the D52 past the ❸ Château de Fougères-sur-Bièvre.

Château de Fougères-sur-Bièvre is a small, fortified castle and marvellous example of medieval architecture softened by a Renaissance gallery.

Continue on through vineyards, following signs to Cheverny ❹, one of the Loire's finest chateaux, in magnificent grounds.

Cheverny has an elaborately decorated interior with Flemish tapestries and old masters. From April to November you can see the grounds either by boat or by electric car (golf-cart style).

From here follow signs to Chambord. Cross the D765, joining the D102 to Bracieux. Turn left onto the D120/D112 through the dense Forêt de Boulogne straight to Chambord ❺.

Chambord (see page 147), is the largest of all the chateaux, with pinnacles, spires, domes and chimneys piercing the skyline.

Now head for Blois ❻ on the D33 and D956.

The palace at Blois (see page 149) is famous for its unusual architecture and its tales of love and intrigue.

From Blois, the N152 on the north bank of the Loire leads to Amboise, past turreted Chaumont ❼ on the south bank.

Set in a spacious park planted with 100-year-old cedars, Chaumont is a very pretty chateau where Catherine de Medici lived briefly after the death of Henri II. Have a look at the stables where the troughs are made of porcelain! From mid-June to mid-October, the chateau hosts an international garden festival, which has a different theme each year. The festival takes place in 25 separate gardens of the chateau's estate.

At Amboise ❽, cross the river to the old town and chateau, one of the most visited in the Loire.

Amboise has one of the truly royal châteaux of the Loire, with an interesting and blood-soaked history. Though still offering plenty to see, the castle has been much diminished over the centuries: It was abandoned by royalty after the blood-letting of

the Amboise Conspiracy of 1560, and large parts were dismantled after the Revolution owing to a lack of funds. At the beginning of the 16th century, François I invited Leonardo da Vinci to live at Amboise, and he spent the last four years of his life there. A museum displays more than 40 models constructed from Leonardo's designs.

Take the D31 through the Forêt d'Amboise and return to Bléré.

BASICS

Château de Fougères-sur-Bièvre
41120, Fougères-sur-Bièvre
☎ 02 54 20 27 18
🕐 Daily 9.30–noon, 2–6, Apr–end Sep; Wed–Mon 10–noon, 2–4.30, rest of year; closed 1 Jan, 1 May, 1 Nov, 11 Nov, 25 Dec
💶 Adult €4.50, under 18 free
www.monum.fr

Château de Cheverny
41700, Cheverny
☎ 02 54 79 96 29
🕐 Daily 9.15–6.45, Jul, Aug; 9.15–6.15, Apr–end Jun and Sep; 9.30–noon, 2.15–5, rest of year
💶 Chateau and park: adult €5.90, child (7–14) €2.80, under 7 free
www.chateau-cheverny.fr

Château de Chaumont
41150, Chaumont-sur-Loire
☎ 02 54 51 26 26
🕐 Daily 9.30–6.30 mid-Mar to mid-Sep; 10.30–5.30, Apr–early May; 10.30–5, rest of year
💶 Adult €5.50, child €3.50. Combined ticket for chateau and garden festival: €12
www.chaumont-jardins.com

Château d'Amboise
37400, Amboise
☎ 02 47 57 00 98
🕐 Daily 9–6.30, mid-Mar to end Jun; 9–7, Jul, Aug; 9–6 Sep, Oct; 9–noon, 2–4.45, Nov–end Feb; 9–noon, 1.30–5.30, 1–15 Mar
💶 Adult €7, child (7–14) €5
www.chateau-amboise.com

*Gardens at the Château
de Chenonceau*

*Château de Chambord, the
Loire's largest castle*

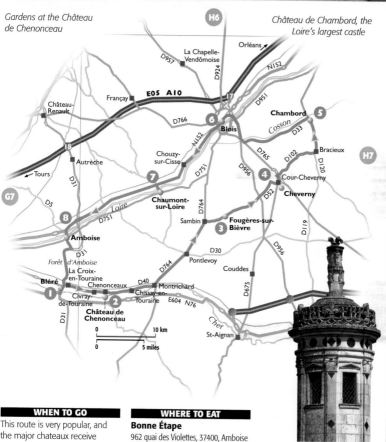

H6

Orléans

La Chapelle-
Vendômoise
D957
D924
N152

Françay
E05 A10
N152
D951

Château-
Renault
D766
6 Blois
Chambord **5**
Cosson D33

I8
Autrèche
Chouzy-
sur-Cisse
NI52
D765
D102
Bracieux
D120
H7

←Tours
D31
7
D751
D956
4
Cour-Cheverny

G7
D5
Loire
**Chaumont-
sur-Loire**
D764
D52
Cheverny

8
D751
Sambin
**Fougères-sur-
Bièvre**
D119

Amboise
3

D31
Forêt d'Amboise
D30
D956

Bléré
La Croix-
en-Touraine
Chenonceaux
D764
Pontlevoy
Couddes

1
Civray-
de-Touraine
2
D40
Chissay-en-
Touraine
Montrichard
E604 N76
D675

D31
**Château de
Chenonceau**
Cher

0   10 km
0   5 miles
St-Aignan

OUT AND ABOUT

WHEN TO GO
This route is very popular, and
the major chateaux receive
incredible numbers of visitors. If
possible, avoid the busy tourist
season of July and August, and
public holidays and weekends
the rest of the year. To avoid the
crowds, you could choose to visit
the less well-known chateaux
rather than the three majors
(Chenonceau, Cheverny and
Chambord). Aim to arrive at any
of the big chateaux half an hour
before the morning opening
time, at midday (if the chateau
does not close) when many
French visitors will be sitting
down for lunch, or late afternoon.

WHERE TO EAT
Bonne Étape
962 quai des Violettes, 37400, Amboise
🕐 Lunch and dinner Thu–Sat and Tue;
lunch Wed and Sun; closed 2–6, Apr, 18
Dec–7 Jan, 4–13 Feb

*Part of the roof of Château de
Chambord (above).
The river Loire at Blois (below)*

ST-BENOÎT-SUR-LOIRE

This walk starts from the superb abbey church of St-Benoît-sur-Loire, one of the most famous Romanesque buildings in France and the final resting place of St. Benedict, regarded as the father of western monasticism. The walk takes you to a 19th-century river port, passing through flat, riverside farmland with raised 15th-century flood protection banks. You'll also see the porch where locals used to exchange village gossip.

OUT AND ABOUT

THE WALK

Length: 9km (5.5 miles)

Allow: 3 hours

Start/end at: The basilica in St-Benoît-sur-Loire

HOW TO GET THERE

St-Benoît-sur-Loire is on the north bank of the river Loire, 40km (25 miles) southeast of Orléans.

The massive basilica ❶, which dominates the village of St-Benoît-sur-Loire and the surrounding countryside, is all that remains of the Benedictine abbey of Fleury, founded in 651. Village life revolves around the abbey church, its services, work and religious celebrations. Six times a day the basilica is filled with the sound of Gregorian chant and prayers dedicated to St. Benedict. Between services, the monks offer guided tours of their magnificent church, with its simple, solid design, built between 1004 and 1218.

From the abbey take the chemin du Port past Hôtel du Labrador, and follow a small sign marking a bicycle path to Sully. Cross a tiny bridge onto a gravel path and turn left, then walk across open farmland until you reach a cluster of buildings called the Hameau du Port ❷.

This attractive hamlet, site of the Port of St-Benoît, was a landing place for river boatmen who lived in the small cottages, which date mainly from the early 19th century.

Turn right, then first left along the waterfront. High water levels are etched on several walls and cottages, recording the years in the early to mid-1800s when severe floods had a devastating impact. Turn left just before the entrance to a campsite, up a path through woodland beside a wooden hut. After a few minutes, the trees clear at a crossing in the path above the farm. Turn right along a raised path ❸, following the curve of the river to your right, with flat farmland to your left.

Such raised banks (*levées*), are common along the Loire. This one was built during the 15th century to prevent flooding.

After about 2km (just over a mile) you reach several buildings on the left-hand side. Turn left, past some farm buildings, onto the chemin de la Levée. Turn right at the T-junction, past a jumble of lovely old stone buildings, and left at the next intersection back towards the abbey. Turn left again at the metal cross, across more farmland until the next crossroads. Turn right and return to St-Benoît. Cross a small bridge and turn first left into tree-shaded place du Grand Arcis, with the village school. Cut diagonally across the small square. Rue Jean de Fleury leads to the main square.

At the corner of this square is a *caquetoir* ❹ (from *caqueter*, to gossip). This covered porch was so called because parishioners used to gather here to exchange their news.

Cross the main square diagonally, turning right down rue Max Jacob, and over another small bridge. Turn immediately left down a path alongside a small *fossé* ❺ (ditch), bright with vivid green weed, which encircles the village. You will pass neat vegetable allotments and rows of private gardens, each accessed by a tiny wrought-iron bridge. Continue along the *fossé* past a large retirement home on the right. The path swings round to the left and returns to the main road. Turn left towards the heart of the village, then second right down the tree-lined avenue de l'Abbaye back to the basilica.

Sculptured capitals in the Abbaye de Fleury

Archways in the Abbaye de Fleury (above)

Shuttered windows at the Abbaye de Fleury (above)

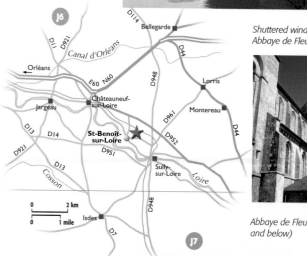

Abbaye de Fleury (above and below)

WHEN TO GO
This walk can be done at any time of year. Even in mid-winter, the riverscapes and the views across fields to the abbey are bleakly beautiful.

WHERE TO EAT
Grand St-Benoît
7 place St-André, 45730, St-Benoît-sur-Loire

Lunch and dinner Tue–Fri; dinner Sat, lunch Sun; closed 25 Aug–3 Sep, 22 Dec–21 Jan

CASCADES DU HÉRISSON

In the heart of the Jura mountains, the Vallée du Hérisson is known for its romantic setting, primeval forests and abundant wildlife, and the area around the Cascades du Hérisson is ideal for exploring on foot. Wear sturdy footwear and be aware that this walk is hilly in places. If time is pressing, the walk can be shortened by driving to Bonlieu, where the falls are signed down a small lane that leads to a parking area at le Saut de la Forge (see below).

THE WALK

Length:	4km (2.5 miles)
Allow:	3 hours
Start/end at:	Ilay

HOW TO GET THERE

Ilay is in the Jura, east of Lons-le-Saunier off the N78.

Hérisson is the name given to the river by a 19th-century cartographer. The original name, Yrisson, means 'sacred water' and has nothing to do with the hedgehog, the present-day translation of *hérisson*. The importance of the valley dates back to the Middle Ages, when three monastic orders fought for control of the river and the right to build various kinds of mills and forges. The area still relies on its abundant natural resources to maintain its way of life. The Jura, one of the most wooded parts of France, is a conservation area. It has a variety of wildlife, much of

Verdant Jura countryside

which, though flourishing there, is endangered in the world as a whole.

At Ilay ❶, there is a large parking area opposite the start of the walk, on the D39 about 100m (109 yards) from a crossroads and behind the Auberge du Hérisson. Follow the signs to Saut Girard ❷, about 500m (550 yards) to the south, via tree-covered pathways and fields.

An ironworks once stood beside the waterfall of Saut Girard; in 1811, 65 tonnes were produced in the village. Half a century later Saut Girard was a marble works. During the Middle Ages and up to 1714, a bridge over the fall linked Lons-le-Saunier with St-Laurent-en-Grandvaux and Geneva beyond, and was used to transport salt, wine and other products.

Next, walk on to Saut du Moulin ❸, beside the ruins of

the mill Le Moulin Jeunet, which can be seen 20m (22 yards) to the right of the path.

Known as the Moulin de Frasnois in 1434, the mill fell into ruin in the 17th century after a war which devastated the lake region. It was rebuilt by Frasnois villagers in 1663. At the end of the 19th century, Séraphin-François Jeunet became the owner and the mill was then named after him.

Le Saut de la Forge ❹, site of another former ironworks, is the next point on the walk; there is a useful orientation board here. Go on to le Gour Bleu, a romantic spot which is reached via a tree-covered path.

The transparent blue waters of the river are so clear that you can see right through to the gleaming river bed. Relax and enjoy the soothing, soft sound of the waterfalls.

OUT AND ABOUT

The river Hérisson flows through the Jura region

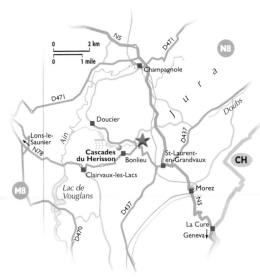

There are plenty of stunning waterfalls

Cross the Hérisson river by the footbridge called Passerelle Lacuzon and climb the steep path to reach la Grotte Lacuzon **5**, at the foot of the waterfalls of le Grand Saut. These falls are best seen from below the towering 60m (200ft) drop. From here, after a 400m (440 yard) hike, you find yourself at the foot of Cascade de l'Éventail **6**.

This is another spectacular waterfall, with the water flowing down for 65m (215ft) over a succession of zigzag steps known as 'the Great Organ'.

You can climb to the summit of l'Éventail **7** via the Sarrazine footbridge, which takes you to the Belvédère des Tuffs and gives a wonderful view of the Hérisson valley and the Cascades du Hérisson. Return the same way.

WHEN TO GO

The falls depend on local rainfall, and so reduce to a trickle in a dry summer. They are also very popular, so July and August are very busy. Spring is a good time to visit when the falls are in full flow and woodland flowers are blooming. If the falls are in fullest flood, wet weather clothing and waterproof boots are essential.

WHERE TO EAT

At Le Saut de la Forge, a chalet sells drinks (mid-April to mid-September) and snacks (June to mid-September). Bring your own food and drinks at other times.

CANAL DE BOURGOGNE

The majestic Burgundy Canal has become one of the most popular waterways in France for boating. In summer, all types of craft jostle for position as they wait to get through the succession of locks that takes them past sleepy villages and up and down the rolling terrain, dotted with grazing cows and sheep. This drive roughly follows the canal between Tonnerre and Flavigny-sur-Ozerain, taking in chateaux, an ancient abbey and a Gallo-Roman site.

THE DRIVE

Length: 90km (56 miles)	
Allow: 1 day	
Start: Tonnerre	
End: Flavigny-sur-Ozerain	

Tonnerre is a former Gallo-Roman settlement. Its tourist office is in the town's major sight, the Hôtel-Dieu **❶**, a 13th-century hospice of awe-inspiring proportions. Its immense beams were cut from local oak forests. Built by Marguerite of Burgundy, today's hospital still receives an income from the provisions of her will, now over 700 years old. The building also houses the town's main museum, the Musée Marguerite de Bourgogne. Another and more unusual sight is a spring called the Fosse Dionne, a water source emerging from a rocky escarpment and almost completely surrounded by the old wash-house. It's a charming spot, with the bluish-green water in the spring's basin overlooked by cottages, trees and the church of St-Pierre.

From Tonnerre, take the D965 to the village of Tanlay **❷**.

Tanlay (see page 169 and pages 314–315) is an unassuming village with a beautiful Renaissance chateau. Built in 1550 for

Carved figure in a church in Flavigny-sur-Ozerain

François de Coligny, the chateau is surrounded by a moat and splendid gardens.

Next stop is Ancy-le-Franc **❸**. To get there continue on the D965 and turn right onto the D12. Alternatively, head back to the canal, crossing it at St-Vinnemer, and pick up the D905 to Ancy-le-Franc.

The Château d'Ancy-le-Franc, built in the mid-16th century, is considered to be one of the finest examples of Renaissance architecture in Burgundy. At various times, it hosted Henri IV, Louis XIII and Louis XIV. The interior, restored and redecorated in the 19th century, is especially interesting.

Continue on the D905 through several villages and Montbard and turn left onto the D32 to the Abbaye de Fontenay **❹**.

L'Abbaye de Fontenay is one of the most beautiful abbeys in France. Set in a cool wooded valley and largely undamaged, it is a perfect example of a Cistercian abbey. The church, with its earthen floor, is often the setting for classical concerts in the summer, and the sculpted cloister is one of the best preserved in France. The gardens are a joy, with their fountain and fish pond. The abbey, a UNESCO World Heritage Site, was once owned by the Montgolfière family, pioneers of hot-air balloon-ing, and is still in private ownership.

Return to the D905 and follow it to **❺** Alise-Sainte-Reine.

Gaulish warriors, led by Vercingetorix, retreated to Alise-Sainte-Reine after their failed attack on Julius Caesar in 52BC (see page 28). Caesar's legions dug double trenches and fortified earthworks around the Gauls' camp to prevent them from escaping and to defend themselves from relief troops coming to save their besieged allies. After six weeks of trying to break through these barriers, Vercingetorix was forced to surrender and was subsequently paraded through the streets of Rome, imprisoned for six years and finally strangled. An imposing statue of the Gaulish leader now dominates the place.

Continue on the D905 and turn left onto D9J (or D9) to Flavigny-sur-Ozerain **❻**.

This tiny hilltop village was once the religious base of the Auxois region. You can see the remains of an important abbey, with a Carolingian crypt. The village's old fortress gates are still standing, as are houses dating from the 13th century. *Anis de Flavigny* (aniseed sweets) have been produced here since the 9th century. The film *Chocolat* (2000) was filmed here.

WHERE TO EAT

If you want to stop for a picnic, there are plenty of good places where the road runs alongside the canal. Just after Lézinnes the road crosses the river and then the canal. Turn immediately right and drive for about 500m (550 yards) to the Port de Lézinnes (this is not signed on the road). There is plenty of space to park, along with picnic tables, benches and a small see-saw for children.

OUT AND ABOUT

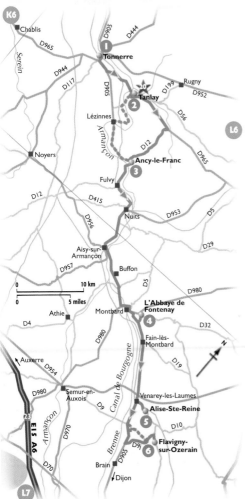

The Château de Tanlay (above). The Canal de Bourgogne at Buffon (above left), west of the Abbaye de Fontenay

BASICS

Tourist information
Hôtel-Dieu, 89700, Tonnerre
☎ 03 86 55 14 48
🕐 Mon–Sat 9–12.30, 2–6, Sun 10–12, 2–5, Apr–end Oct; Mon–Sat 9–12, 2–6, rest of year

Château de Tanlay
See page 169.

Château d'Ancy-le-Franc
89160, Ancy-le-Franc
☎ 03 86 75 14 63
🕐 Guided tours only: Tue–Sun, Easter to mid-Nov
💶 Adult €6, child (7–15) €3
🎫 10.30, 11.30, 2, 3, 4, and 5.30
www.chateau-ancy.com

Abbaye de Fontenay
21500, Montbard
☎ 03 80 92 15 00
🎫 Guided tours at 10, 11, noon and every 30 minutes between 2 and 5, Jul, Aug; 10, 11, noon, 2, 3, 4, 5, Apr to mid-Nov; open 10–noon, 2–5, rest of year (no guided tours)
💶 Adult €8, child (5–18) €4
www.abbayedefontenay.com

Carolingian crypt at Flavigny-sur-Ozerain
🕐 Mon–Fri 8.30–10.30, 2–5
💶 Adult €1, under 12 free

A narrow street in Flavigny-sur-Ozerain

BOAT INFORMATION

Boats can be hired in several places along the canal: Tonnerre and other bases on the Yonne river at the northern end; Montbard near the middle; and St-Jean-de-Losne, Pont d'Ouche and Pouilly-en-Auxois at the southern end. Locks close for lunch daily, all day Wednesday between Dijon and Tonnerre, and all French holidays. Hours vary according to season, so check before setting out. This tour includes a section of the canal from Tonnerre to Flavigny, but there are plenty of other interesting towns and villages to visit if you have time to explore the full length of the canal.

CANALSIDE WALK

This stroll along a stretch of the Canal de Bourgogne also includes a fine example of another of Burgundy's major features, its chateaux.

THE WALK
Length: 4.5km (3 miles)
Allow: 1 hour 30 minutes
Start/end: Tanlay

HOW TO GET THERE
Midway between Auxerre and Dijon in Burgundy, Tanlay is east of Tonnerre on the D965. There is a small parking area between the canal and the tennis courts.

The walk starts at Tanlay ❶, a village known for its fine chateau (see page 169 and below). Set off from the bridge over the Canal de Bourgogne where the D965 approaches the village from the Tonnerre direction.

Walk away from the bridge along rue du Port towards the heart of the village, then branch off to the left along the canal towpath, with the canal on the left.

The Canal de Bourgogne ❷ winds through Burgundy from the Yonne to the Saône, providing a link

Barges and canal boats tied up in the basin of the Canal de Bourgogne, at Tanlay

between the Channel and the Mediterranean. It was once a major highway for freight. Now it carries mainly holiday traffic.

At the first lock gate, cross the canal and continue along the towpath for 1km (just over half a mile) to the next road bridge. Cross the canal here and walk into the village of Commissey ❸.

Just after crossing the canal, look for the wash-house on the left. Turn left at the crossroads in the village to see a small church in Romanesque style, with an unusual stained-glass window in the dome above the altar.

Go straight ahead at place de la Mairie, along rue Haute, and at the crossroads just outside the village carry straight on along a minor road signed for Quincy and Rugny. Walk uphill for 300m (330 yards) to a crossroads, and turn right. Within 100m (109 yards) the surfaced road becomes a rough track.

There are good views from this path into the valley of the Armançon and towards Tonnerre. The landscape is a mixture of cultivated fields and woods.

Follow this track through open countryside for 400m (a quarter of a mile), and about 100m (109 yards) before it enters a wood, turn left on to another, almost invisible track. After 100m (109 yards) the track bears right over stony ground and then becomes a broad path going downhill through a lightly wooded area. Bear left where the path meets a field, and when the path forks near the edge of the wooded area, bear right and continue downhill with a wall to the right.

After another 225m (250 yards) the path meets a road. Turn right along the road and after 100m (109 yards) take the next road to the left, signed for St-Vinnemer and Lézinnes, and return to Tanlay. Opposite rue du Port, turn left into Grande Rue Basse, and after 250m (275 yards) reach the entrance to the Château de Tanlay ❹.

OUT AND ABOUT

This castle was built in the mid-16th century and is an excellent example of French Renaissance architecture. Surrounded by a moat, it is set in a beautiful park and was a Protestant stronghold in the Wars of Religion; tours are available.

Turn right in front of the chateau, following signs to Auxerre and Tonnerre, and walk along an avenue of tall trees. Just past two football pitches turn right along the road towards Tonnerre and walk about 100m (109 yards) to the parking area.

The Canal de Bourgogne is a good place for a bit of peace and quiet

WHEN TO GO

This walk can be done at any time of year. If you'd like to visit the chateau, telephone ahead to establish opening hours as it may be closed in autumn and winter.

WHERE TO EAT

There are several good picnic areas along the route, including the grounds of the chateau, the path down through the woodland, and beside the canal at the end of the walk.

GORGES DU TARN

The gorge of the river Tarn is one of the most beautiful areas in France. This drive explores both the Gorges du Tarn and the Gorges de la Jonte. The route is an arduous one, with narrow, winding roads, the occasional steep section and, in the Tarn gorge, too much traffic if you are there on the wrong day. However, it is a rewarding route with magnificent scenery.

THE DRIVE

Length: 110km (68 miles)
Allow: 1 day
Start/end at: Florac

Florac ❶ is a delightful little town, sitting below the towering cliffs of the Rocher de Rochefort. Its picturesque setting belies its violent history. Occupying a strategic position on the edge of the Causse Méjean, Florac became a local capital and was constantly fought over. Its castle was destroyed and rebuilt several times. The present 17th-century building, now the office of the Parc National des Cévennes, houses displays on the park and its wildlife.

From the middle of Florac, head south, but not by the main N106 that crosses the river. At a roundabout (traffic circle) go straight over to take the D907, signed Meyrueis, Barre-des-Cévennes and St-Jean-du-Gard. After 5km (3 miles) take a right fork signed Vebron, Meyrueis, St-André-de-Vigne and Mont Aigoual, and drive for 10km (6 miles) through a lovely valley to reach les Vanels. Take the D996 to the right, signed for Fraissinet-de-Fourques, Meyrueis, Mont Aigoual and Grotte de Dargilan. There follows a long climb to the Col de Perjuret. At the top go straight on, following signs to Meyrueis ❷, to descend from the col into Meyrueis.

Meyrueis is a popular visitor destination, not least because, at 700m (2,300ft) high, it is relatively cool in the heat of summer. It has managed to remain a quiet place, as a stroll under the old plane trees on quai Sully or around the narrow streets will show. Look out for Maison Belon, with its elegant Renaissance windows. Southwest of Meyrueis, off the D39, the magnificent Grotte de Dargilan is the largest cave in the Cevennes and Causses. It

has huge underground caverns, immense calcium carbonate deposits and crystalline lakes. After a visit to the cave, you emerge on a cliff face with spectacular views of the Gorges de la Jonte.

To leave Meyrueis, return to the D996 at the intersection with the main street and turn left, signed for Millau and Gorges de la Jonte. Take this narrow road out of town, following the road to right and left into the gorge. The gorge itself is attractive and easy to follow.

A wildlife and bird observatory, Le Belvédère des Vautours, by the roadside makes a good stop for ornithologists.

Continue to the western end of the gorge, where there is the tiny village of le Rozier ❸.

Le Rozier is where the Jonte and Tarn rivers meet. The Grand Hôtel de la Muse et du Rozier, a rather strange but interesting building, stands right beside the river. Close to le Rozier, but separated from it by the the river, is Peyreleau, a prettier village, grouped around a modern church and an old tower, the last remnant of a medieval castle.

Continue through le Rozier, bearing right on a short one-way street and then left onto a bridge across the Tarn. On the other side, turn immediately right onto the D907 signed Les Vignes, Sainte-Énimie, Gorges du Tarn and la Muse (this sign indicates the D907, but subsequent signs along the road indicate D907b). Follow the road through the Gorges du Tarn ❹.

The gorge is 50km (30 miles) long and can be followed by car (the easiest), by boat (the most exciting) or on foot (hard but rewarding). The Tarn has no tributaries, but is fed by

the water of more than 40 resurgent springs, with much of the water flowing in as waterfalls. The gorge is never more than 500m (545 yards) wide. Occasionally it narrows to just 30m (33 yards), with sides that are sometimes vertical and occasionally overhanging.

From les Vignes, the views become even more beautiful as the road leads to la Malène ❺.

Beyond les Vignes, the gorge enters its narrowest, most spectacular section. Here are the Pas de Souci, where the Tarn flows over and under huge blocks created by the collapse of part of the gorge walls, and les Détroits, sheer cliffs that are 400m (1,300ft) high. The best way to see these is by boat, which you can take from la Malène.

Next comes a series of tunnels following closely one after the other, then a 1.5km (1 mile) stretch of open road and a final twin tunnel controlled by traffic lights. Take the next (very sharp) turning to the right after this tunnel, signed for St-Chély-du-Tarn. Access to St-Chély-du-Tarn may be difficult in high season when traffic is heavy, as the right turn off the gorge is too tight for medium or large cars unless they swing out left into oncoming traffic. The turn will be impossible for anyone towing a caravan or trailer. The road to the village is about 500m (550 yards) long and very narrow.

St-Chély is a pretty little village on the left bank of the Tarn. The bridge over the Tarn is believed to date from Roman times and the church is unusual as it has an external stairway to its attractive bell tower. Equally charming are the old village houses with their Renaissance chimneys.

OUT AND ABOUT

A dramatic road tunnel

Kayaking along the gorge (above) is one way to avoid the summer traffic.
A typical French village church (left)

OUT AND ABOUT

Retrace the route to the gorge road and turn right (no sign). Follow signs to Ispagnac and Florac to reach Sainte-Énimie **6**.

The village, with its cobbled lanes and delightful old square, is named after St. Énimie, a seventh-century princess and hermit. Legend has it that her leprosy was cured when she bathed in the village's Fontaine de Burle.

Beyond the Sainte-Énimie, the gorge opens up slightly. There are chateaux on each side of the route as it nears Ispagnac **7**.

As the route approaches the end of the gorge, look out for the 16th-century Château de Charbonnières to the right of the road near Montbrun. You also pass Quézac, a village with a Gothic bridge over the Tarn. Delightful Ispagnac, the last village in the gorge, has a 12th-century church.

Continue through Ispagnac and turn right at the N106, signed for Alès and Florac. This road takes you straight back to Florac.

WHEN TO GO
The prime consideration on this tour is the narrowness of the road in places, especially the D907b from le Rozier to Sainte-Énimie. The sides of the gorge are steep so the road can be uncomfortably narrow for caravans and campervans. For this reason, driving this extremely popular route in July and August may result in very slow progress.

If you are going in winter, check with the tourist office at Florac that the Col de Perjuret is passable, as this high point receives heavy snowfall. Ice on the roads is also a major consideration even if the col has been cleared of snow.

WHERE TO EAT
Le Rozier has a choice of bars and restaurants and is an ideal spot for lunch.

THE CAMARGUE BY CAR

The Camargue—the Rhône delta—is huge, and comparatively few roads penetrate its marshy secrets. To see herds of grazing Camargue bulls watched over by their cowboy *gardians,* and far more birds than can be seen from the roads, consider supplementing the drive by taking a boat trip from a town such as Saintes-Maries-de-la-Mer. As with many driving tours of La Camargue, this one begins in Arles, famous for its Roman remains and as the haunt of artist Vincent Van Gogh.

THE DRIVE

Length: 95km (59 miles)	
Allow: 1 day	
Start/end: Arles	

Arles ❶ (see page 173), on the Rhône and north of the Camargue, has exceptionally well-preserved Roman remains and some good art museums containing works by Pablo Picasso, Paul Gauguin and Vincent Van Gogh.

Head west from Arles and cross the Grand Rhône. Take the D570 (signed for Saintes-Maries-de-la-Mer) to Albaron, once a powerful stronghold but now fighting off the sea with pumping stations rather then repelling human invaders. From here take the D37 to Méjanes ❷.

Méjanes is a lakeside village with a small electric railway, a bullring and horse-drawn carriages.

From here, follow the D37 as it runs past the Étang de Vaccarès ❸, the largest of the Camargue's lagoons.

Enjoying the salty views at Salin-de-Giraud

The Étang de Vaccarès is part of a nature reserve called the Réserve Nationale de Camargue, which has its visitor office and headquarters at La Capelière. On this stretch, stop the car at any of the lay-bys (turnouts) and the distinctive smell of marsh immediately becomes apparent—a combination of salt, rotting vegetation and growing plants.

At Villeneuve, turn south towards La Capelière.

It's easy to miss the excellent visitor facility—keep a lookout for the sign and be ready to stop. There are marked nature trails, and the 1.5km (1 mile) path around the building has information boards giving details about the area's plants and animals.

Continue south past Salin-de-Badon, noted for its birds, to Salin-de-Giraud ❹.

Salin-de-Giraud is the best known of the region's salt-producing towns. The tree-lined avenues are dominated by the Solway

refinery, where glittering piles of white salt can be glimpsed through the railings.

Now take the D36 north as it slices through the marshy land to the west of the sluggish Grand Rhône. Eventually it joins the D570, which leads back to Arles.

FLORA AND FAUNA OF THE CAMARGUE

The Camargue is famous for its dazzling white horses and unique black bulls, but this wilderness is also home to countless birds, including ducks, waders and geese. The wide, shallow lagoons provide excellent feeding grounds for swans, avocets and egrets, while the freshwater reed beds are used as nesting sites by bitterns, herons and warblers. Surveys have also recorded 24,000 pink flamingos here, a truly spectacular sight. Perhaps the most remarkable of the creatures that thrive here is the brine shrimp, a crustacean just over 15mm (0.6in) long. It has evolved in such a way that it can live in virtually fresh or very salty water with equal ease, and so is able to survive both floods and droughts.

OUT AND ABOUT

The Camargue is famous for its white horses (left)

Having a snack outside the Roman amphitheatre in Arles (right)

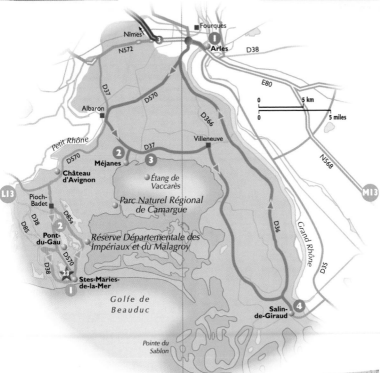

Boats at Saintes-Maries-de-la-Mer (left)

A sign showing some of the activities available around the Étang de Vaccarès (right)

WHERE TO EAT

Restaurant de Méjanes
Domaine de Méjanes, on D37 about 4km (2.5 miles) south of Albaron
☎ 04 90 97 10 51
🄲 Closed Mon
Generous country cooking in the traditional setting of a waterside Camargue *domaine*.

BASICS

Réserve Nationale de Camargue
Centre d'Information de la Réserve Nationale de Camargue, La Capelière, 13200, Arles
☎ 04 90 97 00 97
www.reserve-camargue.org

THE CAMARGUE BY BICYCLE

Bicycling is a good way to explore the flat, sometimes blustery, distances of the Camargue. The *Digue à la Mer* (or sea dike) between the long beach and the Étang de Vaccarès is exclusively for walkers and bicyclists. You'll need to return the way you came if you plan to visit the lighthouse, Phare de la Gacholle, a bracing 12km (7.5 miles) from Saintes-Maries-de-la-Mer, or the flamingo nesting site at Étang du Fangassier; motorists have an easier approach from the Salin-de-Giraud end. This circular route is 20km (12.5 miles) and makes an excellent bicycle tour. There are several places where you can rent bicycles in Saintes-Maries: The tourist office on avenue Van Gogh has a list.

THE TOUR

Length: 20km (12.5 miles)

Allow: 1 hour 30 minutes to 4 hours, depending on how long you spend at the bird reserve and if you do the extra 10km (6 mile) detour to the Château d'Avignon.

Start/end: Saintes-Maries-de-la-Mer

The village of Saintes-Maries-de-la-Mer ❶ is named after the three Marys (Mary Magdalene, Mary Salome the mother of James and John the Apostles, and Mary the sister or sister-in-law of the Virgin) who were said to have landed here by boat from the Holy Land with Sarah, their servant. Sarah is the patron saint of gypsies and there is a large festival in her honour every May. In the crypt of the fortified Romanesque church is the black statue of Sarah, often draped in chiffon.

Flamingos (right) can be seen on the Camargue's marshes

Leave Saintes-Maries on the D85A, a minor road which runs between the Réserve Départementale des Impériaux et du Malagroy on your right and the Étang de Ginès on the left. After 4km (2.5 miles) the road bears left (there's a good view east here near the Mas de Cacharel), while an alternative route branches off right to Méjanes. After 6km

(4 miles) the D85A joins the D570, the main road, at Pioch-Badet. For a longer trip, turn right and cycle 5km (3 miles) to the Château d'Avignon, which has a rich collection of 19th-century furniture. Heading south back towards Saintes-Maries will bring you past the Centre d'Information de Ginès and the Parc Ornithologique du Pont-de-Gau ❷.

The Camargue is a haven for birds, including pink flamingos, ducks, egrets, herons, cranes, geese and swans. For a guaranteed bird sighting, visit the Parc Ornithologique du Pont-de-Gau, where large aviaries show the rarer species.

To return along the Petit-Rhône after the Parc Ornithologique, turn right onto the D85 just

The shore of Étang de Vaccarès (below)

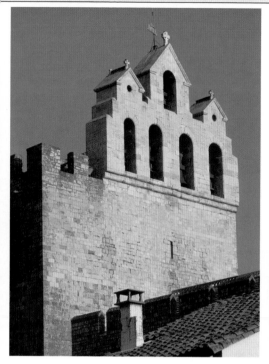

before the Musée de Cire (wax museum) and left onto the D38, which loops back into Saintes-Maries-de-la-Mer around the Étang des Launes.

Church bells in Saintes-Maries-de-la-Mer (above)

The Camargue is a great place to go horse-riding (above)

WHERE TO EAT

Hostellerie du Pont de Gau
Avenue Arles, 13460, Saintes-Maries-de-la-Mer
☎ 04 90 97 81 53
Small hotel with a good, moderately priced restaurant

BASICS

Tourist information
5 avenue Van Gogh, 13460 Saintes-Maries-de-la-Mer
☎ 04 90 97 82 55
🕑 Daily 9–7, May, Jun, Sep; 9–8, Jul, Aug; 9–5 Oct–end Feb; 9–6 Mar, Apr
www.saintesmariesdelamer.com

Château d'Avignon
☎ 04 90 97 58 60
🕑 Guided tours only: Wed–Mon 10–5
🎟 Adult €3, 16–25 €1.50
🚌 Tours every hour from 10am

Parc Ornithologique du Pont-de-Gau
☎ 04 90 97 82 62
🕑 Daily 9–dusk, Apr–end Sep; 10–dusk, rest of year
www.parc-ornitho.com

You can take a boat tour from Saintes-Maries-de-la-Mer (above). Bicycling is a fun way to see the Camargue (below)

THE HEART OF PROVENCE

This tour starts in Aix-en-Provence and takes in the Montagne Sainte-Victoire, which inspired the painter Paul Cézanne, before turning south towards the Massif de la Sainte-Baume, where you'll have a view to Marseille. The roads are narrow in places and hilly in others, but this makes the drive interesting rather than arduous.

THE DRIVE

Length: 135km (84 miles)
Allow: 1 day
Start/end: Aix-en-Provence

The heart of Aix-en-Provence ❶ (see page 172) is the cours Mirabeau, a wide boulevard planted with a double row of plane trees that provide welcome shade from the summer sun. North of here lies Vieil Aix, the oldest and most charming section of the city.

Leave Aix-en-Provence on the D10, signed for St-Marc-Jaumegarde and Vauvenargues, to reach the Barrage du Bimont ❷ after about 8km (5 miles).

The lake behind the Barrage du Bimont dam provides water for local towns.

Continue on the D10 to Vauvenargues ❸.

This pretty village is famous for its Renaissance chateau, inherited by Pablo Picasso in 1958. The artist died here in 1973, and is buried within the extensive park. The park and chateau are not open to the public.

Rejoin the D10 by driving straight through the village (there is only one road). The D10, now signed for Jouques and Rians, runs along the northern flank of the Montagne Sainte-Victoire ❹.

Cézanne loved this mountain and it inspired many of his works.

Go straight on at the next intersection, following the D223, signed for Rians. The road narrows and climbs, but offers good views all the way. At the next intersection, take a left turn onto the D23, signed for Rians and Manosque. This road ends at a T-junction with the D3. Take a right turn, signed for Ollières and St-Maximin-la-Sainte-Baume ❺.

In St-Maximin, turn left at the traffic lights, then right and left again as you traverse St-Maximin.

The basilica in St-Maximin-la-Sainte-Baume is the best example of Gothic architecture in Provence. It was built on the site of a 6th-century church that was, according to local legend, the resting place for the remains of St. Mary Magdalene. Construction of the new basilica started in 1295 and continued until the 16th century, although no belfry was ever built and the west front was unfinished.

The road divides as it leaves the town. Go straight on along the N560, as the main road bears left. This smaller road goes under a railway bridge and is signed for Aubagne, Marseille and St-Zacharie. Continue for 100m, then bear left onto the D83, signed for Rougiers. This road is a slip road that crosses the main road at a STOP sign. Again it is signed for Rougiers. The D83 becomes even narrower after Rougiers.

To reach the village of Rougiers you cross the D1. Go through the village. The road goes uphill towards a ruin and a church that you'll see on top of the hill ahead. It then bears sharp left and goes through an open barrier, before continuing up the valley. Go over a crest and down to an intersection. Turn right onto the D95 (only the back of the signpost is visible, so to check that you are on the right road make sure the wrong side indicates Plan-d'Aups). Go past signs warning of deer, and continue to the ❻ Hôtellerie at la Sainte-Baume.

The Hôtellerie is a 19th-century restoration of a Dominican friars' pilgrim hostel, dating from medieval times. It has now become an international base for spiritual studies.

Continue on the D80 through Plan-d'Aups, after which the road widens a little. At the next intersection, turn right onto a road signed for Auriol, which joins the D45A to make a long, twisty descent around many hairpin bends. When you reach the N560, take a left turn, signed for Aubagne, Auriol and Roquevaire, then immediately turn right (after the Citroën garage) back onto the D45A. At the next crossroads, take a right turn, signed for Moulin de Redon, onto the very narrow D45, going towards St-Zacharie. Turn left, then immediately left again in the heart of the village onto the D85, following signs for Trets and Col du Petit Galibier. Stay on this road and the D12, which climbs giving fine views, to reach ❼ Trets.

Originally Roman, much of the current town now dates from the Middle Ages. You can see the remains of medieval walls, square 14th-century towers, a castle that is 100 years older, and a 15th-century church.

In the middle of the town, turn left onto the D6, signed Aix and Marseille. At the roundabout take the D908 signed Peynier ❽.

The tiny village of Peynier has a pleasant Romanesque church.

Pass through Peynier, and climb up to pass a red-and-white communications tower on the left. Take the D46c to the right, signed for Belcodène, and go through the village, following signs for Fuveau. Go over the autoroute and enter Fuveau. Turn left and right into the main square, then almost immediately, take the first turning on the left, which is the road to Aix-en-Provence and Gardanne. At a roundabout with a central fountain, take the exit signed for Aix and continue to the N96. Turn right and follow this road and the N7 to Aix.

OUT AND ABOUT

*Cézanne's inspiration,
Montagne Sainte-Victoire*

*Eating al fresco on the cours
Mirabeau, in Aix-en-Provence*

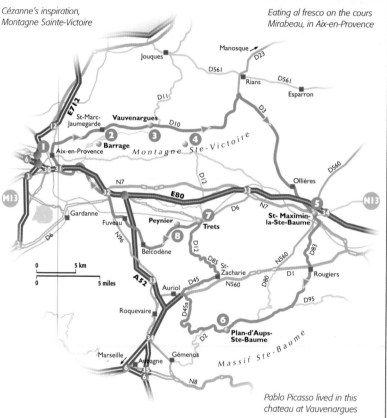

*Pablo Picasso lived in this
chateau at Vauvenargues*

WHERE TO EAT

There are many restaurants and
brasseries in St-Maximin-la-
Sainte-Baume.

BASICS

Hôtellerie la Sainte-Baume
Outside the village of Plan-d'Aups
☎ 04 42 04 54 84

VALLÉE DES MERVEILLES

The Vallée des Merveilles is in the eastern part of the Parc National du Mercantour, in the Alpes-Maritimes region of the Provençal Alps. With the adjoining Parco Naturale dell'Argentera in Italy, it shelters Alpine and Mediterranean flora and fauna. At least 25 of its plant species are not found anywhere else in the world and at least half of all France's flower species are represented. With some of the loveliest scenery in France, it is aptly named the Valley of Marvels. This hike, for which you should be well prepared, takes you past glacial boulders with images of animals and weapons carved by ancient peoples.

BE PREPARED

The only way to reach the Vallée des Merveilles is on foot—not only are there no real roads, but private vehicles are generally banned from this section of the park because it is a protected zone. (Some four-wheel drive visitor vehicles are allowed on the first section to the Refuge des Merveilles.) You need to allow at least a day for this hike and start early in the morning. If you want to stay in the area overnight, options include the *refuges* (Refuge des Merveilles at Lac Long or Refuge de Valmasque at Lac Vert) or one of the hotels at the winter ski resort of Castérino, although not all are open year round. Camping is not allowed. Be aware of sudden storms, plan your hike with the park office in Tende by taking their map with you, wear suitable walking boots, and take food and drinks.

THE WALK

Length: 30km (18.5 miles)
Allow: 1 day
Start/end: Parking area at Lac des Meshes

HOW TO GET THERE

St-Dalmas-de-Tende is in the far south-east of France near the Italian border, off the E74 south of Tende.

The gateway to the Vallée des Merveilles is the little village of St-Dalmas-de-Tende **1**. To reach the start of the walk, drive up the D91 towards Lac des Meshes, passing through peaceful woods with the rocky heights of Cime de la Nauque to the left. At the lake there is a spacious car parking area.

Follow the footpath towards Lac Long **2** which will take several hours. At first the walking is pleasant and easy, winding through wooded slopes, but then the path begins to rise steeply.

Pines surround Lac Long's chilly shores and in spring the area is a wonderful sight as wild flowers bloom. All around is the stony mass of mountains, with Mont Bégo looming to the north. This is the southern end of the Vallée des Merveilles and here is the Refuge des Merveilles **3**. The valley can be sinister in dull light, with the rocks a threatening dark shade.

At this point you join GR52 (GR stands for *Grandes Randonnées* or long-distance path). Climb until you reach Mont des Merveilles, at which point you can start to look for the carvings **4**. As there are few obvious landmarks to describe where they are, refer to the maps from the park offices.

Despite their huge number (more than 100,000), it is easy to miss these ancient carvings, especially in winter when many are covered in snow. It is thought that the oldest date from about 1800BC, with others added in Roman times. No one knows why these intriguing images were carved, although one theory is that Mount Bégo (sometimes called the Magic Mountain) was a sacred site, and the images were etched into the rocks as votive offerings by prehistoric pilgrims. The drawings were not properly studied until the 1890s, when naturalist Clarence Bicknell excavated and catalogued them. He showed how the diagrams of hunting weapons, daggers, animals and mysterious symbols provide a unique insight into the Ligurian culture.

A sign in the Parc National du Mercantour

The footpath continues past a string of lakes through the heart of the valley towards Lac du Basto. Although difficult to find, engravings are littered all along the path, some of them close and others towards the slopes of the mountains. Before Lac du Basto, GR52 heads off to the left, while your path continues towards Valmasque **5**.

There is a *refuge* at Valmasque, near Lac Vert, a lovely place where Mont Sainte-Marie looks down from its imposing height of 2,738m (8,981ft).

Here the path turns northeast for the homeward run. After Mont Peracourte farther on, turn right and head south to Castérino **6**, a tiny resort in an attractive setting on the D91. Taxis cover the final 3km (2 miles) to the car park at Lac des Meshes.

WHEN TO GO

Spring is the best time to come for the wild flowers. It is possible to do the hike all year round, although the *refuges* are not always open. Always book ahead if you are planning to stay or eat in one of the *refuges*.

Vallon de la Minière
Baisse de Vallaurette

Vallée des Merveilles
Refuge des Merveilles
Baisse de Valmasque

Expect beautiful scenery and varied wildlife if you go walking in the Parc National du Mercantour

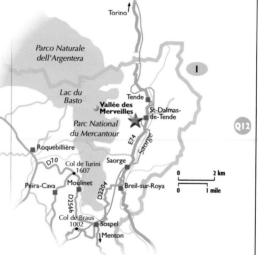

Q12

WHERE TO EAT

You can have meals at the *refuges* if you book ahead. There are seasonal cafés and *auberges* at Castérino; some have terraces with good views.

Refuge des Merveilles
☎ 04 93 04 64 64
📅 Jun to mid-Oct; weekends and French school hols rest of year
www.tendemerveilles.com/merveilles

Refuge de Valmasque
☎ 04 92 20 14 65
📅 Jun–end Sep

BASICS

Maison du Parc National
103 avenue du 16 Sept 1947, 06430 Tende
☎ 04 93 04 67 00

A stunning view in the Vallée des Merveilles (right)

CÔTE D'AZUR AND THE PARC NATIONAL DU MERCANTOUR

There could hardly be a greater contrast than that between the Côte d'Azur coast and the Parc National du Mercantour. One is glitter and bustle, the other peace and unspoiled beauty. This driving tour combines the two, starting in Menton, one of the most pleasant of the Côte d'Azur towns, and then heading north into the hills of Haute-Provence, the foothills of the Alpes Maritimes. Be aware that the roads to the north of the Côte d'Azur tend to be winding and slow.

THE DRIVE

Length: 150km (93 miles)
Allow: 1 day
Start/end: Menton

Menton ❶ describes itself as the warmest town on the Côte d'Azur, and the citrus orchards seem to reinforce this claim. It is a picture-postcard Italian town, which finds itself on the French side of the border. The Musée Jean-Cocteau, at the southern corner of the port, has a collection of works by the artist.

From the middle of town, take the road signed *Autoroute (Nice, Italia)* and *Sospel*. Follow signs for Sospel on the D2566, going under the A8 and passing through Castillon-Neuf. At Sospel, go over the railway crossing and then turn left, following signs for Moulinet and Col de Turini.

The bridge in the pretty village of Sospel ❷ is of 11th-century design, complete with a central tower, but of 20th-century vintage, as the original was destroyed in World War II.

Bear left at a bend onto the D2204 and climb up to Col St-Jean, from where there are superb views back down to Sospel. Go over Col de Braus (1,002m/3,287ft) and descend around hairpin bends almost into l'Escarène. Just after a railway bridge take a right turn, signed for Lucéram and Peïra-Cava.
   Drive through the old village of Lucéram ❸, a haphazard collection of medieval alleys. At the next junction, which is isolated and on a steep hill, bear left, following signs for Turini. The road climbs around 16 hairpin bends and passes through Peïra-Cava ❹.

Peïra-Cava is one of the best viewpoints on the route, with a superb panorama to the Parc National du Mercantour.

Continue to the Col de Turini ❺.

At an altitude of 1,607m (5,271ft), the Col de Turini has fine views. There is a hotel, café and restaurant.

Turn left onto the D70, signed for la Bollène-Vésubie and Nice, carefully descending the long, winding road from the pass. After about 10km (6 miles), look for a chapel ❻ on the left (on a bend) just after the Chapelle-St-Honorat tunnel.

There is a parking place here, and superb views over la Bollène-Vésubie ❼.

Continue through la Bollène. At a T-junction turn left onto the D2565, signed for Nice and St-Martin-Vésubie, to reach a valley bottom. There, follow signs for Lantosque and Nice, going straight on at first, then turning left along the main road. After 1km (half a mile) you can either go right and drive through Lantosque village, or take the bypass. The road through the village rejoins the main road; if you go that way turn right (signed for Nice).
   Continue through St-Jean-de-la-Rivière. About 1km (half a mile) beyond St-Jean take the left fork, the D19, signed *Nice par Levens*—be sure to follow this sign since both directions are signed for Nice. The road narrows and climbs up the side of the Vésubie valley. After you leave the tunnel just before Duranus, there is a viewpoint to the right, the Saut des Français, above sheer cliffs. Continue along the road into Levens ❽.

The attractive main square at Levens has shady gardens and views to the south. The late 18th-century friary Chapelle des Pénitents Blancs stands on the north side, and the Chapelle des Pénitents Noirs, with a fine baroque façade, on the east side. The Maison du Portal gateway is all that is left of the castle. There is a viewpoint at the World War I memorial.

Leave Levens on the D19, signed for Nice. Continue for about 16km (10 miles), passing Tourrette-Levens. Just after St-André you'll pass under the A8. Take a left turn at the traffic lights here, signed for Sospel, cross a river and go straight over at the next set of traffic lights to go back under the A8. Take the next right turn, signed for Route de Turin, crossing the river and a level crossing (grade crossing). Take a left turn at the traffic lights, signed for La Trinité and Drap, and at a roundabout (traffic circle) take the road signed for La Turbie and Laghet. Follow the D2204A up a winding valley to the sanctuary at Laghet. There a hairpin bend takes the road sharply to the right. Pass under the A8 again, and turn left at the next intersection (an *autoroute* slip road, signed for Menton). Turn left again at the next intersection onto a road signed for La Turbie and Monaco. Continue to La Turbie ❾.

The ancient village of La Turbie is on the *Via Julia,* a Roman road built by Julius Caesar to link Genoa with Cimiez, on the northern outskirts of Nice. The triumphal arch, the Trophée des Alpes, was built by Augustus Caesar in about 6BC to celebrate his local supremacy.

Drive through La Turbie and bear left past a hotel, following signs

The Trophée des Alpes, La Turbie

Cows grazing in the hills

for Roquebrune and Menton, and then go downhill. At the bottom, take a right turn at the traffic lights, signed for Nice and Beausoleil. Take a left turn at the next set of traffic lights, signed for Cap Martin. As it leaves the heart of the village, the road veers sharp left. Go straight ahead here, on the road signed for Mayerling and Cap Martin. This road soon reaches the sea. Park here for the start of the walk on pages 328–329.

Follow the coast road back to Menton.

Soothing scenery at the Parc National du Mercantour

WHERE TO EAT

Les Trois Vallées Hotel-Restaurant
Col de Turini
☎ 04 93 04 23 23

There are several bars and restaurants in Sospel.

BASICS

Musée Jean-Cocteau
Le Bastion, Port de Menton, quai Napoléon III, 06500, Menton
☎ 04 93 35 49 71
🕐 Wed–Mon 10–12, 2–6
🎫 Adult €3.50, under 18 free

OUT AND ABOUT

27. WALK

CAP MARTIN COAST

This coastal walk visits what many consider to be the most attractive section of the Côte d'Azur. A long linear walk (you return by train), it is best done in the afternoon, after the heat of the day has passed and the sun is at the best angle for the views. The walk takes you past rhododendrons, cascades of honeysuckle and huge cactus plants to the right, with the turquoise sea to the left and coastal towns ahead. You can extend the walk by continuing into Monaco.

THE WALK

Length: 6km (4 miles)

Allow: 1 hour 30 minutes (longer if you continue to Monte Carlo)

Start: Cap Martin

End: Cabbé or Monte Carlo

HOW TO GET THERE

Cap Martin is to the east of Monaco, in the southeast of France, close to the Italian border.

The thrusting headland of Cap Martin ❶ has long been a lookout point—the ruined tower at its heart was once a fortified medieval watchtower. At the base of the tower are the remains of an 11th-century priory. Legend has it that the prior had an agreement with the local folk that if the tower's bell rang, they would all hurry to the site to defend the

Menton's marina, with the terraced buildings of the old town rising up the steep hillside

monks. One night, just to test the system, the prior rang the bell and was very pleased with the speedy response. The local people were less pleased and a few nights later, when the bell rang again, they did not bother to turn out. But this time it was no trial run, and the priory was sacked by pirates and all the monks killed. Today Cap Martin is a rich suburb of Menton, its mansions set among sweet-smelling mimosas and olive trees.

Start from the parking area at the seaward end of avenue Winston Churchill on Cap Martin. Go back in the direction in which you drove, then pass to the left of the hotel entrance, along a wide footpath at the edge of the sea. The path is marked at its start by a sign for Ville de Roquebrune-Cap Martin, and a list of times for walks. Follow the path skirting the

edge of private gardens and smart hotels. The path heads west along the edge of Cap Martin. There is a superb view of Monaco ahead and the sea is to the left.

The path is named Promenade Le Corbusier ❷ after the highly influential architect of the 1920s, who is connected with this stretch of coast through his association with artist and designer Eileen Gray. Her imaginative house above the shore was designated a historic monument in 1998. The house, hidden from view, lies below the path that continues up the western side of the Cap. Here the path is very close to the railway line.

In several places, steps lead up to the Cap, but the best route continues into Cabbé, from where trains run back into

OUT AND ABOUT

Carnolès. From Carnolès station, head seaward and follow the coastal path back to the car parking area. To extend the walk, you can follow the path into Monte Carlo ❸.

The principality of Monaco (see pages 186–187) has distinct areas, including the commercial hub—La Condamine—and Monte Carlo with its famous casino, hotels, marina, exclusive shops and restaurants. You don't have to be a wealthy player at the gaming tables to appreciate Monte Carlo, as the parks and gardens are a delight and the

waterfront and views over the Mediterranean are superb.

Trains from here also serve Carnolès. This longer walk has the advantage of a glorious entrance to Monaco, but the disadvantage is that the route occasionally strays onto roads.

WHEN TO GO

Before you set off, check there is a suitably timed train from Cabbé to take you back to Carnolès.

WHERE TO EAT

There are expensive, high-quality restaurants in Cap Martin, and less expensive places in Cabbé.

Casino de Monte Carlo, Monaco (above)

OUT AND ABOUT

Swimming in the Lido at Monte Carlo

Provençal herbs on sale in Menton

Menton's seafront (above). Monaco's Palais du Prince (below)

VINEYARDS OF BORDEAUX

Almost every village on this tour through France's greatest wine-producing region has a world-famous name. The drive takes in the beautiful old town of St-Émilion and crosses the river Garonne, which flows through Bordeaux, a thriving city and the wine capital of France.

THE DRIVE	
Length: 120km (75 miles)	
Allow: 1 day	
Start/end: Langon	

Langon ❶, on the banks of the Garonne, is known for its sweet dessert wines. There's a partly Romanesque church with 12th-century frescoes, and 28 menhirs (standing stones), said to be 28 girls turned to stone for missing Mass.

Leave Langon on the N113, signed for Libourne. Just outside the town, turn right after the railway viaduct running parallel with the road, towards St-Macaire ❷.

St-Macaire, a medieval town built on limestone rock, with the impressive church of St-Sauveur, is named after a 6th-century bishop.

Leave St-Macaire by following the N113 northeast for about 500m (quarter of a mile) before turning left onto the D672 towards Sauveterre-de-Guyenne. Pass through le Pian-sur-Garonne and St-André-du-Bois ❸.

In St-André-du-Bois, the Château de Malromé was the final home of the artist Henri Toulouse-Lautrec before his death in 1901, at the age of 37. It contains a rare collection of his drawings. The artist is buried in Verdelais, just southwest of St-André.

Continue to St-Laurent-du-Bois and, shortly after the village, turn left onto an unclassified road (marked with a red-and-white post) that passes through the picturesque hamlet of Le Chantre and emerges onto the D139. Turn left and immediately right onto the D131, through St-Sulpice-des-Pommiers, to rejoin the D672 after this small detour. Turn left and continue on the D672 towards ❹ Sauveterre-de-Guyenne.

This interesting small *bastide* (fortified town) has four large gateways and a castle built by Edward I of England.

Leave Sauveterre-de-Guyenne, following signs to Libourne on the D670, and pass the small town of Le Puch. Continue on the same road, whose sweeping bends demand constant vigilance, and pass through St-Jean-de-Blaignac. Cross the river Dordogne, and go through Lavagnac. Continue through Merlande and Vignonet, arriving at a roundabout (traffic circle) on the D936. Carry straight on (signed Libourne and St-Émilion). About 4km (2.5 miles) farther on, at St-Laurent-des-Combes, take the right turn for St-Émilion ❺.

Medieval St-Émilion (see page 208) perches on a hilltop overlooking the Dordogne valley. The village is famous throughout the world for its wine and locally for its macaroons. St-Émilion's other attractions include its unique monolithic church carved out of solid rock, its catacombs, the medieval Tour du Roi and the delightful frescoes in the simple, elegant Chapelle de la Trinité.

Leave St-Émilion on the same road as you entered by. Cross straight over the D670 onto the D122 (signed for Branne), a narrow, winding road with crumbling edges. After 4km (2.5 miles) turn left onto the D19/D122, signed for Branne, and follow the road over the metal Dordogne bridge into Branne. Leave Branne on the D936, signed Cadillac and Bordeaux. Just under 1km (half a mile) farther on, bear left towards Bordeaux, staying on the D936.

Turn left off the D936 onto the D11, for Targon and Cadillac. Cross over the D128 near Grézillac, continuing on the D11. After about 9km (5.5 miles), turn right onto the main road, the

D671, signed for Targon, and then immediately left, back onto the D11. Follow this into Targon. Leave Targon on the D11 towards Cadillac, following signs to Escoussans. After 6km (4 miles) bear right at the fork on the D11 for Cadillac and then pass through Escoussans. After 2km (just over a mile), at the T-junction, take a right turn for Cadillac and Bordeaux, staying on the D11 which winds downhill through woodland towards Cadillac ❻.

Cadillac is a small fortified town on the banks of the Garonne. It has an impressive 17th-century chateau with vaulted basement rooms once used by tapestry weavers. When the Duc d'Epernon started its construction, King Henri IV, realizing how rich and ambitious the duke was, encouraged him wholeheartedly, hoping the distraction would make him less dangerous. The town was also the home of Chevalier de Lamothe de Cadillac, founder of the city of Detroit, in the US.

As you come into Cadillac follow the signs for the D10 and Bordeaux. After 100m, turn left at the traffic lights, still on the D10 (now signed for the A62 *autoroute*), and go over the bridge across the Garonne. Continue to Cérons ❼.

Cérons is an ancient port on the Garonne, with a Romanesque church that has lovely carvings on the doorway. The village has its own *appellation* for dessert wines, as does nearby Cadillac. In the fishing season, you'll see signs advertising the sale of *alose,* a large freshwater fish abundant along this stretch of the river.

Follow signs to Illats on the A62. Around 2km (just over a mile) after Cérons, where the approach to the A62 veers off to the left, bear right onto the D117, signed

OUT AND ABOUT

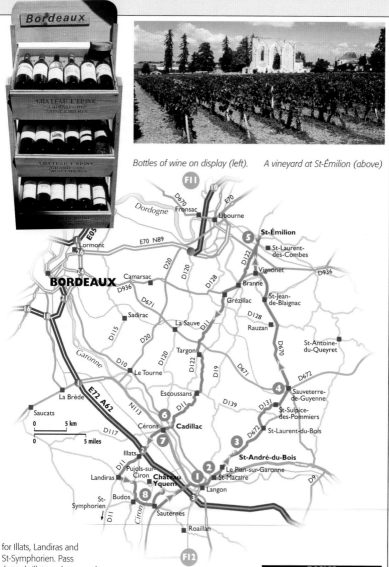

Bottles of wine on display (left).   A vineyard at St-Émilion (above)

OUT AND ABOUT

for Illats, Landiras and
St-Symphorien. Pass
through Illats and stay on the
D11, signed for Landiras and St-
Symphorien. Go through Artigues
and continue to Landiras, where
you turn left onto the D116,
signed for Pujols-sur-Ciron and
Langon. After 3.5km (2 miles)
turn right onto the D118 towards
Budos. In Budos, bear round to
the left onto the D125, towards
Sauternes, crossing the river
Ciron and following this pleasant,
if winding, road through vines
and woods to Sauternes ⑧.

The Maison du Vin, in the
village square here, has wine-
tasting. Just outside Sauternes,
on a hilltop to the north, is
the 12th-century Château

d'Yquem *(not open to the
public)*. It is known for
producing one of France's
most prestigious white wines.

In Sauternes, follow the signs for
Roaillan and Langon. At the next
junction, turn left onto the D8 to
Langon. After 1km (half a mile),
bear right, staying on the D8 to
return to Langon.

WHERE TO EAT
Amelia Canta
Place du Marché, 33330, St-Émilion
☎ 05 57 74 48 03
🕑 Daily 10–7, Feb, Mar, Nov;
9–midnight, rest of year; closed Jan

BASICS
Maison du Vin
14 place de la Mairie, Sauternes
☎ 05 56 76 69 83
🕑 Mon–Fri 9–7, Sat–Sun 10–7

Château de Malromé
33490, St-André-du-Bois
☎ 05 56 76 44 92
🕑 Daily 10.30–5.30, Jul, Aug;
Wed–Sun 2.30–5.30, Apr, Sep, Oct;
Sun 2.30–5.30, Nov–end Mar;
Wed–Sun 2.30–6, May, Jun
🎟 Adult €5, child (10–17) €3.50
www.malrome.com

ROCAMADOUR

Perched high on the rocky plateau known as the Causse du Quercy, the village of Rocamadour seems to defy gravity, occupying an almost vertical site on three main levels. The site of the oldest pilgrimage in France, and a major stop on the pilgrim trail to Santiago de Compostela, it continues to astonish its many visitors with its breathtaking setting. This walk starts from the top of the village, and includes a stroll in the town as well as a circular walk in the Alzou valley, haunt of eagles and other birds of prey, through the surrounding countryside. Owing to the precipitous setting, you should expect some steep ascents and descents.

THE WALK

Length: Village walk: 1km (0.6 mile); country walk: 8km (5 miles)

Allow: Village walk: 1 hour 30 minutes; country walk: 3 hours

Start/end: Rocamadour

Parking: There are free parking areas at the top and bottom of the town.

HOW TO GET THERE

Rocamadour can be approached from the parking areas on two levels: via the D673 from the upper plateau, on foot or by lifts; or from the Alzou valley below, on foot or by a miniature train. Both approaches offer spectacular views.

THE VILLAGE WALK

According to legend, the religious origins of this rocky site go back to the hermit Amadour, whose perfectly preserved body was

The statue of the Black Madonna at the Chapelle de Notre-Dame

discovered in the 12th century. From that time on, miracles began to occur, and crowds of up to 30,000 pilgrims would attend the site on certain holy days.

From the parking area near the chateau **❶**, a coin-operated barrier *(€2.50 per person)* allows access to the ramparts for an unforgettable panorama of the site and its rocky setting. Go down the steeply winding Chemin de Croix, with the Stations of the Cross at each turn of the pathway. Pass through a tunnel under the basilica to arrive in the Cité Religieuse which has seven chapels.

Don't miss Chapelle de Notre-Dame **❷**, to the left of the basilica, which contains the small, much-revered statue of the Black Madonna, blackened by centuries of candle smoke. You can also visit the Musée d'Art Sacré Francis Poulenc **❸**, dedicated to the composer (1899–1963), who had a vision during a visit to the town in 1936 and subsequently composed *Litanies à la Vièrge Noire de Rocamadour*. The museum has an interesting collection of sacred art and artefacts.

Walk down the 223 steps of the Grand Escalier **❹** to visit the village at the lower level. Turn left along the main street (lined with souvenir shops and not very prepossessing) to pass the tourist office, next to the Hôtel de Ville. Just before one of the old town gates, Porte Salmon, turn right down the lane and then descend one of the flights of steps. Go towards the lower car park by the river.

THE COUNTRY WALK

This is marked with an image of a dragonfly *(libellule)* and has a signpost to Fouysselaze at the start.

Cross the river Alzou by the stone bridge, and take the lane on the left. After about 150m (170 yards), a little path on your right leads to the Fontaine de la Fillole. Climb the hill among hazel and oak trees. Once on the plateau, continue between drystone walls past the farm of Fouysselaze on your right.

On the farm of Fouysselaze **❶**, the farmers make the delicious little goats' milk cheeses known as *cabécou*.

When the path meets the tarmac road, turn right and follow the road past the entrance to the farm and a wall on the right where a sheep passage has been made. Skirt the large hollow on your right, known as *Le Cloup de Magès*.

To the left is a dolmen **❷**, at least 4,000 years old.

Leave the road and take the GR46 footpath to Rocamadour, crossing the D32 and following the sign for the Fontaine de Berthiol. There are magnificent views of the village through the trees. Cross the Alzou by the little bridge near the Moulin de Roquefraîche, go straight over the small crossroads, and enter the village by Porte Basse, then pass through Porte Hugon. If you can't face the Great Staircase **❸** again, take the lift and funicular through the rock, back up to the plateau where the walk started.

WHEN TO GO

Rocamadour can be crowded in high season. In late spring the ground is carpeted with meadow flowers.

Perched on a rocky plateau

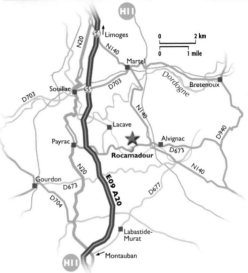

OUT AND ABOUT

WHERE TO EAT

There are plenty of bars and restaurants in the lower level of Rocamadour.

BASICS

Tourist information
46500, Rocamadour
☎ 05 65 33 22 00
www.rocamadour.com

GETTING AROUND

A Petit Train (miniature train) runs from Easter until the end of September, carrying visitors to and from the lower parking areas to the shops and restaurants *(adult return €3.50, child return €2)*. There is also a 30-minute evening tour of illuminated Rocamadour *(adult €5, child €2.50)*. A funicular lift between the top parking area and the religious citadel costs €4 return *(under 8 free)*. Another lift goes between the citadel and the shops and restaurants *(€3 return, under 8 free)*. Opening times for the lifts vary according to season.

Rocamadour is one of France's top sights and attracts crowds of visitors in the summer (top)

One of the many old houses in the village (left)

Vivid religious artwork (below)

BASQUE HILL COUNTRY

Forest and pasture-clad hills paint the Basque country in vivid shades of green. This tour explores some of the best of its scenic delights, with broad vistas and a preview of the Pyrenean peaks marking the French-Spanish frontier. You cross several cols, mostly by good but narrow roads, and with gradients that are generally not too steep.

THE DRIVE

Length: 116km (72 miles)
Allow: 1 day
Start/end: St-Jean-Pied-de-Port

An attractive small town on the river Nive, St-Jean-Pied-de-Port ❶ was formerly the capital of Basse Navarre and a meeting point for thousands of pilgrims making their way to the shrine of Santiago de Compostela in Spain. The old part of St-Jean is contained within the 15th-century fortified walls, while the Citadelle owes its sturdiness to the design of Louis XIV's great military engineer, Vauban. A walk along the ramparts gives views over the town's narrow streets and alleyways.

Leave St-Jean-Pied-de-Port, following directions for St-Palais and Mauléon. After 4.5km (3 miles), turn right in St-Jean-le-Vieux onto the D18, signed for Ahaxe and Mendive. Follow the D18 to begin the long climb to a series of cols, waymarked regularly for bicyclists (with *Col d'Iraty*, the height reached, and the remaining distance). On a green crest about 1km (half a mile) beyond Col d'Haltza, just out of sight on the left of the road, stands the Chapelle St-Sauveur.

The chapel, locked when not in use, is the setting for an annual Corpus Christi pilgrimage. It is barn-like in size and appearance and at first glance would seem to belong to a local hill farm. Surrounding it are 13 small crosses, and a larger stone pedestal with a crucifix stands nearby. A plaque fixed to one wall remembers with gratitude the help given by the Basques of Iraty to Belgian forces in World War II.

Continue to climb among beech woods until you reach Col de Burdincurutcheta (1,135m/

3,723ft), which is 13km (8 miles) from Mendive. Descend for 2.5km (1.5 miles) to a pastureland basin and a small tarn where the road forks. This is an ideal spot for a picnic, with a snack bar on the left open in season. Bear left onto the D19 and shortly afterwards enter the Forêt d'Iraty.

One of the great forests of the Pyrenees, this has mainly beech and yew with some pine. In previous centuries, large quantities of Iraty timber were used for shipbuilding. Today the forest has leafy trails winding through it and picnic areas alongside the Burdincurutcheta-Bagargui road. It is also a great place for cross-country skiing in winter.

Climbing once again through the forest, continue for 7km (4 miles), through les Chalets d'Iraty, until you arrive at Col Bagargui (1,327m/4,353 ft).

During the autumn migrations, millions of birds cross the Basque country. In October, Col Bagargui is a fine vantage point for viewing the flight of birds such as honey buzzards, storks, cranes and kites.

Descend the eastern side of the col (with some tight hairpin bends) to Larrau (13km/8 miles), then 2.5km (1.5 miles) farther on, cross a bridge and pass the buildings of Logibar to the right of the road beside the river. In a little under 15km (9 miles) from Logibar, the D26 meets the D918 at a T-junction. Turn left to reach Tardets-Sourholus ❷.

Tardets is a small town with fine, long views to the frontier mountains. It is a focus of Basque folklore and there is a pilgrimage here twice a year. The Chapelle de la Madeleine stands on a peak high above the valley to the north.

Continue on the D918 for 13km (8 miles) to Mauléon ❸.

Mauléon and Licharre stand on opposite banks of the river Saison, downstream from Tardets. Mauléon is an old feudal town clustered beneath the ruins of its 15th-century castle. On the corner of rue de la Navarre, on the left bank, is a Renaissance chateau with an impressive roof.

Just after passing the entrance sign to Mauléon, turn sharp left (with care), still on the D918, signed for Col d'Osquich and St-Jean-Pied-de-Port. At a small roundabout (traffic circle) 500m (quarter of a mile) later, turn left again and begin a gentle ascent for 13km (8 miles) to Col d'Osquich ❹.

Col d'Osquich (495m/1,624 ft) marks the border between Basse Navarre and the Soule district and offers wonderful views.

Cross the col. At the summit, a small pedestrian track from the lay-by (turnout) on the left leads off to the Chapelle St-Antoine, also known as the Chapelle de la Paix, at a height of 706m (2,316ft). You can see the chapel to the left, high on the skyline, from the road as it descends from the col. Pass by St-Just and Cibits to reach Larceveau. Turn left at the small roundabout (traffic circle) and follow the D933 for 11.5km (7 miles) to St-Jean-le-Vieux ❺.

In the Middle Ages this town was on the Santiago pilgrimage route, and beside the road in nearby Aphat-d'Ospital you can see the near-derelict 12th-century Chapelle St-Blaise, a tiny place of worship used by the pilgrims.

Continue for another 4.5km (3 miles) to return to St-Jean-Pied-de-Port.

OUT AND ABOUT

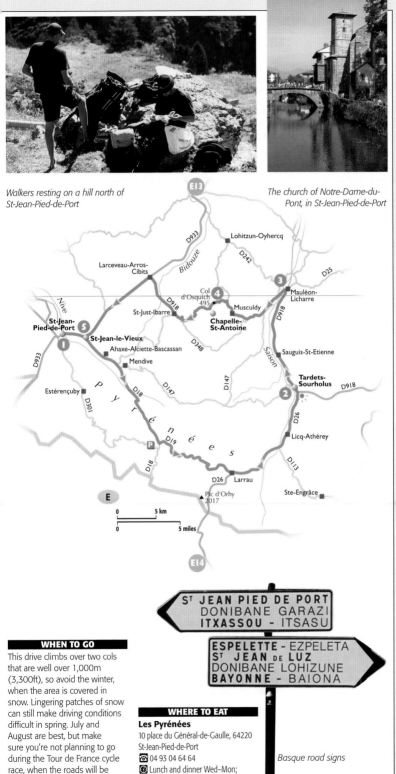

Walkers resting on a hill north of St-Jean-Pied-de-Port

The church of Notre-Dame-du-Pont, in St-Jean-Pied-de-Port

E13

Lohitzun-Oyhercq

D933

D242

Larceveau-Arros-Cibits

D25

Bidouze

Col d'Osquich 495 **4**

Mauléon-Licharre **3**

Nive

St-Just-Ibarre

D918

Musculdy

Chapelle-St-Antoine

St-Jean-Pied-de-Port **5** **1**

St-Jean-le-Vieux

Ahaxe-Alciette-Bascassan

D348

Sauguis-St-Etienne

D918

Mendive

Saison

D933

Estérençuby

D18

D147

D147

Tardets-Sourholus **2**

D918

D301

D19

P

D26

Licq-Athérey

P y r é n é e s

D18

D26 Larrau

D113

▲ Pic d'Orhy 2017

Ste-Engrâce

E

0		5 km
0		5 miles

E14

ST JEAN PIED DE PORT
DONIBANE GARAZI
ITXASSOU - ITSASU

ESPELETTE - EZPELETA
ST JEAN DE LUZ
DONIBANE LOHIZUNE
BAYONNE - BAIONA

WHEN TO GO

This drive climbs over two cols that are well over 1,000m (3,300ft), so avoid the winter, when the area is covered in snow. Lingering patches of snow can still make driving conditions difficult in spring. July and August are best, but make sure you're not planning to go during the Tour de France cycle race, when the roads will be closed to traffic.

WHERE TO EAT

Les Pyrénées
10 place du Général-de-Gaulle, 64220 St-Jean-Pied-de-Port
☎ 04 93 04 64 64
🕐 Lunch and dinner Wed–Mon; closed 5–28 Jan, 20 Nov–22 Dec

Basque road signs

CIRQUE DE GAVARNIE

The Cirque de Gavarnie is a massive, natural amphitheatre of semicircular precipices in three towering limestone tiers, with caves, ice-bridges, rivers of scree, glaciers and waterfalls. This walk in the Parc National des Pyrénées starts in the village of Gavarnie, and includes a strenuous route up into the forest high above the valley path taken by most visitors to the *cirque* and its 423m (1,387 foot) waterfall. Apart from signposts at major path junctions, the route is not waymarked, but the main path is easily discernible: Do not deviate from it. If you prefer not to risk the steep parts of the walk, remain in the valley and go directly to the Hôtel du Cirque.

THE WALK

Length: 10km (6 miles)
Allow: 1 day
Start/end: Gavarnie village
Parking: Park on the lower outskirts of Gavarnie, near the Route de Boucharo.

HOW TO GET THERE

At 1,350m (4,430ft), Gavarnie is the highest village in the Haute-Pyrénées. It is at the end of the D921, south of Lourdes and Argelès-Gazost and close to the Spanish border.

Gavarnie was originally a hamlet inhabited by shepherds. During the Middle Ages, the Knights Templars protected the Bouitabharo Pass on the pilgrim route to Santiago de Compostela. The Templars' headquarters later transformed into a church, which contains an unusual 12th-century statue of the Virgin Mary holding a pilgrim's flask.

From the parking area, walk up to the heart of the village, with its Maison du Parc and church. Continue through the village with the Gave de Gavarnie stream on your left, then follow the track up the valley. At the first bridge, bear left, cross the Gave and turn immediately right. After about 250m (275 yards), you'll see a path on the left next to a small stream, marked with a signpost indicating Parc

National 1 hour, Refuge des Espuguettes 2 hours, Hourquette d'Alans 3 hours 15 minutes, and Barrage des Gloriettes 5 hours 30 minutes. Take this path, the Chemin des Espugues ❶, which rises steeply in a series of zigzags through rocks and bushes, eventually entering the forest. Continue climbing until the path begins to level out and another signpost appears.

This signpost indicates Refuge des Espuguettes 1 hour to the left, Parc National 250m and Cirque de Gavarnie 1 hour to the right. Take the right-hand path, and cross a small wooden bridge across a tumbling stream. This is an idyllic spot for a picnic, with patches of lush meadowland shaded by trees, and glimpses of Gavarnie far below. A few metres farther on, pass the Refuge du Pailha ❷ on your left and follow the path through forest until it enters the national park (via an unusual kind of wooden gate). From here the path follows the contours of the rock face, which rises and sometimes overhangs on the left, with views to the right down through trees to the valley track.

The path leads eventually down to the Hôtel du Cirque ❸, where, from the terrace, the full magnificence of the cirque's panorama is at last revealed. An orientation table

describes (in French) the origins of the cirque and names the peaks and features. In recent years, the site has developed into one of France's main rock-climbing bases.

Follow the path towards the cirque for about 100m, then take the path on the left to go into the cirque.

The limestone rockfaces are nearly 1,500m (5,000ft) high, making the highest peak, Le Marboré, more than 3,000m (10,000ft) above sea level. The main waterfall, la Grande Cascade, is five times the height of the Eiffel tower, and the highest in Europe.

Crossing several streams, continue to the base of La Grande Cascade. Return to the Hôtel du Cirque along the same path. Back at the Hôtel, take the track on the left and follow it down through woods and clearings. At a stream, cross the bridge and pass an information panel on your left. Some 100m farther on, the path forks. Take the left fork and cross the Gave de Gavarnie over another bridge. Follow the path until it reaches a disused bridge over wetland. Take the path that rises on the right and walk across open ground towards the *gave* (stream), now running on your right and below you.

As the path bends to the left, on rising ground to the left is the tomb of Franz Schrader ❹ (d.1924), a geographer and landscape artist, who mapped the Massif de Gavarnie, as well as capturing the area on canvas.

Continue to follow the path along the left bank of the *gave* back to Gavarnie.

OUT AND ABOUT

Walking along the waterside path to the Cirque de Gavarnie (above and above right)

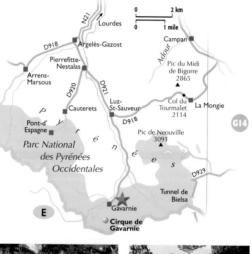

WHEN TO GO

This walk is possible from mid-May through to mid-November, although the waterfall loses its allure as the summer progresses, sometimes reducing to a trickle by autumn. The route most visitors take, which leads directly from the village to the cirque, is walkable at almost any time if you are properly equipped. Weather conditions for the following 24 hours are posted in the window of the tourist information office, or you can ask at the Maison du Parc.

BASICS

Maison du Parc
Gavarnie
☎ 05 62 92 42 48
🕐 Call ahead for opening times

Wild flowers on the walk (right). Typical scenery on the way to the Cirque de Gavarnie (far right)

BONIFACIO

Bonifacio (see page 211), poised above the Mediterranean on white limestone cliffs, is the best-sheltered port in Corsica. Its imposing citadel and fortified old town tower above the active port. Lying in a vast, bare region, Bonifacio is distinct from the rest of Corsica in its customs and its geography. The town has given its name to the narrow, treacherous straits that separate Corsica from Sardinia and controls many of the strategic routes in the western Mediterranean. This two-part walk starts with a stroll around the town followed by a ramble along the coast, taking in churches, beaches, a lighthouse and impressive views of the citadel and even Sardinia.

THE WALK

Length: 10km (6 miles)

Allow: 1 day

Start/end: Bonifacio

HOW TO GET THERE

Bonifacio is in the south of Corsica and is served by Figari-Sud Corse airport, 20km (12 miles) to the north. The main coastal roads, the N196 and N198, both finish in the town. In high summer the town's lack of parking spaces becomes apparent and traffic jams are not unknown.

THE TOWN WALK

Bonifacio was founded by the Tuscans but was seized by Genoa in the 12th century. The indigenous population was expelled and replaced by colonists, who built a new town to a geometric plan. The massive citadel, occupying the western end of the promontory, is set back from the cliffs, but the old town sits precariously on the precipice. Enclosed within the ramparts, the old town has narrow, shady streets with high houses, built as individual fortresses and once accessible only by retractable ladders. Each house had its own courtyard, oven, cistern, olive press, cellar, granary and sometimes a stable. The flying buttresses over the streets are gutters for collecting precious rainwater.

Park near the port and walk to Église St-Érasme ❶. Take the paved ramp to the left of the church up to the Col St-Roch. Continue up a second paved ramp towards the Porte de Gênes and pass through the gate into place d'Armes, enter rue des Deux-Empereurs ❷.

The Habsburg Emperor Charles V (1500–1558), who was also

Charles I of Spain, had a life-long struggle against France. He passed through Bonifacio in 1541, and a plaque in rue des Deux-Empereurs commemorates his visit. It also celebrates the fact that Napoleon Bonaparte, Corsica's most famous son and the Emperor of France, stayed in a house in the street for a few weeks in 1793.

Take the third street on the left, to visit the 13th-century Église Sainte-Marie-Majeure ❸, then take rue Archivolto to the Maison du Podestat, also 13th century. Continue to place Montepagano and pass beyond the citadel walls onto the peninsula, by way of rue St-Dominique and the 13th-century Oratoire Sainte-Croix and Église St-Dominique, the latter one of the few Gothic buildings on the island.

At the far west end of the peninsula, next to a desolate area known as the Bosco, is the marine cemetery ❹. This is a spectacular place with its white mausolea, each topped by a crucifix, leaning together like little houses by the sea. The townlike atmosphere is heightened by an orderly grid of streets which takes you from one end to the other. From here you can look over the turquoise waters of the Mediterranean to Sardinia.

Return to the citadel, passing Église St-Dominique on your right, to visit the limestone steps of Escalier du Roi d'Aragon, via place Carrega.

The 187 steps ❺ hewn from the limestone cliff lead down to the sea. Although the stairway was no doubt an escape route if the port was

blocked, legend says that it was cut overnight by Aragonese invaders in an attempt to capture the city in 1420.

Return to place Montepagano by rue des Pachas and take rue Doria to place Manichella and place du Marché ❻, 65m (215ft) above the sea, with a breathtaking vista. Take ruelle de la Madonnetta back to place d'Armes, then return to the port.

THE COAST WALK

From the port, leave the town and head north along the N196 towards the Site Préhistorique de l'Araguina ❶. Before the campsite, after the garage, turn left and take the hidden path towards plage de l'Arinella. Continue for about 750m (820 yards) towards a small bay with a beach (plage de la Catena) opposite the citadel of Bonifacio. Just above the beach, the path forks. Take the path on the right that leads away from the sea. Continue westwards for about 1.5km (1 mile). The path makes a sharp turn to the left and heads towards the Anse de Fazzio. (The other path continues to plage Paraguano). About 200m (220 yards) farther on, the path reaches plage de Fazzio, opposite a small island ❷.

The path continues around the eastern side of the bay. Follow the coast road towards the lighthouse, Phare de la Madonetta ❸. At the Grotte Marine du Sdragonato sea cave ❹, the path leaves the shoreline for about 100m (109 yards), then rejoins it in a small bay. Follow the marked path and continue around the two small bays approached earlier (plage de l'Arinella and plage de la Catena) back to the port.

OUT AND ABOUT

Typical Corsican coastline (above)

Yachts moor just off the plage Paraguano

Turquoise waters at the plage Paraguano

WHEN TO GO

You can do this walk all year round, but bear in mind that it is an exposed route, so take precautions against the sun in summer.

WHERE TO EAT

Bonifacio has plenty of restaurants. If you are doing the coast walk you might like to take a picnic.

Guided excursions can help you explore France with the added bonus of local knowledge. The trips below are all accompanied and include outdoor sports such as horse-riding, jet-skiing and white water rafting, as well as a wine-tasting vineyard tour.

PARIS

PARIS WALKING TOURS
Tel 01 48 09 21 40
www.pariswalkingtours.com
Take a two-hour walking tour through the city, with English commentary.
🕐 Call ahead for times and itineraries or check the website
💶 Adult €10, child €5

BATEAUX MOUCHES
Tel 01 40 76 99 99 (recorded information in English); 01 42 25 96 10 (reservations)
www.bateaux-mouches.fr
Board at the Pont de l'Alma for a river trip down the Seine in a glass-roofed boat. The tour lasts one hour 10 minutes and there are also dinner cruises.
🕐 Daily every 20–30 min, 10am–11pm, summer; daily 11, 2.30, 4, 6 and 9, winter
💶 Adult €9, child (4–12) €4, under 4 free

NORTHWEST FRANCE

PÉNICHE ST-CHRISTOPHE
2 quai Surcouf, 35605, Redon
Tel 02 99 71 46 03
Boat tours on the Nantes-Brest canal on a 1932 traditional barge. Tours last an hour, two hours, four hours or the whole day, depending on the day of the week.
🕐 Apr–end Sep, not all tours daily
💶 Adult €7–€15, child (5–12) €4.50–€10

LA MAISON DE LA BAIE
Port Est, 35960, Le Vivier-sur-Mer
Tel 02 99 48 84 38
www.maison-baie.com
Guided walking tours of the Baie du Mont-St-Michel. Explore the mussel and oyster beds, as well as the tidal shallows.
🕐 Tours are 2–8 hours and are year round, weather permitting
💶 Adult €9, child (6–12) €6.50

NORTH AND NORTHEAST FRANCE

FUGUES EN FRANCE
'Les Chambertines', Carnot, 21340 Nolay
Tel 03 80 21 71 18
www.bonappetit-france.com
One-day gastronomic tours of the Champagne region from Paris, including tasting at a range of houses. They also do tours of this and other wine regions, lasting 2–15 days.
🕐 Call ahead for times and itineraries or check the website
💶 One-day tour with brasserie lunch €400 per person

SALIENT TOURS
Tel 01249 445075 (UK number), 06 86 05 61 30
www.salienttours.com
Part-day guided tours of the WWI Somme battlefields. Pick up from Albert railway station.
🕐 Tue–Sun, Easter–end Oct
💶 Short tour 3–5.30pm €22, standard tour 10–2pm €29

THE LOIRE

CROISIÈRE SUR LA LOIRE
EURL Ligérienne de Navigation, 56 quai de la Loire, 37210, Rochecorbon
Tel 02 47 52 68 88
50-minute boat tour along the Loire, past the chalk cliffs of Rochecarbon and the Château de Moncontour.
🕐 Daily 4pm and 5pm, Jul, Aug; Sat, Sun 4pm and 5pm, May, Jun and Sep
💶 Adult €8.50, child (under 12) €6

CENTRAL FRANCE AND THE ALPS

ÉCOLE DU SKI FRANÇAIS
Carrefour des Dolomites, 73155 Val d'Isère
Tel 04 79 06 02 34
www.esf-valdisere.com
Guided full-day and half-day ski, cross-country ski, snowboard or snowshoe excursions.
🕐 Ski season early Dec–early May
💶 Guide €270 per day, up to 4 people

SOUTHEAST FRANCE

AQUA VIVA EST
12 boulevard de la République, 04120 Castelanne
Tel 04 92 83 75 74
www.aquavivaest.com
Guided full-day and half-day white-water rafting, canoeing and kayaking trips along the Gorges du Verdon and the Vésubie and Tinée rivers.
🕐 Daily late Apr–late Sep
💶 Full-day (5 hours) €61, half-day (3.5 hours) €50

VISIOBULLE
Ponton Courbet, boulevard d'Aguillon 06600, Antibes (ticket office)
Tel 04 93 74 85 42
www.visiobulle.com
Glass-bottomed boat trip from Juan-les-Pins to the Baie des Millionaires, with views to the seabed.
🕐 4 departures daily Apr–end Jun and Sep; 7 times daily Jul, Aug
💶 Adult €11, child (5–12) €5

SOUTHWEST FRANCE

LES ÉCRURIES DE BOUAU
Quartier de Bouau, 40310, Parlebosq
Tel 05 58 44 30 83
www.horse-trek.com
Guided horse-riding through the Bas-Armagnac area. Treks last 2–6 days and include accommodation, meals and an English-speaking guide.
🕐 Treks all year
💶 Two-day/three-night trek €275

CORSICA

RANDONÉE EN JETSKI
Route de l'Aéroport, 20290, Lucciana
Tel 06 14 62 30 30
www.cls.fr.fm
Jetski tours of the Corsican coast. Trips last from 2–6 days. The cost includes all meals, accommodation and your luggage transfer.
🕐 Mar to mid-Oct
💶 Two-day/one-night tour in low season (May or Oct) €690

OUT AND ABOUT

This chapter lists places to eat and places to stay alphabetically by town within France's regions. In each town, places to eat precede places to stay, although many establishments offer both food and accommodation.

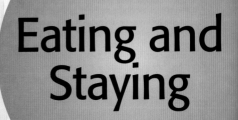

Eating and Staying

FRENCH CUISINE

France loves its food—and regards its top chefs in the same way it treats its famous artists and musicians. Even an office cafeteria will take pride in the quality of the food it serves, and any French citizen with a napkin on their lap and a fork in their hand expects fine ingredients, well prepared. Regional cuisine is seen as a reflection of each corner of the country and while Paris may have the big names and bigger spenders, dinner in a provincial town can eclipse a meal in the capital.

The celebrity chefs, such as Alain Senderens, Paul Bocuse and Joel Robuchon, are the standard bearers of haute cuisine. They and their colleagues Alain Ducasse and Jacques and Laurent Pourcel dictate the food fads of tomorrow. Garlanded with Michelin rosettes and Gault et Millau toques (France's highest culinary awards), they have introduced the concepts of world and fusion foods to the nation. In recent years, a move to lighter dishes and simpler techniques has, belatedly, acknowledged vegetarian tastes, although France's concept of vegetarianism is a little hazy, sometimes involving beef stock, chicken and bacon.

France also has numerous inexpensive North African, Lebanese and Vietnamese restaurants in most towns.

Wherever you dine, remember that fast food is not indigenous. Be prepared to take time over your meal—good food is a way of life and meals are something to be enjoyed, rather than rushed.

RESTAURANTS

Every town has its respected restaurants, quite different from the bistros and brasseries for everyday eating. In these, you'll find a more refined setting, with starched linen, polished glass and silverware and a sense of hushed reverence for the gastronomic offerings to come. Here, families celebrate birthdays and communions, promises are whispered and business deals settled over something even more important than a handshake. Remember to dress smartly and reserve in advance. You can find quality regional food in the dining rooms of Logis de France hotels and there are Michelin-starred establishments across the country, with Paul Bocuse in Lyon, the Pourcel twins in Languedoc and the legacy of the late Bernard Loiseau in Burgundy. The *menu dégustation*, which is only found in the finest restaurants, is a prix-fixe menu offering a sample of the finest dishes accompanied by a selection of appropriate wines. Best value are the midweek set menus at lunchtime, bringing a meal at even the most stellar establishments down to a realistic price.

BRASSERIES AND BISTROS

Brasseries were once brewery bars that served meals. Today, they are friendly informal restaurants that open long hours. Enjoy local special dishes, as well as standards such as *steak-frites* and *choucroute* (sauerkraut). Bistros are often small, independent or family-run restaurants serving traditional cooking, with a modest wine list. In Paris and across France, top chefs are opening bistro annexes to their flagship restaurants. The Pourcels' Jardin des Sens in Montpellier has spawned satellites in other cities, such as Avignon.

CAFÉS AND BARS

Cafés and bars serve coffee, soft drinks, alcohol, snacks and often herbal and traditional teas too. They open from breakfast time until late in the evening and you can expect to pay a little more for your drink if you sit at a table or on the outdoor terrace. You'll notice the locals tend to stand at the bar. Bars often have newspapers and you can linger over your cup of coffee people watching.

CUTTING COSTS

If you are on a budget, have your main meal at lunchtime, when most restaurants serve a *menu du jour*, or daily menu, of two or three courses with a glass of wine for around 50 per cent of the cost in the evening. Many restaurants have prix-fixe meals in the evening, too, with three, four or more courses, the best of which is the *menu gastronomique*.

OPENING TIMES

Most restaurants and bistros keep strict serving times. Restaurants open at 12, close at 2.30, then reopen at 7.30. Except in the bustling heart of a lively city, restaurants stop taking orders between 10pm and 11pm. Many restaurants close Saturday and Monday lunchtimes and on Sunday evenings. Some Paris restaurants may close during July and August, and establishments on the coast often close completely between November and Easter.

ETIQUETTE

Most restaurants include service in the price of dishes, indicated by *service compris* or *s.c.* If the service is exceptional you may like to leave a tip. Although it is only the very top restaurants that may have a dress code, it is usual to dress up when dining in a smarter venue. Address staff as *Monsieur, Madame* or *Mademoiselle,* and never call a waiter *garçon.* By law restaurants must provide a non-smoking section, although this may be a token table by the lavatories.

EATING AND STAYING

THE MEDITERRANEAN

... à la languedocienne: with tomatoes, aubergines (eggplant), *cèpes* (a type of mushroom) and garlic.

... à la niçoise: with olive oil, garlic, tomatoes, onion, herbs, olives, capers, anchovies and tarragon.

... à la provençale: with olive oil, garlic, tomatoes, onion and herbs.

Bouillabaisse: fish stew served with *aïoli* (garlic mayonnaise) or *rouille* (chilli and garlic mayonnaise).

BRITTANY, NORMANDY AND THE LOIRE

Agneau de prés-salés: lamb from animals raised on the salt marshes.

Beurre blanc: butter whipped with white wine vinegar and shallots.

Châteaubriand: a thick cut of tenderloin steak for two people with shallot, herb and white-wine sauce.

Coquille St-Jacques: scallop served hot in its shell in a cream sauce topped with melted cheese or toasted breadcrumbs.

Cotriade: fish stew.

Brandade de morue: paste of salt cod mixed with milk, garlic and olive oil.

Cargolade: stew of snails in wine.

Cassoulet: a thick stew of haricot beans and garlic with goose and pork sausage.

Daube: meat stewed in wine.

Foie gras à la toulousaine: goose liver in pastry.

Pistou: sauce made of ground garlic, basil and cheese bound with olive oil.

Ratatouille: tomatoes, onions, courgettes (zucchini) and aubergines (eggplant) slow cooked in garlic and olive oil.

Salade niçoise: tomatoes, French beans, anchovies, olives, peppers and boiled egg.

Soupe de poisson: a soup of puréed mixed fish.

THE PYRENEES AND THE SOUTHWEST

...à la basquaise: meat served with Bayonne ham, *cèpe* mushrooms and potatoes.

...à la bordelaise: with red wine sauce accompanied by mixed vegetables.

...à la landaise: dishes cooked in goose fat with garlic.

...à la périgourdine: accompanied by a truffle or foie gras sauce, or stuffed with truffles or foie gras.

Confit de canard: pieces of duck that are salted, cooked and then preserved in their own fat.

Foie gras: the enlarged liver of maize-fed geese or ducks, cooked and served in slices hot or cold.

Lièvre à la royale: hare boned and stuffed with bacon cooked in wine and served with a truffle sauce.

Magret de canard: boned duck breast, grilled or fried.

Crêpes and galettes: pancakes with either sweet or savoury fillings.

Far: a thick, sweet tart with prunes, similar to a flan.

Homard à l'armoricaine: lobster served flambéed in a cream and wine sauce.

Moules marinières: mussels in a white wine, shallot and parsley sauce.

Noisette de porc aux pruneaux: loin of pork with prunes.

Plat (assiette ou plateau) de fruits de mer: seafood platter consisting of mixed crayfish (*langouste*), oysters (*huîtres*), prawns/shrimps (*crevettes*), mussels (*moules*), crab (*crabes*) and whelks (*boulots*), served on ice.

Sauce normande: made with cider and cream.

Tarte tatin: upside-down apple tart.

THE NORTH AND ALSACE-LORRAINE

Bäeckeoffe: mixed meat cooked in wine with potatoes and onions.

Carbonnade flamande: beef slow cooked in beer and spices.

Choucroute garnie: pickled cabbage cooked in wine with pork, sausage and smoked ham, served with boiled potatoes.

Chou rouge à flamande: red cabbage cooked with apples in vinegar and sugar.

Jambon en croûte: ham in a pastry case.

Quiche Lorraine: egg custard tart with bacon, onion and herbs.

Salade de cervelas: cold sausage in vinaigrette sauce.

Waterzooi: a soup originating from Belgium, made of a vegetable and cream stew, with either chicken or freshwater fish.

EATING AND STAYING

THE JURA AND THE ALPS

Diots: pork sausages.

Fondue: there are two different types: *au fromage*, cubes of bread dipped into molten cheese mixed with wine (and sometimes kirsch); or *bourguignonne*: cubes of meat cooked in oil, then dipped into sauces.

Gratin dauphinois: sliced potatoes baked in milk with nutmeg.

Gratin savoyard: sliced potatoes with cheese cooked in stock.

CORSICA

Aziminu: a type of *bouillabaisse* (see The Mediterranean).

Brocciu: a sheep's cheese made on Corsica.

Fiadone: cheesecake with lemon.

Fritelles de brocciu: fried doughnuts of cheese and chestnut flour.

Oursins: sea urchins, a local delicacy.

Piverunta: lamb stew with bell peppers.

Raffia: a skewer of roasted lamb offal.

Sanglier: wild or semi-wild pig.

Tianu di fave: pork stew with haricot beans.

BURGUNDY AND THE NORTHERN RHÔNE

Andouille: tripe and pork sausage served cold.

Andouillette: tripe and pork sausage served hot.

Boeuf bourguignon: beef slow cooked with onions and mushrooms in red wine.

Boudin: blood pudding/sausage.

Coq au vin: male chicken with mushrooms and onions stewed in red wine (traditionally Chambertin).

Escargots à la bourguignonne: snails in garlic and parsley butter.

Jambon persillé: ham and parsley in jelly served cold in slices.

Pommes à la lyonnaise: fried sliced potatoes and onions.

Poulet de Bresse: chicken from Bourg en Bresse (considered the best in France).

Poulet (or jau) au sang: chicken in a blood-thickened sauce.

Quenelles de brochet: individual fish mousses with cream sauce.

Saladier à la lyonnaise: cooked sheep's feet and pig's trotters, ox tongue and calf's head served with vinaigrette dressing.

SAUCES

Béchamel: a classic sauce of flour, butter and milk. Often a base of other sauces such as Mornay, with cheese.

Béarnaise: egg yolk, vinegar, butter, white wine, shallots and tarragon.

Diane: cream and pepper sauce.

Chasseur: hunter-style, with wine, mushrooms, shallots and herbs.

Demi-glace: brown sauce of stock with sherry or Madeira wine.

…à la meunière: a method of serving fish, fried in butter then served with lemon juice, butter and parsley.

HOW TO ORDER STEAK

The French taste is for meat to be lightly cooked. Lamb will automatically come rare (unless you demand otherwise). If you order steak, you will be asked how you would like it cooked. The options are as follows:

Bleu: blue, the rarest steak, warm on the outside but uncooked and cool in the middle.

Saignant: bloody, or rare, the steak is cooked until it starts to bleed and is warm in the middle.

À point: literally 'at the point'. The meat is cooked until it just stops bleeding. Many restaurants serve steak *à point* with some blood in the middle. If you want a warm pink middle but no visible blood, ask for steak *plus à point*. It's not an official French term, but good restaurants should oblige.

Bien cuit: 'well cooked', served with only a narrow pink middle. If you want no pink to remain, ask for it *bien bien cuit*, although your waiter may not be impressed.

STAYING IN FRANCE

From palaces to farmyards, the range of places to stay in France depends as much on your taste as your budget. The high quality international hotel chains are found everywhere, although the more 'French' option may be a campsite, _gîte_ or family-run _auberge_.

Hotels are inspected regularly and classified into six categories: no star, 1*, 2*, 3*, 4* and 4*L (Luxury). They must display their rates (including tax) both outside the hotel and in the rooms, and charge per room and not per person. You generally have to pay extra for breakfast and for any additional beds you may want in your room.

There are two ways to get hotels beyond your budget without paying more than you can afford: In Paris and major cities, booking a package with a major tour operator will often allow you to stay in a better class of hotel than you might otherwise consider affordable. The other deal, in some 60 towns and cities (but not Paris), is through the Bon Weekend en Ville promotion. This runs from November until March (year round in around 25 cities) and offers two nights for the price of one at a range of hotels for stays beginning on a Friday or Saturday night. This deal also includes discounts and two-for-one deals on sights and local buses. It's only available from participating tourist offices or via the website www.bon-week-end-en-villes.com.

The increasing number of inexpensive air fares to regional French airports from the UK and other European cities has widened the possibilities for arranging your own holiday package.

LUXURY

If you are looking for a luxury hotel, then France is the right place for you. The traditional haunts of the rich and famous include the fabulous Belle Époque hotels on the Riviera, which offer the full-luxury treatment, and the glitz of the Paris Ritz. These have been joined by new designer hotels such as the Hi-Hotel in Nice, where concept rooms involve rock pools and high-tech plasma screens. Smaller, but no less expensive,

are the boutique hotels, with no more than a couple of dozen rooms styled by fashion gurus. For true luxury (that's truly French), stay at one of the country's many chateaux–former aristocratic and royal residences which now offer paying guests a taste of another era. For more information, look up the website of Relais and Chateaux (_www.relaischateaux.com_).

In most of the luxury options, health and beauty treatments are provided in state-of-the-art spas.

ON A BUDGET

Budget hotels may be something of a luxury. Independent city hotels are often surprisingly smart, although sometimes horribly dated and draughty. Bland international chain hotels and motels are the easy option, and while these may be useful overnight stops on long _autoroute_ journeys south, there are far more interesting options available at similar prices. Best of all are the Logis de France hotels–you can get a full list from the French Tourist Office. These are small, family-run inns and hotels offering a good standards, from basic and comfortable to quaint and charming. Most have their own restaurants, offering traditional local dishes of a high quality. All are regularly inspected and listed on the website www.logis-de-france.com. Some have themed breaks which promote winter sports, fishing or hiking. Some hotels, particularly in more remote areas, offer deals including dinner or all meals. Make sure you check whether room rates include breakfast. In many city hotels, €8 for a croissant and coffee may seem rather expensive, when the café-bar at the corner offers the same for less.

BED-AND-BREAKFAST

Chambre d'hôte is France's answer to the traditional bed-and-breakfast, and local tourist offices have lists of families who offer rooms to visitors. However, the best *chambres d'hôte* are affiliated to the Gîtes de France organization (see below). Graded with one to four ears of corn *(épis)*, depending on the level of comfort and facilities, each region's selection is published in

week or fortnight, and the accommodation is usually simple and decent (bring your own linen or rent on-site), but with a certain rustic charm. Graded from the simple to the very comfortable, the properties are listed in national and regional guides, and may also be found through local tourist offices.

For accredited gîtes see www.gites-de-france.fr.

CAMPING

More than 9,000 fully-equipped campsites, officially graded from 0 to 4*, and 2,300 farm campsites are regularly inspected and graded as carefully as the nation's hotels. Most have excellent facilities, with mobile homes and

a dedicated brochure. Often housed in converted farm buildings or restored watermills, they give you the opportunity to experience French life. Breakfast usually includes home-made treats, from fresh croissants to jams. Since many are run by farmers' wives and vineyard owners, it is worth taking the Table d'Hôte option and dining with the family at least once. In Paris, B&B in private homes is available through www.bed-and-breakfast-in-paris.com.

A deluxe option is bed-and-breakfast with the nobility. Princes and countesses offer rooms in their family chateaux in the Loire and western France. Brochures are available from Bienvenue au Chateau (*2 rue de la Loire, BP 20411, 44204, Nantes; www.bienvenueauchateau.com*).

SELF CATERING

While plenty of holiday companies sell package deals at self-contained holiday parks—with the obligatory kids' club, face painting and live entertainment in season, a popular alternative is to rent a *gîte*. These are self-contained cottages, houses and apartments, often with swimming pools, in small towns and country areas, and are generally administered through Gîtes de France. You can rent *gîtes* by the

pre-pitched tents ready for occupation. Visitors with their own caravans and tents can find inexpensive sites offering electricity, showers and lavatories. In high season (in the north from May–September, and in the south from April to October) it is important to reserve ahead; you may not park your motorhome or put up your tent beside the beach or at the roadside. Police stations have addresses of local campsites in an emergency.

The National Federation of Campsites can be contacted on 01 42 72 84 08 or www.campingfrance.com

TIPS

• The Loisirs Acceuil desk at regional tourist offices arranges themed breaks in each region using local hotels, *gîtes* and *chambres d'hôtes*. These may include extras such as fishing or truffle-hunting excursions with your hosts, farmhouse cookery lessons and craft workshops.
• Paris hotels often charge lower rates during July and August, and provincial and seaside hotels may reduce their prices after mid-September.
• If you are planning a winter sports holiday, remember that after Christmas, many hotels offer huge discounts during school term-time.
• For a little extra, hotels will often put another bed in your room—ideal for families on a budget.
• In cities outside conference season, try asking hotels for a discounted rate.
• If you are planning a hiking tour of a region, you can arrange to have your luggage transported between Logis hotels by prior arrangement. In some regions the hotel may even have donkeys carry your bags.

EATING AND STAYING

HOTEL CHAINS

Name of hotel chain	Description	Website	Phone number
Best Western	The world's largest hotel consortium has more than 150 hotels in France.	www.bestwestern.com	0800 393 130 (UK) 800/780-7234 (US) 0800 904 490 (France)
Campanile	This chain of hotels with restaurants has nearly 500 establishments across France.	www.campanile.fr	0825 003 003 (France)
Châteaux & Hotels de France	An affiliation of luxury hotels and chateaux.	www.chateaux-hotels.com	0820 354 725 (France)
Comfort Inn	This leading limited-service hotel chain claims 'luxury on a budget'.	www.comfortinn.com	0800 444 444 (UK) 877/424-6423 (US) 0800 912 424 (France)
Formule 1	Inexpensive out-of-town hotels, which have fixed-price rooms with 3 beds.	www.hotelformule1.com	0892 685 685 (France)
Golden Tulip	This Netherlands-based hotel group has Golden Tulip hotels (four-star) or Tulip Inns (three-star) in major French cities.	www.goldentulip.com	08705 300 200 (UK) 800/448-8355 (US)
Hilton	Quality hotels in Paris, Lyon, Strasbourg and Cannes.	www.hilton.com	08705 909 090 (UK) 800/HILTONS (US) 0800 907 546 (France)
Ibis	Hotels in this budget chain usually have a restaurant, bar and 24-hour reception.	www.ibishotel.com	0870 609 0963 (UK) 0892 686 686 (France)
Intercontinental/ Holiday Inn	The Intercontinental group includes a range of hotels from luxury Intercontinental through to Holiday Inn and Holiday Inn Express.	www.ichotel.com	0800 405 060 (UK) 800/465-4329 (US) 0800 905 999 (France)
Kyriad	Comfortable, reasonably priced hotels.	www.kyriad.com	0825 003 003 (France)
Marriott	The Marriott hotels in France are in Paris and Monaco.	www.marriott.com	0800 221 222 (UK) 888/236-2427 (US) 0800 908 333 (France)
Mercure	Choose from 3 grades—simple, enhanced comfort and refined.	www.mercure.com	0870 609 0965 (UK) 800/MERCURE (US) 0825 883 333 (France)
Novotel	Comfortable hotels, usually with good-sized bedrooms.	www.novotel.com	0870 609 0961 (UK) 800/NOVOTEL (US) 0825 884 444 (France)
Première Classe	Practical, good-value hotels, which have rooms with 3 beds.	www.envergure.fr	0892 688 123 (France)
Radisson	There are Radisson hotels in Paris, Nice and Cannes.	www.radisson.com	0800 374 411 (UK) 888/201-1718 (US) 0800 916 060 (France)
Relais du Silence	This is an affiliation of peaceful, characterful hotels with good food.	www.relais-du-silence.com	01 44 49 90 00 (France)
Relais & Châteaux	A chain of smart hotels and chateaux.	www.relaischateaux.fr	01 42 99 80 80 (France)
Sofitel	Comfortable hotels with restaurants.	www.sofitel.com	0870 609 0964 (UK) 800/221-4542 (US) 0825 885 555 (France)

Restaurants and Hotels

All the hotels and restaurants listed accept credit cards unless otherwise stated.

🍴 RESTAURANTS
The prices given are for a two-course lunch (L) and a three-course dinner (D) for two people, without drinks. The wine price is for the least expensive bottle. By law all restaurants and cafés have to provide a non-smoking area, although in practice this is often ignored.

🛏 HOTELS
The prices given are the lowest and highest for a double room for one night. Note that rates can vary widely during the year.

PARIS

EATING
In Paris it's possible to sample all of France's great regional dishes without leaving town. The Ambassade d'Auvergne (see this page), near the Centre Georges Pompidou, serves warming feel-good dishes from the heart of France, while Au Trou Gascon (see page 349) is a taste of the gastronomic southwest. Of course, Paris is also the home of chefs with an eye on posterity, so Alain Senderens, Guy Savoy and the other masters of taste dictate today the food fads of tomorrow. Alain Ducasse even has an out-of-town cookery school where visitors can learn his fusion food techniques (at a price), while the Cordon Bleu school in central Paris teaches the rules of classic cuisine. In recent years more restaurants serving food from other countries have appeared.

STAYING
Paris hotels have an (often deserved) reputation for being dated and pokey, but recent years have seen a great improvement in this sector. Small designer boutique hotels are popping up both in the once-inexpensive Marais district and up river to the west, and classic hotels are adding health spas and other forms of pampering. Outside the capital, many farms in Île de France have converted barns to self-catering holiday homes, from where you can take a train into the city.

🍴 ALCAZAR
62 rue Mazarine, 75006
St-Germain-des-Prés
Tel 01 53 10 19 99
www.alcazar.fr
Designer Terence Conran's bar-restaurant is popular with a fashionable Parisian crowd. The key to its success? Some of the best fish in the capital, a vast and elegant dining room and impeccable service. The menu also includes sophisticated non-fish dishes such as grilled lamb. Upstairs there's a lounge bar where international DJs take to the decks. Alcazar is perfect for a pre-dinner drink and is also worth a visit for its excellent Sunday brunch, which comes complete with a relaxing head massage.
🕐 Daily noon–3, 7pm–2am
🍽 L €44, D €90, Wine €16
Ⓜ Odéon

🍴 L'AMBASSADE D'AUVERGNE
22 rue du Grenier St-Lazare, 75003
Le Marais
Tel 01 42 72 31 22
There are rustic surroundings here for robust farmhouse cooking and wines from the mountainous Auvergne. Ingredients are brought in from the region and are used in dishes such as cabbage soup and cassoulet with Puy lentils.
🕐 Daily noon–2, 7.30–10
🍽 L €60, D €80, Wine €15
Ⓜ Rambuteau

🍴 L'APPART
9–11 rue du Colisée, 75008
Champs-Élysées
Tel 01 53 75 16 34
The unusual dining room in this two-floor house is reminiscent of a comfortable library,

with walls lined with bookshelves and beautiful Persian rugs covering the wooden floors. The cuisine is inventive with a Mediterranean accent, offering dishes such as aubergine (eggplant) in a rosemary sauce, cardamom courgettes (zucchini) and pan-roasted veal in a creamy mustard and mushroom sauce. Before the regular Sunday brunch, there is a brunch for children and a pastry workshop, the results of which you can take home.
🕐 Tue–Sat 12.30–2.30, 7.30–11.45; Sun–Mon 12.30–2.30, 7.30–11
🍽 L €40, D €60, Wine €20
Ⓜ Franklin D. Roosevelt

🍴 AU PIED DE CHAMEAU
20 rue Quincampoix, 75004
Les Halles
Tel 01 42 78 35 00
www.aupieddechameau.com
The Arabian Nights surroundings evoke a Moroccan souk. The scene is set by the bright hanks of wool above your head, curios and handicrafts

neatly displayed on carved wooden shelves and the smell of incense. But the show has just begun. It continues with performances by belly dancers, and could end in Casablanca, the nightclub in the basement. The food reflects the North African feel with traditional *tagine* (meat and vegetable stew) and couscous.

Ⓒ Daily noon–2, 8pm–1am
🍴 L €18, D €92, Wine €17
Ⓜ Châtelet

🍴 AU PIED DE COCHON
6 rue Coquillère, 75001
Les Halles
Tel 01 40 13 77 00
www.pieddecochon.com
A Parisian institution that is a blessing for hungry night owls and it has been open daily

around the clock, since it was established in 1946. Take your place in the elegant dining room, feast your eyes on the fresco-covered walls and your palate on one of France's regional dishes. Vegetarians will avoid the house signature dish, pig's trotters, but the seafood is plentiful and the French onion soup a delight.

Ⓒ Daily 24 hours
🍴 L €46, D €100, Wine €17
Ⓜ Les Halles

🍴 AU PIED DU SACRÉ-CŒUR
85 rue Lamarck, 75018
Montmartre
Tel 01 46 06 15 26
www.aupieddusacrecoeur.free.fr
This restaurant is indeed at the foot of the Sacré-Cœur. Warm tones enhanced by indirect lighting and stylish wooden furniture define the elegant, inviting interior. Traditionalists will enjoy dishes such as pan-fried foie gras and grilled steak *au poivre*, while the more adventurous can try innovative creations such as poultry stuffed with prawns. Eat out on the terrace in good weather.

Ⓒ Tue–Sun noon–3, 7.30–midnight
🍴 L €36, D €48, Wine €15
Ⓜ Lamarck-Caulaincourt

🍴 AU TROU GASCON
40 rue Taine, 75012
Bercy
Tel 01 43 44 34 26
This bistro with a turn-of-the-20th-century interior has excellent dishes from the southwest of France. The cassoulet, made with home-made sausages and beans from Tarbes, is one of the best on offer in Paris.

Ⓒ Daily noon–2.30, 7.30–10; closed Aug
🍴 L €72, D €120, Wine €17
Ⓜ Daumesnil

🍴 LE BAR À SOUPES
5 rue Hérold, 75001
Louvre/Palais Royal
Tel 01 45 08 49 84
Close to the Palais Royal and the Louvre, this is the sister venue to the Bastille's Bar à Soupes. The concept is the same, with six fresh soups on offer every day, including curried tomato and red bean and coconut milk and carrot. The interior is like a simple but friendly *cantina*, with wooden tables and chairs, large paintings of vegetables and exposed brick walls.

Ⓒ Mon–Fri noon–3
🥣 Bowl of soup €5
Ⓜ Sentier, Louvre-Rivoli, Les Halles

🍴 BERMUDA ONION
16 rue du Linois, 75015
Grenelle
Tel 01 45 75 11 11
Minutes away from Paris's miniature Statue of Liberty (a copy of the original statue given to America) lies this New York-style restaurant. It has a bright and airy veranda with modern, elegant furniture and a stunning view of the Seine. The cuisine reinterprets French classics. Try duck in vanilla sauce with fresh fruit or pineapple carpaccio with a pina colada sorbet. It's one of the places to be seen, (especially for Sunday brunch) and there's a DJ every night.

Ⓒ Mon–Sat 8pm–2am, Sun noon–4, 8pm–2am
🍴 No lunch, D €64, Wine €16
Ⓜ Charles-Michels

🍴 BISTRO ROMAIN
26 avenue des Champs-Élysées, 75008
Champs-Élysées
Tel 01 43 59 67 83
One of a dozen across Paris, this Bistro Romain has drapes in red, classical-style paintings

and subdued lighting, which set the baroque tone, reminiscent of an Italian opera house. The menu includes bowls of pasta. Those with big appetites will enjoy the carpaccio and the chocolate mousse, which come on an all-you-can-eat basis.

Ⓒ Daily 11.30am–1am
🍴 L €30, D €40, Wine €14
Ⓜ Franklin D. Roosevelt

🍴 LE BISTROT D'À CÔTÉ
10 rue Gustave Flaubert, 75017
Ternes
Tel 01 42 67 05 81
www.michelrostang.com
This restaurant, part of a small chain of bistros created by chef

Michel Rostang, will delight epicureans with its high quality regional cooking. A chalkboard in the dining room displays the daily specials, which vary according to what's available in the market. Hearty dishes include pig's trotters and chicken with mashed potatoes. The interior is typical bistro with an interesting collection of curios and ceramics.

Ⓒ Daily noon–2.30, 7–11
🍴 L €40, D €40, Wine €15
Ⓜ Courcelles

🍴BOFINGER

5–7 rue de la Bastille, 75004
Bastille
Tel 01 42 72 87 82

The interior of this elegant restaurant, in the fashionable Bastille district, is lavish art nouveau, with an impressive stained-glass ceiling, mirrors and carved wood everywhere, as well as lots of plants.
Fans of meat and fish will both find something to enjoy, with beautifully prepared traditional French dishes such as lobster, oysters, duck and sauerkraut on the menu.

🕐 Mon–Fri noon–3, 6.30pm–1am, Sat–Sun noon–1am
🍽 L €40, D €56, Wine €22
Ⓜ Bastille

🍴BRASSERIE FLO

7 cour des Petites Écuries, 75010
Grands Boulevards
Tel 01 47 70 13 59
A wonderful turn-of-the-century interior, with stained-glass panels, green leather booths and wood panels on the ceiling, sets the tone at this Parisian institution, established in 1886, which is now a listed

building. Actress Sarah Bernhardt was once a regular, when performing at the nearby Théâtre de la Renaissance. The menu includes foie gras, shellfish and Alsatian dishes such as sauerkraut, but be sure to leave enough room for the delicious profiteroles.

🕐 Daily noon–3, 7pm–1.30am
🍽 L €50, D €80, Wine €25
Ⓜ Château-d'Eau

🍴BRASSERIE LA LORRAINE

2 place des Ternes, 75008
Ternes
Tel 01 56 21 22 00
www.brasserielalorraine.com
Although the menu is an exploration of regional French cuisine, including sauerkraut and Burgundy snails, seafood is the main attraction of this

Parisian institution. For more than 70 years, fans of sea urchins and oysters have come to the bright, airy dining room or, weather permitting, the terrace. The interior is retro yet elegant, with red padded seats and 1950s-style lighting fixtures. There's also a take-out service at the seafood bar.

🕐 Daily 11.30am–12.30am
🍽 L €120, D €160, Wine €20
Ⓜ Place des Ternes

🍴CAFÉ CASSETTE

73 rue de Rennes, 75006
St-Germain-des-Prés
Tel 01 45 48 53 78
www.perso.wanadoo.fr/cafecassette/

This modern establishment is close to place St-Sulpice and is good for a meal in all weathers. There's a large terrace, a veranda with striking conical orange lighting fixtures, and a bar and salon offering more comfort. The three menus offer restaurant meals

🍴LA COUPOLE

102 boulevard du Montparnasse, 75014
Montparnasse
Tel 01 43 20 14 20
www.coupoleparis.com
Follow in the footsteps of Pablo Picasso, Ernest Hemingway and Man Ray, and enjoy a meal at this elegant art deco brasserie, established in 1927 and a symbol of Montparnasse's

artistic heyday. The bright and airy dining room has fresco-adorned pillars and Cubist floor tiles. All the brasserie classics are on the menu including seafood platters, sauerkraut and steak tartare.

🕐 Sun–Fri 8.30am–1am, Sat 8.30am–1.30am
🍽 L €44, D €60, Wine €20
Ⓜ Vavin

(salmon tartare and grilled steak), café snacks (salads, club sandwiches) and drinks and desserts (try the pancakes and ice cream).

🕐 Daily 7am–1am
🍽 L €26, D €40, Wine €15
Ⓜ St-Sulpice, Rennes

🍴CAFÉ MARLY

93 rue de Rivoli, 75001
Louvre
Tel 01 49 26 06 60

EATING AND STAYING

There are wonderful views of the Louvre pyramid from this elegant brasserie. The interior mingles contemporary minimalism and Napoleon III style, with dark armchairs whose backs are adorned with gold rings, and gilt-edged black-wood panels. The menu has typical brasserie fare with the occasional more modern dish, such as rare tuna in a sesame crust. For dessert there's the inescapable chocolate cake.

🕐 Daily 8am–1.15am
🍽 L €70, D €120, Wine €20
🚇 Palais Royal-Musée du Louvre

🍴 DRAGONS ÉLYSÉES
11 rue de Berri, 75008
Champs-Élysées
Tel 01 42 89 85 10
The high standard of service and the smart address make

this restaurant perfect for a business or more formal lunch. There are both Chinese and Thai dishes such as stuffed crab, spring rolls and Peking-style pork. The unique selling point is the gigantic underfoot aquarium, which contains more than 1,000 fish.

🕐 Daily noon–2.30, 7–11.30
🍽 L €50, D €60, Wine €14
🚇 George V

🍴 LA DURÉE
16 rue Royale, 75008
Madeleine
Tel 01 42 60 21 79
www.laduree.fr

This was Paris's first tea room, established in 1862. Echoes of the Sistine Chapel ceiling and the Garnier opera house can be detected in the lavish interior, dating from 1871, with its fine paintings and gilded panels. In these elegant surroundings you can sample wonderful teas and pastries. The macaroon is a must, with the original tastes (rose petal, Yunnan tea, apricot and ginger), changing seasonally.

🕐 Daily 8.30–7
🍽 Tea €7, 4 mini macaroons €5
🚇 Concorde, Madeleine

🍴 LA FERME ST-SIMON
6 rue de St-Simon, 75007
Invalides
Tel 01 45 48 35 74
www.fermestsimon.com
This 'farm', decorated like an elegant country house, with

exposed beams, candelabra and floral curtains, is in reality surrounded by embassies and ministries. Chef Francis Vendehende's rustic menu, which changes weekly, includes dishes such as smoked salmon and calf's kidney pasta served with foie gras, and roasted sea bass with wild mushrooms and polenta. There are also excellent wines.

🕐 Mon–Fri noon–4, 7.30–10, Sat 7.30–10
🍽 L €56, D €90, Wine €18
🚇 Rue-du-Bac

🍴 LES GRANDES MARCHES
6 place de la Bastille, 75012
Bastille
Tel 01 43 42 90 32
www.lesgrandesmarches.com
The big steps that give the restaurant its name are those of the Opéra Bastille next door, although this building also has its own stylish staircase. The interior design is modern, with plenty of steel surfaces and indirect lighting. Chef Christian

SPECIAL

🍴 GEORGES
Centre Georges Pompidou
Place Georges-Pompidou, 75004
Les Halles
Tel 01 44 78 47 99
With its modern lines and shells of aluminium and vibrant rubber, this restaurant on the top floor of the Centre Georges Pompidou could well be a work of modern art. This is a real Parisian experience with a stunning view over the city and nouvelle cuisine including mushroom cappuccino (a light and foamy soup) and crab millefeuille in puff pastry. The melt-in-the-mouth chocolate cake is one of the house's signature dishes.

🕐 Wed–Mon noon–2am
🍽 L €80, D €100, Wine €20
🚇 Rambuteau

Constant creates innovative French dishes such as Loué chicken with pistachio nuts and mustard, and caramel-coated monkfish with orange juice butter. The restaurant is renowned for its superb seafood platters and wonderful views of place de la Bastille from the first floor.

🕐 Daily noon–midnight
🍽 L €66, D €82, Wine €15
🚇 Bastille

🍴 GUY SAVOY see page 352

🍴 MARKET
15 avenue Matignon, 75008
Champs-Élysées
Tel 01 56 43 40 90
www.market.com
Interior designer Christian Liaigre has created a bare yet polished interior, with soft hues and pale wood furniture punctuated by primitive art. The menu offers a raw bar,

EATING AND STAYING

GUY SAVOY
18 rue Troyon, 75017
Champs-Élysées
Tel 01 43 80 40 61
www.guysavoy.com
Renowned chef Guy Savoy's
motto is that cooking is 'the
art of taking foodstuffs and
transforming them into pure
happiness'. The quality of the
cuisine is high (with prices to
match), with delicacies such
as poached-grilled pigeon
and giblets in a beetroot and
mushroom millefeuille and
split langoustines with citrus
fruit and peas. There is art on
the walls as well as on the
plate, with the many modern
paintings providing a vibrant
contrast to the white linen
tablecloths and black
wooden chairs.
🕐 Mon–Fri noon–2, 7–10.30, Sat
7–10.30
🍴 L €300, D €300, Wine €90
🚇 Charles de Gaulle–Étoile

with a large choice of oysters,
and fusion food by chef Jean-
Georges Vongerichten. Try
black truffle pizza or the 'black
plate', an hors d'oeuvre selection including shrimps on a
skewer, ginger lobster roll, raw
tuna and spiced quail. There is
also brunch at the weekend.
🕐 Tue–Sat noon–3, 7.30pm–12.30am,
Sun–Mon noon–3, 7.30–11.30
🍴 L €64, D €160, Wine €24
🚇 Franklin D. Roosevelt

MAXIM'S
3 rue Royale, 75008
Concorde
Tel 01 42 65 27 94
www.maxims-de-paris.com

Established in 1893 by café
waiter Maxime Gaillard, and
acquired in 1981 by
designer Pierre Cardin, this

Belle-Époque restaurant is a
temple of Parisian social life.
Following its success, other
Maxim's restaurants have
opened across the world (New
York, Beijing and Geneva), but
here you are light years away
from the atmosphere of a
chain restaurant. Attentive
service, refined French cuisine
and a prestigious location all
add up to a unique touch of
class.
🕐 Mon–Sat noon–2.30, 7.30–10
🍴 L €200, D €270, Wine €40
🚇 Concorde

LE PETIT GAVROCHE
15 rue Sainte-Croix de la Bretonnerie,
75004
Le Marais
Tel 01 48 87 74 26
Le Petit Gavroche (the Parisian
urchin, from a character in

Victor Hugo's *Les Misérables*)
is the place for French food
enthusiasts on a budget. The
prix-fixe menu is a bargain,
and has three choices of
appetizer, main course and
dessert. The food isn't fancy
(plates of crudités, meat and
potato pie and the house
tart), but you won't leave
hungry. The retro interior with
old French posters and curios
is an added bonus.
🕐 Mon–Sat 8am–11.30pm
🍴 L €16, D €18, Wine €7
🚇 Hôtel de Ville

LE PROCOPE
13 rue de l'Ancienne-Comédie, 75006
St-Germain-des-Prés
Tel 01 40 46 79 00
www.procope.com
This former Parisian café,
now an elegant dining
room, has quite a history:
Philosophers Voltaire and
Rousseau were regulars, and
Benjamin Franklin is said to
have drafted the American
constitution here. Those great
minds almost certainly did not

witness the candelabra,
drapes and warm yellow and
burgundy painted walls, nor
the food which is now on offer,
which includes grilled beef
and seafood platters.
🕐 Sun–Wed noon–midnight, Thu–Sat
noon–1am
🍴 L €36, D €60, Wine €15
🚇 Odéon

LA RÔTISSERIE D'EN FACE
2 rue Christine, 75006
St-Germain-des-Prés
Tel 01 43 26 40 98
This is the annexe of Jacques
Cagna, the eponymous
gastronomic restaurant across
the street, where the celebrity
chef mans the stoves. You can
expect the same perfection
here, in the relaxed
atmosphere of an elegant
brasserie, which has leather
wall seats and small square
wooden tables. Expect
rotisserie specials like
spit-roasted chicken and
suckling pig.
🕐 Mon–Fri noon–2, 7–11, Sat 7–11.30
🍴 L €46, D €78, Wine €20
🚇 St-Michel

SPOON FOOD AND WINE
14 rue de Marignan, 75008
Champs-Élysées
Tel 01 40 76 34 44
www.spoon.tm.fr
Here you are in elegant,
understated surroundings with
sleek lines, deep purple walls
and pastel chair cushions.
Celebrated chef Alain Ducasse
lets you choose the sauce and
accompaniment to your meal
from a list of French and
Asian delicacies.
🕐 Mon–Fri noon–2, 7–11; closed
26 July–25 August
🍴 L €80, D €110, Wine €35
🚇 Franklin D. Roosevelt

TAILLEVENT

15 rue Lamennais, 75008
Champs-Élysées
Tel 01 44 95 15 01
www.taillevent.com

A highly distinguished restaurant whose master chef Michel Solivérès holds sway. The dining room is discreetly elegant and you can expect the best of French cuisine, with rich dishes such as foie gras, lobster and truffles. There is an exceptional wine cellar.

🕐 Mon–Fri noon–2, 7.30–9.30
💶 L €180, D €220, Wine €24
🚇 Charles de Gaulle–Étoile, George V

LA TAVERNE

24 boulevard des Italiens, 75009
Grands Boulevards
Tel 01 55 33 10 00
www.taverne.com

The menu has Alsatian influences, with dishes such as sauerkraut, monkfish in beer and *tarte tatin* (apple upside-down cake) with cream. To drink, choose from beer and wines from Alsace. The pale wood panels and candelabra give this restaurant a touch of class, while curios such as a bull's head and a massive clock are more evocative of a tavern atmosphere. Some dinner-and-theatre deals are organized with nearby venues.

🕐 Sun–Thu 11am–midnight, Fri–Sat 11am–1am
💶 L €40, D €70, Wine €10
🚇 Richelieu-Drouot, Opéra

THOUMIEUX

79 rue St-Dominique, 75007
Invalides
Tel 01 47 05 49 75

The Thoumieux family proprietors opened this brasserie near near the Eiffel Tower in 1923. Chef Christian Beguet has created a high-quality menu of hearty dishes from southwest France, such as bean and sausage casserole.

🕐 Daily noon–3.30, 6.30–midnight
💶 L €40, D €60, Wine €13
🚇 Invalides

TRÉSOR

7–9 rue du Trésor, 75004
Le Marais
Tel 01 42 71 35 17

In a quiet cul-de-sac in the Marais district, this high-quality Italian restaurant has one of Paris's finest terraces. The chic white and beige interior is a result of a makeover in 2002. Another reason for coming here in the evening is to sneak downstairs for a shiatsu massage. Check out the bathrooms and their goldfish-filled aquariums.

🕐 Food served daily 12–3, 7.30–10, but drinks available all day until 2am
💶 L €60, D €70, Wine €18
🚇 St-Paul, Hôtel de Ville

LE VERRE BOUTEILLE

85 avenue des Ternes, 75017
Étoile
Tel 01 45 74 01 02
www.leverrebouteille.com

This bistro, near the Arc de Triomphe, stays open until the small hours. The traditional interior includes a long bar and wooden tables with wrought-iron legs. Chef Patrick Ameline's aim is to satisfy with simple food cooked to perfection, and he succeeds. Try the warm goat's cheese, country-style croque and chocolate cake. There's also a good selection of wines.

🕐 Daily noon–3, 7pm–5am
💶 L €29, D €60, Wine €18
🚇 Porte Maillot

YUGARAJ

14 rue Dauphine, 75006
St-Germain-des-Prés
Tel 01 43 26 44 91
www.yugaraj.com

Yugaraj is one of Paris's best Indian restaurants. The French and Indian proprietors can lay claim to introducing Indian cuisine to the French with their previous restaurant, which opened in 1971. Alongside traditional curries are crab balls, the house special; the jumbo shrimps marinated in spices are a must.

🕐 Tue–Wed and Fri–Sun noon–2, 7–10pm; Thu 7–10pm
💶 L €70, D €80, Wine €22
🚇 Odéon

LE D'ARTAGNAN

80 rue Vitruve, 75020
St-Blaise
Tel 01 40 32 34 56
www.hostels-in.com

This is France's largest youth hostel, occupying a seven-floor building near Père Lachaise cemetery. Excellent facilities include a bar that opens every evening until 2am, a souvenir shop, four Internet booths, electronic lockers, a cinema, TV lounge and automatic laundry. The rooms are for three to eight people.

💶 €20.60 per person including breakfast
🛏 440 beds
🚇 Porte de Bagnolet

L'ATELIER MONTPARNASSE

49 rue Vavin, 75006
St-Germain-des-Prés
Tel 01 46 33 60 00
www.ateliermontparnasse.com

This three-star hotel pays tribute to 1930s Montparnasse (then an artists' hub), with period furniture and mosaic reproductions of 1930s paintings in the bathrooms. Artists' haunts, such as La Coupole and Le Dôme brasseries, are nearby. Facilities include a laundry service, room service, cable TV, hairdryer and mini-bar. Internet connection is possible in some bedrooms.

💶 €107–€137, excluding breakfast
🛏 17
🚇 Notre-Dame-des-Champs, Montparnasse

AUBERGE DE JEUNESSE JULES FERRY

8 boulevard Jules Ferry, 75011
Canal St-Martin
Tel 01 43 57 55 60
www.hostels-in.com

The dormitories at this youth hostel on Canal St-Martin have up to six beds and there are some bedrooms for couples. Facilities include an automatic laundry, electronic lockers and Internet terminals. There is no kitchen although breakfast is included and there is a microwave that guests can use.

€18.50 per person
100
République

HÔTEL ATLANTIS

4 rue du Vieux-Colombier, 75006
St-Germain-des-Prés
Tel 01 45 48 31 81
www.hotelatlantis.com

Most of the rooms in this two-star hotel face onto picturesque place St-Sulpice, with its fountain and cafés. All are bright and airy, and have been beautifully decorated with fine furniture and quilted bedspreads. They have telephone, satellite TV, Internet connection and hairdryer. There are ornaments in the salon and a grandfather clock in the breakfast room.

€115–€150, excluding breakfast
27
St-Sulpice

HÔTEL DE LA BRETONNERIE

22 rue Sainte-Croix-de-la-Bretonnerie, 75004
Le Marais
Tel 01 48 87 77 63
www.labretonnerie.com

In a 17th-century mansion in the Marais district, this elegant hotel has beamed ceilings, fine fabrics and furniture and some bedrooms

L'HÔTEL

13 rue des Beaux-Arts, 75006
St-Germain-des-Prés
Tel 01 44 41 99 00
www.l-hotel.com

This deluxe four-star hotel, occupying a beautiful 19th-century building, was fully renovated at the turn of the millennium. The exuberantly elegant interior is by Jacques

Garcia and the fully equipped rooms are named after famous people, such as Marco Polo, Mistinguett and Oscar Wilde (he breathed his last at this hotel in 1900). The restaurant (which is closed on Sunday, Monday and for the month of August), has an impressive glass dome.

€260–€343, excluding breakfast
16 rooms, 4 suites
St-Germain-des-Prés

with canopy beds. Facilities in the rooms include satellite TV, safe, minibar and hairdryer and there's a magnificent vaulted ceiling in the breakfast room.

Closed Aug
€108–€140, excluding breakfast
22 rooms, 7 suites
Hôtel-de-Ville

HÔTEL LE BOUQUET DE MONTMARTRE

1 rue Durantin, 75018
Montmartre
Tel 01 46 06 87 54
www.bouquet-de-montmartre.com

The interior of this two-star hotel near Sacré-Cœur is full of character, combining kitsch with classic Louis XVI. The bedrooms have limited facilities (phone but no TV) but have design features such as little alcoves by the beds, candelabra wall lamps or small hanging cupboards. Breakfast is served in a beautiful dining room, with brocade wallpaper and period furniture.

€65, excluding breakfast
36
Abbessess

HÔTEL FRANKLIN ROOSEVELT

18 rue Clément Marot, 75008
Champs-Élysées
Tel 01 53 57 49 50
www.hroosevelt.com

This hotel is ideally placed for the Champs-Élysées and avenue Montaigne. Indirect lighting, thick fitted carpets and rich red fabrics combined with dark woods create a warm atmosphere. If you're looking for a bit of luxury, book the sixth-floor suite, which has a king-size bed and a Jacuzzi. Facilities include a bar, a reading room and a winter garden.

EATING AND STAYING

€175–€205, excluding breakfast
48

Franklin D. Roosevelt, Alma Marceau
RER Pont-de-l'Alma

HÔTEL DU PANTHÉON
19 place du Panthéon, 75005
Latin Quarter
Tel 01 43 54 32 95

PAVILLON DE LA REINE
28 place des Vosges, 75003
Le Marais
Tel 01 40 29 19 19
www.pavillon-de-la-reine.com
It would be hard to find a more perfect setting for a four-star hotel than this 17th-century building on the historic place des Vosges. This was the residence of Anne of Austria, Louis XIII's wife, and the exquisite interior retains

many of its period features, including a particularly imposing fireplace in the salon. Even the vaulted cellar where you can have breakfast has tapestries on the walls. Bedrooms have cable TV and some have canopy beds. Some bedrooms are in a second, more modern building.
€330–€385, excluding breakfast
34

Bastille, St-Paul

This three-star hotel is in the heart of the Latin Quarter. The interior has an 18th-century feel, with gilded panels and fine fabrics. Most of the rooms look onto the Panthéon and have cable TV and a minibar. There is also a laundry service and parking.
€183, excluding breakfast
36

Cardinal Lemoine
RER Luxembourg

HÔTEL DU PARC MONTSOURIS
4 rue du Parc Montsouris, 75014
Denfert-Rochereau
Tel 01 45 89 02 72
www.hotel-parc-montsouris.com
A little way from the main attractions, this two-star hotel is alongside beautiful Montsouris Park. The reception has art deco styling while the bright and airy bedrooms have a desk, cable TV, Internet connection and a hairdryer.
€57–€66, excluding breakfast
35

Porte d'Orléans
RER Cité Universitaire

HÔTEL ST-MERRY
78 rue de la Verrerie, 75004
Le Marais
Tel 01 42 78 14 15
www.hotelmarais.com
This three-star hotel, close to the Centre Georges Pompidou, was once the presbytery of the church of St-Merri. Although it was built during the Renaissance, its highly original interior also includes many late-Gothic features including sculptures, carved woodwork and beamed ceilings. The suite and room nine are particularly distinctive–in room nine you sleep under an impressive flying buttress.
€146–€210, excluding breakfast
10 rooms, 1 suite

Hôtel-de-Ville, Châtelet
RER Châtelet-Les-Halles

RITZ
15 place Vendôme, 75001
Opéra
Tel 01 43 16 30 30
www.ritzparis.com

Nestled between place Vendôme jewellers, this world-famous establishment has been the epitome of luxury and elegance since its opening in 1898. Coco Chanel, Ernest Hemingway and Marcel Proust were all regular guests. The lavish interior is typical of French classicism, with antiques, chandeliers and heavy drapes. The hotel has a club, several restaurants, bars, private salons and the gourmet cookery school, Ritz-Escoffier.
€630–€730, excluding breakfast
135 rooms, 40 suites

Indoor
Tuileries, Madeleine, Concorde

TERRASS HOTEL
12 rue Joseph de Maistre, 75018
Montmartre
Tel 01 46 06 72 85
www.terrass-hotel.com
The terrace of this four-star hotel has one of the best panoramas Paris has to offer, with bedrooms on the fourth floor and above sharing these views. Rooms are decorated in classical French style, warmed up with bright tones from blue and yellow Provençal fabrics. Rooms have satellite TV and the hotel has its own bar and restaurant.
€225–€248
88 (2 non-smoking floors)
Place-de-Clichy

EATING

Seafood is at the heart of almost every meal in sea-washed Brittany and Normandy. Oysters are plentiful and the *belons* from Brittany are often said to be the most popular in France. The north's answer to the *bouillabaisse* (fish stew) of the Mediterranean is the seafood stew *marmite dieppoise*, and its response to the duck terrines of the southwest

comes in the *rillettes*, coarse pâté of pork or mackerel. Crêpes, the fan-folded flat pancakes for which Brittany is justly famous, are the ultimate fast food, with fillings from savoury to wickedly sweet, sold from mid-morning until late at night. Normandy's dairies can rival its fishing fleet, with creams and butters from Isigny acknowledged as some of the best in the world and cheese-lovers can lose themselves in Camembert country. Rustic food includes boudin sausages, *andouille* (pork) sausages and the famous tripe served *à la mode de Caen*. The only dessert that matters is the tarte Tatin, an upside-down apple tart. Countless apple orchards provide the most important drinks in the region—cider, sold at every other farmhouse, and the heady brandy known as Calvados. Locals take it as a *trou normand*, a mid-meal gulp to freshen the palate.

STAYING

Excellent campsites and a number of purpose-built holiday villages cater to the family market in the resorts. Other options include small, family-run hotels or self-catering gîtes. See www.gites-de-france.com to reserve online.

Bretagne

BREST

⑪ AMOUR DE POMME DE TERRE

23 rue des Halles, 29200 Brest
Tel 02 98 43 48 51

The formula is simple at this potato-themed restaurant: Potatoes and every way they can be cooked. The *amour de pomme de terre*, the pièce de résistance, weighing in at 6kg (13lb), is only for the largest of appetites! All plates are enormous and many come with an alcoholic drink and there are also special dishes for vegetarians and children and a good wine list.

🕐 Mon–Fri noon–2, 7.15–11; Sat–Sun noon–2.30, 7.15–11
🍽 L €35, D €50, Wine €12

⑪ LA CHAUMIÈRE

2 rue Émile Zola, 29200 Brest
Tel 02 98 44 18 60

This large, rustic but stylish restaurant has wood panels, a large fireplace, paintings and copper ornaments. Dishes to try include fried sole with fresh mushrooms, *marmite du pêcheur* with four different seasonal fish and Thai-style veal escalope. There are 65 different wines to choose from and dishes for children and vegetarians on request.

🕐 Mon–Sat noon–2, 7.30–9.30; closed 3 weeks in Aug, 1 week at Christmas
🍽 L €26, D €36, Wine €11

⑪ RESTAURANT OCÉANIA

82 rue de Siam, 29200 Brest
Tel 02 98 80 66 66

The restaurant is on the ground floor of the hotel of the same name and the interior is styled like a cruise ship. The presentation of the food is exquisite—so take a good look before digging in. Dishes include steamed monkfish with artichoke ragout and black olives, baked fillet of red mullet with mixed vegetables and rabbit confit with fried shallots and grilled bread.

🕐 Tue–Fri 12.30–2, 7.30–9.30, Sat 7.30–9.30, Sun and Mon 12.30–2; closed 1 week in Jan and 4 weeks from end Jul to end Aug
🍽 L €40, D €74, Wine €14

CAP FRÉHEL

🛏 LE RELAIS DE FRÉHEL

Route du Cap, Plévenon, 22240 Fréhel
Tel 02 96 41 43 02
www.lerelaisdefrehel.com

A great place from which to discover Cap Fréhel. It's in a beautifully renovated *longère*, a typical long and narrow Breton farmhouse and the breakfast room is in a reno-vated stable. The longhouse is surrounded by a large garden with a tennis court. The gener-ous, comfortable rooms are elegantly furnished and sleep up to four people. There are also cottages which sleep three or four people.

🕐 Closed mid-Nov to end Apr
💶 €50
🛏 5 rooms and 2 cottages

CONCARNEAU

⑪ L'AMIRAL

1 avenue Pierre Guéguin, 29900 Concarneau
Tel 02 98 60 55 23

Smart bar-restaurant, stylishly decorated with designer lamps and models of old sailboats. Given the maritime theme, different shades of blue are dominant and the bar is decorated with an underwater scene mosaic. The long room is on the ground floor of a former grand hotel and almost every table has a view of the old fort in the harbour. The menu changes daily and there is always home-made bread. Reserve ahead in summer.

🕐 Daily 12.30–2, 7.30–9.30 in summer; Tue–Sat 12.30–2, 7.30–9.30, Sun 12.30–2, rest of year
🍽 L €34, D €50, Wine €11

⑪ LE PETIT CHAPERON ROUGE

7 place Duguesclin, 29900 Concarneau
Tel 02 98 60 53 32

Small restaurant near the harbour following the Little Red Riding Hood theme with miniature baskets. The dining room has three rows of small red-clothed tables and a large gold lamp-sculpture made out of spoons. In this fairy tale corner of Concarneau (the nearby bar Le Petit Poucet means Tom Thumb), you can treat yourself to sweet and savoury crêpes such as La Blandette (goat's cheese, spinach, ham and cream), La Caramande (pear, caramel,

EATING AND STAYING

butter and grilled almonds) and Mère Grande (banana and honey flambéed with rum).

🕐 Tue–Fri noon–2, 7–9.30, Sat noon–2, 7–10, Sun noon–2; closed 10 days in Jun, 10 days in Mar and 3 weeks in Oct 🍴 L €13, D €16, Wine €9

LE CONQUET

🏨 LA POINTE SAINTE-BARBE

Pointe Ste-Barbe, 29217 Le Conquet
Tel 02 98 89 00 26
www.hotelpointesaintebarbe.com

La Pointe Sainte-Barbe is a large, four-floor hotel on a rock at the entrance to the harbour. The large, modern rooms, which sleep up to four people, have telephone and TV and most rooms have a balcony and a magnificent view of the ocean. The hotel has direct access to the beach and there is a terrace restaurant, a bar and parking.

🕐 Closed mid-Nov to mid-Dec
🛏 €33–€117, excluding breakfast (€7)
🛈 48

DINAN

🍴 CHEZ LA MÈRE POURCEL

3 place des Merciers, 22100, Dinan
Tel 02 96 39 03 80

The exquisite 15th-century building is a twice-listed monument as the 16th-century winding staircase is protected in its own right. The best tables are the round ones near the fireplace which have Louis XIII-style chairs. La Mère Pourcel specializes in lamb fresh from Mont St-Michel, which is available from April to the end of September. Other

temptations are lobster, local fish and scallops in autumn and winter. Reservations are recommended.

🕐 Daily noon–2, 7–10, Jul, Aug; Tue–Sat noon–2, 7–10, Sun noon–2, Mar–Jun and Sep; Wed–Sat noon–2, 7–10, Sun noon–2, Oct–Feb; closed 4 weeks between Feb and Mar
🍴 L €34, D €56, Wine €13

GUIMILIAU

🍴 AR CHUPEN

43 rue du Calvaire, 29400 Guimiliau
Tel 02 98 68 73 63

The restaurant is in an old renovated farmhouse decorated Breton-style with copper pictures and antique furniture. The special dish here is artichokes with different accompaniments. *Fermier* has ham, bacon, mushrooms and cream and *Leonard* and *Royale* are with seafood. There is also a good choice for

vegetarians. Finish your meal with *chouchen,* druid wine served in a horn. When the restaurant fills up, the gregarious chef may come out of the kitchen to play his accordion.

🕐 Daily noon–10, in summer; Sun–Fri noon–2, Sat noon–10 rest of year
🍴 L €30, D €40, Wine €10

🍴 SAVEURS DE GUIMILIAU

41 rue du Calvaire, 29400 Guimiliau
Tel 02 98 68 75 71

Cakes filled with prunes and raspberries, fruit cakes and all the traditional French tarts and gateaux make this tea room a

must. Their specialty is *kouignamann* (a Breton cake of sugar, butter and almonds) which won the 2002 trophy for the best *kouignamann* in Brittany. To go with your cake there is a good choice of teas. The tea room is on the first floor and the shop below is nicely decorated in pastels

that go well with the exhibition of local landscape paintings on the walls.

🕐 Daily 6.30am–7pm, 15 Jun–15 Sep; Sat–Thu, 6.30am–7pm, rest of year
🍵 Tea from €2

HUELGOAT

🍴 CRÊPERIE DE L'ARGOAT

12 rue du Lac, 29690 Huelgoat
Tel 02 98 99 71 72

This small crêperie in an old house has wooden tables and stools and a wooden bar. When the weather is pleasant

you can sit out on the terrace overlooking the lake. Crêpes include the *Pirate* (chitterling sausage and mustard) and the *Océane* (scallops with vegetables).

🕐 Wed–Sun 11–10, Mon 11–2, summer; Wed–Sun 11–8, Mon 11–2, rest of year; closed for 2 weeks in Oct
🍴 L €17, D €25, Wine €6

ÎLE DE BRÉHAT

🍴 L'OISEAU DES ÎLES

Rue du Port, 22870 Bréhat
Tel 02 96 20 00 53

This popular crêperie is in a blue-shuttered building decorated with a large puffin. Inside, the bare pink granite walls complement the blue window and door frames and the white ceiling. The dining room has small square tables or you can eat on the terrace. All the basic crêpes are on offer (ham, cheese, mushroom) as well as specials such as *andouille* (Breton sausage) and salads. Reservations are recommended.

🕐 Mon–Sun noon–2, 7–10, Jul–end Aug; Tue–Sun noon–2, 7–9, Sep–end Dec and Mar–end Jun; closed Jan–Feb
🍴 L €26, D €40, Wine €12

JOSSELIN

🍴 LA MARINE
8 rue du Canal, 56120 Josselin
Tel 02 97 22 21 98

True to its name, La Marine has a blue and white nautical-style interior with a flower-filled terrace which has great views of the chateau and the Oust river. The crêpes reflect the seasons, for instance

L'Automne has sweet chestnut purée and apple and pear jam. The local crêpe, *La Josselinoise*, is filled with black pudding and fried apples. There is a special lunch menu for a crêpe-free meal (unless you want one for dessert), and there are vegetarian and children's options available. Reserve in summer.

🕐 Daily noon–1.45, 7–9, Jul, Aug; daily noon–1.45 and also Sat 7–9, rest of year; closed for 2 weeks in Nov

🍴 L €22, D €32, Wine €10

🛏 LA BUTTE DE ST-LAURENT
La Butte de St-Laurent, 56120 Josselin
Tel 02 97 22 22 09
www.chambres-bretagne.com

Perched on top of the *butte* (hillock), this bed-and-breakfast has a splendid view of the nearby chateau and village and a large garden that is great for children. The comfortable attic rooms, named after the owners' children, have a bathroom with a shower and/or bath. There is also a family room that sleeps up to four people. Credit cards are not accepted.

🕐 Closed mid-Sep to mid-Apr

🛏 €50

🛏 4 rooms (all non-smoking)

LAMPAUL-GUIMILIAU

🍴 L'ESCAPADE
8 place du Villiers, 29400 Lampaul-Guimiliau
Tel 02 98 68 61 27

The only real restaurant in town with two luminous

---

dining rooms spread over two floors of a modern building. The specials are goulash soup and Finistère ostrich steaks. They also serve crêpes, with unusual fillings such as prunes and smoked bacon or *Le Forêt Noir* (cherry, Amarena, chocolate and whipped cream).

🕐 Tue–Fri noon–1.30, 7–8.30, Sat–Sun noon–1.30, 7–9; closed Mon

🍴 L €30, D €62, Wine €12

LOCRONAN

🛏 HOSTELLERIE DU BOIS DU NÉVET
Route du bois du Névet, 29180 Locronan
Tel 02 98 91 70 67
www.hostellerie-bois-nevet.com

This long, modern hotel snakes through the surrounding

gardens. The comfortable rooms might lack charm, but the magnificent setting more than compensates. All rooms have TV, telephone and bathroom, two rooms are fitted for guests with disabilities (including shower) and there are family rooms for up to five people. There is no restaurant but breakfast is served.

🕐 Closed Nov–end Apr

🛏 €51–€59, excluding breakfast (€7)

🛏 35

MALESTROIT

🍴 LE CANOTIER
Place du Docteur Queinnec, 56140 Malestroit
Tel 02 97 75 08 69

The best restaurant in town

---

serves a large and varied menu which specializes in seafood such as red mullet, salmon and scallops. Meat-eaters should try the foie gras fried with honey. The ochre dining room is cosy, with wood panels, and in summer you can eat on the terrace.

🕐 Tue–Sat noon–2, 7–10, high season; Tue–Sat noon–2, rest of year

🍴 L €39, D €55, Wine €8

MORLAIX

🍴 BRASSERIE DE L'EUROPE
Place Emile Souvestre, 29600 Morlaix
Tel 02 98 88 81 15

An elegant brasserie, on the ground floor of the hotel of the same name (see below), with a stylish interior in white and blue. It specializes in fish and seafood, with such dishes as cod in butter with herb and carrot tagliatelle and green lentils, or fried red mullet and foie gras with pineapple. Try the typically Breton *kouigna-mann* (a buttery cake) with apple marmalade for dessert. Reservations are recommended.

🕐 Mon–Sat noon–2, 7.30–9.30

🍴 L €42, D €64, Wine €13

🛏 HÔTEL DE L'EUROPE
1 rue d'Aiguillon, 29600 Morlaix
Tel 02 98 62 11 99
www.hotel-europe-com.fr

This stylish, 200-year-old hotel is filled with antique furnishings and a Bordeaux red-carpeted staircase leads to your room. Rooms are large, tastefully decorated and soundproofed and suites sleep up to four people. A buffet breakfast is served in the Napoleon III dining room and the restaurant next door is connected to the hotel but independently run.

🕐 Closed 22 Dec–5 Jan

🛏 €54–€250, excluding breakfast (€7)

🛏 60 rooms (10 non-smoking)

PERROS-GUIREC

🍴 LA CRÉMAILLÈRE
13 place de l'Église, 22700 Perros-Guirec
Tel 02 96 23 22 08

The two dining rooms are in a 17th-century building, where dark tones, low ceilings and a rustic interior give a warm atmosphere. The menu changes with the seasons and

---

is based around fresh seafood and grilled meat. Dishes to try include scallop kebab with smoked duck breast, roast beef and coffee tart with a citrus marmalade. In summer it's best to reserve a table.

🕐 Tue–Sun noon–2, 7–10, Mon 7-10
🍽 L €29, D €56, Wine €13

🔵 VILLA CYRNOS
10 rue de Sergent l'Hévedere, 22700 Perros-Guirec
Tel 02 96 91 13 36
Halfway between the harbour and the middle of town (about 20 minutes' walk from the beach), this is one of the most expensive bed-and-breakfasts in town—but it's worth it. The large granite mansion has a ship-like veranda with a great view of the harbour. The spacious, comfortable rooms, which sleep up to four people, are tastefully furnished and have a TV. The friendly owner serves a formidable breakfast and there is parking. In case you're wondering, 'Cyrnos' is the Greek name for Corsica.

🕐 Closed mid-Sep to mid-Apr
🍽 €54–€60, excluding breakfast
🛏 5 (all non-smoking)

PLEYBEN

🔴 LA BLANCHE HERMINE
1 place Charles de Gaulle, 29190 Pleyben
Tel 02 98 26 61 29
The chef is an officer of the elite chefs' circle known as the Bouche de la Marmite d'Or, so you can expect quality cooking

here. The restaurant specializes in dishes prepared with cider such as Breton sauerkraut and beef with cider, but classic dishes are also available. There is also an extensive wine list and delicious home-made pastries. It's essential to reserve in summer. The staff speak English, Spanish, Italian and German.

🕐 Daily 11.30–3, 6.30–9.45, 14 Jul–20 Aug; Thu–Mon noon–2.30, 7–9.45, Tue noon–2.30 rest of year; closed 15 Dec–31 Jan
🍽 L €20, D €33, Wine €11

PONT-AVEN

🔴 TAHITI
21 rue de la Belle Angèle 29930, Pont-Aven
Tel 02 98 06 15 93
A small restaurant that draws on the unlikely combination of cuisine from Brittany and Tahiti. The dining room is decorated with fresh flowers

and Polynesian pictures which contribute to the tropical theme. Dishes include Tahitian-style fish and *Tai Pen Lou* (Chinese fondue). Try the Hinano beer, the Tahitian island brew. Reserving is recommended, especially in summer and you can also buy food to take out.

🕐 Wed–Sat 12.15–2, 7.15–9.30, Tue 7.15–9.30 and Sun 7.15–9.30; closed Mon; closed 2 weeks in Nov and 2 weeks in Feb
🍽 L €23, D €40, Wine €10

QUIMPER

🔴 LE CAFÉ DE L'EPÉE
14 rue du Parc, 29000 Quimper
Tel 02 98 95 28 97
The owners claim that this brasserie, in front of the *préfecture* on the banks of the

river, is one of the oldest in France. The interior is art nouveau, with long green

leather benches, polished mahogany tables, balloon-shaped lamps on shiny golden supports, two large 3-D pictures of Quimper and an aquarium with live crabs. Try the duck with sauerkraut and finish with one of their pies if you have room. On Saturday evenings there's an all-you-can-eat seafood buffet for €23.

🕐 Daily noon–2.30, 7–11.30
🍽 L €25, D €32, Wine €13

🔵 HÔTEL DUPLEIX
34 boulevard Dupleix, 29000, Quimper
Tel 02 98 90 53 35
www.hotel-dupleix.com
This hotel is beside the Odet river in Quimper's modern quarter, close to the cathedral and heart of the town. The spacious, modern rooms are quiet and have views of the river and the cathedral towers. There is also a large, comfort-able lounge and terrace. Three rooms have a terrace and there are family rooms for up to six people. Parking is available, but is not free.

🍽 €79–€102, excluding breakfast (buffet breakfast €9)
🛏 29

QUIMPERLÉ

🔴 LE BISTRO DE LA TOUR
20 rue de Brémond d'Ars, 29300 Quimperlé
Tel 02 98 35 09 10
This restaurant and wine cellar is on a street that is itself listed as a monument. There are two dining rooms—the one on the ground floor is art deco in style while the first-floor one is dedicated to paintings by the Pont-Aven school. Dishes to try include oysters or the Breton cassoulet with andouille sausages. Allow yourself enough time to read through the wine list, which has more than 800 entries.

🕐 Mon–Fri 12.15–1.30, 7.30–9, Sat 7.30–9, Sun noon–1.30
🍽 L €34, D €40, Wine €14

RENNES

🔴 LE BOCAL-P'TY RESTO
6 rue d'Argentre, 35000 Rennes
Tel 02 99 78 34 10
Jars (*bocaux*) filled with shells and glass beads give the restaurant its name. An interesting special dish is the pork sautéed in Carambar (a French caramel bar known for

its jokes on the wrapper). Other options include roasted andouille sausage with apple compote or tagliatelle with smoked salmon. Vegetarian options and meals for children are available and reservations are recommended.

🕐 Tue–Fri noon–1.30, 7.30–10.30, Sat 7.30–10.30

🍽 L €20, D €22, Wine €11

Ⓜ République

⊖HÔTEL DES LICES

7 place des Lices, 35000 Rennes
Tel 02 99 79 14 81
www.hotel-des-lices.com

A modern but not soulless hotel close to the heart of the old town. Nearly all rooms have their own balconies and some look out on to the market square, which comes alive for the market on Saturday mornings. Rooms are comfortable and sound-proofed and have satellite TV, minibar and telephone. There is a public car park next to the hotel that costs €2 per night.

🛏 €54–€56, excluding breakfast (€6)

🛌 45

Ⓜ Sainte-Anne

ST-CAST-LE-GUILDO

⊖LES BLÉS D'OR

22380, St-Cast-le-Guildo
Tel 02 96 41 99 93

This pet-friendly campsite is close to the beach of St-Cast. There are large pitches, 30 of which have their own private shower, lavatory and basin. There are electricity hook-ups, a small launderette, a children's playground, table tennis and the site is close to a large supermarket. There are also some mobile homes and cottages available if you don't fancy camping.

🕐 Closed Nov–end Mar

🛏 €12 (€18 with private bathroom)

🛌 135 pitches

ST-MALO

ⓘLES EMBRUNS

120 chaussée du Sillon, 35400 St-Malo
Tel 02 99 56 33 57
www.lesembrunsstmalo.com

Seafood dishes are served here in a salmon-pink painted dining room close to the beach, on Paramé's hotel strip. The menu follows the seasons, but some classics are fat scampi with mayonnaise, lightly salted salmon with

asparagus and lamb's kidneys with purple Brive mustard. Alternatively you can choose your meal from the lobster tank on display. You could come away with more than a good meal as the artwork on the walls is for sale.

🕐 Tue–Sat noon–2, 7–10, Sun noon–2; closed Jan

🍽 L €24, D €35, Wine €13

ⓘLA GALLO

21 rue de Dinan, 35400 St-Malo
Tel 02 99 40 84 17

One of the oldest crêperies in St-Malo set within the historic walled city. Crêpes are prepared in front of you—the most traditional is made with sausage, egg and Roquefort. The *Campagnarde* blends potatoes, onions, sausage, egg and cheese, and the *Iceberg* has chocolate and coconut ice cream and is flambéed with Malibu. Vegetarian options and children's meals are available.

🕐 Tue–Sun noon–11

🍽 L €20, D €32, Wine €4

⊖HÔTEL DES ABERS

10 rue de la Corne-du-Cerf 35400 St-Malo
Tel 02 99 40 85 60
www.abershotel.com

You'll find this hotel within the walls of the old city, behind a flowery 16th-century façade. The staff are friendly and all rooms have queen-sized beds, a private bathroom, satellite TV, a hairdryer and a safe. Some rooms are sound-proofed and there are no family rooms, although baby beds are available. Tea and coffee are freely available in the lobby. There is an Indonesian restaurant attached to the hotel.

🛏 €87–€120, excluding breakfast (continental €10, English €14)

🛌 14 rooms

ST-POL-DE-LÉON

ⓘAUBERGE DE LA POMME D'API

49 rue Verderel, 29250 St-Pol-de-Léon
Tel 02 98 69 04 36

This 16th-century building houses a lovely country inn. The elegant interior reflects the beauty of the exterior, with a large fireplace and exposed stone walls. The food is a treat, but you'd better brush up on your French as dishes are

elaborately concocted and equally elaborately named; *dos de bar, cuit sur peau* (seabass), *légumes oubliés* (forgotten vegetables!) and *cèpes et saucisse de Morteau* (cep mushrooms and smoked sausage). Vegetarian and children's options are available on request.

🕐 Wed–Sat noon–2, 7.30–9, Sun noon–2, Tue 7–9 (spring/summer); closed two weeks in Nov and 3 weeks in Feb

🍽 L €45, D €70, Wine €23

ST-THÉGONNEC

⊖ARS PRESBITAL COZ

18 rue du Gividic, 29410 St-Thégonnec
Tel 02 98 79 45 62

This 250-year-old former presbytery has a huge garden and six large, comfortable rooms with rustic furniture. All rooms have private bathrooms, but no TV. There is a small outdoor terrace for coffee, weather-permitting. A continental breakfast is included; if you reserve before noon, you can join the proprietors for dinner and drink all the wine you like for €15. Credit cards are not accepted.

🛏 €46 including breakfast

🛌 6 rooms (all non-smoking)

VANNES

ⓘLE MARGOT

12 rue Porte Poterne, 56000 Vannes
Tel 02 97 47 18 86

The restaurant is in an attractive granite building built into the ancient city wall. The

EATING AND STAYING

terrace sits in the wall itself, with excellent views of the historic buildings as well as the canal and gardens just outside. Inside are three dining rooms, two on the first floor and one on the second. On the menu are scallops with bacon and andouille, *tartiflette* (a traditional potato and cheese dish from the Alps) and pizza. Reservations are recommended, especially for the terrace.

🕐 Daily noon–2, 7–10.30, Jul to end Aug; Mon noon–2, Tue–Thu noon–2, 7–10, Fri and Sat noon–2, 7–10.30, rest of year; closed Nov

💶 L €18, D €36, Wine €10

🏕CAMPING MUNICIPAL DE CONLEAU

188 avenue du Maréchal-Juin, 56000 Vannes

Tel 02 97 63 13 88

Comfortable campsite, 3km (2 miles) from the middle of town, in a good location near the sea with trees to protect campers from the wind and sun. There are pitches for tents, caravans and camper vans (electricity hook-ups are available) and mobile homes for rent. Other facilities include table tennis, a children's playground and a launderette.

🕐 Closed Oct–end Mar

💶 €10 (2 adults with tent), €13 (2 adults with caravan)

VITRÉ

🍴LA TAVERNE DE L'ÉCU

12 rue Baudrairie, 35500 Vitré

Tel 02 99 75 11 09

If you like dining in historic surroundings then come here to eat. The restaurant is in a beautiful 16th-century building with two dining rooms, each

with a large fireplace and exposed beams. The menu changes with the seasons and everything is made on the premises, even the bread. You

might be tempted by the roasted rabbit leg with white beans and dried Italian tomatoes, boar fillet with salad and spicy apple chutney or catch of the day with preserved tomatoes. There's an extensive wine list, so you're bound to find something suitable to accompany your meal. There are vegetarian dishes and a children's menu.

🕐 Mon and Thu–Sat noon–2, 7.30–9.30, Tue and Sun noon–2

💶 L €30, D €40, Wine €13

Basse-Normandie

ARROMANCHES-LES-BAINS

🏨HÔTEL VICTORIA

24 chemin de l'Église, 14117 Arromanches-les-Bains

Tel 02 31 22 35 37

www.hotelvictoria-arromanches.com

This 19th-century Norman manor/hotel close to the D-Day beaches has period furniture and old paintings. The bedrooms range from large and vibrantly decorated to intimate with beamed ceilings, and look onto either the gardens or the flower-filled courtyard. There is an enclosed parking area.

🕐 Closed Oct–end May

💶 €74–€85, excluding breakfast (€7.50)

🛏 14

BAGNOLES DE L'ORNE

🏨HÔTEL LUTÉTIA-REINE ASTRID

Boulevard Paul Chalvet, 61140 Bagnoles de l'Orne

Tel 02 33 37 94 77

www.lutetiaastrid.com

A Belle Époque-style villa makes an elegant hotel here. Bedrooms have been tastefully decorated with period

furniture and all rooms have TV. You can try local dishes in the pastel-painted dining room or on the terrace, weather permitting. Full board

(including all meals) and half board (including two meals) packages are available. You can relax on lounge chairs in the garden and parking is available.

🕐 Closed Oct–end May

💶 €70–€110, excluding breakfast

🛏 32

🏨MANOIR DU LYS

La Croix Gauthier, 61140 Bagnoles de l'Orne

Tel 02 33 37 80 69

www.manoir-du-lys.fr

This manor house is on the edge of the Andaine forest. Some rooms look out onto the orchard and some onto the

park and are decorated in different styles–classic or modern. Alongside the manor are seven cabins on stilts, each with a sitting room, bedroom and bathroom—perfect for families. There are mountain bicycles for rent, a tennis court and a restaurant serving local cuisine.

🕐 Closed Jan

💶 €57–€185, excluding breakfast (€12.50)

🛏 23 rooms, 7 cabins

🏊 Outdoor

BAYEUX

🍴LE LION D'OR

71 rue St-Jean, 14400 Bayeux

Tel 02 31 92 06 90

A former coach house and courtyard, dating back to the 18th century, provides a lovely

setting for a meal. Chef Patrick Mouilleau cooks dishes of the region. Try rabbit confit with sage and millefeuille of carrots or pan-sautéed salmon cooked in olive oil and thyme and served with thick slices of potato.

🕐 Tue–Fri, Sun noon–2.30, 7.30–10; closed Jan

🍴 L €56, D €88, Wine €18

BRÉVILLE-SUR-MER
🛏 LA BEAUMONDERIE
20 rue de Coutances, 50290 Bréville-sur-Mer
Tel 02 33 50 36 36
www.la-beaumonderie.com
This smart country house on Mont St-Michel bay looks out onto the nearby harbour. Spacious bedrooms with large beds are furnished in a classical style although they sometimes have contemporary decorative items. You can reserve a room or just have dinner in the elegant restaurant with its welcoming open fireplace.

🍴 €50–€135, excluding breakfast
🛏 15

CABOURG
🛏 HÔTEL DU PARC
31–33 avenue Général Leclerc, 14390 Cabourg
Tel 02 31 91 00 82
www.cabourg-web.com/hotelduparc/
This hotel is close to the heart of the city and not too far from the beach. The bright reception area has pink sofas, blue carpets and cheerful red curtains. The simply furnished bedrooms are also decorated in bright tones and have TV, telephone, alarm clock and hairdryer. Free parking is available.

🍴 €40–€60, excluding breakfast
🛏 17

CHERBOURG
🍴 LA RÉGENCE
42 quai de Caligny, 50100 Cherbourg
Tel 02 33 43 05 16
This restaurant overlooks the port and its fishing fleet. Fine bistro-style furniture and tableware give the place a touch of class. The menu includes regional specials, with an emphasis on seafood, including delicious platters. There is a children's menu.

🕐 Daily noon–2.30, 7.30–10
🍴 L €32, D €30, Wine €16

DEAUVILLE
🍴 AUGUSTO
27 rue Désiré Le Hoc, 14800, Deauville
Tel 02 31 88 34 49
www.adeauville.com/augusto.htm
At Augusto, a chic bistro, they claim to be the 'kings of lobster' and they may well be right. The house special is served with a coral sauce and fresh pasta and other incarnations include lobster mousse and lobster broth. Alternatives include good fish and meat dishes such as chicken with morels and wild rice. You can eat outside or inside where the interior decoration is maritime-inspired. There are prix-fixe menus.

🕐 Thu–Mon noon–2.30, 7–10
🍴 L €52, D €128, Wine €18

🛏 HOSTELLERIE DE TOURGEVILLE
Chemin de l'Orgueil Tourgéville, 14800 Deauville
Tel 02 31 14 48 68
www.hostellerie-de-tourgeville.fr
Originally built as a country estate by film director Claude Lelouch, this Norman-style complex of country houses set in beautiful grounds is full of character. You have a choice of rooms named after film stars, or a split-level apartment. There are plenty of facilities and sports available: sauna, tennis courts, swimming pool, billiards room, beach, golf courses and horse-riding stables. The chef, Jean-Louis Farjot, prepares dishes such as snails and seafood risotto.

🕐 Closed Feb
🍴 €100–€280, excluding breakfast (€13)
🛏 25 rooms, 19 apartments
🏊 Outdoor 🌊

HONFLEUR
🛏 L'ABSINTHE
1 rue de la Ville, 14600 Honfleur
Tel 02 31 89 23 23
www.absinthe.fr
You can tell this used to be a 16th-century presbytery by the wooden panels and stained-glass windows in reception. The tranquil atmosphere continues in the bedrooms which have beamed ceilings, heavy drapes and subdued lighting. All rooms have satellite TV and a Jacuzzi and the suite has half-timbered walls. The restaurant and Frog

🍴 LA FERME ST-SIMÉON
Rue Adolphe Marais, 14600 Honfleur
Tel 02 31 81 78 00
www.saint-simeon.com
In the 19th century this mansion was the haunt of artists of the Honfleur school, including Claude Monet. There is a hotel, restaurant and beauty spa with water treatments. The restaurant has a beamed ceiling and

candelabra and the terrace looks onto the sea. The food is excellent with dishes such as langoustines and caviar, lobster risotto, oysters and mussels.

🕐 Wed–Sun 12–2.30, 7.30–9.30, Tue 7.30–9.30
🍴 L €104, D €160, Wine €25

Brasserie are round the corner on the nautically named quai de la Quarantaine.

🍴 €92–€119, excluding breakfast (€10)
🛏 6 rooms and 1 suite

HOULGATE
🍴 HÔTEL RESTAURANT 1900
17 rue des Bains, 14510, Houlgate
Tel 02 31 28 77 77
www.hotel-1900.fr
Dine in style near Houlgate's turquoise-water-fringed beaches. The restaurant of this small hotel has a painted ceiling, wood panels, antique furniture and a garden. The specials are fish and seafood. The local dish is turbot fillet served à la Houlgataise with baby vegetables in rosemary.

🕐 Daily 12–2.30, 7.30–9.30; closed Jan and mid-Nov to mid-Dec
🍴 Prix-fixe menus only, €10–€45 per person, wine from €15

EATING AND STAYING

LISIEUX

🅗 HÔTEL DE LA COUPE D'OR

49 rue Pont Mortain, 14100 Lisieux
Tel 02 31 31 16 84
www.la-coupe-d-or.com

This hotel in the heart of town has rooms which, although not very spacious, are pleasantly decorated in a rustic local style and have cable and satellite TV. The restaurant's vast dining room, with rustic furniture and vibrant tablecloths, serves local dishes.

🍴 €44, excluding breakfast (€6)
🛏 14 (3 non-smoking)

LE MONT ST-MICHEL

🅗 DU GUESCLIN

Grande Rue, 50170 Le Mont St-Michel
Tel 02 33 60 14 10

Set on Mont St-Michel's main street, Du Guesclin has delightful panoramic views across the bay. There's plenty of seafood and the fresh grilled local lamb is highly recommended. There is also a special menu for children.

🕐 Thu–Mon noon–2.30, 7.30–9.30, Tue noon–2.30; open daily in Aug; closed Nov–end-Mar
🍴 L €32, D €66, Wine €16

NOTRE-DAME-D'ESTRÉES

🅗 AU REPOS DES CHINEURS

Chemin de l'Église, 14340 Notre-Dame-d'Estrées
Tel 02 31 63 72 51
www.au-repos-des-chineurs.com

This tea room and hotel is in a former 17th-century coaching inn, with beamed ceilings and an antique tiled floor. *Chineurs* means antique-hunters or dealers which is appropriate as everything here is for sale, from the chest of drawers in your bedroom to the fine china cup you're drinking from. Rooms (some of which have whirlpool tubs) look out onto the surrounding meadows.

🕐 Closed Jan, Feb
🍴 €78–€101, excluding breakfast
🛏 10

PORT-EN-BESSIN

🅗 LA CHENEVIÈRE

Escures-Commes, 14520
Port-en-Bessin
Tel 02 31 51 25 25
www.lacheneviere.com

This elegant 18th-century chateau, in beautiful grounds, has rooms decorated in classical style but with modern amenities such as TV and a

mini bar. Additional facilities include a laundry service, babysitting and Internet access at reception. You can order fresh flowers for your bedroom. The gourmet restaurant, serving seasonal foods, is run by chef Claude Esprabens.

🕐 Closed Dec–end Apr
🍴 €170–€300, excluding breakfast (€15)
🛏 22

ST-VAAST-LA-HOUGUE

🅗 HÔTEL DE FRANCE

20 rue du Maréchal-Foch, 50550 St-Vaast-la-Hougue
Tel 02 33 54 42 26
www.france-fuchsias.com

A delightful country house hotel and restaurant near the harbour of St-Vaast. The rooms are tastefully furnished and most look onto a superb garden, with exotic plants such as banana trees, palm trees and mimosas, the setting for outdoor chamber music concerts in August. Half board packages (including dinner in the Restaurant des Fuchsias) are available.

🕐 Closed Jan, Feb and Mon out of season
🍴 €27–€94, excluding breakfast
🛏 34

Haute-Normandie

CONCHES EN OUCHE

🅗 RESTAURANT ET HÔTEL DU CYGNE

2 rue Paul Guilbaud, 27190 Conches en Ouche
Tel 02 32 30 20 60

This hotel/restaurant is in a two-floor cottage that was formerly a coach house. The dining room, with its beamed ceiling and tiled floor, has a traditional but elegant look. Fresh regional produce is used and the menu changes with the season but always has French classics such as foie gras.

🕐 Tue–Sat 12–2.30, 7.30–9.30, Sun 12–2.30
🍴 L €30, D €54, Wine €14

DIEPPE

🅗 RESTAURANT DE L'HÔTEL WINDSOR

18 boulevard de Verdun, 76200 Dieppe
Tel 02 35 84 15 23
www.hotelwindsor.fr

The contemporary restaurant at the Hotel Windsor has

panoramic sea views and serves local specials, with an emphasis on seafood. The fresh shellfish platter and the foie gras are highly recommended.

🕐 Daily noon–2.30, 7.30–9.30
🍴 L €56, D €98, Wine €24

🅗 LES ARCADES DE LA BOURSE

1–3 arcade de la Bourse, 76200 Dieppe
Tel 02 35 84 14 12
www.lesarcades.fr

This historic building in the heart of town takes its name from its covered arcade. Rooms, which all have TV, are simply furnished and some have balconies with views of the harbour. Hotel facilities include a sauna and Internet access and the restaurant is renowned for its seafood.

🍴 €43–€75, excluding breakfast (€6)
🛏 21

ÉTRETAT

🅗 LE DONJON

Chemin St-Clair, 76790 Étretat
Tel 02 35 27 08 23
www.ledonjon-etretat.fr

Le Donjon is stunningly set in a 19th-century Anglo-Norman-style chateau overlooking the village and cliffs of Étretat. Some rooms have a spa bathtub and all have satellite TV. 'Sydney' has red tones and a four-poster bed while 'Demoiselles' has pastels and period furniture. There is also a restaurant.

🍴 €145–€300
🛏 21
🏊

🅗 DORMY HOUSE

B.P. 2 route du Havre, 76790 Étretat
Tel 02 35 27 07 88
www.dormy-house.com

Perched on top of the cliffs of Étretat, this large mansion has panoramic views from some of the bedrooms. Some rooms mix period furniture with bright tones, while others are more country-style, with floral bedspreads and large wooden chests of drawers. The elegant restaurant has large bay windows overlooking the sea.

🍽 €50–€190, excluding breakfast (€13)

🛏 61

ÉVREUX

🏨 HÔTEL DE FRANCE
29 rue St-Tomas, 27000 Évreux
Tel 02 32 39 09 25
www.hoteldefrance-evreux.com
A large town house gives the Hotel de France plenty of local character. The attractive bedrooms, some with exposed beams, all have satellite TV. In the restaurant, owner-chef Jean-Luc Wantier offers fine traditional cuisine. The hotel has private parking.

🍽 €46–€52, excluding breakfast (€6.50)

🛏 16

FÉCAMP

🏨 HÔTEL NORMANDY
4 avenue Gambetta, 76400 Fécamp
Tel 02 35 29 55 11
www.normandy-fecamp.com
A former post house which was renovated in 1998. Spacious, comfortable and modern rooms all have satellite TV. The interior of the restaurant, La Brasserie Maupassant, evokes the early 19th century. Parking is available.

🍽 €58, excluding breakfast

🛏 30 (5 non-smoking)

FOURGES

🍴 MOULIN DE FOURGES
38 rue du Moulin, 27630, Fourges
Tel 02 32 52 12 12
www.moulin-de-fourges.com
This beautiful, Norman-style mill, is right on the river just a couple of miles away from Giverny. Each room is decorated differently but all have characteristic features such as a fireplace or half-timbered walls. The food in the restaurant makes innovative use of the local produce, but isn't restricted to local recipes. Try the duet of foie gras, one cooked in port, the other marinated in lavender.

🕐 Tue–Sat noon–2.30, 7.30–10, Sun 7.30–10; closed mid-Nov to mid-Apr

🍽 L €64, D €64, Wine €18

LE HAVRE

🍴 VENT D'OUEST
4 rue Caligny, 76600 Le Havre
Tel 02 35 42 50 69
www.ventdouest.fr
Vent d'Ouest is halfway between the city heart and the sea. The lounge and some of the bedrooms have a nautical look, while others have countryside or mountain themes. The hotel doesn't have a restaurant but has a tea room with snacks. There is private parking.

🍽 €75–€100, excluding breakfast (€9)

🛏 35

LYONS-LA-FORÊT

🏨 LA LICORNE
La Licorne, B.P. 4, 27480 Lyons-la-Forêt
Tel 02 32 49 62 02
www.licorne-hotel-restaurant.com
Here, you are in a 17th-century inn in a pleasant village surrounded by Europe's largest beech forest, the Lyons forest. Behind a half-timbered façade, is a quaint interior with rooms tastefully decorated and furnished with antiques. The inviting dining room, with its large fireplace and exposed beams, serves traditional regional dishes.

🍽 €65–€92, excluding breakfast (€10)

🛏 19 (2 non-smoking)

MONTIGNY

🏨 LE RELAIS DE MONTIGNY
Rue du Lieutenant Aubert, 76380 Montigny
Tel 02 35 36 05 97
www.relais-de-montigny.com
This modern hotel, just a couple of miles from Rouen, looks onto a pleasant garden. Rooms, which all have satellite TV, are comfortable and some have a small terrace overlooking the surrounding greenery. The restaurant serves local dishes and you can dine on the terrace in good weather.

🕐 Closed end Dec–early Jan

🍽 €68–€75, excluding breakfast (€9)

🛏 22

ROUEN

🍴 LE CATELIER
134 bis avenue des Martyrs de la Résistance, 76100 Rouen
Tel 02 35 72 59 90
www.lecatelier-restaurant.fr
Dine on local delicacies in this Norman house close to the botanical garden. The dining room is elegant yet

convivial with a large mirror and cane-backed chairs. Chef Marie-France Atinault specializes in seafood. Try scallops from Dieppe, turbot in a white wine sauce or lobster salad with cider-butter and fried apples. Her husband Daniel will help you choose the best wine to go with your meal. There are several prix-fixe menus.

🕐 Tue–Sat noon–2.30, 7.30–10; closed 2 weeks in Aug

🍽 L €70, D €100 wine included

🍴 LA PÊCHERIE
29 place de la Basse Vieille Tour, 76000 Rouen
Tel 02 35 88 71 00
www.lapecherie.fr
They serve generous platters of fish and shellfish, and less common combinations such as lobster in a cider reduction, at this friendly brasserie. A couple of meat dishes and some inventive desserts (spicy pineapple carpaccio and Earl-Grey-scented crème brûlée) complete the picture. In fine weather, tables and chairs are set up on the small terrace.

🕐 Mon–Fri noon–2.30, 7.30–9.30, Sat 7.30–10

🍽 L €29, D €80, Wine €16

🍴 SALON DE THÉ MARIANNE
6 rue Massacre, 76000 Rouen
Tel 02 35 89 33 36
www.chez.com/salondethemarianne
This tea room, at the heart of the historic town, is perfect for breakfast, lunch or an afternoon snack. In this comfortable setting with a beautiful wooden floor, white walls and dark wooden furniture, you can choose from English breakfast, salads, soups, eggs and sandwiches which are served all day. At teatime, the brew of your choice comes with a cake or a small sandwich.

🕐 Mon–Sat 8.30–6

🍽 Breakfast and tea from €5

EATING

The greatest tipple in France is the bubbly one from Reims and Épernay. If you can, visit at least one major champagne house for the grand tour and tasting, as well as a small independent winemaker for a more personal introduction to the region's wines. Alsace has its distinguished white wines, yet the classic taste of the north and east is beer, with micro-breweries in the shadows of the better known huge industrial breweries in Lille and St-Omer. For something different, taste white beer, made with chicory, which finds its way onto many menus in various guises. Fresh vegetables and salads are plentiful as they are grown in the market gardens of the north. Other typical Alsatian treats are *flammeküche*, (a local bar-snack midway between a pizza and a pancake), the classic *choucroute*, (hearty sauerkraut with mixed meats) and *baeckeoffe* (a mutton and beef stew steeped in white wine). Lorraine gave its name to the famed quiche and its heart to the *quetsche* plum that appears in jams and liqueurs. Finally, it shouldn't be forgotten that brasseries, which you can find all over France, originated in Alsace.

STAYING

In the north, look out for *estaminets*, local bars in the front room of a private house—the ultimate in hospitality. In the east, you can dine and sleep in an inn, or *auberge*.

Nord-Pas-de-Calais

AIRE-SUR-LA-LYS

⑪HOSTELLERIE DES TROIS MOUSQUETAIRES

Château du Fort de la Redoute, 62120 Aire-sur-la-Lys
03 21 39 01 11
www.hostelleriedes3mousquetaires.com
The 'Three Musketeers' restaurant is in a 19th-century castle with antique furnishings. The dining room is decorated with ornamental plates and

paintings and has high-backed, padded chairs. On the menu, expect local rustic dishes such

as stuffed pig's trotters in beer sauce and fillet of perch with potatoes and Belgian endive.
🕓 Daily noon–2, 7.30–9.30
🍽 L €60, D €78, Wine €15

ARRAS

⑪LA FAISANDERIE

45 Grand'Place, 62000, Arras
Tel 03 21 48 20 76
www.lafaisanderie.com
Chef Jean-Pierre Dargent is a native of southwest France and prepares the local produce with sophistication and originality. Dine on cep

mousse with oysters followed by sautéed hare at elegant tables under 17th-century vaulted ceilings.
🕓 Tue–Sat noon–2.30, 7.30–10; Sun noon–2.30; closed 2 weeks in Feb and 3 weeks in Aug
🍽 L €50, D €140, Wine €30

⑪LE PETIT THÉÂTRE

7 rue des Petits Viéziers, 62000 Arras
Tel 03 21 51 10 85
This restaurant is perfect for dinner before or after a play, as it is near the theatre. The theatrical theme continues inside, with drapes that frame the window as if it were a stage and beautiful frescoes on the walls depicting dancers and acrobats. The food is Italian, with classics such as pizza, pasta and

Milan-style escalope.
🕓 Mon–Sat noon–2, 7–10
🍽 L €16, D €30, Wine €8

BÉTHUNE

⑪LE MEURIN

15 place de la République, 62400 Béthune
Tel 03 21 68 88 88
www.le-meurin.fr
Marc Meurin's restaurant, with its burgundy and yellow interior has sophisticated dishes that use the best local ingredients. The menu includes Brittany lobster, oysters and quail with lentils, braised endives and buttered green cabbage.
🕓 Wed–Sat noon–1.45, 7.30–9.30, Tue 7.30–9.30, Sun noon–1.45; closed 3 weeks in Aug
🍽 L €70, D €104, Wine €35

BONDUES

⑪AUBERGE DE L'HARMONIE

36 place de l'Abbé Bonpain, 59910 Bondues
Tel 03 20 23 17 02
www.aubergeharmonie.fr
The interior design of this restaurant is elegant in ochre and pink. The traditional cuisine looks and tastes good: pan-fried foie gras served with green and white asparagus and gingerbread croutons, wild sea bass with fennel and a vermouth and green olive reduction.
🕓 Wed, Fri and Sat noon–2.30, 7.30–10, Tue, Thu and Sun noon–2.30
🍽 L €50, D €70, Wine €17

CALAIS

⑪AQUAR'AILE

255 rue Jean Moulin, 62100 Calais
Tel 03 21 34 00 00
www.aquaraile.com
Aquar'aile is on the fourth floor of an apartment building and has expansive sea views. On a clear day you can see as far as the English coast. Sleek lines, pale wood and blue tones keep the three dining rooms contemporary, while the menu remains traditional. Seafood is the theme here: Shellfish platters and Calais sole served with lobster sauce are among the highlights.
🕓 Tue–Sat noon–2.30, 7.30–10; Sun noon–2.30
🍽 L €52, D €84, Wine €18

AU CALICE
55 boulevard Jacquard, 62100 Calais
Tel 03 21 34 51 78
www.lecalice.com
A long wooden bar, swirly
glass lighting fixtures and an
old clock provide the setting
here. Dine on *flamiche au
Maroille* (a quiche made with
local cheese), smoked herrings
or home-made cakes. In
summer you can eat on the
pleasant flower-filled terrace.
There is a good selection of
beers to go with your meal
and a range of whiskies to
conclude it.
⏰ Daily 8am–1am
🍽 L €26, D €32, Wine €14

GOSNAY
CHARTREUSE DU VAL
ST-ESPRIT
1 rue de Fouquières, 62199 Gosnay
Tel 03 21 62 80 00
www.lachartreuse.com
This 19th-century castle was
built on the remains of a
14th-century monastery.

Bedrooms are stylish, with
intriguing period furniture and
moulded ceilings. Four rooms
are big enough for families and
the superior rooms are vast.
There are two tennis courts,
parking and there's a golf
course nearby. There's even a
helipad should you choose to
arrive by helicopter.
🛏 €90–€190
🛈 67 (all non-smoking)
♨

LILLE
ALCIDE
5 rue des débris St-Étienne, 59800 Lille
Tel 03 20 12 06 95
A high-class brasserie that has
been in the middle of town
since 1873. Behind a lovely
half-timbered façade you'll
find 1930s-style furniture,
comfortable bench seats and
a glass ceiling. *Moules frites*
(mussels and chips) and

potjevleesch (cold cuts in
aspic) are just two examples
of the classic brasserie dishes.
⏰ Daily noon–2.30, 7.30–11
🍽 L €40, D €70, Wine €14

LA CAVE AUX FIOLES
39 rue de Gand, 59800 Lille
Tel 03 20 55 18 43
www.cave-aux-fioles.fr
A restaurant could not have a
more romantic setting—at the
heart of Lille's old town on a
cobbled street in an 18th-
century red-brick and wood
house. The owners have
succeeded in creating a cosy,
intimate atmosphere in the
dining room, which has a log
fire and soothing jazz. The
food, served by candlelight,
has inventive interpretations
of local dishes, such as scallops in a light vanilla sauce
and Flemish-style lobster.
⏰ Mon–Fri noon–2.30, 7.30–10,
Sat 7.30–10
🍽 L €40, D €60, Wine €15

LA CHICORÉE
15 place Rihour, 59000, Lille
Tel 03 20 54 81 52
This beautiful brasserie,
named after the vegetable of
the region, is popular because
it is in the middle of town, is
open round the clock and has
an extensive menu of seafood
platters, fish stew, onion soup
and rabbit.
⏰ Open daily 11am–5am
🍽 L €41, D €60, Wine €14

À L'HUITRIÈRE
3 rue des Chats Bossus, 59800 Lille
Tel 03 20 55 43 41
www.huitriere.fr
The restored 18th-century
house has an art deco façade
and inside you'll find pale
oak wood panels, crystal
chandeliers and Aubusson
tapestries. Expect classic
seafood dishes, such as cod
in cream with caviar from
Aquitaine, and a wine cellar
with tens of thousands of
bottles. The restaurant's
fabulous fish shop has mosaics
and stained-glass windows
depicting the sea.
⏰ Mon–Sat noon–2.30, 7.30–10, Sun
noon–2.30
🍽 L €86, D €200, Wine €25

HÔTEL BRUEGHEL
5 parvis St-Maurice, 59000 Lille
Tel 03 20 06 06 69
www.hotel-brueghel.com
You'll be near the station here,
on a traffic-free street that
looks onto a glorious Gothic
church. The hotel is named
after Flemish painter Pieter
Brueghel and its interior pays
homage to his style. Bedrooms
are light, tastefully decorated
and have decorative objects
such as fine paintings.
🛏 €62–€95, excluding breakfast
🛈 66

MONTREUIL-SUR-MER
AUBERGE DE LA
GRENOUILLÈRE
La Madelaine-sous-Montreuil, 62170
Montreuil-sur-Mer
Tel 03 21 06 07 22
www.lagrenouillere.fr
There's a froggy theme to this
inn: Frogs are in frescoes
created by English humorist
Frank Reynolds in the 1930s,
and also appear on the menu.
Other dishes include foie gras
served with figs in a mulled
wine reduction and veal in a
porcini and chicory sauce.
⏰ Thu–Mon noon–2.30, 7.30–10;
closed Jan
🍽 L €90, D €120, Wine €35

HÔTEL DE FRANCE
2 rue Petit Coquempot, 62170
Montreuil-sur-Mer
Tel 03 21 06 05 36
www.janie-hoteldefrance.com
Victor Hugo wrote *Letter to
Adèle* in this 16th-century

building. It is now the canvas
on which Janie, the owner,
lets her imagination run free.
Vibrant fabrics, paintings and
artificial flowers create a
unique interior, alternating
between rococo and kitsch.
Bedrooms are regularly redecorated. There is a restaurant.
🛏 €100–€110
🛈 14

SAILLY-SUR-LA-LYS

⊖LA STATION BAC ST-MAUR

La Gare des Années Folles, 77 rue de la Gare, 62840 Sailly-sur-la-Lys
Tel 03 21 02 68 20
perso.wanadoo.fr/station-bac-saint-maur/

A truly original hotel created inside a perfectly preserved 1930s train wagon in a former railway station. The six cabins each have a washbasin, but the two showers and lavatories in the corridor are shared. The profusion of mahogany inlaid with mother-of-pearl and the general atmosphere evocative of the early 20th-century world of Agatha Christie make this a memorable place to stay.

🕐 Closed Nov–end Mar
🛏 €30–€35, excluding breakfast
🛏 6

Picardie

AMIENS

ⓘLES MARISSONS

Pont de la Dodane, Quartier St-Leu
80000 Amiens
Tel 03 22 92 96 66
www.les-marissons.fr

This restaurant is in a 15th-century shipyard on the bank of the Somme. The interior is the blue and yellow of Picardie and there's a pleasant garden and terrace where you can have dinner in good weather. The seasonal menu has local specials such as eels, either smoked or cooked in aromatic herbs, *pâté de canard en*

croûte (duck pie), and *gâteau battu* (a sugared brioche).
🕐 Mon–Fri noon–2, 7–10, Sat 7–10
🍽 L €38, D €96, Wine €18

COURCELLES-SUR-VESLE

ⓘ CHÂTEAU DE COURCELLES

02220 Courcelles-sur-Vesle
Tel 03 23 74 13 53
www.chateau-de-courcelles.fr

This is a splendid chateau hotel. Oak floors, candelabra

and hunting scenes framed on the walls of the dining room preserve the historic character of this Louis XIV-style castle, built in 1690. The elegant winter garden has wonderful views. The restaurant has a well-stocked wine cellar and exquisite French cuisine: grilled lobster with celery mousse, roast duck with figs and potato millefeuille.
🕐 Daily 12.30–2, 7.30–9.30
🍽 L €80, D €140, Wine €35

LAON

ⓘLE PATIO

26 rue St-Jean, 02000 Laon
Tel 03 23 23 28 29

Inside there's a tiled floor, beamed ceiling, long wooden bar and small tables with bistro chairs; outside there's a patio. A good selection of pizzas, grilled meats and Tex-Mex dishes are on the menu alongside tried-and-tested French dishes such as snails, goat's cheese on toast and steak tartare. They also do pizza to take out.
🕐 Mon and Wed–Sat noon–1.30, 7–9.30, Tue noon–1.30
🍽 L €20, D €30, Wine €8

ⓘRESTAURANT DE L'HÔTEL LA BANNIÈRE DE FRANCE

11 rue Franklin Roosevelt, 02000 Laon
Tel 03 23 23 21 44
www.hoteldelabannieredefrance.com

At the heart of the medieval district, this 17th-century building has been transformed into an elegant hotel and restaurant complete with drapes, soft lighting and wood panels. The cuisine includes refined dishes such as poached trout with champagne and veal with morel mushroom cream sauce and there's a good wine list.
🕐 Daily noon–2, 7–9.30
🍽 L €41, D €90, Wine €17

PLAILLY

ⓘAUBERGE DU PETIT CHEVAL D'OR

48 rue de Paris, 60128 Plailly
Tel 03 44 54 36 33
www.auberge-cheval-or.com

This dining room, in a cottage surrounded by greenery, has exposed stone walls, chandeliers and high-backed chairs. In winter you can sit by the fireplace and in summer, on the veranda that looks

onto the lush garden. In either season, you can enjoy the menu that might include truffle-stuffed pigeon, duck foie gras and salmon with a sorrel sauce.
🕐 Daily noon–2.30, 7.30-10
🍽 L €100, D €180 including wine

SAINTE-PREUVE

⊖CHÂTEAU DE BARIVE

02350 Sainte-Preuve
Tel 03 23 22 15 15
www.chateau-de-barive.com

A 19th-century castle, set in vineyards, makes a refined place. The bedrooms have period furniture, paintings, objets d'art and beamed ceilings—one also has a Jacuzzi bath. There's a swimming pool, sauna, tennis court and a golf course nearby. The restaurant has a regal dining room and a winter garden.
🕐 Closed Jan
🛏 €75–€140
🛏 13
🏊 Indoor

Champagne-Ardenne

ÉPERNAY

ⓘL'ARCHIDUCHESSE

38 rue du Général Leclerc, 51200 Épernay
Tel 03 26 53 20 00

The look of this restaurant is indeed worthy of an arch-duchess. Several dining rooms offer different interiors and atmospheres: candelabra, large mirrors and soft tones in one and a vaulted cellar with bottles lining the walls for another. The classics of French cuisine are on the menu, in addition to rural dishes such as wild boar and sea bass stew.
🕐 Tue–Sun noon–2, 7–11
🍽 L €18, D €34, Wine €10

⊖LE CLOS RAYMI

3 rue Joseph de Venoge, 51200 Épernay
Tel 03 26 51 00 58
www.closraymi-hotel.com

This 19th-century mansion hotel, encircled by a secluded garden, has an exquisite 1930s interior complete with ornaments and paintings reminiscent of the era. The themed bedrooms, with names such as Tuscany,

Colonial, Provence and Champagne, have satellite TV and some have queen-size beds. Breakfast is served on the terrace and there is parking available.

€126–€146

7

REIMS

LA CALABRAISE

4 rue de la Magdelaine, 51100 Reims

Tel 03 26 40 57 22

There's a good choice of pizzas, cooked in the brick, wood-fired oven, at this convivial place. A take-out service is also available.

Mon–Sat noon–2, 7–10

L €16, D €30, Wine €15

LE GRAND CAFÉ

92 place Drouet d'Erlon, 51000 Reims

Tel 03 26 47 61 50

Le Grand Café is like a Parisian bistro, with wrought-iron-legged tables and a large terrace on a lively square. They serve 13 different varieties of mussel–the most exotic infused with saffron. Large bowls of pasta, salads and cakes complete the menu.

Daily noon–2.30, 7–11.30

L €40, D €40, Wine €15

AU VIGNERON

Place Paul Jamot, 51000 Reims

Tel 03 26 79 86 86

www.restaurant-levigneron.com

This restaurant offers a tasty introduction to the region's cuisine amid a profusion of posters, barrels and other paraphernalia dedicated to champagne. Poached egg with Maroilles cheese and duck cooked in champagne are just two examples. There is a pleasant terrace.

Mon–Fri noon–3, 7.30–10.30, Sat 7.30–10.30

L €52, D €100, Wine €16

Lorraine

CHAUMONT-SUR-AIRE

DOMAINE DU MOULIN HAUT

Route de St-Mihiel, 55260 Chaumont-sur-Aire

Tel 03 29 70 66 46

perso.wanadoo.fr/domaine.moulinhaut/

This restaurant is at the heart of a vast vineyard, complete with a pond where sturgeon can be fished. The cuisine is traditional, with no sturgeon in sight: duck magret with mushrooms, pigeon flambéed in prune liqueur and scallops flambéed in aquavit. There is also a whole menu dedicated to the illustrious truffle.

Tue–Sat noon–2.30, 7.30–10; Sun noon–2.30; closed mid-Jan to mid-Feb

L €60, D €80, Wine €18

MÉRÉVILLE

LA MAISON CARRÉE

14 rue du Bac, 54850 Méréville

Tel 03 83 47 08 02

www.maison-carree.com

The vast, square house lies in the countryside on the bank of the Moselle river, and has been a Lorraine institution since it opened in 1945. The seven dining rooms have been elegantly decorated with period chairs, soft tones and paintings. The seasonal menu uses the best produce from the market: Dishes include foie gras in a champagne sauce and fish in a white butter sauce.

Tue–Sun noon–2.30, 7.30–10

L €40, D €50, Wine €12

METZ

HÔTEL DE LA CATHÉDRALE

25 place de Chambre, 57000 Metz

Tel 03 87 75 00 02

www.hotelcathedrale-metz.fr

As the name suggests, this historic hotel is in the middle of town at the foot of the cathedral. It's in a 17th-century town house and has welcomed visitors since 1627. There's an impressive wrought-iron balustrade in the lobby and period furniture, paintings and objets d'art fill the communal areas. The bedrooms all have satellite TV and some have wrought-iron bed frames and beamed ceilings. There is no restaurant.

€70–€80, excluding breakfast

20

NANCY

CUBA FELIZ

11 rue des Maréchaux, 54000, Nancy

Tel 03 83 37 02 41

For a change of scenery and tastes, step into this little corner of Cuba, which serves exotic dishes such as *picadillo* (beef cooked with onion, red pepper, rice and black beans). The warmth of Cuba is well reflected in the orange walls, fireplace and comfortable club chairs. You can eat outside on the small terrace in good weather.

Mon–Sat noon–2, 7.30–midnight

L €30, D €60, Wine €15

LA GROLE

47 rue des Ponts, 54000 Nancy

Tel 03 83 30 27 79

www.lagrole.com

You can recognize this restaurant by the statue of a cow outside. The menu concentrates on the food of the mountainous Savoy region, with various fondues and *braserades* (meat grilled on a hot stone). Though main courses are famously generous, those with a sweet tooth should try to leave room for the Toblerone fondue.

Mon–Fri 7pm–10pm, Sat 7pm–midnight

D €70, Wine €15

LE LEZ'ART

93 Grande Rue, 54000 Nancy

Tel 03 83 37 60 18

This oasis of peace in the heart of town has a bar, a pretty winter garden with teak furniture and a salon complete with library. A wide range of snacks are available, including the local *flammeküche* (thin-crust Alsatian pizza) and an excellent Sunday brunch.

Tue–Sat 10am–1am, Sun 11am–5pm

L €36, D €40, Wine €15

Alsace

COLMAR

KELLER

25 rue du Ladhof, 68000 Colmar

Tel 03 89 20 66 66

www.beausejour.fr

This is a successful family-run restaurant (in the Hotel Beauséjour) which opened

in 1913. It has an elegant interior with soft yellow walls, low lighting, paintings,

EATING AND STAYING

mirrors and antique chairs. The menu has hearty French comfort food.

🕐 Mon–Fri noon–2, 7–8.45, Sat 7–8.45

🍷 L €28, D €90, Wine €20

🏠 LA MAISON DES TÊTES

19 rue des Têtes, 68000 Colmar

Tel 03 89 24 43 43

www.la-maison-des-tetes.com

The beamed ceilings, carved wooden panels, old paintings and high-backed chairs preserve the 17th-century character of this Alsatian house. The menu has novel versions of local dishes such as home-made goose foie gras with Riesling, marmalade of apple in a Muscat jelly and basket of warm raspberries with *Gewürztraminer* zabaglione.

🕐 Wed–Sat noon–2, 7–9.30, Tue 7–9.30, Sun noon–2; closed Feb

🍷 L €55, D €80, Wine €18

🏠 RESTAURANT MEISTERMANN

2a avenue de la République, 68000 Colmar

Tel 03 89 41 65 64

www.meistermann.com

This restaurant has two dining rooms each with its own menu—a brasserie section and a more elegant restaurant. Dishes include seafood, game and Alsatian specials. Don't

miss the *Gewürztraminer* sorbet.

🕐 Tue–Sat noon–2.30, 7.30–10, Sun noon–2.30

🍷 L €40, D €100, Wine €20

🏠 WINSTUB LE FLORY

1 rue Mangold, 68000, Colmar

Tel 03 89 41 78 80

www.restaurant-flory.com

'Winstub' are known for their hearty Alsatian dishes (especially pork) and this one is no exception. It's in a 16th-century Alsatian house

with a half-timbered façade on a picturesque traffic-free street. The interior is typical Alsatian with beamed ceilings, wooden chairs with carved hearts and old carriage wheels suspended as candelabra. Fill up on sauerkraut or braised pork knuckles cooked in Pinot Noir.

🕐 Thu–Mon 11.30–2, 6.30–10

🍷 L €41, D €70, Wine €18

🏠 HOSTELLERIE LE MARÉCHAL

Place des Six Montagnes Noires, 68000 Colmar

Tel 03 89 41 60 32

www.hotel-le-marechal.com

This hotel is at the water's edge and among half-timbered houses in the appropriately named 'Little Venice' district. Inside you'll find beamed ceilings, period furniture and canopied beds in most rooms. The bedrooms also have modern amenities such as satellite TV, powerful showers

and whirlpool bath.

🛏 €95–€215

🚪 30 (3 non-smoking)

♿

ITTERSWILLER

🏠 HÔTEL ARNOLD

98 route des Vins, 67140 Itterswiller

Tel 03 88 85 50 58

www.hotel-arnold.com

An Alsatian house among the vineyards makes an atmospheric place to stay. Most of the comfortable rooms have wonderful vistas of the valley and all have TV. The Winstub restaurant is in an old wine cellar and has a terrace with views of the countryside and vineyards and serves sauerkraut and foie gras. The hotel shop sells gifts and wines from its own vineyards.

🛏 €75–€109, excluding breakfast

🚪 29

MARLENHEIM

🏠 LE RELAIS DE LA ROUTE DU VIN

1 place du Kaufhaus, 67520 Marlenheim

Tel 03 88 87 50 05

www.relais.fr

This inn at the gates of the Alsatian wine route has a restaurant and bedrooms with TV and bathrooms. It certainly feels like a traditional inn, with a rustic interior with candelabra and beamed ceilings. Local wines are the perfect accompaniment to the traditional cuisine, which includes foie gras, smoked ham and the ubiquitous sauerkraut.

🕐 Tue–Sun noon–2.30, 7–10; closed 2 weeks in Mar

🍷 L €26, D €48, Wine €11

OBERNAI

🏠 À LA COUR D'ALSACE

3 rue de Gail, B.P. 64, 67212 Obernai

Tel 03 88 95 07 00

www.cour-alsace.com

The spacious, comfortable guest rooms in this former manor house are decorated in soft tones and with Alsatian furniture. All of the rooms have a minibar, safe and cable TV. Le Caveau de Gail wine tavern and the Jardin des Remparts restaurant, which spills out into the lovely gardens, serve Alsatian dishes.

🕐 Closed Jan

🛏 €132–€149, excluding breakfast

🚪 44 (3 non-smoking)

OSTWALD

🏠 CHÂTEAU DE L'ÎLE

4 quai Heydt, 67540 Ostwald

Tel 03 88 66 85 00

www.chateau-ile.com

This hotel, on the bank of the river Ill, is made up of a 19th-century chateau and a cluster of half-timbered houses. Bedrooms are lavishly decorated with chandeliers, antique furniture, Persian carpets and heavy drapes. The restaurant has three dining rooms—one has an amazing carved wooden ceiling.

🛏 €190–€355

🚪 62 (only 7 are in the chateau)

♿ 🏊 Indoor 🚗

RIQUEWIHR

⊝HÔTEL DE LA COURONNE
5 rue de la Couronne, 68340
Riquewihr
Tel 03 89 49 03 03
www.hoteldelacouronne.com
The hotel is in a 16th-century
house with half-timbered
walls, beamed ceilings and
period furniture. Some of the

bedrooms have original 16th-
century frescoed ceilings, while
others have contemporary
murals depicting flowers and
fruits. In addition to rooms
(which all have TV), there are
apartments suitable for
families. Parking is available.
🛏 €58–€105, excluding breakfast
🛏 40

ROUFFACH

⊝CHÂTEAU D'ISENBOURG
68250 Rouffach
Tel 03 89 78 58 50
www.isenbourg.com
The chateau overlooks the
Vosges forest and vineyards
and has a wonderful view
from the magnificent marble
dining room. The classic,
luxurious rooms have chandeliers, antique furniture and
floral tapestries. The leisure
facilities are excellent and
include sauna, whirlpool
bath, Turkish bath, tennis
courts, mountain bikes and
two pools.
🍽 Closed mid-Jan to end Mar
🛏 €190–€290
🛏 41
🏊 Indoor and outdoor 🚣

STRASBOURG

🍽À L'ANCIENNE DOUANE
6 rue de la Douane, 67000 Strasbourg
Tel 03 88 15 78 78
Discover classic Alsace at its
best in this popular restaurant
on the bank of the river Ill.
Inside you'll find carved
wooden chairs around tables
covered with red and white
checked tablecloths. The menu

has Alsatian specials
sauerkraut, *flammeküche*
(a thin-crust Alsatian pizza)
and Gewürztraminer wine.
🍽 Daily 11.30–2, 6.30–11
🍽 L €30, D €40, Wine €15

🍽LA CLOCHE À FROMAGE
27 rue des Tonneliers, 67000
Strasbourg
Tel 03 88 23 13 19
www.cheese-gourmet.com
With more than 200 cheeses,
this is a cheese-lover's
paradise. However, if you don't
do dairy, your options are
more limited. The resident
cheesemonger, who's mad
about cheese, can advise
you on the large choice of
fondues, meat and fish dishes
(with cheese) and *raclettes*
(melted cheese with cold
meats). There is a good
selection of wines by the glass.
Reserve ahead.
🍽 Thu–Mon noon–2, 7–10.30,
Wed 7–10
🍽 L €49, D €49, Wine €15

🍽AU CROCODILE
10 rue de L'Outre-France, 67060
Strasbourg
Tel 03 88 32 13 02
www.au-crocodile.com
A stuffed crocodile, said to be
a hunting trophy brought back
from one of Napoleon's
Egyptian campaigns, presides
over the dining room and
gives the restaurant its name.
Antique furniture and paintings
framed by heavy drapes and
wood panels set the scene for
chef Émile Jung's inventive
cuisine. Duck liver with
apricots and ginger, lobster
with golden vermicelli and
pink pepper with a citrus
sauce, and black truffle pie
are just a few examples.
🍽 Tue–Sat noon–2.30, 7.30–10; closed
3 weeks in Jul and at the end of Dec
🍽 L €156, D €250, Wine €50

🍽OBERJAEGEROF
Route de l'Oberjaegerhof, 67100
Strasbourg
Tel 03 88 39 63 84
You'll find this 19th-century
country house just ten minutes
from the middle of town, yet
on the edge of a forest. The
three dining rooms all have
traditional Alsatian touches
such as wooden chairs with a
heart motif and beamed
ceilings. The menu is also

⊝HÔTEL DU DRAGON
2 rue de l'Écarlate, 67000 Strasbourg
Tel 03 88 35 79 80
www.dragon.fr
Although this hotel occupies
a 17th-century building, its
style is resolutely contemporary, with grey-on-grey
schemes and modern
furniture designed by Mallet
Stevens, Philippe Starck and
Gaetano Pesce. Some rooms
have a king-size bed,
and all come with a TV and
telephone. You can have
breakfast outside in the
hotel's beautiful paved
courtyard.
🛏 €79–€108
🛏 32 (10 non-smoking)

typically Alsatian, offering
sauerkraut and *flammeküche*.
🍽 Wed–Sun noon–2, 6.30–10
🍽 L €40, D €52, Wine €15

⊝HÔTEL MAISON ROUGE
4 rue des Francs-Bourgeois, 67000
Strasbourg
Tel 03 88 32 08 60
www.maison-rouge.com
This red house is in the heart
of Strasbourg, near place
Kléber. Inside the three-star
hotel you'll find paintings,
trompe l'œil murals and
period furniture such as
typically Alsatian Splinder
marquetry. Rooms are
comfortable and have a safe,
minibar and cable TV.
🛏 €82–€109
💲

TURCKHEIM

⊝AUBERGE DU BRAND
8 Grand Rue, 68230 Turckheim
Tel 03 89 27 06 10
www.aubergedubrand.com
This hotel is in a medieval
town a few kilometres
southwest of Colmar and
surrounded by vineyards. The
rooms are named after local
vintages such as Riesling
and Muscat and have floral
curtains, beamed ceilings
and some antique furnishings.
There is also a restaurant.
🛏 €55–€77, excluding breakfast
🛏 9 (4 non-smoking)

EATING AND STAYING

EATING

The grapes that grow along the banks of the river Loire are turned into crisp, dry white wines such as Muscadet and Sancerre. The river also provides fresh salmon, trout, carp and perch for the many gastronomic restaurants within

the priory, chateau and manor house hotels, perched high above the river. In addition to exploring chateaux during your stay, you can investigate the region's other wines, such as rich, strong Chinon or sparkling Saumur. The caves that keep these effervescent wines cool also contain the famous local mushrooms, cultivated in the dark. Passageways long ago hewn out of the rock created troglodyte dwellings, some of which are now fashionable restaurants, hotels and self-catering *gîtes*.

STAYING

Excellent hotels dot the area, but the region's specialty is rooms in historic buildings. The Royal Abbey of Fontevraud, Richard the Lionheart's last resting place, has a stylish hotel with a cloister in a former leper colony within its walls. Bienvenue au Château, an association of titled and untitled owners of castles and palaces, offers four-poster bed-and-breakfast stays in a grand style.

Pays de la Loire

ANGERS

○HOTEL ANJOU

1 boulevard du Maréchal Foch, 49100 Angers
Tel 02 41 88 24 82
The strength of this hotel is in its diverse interior. The spacious rooms might have art-deco mosaics or 17th- or 18th-century fittings and the

public areas have ornate ceilings and stained-glass windows. Rooms all have satellite TV and there are parking spaces. The restaurant, Le Salamandre, named after the symbol of François I, has high ceilings and is decorated with Renaissance-inspired frescoes. Prix-fixe menus are between €29 and €40 and the children's menu is €19.
€83–€147, excluding breakfast
53 (8 non-smoking)

CHÊNEHUTTE-LES-TUFFEAUX

○PRIEURÉ

49350 Chênehutte-les-Tuffeaux
Tel 02 41 67 90 14
www.prieure.com
This former priory is on a peaceful 24-hectare (60-acre) piece of woodland on a slope above the Loire, 7km (4 miles) northwest of Saumur. It was built between the 12th and the 16th centuries and welcomes guests into capacious, comfortable rooms, which all overlook the river. In summer the sports on offer are swimming, tennis, lawn-bowling and miniature golf. The restaurant serves Anjou-style cuisine in two large dining rooms, with views of the Loire.
Closed Jan, Feb
€180–€275
19 rooms, 2 suites and 15 cottages
Outdoor heated

FONTEVRAUD-L'ABBAYE

○LICORNE

Allée Sainte-Catherine, 49590 Fontevraud-l'Abbaye
Tel 02 41 51 72 49
Next door to the splendid abbey, this restaurant has a unicorn-themed interior. The dining room is decorated in Louis XIV style and there's a lovely terrace. Chef Jean-Michel Bezille cooks prawn and basil ravioli in morel sauce, fillet of beef with smoked pork and shallots and desserts such as warm chocolate tart with pears and lemon-butter sauce. Try a bottle of Saumur from the wine list. Reserve ahead.
Tue–Sat 12.15–1.30, 7.15–9, Sun 12.15–1.30, Apr–end Nov; Tue, Thu–Sat 12.15–1.30, 7.15–9, Wed, Sun 12.15–1.30, rest of year; closed 15 Dec–end Jan
L €60, D €120, Wine €10

HAUTE GOULAINE

○MANOR DE LA BOULAIE

33 rue de la Chapelle St-Martin, 44115 Haute Goulaine
Tel 02 40 06 15 91
In a mansion, with views of the surrounding vineyard, chef Laurent Saudeau takes an innovative approach to cooking. Try crab and celery ravioli or crystalline of aubergine (eggplant) with mascarpone-raspberry sauce. The wine list focuses on Muscadet and Loire wines and has a good selection.
Tue, Thu–Sat 12.15–1.45, 7–9, Wed, Sun 12.15–1.45; closed 29 Jul–22 Aug, 23–31 Dec, 24 Feb–5 Mar
L €60, D €120, Wine €20

LE MANS

○LE BEAULIEU

24 rue Ponts Neufs, 72000 Le Mans
Tel 02 43 87 78 37
Le Beaulieu is in a pre-Renaissance, oak-beamed building in the heart of old Le Mans. Chef Olivier Boussard prefers traditional cuisine: scallops roasted in the shell and fillet of Loué chicken with Vin Jaune (chicken cooked in a sherry-like wine with a creamy tarragon sauce). The wine list has many Loire wines and as the restaurant is popular with locals and visitors, you should reserve in high season.
Mon–Fri 12.15–1.30, 7.15–9; closed 1–10 Mar and Aug
L €50, D €100, Wine €19

○RASCASSE

6 rue Mission, 72000 Le Mans
Tel 02 43 84 45 91
Close to the famous Église de Sainte-Jeanne d'Arc, this is a sound choice for lunch, with a fireplace and art deco furniture which keep the dining room snug and warm. Traditional regional cooking includes *les diableries* (shredded meat and sausage) and succulent fresh fish. For dessert, try the *bugattises*, a chocolate-covered bonbon.
Tue, Wed, Fri, Sat noon–2, 7.30–9.30, Thu and Sun noon–2; closed 1–26 Aug
L €30, D €80, Wine €14

NOVOTEL LE MANS
Boulevard Robert Schuman, 72100
Le Mans
Tel 02 43 85 26 80
www.novotel.com
This Novotel has a modern
façade, although inside it is
more traditional, with stained-
glass windows. Rooms have
TV and minibar and there's
a restaurant (a meal costs
around €25 and children's
meals are €8), a small pool
and a quiet garden close to
the river. You are also free
to bring your dog as pets
are permitted.
€81–€91, excluding breakfast (€10)
94
Outdoor

NANTES
L'ATLANTIDE
Quai Ernest Renaud, 44100 Nantes
Tel 02 40 73 23 23
Both the setting and the
cuisine are contemporary
at this nautically themed
restaurant. It was designed
by Jean-Pierre Wilmotte
and has views of the Loire
and the city. Chef Jean-Yves
Gueho works in an open
kitchen, allowing you to enjoy
his cooking as performance.
Dishes might include Breton
turbot with Cantonese spices
or fillet of bass in *demi-deuil*
(encrusted with truffles).
For dessert try the bananas
braised in local beer. The
wine list is noted for its
Anjou and Muscadet and it's
a good idea to book as it's a
popular place.
Mon–Fri noon–2, 8–10, Sat 8–10;
closed 8–12 May, 7 Jul–26 Aug
L €50, D €120, Wine €16

LES CAPUCINES
1 bis rue Bastille, 44000 Nantes
Tel 02 40 20 41 58
An excellent-value bistro
which has a convivial
atmosphere and is good for
lunch or a quick dinner stop.
The carafe wines, especially
the whites, go well with the
seafood and fish dishes.
Tue–Fri 12.15–1.45, 7.15–8.45, Mon
12.15–1.45, Sat 7.15–8.45; closed 28
Jul–26 Aug, 22 Feb–3 Mar
L €21, D €56, Wine €9

DON GIOVANNI
20 rue Kervegan, 44000 Nantes
Tel 02 40 89 32 39
Locals love this unusual Italian
restaurant on a small street
lined with 17th-century
buildings. Its decoration is
entirely devoted to opera,
(which reflects the chef's
Italian heritage), with posters
and musical paraphernalia
evoking the great European
opera houses.
Daily 12.15–2, 7.15–8.45; sometimes
closes Sun, phone to check
L €25, D €40, Wine €13

GRAND HÔTEL MERCURE
4 rue Couëdic, 44000 Nantes
Tel 02 51 82 10 00
www.mercure.com
A 19th-century façade
contrasts with the modern,
film-themed public rooms.
Although part of a chain, the
hotel has some individual
charm thanks to the large
art deco spaces and grand
staircases. The rooms are a
good size and they all have
a TV and modem point. The
reasonably priced restaurant
serves mainly seafood
prepared in the local style.
€70–€350, excluding breakfast
(€12.50)
152

ST-SYLVAIN D'ANJOU
AUBERGE D'ÉVENTARD
Parc des Expositions, 49480 St-Sylvain
d'Anjou
Tel 02 41 43 74 25
In summer the terrace and
garden come into their own
at this classic countryside inn.
The menu concentrates on
traditional regional dishes and
changes daily depending on
what's available locally.
There's an unusually wide
range of prix-fixe menus, from
affordable to expensive and
the wine list is strong in
Vouvray and Saumur.
Tue–Fri noon–2, 8–9.15, Sat 8–9.15,
Sun noon–2
L €40, D €120, Wine €19

SAUMUR
AUBERGE ST-PIERRE
6 place St-Pierre, 49400 Saumur
Tel 02 41 51 26 25
This inn, in a 15th-century
monastery close to Saumur's
attractions, has three dining
rooms with oak-beamed
ceilings. The menu, which is

strongly influenced by the
region, is good value and the
welcoming service makes
this a pleasant lunch stop. The
wine list has a range of
inexpensive and refreshing
Loire choices.
Tue–Sat noon–2, 7–10; closed
12–26 Mar, 8–22 Oct and 24 Dec–3 Jan
L €25, D €45, Wine €13

LES DÉLICES DU CHÂTEAU
Cour du Château, 49400 Saumur
Tel 02 41 67 65 60
After touring the chateau,
enjoy an evening meal at the
delightful restaurant in the
courtyard. The traditional
menu has especially good
terrines, pâtés and fish dishes.
Mon, Wed–Sat 12.15–1.45,
7.15–8.45, Tue, Sun 12.15–1.45 Apr–end
Sep; Wed–Sat 12.15–1.45, 7.15–8.45,
Tue, Sun 12.15–1.45 rest of year; closed
15 Dec–10 Jan
L €40, D €80, Wine €15

Centre
AMBOISE
BONNE ÉTAPE
962 quai des Violettes, 37400 Amboise
Tel 02 47 57 08 09
This is a reasonably priced
choice for a pleasant lunch or
mid-route evening meal, with
the chateau and lovely river
views of the Île de Jean. The
fish dishes served with

regional sauces are particularly
good and the wine list has a
nice selection of whites.
Children are made to feel

EATING AND STAYING

welcome and their special menu costs €8.

🕐 Thu–Sat, Tue noon–1.45, 7.30–8.45, Wed, Sun noon–1.45; closed 2–6 Apr, 18 Dec–7 Jan, 4–13 Feb

🍴 L €20, D €50, Wine €12

CHOISEUL
36 quai Charles Guinot, 37400 Amboise
Tel 02 47 30 45 45
www.choiseul.com

This is a graceful 18th-century mansion with light and airy public rooms and good-sized, tastefully decorated guest rooms. Children under 12 stay for free and there are pretty

river walks, a swimming pool and tennis courts. The restaurant serves dishes such as pressed duck liver and fillet of roast perch with a sorrel cream sauce and there is a terrace where you can eat out in summer.

🕐 Closed mid-Dec to early Feb

🍴 €180–€267, excluding breakfast (€16–€25)

🛏 28 rooms, 5 suites

🏊 Outdoor

AZAY-LE-RIDEAU
LES GROTTES
23 rue Pineau, 37190 Azay-le-Rideau
Tel 02 47 45 21 04

The two dining rooms here are actually caves carved from

solid rock. They serve good regional cuisine such as smoked *anguille* (fresh water eel), sausage with scrambled

eggs and medallions of duck with sautéed apples. Loire Valley wines form the majority of the wine list.

🕐 Fri–Tue 12.15–1.45, 7.15–8.45, Thu 7.15–8.45 Jul, Aug; Fri–Tue 12.15–1.45, 7.15–8.45, rest of year; closed 2–31 Jan and 17–30 Nov

🍴 L €40, D €63, Wine €10

LA PETITE LOGE
15 route de Tours, 37190 Azay-le-Rideau
Tel 02 47 45 26 05 or 06 81 61 94 07

A small house on a side street, this makes for a good change of pace. The simple rooms each have a separate entrance and a kitchen—welcome facilities for anyone tired of conventional hotels. There is a tidy garden and a barbecue area you can use in summer.

🕐 Closed Dec–end Feb

🍴 €42

🛏 5

BLOIS
AU BOUCHON LYONNAIS
25 rue des Violettes, 41000 Blois
Tel 02 54 74 12 87

This good value restaurant is headed by chef Frédéric Savy and offers regional French dishes including delicious monkfish in pepper sauce and salmon in a paste of balsamic vinegar and roasted nuts. The dining rooms, with oak beams, are open and welcoming. Reserve ahead.

🕐 Tue–Sat noon–2, 7–10, Sun and Mon 7–10 Jul, Aug; Tue–Sat noon–2, 7–10 rest of year; closed 1–10 Sep, 21–29 Oct, 23 Dec–10 Jan

🍴 L €30, D €80, Wine €11

AU RENDEZ-VOUS DES PÊCHEURS
27 rue Foix, 41000 Blois
Tel 02 54 74 67 48

Well-known locally and regionally, this restaurant serves fish and seafood. House specials include crayfish flan with parsley, roast sea bass with a shallot tart in red wine sauce and lobster dishes. The wine list includes excellent, affordable vintages of Cheverny and Montlouis. The children's menu is €14. Reserve ahead.

🕐 Tue–Sat noon–1.30, 7.15–9.15, Mon 7.15–9.15; closed 28 Jul–18 Aug, 2–12 Jan

🍴 L €48, D €128, Wine €21

MERCURE CENTRE
28 quai St-Jean, 41000 Blois
Tel 02 54 56 66 66
www.mercure.com

The chateau and the old town of Blois are within walking distance of this pleasant hotel. It is furnished in a contemporary style and from the floor-to-ceiling windows you can see the Loire flowing swiftly by. The large, sound-proofed rooms all have TV and there is a heated indoor pool, Jacuzzi, exercise room and covered car parking. The restaurant serves local cuisine, such as cured ham and Loire wines.

🍴 €84–€111, excluding breakfast (€10.50)

🛏 84 rooms and 12 suites (48 non-smoking)

🏊 Indoor

BOURGES
ABBAYE ST-AMBROIX
60 avenue Jean Jaurès, 18000 Bourges
Tel 02 48 70 80 00

An airy, ornately decorated former chapel serving excellent food such as ragout of oysters and aromatic mackerel with lightly saffroned aubergine (eggplant). For dessert, try the soft chocolate wafers or ice cream made with almond milk. The sommelier can help you choose from the wine list, which is dominated by Reuilly and Menetou-Salon.

🕐 Daily noon–1.30, 7.30–9.30

🍴 L €85, D €126, Wine €21

BOURBONNOUX
44 rue Bourbonnoux, 18000 Bourges
Tel 02 48 24 14 76

This cheerful restaurant, with its old-fashioned look, is on a small street in the heart of town, making it a good lunch stop. The menu of traditional dishes was designed by chef Jean-Michel Huard, and you get excellent value for money. Lunch might be a cucumber mint gazpacho to start, followed by a fish dish with a glass of Loire white wine.

🕐 Sun–Thu 12.15–1.45, 7.15–8.45, Sat 7.15–8.45, Jul–end Oct; Mon–Thu 12.15–1.45, 7.15–8.45, Sat 7.15–8.45, Sun 12.15–1.45, rest of year; closed 15–22 Mar, 30 Aug–20 Sep and 17–27 Jan

🍴 L €22, D €40, Wine €10

⊙LE BOURBON

Boulevard République, 18000 Bourges
Tel 02 48 70 70 00
www.mercure.com

An 18th-century former abbey
in the middle of Bourges, offering well-lit, comfortable rooms,
all of which have satellite TV.
Some rooms have access for
people with disabilities. The
bar area is impressive and the
Abbaye St-Ambroix restaurant
is in what was once the chapel
(see page 373). Pets are
welcome and there is parking.
🕭 €78–€120, excluding breakfast
(€11)
🛏 59 (29 non-smoking)

BRACIEUX

⊙LE RELAIS BERNARD ROBIN

1 avenue de Chambord, 41250
Bracieux
Tel 02 54 46 41 22
www.theworldwidegourmet.com/relais/
france/centre/robin.htm

This tastefully decorated house
outside the village of Bracieux

offers impeccable service.
Chef Bernard Robin is known
internationally for his
traditional menu and people
flock here from far and wide,
so reserve a table in advance.
Try the crispy lobster with dried
tomatoes or the braised
pork. The wine list has an
extraordinary selection–the
Vouvray and Cheverny are
solid choices.
🕙 Tue–Sat noon–1.30, 7.15–9,
Sun noon–1.30, Dec–end Mar;
Thu–Mon noon–1.30, 7.15–9, rest of
year; closed 15 Dec–mid Jan
🍴 L €120, D €160, Wine €21

CHAMBORD

⊙HOTEL GRAND MICHEL

103 place St-Michel, 41250 Chambord
Tel 02 54 20 31 31

The restaurant is in what was
once the kennels for the
chateau's hounds. It serves a
straightforward menu of

regional dishes. Try the duck
breast in a green peppercorn
sauce or a local pâté. You can
see the chateau from the
dining room and the terrace—
on a moonlit night the view is
breathtaking. Book ahead for
Sundays and holidays.
🕙 Daily noon–2, 7–8.30 Apr to end
Nov; Thu–Tue noon–2, 7–8.30,
Dec–end Mar; closed 12 Nov–20 Dec
🍴 L €30, D €45, Wine €12

CHAUMONT-SUR-LOIRE

⊙LA CHANCELIÈRE

1 rue de Bellevue, 41150
Chaumont-sur-Loire
Tel 02 54 20 96 95

This is a good lunch stop after
a stroll by the river or a visit to
the chateau next door. The
service in the rustic dining
rooms is efficient and friendly
and children are welcome. The
fish dishes are excellent.
🕙 Fri–Tue noon–1.30, 7–8.30; closed
8 Nov–8 Dec, 10 Jan–6 Feb
🍴 L €30, D €60, Wine €15

CHENONCEAUX

⊙HOSTELLERIE LA RENAUDIÈRE

24 rue du Docteur Bretonneau, 37150
Chenonceaux
Tel 02 47 23 90 04

Here you'll find excellent and
affordable food in a simple
setting. The dining room,
veranda and terrace give pretty
views over a park of majestic
trees. The cuisine is regional
French, there are wines
from the Loire valley and a
children's menu for €8.
🕙 Sat, Sun noon–2, 7–9, Thu, Fri, Mon,
Tue 7–9; closed mid-Nov to mid-Dec
🍴 L €38, D €80, Wine €13

⊙HÔTEL DU BON-LABOUREUR ET DU CHÂTEAU

6 rue du Dr Bretonneau, 37150
Chenonceaux
Tel 02 47 23 90 02
www.amboise.com/laboureur

This inn has been welcoming
guests since 1786 and its age

is apparent in the thick-walled
construction. The small
rooms are housed in several
buildings on the manicured
grounds, and have satellite
TV, kitchenettes and a
hairdryer. Reserve early for
the oak-beamed restaurant
that is renowned for its
seafood and regional dishes
such as braised rabbit with
dried fruits. The wine list
is exceptional.
🕙 Closed 15 Nov–20 Dec and Jan
(dates vary)
🕭 €75–€130, excluding breakfast (€9)
🛏 22 rooms, 4 suites (all non-
smoking)
🏊 18 ☀ Outdoor

⊙LA ROSERAIE

7 rue du Docteur Bretonneau, 37150
Chenonceaux
Tel 02 47 23 90 09
www.roseraie.portland.co.uk

An ivy-covered, white stone
hotel and restaurant tucked
away on a small street in the
heart of the village and within
easy walking distance of the
chateau. La Roseraie has all
the strengths of a boutique
hotel: intimate size, pleasant
public spaces decorated
with tasteful antiques and
welcoming staff. The rooms
are small but have all you
need. In the restaurant, owners
Laurent and Sophie Fiorito
offer classic dishes including
magret de canard (breast of
fattened duck) with pears
and cherries, delicious fish
and braised rump steak with
wine-marinated pears. Eat in
the dining room with its large
fireplace or on the terrace
with a view of the green
park behind the hotel. There
is car parking.
🕙 Hotel: closed 21 Nov–end Feb
Restaurant: Wed–Mon 12.15–1.45,
7.15–9, Tue 7.15–9; closed Mon in Mar
🛏 17 (€56–€90, excluding
breakfast €9)
☀ Outdoor

CHEVERNY

⑪ROUSSELIÈRE
41700 Cheverny
Tel 02 54 79 23 02
This old farm has a terrace and a dining room overlooking an 18-hole golf course, once the Chateau de Cherverny's hunting grounds. It's popular for its simple, traditional meals.

Ⓒ Daily 12.15–1.45, 7.15–8.45, Jun to mid-Sep; 12.15–1.45, rest of year; closed 23 Dec–5 Jan
Ⓦ L €20, D €30, Wine €9

CHINON

◯HÔTEL LE CHINON
Digue St-Jacques, 37500 Chinon
Tel 02 47 98 46 46
This clean, modern hotel may not be the most attractive, but the rooms are comfortable. The hotel has a pool, an exercise room and a tennis court. The restaurant serves regional dishes. In summer there's a barbecue buffet on the terrace.
Ⓒ Closed 20 Dec–7 Jan
Ⓦ €74, excluding breakfast (€8)
① 52
▣ Outdoor ▣

COUR-CHEVERNY

◯ST-HUBERT
122 rue Nationale, 41700
Cour-Cheverny
Tel 02 54 79 96 60
Near the middle of town, this pleasant hotel has clean, bright rooms with TV. The restaurant is known for its local wine and food; the prix-fixe menu is €36.
Ⓒ Closed 6–27 Feb
Ⓦ €52, excluding breakfast (€6)
① 20
Ⓢ

ONZAIN

⑪DOMAINE DES HAUTS LOIRE
Route de Herbault, 41150 Onzain
Tel 02 54 20 72 57
www.theworldwidegourmet.com/relais/
france/centre/hauts-loire.htm
Stroll in the gounds of this former hunting lodge after your meal. Chef Rémy Giraud, creates dishes such as scallop viennoise with pears and creamy coconut rice and rabbit with duck foie gras, fondue of red chard and wasabi cream. The wine cellar has superb local wines.
Ⓒ Daily 12.15–1.45, 7.15–9.15, Apr–end Oct; Wed–Sun 12.15–1.45, 7.15–9.15, rest of year; closed Dec–20 Feb
Ⓦ L €160, D €250, Wine €20

ORLÉANS

⑪LES ANTIQUAIRES
2 rue au Lin, 45000 Orléans
Tel 02 38 53 52 35
www.restaurantlesantiquaires.com
The well-known restaurant of chef Philippe Bardau, who prepares contemporary, Mediterranean cuisine. In the warm-toned dining rooms, he serves dishes such as pan-fried asparagus with a creamy morel sauce and sea bass with artichokes and fennel.
Ⓒ Tue–Sat 12.15–1.45, 7.15–8.45, Sun 12.15–1.45 Sep–end Jun; Tue–Sat 12.15–1.45, 7.15–8.45, rest of year
Ⓦ L €60, D €100, Wine €17

⑪EUGÈNE
24 rue Sainte-Anne, 45000, Orléans
Tel 02 38 53 82 64
A popular bistro, near place du Martroi, with a taste of the south of France in its decoration and menu. The convivial atmosphere complements thedaily changing menu.
Ⓒ Tue–Fri noon–2, 7.30–9.30, Mon, Sat 7.30–9.30; closed 5–13 May, 2–19 Aug, 26 Dec–6 Jan
Ⓦ L €50, D €75, Wine €20

⑪JARDIN DE NEPTUNE
6 rue Jean Hupeau, 45000, Orléans
Tel 02 38 62 45 64
Seafood is the highlight at this nautically themed restaurant. The service is friendly and efficient, the atmosphere is bustling and the oysters and mussels are very good.
Ⓒ Tue–Sat 12.15–1.45, 7–8.45; closed 1–18 Aug
Ⓦ L €18, D €35, Wine €10

◯TERMINUS
40 rue République, 45000
Orléans
Tel 02 38 53 24 64
www.terminus-orleans.com
This is a classic small city hotel, with a breakfast salon. The rooms are small but up to date.
Ⓒ Closed 24 Dec–1 Jan
Ⓦ €61–€74, excluding breakfast (€7)
① 47

ROCHECORBON

⑪LES HAUTES ROCHES
86 quai Loire, 37210 Rochecorbon
Tel 02 47 52 88 88
www.leshautesroches.com
Dine in a long, bright room with pale yellow and coral tones in this chateau. The modern cuisine has its roots in Brittany. Dishes include duck foie gras in a Vouvray terrine, a menu of lobster dishes, and stuffed tomato with crumbled crab, lemon liqueur and thyme cream. It's also a hotel, whose troglodyte rooms are built into a bank of the Loire.
Ⓒ Mon–Wed and Sat 7–9, Thu–Fri and Sun noon–2, 7–9, Apr–Oct; Tue–Wed and Sat 7–9, Thu–Fri and Sun noon–2, 7–9, rest of year; closed 20 Jan–21 Mar
Ⓦ L €45, D €110, Wine €21

ROMORANTIN-LANTHENAY

◯HÔTEL LION D'OR
69 rue Clemenceau, 41200
Romorantin-Lanthenay
Tel 02 54 94 15 15
www.hotel-liondor.fr
The Barrat-Clément family runs this Renaissance mansion, built by a friend of François I. The immaculate gardens and sun-washed terraces are marvellous in summer. The rooms are decorated in period style and the restaurant, run by chef Didier Clément, is known for its innovative cuisine. Among the most famous dishes is *langoustines à la graine de paradis* (Breton prawns roasted with paradise seed, a medieval spice reintroduced by the chef).
Ⓒ Closed 15 Feb–end Mar and 25 Nov–5 Dec
Ⓦ €125–€330
① 13
Ⓢ

SACHÉ

⑪ AUBERGE DE XIIEME CENTURY

1 rue du Château, 37190 Saché
Tel 02 47 26 88 77
Novelist Honoré de Balzac liked this half-timbered inn just outside Azay-le-Rideau. Today it is one of the best mid-range restaurants in the Loire Valley. You can eat in the bright and cheery dining room or the flower-bedecked garden. Dishes include salad of pan-fried squab (young pigeon) and foie gras and pan-fried perch with rhubarb. Reservations are recommended on Sundays.
🕐 Wed–Sat 12.15–1.30, 7.30–9.15, Sun 12.15–1.30, Tue 7.30–9.15; closed 3–11 Jun, 2–10 Sep and 8–30 Jan
🍴 L €54, D €90, Wine €11

ST-BENOÎT-SUR-LOIRE

⑪ GRAND ST-BENOÎT

7 place St-André, 45730
St-Benoît-sur-Loire
Tel 02 38 35 11 92
www.hoteldulabrador.fr
This restaurant, in the Hôtel du Labrador, faces a 12th-century Romanesque church. The oak-beamed ceilings contrast with the contemporary furniture in the dining room and in summer, you can sit on the terrace. Seasonal and regional dishes are painstakingly prepared.
🕐 Tue–Fri 12.15–1.45, 7.15–8.45, Sat 7.15–8.45, Sun 12.15–1.45; closed 25 Aug–3 Sep, 22 Dec–21 Jan
🍴 L €40, D €86, Wine €17

ST-OUEN-LES-VIGNES

⑪ L'AUBINIÈRE

29 rue Jules Gautier,
37530 St-Ouen-les-Vignes
Tel 02 47 30 15 29
www.touraine-gourmande.com/english/aubin/fiche.html
North of Amboise and the Loire, this small, rustically decorated dining room is a great place to enjoy the creations of chef Jacques Arrayet. He serves outstanding ravioli of prawns with baby vegetables, and the terrines and beef entrecôte are delicious.
🕐 Mon, Thu–Sat noon–2, 7–9, Tue, Sun noon–2; closed 21–31 Oct, Feb
🍴 L €40, D €100, Wine €17

TOURS

⑪ CHARLES BARRIER

101 avenue Tranchée, 37100, Tours
Tel 02 47 54 20 39
A quick walk across Pont Wilson brings you to one of Tours's famous restaurants. The dining room is an open space, with lots of flowers and subtle lighting. Expect smoked salmon, *boeuf bourguignon* (beef casserole) and *blanquette de veau* (veal in cream sauce).
🕐 Mon–Fri noon–2.30, 7–8, Sat 7–8
🍴 L €45, D €125, Wine €16

⑪ JEAN BARDET'S CHÂTEAU BELMONT

57 rue Groison, 37000, Tours
Tel 02 47 41 41 11
www.jeanbardet.com
International visitors seek out Sophie and Jean Bardet's stately mansion, in flower-filled grounds, for the cuisine served here. Chef Jean Bardet uses produce from his garden in his cooking: tomato tartare with coriander (cilantro) and tomato jam, frog's legs, sautéed lamb's feet and chanterelles and pigeon in a fruit sauce. Reserve ahead. For the hotel, see Special, above right.
🕐 Mon, Tue, Sat 7.30–9.30, Wed–Fri and Sun 12.30–1.15, 7.30–9.30, Apr–end Nov; Wed–Fri 12.30–1.15, 7.30–9.30, Tue and Sat 7.30–9.30, Sun 12.30–1.15, rest of year
🍴 L €100, D €200, Wine €30

VALLIÈRES

⑪ AUBERGE DE PORC VALLIÈRES

On N152, 37230, Vallières
Tel 02 47 42 24 04
www.touraine-gourmande.com/vallier/present.html
On the banks of the Loire, in a former pub for local fishermen, chef Jean-Jacques Thomas cooks hearty regional cuisine such as herb-stuffed cabbage, which is served as an accompaniment to the meat dishes. There are well-priced Loire Valley wines and a special €9 menu for children.
🕐 Sun–Tue noon–2, Thu–Sat noon–2, 7–9; closed Aug 15–Sep 7 and Jan 2–10
🍴 L €18, D €30, Wine €8

⊖ JEAN BARDET'S CHÂTEAU BELMONT

Rue Groison, 37000 Tours
Tel 02 47 41 41 11
www.jeanbardet.com
The 17th-century Touraine mansion, Château Belmont, sits on a hill that was once a vineyard, but is now used as chef Jean Bardet's flower and vegetable garden (see restaurant on this page). The hotel, which has simple and elegant rooms, overlooks the outdoor heated pool and gardens that are perfect for a quiet stroll.
🛏 €115–€229
🛏 16 rooms, 5 suites
🏊 ⊠ Outdoor

VILLANDRY

⑪ L'ORANGERIE

11 route Principale, 37510, Villandry
Tel 02 47 43 56 26
www.traiteur-touraine.com
This pizzeria, next to the chateau known for its fabulous gardens, is excellent value for money. The pizzas from the wood-fired oven are outstanding and the French cuisine is also good. It gets busy in summer with chateau visitors, especially at lunch. There's a children's menu available.
🕐 Daily 12.15–1.15, 7–8.15
🍴 L €22, D €45, Wine €12

⊖ CHEVAL ROUGE

9 rue de la Mairie, 37510, Villandry
Tel 02 47 50 02 07
This century-old property, beside the expansive gardens of Villandry, has small, neat rooms. The restaurant is popular for its regional cuisine, notably the terrine of foie gras or anything from the wood-fired grill. There is parking in front of the hotel.
🛏 €62, excluding breakfast (€7)
🛏 35 (2 non-smoking)

CENTRAL FRANCE AND THE ALPS

EATING

In this part of France they say a meal without wine is like a day without sunshine: The yellow wines of Franche Comté, fruity Beaujolais and those splendid classics from Burgundy might make you agree. To find the best wines, drive along the Côtes de Nuits, where roadmaps read like wine lists. If you visit in autumn, find a wine festival to truly appreciate what wine means to the locals. The world's best known aperitif, Kir, was invented here, blending white wine with the blackcurrant crème de cassis from Dijon. Fields are dotted with lean creamy-white Charolais cows, the inspiration for many Burgundian chefs, who have made *boeuf bourguignon* an internationally recognised dish. The biggest names in gastronomy hold court around Lyon, but budget-conscious diners, hungry for truly local food, should spend the evening in a bistro or *bouchon*. Meats and sauces reign here, but don't forget the cheese course as Auvergne is home to St-Nectaire and the queen of blue cheeses, Roquefort. For a delicious hard cheese, try a well-matured Comté from Franche Comté.

STAYING

If you can, stay in a country inn (Hollywood star Leslie Caron runs La Lucarne aux Chouettes, by the bridge at Villeneuve-sur-Yonne). In the mountains, choose between traditional chalets in smaller villages and large resort hotels with gyms and swimming pools.

Auvergne

LE PUY EN VELAY

🍴BRASSERIE LE MAJESTIC
8 boulevard Maréchal Fayolle, 43000
Le Puy en Velay
Tel 04 71 09 06 30
There's a young, trendy and friendly atmosphere here. It's a perfect place to sit back and relax with a drink and a bite to eat while you admire the paintings and sculptures exhibited by local artists. On the menu there's a big choice of salads, omelettes, meat dishes and pasta as well as desserts, and there are regular music and theme nights.
🕐 Café: Mon–Sat 7am–1am, Sun 10am–1am. Brasserie: Daily noon–2.30, 7.30–10.30
🍽 L €16, D €30, Wine €13

🍴À L'ÉCU D'OR
59 and 61 rue Pannessac, 43000
Le Puy en Velay
Tel 04 71 02 19 36
www.zoom43.fr/alecudor
This restaurant, with vaulted ceilings and murals, is in rooms dating from the 11th to the 15th centuries. There are four prix-fixe menus and an à la carte, with regional dishes including Auvergne salad, guineafowl fricassée with mushrooms and pan-fried trout with garlic.
🕐 Mon–Sat noon–2, 7.30–10, Sun noon–2; closed Wed Oct–end May
🍽 L €26, D €90, Wine €20

🍴L'OLYMPE
8 rue du Collège, 43000
Le Puy en Velay
Tel 04 71 05 90 59
L'Olympe is a small restaurant in the old city. It has a vaulted ceiling and interior decoration typical of the area, with Aubusson-style rugs and paintings. Expect Auvergne dishes such as trout with

verbena, the area's green lentils and *tripoux* (sheep's feet).
🕐 Tue–Fri noon–1.30, 7.30–9.30, Sat 7.30–9.30, Sun noon–1.30
🍽 L €34, D €40, Wine €15

🛏HÔTEL BRISTOL
7 avenue Maréchal Foch, 43000
Le Puy en Velay
Tel 04 71 09 13 38
The Bristol is in a tall, old Auvergne-style building that has been modernized with an annexe next to the garden. The rooms have TV and telephone and there's private parking, a garden and a restaurant.

🕐 Closed 22 Feb–17 Mar
🍽 €41–€71
🛏 24 rooms and 3 apartments
🚭

VICHY

🍴CALIFORNIA
27 rue Jean-Jaurès, 03200 Vichy
Tel 04 70 97 85 05
Hôtel California has a small dining room, with painted wood and a parquet floor, where non-residents are welcome. On the menu are Auvergne dishes including chicken in a *bleu d'Auvergne* (strong local cheese) sauce. In good weather you can eat out in the small terrace garden.
🕐 Daily 12.30–2, 7.30–9; closed 31 Dec–21 Jan
🍽 L €22, D €40, Wine €10

🍴LES JARDINS DE L'EMPEREUR
111 boulevard de L'États-Unis, 03200 Vichy
Tel 04 70 30 82 00
This chic restaurant is in the luxurious Sofitel Les Célestins hotel and thermal spa facility. The haute cuisine chef prepares rich, high-quality dishes, and healthier options.
🕐 Mon–Sat 12.30–7.30; closed 1–26 Dec
🍽 L €72, D €180, Wine €26

🍴LES PLANCHES DE LA ROTONDE
Boulevard de Lattre de Tassigny, 03200 Vichy
Tel 04 70 96 36 97
A Spanish restaurant in the rotunda on the water's edge, with a panoramic view of Lake Allier and the park. Specials include paella and fondue with Bodega sauce. There's music nightly and, usually on Thursday evenings, there's dancing with an orchestra, and a tea dance on Sunday afternoons.
🕐 Wed–Sun 8pm–1am; closed Jan 15–end Feb
🍽 D €40, Wine €15

HÔTEL DE GRIGNAN

7 place Sevigné, 03201 Vichy
Tel 04 70 32 08 11
www.hoteldegrignan.fr
The hotel is in a quiet area of town, close to Parc Napoléon III, the lake and the casino. If you fancy some spa treatments, the hotel runs special deals that combine six days of full board (with all meals) plus six days of treatments at one of the spas. The bedrooms all have bathroom, hairdryer, TV and radio. L'Abecedaire restaurant has a good prix-fixe menu.

🕐 Closed 23 Dec–26 Jan
🛏 €48–€70, excluding breakfast (€6.90)
🛈 115
♿ Restaurant and communal areas

HÔTEL ROYAL

12 rue Président Wilson, 03200 Vichy
Tel 04 70 98 62 14
www.hotel-royal.fr
Two-star hotel overlooking the Parc des Sources and a short walk from the thermal spas. Rooms are simply furnished and have satellite TV and there is parking, although there is no bar or restaurant.

🛏 €32–€64, excluding breakfast
🛈 51 (20 non-smoking)

Bourgogne

BEAUNE

LE CLOS DU CEDRE

10 boulevard Maréchal Foch, 21200 Beaune
Tel 03 80 24 01 01
www.bleumarine-beaune.com
Formerly known as the Bleu Marine, the restaurant is in a 19th-century winegrower's house on the edge of the city heart. Enjoy chef François Dervault's fine Burgundian cuisine on the fire in winter and on the terrace in summer.

🕐 Mon–Sat noon–2, 7.30–9.30
🛏 L €32, D €100, Wine €26

LA GRILLADINE

17 rue Maufoux, 21200 Beaune
Tel 03 80 22 22 36
This restaurant is between boulevard Bretonnière and rue Gardin. Exposed stone, old beams and richly decorated walls give its three dining rooms a warm and cheerful atmosphere. The menu is typical of Burgundy, with dishes as *boeuf bourguignon*,

oeufs en meurette (poached eggs in red wine sauce), snails, and ham with parsley.

🕐 Tue–Sun noon–3, 7–10
🛏 L €23, D €45, Wine €17

HÔTEL GRILLON

21 route de Seurre, 21200 Beaune
Tel 03 80 22 44 25
www.hotel-grillon.fr
This 19th-century house is in a beautiful setting on the outskirts of Beaune. It is fronted by large gates and is hidden from view by leafy chestnut trees. The bedrooms look out onto flowers and greenery and there are plenty of places to relax, including the heated outdoor swimming pool, terrace, lounge and bar decorated in the style of a Burgundy wine cellar. You can have breakfast in the sunny breakfast room and dinner in the Verger restaurant in the grounds.

🕐 Closed Jan–end Mar
🛏 €50–€65, excluding breakfast (€7)
🛈 18 (7 non-smoking)
♿ 🏊 Outdoor

VILLA FLEURIE

19 place Colbert, 21200 Beaune
Tel 03 80 22 66 00
www.lavillafleurie.fr
The hotel, in a house dating from around 1900, was completely renovated when the current owner bought it in the mid-1990s and the interior design and furnishings match

the original style of the house. The bedrooms are beautifully decorated and have period features, a fireplace and TV. Continental breakfast is served in a breakfast room decorated with fruit and flowers and there is a flower-filled terrace, a garden and parking.

🛏 €70–€75, excluding breakfast (€8)
🛈 10

DIJON

MAISON MILLIÈRE

10 rue de la Chouette, 21000 Dijon
Tel 03 80 30 99 99
The façade of this 15th-century building was altered in 1926, and the roof is now adorned with figures of animals (look for the cat on top of one window). Inside you'll find a boutique selling regional produce and gifts, a tea room and a restaurant with a garden. The restaurant has frequently changing menus and the tea room has a choice of 20 different teas to go with its pastries and tarts.

🕐 Tea room: Tue–Sun 10–7
Restaurant: Tue–Thu 12–2, Fri–Sat 12–2, 7.30–10
🛏 L €29, D €46, Wine €13.50

RESTAURANT DE LA PORTE GUILLAUME

Place Darcy, 21000 Dijon
Tel 03 80 50 80 50
www.bourgogne.net/hotelnord
This restaurant, with exposed beams and wooden columns, has Burgundy wines and dishes such as foie gras, oysters and smoked salmon with mustard and honey vinaigrette, roasted salmon with cream and rabbit and guinea fowl with truffles and tagliatelle.

🕐 Daily noon–2, 7–10.45
🛏 L €32, D €64, Wine €18

RESTAURANT STÉPHANE DERBORD

10 place Wilson, 21000 Dijon
Tel 03 80 67 74 64
www.restaurantstephanederbord.fr
An elegant restaurant with pale walls and modern upholstered furniture. The menu concentrates on dishes from the Burgundy region, such as black pudding coated in spiced breadcrumbs with Jura wine caramel, crayfish roasted with ginger, pineapple and red pepper compote

EATING AND STAYING

topped with saffron sauce, and delicious desserts such as pear caramelized in honey with nut and raisin ice cream. The prix-fixe menu costs €23.

ⓒ Wed–Sat noon–1.15, 7.30–9.15, Mon–Tue 7.30–9.15; closed 1 week in Jan, 1 week in Mar and 3 weeks in Aug
🖐 L €46, D €140, Wine €22

⊖HÔTEL DES JARDINS DU GRAND KAF'
5 rue du Château, 21000 Dijon
Tel 03 80 30 51 64
www.grand-cafe-hotel-poste.fr
This modest hotel is in the middle of town and its bedrooms, decorated with a floral theme, look onto a pedestrianized street. Facilities include satellite TV, bar and a 1930s-style brasserie.
🖐 €47–€80, excluding breakfast (€6)
ⓘ 30

⊖HOSTELLERIE DE LA CHAPEAU ROUGE
5 rue Michelet, 21000 Dijon
Tel 03 80 50 88 88
Each of the rooms in this 16th-century building is decorated and furnished in a different style, although they all have satellite TV with some foreign channels, air conditioning, safe

and telephone. Hotel facilities include a bar and a restaurant which serves contemporary cuisine. Buffet breakfast is included in the room price. The hotel is part of the Best Western group.
🖐 €126–€197, excluding breakfast (€13)
ⓘ 26 rooms, 4 suites
Ⓢ

NUITS-ST-GEORGES
⑪LE ST-GEORGES
Carrefour de l'Europe, 21700 Nuits-St-Georges
Tel 03 80 62 00 62
www.le-saint-georges.fr
This hotel and restaurant, in a village famed for its wine, has

rich plum walls, cool white table linen and a terrace. The wines are selected from more than 100 local producers and go well with local dishes such as three-fish terrine with cray-fish and fresh tomato coulis, cream of cauliflower soup with

bacon, black pudding salad and white chocolate mousse with fresh figs.
ⓒ Daily noon–2, 7–9.30
🖐 L €30, D €74, Wine €20

PULIGNY-MONTRACHET
⑪LA TABLE D'OLIVIER LEFLAIVE
Place du Monument, 21190 Puligny-Montrachet
Tel 03 80 21 37 65
www.olivier-leflaive.com
Named after its founder, this restaurant specializes in wine-tasting lunches. In the rustic dining room with exposed beams you have a light lunch and try labels such as Bourgogne Blanc les Setilles, St-Aubin, Puligny-Montrachet and Pommard. There's a €10 supplement for tasting premier cru wines and you must reserve.
ⓒ Mon–Sat 12.30–2, Mar–end Nov
🖐 Lunch including wine €35/€45 per person

Franche-Comté

FRAHIER
⊖LES GROS CHÊNES
70400, Frahier
Tel 03 84 27 31 41
www.amiesenfranchecomte.com
This bed-and-breakfast is in the countryside at the foot of the Ballon d'Alsace. Each of the four rooms has a shower room. Children under 5 go free and there's a discount if you stay for more than four days. You can sit out on the veranda or the furnished terrace and there's a children's play area on site. Within 5km (3miles)

there is hiking, fishing, canoeing and horse-riding.
🖐 €40
ⓘ 4
Ⓢ

VILLERS-ROBERT
⊖LE MOULIN
39120 Villers-Robert
Tel 03 84 71 52 39
A restored mill in a wooded garden offering bed-and-breakfast. The area is ideal for walking and fishing with ponds, forests and a river nearby. The mill itself has three bedrooms and two family rooms all with TV and bathroom, and a separate large bedroom which has a fireplace and its own entrance. There's a communal lounge and dining room that everyone can use and you can have dinner here for about €20.
🖐 €49
ⓘ 6

Rhône-Alpes

ANNECY
⑪BATEAU-MS-LIBELLULE
2 place aux Bois, 74000 Annecy
Tel 04 50 51 08 40
www.annecy-croisieres.com
Why not combine dinner with a boat trip on beautiful Lac d'Annecy? The mini-cruise offers lunch and dinner dances with fantastic views of the lake and mountains, and a commentary in French and English.
ⓒ Mon–Sat noon–2, 8.30pm–12.30am, Mar–end Oct
🖐 L €42, D €68, Wine €20, plus cruise €13.30

⑪BRASSERIE ST-MAURICE
7 and 9 rue de Collège, 74000 Annecy
Tel 04 50 51 24 49
www.stmau.com
Owners Muriel and Stéphane Bouchet offer a warm welcome in this 17th-century building on the edge of pretty Lac d'Annecy. Inside, the lower floor has an antique bar while upstairs is more modern. Fish dishes are popular here, but there are plenty of meat dishes and a special children's menu (€12) too. Outside meal times, it's a great place for a drink or a coffee.
ⓒ Tue–Sat 8am–midnight; lunch noon–2, dinner 7–11
🖐 L €48, D €84, Wine €19

LA MONTAGNETTE
22 Faubourg Sainte-Claire, 74000
Annecy
Tel 04 50 45 88 78
Resembling a mountain chalet,
this small restaurant in the
traffic-free part of town is
decorated entirely with wood.
There are typical mountain
dishes such as fondue,
tartiflette (potato gratin) and
raclette (a melted cheese dish)
as well as meat and fish
dishes. Don't miss the
delicious regional cheeses.
🕐 Daily 12–2, 7.15–11, Jul, Aug;
Mon–Tue and Thu–Fri 12–2, 7.15–11
rest of year
🍽 L €36, D €90, Wine €20

SHIVA
18 avenue de la Mandallaz, 74000
Annecy
Tel 04 50 51 76 25
In a quiet area near the station,
Shiva specializes in curries and
tandoori dishes. Children and
vegetarians are well catered
for and there is an extensive
wine list. Reservations are
advisable, especially for
Saturday evenings.

🕐 Tue–Sat 7–11, Sun noon–2, 7–11
🍽 L €40, D €50, Wine €15

VIEUX NECY
3 rue Filaterie, 74000 Annecy
Tel 04 50 45 01 57
If you like cheese then this
rustic restaurant, with an
interior of exposed wood and
stone, is for you. It specializes
in Savoyard cheese and other
traditional melted cheese
dishes like *raclette* (served
melted), *tartiflette* (potato
gratin) and fondue. Non-
cheese options include grilled
meat and salad.
🕐 Mon–Fri noon–2, 7–10.30, Sat 7–11,
Sun 7–10
🍽 L €25, D €42, Wine €14

HÔTEL DU CHÂTEAU
16 Rampe du Château, 74000 Annecy
Tel 04 50 45 27 66
www.annecy-hotel.com
At the foot of Annecy's hilltop
chateau, this stone-built hotel
has been run by the same
family since it was established
in 1959. It's a short walk from
the lake and has comfortable

rooms which have a bathroom,
and satellite TV. You can have
breakfast in your room, in the
lounge or on the flower-filled
terrace with its panoramic view
over Annecy. There is parking
and free Internet access.
🕐 Closed 15 Nov–15 Dec
🛏 €48–€53, excluding breakfast (€6)
🚪 16

HÔTEL TRÉSOMS
3 boulevard de la Corniche, 74000
Annecy
Tel 04 50 51 43 84
www.lestresoms.com
Built in 1930 in Swiss-chalet
style, this three-star hotel is
between Lac d'Annecy and the
mountains of Semnoz and has
a superb view of the lake. The
comfortable, well-furnished
bedrooms overlook the hotel
garden or the lake and have a
bathroom and satellite TV. The
hotel has plenty of facilities,
including a terrace, disabled
access, private parking, an
outdoor swimming pool,
sauna and beauty room. The
elegant hotel restaurant, La
Rotonde, has prix-fixe menus.
🛏 €95–€209, excluding breakfast
(€14 adults, €6 children)
🚪 49
🏊 Outdoor

ARGENTIÈRE
LA CRÉMERIE DU GLACIER
Chemin de la Glacière, 74400
Argentière
Tel 04 50 54 07 52
www.lacremerie.com
Georges Ravanel built this
small wooden cabin in 1926

and it became a welcome
stop for thirsty walkers. It is
in the forest between ski
runs and is still owned by the
same family, although it has
been completely renovated.
Now the family serves delicious, filling dishes such as
morel mushrooms en croute,
and fondue.
🕐 Thu–Sun 10am–midnight,
Mon–Wed 10–6
🍽 L €32, D €42, Wine €11

CHAMBÉRY
L'ESSENTIEL
183 place de la Gare, 73000 Chambéry
Tel 04 79 96 97 27
www.l-essentiel.com
Wood, rich tones and large
expanses of glass, plus a
terrace for fine evenings,
provide a contemporary rustic
atmosphere. Dishes include
grilled foie gras with cider
caramel and blood orange
sorbet. The prix-fixe menus
(from €35) tend to be better
value than the à la carte menu.
🕐 Tue–Fri noon–2, 7.30–10, Mon,
Sat 7.30–10
🍽 L €114, D €138, Wine €21

LA TABLE DE MARIE
193 rue Croix d'Or, 73000 Chambéry
Tel 04 79 85 99 76
This bistro-style restaurant
has a pleasant atmosphere
and serves traditional
Savoyard specials.
🕐 Thu–Mon noon–2, 7–10, Tue
noon–2
🍽 L €20, D €60, Wine €13

TAVERNE MAÎTRE KANTER
1 rue Sommeiller, 73000 Chambéry
Tel 04 79 62 22 10
www.tavernes-maitre-kanter.com
With its bright red exterior,
this brasserie near the railway
station is hard to miss. There's
plenty of room and service is
uninterrupted from noon until
midnight. Dishes include
sauerkraut, seafood and
Savoyard cuisine and you can
eat in or take out.
🕐 Daily 7.30am–midnight
🍽 L €21, D €45, Wine €12

HÔTEL ART
154 rue Sommeiller, 73000 Chambéry
Tel 04 79 62 37 26
www.arthotel-chambery.com
Hôtel Art is in the middle of
town, close to the railway
station, and has soundproofed
bedrooms with satellite TV,

telephone and bathroom. There is no restaurant, but a cold buffet breakfast is served in the breakfast room. There is also a private garage.

🛏 €43–€50, excluding breakfast (€6)
🔢 36

CHAMONIX

🍽 L'ATMOSPHÈRE

123 place Balmat, 74400 Chamonix
Tel 04 50 55 97 97
www.restaurant-atmosphere.com
Sit on the terrace in the middle of Chamonix and enjoy the majestic view of Mont Blanc. The menu has local dishes including fondue and if you are here in autumn, try something from the game menu.

🕐 Daily noon–2, 7–11
🍴 L €42, D €56, Wine €12

🍽 LA BERGERIE

232 avenue Michel-Croz-Gare SNCF, 74000 Chamonix
Tel 04 50 53 45 04
perso.wanadoo.fr/labergeriechamonix
Once a farm, this restaurant is known for its warm welcome and quality regional cuisine. It is decorated in the local style, with lots of wood panels and an open fire. The long and varied menu includes grilled meats, tomato and mozzarella salad and a red fruit dessert.

🕐 Daily noon–2, 7–10
🍴 L €24, D €48, Wine €15

🍽 LA CALÈCHE

18 rue Paccard, 74000 Chamonix
Tel 04 50 55 94 68
www.restaurant-caleche.com
This old, three-floor wooden house furnished with antiques, serves dozens of Savoyard dishes. Try beef braised in Savoy wine and for fans of cheese, there's *raclette* (melted cheese dish), fondue and *tartiflette* (a baked potato and cheese dish). Naturally, there are plenty of Savoy wines on the wine list. You can get a full evening's entertainment here as there's live folk music and dancing on Thursday evenings and skiing and mountaineering films shown on a big screen.

🕐 Daily noon–2, 7–11
🍴 L €38, D €56, Wine €15

🏨 LE MANOIR

8 route de Bouchet, 74400 Chamonix
Tel 04 50 53 10 77
www.auberge-du-manoir.com
In a pretty Savoyard wooden chalet, this two-star hotel has a white façade and flower-filled balconies. Although you are close to the middle of town, there are mountain and woodland walks less than five minutes' away. There is also a swimming pool and skiing close by. Rooms have great views, a bathroom, satellite TV and a telephone, and many have a balcony. The restaurant, which has a terrace, serves Provençal-style dishes.

🕐 Closed Nov and a period in Jun
🛏 €52–€65, excluding breakfast (€6)
🔢 24
💲

🏕 LES ROSIÈRES

121 clos des Rosières, 74400 Chamonix
Tel 04 50 53 10 42
www.campinglesrosieres.com
This campsite is in a quiet location, 15 minutes' walk from the middle of Chamonix,

with wonderful views of Mont Blanc. Some pitches are in the shade and there are also mobile homes and apartments to rent. The complex is within walking distance of a swimming pool, an ice rink and tennis courts. The campsite's facilities include a laundry room, showers with hot water, bar, restaurant and bicycle rental. There's a grocery store and a bakery within walking distance and a free bus service to the village, as well as ski lifts 50m (55 yards) from the site. Credit cards are not accepted.

🕐 Closed 16 Oct–6 Feb
🛏 €4.70–€5.50 per adult per night, €4 per child, pitch €2.20–€5.50 per night; electricity hook-up €3 per night
🔢 147 pitches

GRENOBLE

🍽 LES ARCHERS

2 rue Docteur Bailly, 38000 Grenoble
Tel 04 76 46 27 76
perso.wanadoo.fr/les.archers
This brasserie reputedly dates from the reign of King Henri IV (1589–1610), when the king's archers trained nearby. It has a gallery with tables overlooking a large downstairs room dominated by a huge painting of bowmen. There are also seats outside with shade provided by trees and a canopy. You will be spoiled for choice by the extensive menu. If you want a late meal, this is the place to come.

🕐 Sun–Mon 11am–1am, Tue–Sat 11am–2am
🍴 L €22, D €30, Wine €10

🍽 LE CAFÉ DES ARTS

36 rue St-Laurent, 38000 Grenoble
Tel 04 76 54 65 31
On the north side of the river, between place de la Cimaise and rue Chevalier, the Café des Arts stages shows with music from Africa to the Andes. The venue has particularly good acoustics thanks to the ceiling's guitar-shaped resonance chamber. Typical dishes include Caesar salad, guinea-fowl in port wine and a chocolate and banana tart. Show times vary–get them at the tourist information office.

🕐 Tue–Sat 8pm–1am; closed mid-Jul to mid-Aug
🍴 D €36, Wine €15

🍽 LES COURS DES MIRACLES

7 bis place Paul Vallier, 38000 Grenoble
Tel 04 38 37 00 10
Les Cours des Miracles, opposite Parc Paul Mistral, is the creation of Thierry Chiaberto and Jean Jerome Bouron. Here, Chiaberto expanded his circus school and Bouron opened a restaurant. The dining room has an international menu. There's circus-themed entertainment every Wednesday night and a magic show on Tuesday evenings and on Saturday at noon. A children's menu is available.

🕐 Tue–Thu noon–2, 7.30–10, Fri–Sat noon–2, 7.30–11; closed 8–26 Aug
🍴 L €26, D €33, Wine €10.50

⑪ LE PRIVILÈGE

13 place Grenette, 38000 Grenoble
Tel 04 76 44 10 74
www.ifrance.com/leprivilege38
Le Privilège is an independently owned pizzeria serving traditional Italian food. It's in

the heart of town on place Grenette, between rue Félix Poulat and rue de la Republique, and has parking and a shaded terrace. The menu includes meat dishes, pasta and salads as well as pizza.
🕐 Daily noon–11
🍴 L €30, D €44, Wine €9

⑪ AUBERGE NAPOLÉON

7 rue Montorge, 38000 Grenoble
Tel 04 76 87 53 64
www.auberge-napoleon.fr
This auberge, opposite the Jardin du Ville, is named after Napoleon, who stayed here in 1815 on his way back from the island of Elba. The dining room is air-conditioned, has subdued lighting and plenty of fresh flowers and plants. The

menu includes regional cuisine as well as luxurious dishes like foie gras and truffles. You can reserve via the website, which also has some recipes.
🕐 Mon–Wed 7.30–9.30, Thu–Sat noon–2, 7.30–9.30; closed 25 Aug–7 Sep, 1–8 May
🍴 L €80, D €120, Wine €25
❖

⊜ GRAND HÔTEL INTERHOTEL

5 rue de la République, 38000 Grenoble
Tel 04 76 44 49 36
www.grand-hotel-grenoble.com
The hotel is in a 19th-century building but the lobby is pure art deco. The bedrooms are less ornate but have a bathroom, hairdryer and satellite TV. The hotel has a 24-hour bar and room service.
🕐 Closed for 3 weeks in Aug
🛏 €75–€88, excluding breakfast (€10)
🛌 50 (20 non-smoking)
❖

⊜ HÔTEL GALLIA

7 boulevard Maréchal-Joffre, 38000 Grenoble
Tel 04 76 87 39 21
www.hotel-gallia.com
A modern two-star hotel offering soundproofed rooms with light wood furniture and bold fabrics. Rooms have satellite TV, minibar, hairdryer, safe and modem point. Parking costs €5.50 per day.
🕐 Closed mid-Jul to mid-Aug
🛏 €40–€46, excluding breakfast (€5.70)
🛌 35

⊜ HÔTEL SUISSE ET BORDEAUX

6 place de la Gare, 38000 Grenoble
Tel 04 76 47 55 87
www.hotel-sb-grenoble.com
Dating from the 19th century, this attractive hotel is on a corner of a square with fountains. Bedrooms have bathroom, telephone with modem point and satellite TV. Breakfast is served in the air-conditioned dining room. The hotel has private car parking.
🛏 €46
🛌 63 (2 non-smoking)

LYON

⑪ L'ASSIETTE DU MARCHÉ

21 Grande Rue de Vaise, 69009 Lyon
Tel 04 78 83 84 90
www.assiette-du-marche.com
A popular restaurant that's great value, so it's a good idea to reserve. There are two dining rooms (one smoking, one not), one of which has exposed stone walls and a typically Lyonnaise wooden ceiling. Access to this dining room and the enclosed terrace (heated in winter) is

through the kitchen, where you can see the chefs at work. The restaurant specializes in fish and unusually there is no formal menu, although there are always two dishes of the day (one meat, one fish).

Dishes might include tuna gratin, fish soup or pikeperch.
🕐 Mon–Sat noon–2
🍴 L €27, Wine €6.50, prix-fixe menus €10.50 or €13.50

⑪ BEL CANTO

2 rue Celu, 69004 Lyon
Tel 04 78 30 04 27
This bistro-style Italian restaurant off the main shopping area of Croix Rousse, serves excellent meals that are good value. Choose from prix-fixe, à la carte or the day's special. There is a selection of more than 35 types of pizza, all cooked in a wood-fired oven, as well as pasta, meat and fish dishes. There's also a children's menu. Booking is recommended.
🕐 Mon–Fri noon–2, 7.15–10.30
🍴 L €24, D €33, Wine €7.50

⑪ BRASSERIE GEORGES

30 cours Verdun, 69002 Lyon
Tel 04 72 56 54 54
Founded in 1836 and decorated in a splendid art deco style, this is a huge restaurant with fast service. Meals include Lyonnaise dishes, sauerkraut, seafood and omelettes.
🕐 Sun–Thu 11.30am–11.15pm, Fri–Sat 11.30am–midnight
🍴 L €35, D €48, Wine €15

SPECIAL
LA BRASSERIE DES BROTTEAUX
1 place Jules Ferry,
69006 Lyon
Tel 04 72 74 03 98
www.brasseriedesbrotteaux.com

Established in 1913, this elegant brasserie is beautifully decorated with antiques, bright tiles, glass and mirrors. The dining room is air conditioned, and you can eat outside in good weather. Opt for one of the wonderful prix-fixe menus or try a salad or the Aberdeen Angus beef.
- Mon–Sat 7.30am–10.30pm
- L €35, D €54, Wine €15

MAI THAI
199 rue Crequi, 69003 Lyon
Tel 04 78 95 40 16
A friendly atmosphere, bright interior and delicious Thai food make this a popular place. The superb food includes a spicy seafood salad, spring rolls and prawns in lime sauce. The small wine list has wines from the Côtes du Rhône region, which are apparently best suited to the food. Reserve ahead.
- Mon–Tue and Thu–Sat noon–2, 8–11, Wed noon–2
- L €24, D €36, Wine €12

NEW DELHI
5 avenue de Doyenne,
69005 Lyon
Tel 04 72 41 96 37
The dining room of this restaurant, specializing in Indian cuisine, is decorated in pale tones with bright swags of material at the windows and a huge map of India on one wall. The owner and his son run the place with gusto and have designed a menu with

SPECIAL
LA REINE ASTRID
26 boulevard de Belges, 69006 Lyon
Tel 04 72 82 18 00
www.warwickastrid.com
In a residential area convenient for Parc Tête d'Or,

this four-star all-suite hotel is within easy walking distance of local shops and restaurants. The suites have soft furnishings in rich red, gold and dark blue and come with one or two bedrooms, bathroom, kitchen, satellite TV and Internet access. There is a cocktail bar, a reading lounge with complimentary newspapers, parking and a restaurant with a terrace.
- €190–€420, excluding breakfast (€15)
- 90 suites (25 non-smoking)

dishes cooked to suit French tastes—the food is not too spicy, but can be spiced up on request. Choose from a multitude of curries (chicken tikka, prawn Madras and biryani dishes), kebabs and breads.
- Tue–Sun noon–2, 7–11, Mon 7–11
- €26, €30, €7

HOTEL ATHENA
45 boulevard Marius Vivier Merle,
69003, Lyon
Tel 04 72 68 88 44
www.athena-hotel.com
As this hotel is right outside the SNCF and TGV railway station, as well as near bus, Métro and tram stations, it's convenient for those who have just arrived in the city. There are also taxis and shuttle buses for Lyon-St-Exupéry and St-Étienne airports. It's a modern, two-star hotel and rooms have satellite TV,

telephone and radio. Parking costs €7 per day.
- €67–€74, excluding breakfast (€7.30)
- 122

LES PRAZ DE CHAMONIX
HÔTEL EDEN RESTAURANT
35 route de Goudanys,
74400 Les Praz de Chamonix
Tel 04 50 53 18 43
www.hoteleden-chamonix.com
This welcoming mountain restaurant has an open fire and permanent exhibitions of photographs and sculptures. A contemporary twist to classic French cuisine has earned acclaim for Swedish chef Frederick Darenius who creates dishes such as beef carpaccio, rock lobster and roast rack of lamb with thyme sauce. Desserts include nougat ice cream and three-chocolate terrine. The maître d'hôtel, Phillippe Bruguet, has an extensive knowledge of wine and can help you to choose the best one to accompany your meal. There are also vegetarian prix-fixe menus.
- Daily 7pm–10.30pm
- D €100, Wine €20

SERVOZ
GORGES DE LA DIOSAZ
74310 Servoz
Tel 04 50 47 20 97
www.hoteldesgorges.com
This restaurant is two minutes from the middle of the village and opposite the post office. The menu includes salmon smoked in-house, foie gras with cherry vinegar, perch with crayfish and bass fillet in a champagne butter. There are fixed price menus and a children's menu. You'll need to give 24 hours' notice if you are going to have the superb seafood platter. Eat inside or on the terrace with wonderful views of the mountain range. Servoz is 1km(1.5 miles) from the A40 motorway.
- Tue and Thu–Sat noon–1.30, 7–9.30, Mon 7–9.30, Sun noon–1.30
- L €46, D €68, Wine €18

EATING

Olive oil, tomatoes, garlic, fresh fish and clumps of wild herbs are the ingredients of classic Mediterranean cuisine. Visit any of the region's markets and you'll see for yourself the fresh ingredients that make Mediterranean dishes so appetizing. Gastronomy does exist, with the Pourcel twins' much garlanded restaurants, but you can best discover the true taste of the area at a table in a simple fishing port on the Thau lagoon or at the quayside of a Riviera village. Dishes follow the Mediterranean coastline from the Italian to the Spanish border, with *salade Niçoise* from Nice, bouillabaisse fish stew from Marseille, Bouzigues oysters and the succulent anchovies of Collioure. Thyme, rosemary, sage and lavender are used in many dishes, and wines range from the tangy Picpoul to the earthier Corbières and Fitou.

STAYING

In the southeast, you can find every type of accommodation possible, from campsites to dinner, bed-and-breakfast in a Corbières wine-grower's village home. In the Cévennes, *chambres d'hôtes* rent out donkeys to carry your bags on a hiking trail that follows in the footsteps of Robert Louis Stevenson. Accommodation is arranged for both walker and donkey at bed-and-breakfast establishments. On the Riviera, luxury hotels such as the Negresco and Carlton are cultural legends, while new design-led hotels such as the futuristic Hi-hôtel in Nice are emerging. Except in coastal resorts, Languedoc has fewer hotels, so consider a modest bed-and-breakfast or self-catering apartment at one of the many family holiday bases.

Languedoc-Roussillon

CARCASSONNE

🍴 LE LANGUEDOC
32 allée d'Iéna, 11000 Carcassonne
Tel 04 68 25 22 17
This classy restaurant has precise, formal service and an

🍴 HÔTEL DE LA CITÉ
Place de l'Église, 11000 Carcassonne
Tel 04 68 71 98 71
www.hoteldelacite.orient-express.com
Queen Elizabeth II has stayed at this super-sumptuous hotel. It has one of the few gardens within the old city, providing a pleasant setting. Suites are themed and cater to every taste—choose anything from a warm Provençal-style room to a neo-Gothic suite with wooden floors and panels. As you would expect of a hotel of this class, every conceivable service and amenity is provided.
🕐 Closed Dec–15 Jan
🛏 €315–€400, excluding breakfast (€28.80)
ℹ 50 rooms, 11 suites
♿ 🏊 Outdoor

extravagant Louis Philippe interior. Meat and poultry form the bulk of the long menu, which includes the classic cassoulet (meat and bean

casserole) and chicken liver mousse. Round off your meal with home-made sorbet or Grand Marnier ice cream.
🕐 Mon–Sat noon–1.30, 7.30–9.30, Sun noon–1.30; Closed Mon out of season, 23 Jun–7 Jul and 24 Dec–22 Jan
🍽 L €45, D €70, Wine €10

MONTPELLIER

🍴 LES BAINS
6 rue Richelieu, 34000, Montpellier
Tel 04 67 60 70 87
This stylish restaurant is named after the public baths that used to occupy the building. It serves a range of modern and traditional Mediterranean dishes with an emphasis on seafood. You

can eat outside on the expansive terrace or in the smart dining room. The €24 prix-fixe menu is excellent value for money and has a decent choice for each of the three courses. The restaurant also serves afternoon tea.
🕐 Mon 7.30pm–10.30pm, Tue–Sat noon–10.30
🍽 L €45, D €60, Wine €10

🍴 BRASSERIE DU THÉÂTRE
22 boulevard Victor Hugo, 34000 Montpellier
Tel 04 67 58 88 80
It's opposite the opera house, so this brasserie is all the rage with the opera set. On a summer evening you can sit out on the gorgeous terrace and hear the music from performances drifting in. The restaurant specializes in seafood, but also has an extensive range of meat and poultry dishes. The €14 prix-fixe menu, of two courses and wine, is excellent value. The interior is a little lifeless, so opt for a table on the terrace if the weather is fine.
🕐 Daily 11am–10pm
🍽 L €40, D €60, Wine €6

🍴 HÔTEL DU PALAIS
3 rue du Palais, 34000 Montpellier
Tel 04 67 60 47 38
In one of the prettiest quarters in the historic town, this two-star, family-run hotel is great value for money. The vine-covered ancient building with its shuttered façade contains small, immaculate rooms decorated in a slightly outmoded style. Each bedroom has a private bathroom, minibar, coffee-making facilities and satellite TV. Some overlook the gorgeous nearby square and the rest have fine views of the traffic-free, cobbled streets.
🛏 €62–€80, excluding breakfast (€9)
ℹ 26
♿

EATING AND STAYING

⊖HÔTEL LE JARDIN DES SENS

11 avenue St-Lazare, 34000 Montpellier
Tel 04 99 58 38 38
www.jardindessens.com

In a quiet residential quarter just a 10-minute walk from central Montpellier, Hôtel le Jardin des Sens has built its reputation on its highly acclaimed eponymous restaurant, which serves some of the finest cuisine in the region. The hotel was established by twins Jacques and Laurent Pourcel and the large, minimalist, contemporary rooms, were designed by Philippe Starck. Most rooms overlook the neat gardens and swimming pool and one suite even has its own pool.

🛏 €150–€450, excluding breakfast
🛎 12 rooms, 2 suites
🔲 🏊 Outdoor

NARBONNE

⊕LE PETIT COMPTOIR

4 boulevard de Marèchal-Joffre, 11100 Narbonne
Tel 04 68 42 30 35

An unimposing façade gives way to a surprisingly lavish dining room decorated with period mirrors and plenty of flowers. It's not easy to predict what you'll find on the menu in this small restaurant (it changes every week according to what is available in the local market), but pasta, casserole and pastry dishes are sure to be on offer.

🕐 Mon–Sat noon–10, Jul, Aug; Tue–Sat noon–10, rest of year
🍽 L €30, D €50, Wine €11.80

NÎMES

⊕LE BOUCHON ET L'ASSIETTE

5 rue de Sauve, 30000 Nîmes
Tel 04 66 62 02 93

This exclusive restaurant is in a lovely old building next to the Fontaine gardens. With prix-fixe menus starting at €15, better value would be hard to find. The cooking brims with creativity, and arrives at the table artistically arranged. Try the lightly grilled foie gras with peppers and grape caramel. In the dining room, simple furnishings offset exposed beams and stone walls.

🕐 Thu–Mon noon–1.30, 7.30–10; closed 1–15 Jan and 3 weeks Aug
🍽 L €40, D €55, Wine €15

⊕LE VINTAGE CAFÉ

7 rue de Bernis, 30000 Nîmes
Tel 04 66 21 04 45

This delightful little restaurant is in a great location at the back of a tiny square with a fountain, between the arena and La Maison Carrée. The dining room is a typical bistro, and doubles as a gallery space for local artists. The menu encompasses meat, seafood and poultry dishes, with daily specials written on the blackboard, and wines can be served by the glass.

🕐 Tue–Fri 11–2.30, 7–11, Sat 7–11; closed 2 weeks Aug
🍽 L €30, D €45, Wine €8

⊖HÔTEL IMPERATOR CONCORDE

Quai de la Fontaine, 15 rue Gaston-Bossier, 30000 Nîmes
Tel 04 66 21 90 30
www.hotel-imperator.com

Although this hotel fronts onto the road, its outstanding beauty and magnificent gardens more than make up for this. Both Ernest Hemingway and Ava Gardner were lured to this wonderful place overlooking Jardin de la Fontaine and place Picasso, to luxuriate in its extravagant rooms. Start your evening with cocktails on the terrace overlooking the fountain and finish it in one of the spacious, well-designed rooms.

🛏 €99–€198, excluding breakfast (€16)
🛎 62
🔲

PERPIGNAN

⊕LES TROIS SOEURS

2 rue Frontfroide, 66000 Perpignan
Tel 04 68 51 22 33

Run by three sisters, Isabelle, Christine and Katrine, this restaurant is on place Gambetta facing the church. Seek out the coolness of the light and airy dining room, or sit on the terrace and soak up the beauty of this undiscovered little square. Seafood fans will appreciate the great choice of wonderfully prepared dishes, while meat classics such as foie gras and entrecôte also make it on to the menu. For a great value meal for a family or a group, order oysters and mussels by the kilo and have them prepared the way you like them.

🕐 Mon–Sat noon–2, 7.30–10
🍽 L €35, D €35, Wine €12

⊖HÔTEL DE LA LOGE

1 rue Fabriques d'en Nabol, 66000 Perpignan
Tel 04 68 34 41 02
www.hoteldelaloge.fr

This small, two-star, family-run hotel is a friendly place to stay. It's on the pretty place de la Loge in the middle of town, close to the canal and its quayside attractions, and is in a delightful 15th-century mansion. The comfortable rooms have TV and private bathroom. There is a small bar which serves drinks, but no restaurant.

🛏 €47–€64, excluding breakfast
🛎 21

Provence-Alpes-Côte-d'Azur

AIX-EN-PROVENCE

⊕L'AIXQUIS

22 rue Victor Leydet, 13100 Aix-en-Provence
Tel 04 42 27 76 16
www.aixquis.com

The setting here, with elegantly laid tables and subtle lighting, is perfect for a romantic dinner. Bouquets of freshly cut

flowers and a tiled floor give the place a Provençal touch. The food is fine Mediterranean cuisine—warm lobster salad with coral vinaigrette is the signature dish.

🕐 Tue–Sat noon–1.30, 7.30–9.30; closed Aug
🍽 L €82, D €106, Wine €18

LE P'TIT PUITS

14 rue des Bernardines, 13100
Aix-en-Provence
Tel 04 42 91 42 77

Named after the little well that sits in its vaulted basement, the dining room here is warm and welcoming. The dark-orange tablecloths complement the tawny walls, and the soft lighting keeps the mood relaxed. The menu is long and includes fondues, hearty stuffed baked potatoes, salads and Provence-style fish.

🕐 Mon–Fri noon–2.30, 7.30–10; Sat 7.30–10
🍴 L €27, D €30, Wine €10

HÔTEL LE PIGONNET

5 avenue du Pigonnet, 13090
Aix-en-Provence
Tel 04 42 59 02 90
www.hotelpigonnet.com

Le Pigonnet is a former country house which is now a four-star hotel. It's right in the middle of town at the end of a tree-lined avenue. From the hotel there's a wonderful view of Mont Sainte-Victoire, the mountain repeatedly depicted by Impressionist painter Paul Cézanne. Inside is refined elegance with antiques and objets d'art—notably some Aix-style chests of drawers. You can have dinner in the elegant gastronomic restaurant Riviera.

💶 €180–€350, excluding breakfast
🛏 48
🏊 Outdoor

ANTIBES

LE BRÛLOT

3 rue Frédéric Isnard, 06600 Antibes
Tel 04 93 34 17 76
www.brulot.com

There's plenty of character at this restaurant, where simplicity and authenticity come together. There's exposed stone, beamed ceilings, an antique baker's oven and a second room in the basement with vaults dating to the 12th century. The cuisine makes good use of the wood oven: grilled steak with Provençal herbs and grilled scampi flambéed with pastis (a local aniseed spirit). Alongside these traditional offerings, there are specials some days of the week such as couscous on Thursdays and ham on the bone on Fridays.

🕐 Thu–Sat noon–2.30, 7.30–10, Mon–Wed 7.30–10
🍴 L €40, D €60, Wine €12

APT

AUBERGE DU LUBÉRON

8 place du Faubourg du Ballet, 84000 Apt
Tel 04 90 74 12 50
www.auberge-luberon-peuzin.com

The inside of this inn is subtly elegant, with old furniture, beautiful drapes and pastel tones for the veranda dining room. From the terrace there are wonderful views of the Apt valley. The Lubéron region

dominates the menu in dishes such as pan-fried duck foie gras served with regional glacé fruits, which is one of the chef's specials. The dessert menu is in keeping with the Provençal tradition of having 13 desserts at Christmas.

🕐 Mon–Tue 7.30–9.30, Wed–Sun noon–2, 7.30–9.30; closed first 2 weeks of Jan
🍴 L €84, D €106, Wine €18

LES ARCS-SUR-ARGENS

LOGIS DU GUETTEUR

Place du Château, 83460
Les Arcs-sur-Argens
Tel 04 94 99 51 10
www.logisduguetteur.com

This three-star hotel is in a beautifully restored 11th-century castle. You can have dinner in the vaulted basement, where a fire crackles in winter, or by the pool in fine weather. The bedrooms are traditional in style with printed fabric bedspreads and wood furniture. Most rooms have panoramic views of the mountains and all have TV.

🕐 Closed mid-Jan to mid-Mar
💶 €99–€108, excluding breakfast
🛏 12
🏊 Outdoor

ARLES

LA GUEULE DU LOUP

39 rue des Arènes, 13200 Arles
Tel 04 90 96 96 69

The tawny walls with pictures contrast beautifully with the exposed stone in this restaurant. The cuisine, though true to the traditions of the Camargue and Provence, bears owner/chef Jean-Jacques Allard's personal touch. For example, eels from the Camargue are served with a leek and chicory fondue in a red wine sauce.

🕐 Tue–Sat noon–1.30, 7.30–9.30, Mon 7–9.30 Mar–end Sep; Closed Jan
🍴 L €24, D €50, Wine €15

LA MAMMA

20 rue de l'Amphithéâtre, 13200 Arles
Tel 04 90 96 11 60
www.lamammaarles.com

This restaurant near the arenas has a rustic feel, with a tiled floor, basket-weave chairs, decorative agricultural items and a massive pizza oven. Expect Italian and regional cuisine such as sautéed beef with olives, crudités with anchovy sauce, and, of course, a range of pizzas.

🕐 Tue–Sat noon–2.30, 7–10.30, Sun noon–2.30
🍴 L €22, D €32, Wine €12

L'OLIVIER

1 bis rue Réattu, 13200 Arles
Tel 04 90 49 64 88
www.restaurant-olivier.com

L'Olivier has a wonderful setting in a 16th-century town house with a courtyard and a fountain. The succession of small dining rooms creates a tranquil, intimate mood and the tones of white and soft brown match the exposed stone. The menu has fine regional cuisine, with some Camargue specials such as beef served with a pepper and anchovy sauce.

🕐 Tue–Sat noon–2.30, 7.30–10; closed Nov and 1–15 Jan
🍴 L €36, D €108, Wine €20

EATING AND STAYING

HÔTEL CALENDAL

5 rue Porte-de-Laure, 13200 Arles
Tel 04 90 96 11 89
www.lecalendal.com

The 17th-century building that houses this two-star hotel is just a stone's throw from the Roman arenas. Some bedrooms face this monument, others overlook the hotel's exquisite garden courtyard. The interior is Provençal in style with a tiled floor, wrought iron and warm tones. In fine weather, you can have buffet-style breakfast and light meals in the shade of the palm trees in the garden.

🕐 Closed Jan
💶 €45–€75, excluding breakfast
🛏 38
♿

AVIGNON

CHRISTIAN ÉTIENNE

10 rue de Mons, 84000 Avignon
Tel 04 90 86 16 50
www.christian-etienne.fr

This elegant restaurant is in a 14th-century palace, which was once the home of the Marshal of the Roman court. The dining room bears traces of this rich history, with

beautiful painted ceilings and frescoes, the rest is Provençal. The wonderful terrace looks onto the Palais des Papes. Christian Étienne, former sous-chef at the luxury Ritz Hotel in Paris, creates exquisite regional dishes with truffles and tomatoes his preferred ingredients–the black truffle omelette is one of the house specials.

🕐 Tue–Sat noon–1.15, 7.30–9.15
💶 L €100, D €140, Wine €16

HÔTEL D'EUROPE

1 place Crillon, 84000 Avignon
Tel 04 90 14 76 76
www.hotel-d-europe.fr

Follow in the steps of Napoleon, Salvador Dalí and Pablo Picasso, who all stayed at the Marquis of Graveson's former house, built in 1580 and turned into a hotel in 1799. There are luxury furnishings throughout, with antiques, candelabra, old paintings and Persian carpets. The suites have a terrace with wonderful views

over the roofs of Avignon and all the rooms have air conditioning and satellite TV. There's a gastronomic restaurant and parking.

💶 €125–€398, excluding breakfast (€20)
🛏 44
♿

LE SIMPLE SIMON

26 rue Petite-Fusterie, 84000 Avignon
Tel 04 90 86 62 70

This place is a little piece of old England in the heart of Avignon. Inside there are beamed ceilings, decorative plates hanging on the walls, a collection of teapots on the shelves and a large round table at the middle of the room where the cakes and

desserts are displayed. During the afternoon it's a great place to enjoy a cup of tea and a scone. At lunchtime, a dish of the day (often of British influence) is served.

🕐 Mon–Sat noon–7
💶 L €30 (lunch only)

BARCELONNETTE

AUBERGE DU CLOS SOREL

Les Molanès, 04400 Pra Loup 1500 Barcelonnette
Tel 04 92 84 10 74
www.clos-sorel.com

This three-star inn, in a restored 17th-century farm at

the Pra Loup 1500 resort, has the atmosphere of a mountain chalet. Beamed ceilings, exposed stonework, and fireplaces (also in one of the guest rooms) give the public rooms a warmth, continued in the bedrooms by the wooden furniture and Provençal fabrics. In winter, a chairlift just 200m (220 yards) from the hotel gives access to Pra-Loup resort slopes and the restaurant opens for dinner. In summer, when the snow has gone, there are aquagym classes to keep you fit.

🕐 Closed May to mid-Jun and Sep–end Nov
💶 €64–€138, excluding breakfast
🛏 11
🏊 Outdoor

LES BAUX DE PROVENCE

OUSTAÙ DE BAUMANIÈRE

13520 Les Baux de Provence
Tel 04 90 54 33 07
www.oustaudebaumaniere.com

Here there's a 16th-century Provençal country house restaurant coupled with a four-star hotel. Dining on the terrace allows you to appreciate the surrounding beautiful forest of cypresses punctuated by rocky outcrops. Inside, all is subtle elegance, with drapes and harmonious

soft tones—the perfect setting in which to enjoy exquisite dishes such as truffle and leek ravioli, pan-fried foie gras with a wine reduction and 'blue' lobster with a herb salad.

🕐 Fri–Tue noon–2, 7–9; Wed–Thu 7–9 Apr–end Dec; closed Jan–end Mar
🍽 L €168, D €220, Wine €40

⊖LE MAS D'AIGRET
13520 Les Baux de Provence
Tel 04 90 54 20 00
www.masdaigret.com
Nestled against a cliff, this three-star hotel has wonderful views and some surprising interiors—the breakfast room, bar, lounge and some of the guest rooms have been carved out of the rock and still display the exposed rockface. The bedrooms are simply but tastefully decorated,

with floral bedspreads and white furniture and there is a restaurant.

🍽 €95–€170, excluding breakfast (€12)
🛏 16
♿ ⛱ Outdoor

BOLLÈNE
⊖LE CHÂTEAU DE ROCHER
156 avenue Emile-Lachaux, 84500 Bollène
Tel 04 90 40 09 09
www.lechateaudurocher.com
This three-star residence is surprisingly good value considering it is in a 19th-century manor, built for the Comte de Rocher. It lies in a

4ha (10-acre) park inhabited by ostriches and peacocks. The rooms are cosy and there is a gastronomic restaurant as well as enclosed car parking.

🍽 €45–€66, excluding breakfast
🛏 19

CABRIÈRES-D'AVIGNON
⊖LA BASTIDE DE VOULONNE
RD 148, 84220 Cabrières-d'Avignon
Tel 04 90 76 77 56
www.bastide-voulonne.com
Behind the ochre façade and blue shutters of this 18th-century former farmhouse is a tastefully decorated interior, where wrought iron, wood, and shades of terracotta dominate. Most of the rooms have king-size beds, there is a garden and an impressive bread oven in the dining room.

🕐 Closed mid–Nov to mid–Dec; Reservations essential in Jan and Feb
🍽 €122–€145, excluding breakfast
🛏 7
⛱ Outdoor

CANNES
⊕ESCALE DE CHINE
58 rue Jean Jaurès, 06400 Cannes
Tel 04 93 99 15 99
www.escaledechine.com
The decoration in this Chinese

restaurant is rich, with a profusion of exotic wood, mirrors, columns and gilded panels, yet manages to avoid kitsch. The cuisine is equally refined, with dishes such as Chinese fondue and Peking-style duck.

🕐 Wed–Sun noon–2.30, 7–11, Mon–Tue 7–11
🍽 L €22, D €38, Wine €11

⊕LA POTINIÈRE DU PALAIS
Square Mérimée, 06400, Cannes
Tel 04 93 39 02 82
The *palais* (palace) refers to the Palais des Festivals, where major events in Cannes take place. But there's more to this restaurant than a choice location. The cooking is exceptionally good and has a lot of fish and classics such as grilled steak and roast chicken. The pleasant room, decorated in yellows and pale greens, is a bonus.

🕐 Mon–Sat noon–2.30, 7.30–10
🍽 L €43, D €60, Wine €16

⊖HÔTEL DE PARIS
34 boulevard d'Alsace, 06400 Cannes
Tel 04 93 38 30 89
www.hotel-de-paris.com
This three-star hotel has a pink 19th-century façade, which contrasts beautifully with the blue of the outdoor pool. Inside, there is antique furniture and even some medieval armour. There are facilities galore, with a private beach, swimming pool, Jacuzzi and hammam (Turkish bath). Bedrooms have satellite TV, a safe and modem connection for laptops.

🍽 €95–€150, excluding breakfast
🛏 50
♿ ⛱ Outdoor

CARNOUX
⊕LE COLOMBIER
2 avenue Claude Debussy, 13470 Carnoux
Tel 04 42 73 62 82
The modern interior design at this restaurant remains true to Provence: Pink, yellow and a lot of blue are used in the large frescoes depicting the seaside. The chef prepares classic dishes such as stuffed mutton tripe and beef slowly cooked in red wine. With cheese and dessert included in all menus, Le Colombier provides good value for money.

🕐 Tue–Sun noon–2.30, 7.30–10
🍽 L €40, D €70, Wine €8

EATING AND STAYING

CHEVAL-BLANC

L'AUBERGE DE CHEVAL BLANC

481 avenue de la Canebière, 84460 Cheval-Blanc

Tel 04 32 50 18 55

Chef Hervé Perrasse prepares the great classics of Provençal cuisine with obvious pleasure. The *escabèche millefeuille* (anchovies in puff pastry) or melt-in-your-mouth Provençal cake made with fresh, local herbs and white wine are excellent choices. There's a pleasant shaded terrace which looks onto a garden, and the dining room has beamed ceilings, wicker chairs and art displays by local artist Christine Darellis.

Mon, Sat 7.30–10, Tue, Thu, Fri and Sun noon–2, 7.30–10

L €32, D €78, Wine €19

LE CRESTET

LE MAS DE MAGALI

Quartier Chante Coucou, 84110 Le Crestet

Tel 04 90 36 39 91

www.masdemagali.com

This restaurant has a lovely setting, in a country house in a 3ha (7.5-acre) park planted with oak trees. You can have dinner on the terrace, or in the

elegant dining room, which is decorated in Provençal style with a romantic twist. Blue and yellow set the tone, and there are vases of flowers, mirrors and subdued lighting. Dishes to try include terrine of foie gras, chicken with a mushroom sauce and zabaglione for dessert.

Thu–Tue 7.30–9; Closed Oct–end Apr

D €48, Wine €12

LA CROIX-VALMER

CHÂTEAU DE VALMER

Route de Gigaro, 83420 La Croix-Valmer

Tel 04 94 55 15 15

www.chateau-valmer.com

This chateau lies at the heart of 5ha (12 acres) of grounds, with its own private beach, tennis court and a large swimming pool, surrounded by century-old palm trees. The bedrooms have Provençal fabrics, marble bathrooms and satellite TV. Some have a canopy bed and certain suites can accommodate up to four people. You can sample Mediterranean cuisine at La Pinède Plage restaurant by the beach. There is private parking.

Closed Oct to mid-Apr

€162–€315, excluding breakfast

42

Outdoor

FORCALQUIER

AUBERGE CHAREMBEAU

Route de Niozelles, 04300 Forcalquier

Tel 04 92 70 91 70

www.charembeau.com

A two-star country inn close to the picturesque village of Niozelles, developed from a restored 18th-century farmhouse. In addition to traditional hotel rooms, some rooms can accommodate up to four people and have a kitchenette. The lovely interiors have Provençal furniture and floral soft furnishings. Some rooms have a balcony, others have a terrace. Bring your racket as there's a tennis court.

Closed mid-Nov to mid-Feb

€54–€106, excluding breakfast

23

Outdoor

FRÉJUS

L'ABRI-COTIER

Quai Marc Antoine, 83600, Fréjus

Tel 04 94 51 11 33

Comfortable wall-seating, floral bouquets, a superb view of the harbour and a heated terrace contribute to the feel-good nature of this restaurant. The food is outstanding, with dishes such as sea bass in a champagne sauce and bay prawns mingling happily on the menu with simple but tasty meals such as pizzas. There's a children's menu.

Thu–Mon noon–2.30, 7.30–10, Tue noon–2.30

L €36, D €48, Wine €15

L'ARÉNA

145 rue Général de Gaulle, 83600 Fréjus

Tel 04 94 17 09 40

www.arena-hotel.com

This charming three-star hotel in the heart of Fréjus has a terracotta façade. There are palm trees in the garden, wooden furniture in the bedrooms and a restaurant that serves Mediterranean cuisine. In summer, you can have breakfast in the garden by the pool. Private parking is available.

Closed mid-Dec to mid-Jan

€95–€115, excluding breakfast (€10)

36

GORDES

HOSTELLERIE LE PHEBUS

Route de Mur Joucas, 84220, Gordes

Tel 04 90 05 78 83

www.lephebus.com

Le Phebus is both a restaurant and a wonderful four-star hotel. Chef Xavier Mathieu's sophisticated regional cuisine includes fillet of sole pan-fried in salt butter with tangy jasmine and vanilla or farmhouse duck foie gras. You can dine

in the elegant dining room, which has beamed ceilings, or you may prefer the terrace and its fantastic views.

Fri–Mon noon–2, 7–9.30, Tue–Thu 7–9.30; Closed mid-Nov to mid-Mar

L €100, D €160, Wine €15

⊖BASTIDE DES CINQ LYS

Les Beaumettes, 84220 Gordes
Tel 04 90 72 38 38
www.bastide-des-5-lys.fr
This 16th-century four-star
manor stands at the end of an
alley planted with cypress trees
and pink oleanders. The soft
tones and subtle lighting in the
bedrooms exude tranquillity
and all of the rooms have an
attractive feature such as a
four-poster bed, a terrace or
even a private garden. You are
spoiled for choice with a
restaurant, tennis court and
golf course. Every Saturday in
July and August there's a piano
bar by the pool.
🅿 €154–€261
🛏 18
🏊 Outdoor

HYÈRES
⊕LA COLOMBE

663 route de Toulon-La Bayorre, 83400
Hyères
Tel 04 94 35 35 16
www.restaurantlacolombe.com
Chef Pascal Bonamy likes to
innovate, mixing the finest
ingredients. His sea bass dish
comes with asparagus and
pearl onions, and he uses
peppers from Espelette, in the
Basque country. The refined
interior, with yellow and blue
tones and cane chairs,
betrays a regional influence.
🕐 Tue–Sat noon–1.30, 7.30–9.30, Sun
noon–1.30, Sep–end Jun; Tue–Fri and
Sun noon–1.30, 7.30–9.30, Sat
7.30–9.30, rest of year
🍴 L €52, D €90, Wine €17

LAURIS
⊕LA TABLE DES MAMÉES

1 rue du Mûrier, 84360 Lauris
Tel 04 90 08 34 66
There are exposed stone
vaulted ceilings, a large
fireplace and soft lighting in

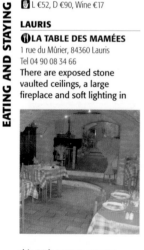

this 14th-century country
house. The cuisine is also full
of character, with dishes such

as duck with olives, garlic and
courgettes (zucchini) and
traditional fish soup. The cellar
contains plenty of local wines.
🕐 Tue–Sat noon–2.30, 7.30–10, Sun
noon–2.30; Closed Mar
🍴 L €40, D €45, Wine €18

MARSEILLE
⊕LES ARCENAULX

25 cours Estienne d'Orves, 13001
Marseille
Tel 04 91 59 80 40
www.les-arcenaulx.com
Numerous books line the walls
of Marseille's majestic former
arsenal, which has a beamed
ceiling and long red wall seats.
Sophisticated regional cuisine
is on the menu, with dishes

such as honey and lemon duck
served with citron-scented
courgette (zucchini) gratin. In
the afternoons, Les Arcenaulx
is a tea room.
🕐 Mon–Sat noon–11
🍴 L €50, D €90, Wine €18

⊕CHEZ FONFON

140 rue du Vallon des Auffes, 13007
Marseille
Tel 04 91 52 14 38
The lively fishing port, now
a conservation area, is the
place to try *bouillabaisse*, the
Mediterranean fish soup for
which Marseille is famous.
Here you are in a different
world, far from the touristy
restaurants of the city's old
port. Chez Fonfon is an
institution in town and has
been run by the same family

for more than 50 years. It has
an elegant, Mediterranean
interior with green basket-
weave chairs, a white and
terracotta tiled floor and
Provençal fabrics.
🕐 Mon 7.30–10, Tue–Sat noon–2,
7.30–10
🍴 L €60, D €80, Wine €15

⊖HÔTEL LE CORBUSIER

280 boulevard Michelet, 3rd floor,
13008 Marseille
Tel 04 91 16 78 00
The hotel is in a block of 300
apartments designed by Le
Corbusier. For this monument
of modern architecture, he
devised a revolutionary
concept—to re-create a city

within a single building. As
such, it comes complete with
play areas, shops, a cinema, a
bar and a library. The simplicity
of the bedrooms is delightful
and they look onto the sea or
the enclosed park and terrace.
There is private car parking and
the nearest Métro station is
Rond-Point du Prado.
🅿 €45–€70, excluding breakfast
🛏 21

⊖HÔTEL HERMÈS

2 rue Bonneterie, 13002 Marseille
Tel 04 96 11 63 63
www.hotelmarseille.com
This two-star hotel is by the
Vieux Port, a picturesque and

animated spot packed with
restaurants and cafés. You
needn't worry about noise, as

EATING AND STAYING

the rooms have been sound-
proofed. Although lacking the
charm of the old, bedrooms
are light and have a TV. Some
have a balcony.

💶 €52–€69, excluding breakfast (€7)
💶 €45–€81
♿

MOUSTIERS-SAINTE-MARIE

🍴FERME SAINTE-CÉCILE
Route des Gorges du Verdon, 04360
Moustiers-Sainte-Marie
Tel 04 92 74 64 18
www.ferme-sainte-cecile.com
The restaurant is in a former
18th-century farm set against
the hillside. It has beamed
ceilings, white wooden chairs,
blue and yellow tablecloths,

and various ornaments. The
menu makes the most of
the local produce: lamb in a
spicy crust, foie gras with a
thyme courgette (zucchini)
marmalade. In fine weather,
opt for the terrace and enjoy
wonderful views of the
surrounding mountains.
🕐 Tue–Sun noon–2, 7–9; Closed mid-
Nov to end Dec and 2 weeks in Feb
🍽 L €40, D €60, Wine €14

⊖LA BASTIDE DE
MOUSTIERS
Chemin de Quinson, 04360
Moustiers-Sainte-Marie
Tel 04 92 70 47 47
www.bastide-moustiers.com
This cottage turned four-star
inn houses one of chef Alain
Ducasse's restaurants. The
12 bedrooms are named
after local produce and each
is decorated according to its
name—yellow and green for
the Olive suite, for example.
Treat yourself to the
Mediterranean cuisine in
the restaurant.
💶 €230–€295, excluding breakfast
🛏 12
♿ 🌳 Outdoor

NICE

🍴L'ÂNE ROUGE
7 quai des Deux-Emmanuel,
06300 Nice
Tel 04 93 89 49 63
www.anerougenice.com
Chef Michel Devilliers likes to
cook fish, and his creations are
tantalizing: succulent scallops

roasted with chorizo, fresh and
dried tomatoes and thyme
flower. The warm, elegant
interior has beamed ceilings,
bright pictures hung on ochre
walls, comfortable high-back
padded chairs and a large fireplace. The flower-filled terrace
has a view of the harbour.
🕐 Mon–Tue and Fri–Sun noon–2.30,
7.30–10, Thu 7.30–10
🍽 L €64, D €102, Wine €18

🍴CHÂTEAU DES OLLIÈRES
39 avenue des Baumettes, 06000 Nice
Tel 04 92 15 77 99
www.chateaudesollieres.com
This former villa was converted
into a chateau by the Russian

Prince Alexeï Lobanov-
Rostowsky in 1885. Works of
art, drapes, candelabra and
period furniture all contribute
to the refined atmosphere. The
cuisine, with local produce
where possible, includes lamb
in an olive crust, crab mousse
on a bed of fresh herbs with a
tomato coulis and a citrus fruit
gratin with orange biscuit.
🕐 Daily noon–2.30, 7.30–9.30;
closed Jan
🍽 L €84, D €128, Wine €15

🍴CHEZ SIMON
St-Antoine-de-Ginestière, 06200, Nice
Tel 04 93 86 51 62
www.restaurantchezsimon.com
Five generations of the
same family have run this
establishment, once a coaching inn. Beamed ceilings,
basket-weave chairs, and a

plough-wheel candelabrum set
the traditional character of the
dining room. In fine weather,
choose the terrace, where you
can dine while watching a
game of *pétanque* (the local
form of bowls). The traditional
Provençal cuisine includes
stuffed mutton tripe and hake.
🕐 Daily 12.30–2, 7.30–10
🍽 L €56, D €56, Wine €15

🍴RESTAURANT BOCCACCIO
7 rue Masséna, 06000 Nice
Tel 04 93 87 71 76
www.boccaccio-nice.com
There are no less than six
dining rooms here, all of which
have a marine theme. One has

a large aquarium, another with
a vaulted wooden ceiling is
reminiscent of the interior of
a caravel (a historic small
ship), and model boats carry
on the theme. The menu
has Mediterranean seafood
dishes such as bass in a salty
crust, bouillabaisse and
seafood platters.
🕐 Daily noon–2.30, 7–11
🍽 L €90, D €90, Wine €24

⊜HÔTEL NEGRESCO

37 promenade des Anglais, 06000
Nice
Tel 04 93 16 64 00
www.hotel-negresco-nice.com
Built in 1912, this palace and
its signature black dome have
been given landmark status.
The interior is an ode to fine
art from the Renaissance to
the modern: In the Salon
Royal, Niki de Saint-Phalle's
'Nana,' an oversized sculpture
of a woman, sits happily
next to classical portraits.
The hotel has its own
private beach.
🍽 €213–€480, including breakfast
🛏 145 rooms, 24 suites
💺

⊜HÔTEL DE LA BUFFA

56 rue de la Buffa, 06000 Nice
Tel 04 93 88 77 35
www.hotel-buffa.com
This two-star hotel is in an
early 20th-century building,
close to the Promenade des
Anglais and the sea. The
unpretentious interior is
inviting and bedrooms have
Provençal fabrics, a minibar,
safe and satellite TV. The
street-facing rooms have
double glazing and there's
private car parking.
🍽 €65–€69, excluding breakfast (€7)
🛏 14
💺

PIOLENC

⊜LA MANDARINE

Le Grand Colombier, 84420 Piolenc
Tel 04 90 29 69 99
www.orangerie.net
Micky and Gérard de la
Roque's guesthouse is in a
lovely Provençal cottage 4km
(2.5 miles) northwest of
Orange. The four bedrooms
have been tastefully decorated
and the style of each is unique,
with souvenirs from Asia in
the Colonial room and the
atmosphere of a boudoir in
the Cézanne room. The hosts
also run L'Orangerie restaurant,
a few miles away.
🍽 €69–€78, excluding breakfast
🛏 4
🏊 Outdoor

ST-ANDIOL

⊜LE BERGER DES ABEILLES

RD74E, 13670, St-Andiol
Tel 04 90 95 01 91
www.berger-abeilles.com
The warmth of the south is
tangible in the fabric of this
two-star hotel in a Provençal
cottage. Typical of the region
are the soft green, yellow
and burgundy hues which
dominate in the bedrooms,
some of which have antique
furniture. All of the rooms are
named after women in the
hosts' family (Alexia, Anaïs,
Maya). There's private parking
and a garden where you can
have dinner.
🕒 Closed Jan to mid-Feb
🍽 €77–€90, excluding breakfast
🛏 8

SAINTES-MARIES-DE-LA-MER

⊜HOSTELLERIE DE CACHAREL

Route de Cacharel, 13460
Saintes-Maries-de-la-Mer
Tel 04 90 97 95 44
www.hotel-cacharel.com
All around are marshes and
ponds inhabited by pink
flamingos, as the hotel lies at
the heart of a nature reserve.
The Camargue is famous for
its horses, and this *hostellerie*

has its own stables. In this
1950s white house, typical of
the region, there's a large
fireplace, tiled floor and fine
furniture in the bedrooms,
which are decorated with
pictures of the surrounding
landscape and don't have TV.
There is no restaurant, but you
can order a dinner platter.
🍽 €125
🛏 16
🏊 Outdoor

ST-RÉMY-DE-PROVENCE

⊜LE BISTROT DES ALPILLES

15 boulevard Mirabeau, 13210
St-Rémy-de-Provence
Tel 04 90 92 09 17
www.bistrotdesalpilles.com
This regional bistro is an
institution in town and has

large paintings of toreadors,
comfortable wall seats and
wooden chairs. The brasserie
food betrays a southern
accent. Try aubergine (eggplant) and goat's cheese
terrine, Mediterranean tuna
with a vegetable reduction
and tapenade or the grilled
beef. For dessert, don't
miss the lavender, thyme
and rose sorbets.
🕒 Daily noon–2, 7.30–10
🍽 L €30, D €60, Wine €15

ST-TROPEZ

⊜LE CAFÉ

Place des Lices, 83990 St-Tropez
Tel 04 94 97 44 69
www.lecafe.fr
Some think the soul of the
real St-Tropez lies within these
four walls. It's on a square in
the heart of the town and has
one of the best terraces. Enjoy
Provençal cuisine while
watching the activity of the

market or a game of boules. Try
monkfish soup with garlic
mayonnaise cream, beef in
vintage port with baby carrots
or pastry nougat glacé.
🕒 Daily 12–2.30, 7.30–11
🍽 L €62, D €84, Wine €18

HÔTEL BYBLOS
Avenue Paul Signac, 83990 St-Tropez
Tel 04 94 56 68 00
www.byblos.com
This palace has true luxury in a Provençal style and is popular with the jet set. Behind an ochre and blue façade is a

sophisticated interior decorated with local materials. You'll find antiques and local fabrics and around every corner, ceramic or wrought-iron artwork. The services are those you would expect from a luxury hotel.
🕐 Closed Nov to mid-Apr
🍴 €350–€660, excluding breakfast (€30)
🛏 52 rooms, 43 suites
🔲 🏊 Outdoor 🎾

SISTERON
LA CITADELLE
126 rue Saunerie, 04200 Sisteron
Tel 04 92 61 13 52
This is a great place to try local dishes, including stuffed mutton tripe, Sisteron lamb and frozen nougat. Chef Jean-François Destremont is a master at cooking fish the Provençal way, with dishes such as sea bass with garlic mayonnaise, and, in season, there's a game menu.
🕐 Daily noon–2.30, 7.30–10; closed Wed Oct–end May
🍴 L €30, D €56, Wine €7

TARASCON
ABBAYE ST-MICHEL DE FRIGOLET
Communauté des Prémontrés, Abbaye St-Michel de Frigolet, 13150, Tarascon
Tel 04 90 95 70 07
www.frigolet.com
At the heart of a 12th-century abbey, still occupied by a monastic community, this restaurant has an exceptional setting. The two dining rooms, one with a beamed ceiling, are both Provençal in style, with

tiled floors and yellow and burgundy tablecloths. In fine weather, you can dine out on the terrace with its wonderful views of the surrounding mountain scenery. The cuisine has a regional accent, and many dishes incorporate the local Frigolet liqueur. Try the red mullet with a basil mayonnaise and Frigolet liqueur crème brûlée.
🕐 Daily noon–1.30, 7–8.45
🍴 L €25, D €37, Wine €10

VILLEFRANCHE-SUR-MER
HÔTEL WELCOME
1 quai Courbet, 06230 Villefranche-sur-Mer
Tel 04 93 76 27 62
www.welcomehotel.com
The Welcome Hotel is in a modern building overlooking the bay. All bedrooms have balconies—their picturesque views once seduced writer and film director Jean Cocteau, a former guest. The interior has a contemporary elegance, with low armchairs.

The bedrooms are bright, some decorated with floral fabrics. There is no restaurant.
🕐 Closed mid-Nov to Christmas
🍴 €155–€290, excluding breakfast (€8)
🛏 37
🔲

Monaco

HÔTEL HERMITAGE
Square Beaumarchais, 98000 Monaco
Tel 377 92 16 40 00
www.montecarloresort.com
This Belle-Époque luxury hotel faces the Mediterranean Sea. It has a panoramic restaurant, Le Vistamar, and you can have breakfast under a glass ceiling designed by Gustave Eiffel. The services are those you

would expect of a luxury hotel, including a helicopter shuttle service between Monaco and Nice airport. There is direct access to Les Thermes Marins de Monaco Spa and Health Resort.
🍴 €480–€750, excluding breakfast (€32)
🛏 229
🔲 🏊 Outdoor 🎾

LE LOUIS XV
Hôtel de Paris, place du Casino, 98000 Monaco
Tel 377 92 16 29 76
www.alain-ducasse.com
The height of luxury, this restaurant is within the majestic Hôtel de Paris, which was built in 1864. Here, Alain Ducasse, one of France's most celebrated chefs, practises his art. The Mediterranean-inspired menu changes with the seasons and is in

themes, including the kitchen garden, hunting, the farm, the sea and rivers. The luxurious Louis XV-style interior provides the backdrop to a feast fit for a king.
🕐 Thu–Mon noon–2, 7.30–9.30; Wed dinner in Jul and Aug; closed 3 weeks Dec and 2 weeks Mar
🍴 L €240, D €272, Wine €90

EATING

Duck breast and goose liver rule the roost in foie gras and *confit de canard* country. Pâté finds its way into almost every dish, as do the wild mushrooms and truffles from the forest floors of Périgord and Limousin. Plums and prunes are staple ingredients of Gascon cuisine and often blend with the farmyard fare served both in rustic inns and gastronomic dining rooms. The woods are home to wild boar, and the hunting season brings game to menus throughout southwest France. Walnuts abound too, and make a superb liqueur, only found at Brive La Gaillard. The most famous of the strong tipples are Armagnac and Cognac, and these too find their way onto the plate almost as often as into the glass, in some unforgettable dishes. Bordeaux is the capital of claret country and you can learn about the classic wines at the city's wine schools and the surrounding estates. Less expensive, but still worth discovering, are the wines of Bergerac.

STAYING

The business activity of Toulouse and Bordeaux guarantees a range of quality hotels in these cities, and the seaside resorts have grand hotels of the old school as well as welcoming budget venues. Holiday villages abound, catering for families and those who like sports, and you are rarely more than 20 minutes from a campsite.

Aquitaine

AGEN

CHÂTEAU LASSALLE
Château de Lassalle, Brimont, 47310 Laplume
Tel 05 53 95 10 58
This 18th-century mansion is now a stylish hotel, with stone houses arranged around a courtyard. It is surrounded by a landscaped park overlooking a valley. Each of the spacious bedrooms is decorated with elegant antiques, and all have park views. The restaurant has an excellent reputation.

Château Lassalle is 7km (4 miles) southwest of Agen via the N21 and D268.
€90–€200, excluding breakfast (€8)
13 rooms, 4 suites
Outdoor

BAZAS

LES REMPARTS
Espace Mauvezin, place de la Cathédrale, 33430 Bazas
Tel 05 56 25 95 24
This cathedral town is home to its own breed of cattle, the Bazadaise, and you'll find beef prepared in a range of ways, including barbecued with vine cuttings. Come to this restaurant for the best *entrecôte à la bordelaise* (steak with shallots), the dish that is synonymous with Bazas, and a panoramic view over the expansive Jardins de Sultan. If you want something other than beef, try the amazing Grignols capon with ceps.
Tue–Sun noon–3, 7.30–midnight, Easter–end Sep; Tue–Sat noon–3, 7.30–midnight, Sun noon–3 rest of year
L €26, D €45, Wine €15

BIARRITZ

HÔTEL MAISON GARNIER
29 rue Gambetta, 64200, Biarritz
Tel 05 59 01 60 70
A small family-run hotel, in a quiet part of town in a restored 19th-century town house. On offer is a large, comfortable lounge with parquet flooring and a log fire. The rooms have cable TV, a shower-room and Internet access.
€80–€110, excluding breakfast (€9)
7

BORDEAUX

LA BEL CANTO
20 allées de Tourny, 33000 Bordeaux
Tel 05 56 81 61 61
Owned by a Neapolitan named Antonio, this trattoria has the area's best Italian cuisine: enormous pizzas, mounds of Parma ham, wonderful tiramisù and a good selection of Italian wines. Best of all, the restaurant is opposite the Grand Théâtre, and on Thursday, Friday and Saturday nights, singers appearing at the theatre come in and perform opera classics for diners.
Daily noon–3, 6.30–1am
L €20, D €60, Wine €10

LE CAFÉ DES ARTS
138 cours Victor-Hugo, 33000 Bordeaux
Tel 05 56 91 07 89
Usually packed with people who come to watch the world go by from the streetside terrace over a cup or two of coffee, this is a good place to grab a meal or a snack at any time of the day. Although the clientele tends to be young and trendy, the menu is traditional, with bistro dishes such as tasty salads, omelettes, steak tartare and scallops.
Daily 8am–2am
L €25, D €35, Wine €8

LE FRANCHOUILLARD
21 rue Maucoudinat, 33000 Bordeaux
Tel 05 56 44 95 86
In the traffic-free heart of Bordeaux, this restaurant has *France à la carte*, with a menu that changes every few weeks so you can sample the cuisine of different regions of the

country. It's reasonably priced and popular with students and a young Bordelaise crowd, and is worth a visit for the atmosphere as much as for the food. The highlight of the evening comes around 11.30, when song sheets are handed out and the entire restaurant sings classic French tunes. A fun, but smoky experience.
Mon–Sat noon–3, 6pm–1am
L €40, D €50, Wine €10

EATING AND STAYING

RESTAURANT DE FROMAGES BAUD ET MILET

19 rue Huguerie,
33000 Bordeaux
Tel 05 56 79 05 77

This small, family-run restaurant is a dairy-lover's paradise, with a selection of more than 200 kinds of cheese. The owner's passion for cheese is infectious and he will readily explain his cheeses to you in detail. The menu has a choice of an all-you-can-eat cheese platter as well as a selection of traditional cheese-based dishes including *tartiflette* (potato gratin with cheese) and *raclette* (melted cheese served with potatoes, pickles and pearl onions).

Mon–Sat 11.30–2, 7–11
L €28, D €40, Wine €10

LA TABLE DU PAIN

Place du Parlement, 33000 Bordeaux
Tel 05 56 81 01 00

With generous portions, long wooden tables, newspapers and lots of young customers, this laid-back patisserie is one of those relaxed breakfast places seldom found outside Paris. For €15 you get a mound of ham, eggs, breads, pastries, yoghurt, coffee, juice and even a glass of wine. The range of pastries is amazing and includes traditional sweets like enormous *pain au chocolat* (chocolate-filled croissants) as well as healthier carrot muffins. This café has sister establishments in Paris and Barcelona.

Daily 8.30–7.30
Brunch €15

HOTEL DE FRANCE

7 rue Franklin, 33000 Bordeaux
Tel 05 56 48 24 11

This basic but clean hotel is a great practical choice for those on a budget. All of the rooms have a private bathroom and

the hotel's position at the edge of the traffic-free quarter in the middle of Bordeaux makes it easy to get to the city's many attractions.

€48, excluding breakfast
20

LES 4 SOEURS

6 cours de XXX Juillet,
33000 Bordeaux
Tel 05 57 81 19 20

A characterful hotel with a great location close to the middle of the city. Some of the rooms are small and basic, but there are a few larger rooms overlooking the square. Some bedrooms sleep up to five people, making them a good choice for families.

€60–€85, excluding breakfast
34

BOULIAC

LE CAFÉ DE L'ESPÉRANCE

10 rue de l'Esplanade,
33270 Bouliac
Tel 05 56 20 52 16

This bistro, on the main road the small village of Bouliac, is attached to the Hôtel St-James, but worth seeking out for a meal even if you are not a resident. Its reputation is well deserved and the wine list is first class. There's a traditional bistro atmosphere, with a fireplace inside and a terrace for the summer, making this a pleasant place to eat.

Daily 12.20–3.30, 7.30–11
L €38 (wine included), D €70, Wine €20

CADILLAC

AU FIN GOURMAND

6 place de la République, 33410
Cadillac
Tel 05 56 62 90 80

Just the location of this restaurant—right in the heart of 13th-century Cadillac, overlooking the town's walled square—makes it worth a visit. The food lives up to the name of the restaurant, with a vast array of regional cuisine and something to suit all tastes and budgets. Traditional dishes of the southwest include foie gras and pigeon in red wine, entrecôte with shallots and seafood.

SPECIAL

HÔTEL ST-JAMES

3 place Camille Hostein,
33270 Bouliac
Tel 05 57 97 06 00
www.saintjames-bouliac.com

A member of the Relais & Châteaux group, this modern hotel is one of the best in the Bordeaux area. The well-kept village of Bouliac is just 15 minutes southeast of Bordeaux, with an amazing view over the city and vineyards. The hotel, built only 10 years ago, was designed by architect Jean Nouvel to be in harmony with the environment. Bedrooms have Bang and Olufsen audio-video equipment, electric blinds and views over the heated swimming pool and the city below. The three restaurants, ranging from bistro to formal, are renowned as being among the best in the area (see left).

€168–€297, excluding breakfast
15 rooms, 3 suites
Outdoor

Tue–Sat noon–3.30, 7–9, Sun noon–3
L €20, D €30, Wine €10

CAMPING MUNICIPAL DU CADILLAC

Rue du Port,
33410 Cadillac
Tel 05 56 62 72 98

This two-star campsite, on the banks of the river Garonne, is a great find. Plenty of shady pitches and a children's play area make it ideal for families. The 13th-century fortified town of Cadillac and its castle are close by. A swimming pool, snack bar and cinema are a short walk away.

Closed Nov–end May
€8 for 2 people, a tent and a car; caravan €3; electricity €1.50
30 pitches

CHAMPAGNE-DE-BELAIR

⊜LE MOULIN DU ROC
24530, Champagne-de-Belair
Tel 05 53 02 86 00
www.moulinduroc.com
On the bank of the river
Dronne 6km (4 miles)
northeast of Brantôme, this
17th-century mill was once
used to produce walnut oil.
Today it is a small, stylish hotel
where each room is named
after food. Stay in Noisette
(hazelnut), Maïs (corn) or
Colza (rapeseed oil). The ivy-
covered building looks out
over an expansive park where
you can swim, go boating, fish
or play tennis. Other activities
such as golf, karting, canoeing
and horse-riding are all nearby.
Alain and Maryse Gardillou are
wonderful hosts, and their
restaurant serves plentiful
amounts of local produce.
🕐 Closed Jan, Feb
💶 €120–€174, excluding breakfast
🛏 10 rooms, 2 suites and 1 apartment
♿ 🏊 Outdoor

GIRONDE-SUR-DROPT

ⓘLES TROIS CÈDRES
33190 Gironde-sur-Dropt, on main
N113 road
Tel 05 56 71 10 70

In an old-fashioned family-run
hotel 4km (2.5miles) west of
La Réole, this restaurant serves
grilled sea bass with superb
fresh pasta on its terrace
shaded by cedar trees. There
are great views of the valley
and the food is simple but
well executed. The relaxed
atmosphere makes a
long lunch an agreeable
proposition.
🕐 Mon–Fri noon–3, 7–10, Sat 7–10,
Sun noon–3; closed 1–15 Jan
💶 L €30, D €45, Wine €15

LÈGE CAP FERRET

ⓘCHEZ HORTENSE
Avenue du Sémaphore, 33970
Lège Cap Ferret
Tel 05 56 60 62 56
Cap Ferret is the most sought
after spot on the Bassin
d'Arcachon. Chez Hortense
is right at the end of the
peninsula, overlooking the
bay, and is best approached
by boat from Arcachon. It's
pricey but excellent and
serves nothing but the
freshest seafood. Specials
include mussels in cream,
lobster with cream and
vermouth, Arcachon Bay
oysters and *chaudrée*, a fish
soup with white wine. A
real experience.
🕐 Daily noon–11, Jun–end Aug;
Sat–Sun noon–11, rest of year
💶 L €60, D €80, Wine €15

MARGAUX

⊜LE PAVILLON DE
MARGAUX
3 rue Georges Mandel,
33460 Margaux
Tel 05 57 88 77 54
This family-run hotel is
excellent value for money and
right in the heart of the pretty,
well-kept town of Margaux,
an ideal base for exploring
the numerous vineyards of the
Médoc. The rooms (nine
superior and five standard) are
all named after different wine

estates, with bottles of that
vineyard's wine in the room.
The restaurant is well priced,
although the wine list can
be expensive. If arriving by car,
take the D2 from Bordeaux
into Margaux. The hotel is in
the middle of town.
💶 €79–€108, excluding breakfast
🛏 14
♿

PAU

⊜HÔTEL LE POSTILLON
Place de Verdun, 10 cours Camou,
64000 Pau
Tel 05 59 72 83 00
www.hotel-le-postillon.fr
A traditional, family-run hotel,
decorated in French provincial
style and with a flower-filled
courtyard. Rooms, which all
have a shower room, are
comfortable and a few have a
balcony overlooking the pretty
courtyard garden. Their
reasonable prices keep the
hotel consistently full (rates
do not change for the
high season), so advance
reservations are advised.
There is no restaurant here
but you'll find plenty nearby.
💶 €42–€51, excluding breakfast (€4)
🛏 28
♿

PAUILLAC

⊜CHÂTEAU CORDEILLAN-
BAGES
Route des Châteaux, 33250 Pauillac
Tel 05 56 59 24 24
www.cordeillanbages.com

Next to the Château Lynch
Bages vineyard, this four-star
hotel, renovated in 1985,
has been decorated in red
and green shades to reflect
the surrounding vineyards.
The spacious rooms are
comfortable, and the
outstanding restaurant, which
has a huge wine list, serves
regional cuisine. The estate has
weekend or five-day wine
tasting courses at the École
du Bordeaux. The hotel can
arrange access to the nearby
swimming pool, tennis court
or golf course and the coast is
less than half an hour away
by car.
🕐 Closed 15 Dec–end Jan
💶 €165–€256, excluding breakfast
🛏 23 rooms and 1 suite
♿

EATING AND STAYING

PUJOLS

🔴 LA TOQUE BLANCHE
La Toque Blanche, 47300 Pujols
Tel 05 53 49 00 30
Set among plum trees, this cosy restaurant provides panoramic views across medieval Pujols, with its beautiful white walls. The restaurant serves some of the most delicate duck dishes imaginable, from grilled with preserved pears to traditional foie gras. The extensive wine list may add to the cost of the final bill.
🕐 Daily noon–3.30, 7–11, Aug; Wed–Sat noon–3.30, 7–11, Sun noon–3.30, Tue 7–11, rest of year
🍽 L €40, D €60, Wine €10

RIBÉRAC

🟢 JANE AND JOHN EDWARDS
Pauliac, Celles, 24600 Ribérac
Tel 05 53 91 97 45
John and Jane lovingly restored this guesthouse, which they have owned for nearly two decades. Each of the rooms has beautiful wooden floors and carefully selected pieces of furniture. Home-cooked meals are served at a huge wooden communal table and vegetarians are catered for. In summer, take a dip in the stone plunge pool in the garden, let the children play in the paddling pool or go walking in the area.
🍽 €46–€53
🛏 5 rooms and 1 suite

ST-ÉMILION

🔴 CHEZ GERMAINE
13 place du Clocher, 33330, St-Émilion
Tel 05 57 74 49 34
Right in the heart of the beautiful village of St-Émilion, this restaurant is right beneath the church bells, with the stone dining room reflecting the architecture of the village. The emphasis is on traditional dishes, including foie gras, sweetmeats, scallops with vegetables, fish soup and coq au vin. The macaroons, a special dish of St-Émilion, are unbelievably light. Prices may seem high, but the different prix-fixe menus are good value.
🕐 Daily noon–3, 6–10
🍽 L €20, D €35, Wine €12

ST-JEAN-DE-LUZ

🟢 LE PARC VICTORIA
5 rue Cepe, 64500, St-Jean-de-Luz
Tel 05 59 26 78 78
www.parcvictoria.com
St-Jean-de-Luz is a pretty coastal town in the Basque region, with a host of things to do, from sport, theatre, galleries and shopping to eating. This is one of the loveliest hotels in the region and is in an unusual 19th-century building with beautiful light and airy rooms with art deco style furniture. The four suites are great for families and have their own garden. The restaurant, with a wonderfully inventive menu, has views over the parkland surrounding the hotel. Nearby there is a spa and the chance to go diving in the Atlantic.
🕐 Closed 15 Nov–15 Mar
🍽 €155–€380, excluding breakfast
🛏 8 rooms, 8 suites
♿ 🏊 Outdoor

ST-JEAN-PIED-DE-PORT

🔴 LES PYRÉNÉES
19 place du Général-de-Gaulle, 64220 St-Jean-Pied-de-Port
Tel 05 59 37 01 01
This family-run restaurant in a luxuriously renovated old coaching inn is worth the expense. The chef is knowledgeable about his craft, and he keeps the menu simple. You'll find plenty of imaginative uses of local produce, from truffles and Pyrenean lamb dishes to anchovies, sardines, cod and tuna from the Bay of Biscay.
🕐 Wed–Mon noon–3, 7–12; closed 5–28 Jan, 20 Nov–22 Dec
🍽 L €76, D €120, Wine €22

TRÉMOLAT

🔴 BISTRO LE VIEUX LOGIS
24510, Trémolat
Tel 05 53 22 80 69
This bistro is part of a luxury hotel which was formerly a tobacco farm. The open kitchen allows you to watch the food being prepared. On a warm evening, you can eat on the terrace under the linden trees. It would be hard to find better food or service at this price and the desserts, such as the enormous portion of delicious chocolate mousse, are amazing. There is also a

small gift shop with food from the Dordogne region. Reservations are essential.
🕐 Daily 12.20–3.30, 7.30–11.30
🍽 L €23, D €30, Wine €12

VITRAC

🟢 LE DOMAINE DE ROCHEBOIS
Route de Montfort, 24200 Vitrac
Tel 05 53 31 52 52
www.rochebois.com
Bedrooms in this beautiful four-star, neoclassical-style hotel give views of the surrounding gardens and the Dordogne valley. Facilities include a nine-hole golf course, swimming pool, fitness area, billiards room and tennis court on site and ballooning and canoeing nearby. The restaurant is home to chef Christophe Ochler's creations. Vitrac is 8km (5 miles) south of Sarlat-la-Canéda.
🕐 Closed Nov–end Mar
🍽 €150–€450, excluding breakfast
🛏 34 rooms, 6 suites
♿ 🏊 Outdoor🌳

Poitou-Charentes

ANGOULÊME

🟢 IBIS ANGOULÊME
Route N10, 16000 Angoulême
Tel 05 45 69 16 16
www.ibishotel.com
This budget hotel, just outside town, makes a good base for exploring Angoulême's ramparts and medieval quarter. It is an excellent budget choice with large, comfortable rooms. The country-style restaurant has an exposed-beam ceiling, and opens onto a garden terrace. The fixed-price menu is €15 and the children's menu is €6.
🍽 €53, excluding breakfast (€6)
🛏 62
♿

ÎLE D'OLÉRON

🔴 AUBERGE DE LA CAMPAGNE
D734, 17310, St-Pierre-d'Oléron
Tel 05 46 47 25 42
You'll find quiet refuge away from the windswept attractions of the island at this rustic restaurant, on the island's main road, the D734. The inn is in converted farm outbuildings, where islanders

and visitors enjoy traditional cuisine and an outstanding wine list. The garden and terrace are good in summer and there's a children's menu at €15.

🕐 Tue–Sat 12.15–1.45, 7.15–9, Sun 12.15–1.45; Closed Apr 15–end Oct

🍴 L €50, D €120, Wine €18

⊖ NOVOTEL THALASSO OLÉRON

Plage de Gatseau, 17370 St-Trojan-les-Bains
Tel 05 46 76 02 46
www.novotel.com

Just outside the town of St-Trojan-les-Bains, the Novotel is set in a quiet pine forest overlooking a beach on the southern coast of Île d'Oléron. It has both ocean and forest views and an idyllic quiet setting. There's a spa, a heated saltwater pool overlooking the sea, exercise facilities, and an excellent restaurant, Le Pertuis. You can also use the complimentary bicycles to travel round the island.

🛏 €120–€150
🛌 80
🔇 🏊 Indoor 🐾

ÎLE DE RÉ

⊖ LE RICHELIEU

44 avenue de la Plage, 17630 La Flotte en Ré
Tel 05 46 09 60 70
www.hotel-le-richelieu.com

In the tradition of grand luxury hotels, the building itself is an attraction, with about half of the guest rooms having terraces that put you right over the sea. There is a spa with water-based therapies, tennis courts, a huge outdoor pool open in summer, and La Brise restaurant.

🕐 Closed 5 Jan–5 Feb
🛏 €140–€415, excluding breakfast (€20)
🛌 40
🔇 🏊 Outdoor

IRLEAU LE VANNEAU

⊖ LE PARADIS CHAMBRE D'HÔTE

29 Sainte-Sabine, 79270 Irleau le Vanneau
Tel 05 49 35 33 95
www.maraispoitevinchambredhote.com

This bed-and-breakfast is in a beautiful old house with blue-painted shutters in the heart of Venise Verte, Marais Poitevin.

It's set in its own grounds where you can fish or take a boat out on the private lake. Each bedroom has a shower room, there's a communal kitchen and a large covered terrace.

🕐 Closed mid-Nov to end Mar
🛏 €42
🛌 5

ROCHEFORT-SUR-MER

🍴 LA CORDERIE ROYALE

Rue Audebert, 17300 Rochefort-sur-Mer
Tel 05 46 99 35 35
www.corderieroyale-hotel.com

On the banks of the Charente river, this restaurant offers a light and breezy dining area with terrific views of the busy river as well as the gardens alongside. There's first-class service and a variety of seafood, meat and poultry dishes, including duck with pan-fried foie gras, clams filled with parsley butter, pan-fried skate with citrus fruit and beef in a chanterelle cream sauce. All of the dishes include ingredients from local markets.

🕐 Mon–Sat noon–2.30, 7–10, Apr–end Nov; Tue–Sat noon–2.30, 7–10 rest of year; closed Feb
🍴 L €36, D €84, Wine €13

LA ROCHELLE

🍴 LA MARÉE

1 avenue de Colmar, 17000 La Rochelle
Tel 05 46 41 19 92

Reserve ahead, as this seafood restaurant is very popular. There are three dining areas: the conservatory overlooking the harbour and the two comfortable dining rooms inside. There are more than a dozen different types of shellfish on offer, plus a wide choice of fish dishes, depending on what's in season.

🕐 Daily 11.30–2.30, 7–11
🍴 L €21, D €21, Wine €12

🍴 LA MARINE

30 quai Duperre, 17000 La Rochelle
Tel 05 46 41 08 68
www.lechaponfin-moissac.com

This brasserie, with wonderful views of the old port, has an early 1900s atmosphere that gives the place a traditional feel. It serves food and drink from early morning to late at night. There's a choice of brasserie cuisine and local seafood dishes. The oysters and *tarte du jour* are recommended.

🕐 Daily 7am–2am
🍴 L €24, D €48, Wine €10

⊖ FRANCE ANGLETERRE ET CHAMPLAIN

20 rue Rambaud, 17000 La Rochelle
Tel 05 46 41 23 99
www.france-champlain.com

Once a private residence, this hotel, near place Verdun, has a great location as the old port, the cathedral and the natural history museum are all easily accessible. The lovely, quiet garden and the superbly furnished and spacious rooms are premier attractions. There is no restaurant, but the bar and foyer are perfect for a late-night drink. Covered parking is available.

🛏 €58–€122, excluding breakfast (€12)
🛌 36 rooms (6 non-smoking), 4 suites
🔇

SAINTES

🍴 LE BISTRO GALANT

28 rue St-Michel, 17100 Saintes
Tel 05 46 93 08 51

Tucked away on a quiet pedestrian street in the middle of town, this cheery, bright little bistro makes an excellent lunch stop. The eclectic menu changes daily and has tasty meat dishes such as sirloin steak with spicy pepper sauce.

🕐 Tue–Sat noon–1.45, 7.15–9, Sun noon–1.45
🍴 L €20, D €40, Wine €12

Limousin

ARGENTAT

⊖CHADIOT
Chadiot, 19400 Argentat
Tel 05 55 28 81 99
If you like fly fishing then this bed-and-breakfast is for you, as the owner runs courses on the Dordogne river. The building itself dates from the 18th century and is in the hollow of a sunny valley. Breakfast is included and you can also have dinner with the family and other guests if you reserve.
€41
3

BLANZAC

⊖ROUFFIGNAC
Rouffignac, RN145, 87300 Blanzac
Tel 05 55 68 02 14
At this bed-and-breakfast on a farm, you are close to the mountains of Mortemart, Bellac and Blond. The rooms are perfect for families as they

all have private bathroom and sleep four or five people. There is a mezzanine over a large sitting room, a TV room and a games room with a billiard table. Meals are generous and use produce from the farm.
€41
5

GENTIOUX

⊖LA COMMANDERIE DE PALLIER
23340 Gentioux
Tel 05 55 67 91 73
www.pallier23.com
History buffs will love this 18th-century knights' fortress, with its living room, TV lounge, library, medieval garden and landscaped grounds. You'll find plenty of outdoor activities within 15km (10 miles). A meal costs about €15.
Closed mid-Nov to mid-Mar
€58
5

Midi-Pyrénées

ALBI

⊖HÔTEL GEORGE V
29 avenue Maréchal Joffre, 81000, Albi
Tel 05 63 54 24 16
www.hotelgeorgev.com
This small hotel in a redbrick house has a welcoming entrance. It's near the station and a short stroll from the cathedral. The garden is a wonderful place to have coffee in fine weather and the spacious, bright rooms have high ceilings and simple decoration.
€32–€39, excluding breakfast (€5.50)
9

CAHORS

⊕MARIE COLLINE
173 rue Georges Clemenceau, 46000 Cahors
Tel 05 65 35 59 96
A wonderful vegetarian restaurant with a great choice of dishes, and seats outside for sunny days. The menu includes at least two daily specials, plus many smaller dishes and desserts. Dishes include *gratin au chèvre* (melted goat's cheese) and *clafoutis aux fruits rouges* (red fruits cake).
Tue–Fri 12.30–3.30; closed Aug
L €30, D €50, Wine €10

LOURDES

⊖CHAMBRE D'HÔTE, MME VIVES
28 route de Bartres, 65100 Loubajac
Tel 05 62 94 44 17
If you have a car and feel like escaping the bustle of Lourdes in high season, this peaceful house, 5km (3 miles) north of town, is ideal. The rooms are modern, with rustic furniture. Most have stunning views of the Pyrenees and some have their own terrace. The dining room has a farmhouse feel, with a fireplace, beams and old furniture. A hearty breakfast and dinner is included in the price.
Closed Nov to mid-Feb
€63
6

TOULOUSE

⊖FOYER DES JEUNES TRAVAILLEURS
2 avenue Yves Brunaud, 31500 Toulouse
Tel 05 34 30 42 80
For great value, stay in Toulouse's answer to a youth hostel, within walking distance of the middle of town. It has clean rooms and studios, a TV and games rooms and a communal kitchen.
€12 per person
42
Jolimont

⊖HÔTEL DES BEAUX-ARTS
1 place du Pont Neuf, 31000 Toulouse
Tel 05 34 45 42 42
www.hotelsdecharmetoulouse.com
An intimate three-star hotel in an 18th-century building with stunning views of the river. Bedrooms have satellite TV and minibar and some rooms, including the junior suite, have views of the Pont Neuf. Dine in the nearby Dix-Neuf restaurant, owned by the same group, and have drinks on the terrace in the summer.
€104–€168, excluding breakfast (€16)
19

Esquirol

TOUZAC

⊕LA SOURCE BLEUE
46700 Touzac
Tel 05 65 30 63 18
Truffle fans will love this 12th-century mill, in extensive grounds once owned by actress Marguerite Moreno, as, in season, truffles feature extensively on the menu. Outside truffle season there are plenty of other regional specials, such as foie gras.
Thu–Tue 12.30–3.30, 6.30–10.30; closed Jan, Feb
L €30, D €50, Wine €10

EATING AND STAYING

EATING

Take the opportunity to discover Corsica's excellent strong cheeses—look out for roadside and market stands selling Fromage de Berger. Hearty winter meat dishes use game, wild boar and pork, although a lot of meat is imported from the mainland. Fish is on every menu and dishes incorporate locally grown figs, olives, peaches, sweet chestnuts and almonds. Hotel wine lists have classic names from around France, but for a true taste of the island, and for an ideal complement to your meal, opt for the lesser-known country wines. You'll find grape varieties here (Nielluccio, Sciacarello and Vermentino) that you are unlikely to find anywhere else in France.

STAYING

The granite cliffs above crystal clear coves of transparent water have not been too spoiled by typical Mediterranean hotel building. Popular choices are family-run inns, specialist holiday villages with experts on hand for watersports, and *gîtes* (see www.gites-de-france.com).

AJACCIO

🍽 LE 20123

2 rue du Roi-de-Rome, 20000 Ajaccio
Tel 04 95 21 50 05
Probably the most popular restaurant in Ajaccio, Le 20123 brings excellent country cooking to the city. There is only one prix-fixe menu each day, but it's worth seeking out to try good Corsican dishes made from the freshest seasonal ingredients. The dining room is rustic and in summer tables fill the small square outside.

🕐 Tue–Sun 7.30pm–9.30; closed mid-Jan to mid-Feb
🍴 D €52, Wine €11

BARBAGGIO

🛏 U CASTELLU PIATTU

Pezzo Brietta, 20253 Barbaggio
Tel 04 95 37 28 64 or 06 24 33 18 32
www.castellu-piattu.fr.st/
This bed-and-breakfast, between St-Florent and Bastia, is in a vineyard in the countryside, with views of Sant Angelo mountain. The rooms are in a stone building near the owners' house and have a bathroom and independent access. They all open onto a patio with a pool. Table d'hôte meals are €18 per person. From St-Florent follow signs to Cathedrale du Nebbio. After 5km (3 miles) turn left towards Brietta, and U Castellu Piattu is 1.3km (about a mile) farther on.

🛏 €75
ℹ 5
🏊 Outdoor

CALENZANA

🛏 SCUZZULATAJO

Route de Calvi, 20214 Calenzano
Tel 04 95 60 15 53 or 06 86 44 88 34
www.calvi-gites.fr.st
A bed-and-breakfast in the countryside, just 5km (3 miles) from Calvi, on the road towards Calenzana. Rooms all have a bathroom and there's a big sitting room with a fireplace, a garden and a veranda. You can have a table d'hôte meal (€22 per person) if you reserve.

🛏 60
ℹ 3

CALVI

🍽 SANTA MARIA

Place de l'Église, 20260 Calvi
Tel 04 94 65 04 19
A popular informal restaurant where the tables tumble out into the church square below the fortress. The menu has French and Italian dishes and is good value. The friendly service and generous portions make this a good choice for family meals.

🍴 L €18, D €30, Wine €10

CENTURI

🍽 LE VIEUX MOULIN

Le Port, 20238, Centuri
Tel 04 95 35 60 15
www.le-vieux-moulin.net
Le Vieux Moulin, at the north-western corner of Cap Corse, is the perfect place for lunch while touring the peninsula.

From the terrace there are panoramic views of the sea and the tiny fishing port of Centuri. The menu concentrates on the freshest seafood brought ashore only a few yards away.

🕐 Daily noon–2.30, 7.30–9.30 Mar–end Oct
🍴 L €60, D €60, Wine €14

ERBALUNGA

🛏 HÔTEL CASTEL BRANDO

20222 Erbalunga
Tel 04 95 30 10 30
www.castelbrando.com
This family-owned hotel is by the sea in the tiny port of Erbalunga, a 19th century artists' colony, with some excellent restaurants and sandy beaches nearby. The three-star hotel is in a 19th-century mansion, with antique furnishings and mature gardens. Rooms are comfortable, although they vary in size.

🛏 €134–€160, excluding breakfast
ℹ 27
🅿 🏊 Outdoor 🖥

QUENZA

🍽 SOLE E MONTI

20122, Quenza
Tel 04 95 78 62 53
www.solemonti.com
Surrounded by a dramatic mountain landscape, this inn is on the road leading to Bavella. The agricultural tools hanging on the walls and wooden ceilings create a country look which is reflected in the food, with local dishes such as wild boar stew and roast trout.

🕐 Wed–Sun noon–1.45, 7.30–9.45 May–end Oct
🍴 L €46, D €70, Wine €10

SUARTONE

🛏 LA RONDINARA

20169 Suartone
Tel 04 95 70 43 15
www.rondinara.fr
A handily campsite, between Porto Vecchio and Bonifacito on the N198, that is close to a beach with water sports.

🕐 Closed Oct to mid-May
🍴 €6 per person, €3 tent, €4 caravan
🏊 Outdoor

Planning

CLIMATE

- **Paris** has cool winters and warm summers. The longest days are in June, when you're likely to find comfortable temperatures and the most sunshine. August can be hot, muggy and stormy.
- **The northwest**, affected by the Atlantic, is often rainy, with mild winters and cool summers.
- **The southwest** has hot summers.
- In **the mountains**, altitude is the main factor which affects the weather. The Vosges are hot in summer, the Massif Central is stormy and the southern Massif is dry. In contrast, the Cévennes get a lot of rain and the Northern Massif can become very hot.
- **The south of France** has hot, dry summers and warm, wet winters. Summer winds are cooling and gentle but the colder and fiercer Mistral, from the north, can swirl around for days, particularly in March and April.
- For up-to-date weather information for your region, look up www.meteo.fr/meteonet.

TIMES ZONES

City	Time difference	Time at 12 noon French time
Amsterdam	0	12 noon
Berlin	0	12 noon
Brussels	0	12 noon
Chicago	-7	5am
Dublin	-1	11am
Johannesburg	+1*	1pm
London	-1	11am
Madrid	0	12 noon
Montréal	-6	6am
New York	-6	6am
Perth, Australia	+7*	7pm
Rome	0	12 noon
San Francisco	-9	3am
Sydney	+9*	9pm
Tokyo	+8*	8pm

Clocks in France go forward one hour on the last Sunday in March, until the last Sunday in October.
* One hour less during Summer Time.

WHEN TO GO

- Spring is a good time to visit Paris, with blossom on the trees and the weather warming up. August is quiet, as many Parisians flee to other parts of France to escape the muggy heat. Some restaurants close for the whole month and there are fewer cultural activities. Autumn can be pleasant but hotel rooms may be hard to find as the trade fair season is in full swing. If you don't mind cooler winter weather, December can be magical, with the streets sparkling with Christmas lights.
- For other parts of France, what you plan to do when you're there will determine the best time to go. January, February and March are the months to go skiing in the Alps; sun-lovers should head to the Mediterranean in July and August; Strasbourg's huge Christmas market is popular; car fanatics go to Le Mans in June for the 24-hour endurance race.
- Tourist office websites (see page 416) should list festivals, activities and hotel prices.
- Many monuments and museums in France close on 1 January, 1 May, 1 November, 11 November and 25 December. Bus and train services are reduced on all national holidays (see page 414).

WHAT TO TAKE

- The key things to remember are travel and health insurance documents, money, credit cards and any medication you'll need. If you plan to drive in France, take your driving licence and, if using your own car, the vehicle registration and insurance certificates.
- If you go skiing, and in the sunnier months, you'll need sunscreen and sunglasses, even in the north.
- You may like to take smarter clothes for going out in the evening. Remember that when visiting churches you'll need to wear suitably modest clothes.
- A small rucksack or shoulder bag is useful for sightseeing. Bear in mind that these are attractive to pickpockets, so keep your money tucked away and an eye on your bag when you're in restaurants and other crowded places, especially in cities.
- Take the addresses and phone numbers of emergency contacts,

PLANNING

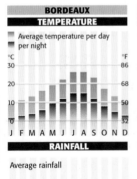

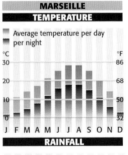

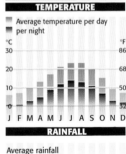

FRENCH EMBASSIES AND CONSULATES ABROAD		
Country	Address	Website
Australia	31 Market Street, St. Martin Tower, Level 26, Sydney, NSW 2000 Tel (02) 92 61 57 79	www.consulfrance-sydney.org
Canada	1 place Ville Marie, Bureau 2601, Montréal, Québec, H3B 4S3 Tel 514 878-4385	www.consulfrance-montreal.org
Ireland	36 Ailesbury Road, Ballsbridge, Dublin 4. Tel 01 260 1666	www.ambafrance.ie
New Zealand	34–42 Manners Street, Wellington, 12th floor, PO Box 11-343 Tel 644 384 25 55	www.ambafrance-nz.org
UK	21 Cromwell Road, London, SW7 2EN. Tel 020 7073 1200	www.frenchembassy.org.uk
US (Los Angeles)	10990 Wilshire Boulevard, Suite 300, Los Angeles, CA 90024 Tel 310/235-3200	www.consulfrance-losangeles.org
US (New York)	934 Fifth Avenue, New York, NY 10021. Tel 212/606-3600	www.consulfrance-newyork.org

including the numbers to call if your credit cards are stolen. Make photocopies of your passport, insurance documents and tickets, in case of loss. Keep a separate note of your credit card numbers in case you need to report a theft to the police.

● Visitors from the UK and US will need adaptors for electrical equipment (see page 404).

● There is a language section on pages 417–422 of this book, but if you are keen to communicate in French you may find a separate phrase book helpful.

● A first aid kit is a useful precaution.

● If you wear glasses, take a spare pair and your prescription.

● Bookshops in the main cities sell English-language books, and news-stands sell English-language papers, but it is generally less expensive to bring your own reading matter.

● Don't forget your camera! Camera film is widely available, but it is probably easier to take at least one film with you.

PASSPORTS AND VISAS

● UK, US and Canadian visitors need a passport, but not a visa, for stays of up to three months. You should have at least six months' validity remaining on your passport. Citizens of EU countries that have National Identity cards need either a passport or National Identity card.

● For more information about visa and passport requirements, look up the French tourist office website (www.franceguide.com) or the French Embassy (www.frenchembassy.org.uk or www.consulfrance-newyork.org).

● Before you travel, check visa and passport regulations since these are subject to change.

● Take a photocopy of the relevant pages of your passport to carry around with you, so you can leave your actual passport in your hotel safe. Always keep a separate note of your passport number and a photocopy of the

page that carries your details, in case of loss or theft.

LONGER STAYS

● UK and other EU citizens who want to stay longer than three months should apply for a *Carte de séjour* from the Préfecture de Police. US and Canadian visitors need a *Carte de séjour* and a visa. For information call the Immigration Department of the French Consulate (see chart).

TRAVEL INSURANCE

● Make sure you have full health and travel insurance before you set off.

● EU nationals receive reduced-cost health treatment with the relevant documentation (form E111 for British visitors), but full health and travel insurance is still advisable. For other visitors, full health insurance is a must.

● Check your insurer has a 24-hour helpline.

CUSTOMS

From another EU country

Below are the guidelines for the quantity of goods you can bring to France from another EU country, for personal use:

- 800 cigarettes
- 400 cigarillos
- 200 cigars
- 1 kg of smoking tobacco

- 110 litres of beer
- 10 litres of spirits
- 90 litres of wine (of which only 60 litres can be sparkling wine)
- 20 litres of fortified wine (such as port or sherry)

From a country outside the EU

You are entitled to the allowances shown below only if you travel with the goods and do not plan to sell them.

- 200 cigarettes or 100 cigarillos or 50 cigars or 250gms of tobacco
- 60cc/ml of perfume
- 250cc/ml of eau de toilette

- 2 litres of still table wine
- 1 litre of spirits or strong liqueurs over 22% volume; or 2 litres of fortified wine, sparkling wine or other liqueurs
- Up to €175 of all other goods

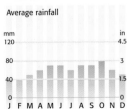

LYON
TEMPERATURE

■ Average temperature per day per night

°C °F
30 86
20 68
10 50
0 32

J F M A M J J A S O N D

RAINFALL

Average rainfall

mm in
120 4.5
80 3
40 1.5
0 0

J F M A M J J A S O N D

PLANNING

PRACTICALITIES

ELECTRICITY
- Voltage in France is 220 volts. Sockets take plugs with two round pins. UK electrical equipment will need an adaptor plug, which you can buy at airport and Eurostar terminals. American appliances using 110–120 volts will need an adaptor and a transformer. Equipment that is dual voltage should need only an adaptor.

LAUNDRY
- There are two options if you need a laundry service—a *laverie automatique* (laundrette) and a *pressing/nettoyage à sec* (dry-cleaners). Dry-cleaners are easier to find, but are more expensive. Some have an economy service, but this is not recommended for your best silk jacket.

MEASUREMENTS
- France uses the metric system. Road distances are measured in kilometres, fuel is sold by the litre and food is weighed in grams and kilograms.

LAVATORIES
- Today's modern unisex public lavatories are a vast improvement on previous facilities. Coin-operated and self-cleaning, you can find them in Paris and most large cities.
- In smaller towns and villages, free public lavatories can normally be found by the market square or near tourist offices, although cleanliness varies.
- The two most reliable options are to take advantage of facilities in museums or other visitor attractions (almost always a good standard) or in restaurants and cafés, though you should be a customer to use the facilities, so be sure to buy a drink.
- Ask for *les toilettes* or *WC* (pronounced *vay, say*).

SMOKING AREAS
- Smoking is banned in public places such as cinemas, buses and Métro stations.
- By law restaurants and cafés should provide a non-smoking section, although in reality it can be difficult to find a dining room, bar or café that is smoke-free.
- Some taxis display a no-smoking sign.

CONVERSION CHART		
From	**To**	**Multiply by**
Inches	Centimetres	2.54
Centimetres	Inches	0.3937
Feet	Metres	0.3048
Metres	Feet	3.2810
Yards	Metres	0.9144
Metres	Yards	1.0940
Miles	Kilometres	1.6090
Kilometres	Miles	0.6214
Acres	Hectares	0.4047
Hectares	Acres	2.4710
Gallons	Litres	4.5460
Litres	Gallons	0.2200
Ounces	Grams	28.35
Grams	Ounces	0.0353
Pounds	Grams	453.6
Grams	Pounds	0.0022
Pounds	Kilograms	0.4536
Kilograms	Pounds	2.205
Tons	Tonnes	1.0160
Tonnes	Tons	0.9842

CHILDREN
- The French *autoroute* system has a network of service stations at approximately 40km (25 mile) intervals, which sell food and have recreation areas. At intervals of about 10km (6 miles), there are *aires*, stopping areas with lavatories and recreation areas but no food or fuel, good for restless children to run around.
- Most restaurants welcome children, although not many have high chairs and children's menus are not common outside family-friendly tourist resorts, so it's probably best to aim for family-style bistros where facilities are better and staff are more helpful.
- If you need special facilities in your hotel, such as a cot, or a child seat in your rented car, reserve them in advance.
- For baby-changing facilities while out and about, try the restrooms in department stores and the larger museums.
- Supermarkets and pharmacies sell nappies (diapers) and baby food, although they are often closed on a Sunday so make sure you stock up.
- Entrance to museums is often free to young children.
- For babysitting services, you could try www.babysittingservices.com. Inter-Service Parents (*tel 01 44 93 44 93*) gives information on baby-sitting agencies and children's activities in Paris.

CLOTHING SIZES		

The chart below indicates how European clothing sizes compare with those in the UK and US.

UK	Europe	US	
36	46	36	
38	48	38	
40	50	40	SUITS
42	52	42	
44	54	44	
46	56	46	
48	58	48	
7	41	8	
7.5	42	8.5	
8.5	43	9.5	
9.5	44	10.5	SHOES
10.5	45	11.5	
11	46	12	
14.5	37	14.5	
15	38	15	
15.5	39/40	15.5	
16	41	16	SHIRTS
16.5	42	16.5	
17	43	17	
8	36	6	
10	38	8	
12	40	10	
14	42	12	DRESSES
16	44	14	
18	46	16	
20	48	18	
4.5	37.5	6	
5	38	6.5	
5.5	38.5	7	
6	39	7.5	SHOES
6.5	40	8	
7	41	8.5	

VISITORS WITH DISABILITIES
- France has made great headway in recent years in providing access and facilities for visitors with disabilities. All new buildings must take the needs of people with special requirements into account, and, where possible, existing buildings such as town halls, airports and train stations must be adapted with ramps and automatic doors.
- However, some visitor offices, museums and restaurants that are in historic, protected buildings are still not fully accessible. A telephone call before going to a restaurant is a good idea to organize a more easily accessible table.
- The Association des Paralysés

PLANNING

Facilities for those with disabilities are improving

Remember that churches are places of worship, as well as visitor attractions

de France (*17 boulevard Auguste Blanvui, 75013, Paris; 01 40 78 69 00; www.apf.asso.fr*) provides information on wheelchair access. For other organizations which give advice to people with disabilities, see page 66.

CAR RENTAL
● Driving is a good way to explore the villages and countryside of France, although driving in Paris is not recommended.
● It is best to reserve a car in advance, making sure that full insurance is included in the package. You can also arrange car rental through some travel agents when you book your travel arrangements.
● See pages 50–54 for information on driving.

PLACES OF WORSHIP
● Some of the most magnificent buildings in France are the great Gothic cathedrals found in the major cities and the tiny parish churches and chapels in towns and villages. They have become so popular as visitor attractions that it's easy to forget that they are still active places of worship. As such, it's important to respect these churches and worshippers by dressing appropriately. Men should wear long trousers rather than shorts and should avoid

sleeveless shirts. Women should keep their knees and shoulders covered and men should remove hats on entering the building.
● Take photos only if it is permitted and don't forget to turn off your mobile phone.

LOCAL WAYS
● Greetings are often quite formal in France. Offer to shake hands when you are introduced

Café society is an enjoyable part of life in France

to someone, and use *vous* rather than *tu*. It is polite to use *Monsieur, Madame* or *Mademoiselle* when speaking to people you don't know. For very young women and teenage girls use *Mademoiselle*, otherwise use *Madame*.

● The continental kiss is a common form of greeting between friends, and the number of times friends kiss each other on the cheek varies from region to region.
● Address waiters and waitresses as *Monsieur, Madame* or *Mademoiselle* when you are trying to attract their attention. Never use *garçon*.
● Communicating in French is always the best option, even if you can manage only *bonjour, s'il vous plaît* and *merci*. The

French are protective of their language and your efforts to speak it will be appreciated. If your knowledge of French is limited, ask the fail-safe *Parlez-vous anglais?* and hope the answer is *oui*.
● Remember that it is traditional to say hello as you enter a shop, bar or café, particularly in small towns and villages, and that you are greeting your fellow customers as well as the proprietor. For a mixed audience, a *bonjour monsieurs dames* is the appropriate phrase. When it is your turn to be served, greet the server with *Bonjour Madame* or *Bonjour Monsieur*, then don't forget to say *merci* and *au revoir* or *bon-journée* as you leave.

CAR RENTAL COMPANIES INCLUDE:		
Name	**Telephone**	**Website**
Avis	01 44 18 10 50	www.avis.fr
Citer	01 44 38 61 61	www.citer.fr
Easycar	01 40 15 60 39	www.easycar.com
Europcar	08 25 358 358	www.europcar.fr
Hertz	01 39 38 38 38	www.hertz.fr
Rent-a-Car	01 43 45 98 99	www.rentacar.fr

MONEY MATTERS

THE EURO
● France is one of 12 European countries that has adopted the euro as the official currency. Euro notes and coins were introduced in January 2002, replacing the former currency, the French franc.

BEFORE YOU GO
● It is advisable to use a combination of cash, traveller's cheques and credit cards rather than relying on only one means of payment during your trip.
● Check with your credit or debit card company that your card can be used to withdraw cash from Automatic Teller Machines (ATMs) in France. It is also worth checking what fee will be charged for this and what number you should ring if your card is stolen.

TRAVELLER'S CHEQUES
● Traveller's cheques are a safer way of bringing in money as you can claim a refund

| TIPS |
● Try to avoid using higher denomination notes when paying taxi drivers and when buying low-cost items in smaller shops.
● Never carry money or credit cards in back pockets, or other places that are easy targets for thieves.
● Keep your spare money and traveller's cheques in your hotel safe (coffre-fort) until you need them.
● Check the exchange rates for traveller's cheques and cash offered in post offices as well as in banks, as banks do not always offer the best rate.
● In France, Mastercard is sometimes known as Eurocard and Visa is known as Carte Bleue.
● Some smaller hotels and inns don't accept credit cards, so find out before you check in.

if they are stolen—but commission can be high when you cash them.

ATMS
● ATMs are common in France, often with on-screen instructions in a choice of languages. Among the cards accepted are Visa, MasterCard and Diners Club. You'll need a four-digit PIN number.
● Your card issuer may charge you for withdrawing cash.

BANKS
● Hours vary, but usual opening hours are Monday to Friday 8.30 or 9–noon and 2–5, although banks in cities may not close for lunch.
● In smaller towns and villages banks often close on Mondays but open on Saturday mornings instead.
● Banks close at noon on the day before a national holiday, as well as on the holiday itself. Only banks with *change* signs change

BANKNOTES AND COINS

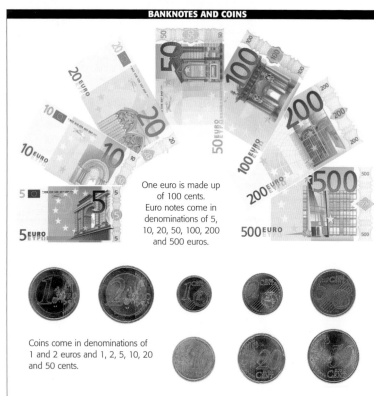

One euro is made up of 100 cents.
Euro notes come in denominations of 5, 10, 20, 50, 100, 200 and 500 euros.

Coins come in denominations of 1 and 2 euros and 1, 2, 5, 10, 20 and 50 cents.

PLANNING

ATMs often give instructions in a choice of languages

traveller's cheques or foreign currency and you'll need your passport to do this.

BUREAUX DE CHANGE
● Bureaux de Change have longer opening hours than banks, but the exchange rates may not be so good. You'll find them across Paris and in all of the major cities.
● Avoid changing large amounts of traveller's cheques at hotels as the rates may not be competitive.

Look for the 'change' sign if you want to exchange money

CREDIT CARDS
● Most restaurants, shops and hotels accept credit cards, although some have a minimum spending limit.
● Before you travel, it's worth finding out how much your card issuer will charge you to withdraw cash from an ATM and the emergency number to call if your card is stolen.

TAXES
● Non-EU residents can claim a sales tax refund *(détaxe)* of 12 per cent on certain purchases, although you must have spent more than €175 in one shop, at one time. Ask the store for the relevant forms, which the trader should complete and stamp. Give these forms to customs when you leave the country, along with the receipts, and they will be stamped. Post the forms back to the shop and they will either refund your credit card account or send you a cheque.
● Remember that you may have to show the goods to Customs when you leave France, so keep them within easy reach.
● Exempt products include food and drink, medicine, tobacco, unset gems, works of art and antiques.
● The company Global Refund offers a reimbursement service (*01 41 61 51 51; www.globalrefund.com*).

WIRING MONEY
● In an emergency, you can have money wired to you from your home country, but this can be expensive (as agents charge a fee for the service) and time-consuming.
● You can send and receive money via agents such as Western Union (*www.westernunion.com*) and Travelex (*www.travelex.fr*).
● Money can be wired from bank to bank, which takes up to two working days, or through Travelex and Western Union, which is normally faster.

CONCESSIONS
● If you are a student or teacher, apply to the International

TIPPING GUIDE

Restaurants	
(service included)	Change *
Hotels (service included)	Change *
Cafés (service included)	Change *
Taxis	10 per cent
Tour Guides	€1–€1.50
Porters	€1
Hairdressers	€1
Cloakroom attendants	30c
Lavatories	Change
Usherettes	30c
* Or more if you are impressed with the level of service	

Student Travel Confederation (*www.isic.org*) in your own country for an International Student Identity Card (ISIC). This entitles you to various reductions during your visit.
● Seniors often get reduced-rate tickets on public transportation and on admission to museums and sights by showing a valid identity card or passport.
● Small children often have free entry to sights.

POST OFFICES
● Most post offices have ATMs.
● Cards accepted are listed on each dispenser and instructions are available in English.
● Money can be wired, through Western Union, via most post offices, and generally takes only a few minutes to receive.
● International Money Orders can be sent from all post offices (a charge is applied).
● Most post offices offer exchange services in the following currencies: American, Australian and Canadian Dollars, the Yen, British Pound Sterling, Swiss Francs and Swedish, Danish and Norwegian Kroners.

PRICES OF EVERYDAY ITEMS (PARIS)		
Takeout sandwich		€2.20–€3.20
Bottle of mineral water	(from a shop, 0.5 litres)	€0.20–€0.40
Cup of coffee	(from a café, espresso)	€1–€1.85
	(Crème, larger cup with milk)	€1.85–€2.25
Beer	(*Un demi*, half a litre)	€1.85–€2.60
Glass of house wine		€1.85–€2.15
French national newspaper		€1–€1.20
International newspaper		€1.50–€2.30
Litre of petrol	(98 unleaded)	€1.03
	(diesel)	€0.81
Métro ticket	(single)	€1.30
	(per ticket, if you buy a *carnet*)	€1
Camera film	(36 pictures)	€7–€8
20 cigarettes	(on average)	€3.50

HEALTH

USEFUL NUMBERS

Emergency medical aid/ambulance
15

General emergencies
112

Police
17

Fire (Pompiers)
18

Anti-Poison Centre in Paris
01 40 05 48 48

FACTS (HIV/Aids advice in English. Mon–Fri 11am–2pm)
01 44 93 16 69

SOS Help (English crisis information hotline. Daily 3pm–11pm)
01 46 21 46 46

BEFORE YOU GO

● EU citizens receive reduced-cost healthcare in France with the relevant documentation. For UK citizens, this is the E111 form, which must be stamped by the post office before you travel. Bring a photocopy with you as well as the original, as this will be kept by the hospital or doctor if you need treatment. Full health insurance is still strongly advised. For all other countries full insurance is a must.

● Make sure you are up to date with anti-tetanus boosters. Bring any medication you need with you and pack a first aid kit. In summer, always bring sun-protection cream.

IF YOU NEED TREATMENT

● The French national health system is complex. Any salaried French citizen who receives treatment by a doctor or public hospital can be reimbursed by up to 70 per cent. The same is true if you are an EU citizen and have a valid E111 form.

● If you are relying only on E111, rather than travel insurance, make sure the doctor you see is part of the French national health service (a *conventionné*), rather than the private system, otherwise you may face extra charges. In any case, you will have to pay up front for the consultation and treatment. To reclaim part of these costs, send the *feuille de soins* (a statement from the

HEALTHY FLYING

● If you are visiting France from the US, Australia or New Zealand, you may be concerned about the effect of long-haul flights on your health. The most widely publicized concern is Deep Vein Thrombosis, or DVT. Misleadingly named economy class syndrome, DVT occurs when a blood clot forms in the body's deep veins, particularly in the legs. The clot can move around the bloodstream and could be fatal.

● Those most at risk include the elderly, pregnant women and those using the contraceptive pill, smokers and the overweight. If you are at increased risk of DVT see your doctor before departing. Flying increases the likelihood of DVT because passengers are often seated in a cramped position for long periods of time and may become dehydrated.

To minimize risk:

Drink water (not alcohol).

Don't stay immobile for hours at a time.

Stretch and exercise your legs periodically.

Do wear elastic flight socks, which support veins and reduce the chances of a clot forming.

A small dose of aspirin may be recommended; this thins the blood before the flight.

EXERCISES

1 ANKLE ROTATIONS	2 CALF STRETCHES	3 KNEE LIFTS

Lift feet off the floor. Draw a circle with the toes, moving one foot clockwise and the other counterclockwise.

Start with heel on the floor and point foot upward as high as you can. Then lift heels high keeping balls of feet on the floor.

Lift leg with knee bent while contracting your thigh muscle. Then staighten leg pressing foot flat to the floor.

Other health hazards for flyers are airborne diseases and bugs spread by the plane's air-conditioning system. These are largely unavoidable, but if you have a serious medical condition seek advice from a doctor before setting off.

doctor) and your E111 to the Caisse Primaire d'Assurance-Maladie (state health insurance office) before you leave the country. Call 0820 904 175 to find the nearest office. You should also attach the labels of any medicine you have to buy.

● If you have to stay overnight in a public hospital, you will have to pay 25 per cent of the treatment costs, as well as a daily charge (*forfait journalier*). These are not refundable. It is far better to have

full health insurance than to rely solely on the E111 form.

● Citizens of non-EU countries must have full health insurance.

● If you are hospitalized and have insurance, ask to see the *assistante sociale* to arrange reimbursement of the costs directly through your insurers.

● In an emergency, dial 15 for Service d'Aide Médicale d'Urgence (SAMU) unit (ambulance). They work closely with hospital emergency units

PLANNING

and are accompanied by trained medical personnel.

• If you are able to get yourself to a hospital, make sure it has a casualty or emergency department (*urgences*).

FINDING A DOCTOR

• You can find a doctor (*médecin*) by asking at the local pharmacy or at your hotel. Appointments are usually made in advance, but few doctors will refuse to see an emergency case.

• Emergency house calls (24-hours) can be arranged in the Paris area by calling SOS Médecins (*tel 01 47 07 77 77*). Otherwise call 15 for emergencies or SOS Help (*tel 01 46 21 46 46*) for practical help in English.

FINDING A HOSPITAL

• Hospitals are listed in the phone book under *Hôpitaux* and round-the-clock emergency services are called *urgences*.

• Private hospitals are a lot more expensive than public ones and treatment is not necessarily better. If you choose a private hospital, check that you are covered for the costs before receiving treatment.

• For ease of communication, English-speakers in Paris may prefer The American Hospital (*63 boulevard Victor Hugo, 92200, Neuilly; 01 46 41 25 25*) or The Hertford British Hospital (*3 rue Barbès, 92300 Levallois-Perret; 01 46 39 22 22*). Both are private hospitals.

DENTAL TREATMENT

• EU citizens can receive reduced-cost emergency dental treatment with form E111, although insurance is still advised. The reclaim procedure is the same as for general medical treatment.

• Other visitors should check that their insurance covers dental treatment. It's a good idea have a dental check-up before your visit.

PHARMACIES

• A pharmacy (*pharmacie*) will have an illuminated green cross outside. Most are open Mon–Sat 9–7 or 8, but they usually post details on the door of another pharmacy that is open later (called the *pharmacie de garde*).

• Pharmacists are highly qualified and provide first aid, as well as supplying medication (some drugs are by prescription, or *ordonnance,* only). But they cannot dispense prescriptions written by doctors outside the French health system, so bring sufficient supplies of any prescribed drugs you need.

• Some pharmacists speak English and can direct you to local doctors or specialists.

• They also sell a range of health-related items, although it is less expensive to go to the supermarket for items such as soap, toothbrushes and razors.

• Some commonly used medicines sold in supermarkets at home (such as aspirins and cold remedies) can only be bought in pharmacies in France.

TAP WATER

• Tap water is safe to drink and restaurants will often bring a carafe of water to the table, although most French people opt instead for bottled water.

• In public places look for the sign *eau potable* (drinking water). Don't drink from anything marked *eau non potable*.

SUMMER HAZARDS

• The sun can be strong in any part of the country between May and September, so pack a high-factor sun block. You may also like to take an insect repellent, although the insect bites you get in France are more likely to be irritating than dangerous.

• If you are planning on doing any high altitude walks take plenty of water, warm clothing and check weather reports before you go, as sudden changes in weather are not unknown.

• Recent hot dry summers have led to forest fires in some areas in the south of France. If you are concerned about this, ask at the nearest tourist information office whether the area you intend to visit is at risk.

ALTERNATIVE MEDICAL TREATMENT

• Alternative medicine, such as homoeopathy, is generally available from most pharmacies.

• Alternative treatment is available and is on the increase, although chiropractics and reflexology are not widespread. Useful websites include www.chiropratique.org (the Association Française de Chiropratique), www.aea-org.com (Association Europe Acupuncture) and www.naturosante.com (a site about alternative medical treatments).

Pharmacies have an illuminated green cross outside. Each town has a 'pharmacie de garde' that stays open late, or even 24 hours

OPTICIANS	
It's always a good idea to pack a spare pair of glasses or contact lenses and your prescription, in case you lose or break your main pair.	
Name	**Website**
Opticiens Krys	www.krys.com
Lissac Opticien	www.lissac.com
Alain Afflelou	www.alainafflelou.com
Optical Center	www.optical-center.com
Optic 2000	www.optic2000.fr

TELEPHONING

French numbers All numbers in France have ten digits. The country is divided into five regional zones, indicated by the first two digits of the phone number (see chart below). You must dial these two digits even if you are calling from within the zone.

International Calls To call France from the UK dial 00 33, then drop the first zero from the ten digit number. To call the UK from France, dial 00 44, then drop the first zero from the area code. To call France from the US, dial 011 33, then drop the first zero from the ten digit number. To call the US from France, dial 00 1, followed by the number.

Call charges For calls within France, peak period is from 8am to 7pm, Monday to Friday. You'll save money if you call outside this time. Numbers beginning with 08 have special rates. 0800 or 0805 numbers are free. 0810 and 0811 numbers are charged at local rate. Other 08 numbers cost more than national calls—sometimes considerably more. Watch for the prefixes 0893, 0898 and 0899, which are particularly expensive.

COUNTRY CODES FROM FRANCE	
Australia	00 61
Belgium	00 32
Canada	00 1
Germany	00 49
Ireland	00 353
Italy	00 39
Monaco	00 377
Netherlands	00 31
New Zealand	00 64
Spain	00 34
Sweden	00 46
UK	00 44
US	00 1

PREFIXES	
00	International
01	Île-de-France (including Paris)
02	Northwest France
03	Northeast France
04	Southeast France
05	Southwest France
06	Mobile telephone numbers
0800/0805	Toll-free
08	Special-rate numbers

USEFUL TELEPHONE NUMBERS
Directory Enquiries
(national)
12
(international)
3212

TIPS
● When reserving show tickets by telephone or calling for tourist information, bear in mind that you may be calling a higher-rate telephone number. This is usually indicated by the prefix 089.

GUIDE PRICES		
Type of Call	**Initial charge**	**Each further minute**
Local, peak	€0.091 (1 min)	€0.033
Local, off-peak	€0.091 (1 min)	€0.018
National, peak	€0.112 (39 sec)	€0.091
National, off-peak	€0.112 (39sec)	€0.061
Calling the UK, off-peak	€0.11 (15 sec)	€0.12
Calling the US, off-peak	€0.11 (27 sec)	€0.15

PAYPHONES

● Nearly all public payphones in France use a phone card (*télécarte*) rather than coins. You can buy these at post offices, *tabacs*, newsagents and France Telecom shops, with 50 or 120 units. Some phones also accept certain credit cards, although this may make the calls more expensive. You do not need to pay if you are calling an emergency number.

● The phone gives instructions in various languages—press the flag button to select your choice. If the phone displays the blue bell sign, you can receive incoming calls.

● Public phones in cafés and restaurants use cards, coins or need to be switched on by staff and you pay after the call. They tend to be more expensive than public payphones. Check the rates for hotel phones, as they can be much higher than from a public payphone.

MOBILE PHONES

● You can usually use your own mobile, but there are a few points to check before leaving:

● Contact your Customer Service department to find out if you have any restrictions on making calls from France.

● Check if you need an access code to listen to your voice mail.

● Make sure the numbers memorized in your directory are in the international format.

● Check the call charges, which can rise dramatically when you use your phone abroad.

Most public payphones in France take phone cards

SENDING A LETTER

● You can buy stamps (*timbres*) for a letter (*lettre*) or a postcard (*carte postale*) at post offices and *tabacs*. Write *par avion* (by air) on the envelope or postcard.

● If you want registered post, ask at the post office for the letter to be sent *recommandé*. For a parcel (*colis*), you can choose either *prioritaire* (priority) or the less expensive, but slower, *économique*.

● Mailboxes are yellow. In Paris,

POSTAGE RATES FOR LETTERS	
Within France	€0.50
To Western Europe	€0.50
To Eastern Europe	€0.75
To America	€0.90
To Africa	€0.75
To Asia	€0.90
To Australia	€0.90

some have two sections, one for Paris and the suburbs (*Paris–Banlieue*), and another for national and international mail (*autres départements/ étranger*). Mail sent from France should take between two and five days to arrive, but can take longer.

POST OFFICES
● Post offices (*bureaux de poste*) are well signposted. The postal service is known as La Poste.
● Opening hours are generally Monday to Friday 8–5 or 6, Saturday 8–noon. Some branches close for lunch and some stay open longer. Queues tend to be worst during lunch hours and in the late afternoon.
● Facilities usually include phone booths, photocopiers, fax

Mailboxes in France are an easy-to-spot yellow

(*télécopieur*) and access to the Minitel directory service. *Poste Restante* services are also available for a fee.
● Money can be wired through Western Union via most post offices and international money orders can be sent from post offices (a charge is payable). Many also have exchange services in the following

currencies: American, Australian and Canadian Dollars, Yen, British Pound Sterling, Swiss Francs, Swedish, Danish and Norwegian Kroner.

INTERNET ACCESS
● Internet cafés are popular in Paris and major towns, although they are quite expensive. Some hotels and libraries have Internet terminals, as do many post offices.

LAPTOPS
● Most hotels of two stars and above provide modem points. You can easily connect to the Internet providing this service is supported by your ISP (Internet Service Provider). Local telephone charges will apply. Remember that you may need a modem plug adaptor.

FINDING HELP

Most visits to France are trouble-free, but make sure you have adequate insurance to cover any health emergencies, thefts or legal costs that may arise. If you do become a victim of crime, it is most likely to be at the hands of a pickpocket, so always keep your money and mobile phones safely tucked away.

PERSONAL SECURITY
● Take a note of your traveller's cheques numbers and keep it separate from the cheques themselves, as you will need it to make a claim in case of loss.
● Don't keep wallets, purses or mobile phones in the back pockets of trousers, or anywhere else that is easily accessible to thieves. Money belts and bags worn around the waist are targets, as thieves know you are likely to have valuables in them. Always keep an eye on your bags in restaurants, bars and on the Métro, and hold shoulder bags close to you, fastener inwards, when you are walking in the streets.
● Thieves and pickpockets are especially fond of crowded Métro trains, airports, the Gare du Nord Métro station in Paris, markets, tourist hotspots and the south coast, particularly the Côte d'Azur. Beware if someone bumps into you—it may be a ploy to distract

EMBASSIES AND CONSULATES IN PARIS		
Country	**Address**	**Website**
Australia	4 rue Jean-Rey, 75015; tel 01 40 59 33 00	
Canada	35 avenue Montaigne, 75008	www.amb-canada.fr
	tel 01 44 43 29 00	
Germany	13–15 avenue Franklin Roosevelt,	www.amb-allemagne.fr
	75008; tel 01 53 83 45 00	
Ireland	4 rue Rude, 75116; tel 01 44 17 67 00	
Italy	51 rue de Varenne, 75007	www.amb-italie.fr
	tel 01 49 54 03 00	
Spain	22 avenue Marceau, 75008	www.amb-espagne.fr
	tel 01 44 43 18 00	
UK	35 rue du Faubourg-St-Honoré,	www.amb-grandebretagne.fr
	75008; tel 01 44 51 31 00	
US	2 avenue Gabriel, 75008	www.amb-usa.fr
	tel 01 43 12 22 22	

you while someone else snatches your money.
● If you are the victim of theft, you must report it at the local police station (*commissariat*) if you want to claim on your insurance. Keep hold of the statement the police give you. You must also contact your credit card company as soon as possible to cancel any stolen cards.
● Keep valuable items in your hotel safe (*coffre-fort*).
● Theft of cars and theft from cars are significant problems in France. When you park your car, don't leave anything of value inside. It's even risky leaving anything at all in view that may attract the interest of a thief.

Carry your belongings with you or leave them in your hotel.
● On trains, try to keep your luggage where you can see it.

LOSS OF PASSPORT
● Always keep a separate note of your passport number and a photocopy of the page that carries your details, in case of loss or theft. You can also scan the relevant pages of your passport and then e-mail them to yourself at an e-mail account that you can access anywhere (such as *www.hotmail.com*).
● If you do lose your passport or it is stolen, report it to the police and then contact your nearest embassy or consulate.

POLICE

- There are various types of police officer in France. The two main forces are the *Police Nationale,* who are under the control of the local mayor, and the *Gendarmerie Nationale,* who you often see at airports.
- You are likely to encounter the armed CRS riot police only at a demonstration.
- In Paris each *arrondissement* has several police stations.

- In France, the police have wide powers of stop and search. It is wise to carry your passport in case a police officer stops you and requests your ID.

FIRE

- The French fire brigade deals with a number of emergencies in addition to actual fires. These range from stranded cats to road accidents and gas leaks. They are trained to give first aid.

EMERGENCY NUMBERS
112
General emergency number
15
Ambulance
17
Police
18
Fire

HEALTH EMERGENCIES
See pages 408–409.

MEDIA

TELEVISION

- France has five non-cable television stations, the nationally owned and operated channels 2 and 3, the privately owned 1 and 6, and the Franco-German ARTE (channel 5). Almost all the shows are in French. There are adverts on all terrestrial channels except ARTE.
- **TF1** has news, recent American and French films, soaps and shows.
- **France 2** has news, recent French and foreign films, soaps, shows and documentaries.
- **France 3**, a regional and national channel, has regional and national news, regional shows, documentaries, mostly French films and, once a week, a film in its original language.
- **ARTE** is a Franco-German channel operating from 7pm every evening with shows in French and German. International films are shown in their original language and there are also cultural documentaries.
- **M6** shows a lot of low-budget films and past American sitcoms and soaps. There are also some interesting documentaries.
- Digital television has now taken off in France. More than 100 channels are on offer either through satellite or cable.
- If the TV listings mention VO (*version originale*), the show or film will be in the language in which it was made, with French subtitles (Channel 3 usually screens a good film in VO every Sunday at around midnight).
- Note that French television channels do not always keep exactly to schedule.
- Most hotels have at least a basic cable service, which is likely

to include BBC World and CNN. Cable channels now offer multilingual versions of some shows. Ask at your hotel how to use this option as the mechanics vary. The commercial-free ARTE usually offers a choice between French and German for its cultural shows.

RADIO

- French radio stations are available mainly on FM wave lengths, with a few international stations on LW. All FM stations are in French.
Stations (with their Paris frequencies) include:
- **Chérie FM:** 91.3 FM; French mainstream pop, news, reports.
- **France Infos:** 105.5 FM; news bulletins every 15 minutes.
- **France Musique:** 91.7 FM; classical and jazz music, concerts, operas, news.
- **NRJ:** 100.3 FM; French and International pop, techno, rap, R'n'B.

- **Radio Classique:** 101.1 FM; classical music.
- **Skyrock:** 96 FM; rap, hip-hop, R'n'B.
- **BBC Radio 4** 198 kHz MW; news, current affairs, drama.
- **BBC Five Live** 909 kHz MW; news and sport.
- **BBC World Service** 648 kHz LW.

NEWSPAPERS

- In tourist areas and the major cities, you can buy the main English dailies, sometimes a day old, at a price premium.
- *The Economist, USA Today* and *The Wall Street Journal* can be found at news-stands in cities, along with *The European,* which presents a pan-European perspective in English, and the *International Herald Tribune,* which reports international news from a US standpoint.
- You may be disappointed to find an international edition of your preferred paper rather than

CABLE TV	
Depending on what cable option your hotel has, you may have some of the following channels:	
BBC Prime	With a mix of BBC shows, old and new
Canal+	Shows recent films (some in the original language)
MTV	Contemporary music channel
MCM	The French version of MTV
Eurosport or Infosport	For major sporting events
Planète	Nature and science documentaries
RAI Uno	Italian
TVE 1	Spanish
Euronews	A European all-news channel
LCI	All news in French
Canal Jimmy	Shows some British and American shows like *Friends* and *NYPD Blue* in English or multilingual versions
Paris Première	A cultural channel with some films in English
Canal J	With children's shows until 8pm
Téva	A women's channel that runs some English-language shows such as *Sex in the City*

A newspaper stand outside the Gare Du Nord, Paris

the one you would get at home.
● Most French cities and regions have their own newspapers, such as *Le Progrès* in Lyon, *Breton Ouest-France* in Brittany or *Le Populaire* in central France.
● Leading local newspapers play an active part in pressure politics in their area, though the issues of some may seem parochial to the outsider.
● If you want to find out what's happening in a French city during your stay, consult the 'what's on' supplements, which are issued with some newspapers.

● Major cities also produce one or more monthly magazines with listings of live performances, exhibitions and cinema. In the capital there's *Pariscope,* Lyon has *Lyon Poche* and in Nantes there is a booklet called *Les Mois Nantais.* Free listings publications can be picked up at tourist offices, music stores or cafés.
● Weekly news magazines include *Le Nouvel Observateur, Le Point* and *L'Express.*
● For women's fashions, options include *Elle, Vogue* or *Marie Claire.*
● When you want celebrity gossip and lots of pictures, buy *Paris Match, Voici* or *Gala.*

NEWSPAPERS
French daily newspapers have clear political leanings.
Le Monde This stately paper, left-of-centre, refuses to run photos and uses illustrations.
Libération This lively youth-focused paper is more clearly leftist.
L'Humanité Left wing.
Le Figaro Mainstream conservative daily.
Le Parisien This tabloid paper is written at a level of French that makes it fairly easy for non-native readers to understand.
Journal du Dimanche Sunday newspaper.

OPENING TIMES AND TICKETS

OPENING TIMES		
Banks	Usual opening hours are Monday to Friday 9–12, 2–5, but these can vary.	Banks close at noon on the day before a national holiday, as well as on the holiday itself.
Shops	Food shops are open Tuesday to Friday 7 or 8am–6.30 or 7.30pm.	Some close all day Monday while others will open in the afternoon only. On Saturday and Sunday they may open mornings only. Smaller shops tend to close at lunchtime from 12–2. Bakers (*boulangerie*) open on Sunday mornings and supermarkets and hypermarkets are open six days a week and have long business hours, opening at about 9am and staying open until 9 or 10pm, but closing on Sundays. Some also remain closed on Monday mornings.
Museums	In Paris, most national museums close on Tuesdays—the Musée d'Orsay is a notable exception, closing on Mondays. Municipal museums in Paris usually close on Tuesdays.	Entrance to some museums is free on the first Sunday of the month, although this can lead to crowds. If you plan to travel a long distance to see a particular museum, ring in advance as opening hours can be idiosyncratic (some museums open on public holidays and some do not and the renovation craze has not helped).
Restaurants	Lunch is generally served from 12–2 or 2.30 and dinner from 7.30–10 or 11.	Brasseries tend to serve food all day. Some restaurants in Paris close for the whole of August for staff to have their annual vacation. Some restaurants on the coast close from November to Easter.
Post offices	These generally open Monday to Friday 8–5, 6 or 7 weekdays and 8–noon on Saturday.	Small branches may close for lunch.
Pharmacies	Most are open Monday to Saturday 9–7 or 8.	They all display a list of local pharmacies that open later and on a Sunday.

PLANNING

TICKETS

- Tourist information offices in French cities often sell a pass that gives entry to the main sights at a reduced rate. For example, the Lyon City Card entitles you to entry to 19 museums, guided and audio city tours, river cruises, lunchtime classical concerts, public transportation within the city and a 10 per cent discount on purchases at Galeries Lafayette. It's worth investing in one of these if you plan on spending a few days in one city.
- For information on transportation tickets, see pages 55–66.

- Students with an International Student Identity Card (ISIC) and seniors get reduced-price entry at some museums.
- For information on show and concert tickets, see page 219.

TOURIST OFFICES

IN PARIS

- The Paris tourist office (*www.paris-touristoffice.com*), due to move to rue des Pyramides in May 2004, is a handy source of information on anything from sightseeing and accommodation to exhibitions and children's activities. You can also buy the *Carte Musées-Monuments* pass and the *Paris Visite* bus and Métro pass.
- In the summer there are also information kiosks at various sites around the city.
- The regional tourist office, the Comité Régional du Tourisme—Paris Île-de-France, has offices at the Carrousel du Louvre and Disneyland Resort Paris. It covers the whole of the Île de France, including Versailles and Fontainebleau.

Head to the tourist office when you arrive

TOURIST OFFICES

Bordeaux
12 cours du 30 Juillet, 33080, Bordeaux
Tel 05 56 00 66 00
Open: Mon–Sat 9–7, Sun and public hols 9.30–6.30, May, Jun, Sep, Oct; Mon–Sat 9–7.30, Sun and public hols 9.30–6.30 Jul, Aug; Mon–Sat 9–6.30, Sun and public hols 9.45–4.30 rest of year; closed 25 Dec, 1 Jan

Dijon
Place Darcy and 34 rue des Forges, 21000, Dijon
Tel 03 80 44 11 44
Open: place Darcy: daily 9–7 Jun–end Aug; 10–6 rest of year; rue des Forges: Mon–Sat 9–12, 2–6

Lille
Palais Rihour, place Rihour, 59002
Tel 03 20 21 94 21
Open: Mon–Sat 10–6, Sun 10–noon, 2–5

Lyon
Place Bellecour, 69002
Tel 04 72 77 69 69
Mon–Sat 9–7 Sun and hols 9–6 mid-Apr to mid-Oct; Mon–Sat 10–6 Sun and hols 10–5.30 rest of year; closed 25 Dec, 1 Jan and 1 May

Marseille
4 La Canebière, Marseille
Tel 04 91 13 89 00
Open: Mon–Sat 9–7, Sun 10–5. Longer hours in peak season

Monaco
2a boulevard des Moulins
Tel 92 16 61 16 (country code 377)
Open: Mon–Sat 9–7, Sun 10–12

Nice
5 promenade des Anglais, 06000
Tel 0892 707 407
Open: Mon–Sat 8am–8pm, Sun 9–6, summer; Mon–Sat 9–6, rest of year

Paris
25–27 rue des Pyramides, 75001
Tel 0892 683 000 (€0.34 per minute)
Open: daily 9–8 May–end Oct; 10–7 rest of year. Closed 1 May, 25 Dec
Métro: Pyramides
www.paris-touristoffice.com

Reims
2 rue Guillaume de Machault, 51100
Tel 03 26 77 45 25
Open: Mon–Sat 9–7, Sun 10–6, mid-Apr to mid-Oct; Mon–Sat 9–6, Sun 11–5 rest of year

Rennes
11 rue St-Yves, 35064
Tel 02 99 67 11 11
Open: Mon–Sat 9–6, Sun 11–6

Rouen
25 place de la Cathédrale, BP 666, 76008
Tel 02 32 08 32 40
Open: Mon–Sat 9–7, Sun and public hols 9.30–12.30, 2–6, May–end Sep; Mon–Sat 9–6, Sun and public hols 10–1, Oct–end Apr

Strasbourg
17 place de la Cathédrale, 67082
Tel 03 88 52 28 28
Open: Mon–Sat 9–7, Sun 9–6

Toulouse
Donjon du Capitole, 31080, Toulouse
Tel 05 61 11 02 22
Open: Mon–Sat 9–7, Sun 9–1, 2–5.30 May–Sep; Mon–Fri 9–6, Sat 9–12.30, 2–6, Sun 10–12.30, 2–5 rest of year

PLANNING

FILMS, BOOKS AND MAPS

FILMS

● Watching a French film is a good way to get the feel of the place before you visit.
● For a classic, try *Les Enfants du Paradis* (1945) directed by Marcel Carné. For *nouvelle vague* (new wave) cinema—often filmed with a hand-held camera—try *Jules et Jim* (1962) directed by François Truffaut and starring Jeanne Moreau, or *À Bout de Souffle* (1959), directed by Jean-Luc Godard. The surreal *Belle de Jour* (1967), starring Catherine Deneuve, caused a scandal at the time due to its erotic subject matter. The 1987 weepie *Au Revoir les Enfants* tells the story of a Jewish boy in occupied France in World War II.
● No reference to French movies would be complete without mentioning Gérard Depardieu, the actor who conquered France and then Hollywood. His best known works include *Cyrano de Bergerac* (1990) and *Jean de Florette* (1986). The sequel to this, *Manon des Sources* (1986), stars Emmanuelle Béart, one of France's leading actresses.
● Jean-Pierre Jeunet's *Delicatessen* (1991) turns the controversial subject of cannibalism into a black comedy.
● For a French feel with a Hollywood budget, watch a film directed by Luc Besson, such as *The Fifth Element* (1997) or *Léon* (1994), known for the

understated performance of Jean Reno.
● The quirky and hugely successful *Amélie* (2001) is set in Montmartre, Paris. *Les Rivières Pourpres* (*The Crimson Rivers*; 2000) is directed by Matthieu Kassovitz, the actor who played the love interest in *Amélie*. It's an action thriller set in the French Alps, worth watching for the atmospheric scenery alone, and starring two of the best French actors of the moment, Jean Reno and Vincent Cassel.
● If you're looking for beautiful countryside, *French Kiss* (1995), with Hollywood's Meg Ryan, is a good start. Another English-language movie set in France is *Chocolat* (2000), starring Juliette Binoche.
● Cannes hosts Europe's most prestigious film festival in May. It attracts top international actors, directors and producers, as well as hundreds of starlets and self-promoting wannabes whose antics contribute much to the atmosphere of the festival. Millions of euros of business is conducted during the 12 days of the festival. For more details, look up www.festival-cannes.fr.

BOOKS

● For those who prefer to find their atmosphere on the page, there is no shortage of choice.
● Books written from a foreigner's perspective range

from Charles Dickens' view of the French Revolution in *A Tale of Two Cities* (1859) to Peter Mayle's experiences in the southeast of France in *A Year in Provence* (1989). English actress Carol Drinkwater recounts her Provençal experiences in *The Olive Farm* (2001) and *The Olive Season* (2003).
● Classic literature set in Paris includes Victor Hugo's *The Hunchback of Notre Dame* (1831) and George Orwell's *Down and Out in Paris and London* (1933), which describes the difficulties of surviving penniless in the capital in the 1930s. Adam Gopnik's essays in *Paris to the Moon* (2000) provide one American's view of life in the French capital in the 21st century. Ernest Hemingway's *A Moveable Feast* (published in 1964) and Gertrude Stein's *The Autobiography of Alice B. Toklas* (1933) describe a more romantic era in the early 20th century, when a young couple could live on $5 a day and an art collector could snap up works by Pablo Picasso and Henri Matisse for a song.

MAPS

The AA (UK) produces a French road atlas and touring atlas, as well as 16 regional road sheet maps of France. To order a copy, look up www.theAA.com.

PLANNING

USEFUL WEBSITES

www.aeroport.fr
Information on all of France's airports. (French)

www.fodors.com
A comprehensive travel-planning site that lets you research prices, reserve air tickets and put questions to fellow visitors. (English)

www.franceguide.com
Practical advice from the French Tourist Office on everything from arriving in France to buying a property. The site also has features on holidays and attractions. (French, English, German, Spanish, Italian, Dutch, Portuguese)

www.francetourism.com
The official US website of the French Government Tourist Office. (English)

www.intermusees.com
The organization that runs the *Carte Musées-Monuments* pass for Paris. (French and English)

www.lemonde.fr
Catch up on current events on the site of *Le Monde* newspaper. (French)

www.meteo.fr/meteonet
Weather forecasts for France. (French, English and Spanish)

www.monum.fr
Find out more about some of France's most historic monuments, on the site of the Centre des Monuments Nationaux. (French and English)

www.parisdigest.com
An independent site that guides you to the best Paris has to offer, whether you want to sightsee, shop or eat out. (English)

www.pagesjaunes.fr
France's telephone directory, online. (French and English)

www.paris-touristoffice.com
The website of the Paris Tourist Office is packed with information on sights, restaurants, shops, hotels, transportation and events. It also has useful links to other sites. (French and English)

The Internet is a great way to find out more about France

www.radio-france.fr
News, music and sport. (French)

www.ratp.fr
The site of Paris's Métro and bus operator, with lots of information about getting around in Paris. (French and English)

www.skifrance.fr
Search for a resort, find out the latest snow conditions and see the slopes in real time via webcam. (English and French)

www.theAA.com
The AA website contains a route planner, helpful if you are driving in France. You can also order maps of the country. (English)

www.tourist-office.org
Lists details of every tourist information office in France. (French)

Other websites are listed alongside the relevant sights and towns in the Seeing section, and in the On the Move section.

KEY SIGHTS QUICK WEBSITE FINDER		
Sight/Town	**Website**	**Page**
Aix-en-Provence	www.aixenprovencetourism.com	172
Arles	www.tourisme.ville-arles.fr	173
Avignon	www.ot-avignon.fr	174
Battlefields of Picardie	www.somme-tourisme.com	125
Bordeaux	www.bordeaux-tourisme.com	196–199
Caen	www.ville-caen.fr	99
Colmar	www.ot-colmar.fr	128
Corsica	www.corsica.net	209–214
Dijon	www.dijon-tourism.com	160–161
Disneyland Resort Paris	www.disneylandparis.com	73
Lille	www.lilletourism.com	132–135
Lyon	www.lyon-france.com	164–167
Marseille	www.marseille-tourisme.com	182–185
Monaco	www.visitmonaco.com	186–187
Mont St-Michel	www.monum.fr	110–111
Montpellier	www.ot-montpellier.fr	181
Musée d'Orsay	www.musee-orsay.fr	85
Musée du Louvre	www.louvre.fr	82–83
Nice	www.nice-coteazur.org	188
Reims	www.tourisme.fr/reims	138–139
Rennes	www.tourisme-rennes.com	114–115
Rouen	www.rouen.fr	116–119
St-Malo	www.saint-malo-tourisme.com	121
Strasbourg	www.ot-strasbourg.fr	140–143
Toulouse	www.ot-toulouse.fr	206–207
Tour Eiffel	www.eiffel-tower.com	92–93

PLANNING

WORDS AND PHRASES

Even if you're far from fluent, it is always a good idea to try to speak a few words of French while in France. The words and phrases on the following pages should help you with the basics, from ordering a meal to dealing with emergencies.

CONVERSATION

What is the time?
Quelle heure est-il?

When do you open/close?
A quelle heure ouvrez/ fermez-vous?

I don't speak French.
Je ne parle pas français.

Do you speak English?
Parlez-vous anglais?

I don't understand.
Je ne comprends pas.

Please repeat that.
Pouvez-vous répéter (s'il vous plaît)?

Please speak more slowly.
Pouvez-vous parler plus lentement?

What does this mean?
Qu'est-ce que ça veut dire?

Write that down for me please.
Pouvez-vous me l'écrire, s'il vous plaît?

Please spell that.
Pouvez-vous me l'épeler, s'il vous plaît?

I'll look that up (in the dictionary).
Je vais le chercher (dans le dictionnaire).

My name is…
Je m'appelle…

What's your name?
Comment vous appelez-vous?

This is my wife/husband.
Voici ma femme/mon mari.

Voici ma fille/mon fils.
This is my daughter/son.

This is my friend.
Voici mon ami(e).

Hello, pleased to meet you.
Bonjour, enchanté(e).

I'm from …
Je viens de …

I'm on holiday.
Je suis en vacances.

I live in …
J'habite à …

Where do you live?
Où habitez-vous?

Good morning.
Bonjour.

Good evening.
Bonsoir.

Goodnight.
Bonne nuit.

Goodbye.
Au revoir.

See you later.
A plus tard.

How much is that?
C'est combien?

May I/Can I?
Est-ce que je peux?

I don't know.
Je ne sais pas.

You're welcome.
Je vous en prie.

How are you?
Comment allez-vous?

I'm sorry.
Je suis désolé(e).

Excuse me.
Excusez-moi.

That's all right.
De rien.

USEFUL WORDS

Yes	**Oui**	Who	**Qui**	Open	**Ouvert**
No	**Non**	When	**Quand**	Closed	**Fermé**
		Where	**Où**	Why	**Pourquoi**

There	**Là-bas**	How	**Comment**
Here	**Ici**	Later	**Plus tard**
		Now	**Maintenant**

Please	**S'il vous plaît**
Thank you	**Merci**

SHOPPING

Could you help me, please?
(Est-ce que) vous pouvez m'aider, s'il vous plaît?

How much is this?
C'est combien?/Ça coûte combien?

I'm looking for …
Je cherche …

When does the shop open/close?
A quelle heure ouvre/ferme le magasin?

I'm just looking, thank you.
Je regarde, merci.

This isn't what I want.
Ce n'est pas ce que je veux.

This is the right size.
C'est la bonne taille.

Do you have anything less expensive/smaller/larger?
(Est-ce que) vous avez quelque chose de moins cher/plus petit/plus grand?

I'll take this.
Je prends ça.

Do you have a bag for this, please?
(Est-ce que) je peux avoir un sac, s'il vous plaît?

Do you accept credit cards?
(Est-ce que) vous acceptez les cartes de crédit?

I'd like ….grams please.
Je voudrais …grammes, s'il vous plaît.

I'd like a kilo of …
Je voudrais un kilo de …

What does this contain?
Quels sont les ingrédients?/Qu'est-ce qu'il y a dedans?

I'd like … slices of that.
J'en voudrais … tranches.

Bakery
Boulangerie

Bookshop
Librairie

Chemist
Pharmacie

Supermarket
Supermarché

Market
Marché

Sale
Soldes

NUMBERS

1 un	6 six	11 onze	16 seize	21 vingt et un	70 soixante-dix
2 deux	7 sept	12 douze	17 dix-sept	30 trente	80 quatre-vingts
3 trois	8 huit	13 treize	18 dix-huit	40 quarante	90 quatre-vingt dix
4 quatre	9 neuf	14 quatorze	19 dix-neuf	50 cinquante	100 cent
5 cinq	10 dix	15 quinze	20 vingt	60 soixante	1000 mille

POST AND TELEPHONES

Where is the nearest post office/mail box?
Où se trouve la poste/la boîte aux lettres la plus proche?

How much is the postage to…?
A combien faut-il affranchir pour …?

I'd like to send this by air mail/registered mail.
Je voudrais envoyer ceci par avion/en recommandé.

Can you direct me to a public phone?
Pouvez-vous m'indiquer la cabine téléphonique la plus proche?

What is the number for directory enquiries?
Quel est le numéro pour les renseignements?

Where can I find a telephone directory?
Où est-ce que je peux trouver un annuaire?

Where can I buy a phone card?
Où est-ce que je peux acheter une télécarte?

Please put me through to…
Pouvez-vous me passer …, s'il vous plaît?

Can I dial direct to …?
Est-ce que je peux appeler directement en …?

Do I need to dial 0 first?
Est-ce qu'il faut composer le zéro (d'abord)?

What is the charge per minute?
Quel est le tarif à la minute?

Have there been any calls for me?
Est-ce que j'ai eu des appels téléphoniques?

Hello, this is …
Allô, c'est … (à l'appareil)?

Who is speaking please …?
Qui est à l'appareil, s'il vous plaît?

I would like to speak to …
Je voudrais parler à …

DAYS/MONTHS/HOLIDAYS/TIMES

Monday **lundi**	January **janvier**	August **août**	spring **printemps**	morning **matin**	day **le jour**
Tuesday **mardi**	February **février**	September **septembre**	summer **été**	afternoon **après-midi**	month **le mois**
Wednesday **mercredi**	March **mars**	October **octobre**	autumn **automne**	evening **soir**	year **l'année**
Thursday **jeudi**	April **avril**	November **novembre**	winter **hiver**	night **nuit**	
Friday **vendredi**	May **mai**	December **décembre**	holiday **vacances**	today **aujourd'hui**	
Saturday **samedi**	June **juin**		Easter **Pâques**	yesterday **hier**	
Sunday **dimanche**	July **juillet**		Christmas **Noël**	tomorrow **demain**	

HOTELS

Do you have a room?
(Est-ce que) vous avez une chambre?

I have a reservation for … nights.
J'ai réservé pour … nuits.

How much each night?
C'est combien par nuit?

Double room.
Une chambre pour deux personnes/double.

Twin room.
Une chambre à deux lits/ avec lits jumeaux.

Single room.
Une chambre à un lit/pour une personne.

With bath/shower/lavatory.
Avec salle de bain/ douche/WC.

Is the room air-conditioned/ heated?
(Est-ce que) la chambre est climatisée/chauffée?

Is breakfast/lunch/dinner included in the cost?
(Est-ce que) le petit déjeuner/le déjeuner/le dîner est compris dans le prix?

Is there a lift in the hotel?
(Est-ce qu')il y a un ascenseur à l'hôtel?

Is room service available?
(Est-ce qu')il y a le service en chambre?

When do you serve breakfast?
À quelle heure servez-vous le petit déjeuner?

May I have breakfast in my room?
(Est-ce que) je peux prendre le petit déjeuner dans ma chambre?

Do you serve evening meals?
(Est-ce que) vous servez le repas du soir/le dîner?

I need an alarm call at…
Je voudrais être réveillé(e) à… heures.

I'd like an extra blanket/pillow.
Je voudrais une couverture/ un oreiller supplémentaire, s'il vous plaît.

May I have my room key?
(Est-ce que) je peux avoir la clé de ma chambre?

Will you look after my luggage until I leave?
Pouvez-vous garder mes bagages jusqu'à mon départ?

Is there parking?
(Est-ce qu') il y a un parking?

Where can I park my car?
Où est-ce que je peux garer ma voiture?

Do you have babysitters?
(Est-ce que) vous avez un service de babysitting/garde d'enfants?

When are the sheets changed?
Quand changez-vous les draps?

The room is too hot/cold.
Il fait trop chaud/froid dans la chambre.

Could I have another room?
(Est-ce que) je pourrais avoir une autre chambre?

I am leaving this morning.
Je pars ce matin.

What time should we leave our room?
A quelle heure devons-nous libérer la chambre?

Can I pay my bill?
(Est-ce que) je peux régler ma note, s'il vous plaît?

May I see the room?
(Est-ce que) je peux voir la chambre?

Swimming pool.
Piscine.

No smoking.
Non fumeur.

Sea view.
Vue sur la mer.

Where is the information desk?
Où est le bureau des renseignements?

Where is the timetable?
Où sont les horaires?

Does this train/bus go to…?
Ce train/bus va à…?

Do you have a Métro/bus map?
Avez-vous un plan du Métro/des lignes de bus?

Please can I have a single/ return ticket to…?
Je voudrais un aller simple/ un aller-retour pour…, s'il vous plaît.

I'd like to rent a car.
Je voudrais louer une voiture.

Where are we?
Où sommes-nous?

I'm lost.
Je me suis perdu(e).

Is this the way to…?
C'est bien par ici pour aller à…?

I am in a hurry.
Je suis pressé(e).

Where can I find a taxi?
Où est-ce que je peux trouver un taxi?

How much is the journey?
Combien coûte la course?

Go straight on.
Allez tout droit.

Turn left.
Tournez à gauche.

Turn right.
Tournez à droite.

Cross over.
Traversez.

Traffic lights.
Les feux.

Intersection.
Carrefour.

Corner.
Coin.

No parking
Interdiction de stationner

Train/bus/Métro station
La gare SNCF/routière/ la station de Métro.

Do you sell travel cards?
Avez-vous des cartes d'abonnement?

Do I need to get off here?
(Est-ce qu') il faut que je descende ici?

Where can I buy a ticket?
Où est-ce que je peux acheter un billet/ticket?

Where can I reserve a seat?
Où est-ce que je peux réserver une place?

Is this seat free?
(Est-ce que) cette place est libre?

Where can I find a taxi?
Où est-ce que je peux trouver un taxi?

Is there a bank/currency exchange office nearby?
(Est-ce qu') il y a une banque/un bureau de change près d'ici?

Can I cash this here?
(Est-ce que) je peux encaisser ça ici?

I'd like to change sterling/ dollars into euros.
Je voudrais changer des livres sterling/dollars en euros.

Can I use my credit card to withdraw cash?
(Est-ce que) je peux utiliser ma carte de crédit pour retirer de l'argent?

What is the exchange rate today?
Quel est le taux de change aujourd'hui?

brown	blue
marron/brun	**bleu(e)**
black	green
noir(e)	**vert(e)**
red	yellow
rouge	**jaune**

I'd like to reserve a table for … people at …
Je voudrais réserver une table pour … personnes à …heures, s'il vous plaît.

A table for …, please.
Une table pour …, s'il vous plaît.

We have/haven't booked.
Nous avons/n'avons pas réservé.

What time does the restaurant open?
A quelle heure ouvre le restaurant?

We'd like to wait for a table.
Nous aimerions attendre qu'une table se libère.

Could we sit there?
(Est-ce que) nous pouvons nous asseoir ici?

Is this table taken?
(Est-ce que) cette table est libre?

Are there tables outside?
(Est-ce qu') il y a des tables dehors/à la terrasse?

Where are the lavatories?
Où sont les toilettes?

Could you warm this up for me?
(Est-ce que) vous pouvez me faire réchauffer ceci/ça, s'il vous plaît?

Do you have nappy-changing facilities?
(Est-ce qu') il y a une pièce pour changer les bébés?

We'd like something to drink.
Nous voudrions quelque chose à boire.

Could we see the menu/ wine list?
(Est-ce que) nous pouvons voir le menu/la carte des vins, s'il vous plaît?

Is there a dish of the day?
(Est-ce qu') il y a un plat du jour?

What do you recommend?
Qu'est-ce que vous nous conseillez?

This is not what I ordered.
Ce n'est pas ce que j'ai commandé.

I can't eat wheat/sugar/salt/pork/beef/dairy.
Je ne peux pas manger de blé/sucre/sel/porc/bœuf/produits laitiers.

I am a vegetarian.
Je suis végétarien(ne).

I'd like…
Je voudrais …

Could we have some more bread?
(Est-ce que) vous pouvez nous apporter un peu plus de pain, s'il vous plaît?

How much is this dish?
Combien coûte ce plat?

Is service included?
(Est-ce que) le service est compris?

Could we have some salt and pepper?
(Est-ce que) vous pouvez nous apporter du sel et du poivre, s'il vous plaît?

May I have an ashtray?
(Est-ce que) je peux avoir un cendrier, s'il vous plaît?

Could I have bottled still/sparkling water?
(Est-ce que) je peux avoir une bouteille d'eau minérale/gazeuse, s'il vous plaît?

The meat is too rare/overcooked.
La viande est trop saignante/trop cuite.

The food is cold.
La nourriture est froide.

Can I have the bill, please?
(Est-ce que) je peux avoir l'addition, s'il vous plaît?

The bill is not right.
Il y a une erreur sur l'addition.

We didn't order this.
Nous n'avons pas commandé ça.

I'd like to speak to the manager, please.
Je voudrais parler au directeur, s'il vous plaît.

The food was excellent.
La nourriture était excellente.

Breakfast **Petit déjeuner**	Sugar **Sucre**	Mushroom soup **Soupe aux champignons**	Casserole **Plat en cocotte**	Tomatoes **Tomates**
Lunch **Déjeuner**	Wine list **Carte/liste des vins**	Sandwiches **Sandwichs**	Roast lamb **Gigot**	Fruit **Les fruits**
Dinner **Dîner**	Main course **Le plat principal**	Ham sandwich **Sandwich du jambon**	Mixed cold meat **L'assiette de charcuterie**	Apples **Pommes**
Coffee **Café**	Dessert **Dessert**	Dish of the day **Plat du jour**	Potatoes **Pommes de terre**	Strawberries **Fraises**
Tea **Thé**	Salt/pepper **Sel/poivre**	Fish dishes **Les poissons**	Cauliflower **Chou-fleur**	Peaches **Pêches**
Orange juice **Jus d'orange**	Cheese **Fromage**	Prawns **Crevettes roses/bouquet**	Green beans **Haricots verts**	Pears **Poires**
Apple juice **Jus de pomme**	Knife/fork/spoon **Couteau/Fourchette/Cuillère**	Oysters **Huîtres**	Peas **Petits pois**	Fruit tart **Tarte aux fruits**
Milk **Lait**			Carrots **Carottes**	Pastry **Pâtisserie**
Beer **Bière**	Soups **Soupes/potages**	Salmon **Saumon**	Spinach **Épinards**	Chocolate cake **Gâteau au chocolat**
Red wine **Vin rouge**	Vegetable soup **Soupe de légumes**	Haddock **Aiglefin**	Onions **Oignons**	Cream **Crème**
White wine **Vin blanc**	Chicken soup **Soupe au poulet**	Squid **Calmar**	Lettuce **Laitue**	Ice cream **Glace**
Bread roll **Petit pain**	Lentil soup **Soupe aux lentilles**	Meat dishes **Viandes**	Cucumber **Concombre**	Chocolate mousse **Mousse au chocolat**
Bread **Pain**		Roast chicken **Poulet roti**		

Where is the tourist information office, please?
Où se trouve l'office du tourisme, s'il vous plaît?

Do you have a city map?
Avez-vous un plan de la ville?

Where is the museum?
Où est le musée?

Can you give me some information about…?
Pouvez-vous me donner des renseignements sur …?

What are the main places of interest here?
Quels sont les principaux sites touristiques ici?

Please could you point them out on the map?
Pouvez-vous me les indiquer sur la carte, s'il vous plaît?

What sights/hotels/restaurants can you recommend?
Quels sites/hôtels/restaurants nous recommandez-vous?

We are staying here for a day.
Nous sommes ici pour une journée.

I am interested in…
Je suis intéressé(e) par…

Does the guide speak English?
Est-ce qu'il y a un guide qui parle anglais?

Do you have any suggested walks?
Avez-vous des suggestions de promenades?

Are there guided tours?
Est-ce qu'il y a des visites guidées?

Are there organised excursions?
Est-ce qu'il y a des excursions organisées?

Can we make reservations here?
Est-ce que nous pouvons réserver ici?

What time does it open/close?
Ça ouvre/ferme à quelle heure?

What is the admission price?
Quel est le prix d'entrée?

Is there a discount for senior citizens/students?
Est-ce qu'il y a des réductions pour les personnes âgées/ les étudiants?

Do you have a brochure in English?
Avez-vous un dépliant en anglais?

What's on at the cinema?
Qu'est-ce qu'il y a au cinéma?

Where can I find a good nightclub?
Où est-ce que je peux trouver une bonne boîte de nuit?

Do you have a schedule for the theatre/opera?
Est-ce que vous avez un programme de théâtre/ d'opéra?

Should we dress smartly?
Est-ce qu'il faut mettre une tenue de soirée?

What time does the show start?
A quelle heure commence le spectacle?

How do I reserve a seat?
Comment fait-on pour réserver une place?

Could you reserve tickets for me?
Pouvez-vous me réserver des billets?

I don't feel well.
Je ne me sens pas bien.

Could you call a doctor?
(Est-ce que) vous pouvez appeler un médecin/un docteur, s'il vous plaît?

Is there a doctor/pharmacist on duty?
(Est-ce qu') il y a un médecin/docteur/une pharmacie de garde?

I feel sick.
J'ai envie de vomir.

I need to see a doctor/dentist.
Il faut que je voie un médecin/docteur/ un dentiste.

Please direct me to the hospital.
(Est-ce que) vous pouvez m'indiquer le chemin pour aller à l'hôpital, s'il vous plaît?

I have a headache.
J'ai mal à la tête.

I've been stung by a wasp/bee/jellyfish.
J'ai été piqué(e) par une guêpe/abeille/méduse.

I have a heart condition.
J'ai un problème cardiaque.

I am diabetic.
Je suis diabétique.

I'm asthmatic.
Je suis asmathique.

I'm on a special diet.
Je suis un régime spécial.

I am on medication.
Je prends des médicaments.

I have left my medicine at home.
J'ai laissé mes médicaments chez moi.

I need to make an emergency appointment.
Je dois prendre rendez-vous d'urgence.

I have bad toothache.
J'ai mal aux dents.

I don't want an injection.
Je ne veux pas de piqûre.

Help!
Au secours!

I have lost my passport/ wallet/purse/handbag.
J'ai perdu mon passeport/ portefeuille/porte- monnaie/sac à main.

I have had an accident.
J'ai eu un accident.

My car has been stolen.
On m'a volé ma voiture.

I have been robbed.
J'ai été volé(e).

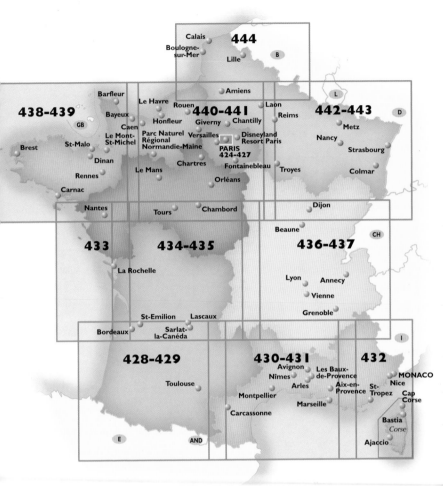

Calais
Boulogne-sur-Mer
444
Lille
B

Amiens

Barfleur
Le Havre Rouen
440-441
Laon
L

438-439
Bayeux
Honfleur Giverny Chantilly Reims
D

GB
Caen
Le Mont-St-Michel
Parc Naturel Versailles Disneyland Resort Paris
Metz
Nancy

Brest
St-Malo
Régional Normandie-Maine
PARIS **424-427**
Strasbourg

Dinan
Chartres
Fontainebleau
Troyes
Colmar

Rennes
Le Mans
Orléans

Carnac

Nantes
Tours
Chambord
Dijon

433
434-435
Beaune
CH

La Rochelle
436-437

Lyon Annecy
Vienne

St-Emilion Lascaux
Grenoble

Bordeaux
Sarlat-la-Canéda
I

428-429
430-431
432

Avignon
MONACO

Toulouse
Nîmes
Les Baux-de-Provence
Nice

Arles
Aix-en-Provence
St-Tropez
Cap Corse

Montpellier
Marseille

Carcassonne
Bastia
Corse

E
AND
Ajaccio

=== Toll motorway (Turnpike)

=== Motorway (Expressway)

❷ ● Motorway junction with and without number

National road

Regional road

Railway

International boundary

Administrative region boundary

■ City / Town

National park

● Featured place of interest

✈ Airport

621
▲ Height in metres

⌂— Port / Ferry route

Mountain pass

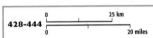

428-444
0   25 km
0   20 miles

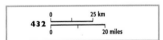

432
0   25 km
0   20 miles

Maps

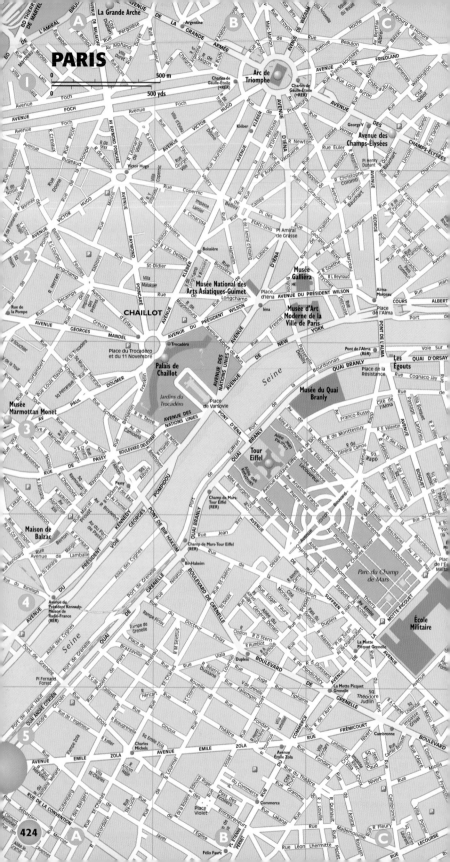

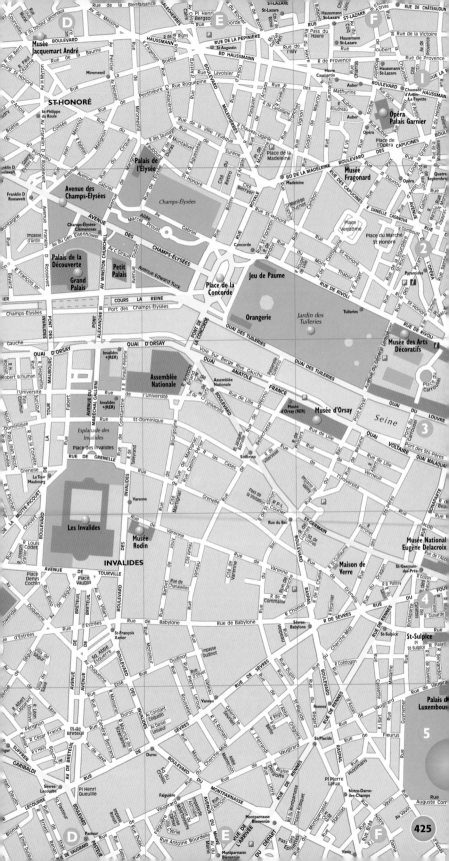

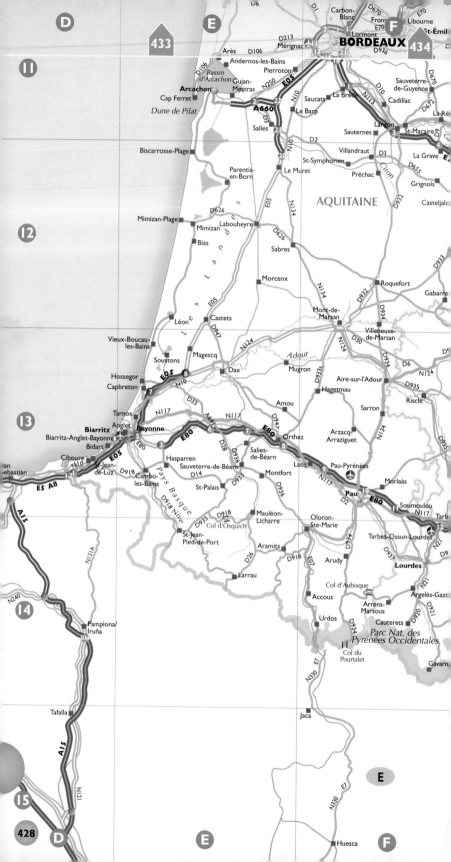

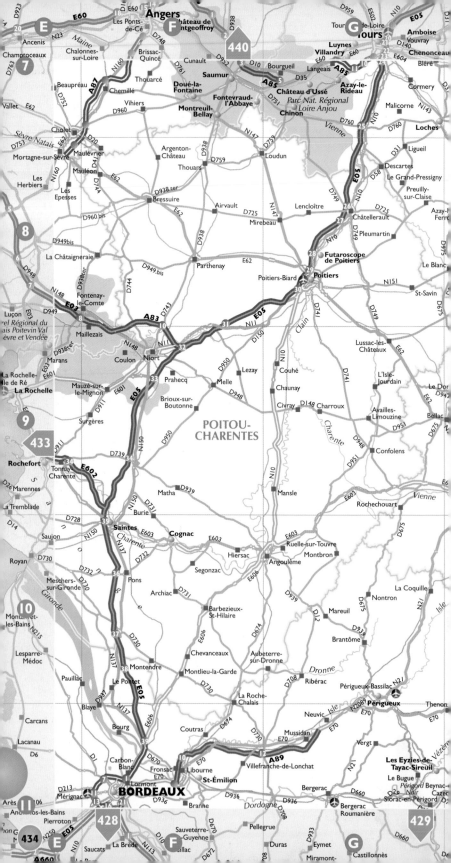

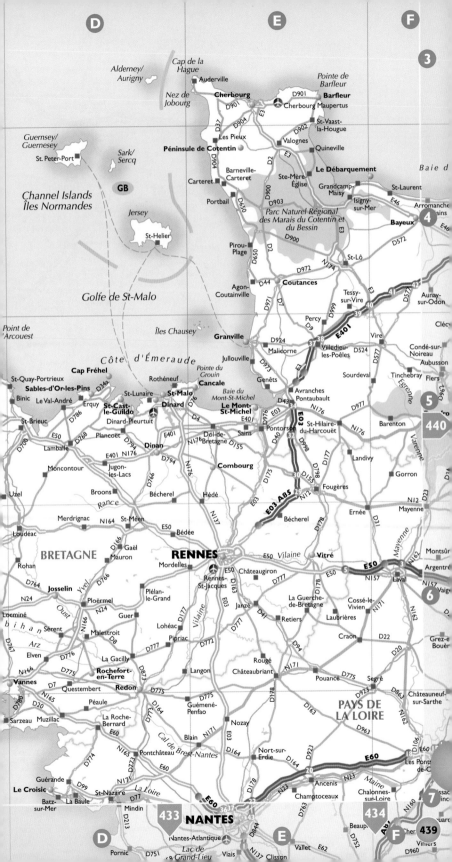

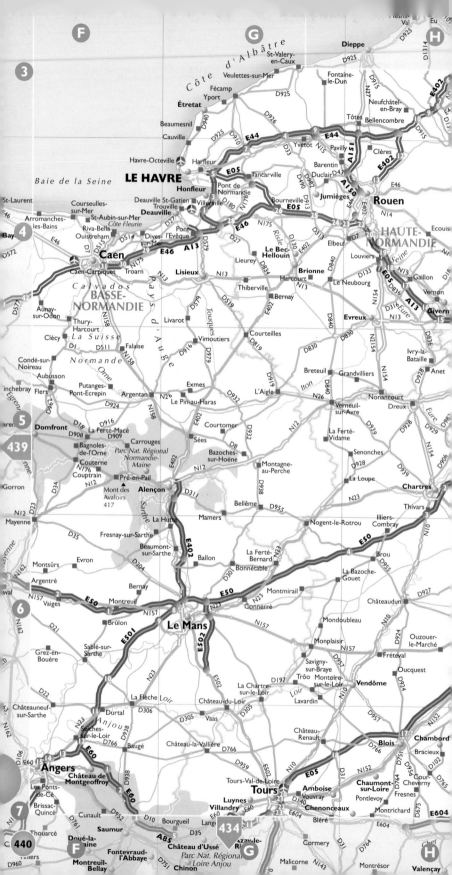

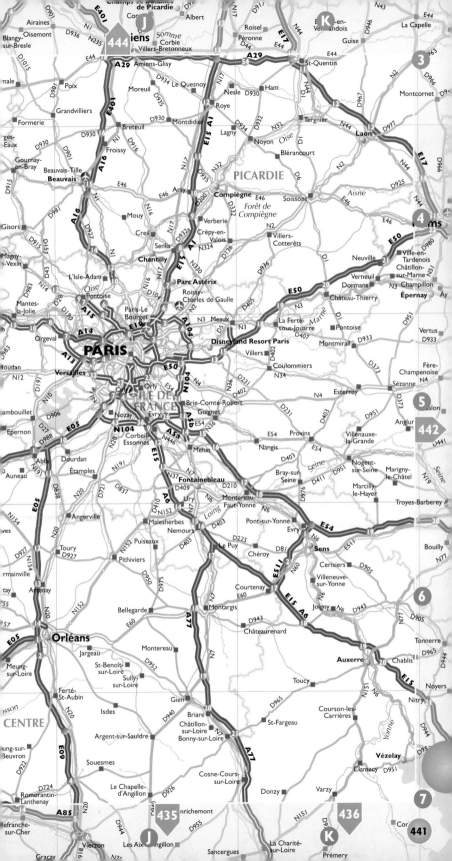

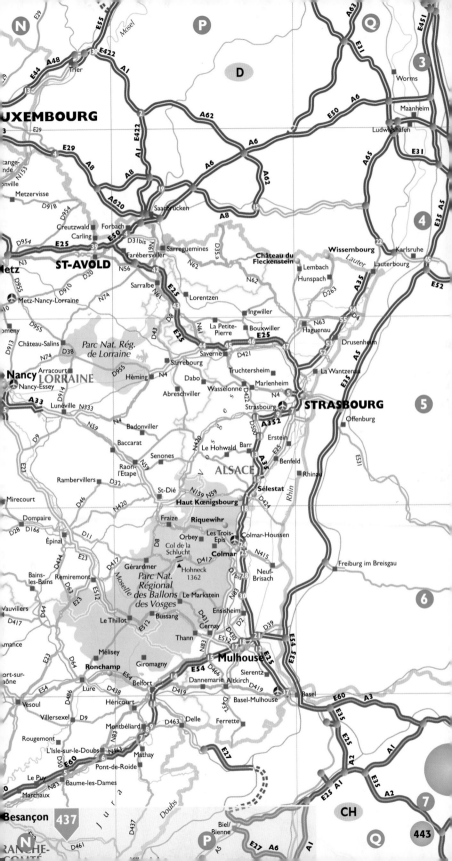

Nozay 441 J5
Nyons 431 M12

O

Oisemont 444 H3
Olargues 430 K13
Olette 430 J15
Olliergues 436 K10
Oloron-Ste-Marie 428 F14
Orange 431 M12
Orbey 443 P6
Orgeval 441 J5
Orléans 441 H6
Orly 441 J5
Orthez 428 E13
Oucquest 440 H6
Ouistreham 440 F4
Ouzouer-le-Marché 440 H6
Oyonnax 437 N9

P

La Pacaudière 436 L9
Paimpol 438 C5
Le Palais 438 C7
Palavas-les-Flots 430 L13
Pamiers 429 H14
Paray-le-Monial 436 L8
Parc Astérix 441 J4
Parentis-en-Born 428 E12
Paris 441 J5
Parthenay 434 F8
Pas-en-Artois 444 J3
Patay 441 H6
Pau 428 F13
Pauillac 434 F10
Pavilly 440 G4
Péaule 439 D7
Peïra-Cava 432 Q12
Pellegrue 429 F11
Péninsule de Cotentin 439 E4
Pentrez-Plage 438 B6
Percy 439 E5
Périgueux 434 G10
Péronne 444 K3
Pérouges 436 M9
Perpignan 430 K14
Perros-Guirec 438 C5
Pertuis 431 N13
La Petite-Pierre 443 P5
Pézenas 430 K13
Piana 432 P14
Pierre-de-Bresse 436 M8
Pierrefort 435 J11
Pierrefort 442 N5
Les Pieux 439 E4
Piney 442 L5
Pinols 436 K11
Pipriac 439 D6
Pirou-Plage 439 E4
Pithiviers 441 J6
Plabennec 438 B5
Plage-en-Ré 433 E9
Plancoët 439 D5
Plélan-le-Grand 439 D6
Pleumartin 434 G8
Pleyben 438 B5
Ploërmel 439 D6
Plouay 438 C6
Ploudalmézeau 438 B5

Plouescat 438 B5
Plougasnou 438 C5
Plougastel-Daoulas 438 B5
Plouha 438 C5
Plouigneau 438 C5
Ploumanac'h 438 C5
Plouray 438 C6
Pluvigner 438 C6
Poissons 442 M5
Poitiers 434 G8
Poix 441 J3
Poix-Terron 442 L3
Pons 434 F10
Pont du Gard 431 L12
Pont l'Evêque 440 G4
Pontailler-sur-Saône 442 M7
Pont-à-Mousson 442 N5
Pontarlier 437 N8
Pontaubault 439 E5
Pont-Aven 438 B6
Pontcharra 437 N10
Pontchâteau 439 D7
Pont-Croix 438 B6
Pont-d'Ain 437 M9
Le Pont-de-Beauvoisin 437 N10
Pont-de-Roide 443 P7
Pont-de-Vaux 436 M8
Le Pontet 434 F10
Pontgibaud 435 J9
Pontivy 438 C6
Pont-l'Abbé 438 B6
Pontlevoy 440 H7
Pontoise 441 J4
Pontoise 441 K5
Pontorson 439 E5
Pontrieux 438 C5
Pont-sur-Yonne 441 K6
Les Ponts-de-Cé 440 F7
Pornic 433 D7
Porquerolles 432 N14
La Porta 432 Q14
Portbail 439 E4
Port-de-Bouc 431 M13
Port-Grimaud 432 P13
Porticcio 432 Q15
Port-Joinville 433 D8
Port-Louis 438 C6
Port-Manech 438 B6
Port-Navalo 438 C7
Porto 432 Q14
Porto-Vecchio 432 Q15
Port-sur-Saône 443 N6
Pouancé 439 E6
Pouilly-en-Auxois 436 L7
Le Pouldu 438 C6
Pouyastruc 429 F13
Pradelles 430 L11
Prahecq 434 F9
Prats-de-Mollo-la-Preste 430 J15
Préchac 428 F12
Prémery 436 K7
Preuilly-sur-Claise 434 G8
Privas 431 L11
Propriano 432 Q15
Provins 441 K5
Prunete 432 Q14
Puiseaux 441 J6
Putanges-Pont-Ecrepin 440 F5
Le Puy 441 J6

Le Puy 443 N7
Puy de Dôme 435 K10
Puy-l'Evêque 429 H12
Le Puy-en-Velay 436 L11

Q

Le Quesnoy 441 J3
Le Quesnoy 444 K3
Questembert 439 D6
Quiberon 438 C7
Quillan 430 J14
Quillins 436 M10
Quimper 438 B6
Quimperlé 438 C6
Quineville 439 E4
Quingey 437 N7
Quissac 430 L12

R

Rabastens-de-Bigorre 429 F13
Rambervillers 443 N5
Rambouillet 441 H5
Randan 436 K9
Raon-l'Etape 443 P5
Réalmont 430 J13
Recey-sur-Ource 442 M6
Redon 439 D6
Reignier 437 N9
Reims 442 L4
Remiremont 443 N6
Rennes 439 E6
La Réole 428 F11
Réquista 430 J12
Rethel 442 L4
Retiers 439 E6
Reuilly 435 J7
Rhinau 443 Q5
Ribérac 434 G10
Rieumes 429 H13
Rieux 429 H13
Rignac 430 J12
Riom 435 K9
Riquewihr 443 P6
Riva-Bella 440 F4
Rivedoux-Plage 433 E9
Roanne 436 L9
Rocamadour 429 H11
La Roche-Bernard 439 D7
La Roche-Chalais 434 F10
Rochechouart 434 G9
Rochefort 433 E9
Rochefort-en-Terre 439 D6
La Rochelle 433 E9
La Roche-sur-Foron 437 N9
La Roche-sur-Yon 433 E8
La Rochette 437 N10
Rodez 430 J12
Rogliano 432 Q14
Rohan 439 D6
Roisel 444 K3
Romorantin-Lanthenay 441 H7
Ronchamp 443 N6
Roquebillière 432 Q12
La Roquebrussanne 431 N13
Roquefort 428 F12
Roquefort-sur-Soulzon 430 K12
La Roque-Gageac 435 H11
Rosans 431 M12
Roscoff 438 B5

Rosporden 438 B6
Rostrenen 438 C5
Rothéneuf 439 D5
Roubaix 444 K2
Rouen 440 H4
Rougé 439 E6
Rougemont 443 N7
Roussillon 431 M12
Rouvres-en-Xaintoi 442 N5
Royan 433 E10
Roybon 437 M10
Roye 441 J3
Royère-de-Vassivière 435 H9
Le Rozier 430 K12
Rue 444 H2
Ruelle-sur-Touvre 434 G10
Ruffieux 437 N9
Rumigny 442 L3

S

Les Sables-d'Olonne 433 D8
Sables-d'Or-les-Pins 439 D5
Sablé-sur-Sarthe 440 F6
Sabres 428 E12
St-Amand-Montrond 435 J8
St-Aubin-sur-Mer 440 F4
St-Avold 443 N4
St-Benoît-sur-Loire 441 J6
St-Brieuc 439 D5
St-Cast-le-Guildo 439 D5
St-Cirq-Lapopie 429 H12
St-Claude 437 N8
St-Denis-d'Oléron 433 E9
St-Dié 443 P5
St-Dizier 442 M5
Sainte-Lucie-de-Tallano 432 Q15
Ste-Mère-Église 439 E4
St-Émilion 434 F11
Ste-Enimie 430 K12
Saintes 434 F10
Stes-Maries-de-la-Mer 431 L13
St-Étienne 436 L10
St-Étienne-de-Tinée 432 P12
St-Fargeau 441 K7
St-Florent 432 Q14
St-Florent 435 J8
St-Flour 435 K11
St-Guénolé 438 B6
St-Hilaire-du-Harcouët 439 E5
St-Jean-de-Luz 428 D13
St-Jean-Pied-de-Port 428 E14
St-Laurent 439 F4
St-Lizier 429 H14
St-Lô 439 E4
St-Lunaire 439 D5
St-Macaire 428 F11
St-Malo 439 D5
St-Martin-d'Ardèche 431 L12
St-Maximin-la-Ste-Baume
    431 N13
St-Méen 439 D6
St-Nazaire 439 D7
St-Omer 444 J2
St-Paul 432 P13
St-Pierre-le-Moûtier 435 K8
St-Pierre-sur-Mer 430 K14
St-Pol-de-Léon 438 B5
St-Quay-Portrieux 439 D5
St-Quentin 441 K3

ACKNOWLEDGMENTS

Abbreviations for the picture credits are as follows:
AA = AA World Travel Library, **t** (top), **b** (bottom), **c** (centre), **l** (left), **r** (right), **bg** (background)

UNDERSTANDING FRANCE

4cl AA/I Dawson; **4c** AA/R Moss; **4c** AA/J Edmanson; **5cl** AA/M Short; **5c** AA/C Sawyer; **5cr** AA/P Kenward; **5br** AA/P Enticknap; **6tl** AA/T Souter; **6cl** AA/J White; **6c** AA/K Reynolds; **6cr** AA/B Toms; **6br** AA/P Kenward; **7bl** AA/R Strange; **8tl** AA/C Sawyer; **8tr** AA/J A Tims; **8ctr** AA/I Dawson; **8cbr** AA/R Strange; **8br** AA/D Robertson; **9tl** AA/R Moore; **9cl** AA/R Strange; **9cr** AA/T Teegan; **9bl** AA/R Strange; **10cl** AA/R Moore; **10tr** AA/P Bennett; **10cr** AA/C Sawyer; **10br** AA/B Rieger.

LIVING FRANCE

11 AA/M Jourdan; **12/3bg** AA/C Sawyer; **12tl** AA/C Sawyer; **12tr** AA/R Moore; **12cl** AA/R Strange; **12c** AA/T Teegan; **12cr** AA/R Strange; **12br** AA/N Setchfield; **13tl** AA/J Edmanson; **13tc** AA/A Baker; **13c** AA/R Moss; **13tr** AA/D Ireland; **14/5bg** AA/K Glendenning; **14tl** AA/M Jourdan; **14/5** AA/K Paterson; **14cl** AA/I Dawson; **14c** AA/I Dawson; **14cr** AA/M Jourdan; **14bl** Rex Features Ltd; **15tl** AA/R Moore; **15cl** AA/C Sawyer; **15cr** AA/B Smith; **15c** Rex Features Ltd; **16/7bg** AA/C Sawyer; **16tl** AA/C Sawyer; **16tr** AA/M Adleman; **16cl** AA/R Strange; **16cr** AA/T Oliver; **16b** AA/R Moore; **17tl** AA/P Kenward; **17cl** AA/M Jourdan; **17cr** AA/C Sawyer; **18/9bg** AA/N Setchfield; **18tl** AA/J Edmanson; **18tr** AA/R Day; **18cr** AA/C Sawyer; **18b** AA/M Jourdan; **19tr** AA/J A Tims; **19cl** AA/K Paterson; **19cr** AA/J A Tims; **20/1bg** AA/N Setchfield; **20tl** AA/N Setchfield; **20tr** AA/N Setchfield; **20cl** AA/C Sawyer; **20c** AA/J Wyand; **20cr** AA/B Smith; **20b** AA/R Moore; **21tl** AA/N Setchfield; **21tc** AA/N Setchfield; **21cl** AA/I Dawson; **21c** AA/N Setchfield; **21cr** AA/N Setchfield; **22/3bg** Comité Regional du Tourisme, Pays de la Loire; **22tl** AA/M Jourdan; **22tc** AA/C Sawyer; **22tr** AA/D Noble; **22cr** AA/R Strange; **22br** Comité Regional du Tourisme, Pays de la Loire; **23tl** AA/R Strange; **23tc** AA/R Strange; **23cl** AA/J Wyand; **23cr** AA/A Kouprianoff; **23c** Corbis; **24/5bg** AA/R Moore; **24cr** Rex Features Ltd; **24tl** AA/R Moore; **24tc** AA/P Bennett; **24cl** AA/M Short; **25cl** Rex Features Ltd; **25tr** Renault Formula 1; **25c** Comité Regional du Tourisme, Pays de la Loire; **25cr** Rex Features Ltd; **26bg** AA/C Sawyer; **26cr** AA/C Sawyer; **26tc** AA/N Setchfield; **26tr** AA/C Sawyer; **26c** AA/C Sawyer; **26cl** Rex Features Ltd.

THE STORY OF FRANCE

27 AA/R Moore; **28/9bg** AA/A Baker; **28cl** AA/A Baker; **28cr** AA; **28bl** AA/A Baker; **28bc** AA; **28/9c** AA; **28/9b** AA/A Baker; **29cl** AA; **29c** AA; **29cr** AA; **29bc** AA/B Smith; **29br** AA/A Baker; **30/1bg** AA/D Roberston; **30cl** AA; **30c** AA; **30cr** AA; **30bl** AA; **30/1** AA/D Robertson; **31cl** AA; **31c** AA; **31cr** AA; **31bl** AA/R Moore; **31br** AA/J Edmanson; **32/3bg** AA; **32cl** AA/J Edmanson; **32c** AA/C Sawyer; **32b** AA; **32/3** AA/R Moore; **33ct** AA; **33cr** AA; **33cl** AA; **33cr** AA; **33cb** AA; **34/5bg** AA; **34cl** AA/D Noble; **34cr** AA; **34bl** AA/D Noble; **34/5** AA/J A Tims; **35cl** *Louis XIV* (1638-1715 of France in the costume of The Sun King in the ballet 'La Nuit' c. 1665 (litho), French School (19th century)/Bridgeman Art Library; **35c** AA; **35cr** AA; **35bc** *Portrait of Jean-Baptiste Colbert de Torcy* (1619-83) 1666 (oil on canvas), Lefebvre, Claude (1632-75), Château de Versailles, France/Bridgeman Art Library; **36/7bg** AA; **36cl** Mary Evans Picture Library; **36cr** AA; **36bl** AA; **36/7** AA; **37cl** AA; **37c** AA; **37cr** AA; **37c** AA; **37cr** AA; **37bl** AA; **38/9bg** AA; **38cl** AA; **38ctc** *Winter in Nice* poster advertising P.L.M. trains (colour litho), Alesi, Hugo d' (1849-1906) Bibliotheque–Musée Forney, Paris, France/Archives Charmet/Bridgeman Art Library; **38cr**

Illustrated London News; **38c** AA; **38bl** Illustrated London News; **38/9** Illustrated London News; **39cl** AA; **39c** Illustrated London News; **39cr** AA; **39br** AA/A Baker; **40/1** AA; **40cl** Illustrated London News; **40cr** Mary Evans Picture Library; **40bl** Illustrated London News; **40blc** AA; **40brc** AA; **40br** Illustrated London News; **41cl** AA/M Jourdan; **41c** Mary Evans Picture Library; **41cr** Illustrated London News; **41bl** Hulton Archives/Getty Images; **41b** AA/R Moore; **41br** Rex Features Ltd; **42bc** AA/N Setchfield; **42cl** Rex Features Ltd; **42cr** Rex Features Ltd; **42bl** AA/N Setchfield; **42br** AA/C Sawyer; **42b** AA/N Setchfield.

ON THE MOVE

43 AA/M Jourdan; **44/5** Digital Vision; **46** Digital Vision; **47** Eurostar; **48t** AA/S L Day; **48l** AA/I Dawson; **49t** AA/B Rieger; **49cr** AA/M Adelman; **49br** AA/C Sawyer; **50/1** AA/P Kenward; **51** AA/R Strange; **52/3** AA/P Kenward; **52** AA/P Kenward; **53t** AA/K Glendenning; **53tc** AA/J Wyand; **53tr** AA/A Baker; **53cl** AA/R Strange; **53c** AA/N Setchfield; **53cr** AA/R Moore; **53bl** AA/C Sawyer; **53bc** AA/K Glendenning; **53br** AA/A Baker; **54t** AA/P Kenward; **54c** AA/N Setchfield; **55t** AA/C Sawyer; **55c** AA/C Sawyer; **56/7** AA/C Sawyer; **57** AA/N Setchfield; **58t** AA/C Sawyer; **58c** AA/ Setchfield; **59t** AA/K Paterson; **59c** AA/M Jourdan; **60/1** AA/C Sawyer; **62/3** AA/C Sawyer; **62l** AA/C Sawyer; **62r** AA/M Jourdan; **63** AA/C Sawyer; **64/5** AA/M Jourdan; **64** AA/J Wyand; **65c** Lille Metro; **65b** AA/N Setchfield; **66** AA/C Sawyer.

THE SIGHTS

67 AA/P Enticknap; **68/9bg** AA/J Edmanson; **69** AA/M Jourdan; **70** AA/M Jourdan; **71** AA/T Souter; **72l** AA/K Glendenning; **72r** AA/T Souter; **73** © Disney; **74** AA/M Jourdan; **75l** AA/J A Tims; **75r** AA/K Paterson; **75b** AA/J A Tims; **76tl** AA/M Jourdan; **76br** AA/K Paterson; **77t** AA/B Rieger; **77cr** AA/K Paterson; **78t** AA/M Jourdan; **78lc** AA/M Jourdan; **78b** AA/M Jourdan; **79tl** AA/T Souter; **79br** AA/M Jourdan; **80l** AA/K Paterson; **80r** AA/M Joudan; **81l** Musee D'Art et D'Histoire du Judaisme; **81r** AA/M Jourdan; **82t** AA/J A Tims; **82l** AA/J A Tims; **82c** *Mona Lisa*, c.1503-6 (oil on panel) by Leonarado da Vinci, Louvre, Paris/Bridgeman Art Library; **82r** AA/M Jourdan; **83t** AA/M Jourdan; **83b** AA/J A Tims; **84l** *Promenade near Argenteuil*, 1873 (oil on canvas) by Claude Monet, Musee Marmottan, Paris/Bridgeman Art Library © ADAGP, Paris and DACS, London 2004; **84r** AA/K Paterson; **84b** AA/J A Tims; **85** AA/P Enticknap; **86l** AA/M Jourdan © Succession Picasso/DACS 2004; **86r** AA/M Jourdan; **87tl** AA/M Jourdan; **87r** AA/M Jourdan; **88l** AA/K Paterson; **88r** AA/M Jourdan; **89l** AA/C Sawyer; **89r** AA/M Jourdan; **90l** AA/M Jourdan; **90c** AA/B Rieger; **90r** AA/M Jourdan; **91l** AA/K Paterson; **91r** AA/J A Tims; **92** AA/T Souter; **93t** AA/T Souter; **93r** AA/M Jourdan; **94** AA/M Jourdan; **96l** AA/C Sawyer; **96r** AA/I Dawson; **97l** AA/R Moore; **97r** AA; **98l** Office de Tourism de Belle-Ile/Benjamin Azouze; **98r** AA/B Smith; **99t** AA/I Dawson; **99r** AA/I Dawson; **100l** AA/R Victor; **100r** AA/R Strange; **101l** AA/I Dawson; **101r** AA/R Strange; **102l** AA/R Victor; **102r** AA/I Dawson; **102b** AA/I Dawson; **103t** AA/I Dawson; **103r** AA/I Dawson; **104l** AA/R Moore; **104r** AA/S L Day; **105tl** AA/B Smith; **105tc** AA/A Baker; **105tr** AA/R Moore; **105b** AA/R Strange; **106l** AA/R Moore; **106l** AA/I Dawson; **107tl** AA/R Moore; **107tr** AA/I Dawson; **107b** AA/I Dawson; **108l** AA/I Dawson; **108r** AA/I Dawson; **109l** AA/P Kenward; **109r** AA/R Strange; **110t** AA/I Dawson; **110cl** AA/I Dawson; **110cr** AA/I Dawson; **111** AA/I Dawson;

Abbreviations for the picture credits are as follows:

AA = AA World Travel Library, t (top), b (bottom), c (centre), l (left), r (right), bg (background)

112l AA/R Strange; 112r Parc National Regionale Normandie-Maine; 113l AA/R Victor; 113r AA/A Baker; 114t AA/S L Day; 114cl AA/S L Day; 114cr AA/B Smith; 114bl AA/S L Day; 115l AA/R Victor; 115r AA/S L Day; 116t AA/R Moore; 116cl AA/I Dawson; 116c AA/I Dawson; 116cr AA/R Moore; 117 AA/R Moore; 118 AA/R Moore; 119t AA/I Dawson; 119b AA/I Dawson; 120tl AA/R Strange; 120tr AA/S L Day; 120b AA/S L Day; 121t AA/S L Day; 121r AA/R Victor; 122l AA/R Strange; 122c AA/R Strange; 122r AA/S L Day; 122b AA/R Victor; 124l AA/R Day; 124r AA/R Day; 125 AA/D Roberston; 126l AA/R Day; 126r AA/R Day; 127l World Pictures; 127r AA/C Hatley; 128t AA/B Smith; 128cl Colmar Office de Tourisme; 129l AA/R Day; 129r Office de Tourisme Douai; 130l AA/T Oliver; 130r AA/R Day; 131l Office de Tourisme Mulhouse; 131r AA/B Smith; 132t AA/R Day; 132cl World Pictures; 132c World Pictures; 132cr World Pictures; 133 AA/R Day; 134 World Pictures; 135l AA/R Day; 135c World Pictures; 135br AA/D Roberston; 136tl AA; 136tr AA/R Day; 136b Robert Harding Picture Library; 137tl AA/D Roberston; 137tr AA/D Robertson; 137b AA; 138t AA/R Day; 138cl AA/R Day; 138c World Pictures; 138cr World Pictures; 139t AA/R Day; 139b AA; 140t AA/T Oliver; 140cl World Pictures; 140c World Pictures; 140cr World Pictures; 141 World Pictures; 142 World Pictures; 143l World Pictures; 143c World Pictures; 143r World Pictures; 144l C Follett; 144r AA/B Smith; 146r AA/R Moore; 146l AA/D Noble; 147l AA/J Edmanson; 147r AA/R Moore; 148l AA/J Edmanson; 148c AA/J Edmanson; 148r AA/R Moore; 149r Chateau d'Usse; 149l AA/J Edmanson; 150l AA/R Moore; 150c AA/R Moore; 150r AA/J Edmanson; 151l AA/R Moore; 152 AA/N Setchfield; 153 AA/R Day; 154tl AA/B Smith; 154tr AA/R Moore; 154bl AA/P Aithie; 156; AA/M Short; 156r AA/B Smith; 157tl AA/M Short; 157tr AA/M Short; 157b AA/J Wyand; 158tl AA/R Strange; 158tc AA/B Smith; 158tr AA/R Strange; 158bl AA/T Teegan; 159tl World Pictures; 159tr Evain Office de Tourisme; 159bl AA/M Short; 160t AA/M Short; 160cl AA/J Wyand; 160c AA/J Wyand; 160cr AA/J Wyand; 161l AA/J Wyand; 161r AA/M Short; 162l AA/R Strange; 162r Grenoble Office de Tourisme; 163l AA/J Wyand; 163c AA/J Wyand; 163r AA/J Wyand; 163bl AA/M Short; 164t AA/J Wyand; 164cl AA/J Wyand; 164c AA/J Wyand; 164cr AA/J Wyand; 165 AA/J Wyand; 167 AA/J Wyand; 168l AA/T Oliver; 168c AA/T Oliver; 168r AA/M Short; 169tl AA/M Short; 169tr AA/M Short; 169b AA/M Short; 170l Vichy Office de Tourisme; 170r AA/J Wyand; 172 AA/R Strange; 173t AA/R Strange; 173r AA; 174t AA/R Strange; 174l AA/A Baker; 175l AA/A Baker; 175r AA/R Moore; 176l AA/R Strange; 176r AA/N Setchfield; 177l Castres Office de Tourisme; 177c AA/N Setchfield; 177r AA/A Baker; 178tl AA/A Baker; 178tr AA/R Strange; 178bl AA/C Sawyer; 179tl AA/A Baker; 179tc AA/N Setchfield; 179tr AA/A Baker; 179br AA/C Sawyer; 180tl AA/A Baker; 180tc AA/A Baker; 180tr AA/R Strange; 180br AA/R Strange; 181t AA/N Setchfield; 181r AA/N Setchfield; 182t AA/C Sawyer; 182cl AA/A Baker; 182c AA/A Baker; 182cr AA/C Sawyer; 172bl AA/A Baker; 183 AA/A Baker; 185 AA/C Sawyer; 186t AA/R Strange; 186cl AA/A Baker; 186c AA/C Sawyer; 186cr AA/R Strange; 186bl AA/R Strange; 187 AA/A Baker; 188t AA/R Moore; 188l AA/C Sawyer; 189l World Pictures; 189r AA/A Baker; 190l AA/S Setchfield; 190r AA/R Strange; 190b AA/R Strange; 191l AA/A Baker; 191r AA/A Baker; 192tl AA/A Baker; 192tc AA/A Baker; 192tr AA/A Baker;

192bl AA/B Smith; 194tl AA/N Setchfield; 194tc AA/N Setchfield; 194tr AA/N Setchfield; 194bl AA/N Setchfield; 195l AA/N Setchfield; 195c AA/N Setchfield; 195r AA/N Setchfield; 195b AA/N Setchfield; 196t AA/N Setchfield; 196cl AA/N Setchfield; 196c AA/N Setchfield; 196cr AA/N Setchfield; 196bl AA/P Kenward; 197 World Pictures; 199 AA/N Setchfield; 200tl AA/N Setchfield; 200tc AA/B Smith; 200tr World Pictures; 201l AA/P Kenward; 201r AA/A Baker; 202l World Pictures; 202c AA/N Setchfield; 202r AA/N Setchfield; 203l AA/B Smith; 203r AA/P Kenward; 204r AA/M Ratcliffe; 204l AA/N Setchfield; 205l AA/N Setchfield; 205r AA/B Smith; 206t AA/N Setchfield; 206cl AA/N Setchfield; 206/7c AA/N Setchfield; 206cr AA/N Setchfield; 207 AA/N Setchfield; 208l AA/N Setchfield; 208r AA/B Smith; 210 World Pictures; 211l K Lockley; 211r World Pictures; 212l World Pictures; 212r AA/R Moore; 212bl World Pictures; 213l AA/B Toms; 213r AA/B Toms; 213bl World Pictures; 214l World Pictures; 214r World Pictures; 214b World Pictures.

WHAT TO DO

215 AA/C Sawyer; 216/7 AA/K Paterson; 218t AA/K Paterson; 218bl AA/K Paterson; 218cr AA/C Sawyer; 219t AA/P Enticknap; 219r Digital Vision; 220t AA/T Oliver; 220c Brand X Pics; 221t AA/P Kenward; 221bl AA/T Teegan; 222/3 AA/P Kenward; 222bl AA/R Victor; 223cl Kart'in; 224t AA/M Lynch; 224cr Parc Asterix; 225t AA/J A Tims; 225bl AA/C Sawyer; 225bc AA/C Sawyer; 226/7t AA/J A Tims; 226cl AA/C Sawyer; 226cr AA/C Sawyer; 226br AA/K Paterson; 227cr AA/T Souter; 228/9t AA/J A Tims; 228cl AA/T Souter; 228c AA; 229c AA/B Rieger; 230/1t AA/J A Tims; 230c Le Nouveau Casino, Paris; 231br Printemps; 232t AA/J A Tims; 232b Photodisc; 233t AA/R Victor; 233l AA/R Strange; 234/5t AA/R Victor; 234c AA/B Smith; 236/7t AA/R Victor; 236b Les Planches; 236cr Chateau du Breuil; 237cl AA/r Moore; 237bl Golf Barrière de Deauville; 237c Karting 61; 238/9t AA/R Victor; 238br Digital Vision; 239c AA/P Kenward; 240/1t AA/R Day; 240bl Ould Shebeeb; 240tr Char À Voile Club de la Côte D'Opale; 241br Golf du Touquet; 242/3t AA/R Day; 243c Patisserie Confiserie Kubler; 244/5t AA/B Sm ith; 244c; AA/R Moore; 244br AA/R Moore; 245bl AA/N Setchfield; 245c Le Lieu Unique; 246/7t AA/B Smith; 246bc AA/R Moore; 247cr AA/A Baker; 248t AA/B Smith; 248c AA/R Moore; 248bc AA/M Lynch; 248cr AA/D Noble; 249t AA/T Teegan; 249b AA/C Sawyer; 250/1t AA/t Teegan; 251bl Annecy Office de Tourisme; 252/3t AA/T Teegan; 252bc AA/J Edmanson; 252br AA/B Smith; 253cr AA/J Wyand; 253br L'Opéra Nationale de Lyon; 254t AA/T Teegan; 254br AA/R Strange; 255t AA/R Strange; 255br AA/N Setchfield; 256/7t AA/R Strange; 256cl AA/R Strange; 256tc AA/P Kenward; 257bl AA/C Sawyer; 257cb AA/C Sawyer; 258/9t AA/R Strange; 258cl AA/C Sawyer; 258bl AA/C Sawyere; 259c AA/C Sawyer; 259cr AA/C Sawyer; 260/1t AA/R Strange; 260tc Cap Rando; 261ct AA/A Baker; 261cb AA/C Sawyer; 261cr AA/C Sawyer; 262/3t AA/R Strange; 262ct AA/R Strange; 262cb AA/A Baker; 263tl AA/C Sawyer; 263bc AA/A Baker; 264/5t AA/P Bennett; 264l AA/B Smith; 264r AA/B Smith; 265 Bradley;s Bookshop; 266/7t AA/P Bennett; 266 AA/P Kenward; 267bl AA/P Kenward; 267bc AA/P Kenward; 268/9t AA/P Bennett; 268tl AA/B Smith; 270/1t AA/P Bennett; 270br AA/M Short; 272y AA/P Bennett; 272tc AA/P Kenward; 272cb AA/M Langford; 272cr AA/N Setchfield; 273 AA/N Setchfield; 274t AA/N Setchfield.

Abbreviations for the picture credits are as follows:
AA = AA World Travel Library, **t** (top), **b** (bottom), **c** (centre), **l** (left), **r** (right)

OUT AND ABOUT

275 AA/S L Day; **278b** AA/S L Day; **279tl** AA/S L Day;
279tc AA/S L Day; **279tr** AA/S L Day; **279br** AA/S L Day;
280b AA/R Strange; **281tl** AA/R Victor; **281tr** AA/R Victor;
281bl AA/R Strange; **281br** AA/R Strange; **282b** AA/P Bennett;
283tl AA/P Bennett; **283tr** AA/P Bennett; **283cr** AA/P Bennett;
283br AA/P Bennett; **284c** AA/I Dawson; **285tl** AA/I Dawson;
285tr AA/I Dawson; **285bc** AA/I Dawson; **285br** AA/I Dawson;
286bl AA/C Sawyer; **287t** AA/R Moore; **287cr** AA/I Dawson;
287br AA/R Moore; **288b** AA/S L Day; **289tl** AA/S L Day;
289tc AA/R Victor; **289tr** AA/S L Day; **289br** AA/S L Day;
290b AA/I Dawson; **291t** AA/R Moore; **291cr** AA/I Dawson;
291br AA/I Dawson; **292br** C Follett; **293tl** AA/D Robertson;
293tc AA/D Robertson; **293tr** AA/D Robertson; **293br** AA;
294bl Phototheque Office de Tourisme de Gerardmer;
295tl C Follett; **295tr** Phtotheque Office de Tourisme de
Gerardmer; **295br** Phototheque Office de Tourisme de
Gerardmer; **296b** AA/I Powys; **297tl** C Follett;
297tr Phototheque Office de Tourisme de Gerardmer;
297cr Phototheque Office de Tourisme de Gerardmer;
297br Phtotheque Office de Tourisme de Gerardmer;
298b AA/R Day; **299tl** AA/R Day; **299tr** AA/R Day;
299cr AA/R Day; **299br** AA/R day; **300bl** AA/T Oliver;
301tl AA/B Smith; **301tc** World Pictures; **301tr** AA/R Day;
301cr AA/D Roberston; **301br** World Pictures;
302bl AA/R Moore; **303tl** AA/J Edmanson; **303tr** AA/R Moore;
303cr AA/R Moore; **303br** AA/R Moore; **305tl** AA/R Moore;
305tl AA/R Moore; **305tr** AA/R Moore; **305br** AA/J Edmanson;
307tl AA/J Edmanson; **307tr** AA/J Edmanson;
307cr AA/R Moore; **307br** AA/R Moore; **308bl** AA/J Edmanson;
309tl AA/J Edmanson; **309tr** AA/J Edmanson;
309cr AA/J Edmanson; **309br** AA/J Edmanson; **310bl** Corbis;
311t AA/I Powys; **311cr** AA/M Short; **311cr** AA/T Oliver;
311br AA/I Powys; **312bl** AA/M Short; **313tl** AA/M Short;
313tr AA/J Lloyd; **313br** AA/M Short; **314b** AA/J Lloyd;
315t World Pictures; **315cr** World Pictures; **315br** AA/C Sawyer;
317tl AA/N Setchfield; **317tc** AA/ Setchfield; **317tr** AA/N
Setchfield; **318b** AA/C Sawyer; **319tl** AA/C Sawyer;
319tr AA/C Sawyer; **319bl** AA/C Sawyer; **319br** AA/C Sawyer;
320c AA/C Sawyer; **321b** AA/C Sawyeer; **321cr** AA/C Sawyer;
321l AA/C Sawyer; **321tr** AA/C Sawyer; **321br** AA/C Sawyer;
323tl AA/C Sawyer; **323tr** AA/C Sawyer; **323br** AA/C Sawyer;
324br AA/C Sawyer; **324tl** AA/C Sawyer; **324tr** AA/C Sawyer;
324cl AA/C Sawyer; **324bl** AA/C Sawyer; **327tl** AA/C Sawyer;
327tr AA/C Sawyer; **327bl** AA/C Sawyer; **328bl** AA/A Baker;
329bl AA/A Baker; **329bc** AA/A Baker; **329br** AA/R Strange;
329cr AA/A Baker; **329t** AA/A Baker; **331tl** AA/N Setchfield;
331tr AA/N Setchfield; **323bl** AA/N Setchfield; **333tl** AA/N
Setchfield; **333tr** AA/N Setchfield; **333c** AA/N Setchfield;
333br AA/N Setchfield; **335tl** AA/N Setchfield; **335tr** AA/P
Bennett; **335br** AA/N Setchfield; **336bl** AA/N Setchfield;
337tl AA/N Setchfield; **337tr** AA/N Setchfield; **337bc** D Halford;
337br D Halford; **339t** KLockley; **339b** K Lockley;
339b K Lockley; **340tr** AA/K Paterson; **340tc** AA/R Moore;
340tr AA/R Moore.

EATING AND STAYING

341 AA/P Kenward; **343cl** AA/M Short; **343c** AA/B Smith;
343cr AA/J Edmanson; **344cl** AA/M Short; **344c** AA;
344cr AA/R Moore; **343b** AA/P Kenward; **345bl** AA/A Baker;
345tr AA/P Kenward; **346cl** AA/C sawyer; **346c** AA;
246cr AA/C Sawyer; **346bl** AA/R Moore; **348tr** AA/C Sawyer;
348br AA/C Sawyer; **349cl** AA/C Sawyer; **349tr** AA/C Sawyer;

349br AA/C Sawyer; **350tl** AA/C Sawyer; **350tc** AA/C Sawyer;
350bc AA/C Sawyer; **350cr** AA/C Sawyer; **350br** AA/C Sawyer;
351cl AA/C Sawyer; **351bl** AA/C Sawyer; **351c** AA/C Sawyer;
351cr AA/C Sawyer; **352bl** AA/C Sawyer; **352c** AA/C Sawyer;
352tr AA/C Sawyer; **353cl** AA/C Sawyer; **353tc** AA/C Sawyer;
353br AA/C Sawyer; **354bl** AA/C Sawyer; **354ct** AA/C Sawyer;
354cb AA/C Sawyer; **354cr** AA/C sawyer; **354br** AA/C Sawyer;
355cl AA/C Sawyer; **355ct** AA/C Sawyer; **355tr** AA/C Sawyer;
356l AA/A Baker; **362** AA/R Moore; **369c** AA/T Oliver;
371 AA/J Edmanson; **372tr** AA/J Edmanson; **385** AA/C Sawyer;
386bl AA/C Sawyer; **386c** AA/C Sawyer; **387bl** AA/C Sawyer;
387c AA/C Sawyer; **387bc** AA/C Sawyer; **387cr** AA/C Sawyer;
388tl AA/C Sawyer; **388cl** AA/C Sawyer; **388c** AA/C Sawyer;
389tr AA/C Sawyer; **389br** AA/C Sawyer; **390tc** AA/C Sawyer;
390bc AA/C Sawyere; **390cr** AA/C Sawyer; **390br** AA/C
Sawyer; **391bc** AA/C Sawyer; **391cr** AA/C Sawyer;
391br AA/C Sawyer; **392c** AA/C Sawyer; **392br** AA/C Sawyer;
392br AA/C sawyer; **393tl** AA/C Sawyer; **393tr** AA/C Sawyer;
393br AA/C Sawyer; **400** AA/R Moore.

PLANNING

401 AA/M Jourdan; **405tl** AA/C Sawyer; **405tr** AA/J A Tims;
405c AA/P Kenward; **407tl** AA/C Sawyer; **407bl** AA/R Strange;
409 AA/R Strange; **410** AA/I Dawson; **411** AA/C Sawyer;
413 AA/K Paterson; **414** AA/C Sawyer; **415** AA/C Sawyer.

The editors would like to acknowledge the contribution of
Fiona Dunlop and Adam Ruck.

Project editors
Kathryn Glendenning, Cathy Hatley, Isla Love

AA Travel Guides design team
David Austin, Glyn Barlow, Alan Gooch, Kate Harling, Bob Johnson,
Nick Otway, Carole Philp, Keith Russell

Additional design work
Nautilus Design, Jo Tapper

Picture research
Kathy Lockley, Carol Walker

Internal repro work
Susan Crowhurst, Ian Little, Michael Moody

Production
Lyn Kirby, Caroline Nyman

Mapping
Maps produced by the Cartography Department of AA Publishing

Main contributors
Lindsay Bennett, Colin Follett, Kathryn Glendenning, David and June Halford,
Cathy Hatley, Isla Love, Michael Nation, Lyn Parry, Josephine Perry, Laurence Phillips,
Alwyn Sambrook, Andrew Sanger, The Content Works

Copy editor
Audrey Horne

Published by AA Publishing, a trading name of Automobile Association Developments Limited,
whose registered office is Millstream, Maidenhead Road, Windsor, Berkshire, SL4 5GD. Registered
number 1878835.

A CIP catalogue record for this book is available from the British Library.

ISBN 0 7495 4004 4

Binding style with plastic section dividers by permission of AA Publishing.

Colour separation by Keenes
Printed and bound by Leo, China

Find out more about AA Publishing and the wide range of travel publications and services the AA
provides by visiting our website at www.theAA.com

A01517
Mapping in this title produced from:
France data © Tele Atlas N.V. 2003
Mapping © GEOnext (Gruppo De Agostini) Novara
Relief map images supplied by Mountain High Maps ® Copyright © 1993 Digital Wisdom, Inc
Weather chart statistics supplied by Weatherbase © Copyright 2003 Canty and Associates, LLC
TCS assistance with distance/time charts gratefully acknowledged

We believe the contents of this book are correct at the time of printing.
However, some details, particularly prices, opening times and telephone numbers do change.
We do not accept responsibility for any consequences arising from the use of this book.
This does not affect your statutory rights. We would be grateful if readers would advise us of
any inaccuracies they may encounter, or any suggestions they might like to make to improve
the book. There is a form provided at the back of the book for this purpose, or you can
email us at Keyguides@theaa.com

COVER PICTURE CREDITS
Front Cover: Corbis **Back Cover, top to bottom:** AA/I Dawson; AA/M. Short; AA/S.L. Day; AA/M. Adelman **Spine** Corbis

Dear Key Guide Reader

●

Thank you for buying Key Guide France.
Your comments and opinions are very important to us, so please help us to
improve our travel guides by taking a few minutes to complete this
questionnaire.

You do not need a stamp (unless posted outside the UK). If you do not want to
cut this page from your guide, then photocopy it or write your answers on a plain
sheet of paper.

Send to: **Key Guide Editor, AA World Travel Guides**
FREEPOST SCE 4598, Basingstoke RG21 4GY

ABOUT THIS GUIDE Where did you buy it?_____

_____

When? _ _ month/ _ _ year

Why did you choose AA Key Guide France?
❏ Price
❏ AA Publication
❏ Used this series before; title_____
❏ Cover
❏ Other_____

_____

Please rate how helpful the following features of the guide
are to you: very helpful (**VH**), helpful (**H**) or little help (**LH**)

Size	**VH**	**H**	**LH**
Layout	**VH**	**H**	**LH**
Photos	**VH**	**H**	**LH**
Excursions	**VH**	**H**	**LH**
Entertainment	**VH**	**H**	**LH**
Hotels	**VH**	**H**	**LH**
Maps	**VH**	**H**	**LH**
Practical info	**VH**	**H**	**LH**
Restaurants	**VH**	**H**	**LH**
Shopping	**VH**	**H**	**LH**
Walks	**VH**	**H**	**LH**
Sights	**VH**	**H**	**LH**
Transport info	**VH**	**H**	**LH**

continued on next page…

What was your favourite sight, attraction or feature listed in the guide?

Page _____

Please give your reason _____

_____

Which features in the guide could be changed or improved, or any other comment you would like to make:

_____

_____

ABOUT YOU   Name (*Mr/Mrs/Ms*) _____

Address _____

_____

_____ Postcode _____

Daytime tel nos _____

Which age group are you in?

Under 25 ❏ 25–34 ❏ 35–44 ❏ 45–54 ❏ 55+ ❏

How many trips do you make a year?

Less than one ❏ One ❏ Two ❏ Three or more ❏

Are you an AA member? Yes ❏ No ❏

ABOUT YOUR TRIP   When did you book? _ _ month/_ _ year

When did you travel? _ _ month/_ _ year

Were you travelling for business or leisure? _____

How many nights did you stay? _____

How did you travel?

Individual ❏ Couple ❏ Family ❏ Group ❏

Did you buy any other travel guides for your trip? _____

If yes, which ones? _____

_____

_____

Thank you for taking the time to complete this questionnaire. Please send it to us as soon as possible, and remember, you do not need a stamp (*unless posted outside the UK*).